Chesapeake Politics, 1781–1800

Chesapeake Politics
1781–1800

NORMAN K. RISJORD

New York   COLUMBIA UNIVERSITY PRESS   *1978*

LIBRARY OF CONGRESS CATALOGING IN PUBLICATION DATA

RISJORD, NORMAN K.
    CHESAPEAKE POLITICS, 1781–1800.

    INCLUDES BIBLIOGRAPHICAL REFERENCES AND INDEX.
    1.   POLITICAL PARTIES—MARYLAND—HISTORY.   2.   POLITICAL
PARTIES—VIRGINIA—HISTORY.   3.   POLITICAL PARTIES—NORTH
CAROLINA—HISTORY.   I.   TITLE.
JK2295.M32R57   309.1′75′03   78-7996
ISBN 0–231–04328–7

COLUMBIA UNIVERSITY PRESS
NEW YORK AND GUILDFORD, SURREY

TO

*The University of Wisconsin
with solemn thanks
for the intellectual environment
that made this book possible*

Preface

THIS IS THE STORY of political developments after the American Revolution in three states—Maryland, Virginia, and North Carolina. Similar in economic and social structure, tied together by the Chesapeake Bay, these states formed a regional unit. And they were important enough to have a decisive impact on the national politics of the period. By examining three states I hoped to avoid the provincialism that characterizes most studies of individual states. At the same time, the focus on one region of the country permitted a close, detailed examination of the way in which government functioned in the formative years of the republic.

Because the three states were similar in agricultural development, trade patterns, and social structure, they easily lent themselves to comparative treatment. Each faced similar problems in the post-Revolutionary era—debt, depression, and western uprisings. Each wrestled with church disestablishment, public education, and demands for the amelioration of slavery. A comparison of the way each reacted to these questions offers a new dimension to the story of early American politics.

The basic theme is the evolution of political parties after the Revolution. I am not concerned with the subtle distinction between "party" and "faction"; nor am I concerned with pinpointing a moment when a modern "party" can be said to exist. I feel that party development was an evolutionary process, from nebulous groups of like-minded legislators to full-time professional organizations. There were various elements or stages in this process, though they did not necessarily appear in this order:

—The appearance of two or more identifiable groups of like-minded legislators, who agree with one another 70 to 75 percent of the time on a variety of issues. This level of cohesion suggests more than chance agreement; it suggests a common ideology. Agreement scores of 80 percent or better indicate internal lines of communication and perhaps some form of party discipline.
—The legislative parties differ from each other on a substantial number of (but not necessarily all) significant issues, and the differences involve policies, rather than personalities.
—The perception, at least among party leaders, of an interrelationship among various issues, leading to a public announcement of a program or platform.
—Appeals to the public for support, based upon a candidate's or a party's stand on certain issues, followed by efforts to influence public opinion and mobilize voters.
—The spread of party influence beyond the legislative halls—such as a test of party loyalty as a condition for executive or judicial preferment.
—The appearance of a party apparatus: legislative whips, nominating committees, or "juntos" that coordinate statewide activities.

There are, of course, other criteria that might be demanded, but these seem to be the basic elements of the first party system. By 1801, when the narrative is brought to an end, all these elements are present, at least to some degree, in the politics of the Chesapeake.

The dedication and the acknowledgments express only a few of my many obligations. My debts to librarians and archivists are too extensive to bear enumeration in this short space. But there are a few obligations that require notice. The roll call analysis of the Virginia and North Carolina assemblies, as well as the collection of tax data for those states, was done in collaboration with Dr. Gordon Den Boer and Mr. Richard Leffler. We shared our data freely while developing our own interpretations. Den Boer's dissertation, "The

House of Delegates and the Evolution of Political Parties in Virginia, 1782–1792" (1972) remains the best study of Virginia politics in this period. Leffler's work on North Carolina is still in progress, but holds similar promise.

My wife Constance, in addition to bearing the usual trials of the pedant's spouse, helped substantially with the research, notably in tracking down the biographical minutiae of a thousand Maryland and Virginia legislators.

Finally, my apologies to the many readers who will be told more in these pages than they ever wanted to know about the politics of the Chesapeake. I'm sure that they will share my hope that the story will not have to be told again for some time to come.

Madison, Wisconsin   NORMAN K. RISJORD
May 1978

Acknowledgments

Research for this book was made possible by grants from the following sources:

American Council of Learned Societies
American Philosophical Society
Society of Sigma XI
The Graduate School, University of Wisconsin

Maps were drawn by
The Cartography Laboratory
The University of Wisconsin, Madison

Contents

Maps

PART ONE

The Chesapeake Landscape

CHAPTER ONE

The Landscape and the People, from the Susquehanna to the Rappahannock

CHESAPEAKE BAY is the dominant feature of the region. It shaped the economy, the society, and much of the history of Maryland, Virginia, and even North Carolina. It quite literally divided Maryland in two, and its many estuaries knifed into the heart of Virginia. Settlement followed the water ways, and each great river valley draining into the bay—the Susquehanna, Patuxent, Potomac, Rappahannock, York, and James—had a distinctive style of life and agriculture. The Eastern Shore, though in many respects indistinguishable from other parts of Maryland and Virginia, considered itself a separate entity.

Ready access to water conditioned the bay economy from the earliest settlements. Planters often maintained direct contact with merchant houses in London or Glasgow, sending their tobacco on consignment and receiving in return goods or bills of exchange. The wealthiest owned their own ships; others used the many vessels that poked along the rivers looking for consignments. The most

3

important goods were brought directly from Britain; lesser items and perishables were bought in riverside market towns. Such settlements as Chester Town on the Choptank, Upper Marlborough on the Patuxent, Port Tobacco and Dumfries on the Potomac, or Rappahannock, Yorktown, Bermuda Hundred, all held a dozen dwellings, a store or two, and a tobacco warehouse on the water's edge. Trade was utterly decentralized; there was no central marketplace anywhere in the Chesapeake.[1]

The Revolution disrupted the consignment trade and presented new opportunities to American merchants. Enterprising communities like Baltimore and Annapolis moved to fill the gap. Norfolk, nearly destroyed at the beginning of the war, recovered rapidly when the fighting ended. Alexandria and Georgetown blossomed in the 1780s when improvements in the Potomac opened their hinterland. American merchants replaced British factors after the Revolution, but Chesapeake trade remained decentralized. No port rose to the dominant position of, say, New York or Philadelphia. Chesapeake society was predominantly rural, and this was perhaps the biggest single factor in shaping Chesapeake politics.

The region was also socially homogeneous. About 85 percent of the population originated in the British Isles. Of those who came from non-English-speaking countries, only the Germans (10 percent) were of importance. Ethnic variations were similar in all three states, as indicated by table 1.1, compiled from surnames in the census of 1790. The major differences are the substantially higher proportion of Scots in North Carolina, a reflection of the Highland migration to the Cape Fear Valley on the eve of the Revolution, and the number of Germans in Maryland, no doubt a migratory spillover from neighboring Pennsylvania. Even so, the variations are fairly minor. In no other part of the union—not even in New England—were there three states so similar in their ethnic composition.

Percentages reveal the relative contributions of national stocks, but, because of wide variations in the total populations of the three states, they hide some interesting comparisons. Despite the relatively high proportion of Germans in Maryland, Virginia had more in more actual numbers (ca. 28,000 as against 24,000).

TABLE 1.1   ETHNIC STOCKS OF WHITE POPULATION BY
CENSUS OF 1790 (PERCENTAGES)

	Maryland	Virginia	No. Carolina
English	64.5	68.5	66.0
Scots	7.6	10.2	14.8
Scots-Irish	5.8	6.2	5.7
Irish	6.5	5.5	5.4
German	11.7	6.3	4.7
Dutch	.5	.3	.3
French	1.2	1.5	1.7
Swedish	.5	.6	.2
Unassigned	1.7	.9	1.2

SOURCE: American Council of Learned Societies, "Report of Committee on Linguistic and National Stocks in the Population of the United States [by the census of 1790]," *Annual Report of the American Historical Association for 1931* (Washington, 1932), I, 124.

Indeed, Virginia housed more Germans than any other state except Pennsylvania. Virginia similarly possessed more Scots than North Carolina (ca. 45,000 to 43,000). And, despite Maryland's early reputation as a Roman Catholic refuge, both Virginia and North Carolina surpassed her in the number of southern Irish.[2] In spite of the apparent homogeneity, ethnic minorities were sizable enough to retain a conscious identity. Although there is no evidence of ethnic bloc voting, political practitioners in all three states, as will be seen in the course of the narrative, were conscious of national and linguistic groups.

Religious variations closely followed the ethnic variances. Scots and Ulster Irish were nearly all Presbyterians; Germans were either Lutheran ("Church Germans") or sectarian—Dunkards (Baptists), Menonites, and the like. People of English origin were Anglicans, except for those who had joined the Methodist or Baptist faiths during the religious awakening. The proliferation of faiths enlivened the society, but, except in moments of religious controversy, did not much affect politics. James Madison had a sizable number of Baptists in his Orange County constituency, and he was not above reminding them at election time of his role in the fight for separation of church and state. But Madison was a rarity. Most other political leaders seemed content to vote the interests of the religious majority when they were involved, and ignore the subject the rest of the time.

Within this predominantly rural, Anglo-Saxon society, however, there were wide variations of interest and outlook. Ethnic and religious minorities, for instance, were not distributed evenly. They were concentrated in certain areas, and even within regional units there were ethnic pockets. In the Shenandoah Valley, for instance, Germans and Scots-Irish separated themselves from town to town. The ethnic presence—in some places it even constituted a majority—was a source of regional identity. Moreover, the topography of the landscape and the fertility of soil varied greatly from the Susquehanna bottoms in the north to sandy Cape Fear in the south. In the west the mountains were the major determinant in settlement patterns and trade. So great were the variations that each subregional unit had an identity of its own. Such, for instance, was the Eastern Shore, or the thinly populated counties at the head of the bay. The Patuxent Valley, with the finest tobacco lands in Maryland, was a society unto itself. So were the Potomac, the Piedmont, and the lower James. In North Carolina, Albemarle differed from the Cape Fear Valley in export staples, trade patterns, ethnic origins, and religion as much as England differed from Scotland. Like those great insular rivals, Albemarle and Cape Fear shared little but a common language.

Variations in ethnicity, levels of development, quality of soil, and access to markets contributed to regional rivalries, which became the main dynamic in Chesapeake politics after the Revolution. The rivalries were fought within the state assemblies, but interests of geographical groups commonly transcended state boundaries. The inhabitants of western Maryland had more in common with the Great Valley of Virginia than they had with the seaboard planters. The Potomac Valley—once the Maryland shore caught up in development with Virginia's Northern Neck—was an economic unit, and its residents viewed with considerable suspicion the commercial pretensions of Baltimore. Farther south, the Dan

River–Roanoke complex united Virginia's Southside (the counties south of the James River) with the Carolina Piedmont. Much of the trade of this area went overland to Petersburg or Norfolk. Yet a few miles further south, past another hilly divide, the farmers of the Yadkin and Catawba rivers sent their surplus all the way to Charleston, South Carolina. These interstate contacts, though they complicated the politics of each assemby, did promote regional unity. And they ultimately contributed to the establishment of the federal government in 1788.

Before launching into the story of Chesapeake politics after the Revolution, let us examine these social and topographical variations in more detail.

MARYLAND'S NORTHERN FRONTIER

The traveler heading south from Philadelphia in 1783 had to make a choice of routes shortly after leaving Christiana, Delaware. The left fork turned south along Maryland's Eastern Shore to Chester Town. From there he could take a ferry across the bay to Annapolis. The other fork continued west around the upper end of the bay, through Cecil and Harford counties, and on to Baltimore. Shortly after entering Maryland on this road the traveler came upon the village of Elkton on the Elk River. Almost exactly halfway between Philadelphia and Baltimore, Elkton was a common stopover for both passengers and freight. During the war, when British warships hampered coastal traffic, Elkton became a distribution center for Eastern Shore wheat and corn. Carried to Elkton in small boats, grain or flour went from there by wagon twelve miles to Christiana. There it was loaded on boats again and sent up the Delaware River to Philadelphia. With the war over, Elkton's future was uncertain. The Hollingsworth brothers, principals in the flour trade, tried their best to promote the town. In 1787 they even managed to move the Cecil County seat there from Charlestown, but the village withered anyway, unable to compete with bustling Baltimore. In 1795 an English tourist called it "a dirty, straggling place" with about ninety "indifferent" houses.[3]

Charlestown fared little better. Some eight miles west of Elkton, on the west bank of the Northeast River (itself simply an arm of Chesapeake Bay), Charlestown even in 1777 was described as "much decayed." It served as the county seat from 1783 to 1787, but then it lost to Elkton even that distinction.[4]

The ride across Cecil County by horseback from Elkton to the Susquehanna River took three hours, and every traveler set it down as a dreary trip. In contrast to Delaware's tidy fields of wheat and corn, Cecil was wild and empty, a nearly unending forest of oak and white ash.[5] It is true, of course, that in this bay-oriented society the better plantations were near the water, and since the post roads stuck to high ground for drainage, travelers were looking at the "back forties," as it were. The clearings they did encounter were those of the poorer, landlocked farmers. Even so, in this part of Maryland there was a general appearance of poverty and dilapidation. Charlestown was on the water, yet the lands around it were "but little cultivated," one visitor observed, and another who passed through the village in 1784 noted that merchants had set up a "country fair," but no one had any money to buy.[6]

Just beyond Charlestown the road to Baltimore crossed Principio Creek. The lands from there to the Susquehanna were part of Susquehanna Manor, one of the estates of Henry Harford, heir (in 1779) to the Baltimore proprietary. The manor was confiscated by the state, along with Harford's other properties, during the war. This was the most valuable of his estates because it contained the Principio furnace, largest of Maryland's ironworks. Iron appeared in patches throughout the northern part of the state, though the ore mined was not especially rich. Hence there were a number of small furnaces producing pig iron in Baltimore, Harford, and Cecil counties. Principio was by far the largest, in extent and in capitalization. The furnace was owned by the Principio Company, a joint stock enterprise that included Henry Harford and a number of American investors, among them Augustine Washington, half-brother of George. In 1782, Thomas Russell, one of the original shareholders, purchased the confiscated portion from the state. At that time it amounted to 7,600 acres and 42 slaves appraised at £5,550.[7] It was clearly the biggest business operation in that part of Maryland.

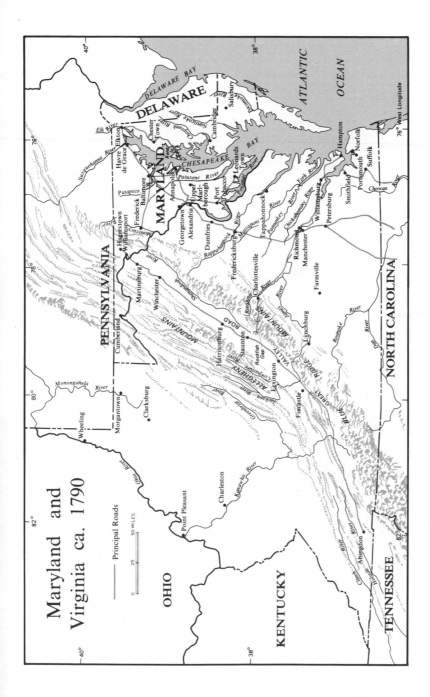

Maryland and
Virginia ca. 1790

——— Principal Roads

0   25   50 MILES

At the Susquehanna crossing (Perryville) the weary traveler encountered the first bright prospect since leaving Philadelphia. John Rodgers' tavern was considered one of the best public houses in the South. Even General Washington, who never lacked for private hospitality, occasionally stayed there. The proprietor's standing in the community was such that he married his daughter to Harford County's most promising young attorney, William Pinkney.[8]

Once the traveler crossed the river and resumed his southwesterly trek, he found the Harford County landscape as forbidding and undeveloped as Cecil's. For Harford there exist some population figures to complement the recorded reactions of travelers. Of the various censuses and statewide tax assessments in this period, only three survive—a state census of 1776, a tax assessment in 1783, and the federal census of 1790. Of all Maryland's counties only Harford's records survive for all three. Although the methods of head-counting are quite different—a census of all whites in 1776, from which heads of households have to be inferred, a list of taxpayers in 1783, and a census of heads of households in 1790—the similarity of results suggests that the three are comparable, and a comparison of them offers a unique glimpse of the county's social structure and growth rate (table 1.2).[9]

The 1776 returns, it should be noted, are incomplete, so there is less population growth during the war than the table suggests and almost none at all the 1780s. The stability in wealth variations

TABLE 1.2   WEALTH DISTRIBUTION, HARFORD COUNTY, MARYLAND, 1783–1790

	Heads of Households					
Slaves Held	1776		1783		1790	
0	559	68%	1,444	72%	1,461	70%
1–4	116	14	329	16.5	346	17
5–12	99	12	174	9	185	9
13–24	33	4	36	2	42	3
25–49	13	2	9	0.5	15	1
50–99	2	0	0	0	3	0
	822	100%	1,992	100%	2,052	100%

suggests that there was no per capita improvement either. Harford remained throughout this period an underpopulated frontier in which the vast majority of farms were small and semi-subsistence. In the tax list of 1783, 966 or 50 percent of all the heads of households owned no land at all.

If these people were tenant farmers, the landlords resided outside the county, for there is no wealthy elite of any substance in it. Nor was there a political elite. Harford's four delegates to the assembly in 1783 were planters of middling wealth, above average but not unusual. John Love had 864 acres and 10 slaves, Ignatius Wheeler, Jr., owned 1,385 acres and 35 slaves, Benjamin Norris 264 acres and 4 slaves, and John Taylor 510 acres with 7 slaves. All four favored debtor-relief measures in the House of Delegates, disliked taxes, and voted against officials' salaries. And they apparently reflected the wishes of the electorate. All served several terms in the assembly; two, Love and Norris, represented the county throughout the 1780s.

Maryland's upper bay counties were capable of development. They had sizable iron deposits (Harford was an iron producer until the Civil War), and the soil was a light-brown loam of good fertility.[10] But down to 1790, and probably for some time thereafter, the region was an underdeveloped frontier with an atmosphere of idle poverty. And this showed in the political behavior of its representatives.

THE EASTERN SHORE

Travelers who turned south at the Delaware state line and followed the eastern shore of Chesapeake Bay found a considerably more developed landscape. La Rochefoucauld-Liancourt, who traveled the road in the mid-1790s, noted that the forest cover had been almost completely removed. Where farther to the north Maryland suffered in comparison with Delaware, on the Eastern Shore the prospect brightened on crossing the Maryland line. Farms were larger than in Delaware and appeared to be more prosperous.[11] The upper counties—Queen Anne's, Talbot, and

Caroline—seemed as wealthy as any in Maryland. Their soil, predominantly Sassafras loam, was considered some of the best tobacco-growing land in the state. The Eastern Shore was abandoning tobacco, not because of soil exhaustion (the same soil produced good crops of tobacco on the Western Shore for many years after the Revolution), but because grain yielded more profitable returns.[12] By the mid-1780s its main exports were wheat, corn, and cattle.

Shortly after entering Maryland the traveler crossed the upper reaches of the Sassafras River and about ten miles farther on reached the Chester River. Chester Town, county seat of Kent, was a village of a hundred-odd wooden houses, some 35 miles from the bay. The river was navigable to that point for ocean-going vessels of 80–90 tons. Smaller boats could reach some ten miles farther.[13] Commercial center for the upper Eastern Shore, Chester Town straddled the economic tension line between Baltimore and Philadelphia. Planters who lived to the west of it in Kent or on Kent Island traded across the bay to Baltimore. Those to the north usually sent their produce to Philadelphia. Chester Town itself had about a dozen storekeepers with contacts in both cities.[14]

South of the Chester River, Queen Anne's, Talbot, and Caroline counties were as well developed as Kent. In the 1790s Queen Anne's farmers explained to Rochefoucauld that their oversized fields were due to the scarcity of wood for fencing.[15] Records of the 1776 census survive for both Queen Anne's and Talbot, and while the 1783 tax lists have unfortunately disappeared, the results can be compared with the federal census of 1790 (table 1.3).[16]

Because the 1776 returns are only partial, the figures do not reveal population growth. Totals for Talbot in 1776 have survived, however—6,643 whites, 149 free blacks, and 4,095 slaves. Comparable totals for 1790 are 8,665 whites, 1,076 free blacks, and 4,777 slaves. The growth is not as great as that of more primitive Harford County, but it is nonetheless substantial. More importantly, these Eastern Shore counties were substantially richer than Harford at the outset of the Revolution, and they gained in wealth over time, despite wartime dislocation and postwar depression. Slaveholding

TABLE 1.3   WEALTH DISTRIBUTION ON THE UPPER EASTERN SHORE,
1776–1790

	Heads of Households						
	Queen Anne's				Talbot		
Slaves Held	1776		1790		1776		1790	
0	298	54%	746	47%	268	55%	772	54
1–4	125	23	410	26	103	21	377	26
5–12	91	16	280	18	83	17	181	13
13–24	28	5	94	6	20	4	66	5
25–49	9	2	33	2	9	2	20	1
50–99	0		10	1	3	1	10	
100+	0		0		0		1	0
	551	100%	1,573	100%	486	100%	1,427	100

increased among all elements of the population, despite an apparent rise in the number of manumissions.[17]

South of Talbot and Caroline the landscape changes dramatically. The soil is sandy, and varieties of southern pine replace the hardwood forests. Dorchester, Somerset, and Worcester counties, though long known to Maryland and Virginia pioneers, were still largely uninhabited at the end of the Revolution. There were no towns of substance in the entire area, and trade went directly from riverside dock to Baltimore, Norfolk, Philadelphia, or the West Indies. Yet the three counties were well served by large rivers—the Nanticoke, the Wicomico, and the Pocomoke. Arising in the marshes that separated southern Delaware from Maryland, the rivers were too shallow for anything but lumber rafts, but they quickly opened up into broad estuaries of the bay.[18] No part of Maryland was better served by water communication, and its exports of lumber and barrel staves went to far-flung seaports. The landscape was primitive, but important changes were under way at the end of the Revolution. Unfortunately, only Worcester's records are complete enough to permit comparative examination.[19] Worcester was the most remote, and in some ways the most interesting of the three. It had no frontage on the bay. Indeed, its only contact was by long journey down the Pocomoke River. On the Atlantic side shipping was blocked by the long sandy spit of Assateague Island, which extended from Delaware to Virginia. During the 1780s the county was in the anomalous position of losing population and gaining per capita wealth (table 1.4).

Because the 1783 returns for Worcester are incomplete, the number of householders is understated; hence the population loss was even greater than appears in the table. Those who left were evidently the poor; indeed, the decline in the number of nonslaveholders alone nearly accounts for the total loss. The wealthy gained both relatively and in absolute numbers. Since it is unlikely that rich planters were moving into the county, in view of the exodus of everyone else, the new wealthy probably came from the lower classes. Thus there is evidence of fairly dramatic increases in per capita wealth in the six-year period. Worcester, in short, was a county undergoing rapid development. There is no contemporary comment on it, but lumbering, the spread of farmland, and the rise of commercial agriculture (which all went together) probably account for the change.

Worcester, like her neighbors, was consistently "creditor" (that is, against legislative debtor-relief measures; see chapters 3 and 4)

TABLE 1.4 WEALTH DISTRIBUTION ON THE
LOWER EASTERN SHORE:
WORCESTER COUNTY, 1783–1790

	Heads of Households			
Slaves Held	1783		1790	
0	1,252	63%	786	57%
1–4	428	22	336	24
5–12	247	12.5	198	14
13–24	38	2	51	4
25–49	6	.5	11	1
50–99	1		2	
	1,972	100%	1,384	100%

SOURCE: Worcester County Tax List, 1783, MdHS; U.S. Census, 1790, Maryland.

in its political stance during the 1780s, and Federalist from 1788 to 1800. It differed from "debtor" Harford in three interesting ways. One is the growth in per capita wealth, compared with Harford's stagnation. Second, Worcester had fewer paupers and tenant farmers. Slaveholding was more widespread and on the rise. Worcester's landless households numbered 556 in 1783, about a fourth of the total, whereas they were half the total in Harford. And finally, Worcester politics was dominated by a wealthy elite. The richest man in the county, Colonel Joseph Dashiell (over 2,000 acres and 68 slaves) was its assembly delegate from 1781 to 1785. Other frequently elected servants were William Morris (1780–84), 33 slaves, John Pope Mitchell (1785–87), 21 slaves, and William Purnell (1785–88), 24 slaves. It is possible that in taking a creditor stand in the assembly these men were serving their own interests rather than their constituents', but the overall growth in per capita wealth suggests that the two were blended.

BALTIMORE: COUNTY AND TOWN

The wayfarer who came along the north shore of the bay through Cecil and Harford counties crossed into Baltimore County at the Gunpowder River, just below the spectacular Gunpowder Falls. The countryside quickly assumed a more prosperous and substantially more populated appearance. But the visitor who assumed this to be characteristic of the county as a whole was quite mistaken. Most of the population and the wealth of the county was concentrated in the more southerly hundreds near the bay, and along the road leading to the city. A few of these hundreds, such as Middle River and Back River, have since been incorporated into the city of Baltimore. In the interior of the county, on the other hand, north and west toward the Pennsylvania line, there were vast stretches of thinly populated forest. Back-country Baltimore County had much the appearance of Harford and Cecil. Through much of the 1780s it also shared their voting habits.

The variations in wealth and population density of Baltimore County are reflected in table 1.5,[20] compiled from the 1783 tax assessment list of hundreds. Several hundreds were omitted for lack

TABLE 1.5 BALTIMORE COUNTY: VARIATIONS IN POPULATION AND WEALTH, 1783

	Bay Hundreds			Middling Interior			North & West	
	Middle River Lower	*Back River Lower*	*Patapsco Lower*	*Middle & Back Upper*	*Gunpowder Upper*	*Mine Run*	*North Hundred*	*Pipe Creek*
Acres	27,627	21,597	26,662	68,728	35,334	30,784	38,816	40,283
Value	£37,022	£27,399	£41,038	£72,455	£38,026	£24,435	£19,704	£17,636
Whites	950	948	891	2,123	1,592	1,566	1,588	1,292
Slaves	369	252	430	1,244	680	360	99	85

SOURCE: Baltimore County Tax List, 1783, MdHS.

of space, but, except for the city hundreds, they were similar to those included in the table. The list itself, however, is not representative, for it omits a number of northern and western hundreds, thereby concealing the less developed part of the county.[21]

Baltimore city was built on the grain trade. Located on the Patapsco River, whose estuary formed a natural harbor, Baltimore had been a village of no importance until 1744 when a road was cut west into the Monocacy Valley. This enabled the town to become an entrepôt for the wheat-growing farmers of central Maryland. As it constructed flour mills and established contacts with the West Indies, it attracted shipments from Pennsylvania, by way of the Susquehanna. When Maryland planters began shifting to wheat on the eve of the Revolution, Baltimore blossomed into the leading city in the colony. The market for flour was pretty well confined to the West Indies, largely because of Britain's imperial regulations, but after the war Baltimore merchants moved into the European continent.[22]

They did not totally ignore tobacco. Circularizing European mercantile houses at the end of the war, the firm of Samuel and John Smith pointed out that Baltimore handled sizable amounts of Virginia tobacco (Europeans considered Maryland tobacco inferior) because Baltimore was the only port on the bay where planters could sell their crop for cash. But tobacco never attained the importance of grain. In 1782, 8 ships cleared the port loaded with tobacco, while 127 sailed with wheat and flour. But the traders remained ever alert for new outlets. They even sent a little-heralded vessel to China just about the time that the New York syndicate was dispatching the *Empress of China* to open contact with that vast market. The Baltimore vessel returned from Canton in August 1785 with a cargo of tea.[23]

The wartime demand for flour and Baltimore's relative immunity from attack sparked rapid growth during the war. The city numbered about 12,000 people in 1783, and every visitor was impressed with the atmosphere of bustling enterprise. The street plan was similar to Philadelphia's. Market Street (now Baltimore Street), a few blocks up from the waterfront, was a mile long and paved with cobblestones by the end of the war. The lower part of almost every house on this street was a store, with the merchant and his family living upstairs. Almost all were of brick, "and a great many of them very handsome," added one visitor. Street lighting was installed at the end of the war, and a force of constables (3 in daytime, 14 at night) patrolled the streets. Wharves and warehouses were located at Fell's Point, a neck of land poking into the bay a few miles southeast of the city.[24]

THE WESTERN SHORE

The southbound traveler had to ride west out of Baltimore for about ten miles to reach the ferry across the Patapsco. Near the ferry was another sign of Baltimore enterprise—Ellicott's mills. Built by the brothers Joseph and Andrew Ellicott just before the Revolution, these were among the many water-powered flour mills in Maryland. Most were small operations serving local planters, but the Ellicotts planned international sales, using Baltimore's port facilities. They even built a road to Baltimore at their own expense, and it was they, allegedly, who started the rush toward wheat growing when they persuaded Charles Carroll of Carrollton, biggest planter in the province, to make the switch.[25]

Beyond the river, the traveler had several options. He could continue west toward Frederick across dreary Baltimore County, a land where, even in June, one voyager complained, "The earth seems to be covered only with tatters."[26] Alternative routes were to proceed southwest to Bladensburg on the Potomac or southeast to Annapolis. Both roads led across Anne Arundel County, which seemed at first much like Baltimore. One diarist described the journey from Baltimore to Bladensburg as "monotonous woods, very little cultivated land to be seen along the road," while another noted that the Annapolis road was sandy and the countryside "barren, producing only shrubs and pines."[27] A modern soil map of Anne Arundel bears out both descriptions. The northern portion of the county is Norfolk sand, a soil that was not very fertile, even in its virgin condition.[28]

Annapolis, capital of the state, lay on the Severn River, whose estuary formed a natural harbor, much like the Patapsco at Baltimore. But, unlike the Patapsco, which sometimes froze over in winter, the Severn was always ice-free. Annapolis boomed during the war, changing from provincial capital and shopping center for the wealthy to an international seaport. The chief reason was that several enterprising merchant firms, led by Wallace, Johnson, and Muir, moved into the consignment tobacco trade in place of the British.[29] The trade flourished for a few years after the war and then declined. Annapolis lost business to the more versatile Baltimore, while Georgetown took over the Potomac traffic. By 1790 Annapolis was once again a provincial capital and country market town.

Despite its flourishing trade, the 1783 tax list indicates that Annapolis was essentially a government town. About 20 percent of the heads of households had government-related jobs, while shopkeepers and tavern owners (another 25 percent) relied on court days and assembly sessions for a good part of their profits. Only about 9 percent of the heads of households were ship captains or sailors. The remainder were employed at a variety of crafts and service trades, but no single industry predominated.[30] The city's delegation in the assembly reflected its blend of politics and service. Samuel Chase, lawyer, speculator, and flamboyant politician, was a perennial choice until he moved to Baltimore in 1786. The other seat invariably went to Chase's good friend, Allan Quynn, a wealthy shoemaker who sat in the House of Delegates for the rest of the century.

South of Annapolis the road remained sandy but the countryside was better developed. Meadows and cornfields were the rule, with only occasional patches of woods. Farmers in that area had built cattle fences, which occasioned numerous gates in the road. Travelers complained about the gates, but the fences were an important sign of progress. Fenced cattle could be checked for disease, intelligently fed, and selectively bred.[31]

Further west lay the valley of the Patuxent River, which separated Anne Arundel from Prince George's County. The soil of this valley was Sassafras loam, as on the Eastern Shore, enriched with alluvial deposits. Tobacco was still the main crop of this valley—or at least the principal export staple—and remained so at least until the Civil War. That it persisted so long was testimony to the quality of the land and the care that Maryland planters gave it.[32] Patuxent tobacco, moreover, was the only Maryland strain could compete in the European market with Virginia tobacco. Most Maryland tobacco was of the Orinocco variety, a heavier, harsher tobacco than the sweet-scented variety for which Virginia's James River was famed. The English scorned Maryland tobacco, and after the Revolution most of it was sent to France.

The Patuxent was the dominant physical feature not only of Anne Arundel and Prince George's, but of Calvert County as well. A thin neck of land between the bay and the Patuxent estuary, Calvert was the most tobacco-minded county in Maryland. It was, moveover, completely dependent on the river because its bay shore had steep banks and no harbors. The soil is a Norfolk loam, similar to that of the lower James Valley in Virginia, the finest natural tobacco soil.[33] A tax list of 1782 reveals Calvert to be a county of large plantations (4 percent of the planters owned more than half the land) and high concentration of slaveholding—highest, in fact, in Maryland. Neighboring Anne Arundel, slightly less wealthy, was more akin to the counties across the bay (table 1.6).[34]

Calvert was clearly the more homogeneous of the two. A good majority of its families were slaveowners, but, though plantations were sizable, no one in the county owned more than 50 slaves (although it is likely that by 1790, when the Anne Arundel figures were taken, there were a couple in Calvert in this class). The two counties differed to about the same degree in their political behavior. Their assembly delegates were, for the most part, drawn from the wealthiest segment, but those from Anne Arundel frequently favored debtor-relief legislation, while Calvert's were generally creditor-minded.[35]

Across the Patuxent was Prince George's County. Once the road wound up out of the rich river valley, the landscape again became sandy and hilly. Pine forest predominated until one neared Bladensburg, a tiny tobacco port on a branch of the Potomac. The

TABLE 1.6 WEALTH DISTRIBUTION ON
THE WESTERN SHORE:
CALVERT (1782) AND ANNE ARUNDEL
(1790)

A. Size of Farms (acres)	Heads of Households Calvert County	
0	404	49%
1-24	7	1
25-99	117	14
100-299	184	22
300-599	83	10
600-999	21	2.5
1,000+	12	1.5
	828	100%

B. Slaves Held	Calvert		Anne Arundel	
0	369	44%	1,022	53%
1-4	243	30	360	18
5-12	135	16	297	15
13-24	67	8	116	6
25-49	14	2	105	5
50-99	0	0	14	1.5
100+	0	0	5	.5
	828	100%	1,919	100%

SOURCE: Calvert County Tax List, 1782, MdHS; U.S.
Census, 1790, Maryland.

country around Bladensburg, and from there to Georgetown on the
Potomac, was extensively cultivated, a mixture of tobacco and corn
fields, with an occasional woodlot.[36]

Georgetown, founded about mid-century, was built on
tobacco. The petition asking the assembly to erect a town requested
a location adjacent to the tobacco warehouse at the mouth of Rock
Creek. Most of the early inhabitants were Scottish factors who
consigned hogsheads to their Glasgow masters.[37] The war interrupted this trade and put many of the Scots to flight, but indigenous
merchants picked up the trade after the war. In 1784 Georgetown
was exporting some 2,000 hogsheads of tobacco annually, and such
enterprising mercantile firms as Forrest and Stoddert were begin-

ning to steal from Annapolis much of southern Maryland's consignment trade.[38] Georgetown prospered throughout the 1780s as the upper Potomac developed, but in the succeeding decade it gave way to Alexandria across the Potomac.

The Potomac Valley was famous for its fertile soil both above and below Georgetown.[39] To the southeast, Charles and St. Mary's counties contained the state's oldest settlements, and, like the Eastern Shore, they were rapidly abandoning tobacco culture. Travelers after the war reported a sort of mixed agriculture—corn, wheat, enclosed pastures, and woodlots. But the countryside retained an atmosphere of tidy prosperity, similar to neighboring Calvert. Riding from Georgetown to Port Tobacco, one diarist commented on the "pretty farmhouses" along the road.[40] Port Tobacco, county seat of Charles, had grown up about the tobacco warehouse on a sharp bend of the Potomac. A short distance below the town was a ferry across the Potomac that lay on the main route to Fredericksburg and Richmond, Virginia. Highway traffic apparently kept its economy sprightly, despite the decline of tobacco, because several inns and ordinaries were built there in the 1780s.[41] The ferry also permitted considerable contact between the lower Potomac counties of Maryland and the Northern Neck of Virginia. People frequently crossed over to Dumfries and Colchester for suppers and dances. Writing during the war from Nomini Hall, Westmoreland County, Robert Carter told his friend Charles Carroll, "There is an intercourse between the people here and those residing in St. Mary's County, Maryland, except during the winter season. Letters to me forward to Leonard Town in St. Mary's will seldom lay long there."[42]

VIRGINIA'S NORTHERN NECK

By "Northern Neck" Virginians originally meant the narrow peninsula between the estuaries of the Potomac and Rappahannock rivers, but in time it came to mean all the territory between the two rivers as far west as the Blue Ridge Mountains. Although the topography of this northern third of the state varied greatly, from the level Tidewater to the rolling Piedmont, it had a common history. In the seventeenth century King Charles II granted it as a proprietary to Governor Thomas Culpeper, and it descended by marriage into the Fairfax family. Lord Fairfax disposed of his land through agents, and these often served themselves as well as their master. When one of Fairfax's agents, Robert "King" Carter, died in 1732 he left to his numerous progeny a princely domain of over 100,000 acres. Lees and Washingtons also benefited from the Fairfax connection. These fortunate few dictated the political and social temper of the Northern Neck into the Revolution and for some time thereafter.

Westmoreland County, directly across the Potomac from St. Mary's and home of numerous Carters, Lees, and Washingtons, was probably the wealthiest of the older counties, but Richmond on the Rappahannock was perhaps more typical. Even that county, as evidenced by table 1.7, had a higher concentration of landholding and greater incidence of slaveholding than any county herein examined.[43] Nowhere else in the Chesapeake is there such a concentration of landed wealth at the end of the Revolution. Modern censuses indicate about 122,880 acres in the county. Thus the top 10 percent of the planters owned at least 30 percent of the land, whereas some 30 percent of the taxpayers owned no land at all.[44] Slaveholding was less concentrated; indeed, about five-eights of all taxpayers held slaves, as against slightly more than half in the richest Maryland county examined. The relatively broad distribution of slave wealth seems inconsistent with the dominant position of the landed wealthy, but politically the two probably complemented one another. The rich and the middling alike seemed well off at the end of the Revolution, and this no doubt accounts for the generally creditor stance taken by the Northern Neck in the assembly.[45]

Despite some increase in the number of small farmers over time, the landed wealthy retained their vast estates. But slaveholding—perhaps a better index of prosperity because it represented invested capital—underwent some significant shifts. Slaveholding declined dramatically among the wealthy and middling planters in the 1780s, and there was an equally dramatic increase in the number of small slaveholders and free farmers. A shift in crop production from tobacco to the less labor-intensive wheat may

TABLE 1.7   WEALTH DISTRIBUTION IN THE NORTHERN NECK:
RICHMOND COUNTY, 1782–1800

	Heads of Households					
A. *Size of Farms (acres)*	*1782*		*1790*		*1800*	
1–24	2	.5%	2	.5%	7	2%
25–99	84	23	92	25	111	30
100–299	180	51	172	47	157	41
300–599	53	15	64	17.5	65	17
600–999	18	5	21	5	20	5
1000+	21	5.5	19	5	23	5
	358	100%	370	100%	383	100%
B. *Slaves Held*	*1783*		*1790*		*1800*	
0	191	37.5%	261	40%	269	47%
1–4	149	27	244	37	191	33
5–12	93	19	105	16	82	14.5
13–24	47	10	32	5	23	4
25–49	25	5	11	2	8	1.5
50–99	4	1	1		1	
100+	2	.5	1		1	
	511	100%	655	100%	575	100%

SOURCE: Richmond County Land Books, 1782, 1790, 1800 and Personalty Books, 1783, 1790, 1800, VaSL.

account for part of this decline, but the increase in the number of landless (to 43 percent) suggests that the county was experiencing hard times as well.[46] The ranks of the affluent continued to thin in the 1790s, though at a somewhat slower rate. Landless taxpayers dropped to 33 percent, but the increase in the number of nonslave-holders suggests that the poor were not prospering any more than the rich. The decline in total population indicates substantial out-ward migration, probably by all economic levels. Politically, Rich-mond County, along with others in the lower Neck, frequently voted debtor in the mid-1780s, though they all favored the Consti-tution. With the exception of Westmoreland, they moved into the Jeffersonian Republican Party in the mid-1790s.

The soil of the lower Northern Neck is mainly Sassafras sandy loam in the uplands, similar to that across the bay. Along the rivers is a silt loam, similar to the soils of the North Carolina coast (Metapeake, Bertie, and Craven soils). Both types are considered to be of medium fertility and are highly acidic. They thus required frequent applications of lime to maintain production. The Eastern Shore planter John Beale Bordley pointed out the value of lime and marl fertilizers just prior to the Revolution, but how widely the information was disseminated is not known. Even when they did learn about fertilizers many farmers found it cheaper simply to move west.

Though once an extremely wealthy region, the Northern Neck had clearly reached its peak by the time of the Revolution. By the 1780s its lands probably required substantial treatment to maintain fertility, and in any case they could not compete with newly opened lands to the west. The slave population declined in the 1780s, and in the succeeding decade the whites began moving out. By contrast, the Piedmont part of the Northern Neck (Fairfax, Loudoun, and Fauquier counties) was thriving, benefiting, perhaps, from the exodus. Table 1.8 gives some data on booming Fairfax, adjacent to the city of Alexandria.[47]

Fairfax grew dramatically after the Revolution, nearly doubling its population in a twenty-year period. There was some increase in the percentage of small freeholders (owning under 100 acres), but in general the county absorbed the population increase without substantial change in its social structure. All economic levels were able to acquire land and slaves at about the same rate. Even the percentage of landless was the same in 1800 as in 1782 (64 percent). The exception is the decline in the number of large slaveholdings. This probably reflected the shift to wheat, rather than hard times among the rich.

A large county in area, Fairfax had a wide variety of soil types that demanded a diversified agriculture. Tobacco probably never had much of a hold in the county, and it was rapidly disappearing as a crop by the end of the Revolution. In 1787 Washington announced that he had "wholly discontinued the cultivation of Tobacco," and his friends were experimenting with a variety of cattle and hog feeds that would enable them to keep animals over the winter.[48] The southern third of the county was hilly and largely

TABLE 1.8   WEALTH DISTRIBUTION IN THE NORTHERN NECK: FAIRFAX COUNTY, 1782–1800

	Heads of Households					
A. *Size of Farms (acres)*	*1782*		*1790*		*1800*	
1–24	7	2%	10	3%	33	7%
25–99	27	9	36	10	39	8
100–299	128	43	168	48	209	45
300–599	69	24	66	19	99	20
600–999	28	9	40	11	36	8
1,000+	38	13	40	11	54	12
	297	100%	349	100%	470	100%
B. *Slaves Held*	*1782*				*1800*	
0	413	50%			736	54%
1–4	216	26			359	27
5–12	120	14			190	14
13–24	59	7			37	3
25–49	15	2			15	1.5
50–99	5	.5			2	.25
100+	3	.5			2	.25
	831	100%			1,341	100%

SOURCE: Fairfax County Land Books, 1782, 1790, 1800, and Personalty Books, 1782, 1800, VaSL.

wooded, but the rest was well cultivated.[49] The predominant soil in the eastern part was a Beltsville-Sassafrass series, ranging in fertility from "fair" to "some of the best land in the county."[50] In the western part of the county, Glenelg is the predominant soil type, considered as fertile as Sassafras and particularly suited to corn and grain.

Contributing to Fairfax's growth, no doubt, was its proximity to Alexandria. The city offered an immediate market for its products and thus encouraged a diversified agriculture. The city, moreover, grew even faster than the county. At the end of the war it numbered about 2,000 inhabitants, black and white, and it jumped to 3,000 by 1790. Travelers in the mid-1780s recorded construction activity similar to Baltimore's and great expectations from the clearing of the Potomac for navigation. In 1786 the city was still exporting some 10,000 hogsheads of tobacco a year, but wheat and flour were gaining. A decade later it shipped ten times as much flour as tobacco.[51] Alexandria's growth is depicted in the land tax books, which show the explosion in the city's rent rolls (for both commercial sites and private dwellings):[52]

1787	£12,199	1795	£ 16,394
1788	£ 7,019	1796	£ 20,038
1789	£ 5,832	1798	£ 28,504
1790	£ 6,265	1799	£ 35,014
[records missing]		1800	£ 38,858

The missing records might have revealed, through chronological association, which factor was primarily responsible for the growth—the transfer of the nation's capital to Washington, the outbreak of war in Europe (with a concomitant demand for flour), or the opening of the Potomac. As it is, the most that can be said is that all three were operative. The sag in total rents in the late 1780s probably resulted from the postwar depression. Because of the contractual nature of rents, it is not surprising to find them lagging behind the business cycle.

Alexandria and its hinterland were solidly creditor in the 1780s and Federalist through the 1790s. Prosperity was only part of it. In both city and county the wealthy were in a peculiarly dominant position. Alexandria's assembly seats were regularly filled by prominent merchants and lawyers, and it was generally felt that this elite governed the town. George Mason (hardly "poor" himself) and other Fairfax farmers periodically complained that merchants controlled the city by intimidating the poor and manipulating "Sailors & other Itinerants."[53] The position of the wealthy in the county is evident from table 1.8. Householders who did not own land—and were therefore not qualified to vote—made up nearly two-thirds of all county taxpayers. Among the propertied, nearly half (46 percent in 1782, 40 percent in 1800) owned 300 acres or more. In no other county examined was the "middle order" (100 to 300 acres) so tiny. Fairfax was controlled by the rich.

Fairfax's neighbors to the south, Prince William, Stafford, and King George counties, were more divided politically and less affluent. Gaps in their tax records prevent close analysis, but the white population in all appears to have risen only slightly over the twenty-year period, while the number of blacks remained stable or perhaps declined. Washington's friend and agricultural informant, David Stuart, felt that the soil in Prince William was as good as that of Fairfax, but the farmers, even in 1791, were "more attached to tobacco." At that date about half the county was still under forest cover.[54]

On the other hand, Stuart considered Loudoun County to the west "perhaps the best farming County in the State, being thickly settled with Quakers and Germans from Pennsylvania."[55] Blessed with rich soil, especially along the Potomac (where bottom lands sold for £3 to £5 an acre in 1791), and an industrious population, Loudoun had a bright future, but it was still undeveloped in 1782. Its surviving tax records are also incomplete, but the adult white male population increased by half (from 2,075 to 3,110) between 1782 and 1787. Slave numbers did not increase at the same pace, however, doubtless because of the aversion to slavery among both Quakers and Germans. Loudoun had its growth spurt in the 1790s when the arrival of the federal capital and the opening of the Potomac widened its markets.[56] In that respect, it bore a closer resemblance to its Maryland neighbors, Frederick and Montgomery counties, than it did to the rest of the Northern Neck.

WESTERN MARYLAND

Montgomery County, across the Potomac from Fairfax, developed somewhat differently in the 1780s, but the political result was similar. Except for the Potomac bottom lands, where wealthy planters like Daniel Carroll raised tobacco for the Georgetown market, the soil of Montgomery was thin and poorly managed.[57] Just emerging from frontier conditions, the county grew rapidly during the Revolution. It continued to grow in per capita wealth in the postwar decade, but, curiously, it lost white population (table 1.9).[58]

Other counties with rising per capita slaveholding, such as Queen Anne's or Fairfax, were also attracting immigrants. So Montgomery is an anomaly. It seems unlikely that all the land of this

TABLE 1.9 WEALTH DISTRIBUTION IN
WESTERN MARYLAND:
MONTGOMERY COUNTY, 1783–1790

Slaves Held	Heads of Households			
	1783		1790	
0	1,470	64%	1,139	55%
1–4	522	22	460	22
5–12	273	12	352	17
13–24	57	2	89	4
25–49	7	0	22	2
50–99	1	0	2	0
	2,330	100%	2,062	100%

SOURCE: Montgomery County Tax List, 1783, MdHS;
U.S. Census, 1790, Maryland.

relatively new county (established in 1776) was engrossed. But it is possible that the good lands along the river were taken (Daniel Carroll alone owned thousands of acres), and when the interior soils wore out the population moved west. The increase in slaveholding, then, may have reflected only Potomac prosperity.

Montgomery's political posture in the 1780s was consistently debtor, which suggests that some of the voters were not sharing in the prosperity. In 1788 it supported the Constitution and remained Federalist thereafter. Expansion of Georgetown, improvements in the Potomac, and arrival of the nation's capital were factors in its later Federalism. But the census figures for 1790 also indicate that, like Fairfax across the river, Montgomery had come under the domination of a wealthy elite.

North and west of Montgomery, across the Catochtin hills, was Frederick County. Its predominant feature was the Monocacy River, which rose in southern Pennsylvania and flowed some forty miles south to the Potomac. The hills on each side were still under forest cover, but the river valley, one visitor remarked in 1784, was "well cleared and rather thickly settled." The land seemed fertile, he added, and there were "many fine farms." Another journalist, coming west from Baltimore, noted the sharp contrast between western Baltimore County and the lush meadows of the Monocacy Valley. Ex-governor Thomas Johnson, who surveyed the agriculture of western Maryland in 1791, thought that wheat was the main market crop, but travelers commented on the large numbers of tobacco fields.[59] The market, in any case, was not important because of transportation costs. Frederick Town, the county seat, was about equidistant (forty miles) from Baltimore and Georgetown. Until improvements were undertaken the Monocacy could not support shipping. Flour and tobacco thus had to be sent overland at a cost that Governor Johnson estimated at £3 a ton. Only in the best of times would Frederick's products be competitive, and through much of the postwar period the county remained isolated and debtor-minded.

It is impossible to get a meaningful wealth analysis of Frederick because the aversion to slavery among westerners, especially Germans and Quakers, makes that an unreliable index. A French traveler in 1791 recorded the following conversation with the wife of a western Maryland farmer, without noting her name or the family religion. The woman opened the exchange with the observation that the family owned more land than the husband could cultivate, but they would not own slaves "even if we were richer." Her argument was that Negroes were understandably unwilling to work because they did not get paid. A master thus had the choice of feeding and clothing the slave without demanding labor or beating him to force him to work. The first alternative would create "an additional expense to no purpose," and with the second "we should have to give up the peace which embellishes this simple cottage."[60] It was an argument derived from common sense, not religion.

West of Frederick, across the South Mountain (an extension of Virginia's Blue Ridge), lay Washington County. Like Frederick, it centered on a broad, rolling valley, drained by Antietam Creek and the Conococheague River, both tributaries of the Potomac. The urban center was Hagarstown, founded in 1739 and, at 2,000 people, about the size of Frederick. A link in the valley complex that extended from Pennsylvania to Tennessee, this part of Maryland was on the main route of population drift from the Cumberland Valley of Pennsylvania to the Shenandoah Valley of Virginia. The population was thus mainly German and Scots-Irish, with a sprinkling of emigrés from the Tidewater.

The migrants from Pennsylvania commonly kept to themselves, and each community had a distinct ethnic character. For instance, the Leitersburg district, on the upper Antietam near the Pennsylvania border, was almost exclusively German. So was Hagarstown on the Conococheague. Along the Potomac, one traveler observed, nearly all the farmers were Irish.[61] The differentiation, however, apparently bred no hostility. In one town of mixed nationalities and only 26 houses, the sole church was deliberately kept open to all sects because the residents preferred to listen to a preacher with whom they disagreed than hear none at all. "Nearly all the sects tolerate each other," one visitor observed, "and the sectarians respect each other."[62] Primitive facilities bred an informal ecumenicism, and the interchange doubtless contributed to understanding. Neither religion nor ethnicity was an important political factor at the end of the Revolution. Even so, political leaders took care not to offend sensibilities in either area.

The Antietam Valley had a limestone floor and a rich, black soil. The Conococheague, resting on slate, was slightly less fertile, but both valleys were well suited to cereal grains. The common farm, observed one traveler, appeared to be about 250 acres, and farmers concentrated on grains, growing corn, wheat, and rye in rotation, followed by a fallow year. The wheat was ground into flour at Hagarstown mills and shipped by wagon to Baltimore. Corn and rye, too low-priced to offset the costs of overland transportation, were fed to livestock or made into whisky. In the latter form they were valuable enough to warrant shipment. Whisky was thus an important cash crop for many westerners, and with money chronically scarce it even served as a medium of exchange. So used, it was valued at a shilling a gallon.[63]

West of the North Mountain was a jumble of ridges and narrow valleys. Bottom lands were fertile enough and occasional clearings contained fields of corn and rye. But most of the country was still forest at the end of the Revolution. The one important settlement was Cumberland on the North Branch of the Potomac. A fort at this site dated from before the French and Indian War, but there was no permanent settlement there until the Revolution. When a town was authorized by the assembly and officially laid out in 1786, it contained some 35 families. West of the main route for Pennsylvania migrants, Cumberland was initially settled by Marylanders from the east. So were the lands to the west of it, which had been reserved by the assembly during the war as compensation for its soldiers. With a mixture of veterans and other migrants, the western valleys filled rapidly after the war. When the region west of North Mountain was established as Allegany County in 1790 it contained a population of 5,000.[64] Its first assembly delegation was solidly Federalist.

THE SHENANDOAH VALLEY OF VIRGINIA

The dynamics of the Chesapeake frontier followed a north-south axis. The counties of northwestern Virginia were more akin, in appearance, in population, and in outlook, to Maryland and Pennsylvania than to their own state. Economically and socially, the Shenandoah and South Branch valleys were extensions of the Susquehanna and Ohio watersheds of Pennsylvania. The main road southwest from Pennsylvania's Cumberland Valley crossed the Potomac at Williams' Ferry (christened Williamsport in 1787) and meandered through Berkeley County to Martinsburg. The first whites to trace this path were Pennsylvania Germans who came in 1732. The main communities at the end of the Revolution, Martinsburg and Mecklenburg (later Shepherds Town) were predominantly German. Scots-Irish, arriving a bit later, pushed farther on up the valley. Virginians, who moved across the mountains into Berkeley during the war, established their own community at Charles Town.[65] In Frederick County, to the south, the pattern was much the same. In Stephensburg, founded in 1758, German was still heard on the streets in the 1780s. Strasburg, on the border of Shenandoah County, was exclusively German, while Staunton in Augusta was Irish. Winchester, county court for Frederick, was founded by Germans, but the Scots-Irish, along with native Virginians, soon became dominant. A French visitor reported in 1791 that "nearly all the inhabitants of Winchester are Presbyterians."[66]

This ethnic pattern of settlement retarded the social homogenization that would normally have resulted from such spatial mobility. Instead of mixing when they moved into new lands, ethnic groups seemed to cling together, developing, one might suppose, a sort of frontier ghetto, internally directed and suspicious of outside authority. A government as distant as Richmond, dominated by eastern planters, seemed nearly as alien as one in New York or Boston. Among Quakers, there were additional ties to Pennsylvania, for the Philadelphia Yearly Meeting was the only institutional organization they had.[67] To be an eastern Virginian was to share in a mystique; among people of the Great Valley it was a residential address.

Valley trade patterns in the 1780s reinforced the Pennsylvania connection. Until the Potomac was cleared, Valley trade followed the Great Philadelphia Wagon Road to its terminus at Lancaster, though increasingly some of this overland traffic was siphoned off by Baltimore. Alexandria merchants did their best to penetrate the Valley, even to the extent of sending German-speaking agents, but they did not do well until a road was opened across Loudoun County to Winchester in the 1790s.[68]

The Valley had a limestone floor that yielded a slightly alkaline soil ideal for pasture and grains. Berkeley County, reported Washington's roving observer David Stuart, "in point of fertility is without doubt the richest in the state." Even the worst lands fetched better than £1 per acre in 1791 (about equal to the state average) and the best went for £4 or £5. Lands throughout the lower Valley were valued at double those east of the Blue Ridge once river and road outlets were opened in the 1790s.[69] The explosive growth of the Shenandoah between the end of the Revolution and 1800 is shown in table 1.10, derived from Frederick County tax lists.[70] Like Fairfax across the mountains, Frederick grew very rapidly in the 1780s, increasing its population by half, and though the rate slowed somewhat in the succeeding decade, it was still impressive. Like Fairfax it grew in wealth as fast as in population, as indicated by the

TABLE 1.10   WEALTH DISTRIBUTION IN THE SHENANDOAH VALLEY: FREDERICK COUNTY, 1782–1800

	Heads of Households					
A. Size of Farms (acres)	1782		1790		1800	
1–24	4	1%	21	2%	69	5%
25–99	46	7	83	9	167	13
100–299	353	54	506	55	710	53
300–599	180	29	222	25	272	20
600–999	34	5	45	5	66	5
1,000+	31	4	34	4	44	4
	648	100%	911	100%	1,328	100%
			1790		1800	
B. Slaves Held	1782		(50% sample)		(50% sample)	
0	1,021	80%	810	82%	914	80%
1–4	136	10.5	116	11	145	13
5–12	78	6	44	4	54	5
13–24	27	2	7	1	18	2
25–49	18	1.5	7	1	3	
50–99	4		0		1	
	1,284	100%	974	100%	1,135	100%

SOURCE: Frederick County Land and Personalty Books, 1782, 1790, 1800, VaSL.

increase in the number of landed wealthy. The number of landless taxpayers, a comparatively high 40 percent of all in 1782, rose to 50 percent in 1790, but then dropped to 30 percent in 1800. That four-fifths of all farmers remained slaveless, despite increases in wealth, suggests again the aversion to the institution among westerners.

Frederick and Berkeley, it must be admitted, were richer than most Valley counties. Blessed with an extraordinary soil and an industrious people, and serving the urban needs first of Winchester and later of Alexandria, they had unique advantages. Rockingham County, at the headwaters of the Shenandoah, was laced with ridges, the highest of which (Massanutten Mountain) split the county in two. Comparatively little of Rockingham was tillable, and as late as 1795 a traveler described it as heavily forested with large numbers of cattle roaming the woods. It grew at about the same pace as Frederick, from 1,500 tithables in 1781 to 2,100 in 1790 and about 2,400 in 1800, but there was not the same evidence of wealth. The slave population grew from 25 percent to 30 percent of the total in Frederick, but it remained about 10 percent in Rockingham.[71]

Moving north into Shenandoah County, the same traveler noted that more of the land was under cultivation, and more farmers were growing wheat. But there was still no comparison with Frederick. In Frederick farm buildings were tidy, crops were varied, fields manured, and cattle penned.[72] Frederick and Berkeley also seemed to differ from their neighbors in having a sizable tenant class. Frederick's landless class, totaling 40 to 50 percent of the population, was unusually high for the west, and travelers commented on the number of tenants in the lower Valley. They were actually sharecroppers, because of the shortage of currency; the landlord simply got one-third of each tenant's produce.[73] Tenantry was probably a carryover from the Fairfax proprietary, where lands were more often rented than sold. The proportion of landless was higher in the Northern Neck and lower Valley than elsewhere in Virginia.

Like western Maryland, the Shenandoah Valley voted debtor through much of the 1780s and then supported the Constitution in 1788. Frederick and Berkeley remained firmly Federalist until the end of the 1790s; Shenandoah and Rockingham drifted rather early into the Republican column.

THE WESTERN VALLEYS

West of the Great Valley there were only two patches of settlement at the end of the Revolution—the South Branch of the Potomac and the Greenbriar Valley in central West Virginia.[74] The Potomac River forks just below Cumberland, Maryland. The state boundary follows the North Branch to its "first fountain," as per Maryland's colonial charter. The South Branch drains a narrow but rich valley across the North Mountains from the Shenandoah, embracing Hampshire, Hardy, and Pendleton counties. West of the Allegheny divide there were some settlements on the Monongahela and its tributary, the Cheat River, but these generally looked downriver toward Pittsburgh, or traded overland via Braddock's Road with Cumberland, Maryland. At the end of the war the assembly appropriated funds for a road from Winchester to Romney in Hampshire County and on to Morgantown on the Monongahela, but it was some years before it could carry wagon traffic.[75]

The South Branch had a limestone soil ideal for grass and grain. Since wheat production was out of the question until the Potomac was cleared for flour rafts, South Branch residents turned to cattle raising. Indeed, the valley was famed for its cattle. Shortly after the war Matthew Patton purchased some English long-horned cattle, which he crossed with local stock. The resulting "Patton stock" became a favorite among western cattlemen for its size and milk capacity.[76] But even before Patton's innovation, the valley was raising huge quantities of beef cattle. A Hampshire tax list of 1784 gives a total of 10,631 cattle for the county, and the distribution of them may be the best index of social structure. The same tax list contains only 530 slaves. In a ranching economy, except for the very biggest operations, slaves were probably not worth the investment (table 1.11).[77]

Assuming that four cattle were enough to keep an ordinary family in milk and meat, a reasonable inference is that those possessed of more than four were raising for the market. Involved in the market, then, were some 60 percent of all Hampshire county farmers. The western valleys were not as remote and isolated as

TABLE 1.11   WEALTH DISTRIBUTION IN THE SOUTH
BRANCH:
HAMPSHIRE COUNTY, 1784

Cattle	Taxpayers		Slaves	Taxpayers	
0	88	8%	0	921	87%
1–4	355	34	1–2	66	7
5–12	421	41	3–4	33	3
13–24	125	11.5	5–7	16	1.5
25–49	53	4.5	8–12	13	1.5
50–99	9	1	13–24	3	
100+	1				
	1,052	100%		1,052	100%

SOURCE: Hampshire County Personalty Book, 1784, VaSL.

they might appear from a map. Moreover, once the Potomac was cleared, wheat became a major crop, with flour boated down the South Branch on the spring flood.[78] Commercially dependent on Alexandria and later Washington, D.C., populated by migrants from the North, its perception of Virginia filtered through Federalist Winchester, the South Branch politically was the most firmly Federalist part of the state. It was still sending Federalists to the assembly in the War of 1812.

The Greenbriar River arose just across the ridge from the upper springs of the South Branch. It flowed south at first until, joining the New River, it turned northwest to the Kanawha. The valley is narrow and rocky, in places a mere gorge. Its only contact with the outside world was by road, past the warm springs, to Staunton in the Great Valley. Until transportation facilities were improved, cattle raising and horses seem to have been the main occupation. A tax list of 1783 credits the county with 7,941 cattle in a population of some 1,400 taxpayers. Both the number of slaves (a mere 345) and the distribution of cattle suggests more poverty here than in the South Branch. Fifteen percent of the Greenbriar taxpayers possessed no cattle at all, and a mere 2 percent owned more than 25 (as against 5.5 percent in Hampshire). On the other hand, 67 percent owned 5 cattle or more, and presumably drove the surplus east to market. The list specifically described the cattle as "neat," which were horned animals raised for beef.[79]

Greenbriar at the end of the Revolution was still raw frontier subject to Indian raids. Nor was it growing much. The census of 1790 credited it with a mere 319 slaves and 6,015 inhabitants.[80] Like Maryland's northern frontier, Greenbriar's development lay in the distant future. Politically, it voted debtor through the 1780s, backed the Constitution (probably in the hope of getting federal aid against the Indians), and divided its vote thereafter.

LAND VALUES AND POLITICS

The pattern for the northern Chesapeake is fairly clear. Those regions with certain natural endowments—fertile soil, cheap transportation, proximity to urban markets—usually elected assembly delegates who were fiscally orthodox. Those lacking these advantages were debtor-minded. Their delegates often voted to postpone taxes, delay debt collection, or inflate the money supply. Land values were the common denominator of endowments, and the correlation between land values and voting behavior was quite extraordinary.

There were, however, additional factors. In some counties, such as Worcester and Montgomery, Maryland, or Fairfax, Virginia, control by a wealthy elite was probably more important than overall growth. Immigrant populations, such as in the Shenandoah and South Branch valleys, were more cosmopolitan in outlook and less loyal to their state of residence. Westerners in general viewed the east with suspicion, and often looked to the national government for help.

In general, these same factors shaped voting attitudes in the tobacco country south of the Rappahannock.

CHAPTER TWO

The Landscape and the People, from the Rappahannock to Cape Fear

SOUTH OF THE RAPPAHANNOCK RIVER was tobacco country. Northern Virginia had virtually abandoned tobacco by the end of the Revolution. The Piedmont would give it up in the 1790s. But in the valley of the James River, and southward from there into the Carolina Piedmont, tobacco remained the cash crop. Tobacco from the region had long commanded a higher price than that grown in northern Virginia or Maryland. As a result, it competed successfully with wheat. That region is still the nation's "tobacco belt" today.

Table 2.1 is derived from export statistics kept by the governor's office after the Revolution. They show the overwhelming importance of tobacco in Virginia's trade, even when its price was declining. The price decline was due less to depression (which apparently did not affect commodity prices before 1786) than to the fact that tobacco was overpriced at the end of the war.[1] North Carolina products, shipped out through Petersburg and Norfolk,

TABLE 2.1 VIRGINIA EXPORTS IN THE 1780s

pril–April bacco	1783–1784	1784–1785	1785–1786	1790–1791
Hogsheads	4,957	11,161	10,486	56,288
Price/unit	£20	£15	£12	(est.) £10
Value	£99,140	£167,415	£125,796	(est.) £562,880
% total value	68%	67%	44%	(est.) 54%
ur				
Barrels	12,532	19,020	25,622	76,350
Price/unit	£2	£2	£2	(est.) £2
Value	£25,064	£38,040	£51,244	(est.) £152,700
% total value	17%	15%	18%	(est.) 15%
eat				
Bushels	34,726	102,906	93,396	305,070
Price/unit	7s.	7s.	7s.	(est.) 7s.
Value	£12,154	£36,017	£32,688	(est.) £106,774
% total value	8%	14%	11%	(est.) 10%
n				
Bushels	31,950	11,882	37,484	387,142
Price/unit	5s.	5s.	6s.	(est.) 6s.
Value	£7,888	£2,970	£11,245	(est.) £116,142
% total value	5%	1%	4%	(est.) 11%
er Exports				
Value	£1,924	£7,250	£67,828	(est.) £105,493
% total value	2%	3%	23%	(est.) 10%
al Value	£146,170	£251,692	£288,801	£1,043,989 ($3,132,000)

RCES: *Calendar of Virginia State Papers and Other Manuscripts,* 11 vols. (Richmond, 5–93), III, 575, IV, 121; *American State Papers,* Class IV, Commerce and Navigation, Is. (Washington, 1832–34), I, 148–55.

inflate the statistics to some extent. The steady increase in "other" exports (mainly turpentine, lumber, and pork) probably reflects increases in North Carolina output. Down to 1786, when the governor's office unaccountably stopped keeping statistics, Virginia had an annual trade surplus. Because most of its goods moved in foreign ships, however, the state's total balance of payments was probably about even. Tobacco, so often denounced as the ruin of Virginia, was in fact its salvation.[2]

Travelers who were accustomed to the tidy countryside of Europe found the Chesapeake landscape wild and desolate. Abandoned fields, full of half-grown trees and brush, were considered signs of American ignorance and laziness. Travelers blamed tobacco for exhausting the soil, and they blamed planters for failing to restore it with manure. In fact, the agricultural system was more complex than they suspected, and, though untidy in appearance, it was efficient.

The red and yellow clay soils of southern Virginia and North Carolina were reasonably fertile, but they needed care. The warm climate meant a long growing season, but that left little time for the land to rest so that worms and microorganisms could restore its fertility. Predominantly clay, the soils were short of organic matter, or humus, and minerals easily washed through (or "leached"). This left the soil more acidic, which, in turn, discouraged bacterial activity. The result was a downward cycle, called podzolization.

Lime and manure could restore the land, but the virtues of lime ("marl") were not yet widely known. And it simply did not pay to collect manure. It was not, as travelers suspected, that Americans were too lazy. Clearing new land, after all, was harder work than collecting manure (land clearers in the 1790s charged £1 an acre). Manure collection required penning cattle, and that would have involved clearing additional lands for pasture and hay. It was cheaper to abandon worn-out fields and pasture the cattle on the resulting brush. Worn-out fields, moreover, did not stay worn out. They gradually recovered fertility and could be cultivated again after a few years. In the meantime, cattle grazing held back the forest.[3]

Tobacco consumed labor, not land. Even the largest estates put

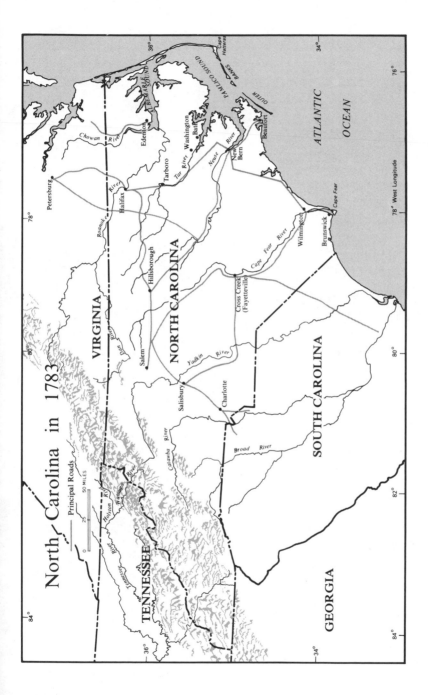

North Carolina in 1783

Principal Roads

0   25   50 MILES

only about 20 acres annually into tobacco, and even that amount took the labor of 20 slaves. By common estimate, a slave could cultivate an acre of tobacco a year, though this probably referred to a productive effort that was in addition to the cultivation of corn and garden crops needed to sustain him/her. An acre produced, on the average, a hogshead (1,000 pounds) of tobacco.

Because of the time and labor involved in clearing land, only a small fraction of each plantation was under cultivation. And most of that was devoted to corn, cereals, cotton, flax, and garden crops needed to sustain the labor force. Meadows were unknown, except in areas where Indians had created prairie by burning.[4] Cattle and hogs roamed freely in the woods. Because of the mild winters there was no need even to store hay for them. All this made the Virginia-Carolina countryside appear unkempt, but the system had its own internal logic.

Travelers usually accompanied their report on the landscape with observations on the poverty of the people, often associating the two.[5] Poverty was more prevalent in the country south of the Rappahannock, but the reason was not laziness or soil exhaustion: it was isolation. Except in the lower reaches of the great rivers, the inhabitants of southern Virginia and North Carolina had no ready access to markets. Rivers were shallow and rocky. Most transport went overland at high cost. As a result, money was scarce. People, for the most part, were debtor-minded and provincial.

MIDDLE TIDEWATER, FROM THE RAPPAHANNOCK TO THE JAMES

Virginia's great rivers—the Potomac, Rappahannock, York, and James—widen into estuaries of Chesapeake Bay. Ocean-going vessels can sail them for more than a hundred miles to ports at the head of navigation, the falls of the rivers. Alexandria, Fredericksburg, Richmond, and Petersburg were all located on the "fall line" that separated the interior from the sea. Below the fall line the rivers drift so gently into the sea that they are affected by tides for many miles inland. Thus the coastal plain between the rivers is commonly called the Tidewater.

The Tidewater counties along the James closely resembled the Northern Neck. Although it was the oldest settled portion of Virginia, it was still under extensive cultivation in the 1780s. Planters here apparently found it was more profitable to care for their lands than abandon them. Unlike the Northern Neck, however, James River planters were still growing tobacco. Their soil yielded a special "sweet scented" variety that was especially prized for snuff. As a result, it commanded about two shillings per hundredweight more than any other kind. The price of bottom lands along the James (£4 to £6 an acre) was higher than anywhere else in Virginia, except the lower Shenandoah Valley (Frederick and Berkeley lands commonly went for £6 to £11 an acre).[6]

Long settled and extensively developed, the lower James was not expanding in population, but the level of wealth was high. Elizabeth City County, which included the village of Hampton, had 252 taxables in 1783 and 265 in 1787. Of its planters, 74 percent owned slaves, the highest proportion anywhere in the Chesapeake. Yet plantations were not large. No one owned more than 50 slaves, and only the Cary family had more than 1,000 acres. Slaveholding declined a bit over the decade, but in 1790 it was still 70 percent. The York River counties to the north were nearly as prosperous. In Gloucester, 68 percent of the planters owned slaves in 1782, and 2 percent had more than 50.[7] Like the planters in similar circumstances in the Northern Neck and in Maryland, the men of the lower Tidewater were creditor-minded and Federalist.

To the north and west toward the fall line the countryside appeared less developed. Travelers along the road from Fredericksburg to Richmond reported that the soil was sandy and the forest cover mostly pine. To people with an eye for land (George Washington, for instance) pines were a sign of poor soil. They seemed to be the only tree that could survive in sand barrens, and where they took root in good land they soaked up the nutrients, leaving it acidic and infertile. Hanover Court House, the only market town between Fredericksburg and Richmond, lay on a tributary of the York River. Because the river could handle only small vessels, Hanover sent its tobacco overland. Occasionally hogsheads were carried by wagon, but most often they were rolled along the roads, with poles driven through the casks to serve as axles. A German visitor noted that Hanover shippers used mules for the purpose, adding that Americans liked these animals "because they are so perfectly adapted for the American economy, thriving with scant attention and bad feed."[8]

An enterprising student of Hanover history has left us a valuable means of examining the county's development. He listed all the taxpayers in one of the county's parishes between 1782 and 1815, and he traced the personalty holdings of each through those years.[9] This valuable work makes it possible to look at social mobility in the decades with which we are chiefly concerned, the 1780s and 1790s. Using slaveholding as the principal index of wealth, a total of 184 (23 percent) Hanover planters improved their lot in the course of the 1780s, 335 (43 percent) stayed the same, and 267 (34 percent) lost slaves. In the following decade, when the nation as a whole was more prosperous, 281 (32 percent) improved their lot, 449 (51 percent) stayed the same, and 147 (17 percent) lost. These figures are the more remarkable when it is noted that the county as a whole seemed to be expanding. The number of taxables increased from 780 in 1782 to 1,217 in 1786 and 1,402 in 1788. Slaves over the age of 16 rose from 3,415 in 1783 to 3,653 in 1788.[10] With opportunities so limited one might have expected a greater outmigration. It does show, however, that in a long-settled rural society there was little or no improvement in per capita wealth, even in good times.

The stability may also explain why this part of the Tidewater was evenly divided politically during the 1780s. Of the men who represented Hanover in the House of Delegates during the decade, only one improved his fortune. Three lost ground during the 1780s; four remained the same. Unfortunately, only one (a debtor party man) voted enough times to be identified politically. The wealthy generally were either declining or holding their own in the 1780s. Most of those who improved their lot were small slaveholders. And most who seemed to stay the same were nonslaveholders. These changes affected the social structure of the county. In 1784 60 percent of the taxpayers owned slaves. In 1790 72 percent were slaveholders. Yet the wealthy (those owning 13 slaves or more) declined from 11 percent of the total in 1784 to 4 percent.[11] It may well be that in this part of the Chesapeake, the rich were the debtor-minded.

THE VIRGINIA PIEDMONT

West of the fall line the land became more hilly as it rose toward the Blue Ridge. Oak and other hardwoods ruled the landscape. Even in the 1790s a traveler reported that three-fourths of Orange County, Madison's home, was "in a state of nature." Rivers were swift and narrow, navigable only for canoes, which were lashed together to carry tobacco hogsheads. The rivers carved their way through the hills, so bottom lands were scarce. Because tobacco grown on the uplands was considered inferior, those soils were given to wheat and corn. When the bottom lands wore out at the end of the 1780s, tobacco culture was abandoned.[12]

For an analysis of Piedmont social structure, Albemarle County, Thomas Jefferson's home, may be taken as typical. Before the Revolution it had grown rapidly, reflecting the overall development of the Piedmont. Tax lists surviving from the 1760s suggest that around 25 percent of its planters owned fewer than 100 acres; only 5 percent were in the 1,000-acre bracket.[13] In 1782, a mere 7.5 percent possessed fewer than 100 acres, while 10 percent owned 1,000 or more. But such per capita improvement slowed to a halt in the 1780s. The distribution of lands remained substantially the same. Slaveholders lost ground. In 1782, 54 percent of the taxpayers owned slaves; by 1790 the number had slipped to 50 percent. Those owning more than 12 slaves declined from 9 percent in 1782 to 4 percent in 1790. The total number of slaves in the county fell from 4,409 in 1782 to 2,797 in 1787. Nearly everyone in Albemarle, it would seem, was selling slaves in the 1780s.[14] Albemarle, together with the rest of the Piedmont, voted debtor in the assembly.

THE SOUTHWEST

Land prices in Augusta County, across the Blue Ridge from Albemarle, were double those of the Piedmont, apparently because the soil was richer. Like the Shenandoah region to the north, this part of the Great Valley had a limestone floor with soil ideal for grains and grasses of all kinds. But it also had serious transportation problems. Augusta and its neighbors, Bath and Rockbridge, contained the headwaters of the James, a succession of tributaries (Maury, Jackson, Cowpasture, Calfpasture, Bullpasture) each with its own narrow valley. The rivers were swift and deep, but the watergap at the Peaks of Otter, where the James broke through the Blue Ridge, was too rocky for anything but skillfully paddled canoes. Valley farmers with a market surplus shipped it overland to Richmond. Hemp was the favored cash crop. Tobacco was considered too risky because an entire year's effort could be lost in the hazardous overland trek.[15] Even hemp had its risks. Zachariah Johnston, Augusta's most prominent citizen, lost the better part of his crop one year when heavy rains soaked it on the road to Richmond and it rotted.[16]

The southwest, like the Shenandoah Valley, was settled in ethnic patches. Augusta and Rockbridge were predominantly Scots-Irish and native Virginian, with only a sprinkling of Germans (most in the northern half of Augusta). Farther to the southwest, Botetourt, Wythe, and Montgomery counties were predominantly German. The southwestern counties were the most remote of all, for even the water outlets—the Roanoke, the Holston, and the Clinch—flowed into North Carolina or Tennessee. The Germans clung to the valley, though, because they were familiar with black limestone soils. Migrants from Pennsylvania, most of them, they did not know what to do with the red clay of the Piedmont.[17]

Valley delegates normally voted with the debtor party in the 1780s, but they had little in common with the debtor delegates from east of the mountains. Valley residents maintained commercial contact with Pennsylvania via the Great Wagon Road, and they looked to Philadelphia for religious leadership. They supported the Constitution in 1788, and remained Federalist thereafter. Heavily German Botetourt, Bedford, and Wythe counties were still sending Federalists to the assembly in 1812.

A 1788 tax list for Russell County at the southwestern tip of Virginia reveals a society of poor farmers. Half the landowners possessed from 1 to 300 acres. Only 5 percent owned more than

1,000. The list also reveals a huge landless population, probably squatting on the estates of nonresident speculators. A comparison of personalty and realty lists indicates that 61 percent of the taxpayers owned no land. There were only a half dozen slaves in the entire county.[18] A recent study of neighboring Montgomery County throws more light on society in the southwestern valleys. Netti Schreiner-Yantis found that 60 percent of the persons paying taxes in 1788 had arrived in the county after 1782. From 1788 to 1789 total population stayed about the same, but there was enormous turnover. Ten percent of the families moved away every year and another 10 percent moved in. A fifth of those who departed had no taxable property, not even a horse. In a number of cases the tax list recorded their destination—73 went to North Carolina, 29 moved elsewhere in Virginia, 7 went to South Carolina or Georgia, and 5 went to Kentucky.[19]

If Montgomery and Russell were typical, the extreme southwest was a society governed by the few. The majority of people were landless or transient. Six men represented Russell County in the House of Delegates between 1787 and 1795. All six resided in the county when it was formed and remained there for the succeeding decade. All were substantially wealthier than the county average. Not one owned less than 300 acres, and two held over 1,000. Three increased their holdings over the decade, three stayed the same. Yet they reflected the interests of their less well-to-do constituents. Only one (the wealthiest) became a Federalist; the rest were Antifederalists in 1788 and Jeffersonian Republicans thereafter.

VIRGINIA'S SOUTHSIDE

The counties south of the James River were Virginia's poverty belt. The land was hilly and easily eroded; the soil was thin and fragile. The German farmers who stayed in the western valley, despite their remoteness, knew their land. Even in mountainous Botetourt, the price of farmland was four times what it was in Campbell County east of the Blue Ridge.[20] George Washington who toured the region in 1791, noted a marked deterioration in the landscape on crossing the James. From Richmond to Petersburg the road passed through "a poor country principally covered with pine, except the interval lands along the river." The inhabitants informed him that pine when mixed with oak and hickory did not necessarily indicate poor land, but Washington was unconvinced. "From Petersburg to Halifax," he continued, "are but few good houses, with small appearance of wealth. The lands are cultivated in tobacco, corn, wheat, & oats, but tobacco & the raising of pork for market seems to be the principal dependence of the Inhabitants."[21]

Tobacco was indeed the main market crop, and it remained so. In 1796, when the Tidewater and northern Piedmont had long since abandoned tobacco, inspectors in one Campbell County warehouse claimed they handled more tobacco than any other warehouse in the state. As late as 1845, tiny Farmville, county seat of Prince Edward, claimed to be the fourth largest tobacco market in the state. and even at that date it was still shipping the crop by wagon to Richmond.[22]

Except for the James, the rivers of the Southside were too small to be of use. Farmville was on the Appomatox River, but it was 140 miles from there to Petersburg by water and one stretch of the river contained a mile and a half of rocks. The Appomatox was not cleared even for flatboats until 1801.[23] The Roanoke River was navigable, except for the falls at Halifax, North Carolina, but it flowed southeast into Albemarle Sound, which had only limited access to the sea because of the Outer Banks. Other streams, such as the Meherrin and the Nottoway, served only to separate counties and delay overland travelers. Thus the Southside's two main sources of income, pork and tobacco, had to be shipped overland, and the cost took a heavy toll of profits. From Pittsylvania County on the Carolina border to Manchester on the James (opposite Richmond) the cost of hauling a hogshead of tobacco in 1784 was £3 3s. 7½ d.—about 25 percent of the value of the hogshead.[24] The poorer farmers rolled their own tobacco, but that took time. From Henry County, to the west of Pittsylvania, it was a hundred miles by road to Lynchburg on the James. The round trip by horse required several weeks.[25]

Iron ore was mined in several places south of the James, and there was a large bed of coal in Chesterfield County, just twelve miles from Richmond. It was apparently used for home heating, for one sensitive traveler complained that the whole city smelled of coal smoke.[26] Richmond, situated at the falls of the James, was the hub that joined Tidewater, Piedmont, and Southside. It contained 280 houses and about 2,000 inhabitants at the end of the Revolution. Because of its strategic location, the site had been peopled since the beginning of the century, but the city was not formally incorporated until 1782. The capital had been moved there from Williamsburg during the war. Its unpaved streets were muddy in wet weather and dusty the rest of the time. The tobacco warehouse handled 15,000 hogsheads annually, but Richmond itself was not a port. Ocean-going vessels could sail only to Bermuda Hundred, a few miles below the falls of the James. That depot handled the trade of both Richmond and Petersburg. Federal export statistics, beginning in 1790, indicate that it was the busiest port in the state (handling a third of all Virginia exports), with Norfolk second and Alexandria third.[27]

Petersburg, at the falls of the Appomatox River, was slightly larger than Richmond at the end of the Revolution, boasting about 300 houses and 2,500 inhabitants. Its trade radius extended into the North Carolina Piedmont; hence it was the largest tobacco market in the nation. Its warehouse annually inspected 20,000 to 25,000 hogsheads in the 1780s. Most of its trade went through Bermuda Hundred, however, for only small vessels capable of carrying 60 hogsheads could get up the Appomatox.[28]

East of Petersburg, the road to Smithfield, the next town of any size, passed through a pine woods. The sandy soil had long since become exhausted and returned to forest. Corn and wheat were grown in the bottom lands along the river. These still sold for £4 to £6 an acre; all else went for 5 to 10 shillings. Smithfield, located on a small tributary of the James, still had a tobacco warehouse at the end of the Revolution, but its main exports were tar, pitch, and turpentine.[29] Suffolk, twenty miles south of Petersburg, and only sixteen miles from the North Carolina line, subsisted on the North Carolina trade. The Nansemond River was navigable for small vessels to that point, and it handled annually some 8 to 10 thousand barrels of tar and turpentine. Both it and Smithfield also exported large amounts of North Carolina pork.[30]

Norfolk, commanding the mouth of the James River as well as the entrance to Chesapeake Bay, was a bustling seaport. The Elizabeth River, where its docks lay, was deep enough to accommodate the largest of vessels. The smaller vessels that plied the rivers and inlets of the southern coast usually brought their cargoes there for transhipment. It dominated the coastal trade from the Rappahannock to Cape Fear. It had been hard hit by the war, however, burned by both sides. Many of the Scottish merchants who dominated its trade before the war had fled. At 2,000 inhabitants in 1782, it was about the size of Richmond.[31] The city was rebuilt rapidly after the war, however, and by 1790 its commerce was thriving. Together with its neighbor to the east, Princess Anne, Norfolk County consistently took a creditor stance in the assembly and supported the Federal Constitution in 1788. Princess Anne prospered during the Revolution, possibly because of wartime trade. A surviving 1775 tax list for Princess Anne offers a rare look at wartime growth. In 1775 only 33 percent of the residents owned slaves, and a mere 2 percent held 13 or more. In 1782, 44 percent were slaveowners, and 6 percent held 13 or more. The number of small slaveholders (owning 5 to 12) increased by half during the war.[32] Growth continued in the 1780s, but at a slower pace. Slightly more than half the planters were slaveowners in 1790. Norfolk and Princess Anne were rare success stories, however. The rest of the Southside was on the decline.

Let us use Charlotte County for a closer examination of wealth distribution and economic development in the Southside. Located some forty miles southwest of Richmond, it was neither in the oldest-settled area nor the newest. Gross figures given by the tax collectors indicate a steady growth in population, both white and black. The number of slaves over the age of 16 increased from 1,626 in 1783 to 2,189 in 1790 and 2,770 in 1800.[33] Most other counties south of the James experienced similar population growth.

Economic growth did not match population growth, however. In Charlotte there was a slight increase in the number of small landholders (see table 2.2), but most of the newcomers (including

TABLE 2.2 WEALTH DISTRIBUTION IN VIRGINIA'S SOUTHSIDE:
CHARLOTTE COUNTY, 1783–1800

	Heads of Households					
1. Size of Farms (acres)	1783		1790		1800	
1–99	58	8%	79	11%	135	16°
100–299	329	48	318	44.5	423	49
300–599	180	26	199	28	187	22
600–999	74	11	68	9.5	54	6
1,000+	47	7	48	7	57	7
	688	100%	712	100%	856	100°
2. Slaves Held	1783		1790		1800	
0	261	36.5%	486	46%	478	42°
1–4	204	29	294	28	406	36
5–12	169	24	246	23	206	18
13–24	54	7.5	26	2	39	3.
25–49	21	3	4	1	6	.
50–99	1		1		1	
	710	100%	1,057	100%	1,136	100°

SOURCE: Charlotte County Land and Personalty Books, 1783, 1790, 1800, VaSL.

young men coming of age) were unable to obtain land. The number of landless, a paltry 3 percent in 1783, rose to 33 percent in 1790. There was a similar rise in the number of nonslaveholders. While the poor failed to gain, the wealthy actually slipped backward. Planters owning 13 slaves or more made up 10 percent of the population in 1783 but only 3 percent in 1790. The acreage figures suggest that they were not selling land or moving away, but they were selling slaves. The middling planters, their ranks swelled by the fallen rich, held their own during the 1780s, but the general picture is one of economic depression. If Charlotte was typical of Southside counties, it is little wonder that the cry for debtor relief was so loud in that area. It came from the most vocal segment of the population—the wealthy. The situation stabilized somewhat in the 1790s. The number of landless declined to 25 percent, and the number of small slaveholders increased sharply. But the wealthy barely held their own. Charlotte clearly reached the peak of its development by the end of the Revolution (perhaps before). Growth thereafter was slow, and in times of depression it was sharply reversed.

RELIGIOUS SECTIONALISM IN VIRGINIA

There was one other factor contributing to sectional differentiation in Virginia—religion. We have already noted that religion reinforced the ethnic consciousness of the Shenandoah Valley. It also helped distinguish Tidewater from Piedmont and both from the Southside. At the end of the Revolution there were only 91 Anglican clergymen in the entire state, even though Anglicanism was the church established by law. The Church of England almost completely disappeared in the counties south of the James. Anglican ministers either left the area or called themselves "Independents." One held on in Lunenburg for a time, but even members of his own vestry refused to attend services.[34]

Most Anglican churches after the Revolution were in the Tidewater, but a few lingered in the Piedmont. Louisa County had three Episcopal churches functioning in the 1780s, and so did Goochland.[35] In Orange, on the other hand, all four Anglican ministers departed. In 1786, one of the vestries, headed by James Madison, Sr., asked a Presbyterian minister to conduct services. He did so for two years.[36]

The Tidewater not only clung to the Anglican Establishment; it resisted dissenting churches. Reverend Samuel Davies brought Presbyterianism to eastern Virginia before the Revolution, but his "Hanover revival" did not win much support below the fall line. Even in heavily Scottish Norfolk, there were only two churches at the end of the Revolution, both Anglican.[37] Quakers and Methodists came over from the Eastern Shore of Maryland, but their influence was spotty.[38]

The Piedmont was more mixed in religion. Along with its three Episcopal churches, Louisa had one Presbyterian and two Baptist churches and a Quaker meetinghouse. Goochland's three Anglican congregations competed with three Baptist ones. In addition to its Presbyterian/Episcopal congregation, Orange had a sizable contingent of Baptists, all in one section of the county.[39]

The region south of the James belonged to Methodists and Baptists. The Brunswick Circuit, organized in Petersburg in 1774, was the first formal Methodist organization in America. It sent itinerant ministers throughout south-central Virginia and along the Roanoke Valley of North Carolina. Within two years it claimed 1,600 communicants. Methodist churches were built throughout southern Virginia during the war.

The Baptists were descendants of the Great Awakening, "new light" Presbyterians and Congregationalists who had embraced adult baptism as a symbol of spiritual rebirth. Baptist itinerants appeared in Virginia as early as the 1760s, but their converts were slow to organize. Greensville County, for instance, had two Methodist churches by 1783, but no Baptist church was built until 1787.[40] The Baptists spread rapidly after the Revolution, however, and by 1790 they claimed 200 congregations and 20,000 communicants.[41] The majority, it seems likely, were south of the James.

An early historian of the Great Awakening claimed that Baptists were traditionally opposed to government because the colonial regime had denied them religious freedom.[42] That may have been true, but there is no direct evidence linking Baptists or Methodists with Antifederalism. The areas where they were strongest—Piedmont and Southside—were debtor-minded and localist, but for other reasons. Religion, however, probably reinforced regional consciousness and thus contributed indirectly to the political tensions within the state.

NORTH CAROLINA'S SEACOAST AND TRADE

"More churches than anywhere else in America." That was the best thing that one traveler could say about the road south from Smithfield into North Carolina. Otherwise the landscape was an "ocean of trees." Dwellings and patches of cultivation were "scattered about in these woods at various distances, 3–6 miles, and often as much as 10–15–20 miles apart."[43] There was no relief from the never-ending pine forest until the wayfarer reached the town of Edenton on the northwest corner of Albermarle Sound. The road from Williamsburg to Edenton was, until the Revolution, the main overland artery between the north and Charleston, South Carolina. At Edenton the traveler took ship across Albemarle Sound, and on the south shore picked up a stage to Wilmington. From there a packet vessel carried him on to Charleston. The route was tedious, however, because of the numerous estuaries of the Carolina coast. One traveler complained that a trip from Petersburg to Wilmington scheduled to take eight days actually required thirteen, and the stage was so unreliable that he had to rent horses much of the way.[44]

After the Revolution, overland trade shifted to the west to avoid the widest part of the Carolina rivers. The Southern Stage, established in 1786, ran from Richmond to Wilmington by way of Halifax and Tarboro, North Carolina.[45] Because of swamps along the coast, the only route from Wilmington to Charleston, South Carolina, was by ship. Those determined to avoid the sea veered west to Fayetteville to pick up a road to Charleston.

Bad as the overland routes were, they were still the best contact North Carolina had with the world. Its seacoast was blocked by a narrow strip of sand reef that extended from near the Virginia line to treacherous Cape Hatteras. Inside these Outer Banks lay the major sounds, Albemarle and Pamlico. The sandy reef was broken in several places, but the only inlets capable of handling seagoing vessels were "Old Topsail" and Ocracoke, each with a draft of about nine feet. Any ship that drew more than that had to unload part of its cargo at the inlet, from whence it was "lightered" into port by smaller vessels. The enterprising Blount brothers built a warehouse at the inlet, but even so the transfers added considerably to freight charges. Located at the southern end of the reef, the inlets were convenient enough for ports on Pamlico Sound, but they were 180 miles from Albemarle. Edenton merchants claimed that it took as long to reach the Atlantic at Ocracoke as it did to sail from there to New York or the West Indies.[46] As a result, most of Albemarle's trade went overland to Virginia.

Along the coast of both Albemarle and Pamlico sounds are

TABLE 2.3   EXPORTS FROM THE CHESAPEAKE, OCTOBER 1790–
SEPTEMBER 1791

	Maryland	Virginia	North Carolina
Tobacco			
(hhds.)	25,000	56,000	4,700
		(41,000)	(19,700)
Wheat (bu.)	205,000	305,000	1,780
Flour (bbls.)	151,000	76,000	3,000
Corn (bu.)	205,000	387,000	213,000
Tar, pitch, turpentine			
(bbls.)	7,000	17,000	32,000
Barrel staves	1,500,000	9,000,000	2,000,000
Shingles	1,900,000	23,700,000	24,700,000
Pine boards			
(ft.)	283,000	1,900,000	3,800,000
Total value	$2,200,000	$ 3,100,000	$ 500,000

SOURCE: *American State Papers,* Class IV, Commerce and Navigation, VII, 148–55.

vast marshes with peat soils unfit for farming. Beyond the marshes, a broad, flat coastal plain extends fifty to eighty miles into the interior, rising imperceptibly to one hundred feet above sea level at the fall line. The forest cover of the coastal plain was principally loblolly and longleaf pines, an extension of the great southern pine forest that reaches all the way to Florida and Louisiana.[47] Longleaf pines are especially rich in resin; hence they were ideal for tar and turpentine. Table 2.3, drawn from statistics compiled by the federal government in 1790, gives an idea of the importance of pine products in North Carolina's trade, as well as a comparison with its neighbors to the north. The figures are somewhat deceptive because so many of North Carolina's exports went through Virginia. One traveler, for instance, reported that the Roanoke Valley annually shipped 10,000 hogsheads of tobacco overland to Norfolk.[48] If the Piedmont sent half that much to Petersburg, North Carolina was accounting for about a fourth of the tobacco exports of those two ports. These estimates are included in parentheses in the table. There is no way of estimating the amount of naval stores or lumber exported through Virginia. Pork, which apparently was consumed in Virginia or sent to the northern states, was not a very important export item. Most of the exports credited to North Carolina went out through Wilmington, the state's one deep-water port, at the mouth of the Cape Fear River. And most of the products went to the West Indies.

The table also demonstrates how tiny North Carolina's foreign trade was. Its commerce with other states was undoubtedly much larger because its ports could handle the smaller vessels that plied the coastal trade. Even so, it is clear that North Carolina was the most isolated of all the thirteen states. And commercial isolation bred a provincial intellect. North Carolina's political elite was the equal of any in the nation, but the vast majority of citizens had little interest in external affairs. Even in Albemarle, astride the high road to the north, the inhabitants, complained one disgusted traveler, were "the most wretchedly ignorant of any I ever met with." They could not even tell him the name of the place they lived, to say nothing of adjacent places.[49] Except among groups that deliberately maintained interstate contacts—such as the Germans and Quakers of the western Piedmont—North Carolina's localism was endemic and enduring. As in Virginia, however, there were regional variations that affected the course of North Carolina politics.

NORTH CAROLINA'S ALBEMARLE

The traveler who took the western highway south from Petersburg to Halifax encountered some of the finest lands in North Carolina shortly after crossing the border. The lands along the Roanoke River were black and fertile, with topsoil several feet thick. The principal crop of the valley was tobacco, which was shipped overland to Petersburg. An English visitor who had toured a good part of the country looking for investments bought a farm on the Roanoke as soon as he saw it. For 100 acres of good bottom land he paid £200. For an adjacent tract of 450 acres he paid a more normal £50.[50] Even the relatively high price of £2 per acre reflected the area's transportation problems. Similar land on the Potomac was selling for £10 an acre.

This same Englishman described Halifax, just below the falls of the river, as "a pretty town" of about 50 houses. The river at that point was a quarter of a mile wide and deep enough to float sloops and schooners capable of carrying 200 barrels of tar or pork.[51] The river traffic was destined for the West Indies, but most of Halifax's intercourse—social as well as commercial—was with Virginia. Indeed, Virginia paper money, which was received for goods shipped to Petersburg, was the principal currency in the town.[52] In and around Halifax lived some of the most prominent creditor-nationalists in the assembly—General Allen Jones, Whitmell Hill, William R. Davie, and Benjamin Hawkins. Hawkins, a close friend of Madison's, maintained political contact with the Virginia nationalists.

On Albemarle Sound, some seventy miles below Halifax, was Edenton, conveniently situated near the mouths of both the Roanoke River and the Chowan. A village of 1,000 to 1,500 people, Edenton had prospered during the war precisely because it was safe from British naval attack. Its customary trade with the West Indies in pork and naval stores went on without interruption. After the war it began to decline, however. West Indies vessels often preferred to continue up the Roanoke to trade with wealthy Halifax. In the other direction, the Chowan River channeled local products toward Norfolk and Portsmouth. In production of naval stores Edenton yielded to ports on Pamlico Sound with more convenient access to the Atlantic.[53]

Among the long-settled counties on the north shore of Albemarle Sound the chief source of income was livestock. Cattle and pigs roamed half wild in the woods, eating pine cones and the sprouts of hardwoods. Some farmers tried to establish ownership by branding, but the animals were so plentiful there was no need. In late summer they were attracted to the settlements with corn and captured. They were then fed corn for five or six weeks before marketing. The wealthy processed their own slaughterhouses. Whitmell Hill, owner of 162 slaves, put up 800 barrels of salt pork a year, and sent them by ship to Norfolk and Baltimore. The poor drove them overland in vast herds to Suffolk, Portsmouth, and Norfolk. Sometimes professional "cattle handlers" bought them from farmers and drove them into Virginia.[54]

Albemarle was the oldest settlement in North Carolina. Surnames were mostly English; most families had come originally from Virginia. Religious persuasion was also similar to southern Virginia. Northampton County, for instance, had an Episcopal church with a withering congregation (services ending in 1800), two Baptist churches, a Methodist church, and a Friends' meetinghouse.[55] But in economic development, especially in the fertile Roanoke Valley, Albemarle differed substantially from southern Virginia.

Only a few eighteenth-century North Carolina tax lists have survived, but there are good series for two Albemarle counties, Bertie and Gates. The Bertie series even includes a pre-Revolutionary list. Bertie was a rich tobacco-growing county on the Roanoke, downriver from Halifax. Gates lay in the turpentine forest in the upper reaches of the Chowan River (see table 2.4).[56] Bertie was comparatively wealthy when the Revolution began, remained stable during the war, and then improved steadily through the 1780s and 1790s. Moreover, it grew in per capita wealth, a phenomenon rare anywhere in the Chesapeake. The growth was reflected in the acquisition of slaves; landholding changed little over the years. The landless (for whom there was a special category in North Carolina lists) were 28 percent of the total in 1784 and 30 percent in 1800. Those possessing more than 1,000 acres were 6 percent throughout the period.

Gates County was formed in 1779. It was a still-developing frontier at the end of the Revolution, and it continued to develop both in increased population and in per capita wealth. Landholding also increased, although not at the same rapid pace. The landless were 23 percent of the population in 1784 and 20 percent in 1800. Planters with 500 acres or more numbered 10 percent of the total in 1784 and 14 percent in 1800.

The long-settled counties situated on Albemarle Sound were not growing at the same rate, but they were holding their own. Table 2.5 gives a brief summary in terms of slaveholding for the two counties with the longest series of lists. Taken as a whole, the Albemarle region was the most densely settled and prosperous part of North Carolina. It was also the most firmly creditor in its political orientation during the 1780s and the only region that supported the Federal Constitution in 1788.

TABLE 2.4 SLAVE DISTRIBUTION IN UPPER ALBEMARLE:
BERTIE AND GATES COUNTIES

Bertie County								Heads of Households					
Slaves Held	1774		1784		1792		1800	
0	56%		557	58%	513	53.5%	433	46%
1–4	31		295	31	302	32	332	36
5–12	11		87	9	106	11	142	15
13+	2		21	2	36	3.5	30	3
	100%		961	100%	958	100%	937	100%

Gates County			Heads of Households					
Slaves Held	1784		1792		1800	
0	306	60.5%	321	52%	284	49%
1–4	146	30	222	36	204	36
5–12	48	9.5	65	10.5	76	13
13+	6	1	11	1.5	12	2
	506	100%	619	100%	576	100%

SOURCES: Bertie County Tax Lists, 1784, 1792, 1800; Gates County Tax Lists, 1784, 1792, 1800, Treasurer's and Comptroller's Papers, NCDH. The 1774 figures are from Merrens, *Colonial North Carolina*, pp. 76–77. I have adjusted his figures slightly to fit my categories of slaveholding.

TABLE 2.5 SLAVEHOLDING IN OLD ALBEMARLE:
CHOWAN AND PASQUOTANK COUNTIES
(SLAVEHOLDERS AS A PERCENTAGE OF TOTAL
TAXPAYERS)

Chowan	1766	1788	1794	1800
	52	51	58	49
Pasquotank		1785	1793	1801
		34	37	34

SOURCES: Chowan County Tax Lists, 1788, 1794, 1800;
Pasquotank Tax Lists, 1785, 1793, 1801, Treasurer's and
Comptroller's Papers, NCDH. The Chowan list for 1766 is
from Merrens, *Colonial North Carolina*, pp. 76–77.

TARHEELS OF PAMLICO

President Washington did not like pine trees. The road from
New Bern along Pamlico Sound to Wilmington passed through
"the most barren country I ever beheld," he recorded in his diary.[57]
But Washington was a farmer. The inhabitants of Pamlico were, for
the most part, woodsmen, and the pine tree was their living.

Turpentine was obtained by making slashes ("boxes") in the
pine trees, which bled sap during the spring and summer months.
Twice a month the flow was "dipped" from the cuts and the cuts
reopened with an ax. Most of the work was done by slaves. A single
laborer could tend 3,000 boxes spread over some 12 to 15 acres of
woods. That amount produced 100 barrels of turpentine a year.[58] If
these figures, carefully recorded by a German visitor, are correct, a
slave in the turpentine forests brought an annual cash return of £80
(at 16 s. per barrel), considerably more than the return from
tobacco growing in Virginia. The price of timberlands, moreover,
was considerably less than prime tobacco land. Pine forest sold for
£10 to £12 per hundred acres in 1783.[59]

Tar was obtained by baking a felled tree in a clay pit. "Sweated
out" of the wood, it ran through wooden pipes into buried casks.
Pitch was made by heating the tar in large iron cauldrons, three
casks of tar yielding two of pitch. Given the amount of meticulous
labor required, it is unlikely that there were any economies of scale.
A tarmaker with a couple of slaves was probably just as efficient,
worker for worker, as the operator with a hundred.[60]

Profitable though production of these naval stores seems, the Pamlico was not a rich area. Neither population nor slaveholding were on the increase; most of the towns in the region were declining. Surviving tax lists, of which there are few, indicate that three-fourths of the population in most counties had no slaves. About a fourth of all taxpayers owned no land. Onslow county on Pamlico Sound had 654 polls (who paid a capitation tax) in 1787, 629 in 1800. In 1787, 63 percent of the taxpayers had no slaves and only 5 owners had more than twelve. In 1800 the same categories were 69 percent and 2.[61]

Pamlico's problem was transportation. Its rivers were so shallow they could carry nothing but flatboats and canoes. Flatboats, little more than rafts, had to be poled because of the slow current, at a pace no faster than land travel. Canoes were made of hollowed cypress logs. Some were large enough to carry several casks of tar and even horses. The perriauger, a freight canoe enlarged by adding planking to a split and hollowed log, could carry up to 80 or 100 barrels of tar, which was also the capacity of a flatboat. Tarmakers who lived at a distance from a river rolled their casks overland to a river port, such as Tarboro.[62] At villages such as Washington at the mouth of the Tar River, the naval stores were transferred to small schooners bound for the northern states or the West Indies. Such vessels were capable of handling about 400 casks, together with some shingles (made from swamp cedars) and pine boards. Everything was thus done on a small scale, and the loading and unloading added to costs. Even with a fairly good price for naval stores, there was little incentive for investment or expansion.

Washington and the related villages on Pamlico Sound were all in a state of decline by the end of the Revolution, largely for lack of a prosperous hinterland.[63] New Bern, at the junction of the Neuse and Trent rivers, was the exception. The Neuse was navigable for small sailing ships for some fifty miles inland, thus giving it access to the interior. A public works project—the construction of Governor William Tryon's palace—started a growth cycle in the 1760s. The construction effort and the prospect that the town would become the seat of government attracted importing merchants and shopkeepers. With some 2,000 inhabitants at the end of the Revolution, New Bern was the largest town in the state, and it was still the largest in 1800.[64] Customs house accounts give an idea of the city's trade, as well as that of the entire region. In a six-month period in 1788, 75 vessels entered and cleared the port. About 30 were in the West Indies trade; only 3 sailed for Europe. The remainder headed for northern ports.[65] An exchange between William Blount of New Bern and Tench Coxe, merchant of Philadelphia, reveals the nature of this coastal trade. Coxe had sent Blount linen imported from Russia, which the New Bern merchant bartered for 75 barrels of pork. That was on its way to Philadelphia, and Blount was undertaking to collect 1,433 barrels of tar, which Coxe had ordered.[66]

Merchants such as William Blount and his brothers, Thomas of Tarboro and John Gray of Washington, were active in politics and usually took a creditor-nationalist position. But most other delegates from the Pamlico were debtor-minded and antinationalist.

CAPE FEAR RIVER VALLEY

Wilmington, declared one unhappy tourist, "without exception is the most disagreeable, sandy, barren town I have visited on the continent—consisting of a few scattered wood and brick houses, without any kind of order or regularity." The land around it, extending north toward Pamlico Sound, said another visitor, was "miserably poor, being nothing but a sand bank covered with pines."[67] Wilmington and its surroundings also suffered considerable damage during the war, both from British forces and from civil war among Americans. Moore's Creek Bridge, site of the 1776 battle between Patriots and Loyalists, was only a few miles upriver from Wilmington. The city's prewar merchant class, mostly Scots, fled to Charleston or Bermuda, and fear of reprisals made them slow to return.

Though wrecked by the war, Wilmington had advantages no other Carolina city could boast—a rich hinterland and access to it. It lay at the forks of the Cape Fear River, whose branches, the Northeast and the Northwest, penetrated deep into the Carolina Piedmont. Oceanic vessels drawing sixteen feet of water could clear the bar of the Cape Fear River, and those drawing ten feet could get into Wilmington. Before the Revolution Wilmington suffered competition from Brunswick at the mouth of the river. But Brunswick was burned during the war and never recovered. Wilmington was in better position to intercept the cargoes coming down the river. By 1785 exports of naval stores were back to prewar levels, and shipping was double the prewar amount.[68]

The landscape from Pamlico south to Wilmington was a succession of sand dunes covered with pines, but above Wilmington the Cape Fear Valley was broad and rich. Naval stores and lumber were its main products and hence Wilmington's chief exports. The scale of operations, in general, was larger than in Pamlico. The lumber plantation of John Rutherford had a saw mill capable of cutting 3,000 boards a day. The boards were shipped downriver on rafts, which were broken up for lumber at their destination. One craft could carry 50,000 boards along with 200 barrels of tar.[69] Farther upriver was good farming country, good for corn, hemp, flax, and all varieties of grain. If wheat was not yet the chief market crop in 1783, it soon would be. When the Hessian fly struck in the 1790s, the district's congressman wrote: "Should we loose [sic] our Wheat it is God and God alone can determine the fate of many in the Lower parts of our State."[70]

The Northwest was the more important of the two branches of the Cape Fear River. Small sailing vessels, displacing 18 to 20 tons, could navigate as far as Fayetteville, 115 miles from Wilmington. Known as Cross Creek until its name was changed in 1784, Fayetteville was the center of Scots immigration before the war. There may have been as many as 10,000 Scots, mostly Highlanders, in the upper Cape Fear Valley at the outset of the Revolution, and the great majority of them had remained loyal to the crown during the war. But they were also industrious farmers, and Fayetteville was a thriving market town. Its trade was one of the main reasons for Wilmington's prosperity.[71]

Besides being on the river, Fayetteville was strategically situated for overland commerce. It was the crossroads of the state, and it straddled the main route into South Carolina (which bent inland to avoid the swamps south of Wilmington). Roads coming from

Salisbury and Charlotte in the west, Hillsborough to the north, and Wilmington in the southeast all converged on Fayetteville. As a result, it was the principal market for the whole southern Piedmont. Even residents of the far western valleys, who had sent goods downriver to Charleston before the war, began shipping through Fayetteville in the 1780s. One writer reported that 40 or 50 wagons a day came into the village. Tobacco, wheat, and flour were the staples sent on to Wilmington.[72]

There are too few surviving tax lists for Cape Fear counties to form an estimate of economic development. The lists that are available portray a land of small farmers. The landless population (about 20 percent) was smaller than anywhere else in the eastern part of the state, but only about a fourth of all taxpayers owned slaves. Only about 1 percent—6 to 10 planters per county—owned more than a dozen slaves. The exception was Wilmington and its vicinity. In New Hanover County 56 percent of the taxpayers were slaveowners, and 12 percent had more than a dozen. This was the area of highly developed naval stores production. The Wilmington district of New Hanover (i.e., the village and its environs) was the most highly developed of all. Around 75 percent of its taxpayers were slaveowners, and 16 percent had more than a dozen. It was also the most socially stratified part of North Carolina. About 25 percent of all taxpayers owned more than 1,000 acres, while 37 percent possessed neither land nor town lots.[73] Wilmington and Fayetteville were creditor-nationalist in political orientation during the 1780s; the remainder of the Cape Fear region was predominantly debtor.

THE CAROLINA PIEDMONT

The Piedmont was the most isolated—and the most provincial—part of North Carolina. Two lengthy rivers drained the eastern half of the Piedmont—the Haw, which was part of the Northwest Branch of the Cape Fear, and the Dan, a tributary of the Roanoke. Both were too shallow for anything but the smallest canoes and rafts. Piedmont traffic was almost all overland. The principal highway, still called the "great trading path" because of its importance in the early fur trade, ran southwest from Petersburg, Virginia, to Hillsborough, then west to Salisbury and south to Charlotte. Another road ran from Salisbury southeast to Fayetteville and Wilmington. The main products of the Piedmont—tobacco, flour, cattle, and hogs—sometimes had to go hundreds of miles to reach a suitable market in Petersburg or Wilmington.[74]

Travelers coming down the "great trading path" from Virginia considered the Piedmont fertile and the farms "very fine." The forest cover was a mixture of oak, hickory, and Virginia pine (a shortleaf variety not suitable for tar or turpentine). Orange County, for which there is a modern soil survey, is probably typical of the region. About 40 percent of the county is a fine textured clay with low organic content, a soil common throughout the Chesapeake states. It is good for pasture, but easily wears out and erodes if plowed. About 20 percent of the county was a rich loam, good for corn or cereal grains. Only about 15 percent of the county had soil suitable for tobacco culture. The remaining fourth of the county was too rocky or steep for cultivation.[75]

Orange was a land of small farmers. Only one-sixth owned slaves at the end of the Revolution, and while the number of slaveowners increased over the years, there is no other evidence of per capita growth. Table 2.6 summarizes the results of four surviving tax lists for the county.

Orange was probably more prosperous than other Piedmont counties, because of its urban center, Hillsborough. Only one other county, Caswell, has enough surviving tax lists to measure change,

TABLE 2.6   DEVELOPMENT IN THE CAROLINA PIEDMONT: ORANGE COUNTY

	1755	1785	1794	1801
Slaveowners	9%	16%	25%	31%
Over 12 slaves	0	(2 polls)	.25%	1%
Landless	—	29%	25%	25%
Over 1,000 acres	—	3%	3%	3%
Total polls	—	1,488	1,747	1,699

SOURCE: Orange County Tax Lists, 1785, 1794, 1801, Treasurer's and Comptroller's Records, NCDH; Merrens, *Colonial North Carolina*, pp. 76–77.

and its growth was even slower. The number of slaveowners in Caswell increased from 29 percent in 1784 to 37 percent in 1796, but there was no other change in the distribution of land or slaves.[76] The best that could be said for the Carolina Piedmont was that, unlike southern Virginia, it was not in decline.

Persons of English extraction were in the majority in the Piedmont, as they were elsewhere in the state, but there were more Scots-Irish and Germans than in the eastern counties. And the number of Germans and Scots-Irish increased the farther west one went. Most had come south from Pennsylvania and Virginia, via the Great Valley route, and in some of the far western counties each group claimed about 30 percent of he population.[77] Relatively recent arrivals in America, the Germans in particular clung to their cultural traditions. For a decade after the Revolution, Germans in the western Piedmont imported both teachers and pastors from Europe. In 1789 a German minister warned his flock not to marry among the English or Irish so that "German blood and the German language be preserved and more and more deciminated [sic]."[78] Other groups in the western Piedmont remained in close contact with the North. The Germans who founded Salem in 1766 were an offshoot of the Moravian community at Bethlehem, Pennsylvania. They looked to Pennsylvania for organizational leadership, as did the numerous Quakers in the region.[79]

The Scots-Irish assimilated more easily than the Germans, of course, but neither group had much in common with the people of eastern Carolina. The west, though it was the most remote part of the state, was also, in a sense, the most cosmopolitan. The effect of this factor is difficult to gauge. But it may be significant that counties with the heaviest non-English population—Surry, Rowan, Lincoln, Mecklenburg—were the only counties in the Piedmont that lent support to the Federal Constitution in 1788–89. Lincoln, probably the most heavily German of all, was the only county outside of Albemarle that favored the Constitution in both of the state's ratifying conventions.

The western Piedmont was hilly country, but the valleys were broad and fertile. George Washington, returning from South Carolina, noticed an improvement in the landscape as soon as he crossed the line into Mecklenburg County. "The lands between Charlotte and Salisbury are very fine," he wrote, "of a reddish cast and well timbered, with but very little underwood. Between these two places are the first meadows I have seen on the Road since I left Virginia & here also we appear to be getting into a Wheat country." The Yadkin Valley, in short, looked like Washington's own Northern Neck. There are those today who claim that the soil of the Yadkin Valley is among the best in the state.[80] The meadows that Washington saw were probably the remnants of early prairies created by Indian burnings. Travelers called these western grasslands "savannahs," and cattle grazing probably helped preserve them. Besides cattle, the principal product of the western counties was corn, though farmers also raised other grains and small amounts of tobacco. The Moravians, and perhaps other German immigrants as well, specialized in wheat. They were more familiar with its culture, and they preferred wheat bread to cornbread.[81]

A surviving tax list for Iredell County, compiled for the special assessment (direct tax) of 1798, offers a rare look at land values. The act authorizing the tax stated that land was to be rated at its current market value. "Wild lands," valued at 25¢ an acre, embraced about 50,000 acres, one-sixth of the county's total. The best improved lands were valued at $3.00 to $2.50 an acre. There were 996 farms in the county distributed as shown in table 2.7. The small

TABLE 2.7   SIZE OF FARMS IN THE
WESTERN PIEDMONT:
IREDELL COUNTY, 1798

Acres	Landowners	
1–99	63	6%
100–299	546	55
300–599	279	28
600–999	79	8
1,000+	29	3
	996	100%

SOURCE: Hugh Hill Wooton, "The Land Valuations of Iredell County in 1800," *North Carolina Historical Review,* 29 (1952), 523–39.

TABLE 2.8   ECONOMIC DEVELOPMENT IN THE WESTERN
PIEDMONT:
STOKES COUNTY, 1790–1800

	1790	1800
Landless	24%	24%
Owning 1,000+ acres	2%	1.5%
Slaveowners	14%	16%
Polls with more than 12 slaves	2	1
Total polls	1,092	1,383

SOURCE: Stokes County Tax Lists, 1790, 1800, Treasurer's and Comptroller's Papers, NCDH.

farm containing a couple of hundred acres was clearly the county norm. Tax lists for other western counties reveal a similar society. Some 20 to 25 percent of the polls were without land. About the same proportion held slaves, but no one owned very many. In most counties only one or two taxpayers owned more than a dozen slaves. Unfortunately, there are not enough surviving lists for an assessment of growth, except for Stokes County in the northwest corner of the state, shown in table 2.8. Even in the prosperous 1790s Stokes was going nowhere. The political stance of Stokes County in the 1780s cannot be determined because it was not organized until the end of the decade. Suffice it to say that the northwest was the most consistently debtor-minded part of the state in assembly voting.

The western rivers were broad and swift, but in need of clearing. The Yadkin, which linked the two principal western towns, Salisbury and Charlotte, became the Great Peedee in South Carolina, and flowed into the Atlantic at Georgetown. The Catawba River to the west became the Wateree in South Carolina and eventually helped to form the Santee. Farther west still, the Broad River was another tributary of the great Santee system. Without improvements, these rivers could carry only rafts and flatboats, but there was considerable traffic. Settlers on the Broad River sent their goods to Columbia, South Carolina; those on the Yadkin traded all the way to Charleston. Tobacco, peach brandy, and cattle were the principal exports. In Charleston these were exchanged for salt, ironware, and household goods.[82] Although the distance was great (about 300 miles), a deep-water port lay at the end of the journey, and for many it was probably worth the trip once a year.

Some goods were shipped overland from the west, though it is difficult to assess the amount of this traffic. The crossroads village of Salisbury sent wagons to both Wilmington and Petersburg, Virginia. The Moravians, who had a number of splendid four mills, shipped most of their produce by wagon. They calculated that it took a wagon loaded with flour barrels two weeks to reach Fayetteville, four to get all the way to Charleston.[83]

The western half of North Carolina exhibited a great deal of variety—in ethnic composition, in landscape, and in trading patterns. And these variations occasionally made themselves felt in politics. Remote and short of cash, the Piedmont and the west were generally debtor-oriented through the 1780s, and in the succeeding decade the area was predominantly Jeffersonian. The Yadkin Valley, however, with a heavy concentration of Germans and Scots and interstate commercial contacts, was more nationalist in temperament, especially when national questions were at the center of public attention.

Throughout the Chesapeake there were substantial variations in population and environment, and the resulting tensions affected political behavior. The clash of regional interests was the principal dynamic in the politics of the Chesapeake after the American Revolution.

PART TWO

The Beginnings of
Political Parties, 1781–1787

CHAPTER THREE

The Politics of Personalities, 1781–1783

THE WAR came late to the Chesapeake, but it came with a vengeance. Coastal plantations in Virginia and North Carolina suffered substantial damage, while military actions and Loyalist removals displaced population. British ships at the entrance to the bay effectively strangled trade and left planters desperately short of cash. But the emergency did force an end, at least temporarily, to political disputes, and in all three states there was general agreement on the need for debtor relief, even as the fighting died down after the fall of Yorktown.

Powerful personalities who had come to the forefront during the war dominated the political scene in each state—Samuel Chase and Charles Carroll in Maryland; Patrick Henry, Richard Henry Lee, and Benjamin Harrison in Virginia; Samuel Johnston and Willie Jones in North Carolina. Each was thought to command a personal following, though not one could claim control of his assembly. During the war these leaders had clashed frequently, sometimes violently, but in the final emergency their differences were composed. In the last months of the war all three states issued

71

paper money to finance military operations, and after the fighting ceased the assemblies listened sympathetically to cries for relief. They enacted stay laws that retarded debt collection through the courts, and they either postponed taxes or permitted payment in kind. Because the distress was general, the benefits from this legislation were spread among all classes. Wealthy planters in debt to foreign merchants took advantage of opportunities to delay payments as frequently as small farmers in debt to village shopkeepers. Only a handful of merchants and lawyers objected to the relief laws, and their position seemed to stem from principle as much as self-interest.

While the fighting continued, relief could be defended as patriotic; when the war ended, better times seemed ahead. Not until the postwar depression, which began in 1784, did proposals for debtor relief become controversial and socially divisive. And not until then did the first recognizable parties appear. In Maryland and in several northern colonies there were blocs of legislators who consistently agreed with one another before and even during the Revolution. But these could not be called parties because they lacked permanence, they lacked constituencies, and they lacked a body of principle that covered a range of issues. Under pressure of the depression, the legislative blocs of the 1780s eventually developed all three.

In the Chesapeake, Maryland, which before the war had the best-organized legislative blocs, led the way. Throughout the war there was a core of men in the House of Delegates who agreed with one another fairly consistently, and by 1784 there were two well-defined, regionally based factions. In Maryland political issues were always more important than personalities. In North Carolina the personalities were nearly all on one side and the numbers on the other. A small, closely knit circle of lawyers and merchants did battle for fiscal responsibility against an amorphous, inarticulate, but overwhelming majority, made up mostly of middling farmers. Virginia was the slowest of all to develop a party system. Its assembly was a kaleidoscope of shifting alliances among a small group of acknowledged leaders, whose behavior seemed to be dictated by prejudice as often as principle. Not until James Madison returned from Congress in 1784 with a comprehensive program of political reform did interest groups replace personalities and a party system begin to form.

THE NEBULAE OF PARTIES IN MARYLAND

The framers of Maryland's government in 1776 seemed most concerned with defending the interests of property and insulating the regime from popular influences. The only officeholders chosen by voters were county sheriffs (who were required to possess property worth £1,000) and members of the lower house of the assembly. Each county was entitled to four delegates in the lower house; the towns of Baltimore and Annapolis sent two each. Elections were annual, and anyone owning a fifty-acre freehold or £30 current money could vote. The land qualification was low (only Pennsylvania and North Carolina, which permitted all male taxpayers to vote, had lower ones), but the freehold requirement did exclude tenant farmers from the franchise. Every five years the voters chose a group of electors, who in turn selected the 15-member Senate (9 from the Western Shore, 6 from the Eastern). Senators, like sheriffs, had to possess £1,000 current money in real or personal property.

The authors of the constitution intended the Senate to serve as the bastion of the wealthy elite, but in reality there was little difference between the houses. Both were in the firm control of the seaboard gentry. The explanation lay less in the elitist features of the constitution than in the geographical homogeneity of the state. Unlike Virginia and North Carolina, Maryland had no Indian frontier, and its sparsely populated mountain region was a tiny finger of land wedged between the Mason-Dixon Line and the Potomac. Nearly all the state's counties and 90 percent of its population lay in the Tidewater region around the bay. The only regional variations were the upper Potomac (Montgomery, Frederick, and Washington counties) and the head of the bay (Baltimore, Harford, and Cecil counties), areas still thinly populated with small landowners at the end of the war. These variations contributed to the formation of legislative parties in the early 1780s.

Throughout the latter years of the war, Charles Carroll of Carrollton, the dominant figure in the Senate, had been feuding with Samuel Chase, the acknowledged leader of the lower house. An enormously wealthy Roman Catholic, educated in Jesuit colleges in Europe and trained in the law at London's Middle Temple, Carroll was a most unusual revolutionary. He was active in the Patriot cause from the beginning, serving on the council of safety in 1775 and signing the Declaration of Independence in 1776, yet he devoted his life to the preservation of the status and powers of the elite. In tones that sometimes verged on hysteria, he denounced every political upheaval of the age, from the tenant riots of the Revolution to the election of Jefferson in 1800. He retired from politics in 1800 still trembling over "an approaching revolution which will subvert . . . our social order and the rights of property."[1]

Carroll did not so much lead the Senate as blend with it. On some matters of great importance to him, such as his feud with Samuel Chase, Carroll often found himself in a minority. But on federal issues and economic policies, Carroll and his fellow legislators invariably agreed. In the great paper money controversy of the middle years of the decade the Senate's stand was always unanimous. Of the 27 individuals who served in the Maryland Senate between 1781 and 1790 (the second and third Senates), not one opposed the Constitution.[2] And of those who still served in the year 1800, not one could bring himself to support Thomas Jefferson.

The most prominent personage in the House of Delegates, all agreed, was Samuel Chase. Son of an Anglican minister, educated by his father, and trained in the law by apprenticeship, Chase was in every way the antithesis of the aristocratic Carroll. He joined the revolutionary movement as early as the Stamp Act riots and served as a delegate to the First Continental Congress. An opportunist who made money out of the war, Chase was feared by many, respected by some, and loved by very few.

His political home was the House of Delegates, but he did not control that body any more than Carroll controlled the Senate. He moved with the creditor-nationalist majority, but when he deviated from the preconceptions of that group, as he did on matters of

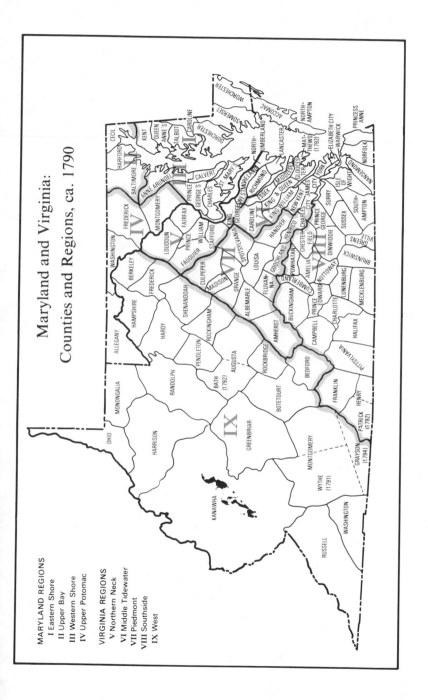

Maryland and Virginia:
Counties and Regions, ca. 1790

MARYLAND REGIONS
I Eastern Shore
II Upper Bay
III Western Shore
IV Upper Potomac

VIRGINIA REGIONS
V Northern Neck
VI Middle Tidewater
VII Piedmont
VIII Southside
IX West

public debt and paper money, he carried with him only a tiny band of interested followers. At the same time, Chase's espousal of paper money—the issue that caught the most public attention—co-opted the debtor interest and overshadowed more legitimate representatives of the hinterland farmers. Like Patrick Henry in Virginia and Willie Jones in North Carolina, Chase adopted enough debtor-relief measures to suit his own purposes, and more than enough to alarm fiscal conservatives such as Carroll, Washington, and Iredell. Chase, Henry, and Jones were considered popular leaders, but in reality they blocked the appearance of genuine spokesmen for the poor. In all three states the provincial, debt-burdened majority remained for the most part silent and invisible.

Chase and Carroll dominated Maryland politics through much of the war because they embroiled the two houses of the assembly in a personal feud. The dispute originated in Chase's nearly insatiable appetite for profiteering. Early in the war he persuaded the House of Delegates that confiscation and sale of Loyalist property would promote the war effort by silencing dissent and replenishing the treasury. Such a trespass on the rights of property alarmed the Senate, and Carroll, organizing the opposition, hinted that Chase was motivated by self-interest. Chase reacted by accusing Carroll of being "the advocate of the disaffected tories and refugees," but the Senate held firm.

Sent to Congress in 1778, shortly after Benjamin Franklin negotiated the treaty of alliance with France, Chase organized a corner on the market in cereal grains and flour in anticipation of the arrival of a hungry French fleet. Alexander Hamilton exposed this operation in three public letters signed "Publius," and in 1779 an assembly resolution accused Chase of using his position to improve his fortune. For the next two years Chase was omitted from the state's congressional delegation. In the summer of 1781 Chase struck back through the newspapers in letters declaring his innocence and blaming Carroll for the assembly's action. The senator, in a move that virtually confessed his complicity in the attack, published what information he had on Chase's financial activities and accused him of "betraying the secrets of Congress." The material was furnished to him by Hamilton's friend James McHenry.[3]

In the fall of 1781 the assembly sent Chase back to Congress. Eastern Shore delegate John Cadwalader, who had opposed both confiscation and paper money, sought to have Chase's election voided on grounds that he had previously betrayed his position, but the move failed. With Chase recovering his popularity, Carroll evidently decided to back away. On January 8, 1782, he wrote Chase to suggest that they settle their quarrel privately. A week later the House of Delegates cleared Chase of any wrongdoing, and on February 3 Chase agreed to "drop all further publications."[4] There the affair ended, until the currency crisis a few years later resurrected their differences on a related matter, paper money.

Although it attracted a great deal of attention, the Chase-Carroll feud had no lasting impact on Maryland politics. It did not even pit the two houses of the assembly against each other, except on the related problems of confiscations and paper money, and by the end of 1781 even these were temporarily resolved. The two branches remained at odds through 1782, but the contest was not one of personalities. It was a conflict of two interest groups. On the one side were delegates who tended to be creditor oriented, concerned for the condition of the treasury, yet willing to pay officials adequate salaries, and inclined to favor the prompt payment of private debts. The other side generally supported relief laws, low salaries, and tax postponement. The battle was not as ferocious as it would become in the depression years and the lines were ill-defined, but the debtor element usually had its way in this year of half-war, half-peace. And that is what provoked disputes with the creditor-dominated Senate. Chase actually voted with the creditor faction, as he did throughout the postwar period.

The cluster-bloc matrix printed as table 3.1 shows the bare beginnings of these factions in the House of Delegates. For a description of the system used in constructing the matrix see the appendix.[5]

To enter the matrix a legislator had to agree with at least one other legislator at least 70 percent of the time. Less than half were able to meet that criterion, and those who did seldom agreed with very many others. As a result the clusters apparent in the table are full of holes. Nevertheless, the clusters do represent at least th nebulae of opposing parties. Most of the roll calls (57 of 69) involved economic interests, such as taxation, salaries, or debtor relief, and it was differences over these that formed the division.[6] The larger cluster, containing 10 men (excluding Rowland of Cecil),[7] was the debtor element. It favored lower taxes, and it wanted them paid in commodities, tobacco, wheat, or pork. When it came to spending money, these men were inclined to be niggardly with salaries for executive and judicial officials, though they were a bit more generous with the army. They also favored paper money, opposed court reform that might make collection of debts easier, and mistrusted the Continental Congress.

The other bloc of 9 was the creditor element, of whom Chase was the most prominent member. These generally voted the reverse on all the above items, with the exception of paper money.[8] On this matter Chase and a few of his friends voted with the debtor group, for reasons that will be explained in the next chapter. The blocs were tiny and incohesive, but the most significant feature of the table is that there were only *two*. One might have expected a number of blocs, each representing an interest or the following of some individual. Americans commonly employed terms like Whig and Tory or "court" and "country" to describe their political rivalries, terms which implied a political duality, but they also assumed that politics was dominated by personalities. The eighteenth-century concept of representation presumed a great deal of independence on the part of elected delegates, but gentlemen of wealth and reputation were also expected to act for the common good. Groups that pursued private interests at the expense of the general welfare were denounced as "parties" or "factions." Thus, no one set out consciously to form a party system, but the presence of two rival corps, each voting the opposite of the other on a variety of issues, suggests the rudiments of one.

That the contest involved issues, rather than personalities, is evident from the fact that it was basically a regional division. Of the 11 debtor delegates, 7 represented the more remote upper Potomac counties; the rest came from the upper Western Shore. Of the creditor delegates, 4 came from the cities of Baltimore and Annapolis; all but one of the rest lived on the wealthy Eastern Shore. This

TABLE 3.1 MARYLAND HOUSE OF DELEGATES, 1782: CLUSTER-BLOC MATRIX (SHOWING DEBTOR PARTY)*

	OGLE THFR	SHRI VRFR	STUL LJWA	EDWA RDMO	ONEA LEMO	BURG SEMO	SENY JOQA	GRIF FHMO	WORT HNAA	ROWL NDCE	MGUD RJPG	BROG DNAA	MILL RWCE	WHEE LRHA	WEEM SJCA	DUVA LSFR	WORT HBAA
OGLETHFR	—	93	84	83	78	77	76	72	71	71	71						
SHRIVRFR	93	—	81	80	81			71	76		75	81	76	71	71	70	
STULLJWA	84	81	—	86			74	81			79						
EDWARDMO	83	80	86	—	79		72	80			79	72		71	76	70	
ONEALEMO	78	81	86	79	—	81	79	80	73		75						
BURGESMO	77				81	—		77	71		84						
SENYJOQA	76		74	72	79		—	71			71						
GRIFFHMO	72	71	81	80	77		71	—	76						72		
WORTHNAA	71	76			73	71		76	—		83	80					92
ROWLNDCE	71									—							
MGUDRJPG	71	75	79	79	75	84	71		83		—	74	80				81
BROGDNAA		81		72					80		74	—					75
MILLRWCE		76									80		—	80			
WHEELRHA		71		71									80	—			
WEEMSJQA		71		76				72							—		
DUVALSFR		70		70												—	
WORTHBAA									92		81	75					—
CHAPLNWA					70						74						
PEARCEKE							74										
TAYLRJHA								78						83			
WIEKNWCH								77							74		
HALLJOAA									71			73					72
BREVADCE										70							
NORRISHA														85		71	
BONDTHSM																74	
DENTGECH																	
DASHJSWO																	
CHASESAN																	
QUYNNAAN																	
KENTJAQA																	
MCMECHBT																	
HINDMNTA																	
FELLXWBT																	
HOPPERCR																	

MARYLAND HOUSE OF DELEGATES, 1/82: CLUSTER-BLOC MATRIX (SHOWING CREDITOR PARTY)

	CHAP LNWA	PEAR CEKE	TAYL RJHA	WIEK NWCH	HALL JOAA	BREV ADCE	NORR ISHA	BOND THSM	DENT GECH	DASH JSWO	CHAS ESAN	QUYN NAAN	KENT JAQA	MCME CHBT	HIND MNTA	FELL XWBT	HOPP ERCR
OGLETHFR																	
SHRIVRFR																	
STULLJWA																	
EDWARDMO																	
ONEALEMO	70																
BURGESMO																	
SENYJOQA		74															
GRIFFHMO																	
WORTHNAA			78	77													
ROWLNDCE					71	70											
MGUDRJPG	74																
BROGDNAA					73												
MILLRWCE																	
WHEELRHA			83	74			85										
WEEMSJQA							71										
DUVALSFR					72												
WORTHBAA			86					74									
CHAPLNWA	—						77										
PEARCEKE	86	—				71											
TAYLRJHA			—														
WIEKNWCH				—			83		75								
HALLJOAA					—												
BREVADCE		71				—											
NORRISHA	77		83				—										
BONDTHSM								—									
DENTGECH									—	79	78	74	74	74	82		
DASHJSWO									79	—	87	85		77			
CHASESAN									78	87	—	88		80		80	72
QUYNNAAN									74	85	88	—				71	71
KENTJAQA									74				—				84
MCMECHBT									74	77	80			—	78	91	
HINDMNTA										82				78	—	71	73
FELLXWBT														91	71	—	
HOPPERCR															73		—

*Explanation of name code: the first six letters are an abbreviation of the delegate's last name, including in some cases his first initials. The last two letters are the abbreviation of the county he represented. Those who wish to identify delegates more fully can trace them in Edward C. Papenfuse et al., *Directory of Maryland Legislators, 1635–1789* (Annapolis, 1976).

TABLE 3.2   MARYLAND HOUSE OF DELEGATES:
VOTES ON SALARIES AND TAXATION, 1782

	Creditor	Debtor	Middle
Eastern Shore	11	2	7
Upper bay	0	4	5
Western Shore	4	5	7
Upper Potomac	0	8	2
Urban	4	0	0
	19	19	21

sectional division, though barely evident at this point, would remain the basis of the first party system in Maryland right down to the election of Jefferson in 1800.

Manual comparisons help to clarify this regional split, though they risk losing some of the objectivity offered by the computer. Questions of salaries and taxation, which generated 32 roll calls, produced the most consistent voting behavior. Perhaps on these matters the issues were most clearly presented and interests least confused. The records of the most consistent members of each faction can be used to construct a model of ideal creditor or debtor voting behavior. Regional breakdowns for these are shown in table 3.2.[9] In order to include those who voted consistently but infrequently, the minimum participation is set at 5 roll calls and an agreement threshold of 75 percent (i.e., 4 out of 5, 6 out of 8, etc.) is required for party identification.

Although the increase in numbers clarifies the regional division, the uncommitted are still the largest group. Expressed in another way, two-thirds of those legislators who voted enough to be identified at all associated themselves with one side or the other. As the party system matured, this figure would approach 80 percent.

No such division existed in the Senate. There were 11 roll calls in the Senate in the fall session, but they followed no pattern. The Senate was fiscally conservative, however, and it did engage in a number of fights with the lower house on taxation and pay allowances. But these had nothing to do with the old feud between Carroll and Chase. On the matter of confiscated property, Carroll even voted in favor of a House-passed resolution, leaving McHenry to oppose it alone.[10] Such conflict as there was between the two branches stemmed from the fact that the debtor element had its way in the lower house on most votes. Though the situation was still very confused, even in the House of Delegates, the politics of personalities had yielded to the politics of issue-conscious regional alignments by the end of the war. In this respect Maryland was far ahead of her neighbors to the south.

VIRGINIA: FRIENDLY RIVALRIES AMONG GENTLEMEN

In analyzing the 1783 Virginia assembly, Attorney General Edmund Randolph discerned three "corps," belonging to Patrick Henry, Richard Henry Lee, and Speaker John Tyler. Henry's was easily the most numerous, and support for the Speaker, he thought, was "but a temporary bubble."[11] Vague as that description is, the historian is hard pressed to improve on it. Unlike Maryland, the Virginia assembly seldom held roll call ballots. The House of Delegates averaged about 15 per session, the Senate no more than half that. By combining sessions (1782–83–84, for instance), it is possible to assemble enough roll calls on related issues to discern whatever blocs there were, but this procedure is complicated by the high annual turnover in membership. About 35 to 40 percent of the House of Delegates were new men in each session.[12] Members of the House of Delegates were elected annually (in the spring) on virtually the same suffrage qualifications that existed in Maryland. Each county was entitled to two delegates, and the cities of Richmond, Williamsburg, and Norfolk had one each. Because of the enormous number of counties in the state (74 at the beginning of our period and 90 at the end), the House was potentially very large, but there was a great deal of absenteeism.

The Senate was also elected annually, on the same suffrage requirements as the lower house. For the purposes of Senate representation, the state was divided into multi-county districts roughly equal in population, each of which was entitled to four senators. Because the electoral requirements were essentially the same, the Senate did not differ materially from the lower house in social composition. It had few powers, however, except to delay legislation, and ambitious politicians shunned it.

The politician with one of the worst attendance records in the assembly was the one generally accorded to be the most influential—Patrick Henry. Henry was a popular favorite in Virginia from the beginning of the crisis with Britain when he lent his silvery voice to the radical cause. Elected the first governor of the state, he served three annual terms and then retired to his first home, the House of Delegates. There he endorsed such popular causes as debtor relief and paper money—or so his enemies said, for there is little evidence of his beliefs in the surviving record. In the six sessions during 1782–84 Henry was present on only ten roll calls, so it is not possible to ascertain the strength of his following.

There were six votes during these years that involved domestic debts and taxation; Henry participated in four of them.[13] Insofar as it is possible to determine the issues at stake in each roll call, a total of 34 delegates voted debtor at least 75 percent of the time (with a minimum participation of 3 out of 3 or 3 out of 4 votes). Over half came from Henry's own country south of the James River, but every region of the state was represented. The group even included three merchants. More significantly, not a single delegate voted on the other side as much as 75 percent of the time. It is clear that debtor relief commanded broad support in the Virginia assembly. If Henry possessed influence, it was because he reflected the views of the vast majority of delegates. How much leadership he might have exerted we shall never know, because he never tried. Assaying the chances that the assembly might approve the congressional impost in 1783 (see chapter 9), Jefferson reported that "Henry as usual is involved in mystery: should the popular tide run strongly in either direction, he will fall in with it. Should it not, he will have a struggle between his enmity to the Lees, and his enmity to everything which may give influence to Congress."[14]

Edmund Randolph was correct in his estimate of John Tyler's strength. It was at best a small circle of friends, probably from Tyler's neighborhood in the lower James Valley. Tyler and General Thomas Nelson, who had a circle of influence in the same area

(Nelson lived at Yorktown), were generally considered allies of Patrick Henry.[15] Tyler became Speaker of the House in 1781, and he was reelected in 1782 and 1783 after being nominated by Henry. As Speaker he did not participate in any roll calls, so it is difficult to define his politics. He named two of his children after Henry, and his old-age recollections recorded by William Wirt were full of admiration for Henry.[16]

In the 1783 contest for Speaker, Tyler's opponent was Richard Henry Lee. Tyler won, 60 to 20, and that vote may have defined the extent of Lee's following.[17] Lee, like Henry, was a leader of prewar radicals. During the war he alternated between Congress (1776–79) and the House of Delegates (1780–84). In Congress Lee engaged in a running battle with Philadelphia merchant Robert Morris, a fight that began in 1778 when his brother Arthur Lee accused Silas Deane (an agent of Morris's) of profiteering while serving as commissioner to France. Morris's business methods had made numerous enemies, and the conflict took on national significance when Morris became Secretary of Finance in 1780. At his urging, Congress sent to the states an amendment to the Articles of Confederation authorizing Congress to collect customs duties. That move changed a factional feud into a question of federal power.

Lee fought the impost amendment in the Virginia assembly, covering his antipathy to Morris with a shroud of sectionalism. Federal customs duties, he told a Northern Neck neighbor, would "strangle our infant commerce on its birth, make us pay more than our proportion and sacrifice this country [Virginia] to its northern brethren."[18] In the assembly Lee favored the speedy collection of taxes so that the state could comply with congressional requisitions. This, he evidently hoped, would forestall the need for an impost. On matters of domestic economy, however, Lee usually sided with the debtor majority.[19]

Other groups fulfilled the eighteenth-century conception of self-serving factions. The brothers James and John Francis Mercer spent a good deal of time lining up support in the assembly to further their own careers (James was a judge of the General Court, John a member of Congress, 1783–85). The brothers were old enemies of Richard H. Lee, whom they blamed for the fall of their brother George, a victim of the Stamp Act Riots in 1765. That breach seems to have healed by the end of the war, however, and the Mercers even relied on Lee for patronage.[20] In the House of Delegates (1782–83) John Mercer voted with the debtor majority. In Congress he sought one appointment after another so shamelessly that Jefferson finally concluded: "Vanity and ambition seem to be the ruling passions of this young man and as his objects are impure, so also are his means. Intrigue is a principal one on particular occasions as party attachment is in the general."[21]

What little opposition there was to Patrick Henry within the House of Delegates gathered around Henry Tazewell, a lawyer from Williamsburg. A genial, courtly gentleman, Tazewell was one of the most popular figures in the House, and his role as opposition leader was an unobtrusive one. Nevertheless, he appeared regularly, offering a motion here, an amendment there as he chipped away at the debtor-relief policies of the Henryite majority. Absenteeism and the paucity of roll calls prevent any accurate assessment of his strength, but there were perhaps a dozen delegates who sided wtih him regularly.[22] Among them were such creditor-minded nationalists as John Marshall (1782 only), Alexander White, and Joseph Prentis, but on the other side were the westerner Archibald Stuart and the Alexandria merchant Alexander Henderson, both later Federalists. If Tazewell's group was a foundation on which a creditor-nationalist party could be built, it was nothing more. Tazewell was not an organizer, and he never tried to combine his isolated actions into a comprehensive system. Politically he functioned within the old rules of interpersonal relationships.[23] He found his home when the assembly in 1785 placed him on the state's highest court.

As a result of Tazewell's limitations, the most vocal opposition to Patrick Henry lay outside the assembly. It consisted of a tiny band of men who shared similar views on public finance and private credit. Although they held important positions in state and continental government, they had almost no influence on Virginia politics in the immediate postwar years. For the moment they had to content themselves with establishing lines of communication and preparing allies. The central figure, because of his fame and influence, was George Washington. Though he retired to Mount Vernon after overseeing the demobilization of his army, Washington remained intensely interested in public affairs, fretful to the many signs of demagoguery and disorder, and quick to offer advice. His circle of friends in Maryland and his many contacts among northern leaders opened channels of communication for his Virginia friends, and his prestige was such that his support was critical to any political program. He refused active public service, however, until he agreed to attend the Federal Convention in 1787. He left to others the task of translating his ideas into political action.

So long as Washington remained in retirement, the elder patron of the group was Joseph Jones of Fredericksburg, one of the most respected attorneys in the state. Educated at the Inns of Court, he was King's Attorney for Fredericksburg and represented the town in the House of Burgesses before the Revolution. During the war he served briefly in Congress and then returned to become a judge of the General Court. In 1780 the assembly sent him back to Congress, and along with him went his young protégé, James Madison. Nephew of an Anglican bishop of the same name who was president of the College of William and Mary, Madison was newly graduated from Princeton when the Revolution began. Although only 25 years old, he was made a colonel of Orange County militia and elected to the Virginia convention of 1776, thereby beginning a career of public service that was to last virtually without interruption for the next forty years. Despite his youth, Madison had important political connections, among them Edmund Pendleton, president of the Convention and an intimate friend of his father's, and Pendleton's neighbor and fellow attorney from Fredericksburg, Joseph Jones. When Madison was defeated for reelection in 1777, partly because he refused to distribute free whiskey to the voters, the legislature placed him on the Executive Council. There he became acquainted with Thomas Jefferson when the latter was made governor in 1779. At the end of that year Madison was elected to Congress, where he remained until December 1783. In Congress he sided consistently with the band of nationalists from the middle states, who were trying to put congressional finances in order, expand the powers of Congress, and establish some rudimentary executive offices.

When Madison retired, having served the three years permitted by the Articles of Confederation, the assembly replaced him with James Monroe. The youngest recruit to the Washington circle, Monroe was a student at William and Mary when the war broke out. He promptly joined the army and served with some distinction in the New Jersey campaigns. Finding promotion too slow, he left the army in 1778 and returned to William and Mary to study law. With the help of his uncle Joseph Jones, he became acquainted with both Madison and Governor Jefferson. In 1782 he was elected to the House of Delegates, and after only a year's legislative service he was sent to Congress. He remained there until 1786, keeping the budding nationalist party in Richmond informed of the travails of Congress.

The most strategically placed member of the group was Attorney General Edmund Randolph. The son of Sir John Randolph, King's Attorney for the colony who fled to England at the outset of the war, Edmund was given his father's position in 1776 and held the office for the next decade. From his listening post in Richmond, Randolph kept his friends informed of the assembly's activities and relayed advice to the congressional delegates. Randolph regarded Governor Benjamin Harrison (1782–84) as an ally, but the governor had no discernible political beliefs. His chief concern seems to have been a rivalry with his neighbor John Tyler. Since Tyler was allied with Patrick Henry, Randolph may have been led to hope for some support in the executive. Harrison's position was a weak one, however, for under the Virginia constitution the governor was a mere figurehead, deprived of any substantial powers.

On the edge of this circle were Thomas Jefferson and George Mason. Emerging from retirement after his brief and disastrous term as governor in 1780, Jefferson served briefly in Congress (1783–84) and then departed for Paris, where he remained for the rest of the decade. Through his extensive correspondence Jefferson received an enormous amount of political intelligence, but he seldom offered advice of his own, except on matters concerning his foreign ministry. He favored the payment of foreign debts but hedged on questions of domestic debts and taxation. He approved of schemes to open trade routes to the West but said little about the responsibility of government in the matter. He advocated giving

Congress the power to regulate foreign trade but had misgivings about broad schemes to revamp the central government. Madison nevertheless regarded him as a friendly listener. Their letters reveal a set of common assumptions and shared views, evidence of many private conversations when both men served in Congress.

George Mason was a more difficult ally because he devoted himself to republican principle as a medieval saint adhered to Christian dogma. A Northern Neck aristocrat of enormous wealth, Mason possessed nearly as much symbolic importance as Washington or Jefferson. His Declaration of Rights of 1776 was a distillation of seventeenth-century Whig principles adapted to the uses of American republicanism. Ever afterward he considered himself the watchdog of liberty, viewing with suspicious eye liberty's natural enemy—government.

Conservative in temperament, Mason felt that contractual obligations should be met and debts should be paid. He could become apoplectic at the mere mention of "paper money." Yet for him it was a matter of private integrity, not a concern of government or of legislative regulation. In the spring of 1783 he drafted for a popular meeting in Fairfax County a set of instructions to its delegates in the assembly. The freeholders demanded that the delegates oppose paper money, remove the legal obstacles to the payment of British debts, and avoid unnecessary delays in the collection of taxes. But Mason's resolves also rejected the congressional request for tax power because it appeared to "exhibit strong proofs of lust for power."[24] Mason was among the first to link the various debt and tax-relief issues into a comprehensive creditor program. But he shied from any appeal to federal authority. The battle was to be fought exclusively in the states. When others—Madison in Virginia and James Iredell in North Carolina—reached the conclusion that fiscal orthodoxy and a viable national authority went hand in hand, Mason adhered to his philosophical distinction. He was too influential to be alienated or ignored, but he caused Madison many an anxious moment.[25]

At the end of the war an intermittent correspondence and certain ill-defined assumptions bound the creditor circle together. But in Congress Madison was rapidly maturing, and the experience had an enormous effect on his political attitudes. When his congressional term expired, he took a seat in the state assembly in the spring of 1784. Almost immediately there was a surge of legislative activity, and by the end of that year his circle of friends had developed a coherent program that combined fiscal orthodoxy with government promotion of the economy at both state and national levels. The collection of delegates he mustered in support of this program was Virginia's first political party.

NORTH CAROLINA: LAWYERS VS. FARMERS

The war wrought more damage in the Carolinas than in any other part of the American union. Although fighting reached the area late in the war, British armies were unusually destructive. The war in the Carolinas, more so than anywhere else, was a civil war. British sympathizers, quiescent after a defeat at Moore's Creek Bridge at the beginning of the conflict, resurfaced when British armies arrived in the South in 1779. Lord Cornwallis recruited entire regiments of Loyalists and placed them under separate command. The fighting that ensued was some of the most vicious of the war. Beset by guerrilla warfare, pursued relentlessly from town to town by British armies, the North Carolina assembly suspended tax collections and financed the war with paper money, backed by nothing but the assembly's promise to redeem. After General Nathaniel Greene chased the last British troops out of the state in the fall of 1781, the legislature returned to order with vivid memories of this traumatic experience. There was near unanimous support for further postponement of taxes and debt settlements, and a lively hostility to everything that was British.

The acknowledged spokesman for this viewpoint was Willie Jones of Halifax. Of old Welsh ancestry and born to wealth, Jones spent several years traveling in England in his youth and reputedly attended Eton for a time. Returning to North Carolina about 1760, he expanded his wealth by combining planting and retailing. His plantation "The Grove" covered several square miles of the fertile Roanoke Valley, and he possessed a store in the town of Halifax.

Still in his mid-thirties when the Revolution came, Jones was a delegate to all five Provincial Congresses between 1774 and 1776, and fellow delegates gave him credit for writing much of the North Carolina constitution. This document, because of the low property qualifications it set for voting (all adult white male taxpayers for the Commons, 50-acre freeholders for the Senate) and holding office (100 acres for members of the Commons, 300 for senators) and its apportionment of representation in a manner that virtually guaranteed back-country control of the assembly, was one of the most democratic of the Revolutionary state constitutions. It earned Jones a reputation as spokeman for popular interests.

During the war Jones served continuously in the assembly, except for a brief tour in the Continental Congress, but when the war ended he retired from politics. Except for two brief appearances in the state Senate (1784 and 1788), his only public role was in the 1788 convention that rejected the Federal Constitution. He was far from idle, however, for his private fortune increased enormously in those years, despite the depressed economy. The Grove expanded from 1,894 acres and 24 slaves in 1784 to a princely domain of 9,477 acres and 78 slaves in 1787, and he picked up another 5,000 acres in Tennessee.[26] Yet he remained the idol of the assembly, living, like Patrick Henry, on his reputation for supporting popular causes.

The man who led the rural majority in the assembly was Thomas Person of Granville, a central Piedmont county lying on the Virginia border. Person was thus a not-too-distant neighbor of Patrick Henry's, but there is no surviving record of contact between the two. Person's father, a surveyor for the Granville proprietary, amassed an empire of 82,000 acres in ten counties. Young Thomas, as future owner of much of western Carolina naturally became a spokesman for its interests. He was tried for complicity in the Regulation of 1770–71 but acquitted, and the experience made him a popular hero. It also made him a lifelong opponent of governmental authority. In the Provincial Congresses of 1774–76 he and Willie Jones were natural allies. The first state legislature made him a general of militia, but though he was styled "General" ever after there is no record that he saw active service. Instead he spent the war in the assembly, serving continuously until 1785 and intermittently thereafter until his death in 1800.

If Person was a man of dynamic personality, there is little evidence of it in the record. Hardly a scrap of personal correspondence survives, and even opponents seldom bothered to mention him. Yet his deeds are spread across the pages of the assembly journal. He derived his authority from the fact that he was so much like the rural majority that he led—hard-headed, inarticulate, provincial. He may also have won his position by default, for there were few among the rural element who made any sort of mark on the historical record. The only ally of Person's mentioned with any frequency was former governor Abner Nash, a lawyer from New Bern who had served in the assembly at various times since the 1760s. As governor during the trying year of 1780, he developed a deep hatred for Loyalists and British merchants. But then in 1782 the assembly sent him to Congress, and there his horizon broadened and his views changed. The North Carolina delegation was as firmly nationalist as those from Maryland and Virginia in these years, and Nash returned in 1784 a firm advocate of moderation and fiscal orthodoxy.[27]

Actually the leading Tory-baiter in the House of Commons was Timothy Bloodworth, who came from the Black River district of New Hanover County, the piney woods north of Wilmington. Bloodworth had tried a number of occupations, from cobbler to minister to wheelwright, but with the Revolution he seems to have found his true vocation—politics. He may have been the nation's first professional politician. From the outset of the Revolution until his death in 1814 there was not a year in which he failed to hold state or federal office.[28] His district was much ravaged, first by Loyalists and then by the British occupation force in Wilmington. Serving in the Commons throughout the war, he was the leading advocate of proscription and confiscation.

The man who emerged from the Revolution with the most bitter memories of all was the popular leader in the Senate, General Griffith Rutherford. A Scot from western Rowan County, Rutherford sprang to early prominence in the war as an organizer of militia. Until Cornwallis invaded the state in 1780 he was mainly occupied with suppressing Tory uprisings. Taken prisoner at the battle of Camden, he was subsequently exchanged and spent the closing years of the war besieging a British-Loyalist force in Wilmington. Rutherford served continuously in the state senate from 1777 to 1786 where he waged political war on the North Carolina Loyalists with the same gusto that had characterized his movements on the field of battle.[29]

The rural element dominated the legislature throughout the Revolutionary period and the legislature controlled the government. It chose both the governor and the judiciary, and it rarely chose men of strong will or independent mind. Perhaps it did not matter, for the governor had little power anyway. The role only frustrated those who brought any ability to the office. Richard Caswell, who presided over the Provincial Congress that wrote the state constitution, served as governor until 1780. He worked closely with the assembly leaders Jones and Person and left office before the fighting reached the state. His successor, Abner Nash, spent most of his term battling the assembly and its Board of War. When he retired, unlamented, the assembly elected Thomas Burke, who shortly thereafter was captured by the British. Though Burke eventually escaped, he refused reelection, and in 1782 the assembly turned to Alexander Martin. A Piedmont tobacco planter,[30] Martin was popular with the assembly because he catered to it. His messages were couched in the humblest terms, and though he verbally supported such unpopular causes as leniency toward Loyalists he never exercised any leadership. Having made no enemies, he was reelected in 1783. When he left office, the assembly returned to its old friend, Richard Caswell.

The rural element controlled the state by sheer weight of numbers. There is no evidence of organization, or even of collaboration, among its leaders. Indeed, the leaders themselves can be identified only from references by their opponents. Though among the wealthiest men in the state, they had no gift for expressing themselves. Their few surviving letters are barely literate; the writing is labored and there are numerous spelling errors. Willie Jones, like his young protégé Nathaniel Macon, arbitrarily inserted a comma about every third or fourth word and made no particular distinction between commas, periods, and dashes. Perhaps the technical difficulty of writing explains why they communicated so seldom. Nor is there any evidence that they had verbal communications outside assembly meetings. In a state of such vast distances, any sort of get-together required considerable advance planning, but there is no hint in the correspondence even of social visits.[31] There was nothing in their situation that demanded a conscious group identity. They led an overwhelming popular majority, and they held their position because they shared its intellectual limitations and its prejudices.

Their opponents were far more articulate, and, being in a tiny minority, far more aware of their group identity. They corresponded regularly, published their views in political broadsides, and collaborated on a legislative program. From their efforts emerged, eventually, the state's first political organization. Let us call them, for lack of a better name, the Lawyers' party, for nearly all the more prominent members were attorneys.[32] They were closely associated with merchants in the coastal towns, and they often represented British clients in matters involving confiscated property and prewar debts. Hence they scorned the "Group of Farmers and Mechanicks" who faced them in the assembly, and battled the legal hacks whom the assembly placed on the bench.[33] The State Superior Court, which traveled among the principal towns to hold its sessions, had three judges, all paid annually by the legislature. The Lawyers approved of one of them, John Williams of Granville County (later a Federalist), but they fought constantly with the other two, Samuel Ashe (New Hanover) and Samuel Spencer (Anson), both later prominent in the fight against the Federal Constitution.

The outstanding figure in the Lawyers' faction was Samuel Johnston, a Scot who had come to the colonies in 1736. The proceeds from his successful law practice went to the acquisition of a gentlemanly estate, and by the end of the Revolution he possessed 6,137 acres and 48 slaves. By 1800 he had doubled that and possessed plantations in seven counties.[34] Though he held various offices in the colonial government, he early joined the Revolution-

ary movement, serving in all four Provincial Congresses and presiding over the third and fourth. He was in the Continental Congress
during North Carolina's years of trial, 1780–82. Thereafter he
tended his law business, seldom emerging onto the political stage,
except when momentous events seemed to demand his presence.
Even in retirement he remained an oracle for political conservatives
concerned for orderly government and the rights of property.

Almost equally influential, and even more retiring politically,
was James Iredell. Born in England the son of a Bristol merchant,
Iredell moved to North Carolina in 1768, studied law under Johnston, and eventually married Johnston's sister. He remained aloof
from the Revolutionary movement, was slow to approve the idea of
independence, and stuck to his law practice through the war. In
1783 his house in Edenton was staffed by seven slaves, and he
possessed plantations in neighboring counties totaling 3,830
acres.[35] Though constantly importuned by friends to stand for
office, Iredell emerged only once into the political arena—in the
ratifying convention of 1788. But his sage advice, constantly solicited by numerous correspondents, and drafts of "anonymous" resolutions periodically adopted by "popular" meetings made him one
of the key intellectual and literary personages in the Lawyers'
faction.

The Lawyers' leading assemblyman at the end of the war was
Archibald Maclaine, an outspoken, crotchety attorney from Wilmington. A native of northern Ireland, Maclaine made himself the
spokesman for the interests of Loyalist exiles both in and out of the
assembly. He defended their property in the courts and advocated
repeal of the confiscation acts in the Commons. But in the charged
atmosphere of war hatred and demands for tax relief, Maclaine was
a solitary figure. Wealthy land speculator William Blount, who
often sided with the lawyers, returned from Congress in 1783 and
promptly sponsored a bill for a new emission of paper money. It
whipped through the assembly without even a roll call.[36] When that
session ended in late May, Maclaine complained to a Tory friend: "I
attempted every thing I possibly could to make some reform in our
public affairs; but there are so many bad men in the assembly, and
so many unconstitutional members [evidently those who failed to

TABLE 3.3   NORTH CAROLINA COMMONS:
TAXATION AND DEBT ISSUES, 1782–1783

	Maclaine	Person	Middle
Albemarle	4	2	10
Pamlico	5	2	11
Cape Fear	2	1	2
Piedmont	0	8	21
West	2	2	5
	13	15	49

meet the property qualifications], that it was beyond the power of any single man, and I was very slenderly supported."[37] On the surface, Maclaine seemed to be correct. The assembly refused to provide relief for Loyalists or British creditors, it authorized printing of more paper money, and it approved a stay law that effectively prevented court-enforced debt collection for a year.

Roll call analysis of the assembly in North Carolina encounters as many difficulties as it does in Virginia. The number of roll calls and turnover in each session were similar and absenteeism was considerably worse. By 1783 the state had fifty-five counties and six towns. Since each county was entitled to four representatives and each town two, a full House would have contained 232 members. Only a third of that number was present on any given roll call. Thus any attempt to combine sessions in order to obtain enough roll calls to permit identification of attitudes inevitably eliminates most of the members. In addition, the issues at stake in roll calls are not always clear from the Commons *Journal*. Since Maclaine's position is clear from his correspondence, the only solution is to use his voting record as a model of "creditor" behavior. And since he regarded Person as an arch-foe, those who voted against him can be considered Person's allies. The results are given in table 3.3 (with a minimum agreement threshhold of 75 percent).[38]

Except for the regional pattern, the voting was virtually random. Neither Maclaine nor Person commanded consistent support. Maclaine was probably too sour to command a following, and Person lacked the drive. On the other hand, there was no third grouping associated with another leader. What appear, then, are the bare nuclei of opposing parties, unorganized and unled—merely fortuitous agreement among men of similar interests. One was centered in the Albemarle-Pamlico region, the other in the Piedmont, with the Cape Fear and the west divided. By 1784, under the stimulus of economic hard times and the organizational efforts of the Lawyers, the regional pattern would become clearer.

The debtor legislation of 1783 greatly alarmed the Lawyers. During the summer Iredell drafted a manifesto, which was approved by a popular meeting in Edenton on August 1. It endorsed the congressional impost and demanded that the state put its own fiscal house in order by redeeming its paper money and collecting back taxes. It asked the assembly to repeal the laws that suspended suits for the collection of debts, and it suggested that liberal salaries and longer tenure would secure a more learned and independent judiciary. Finally, Iredell pointed out that the future prosperity of the state would depend on the development of commerce and manufactures, and he suggested that this could best be done by removing the threat of political persecution of Loyalist merchants and encouraging their return.[39]

Iredell's manifesto was a litany of creditor-nationalist reforms, put into a comprehensive program for the first time. Men of Iredell's persuasion had been battling for such laws in all three states since 1780, but hitherto they had fought for them piecemeal. By linking them Iredell laid the foundation for a political ideology, and he pointed out the need for organization. As the concept spread—and by mid-1784 Madison and Washington were discussing a similar program—it gave birth to the first political parties.

CHAPTER FOUR

Debtor Relief for Rich and Poor

THE MARCH of British armies and the forays of Loyalist raiding parties evoked cries of agony from Chesapeake planters in the last years of the war, but the damage was less than it seemed. Lord Cornwallis's year-long march from Camden northward into Virginia, and Banstre Tarlton's spectacular raids into the hinterland, flushing the frightened Virginia legislature even in remote Charlottesville, crushed American morale, but neither army cut a Sherman-style swath of destruction. The worst damage was confined to a relatively small area—Wilmington in North Carolina, the Norfolk-Portsmouth area in Virginia. Back-country farmers suffered from the civil war in North Carolina, and Benedict Arnold's raiding parties burned coastal plantations in Maryland and Virginia, but elsewhere people never saw enemy soldiers or heard an angry shot.

Economic dislocation caused more widespread hardship. The British naval blockade was thin and sporadic, but effective because of the peculiar geography of the region. British occupation of

96

Wilmington and Norfolk stoppered North Carolina's most important outlets to the sea. A few hosile vessels roaming Chesapeake
Bay brought the trade of Maryland and Virginia to a standstill. One
resident of Maryland's Eastern Shore complained that he could not
even get across to Annapolis without danger of "falling into the
hands of the British."[1] Since foreign trade was the major source of
hard currency, merchants and planters found themselves strapped
for funds. For a time the only source of specie in the entire area was
the French army in Virginia, and it went home after Yorktown.

The shortage of coin meant that domestic exchange depended
more than ever on paper money, but when the fighting ended this
source of currency also dried up. Eighteenth-century monetary
theory, such as it was, considered paper money a temporary expedient, justified only in a military emergency, and something to be
retired as soon as the emergency was ended. Adhering to this
concept, all three states undertook to redeem the paper they had
issued during the war, with little notion of what a drastic contraction of the money supply might do to their economies.

Congress set the example. In an effort to put its own fiscal
affairs in order, Congress in March 1780 ordered the paper issued
since the beginning of the war to be revalued at 40 dollars of paper
to 1 Spanish silver dollar, thereby scaling down the national debt by
that ratio. It proposed to replace the old paper with a new emission
of 10 million dollars, which, it was hoped, would retain its value.
Simultaneously, in recognition of the depreciation of state issues, it
recommended that the states deprive their paper of its legal tender
status. No longer acceptable in discharge of debts, it would cease to
disrupt the economy and eventually disappear from circulation.[2]

The southern delegations voted against the congressional
revaluation because they were busy printing new issues of their
own to finance the struggle with Cornwallis. But they eventually
adopted both Congress's example and its advice. In Virginia the
congressional action encouraged fiscal conservatives who had
become alarmed at the quantity of paper in circulation. In the May
1780 session of the assembly George Mason and Richard Henry
Lee tried to secure assembly approval of the congressional revalua-

tion. Patrick Henry objected, however, and the House of Delegates defeated the Mason-Lee resolutions, 25 to 59. Later in the session, after Patrick Henry departed for home, Mason and Lee persuaded the House to reverse itself and approve the resolutions.[3]

In the fall of 1780 Henry's forces retaliated with a bill making Virginia paper money legal tender for all debts at the ratio of 40 paper dollars to 1 Spanish milled dollar. The measure was designed to bolster the value of Virginia paper and at the same time relieve debtors (because the market value of Virginia currency was actually about 150 to 1). In the spring of 1781, with the military situation in the Carolinas deteriorating further, the assembly authorized another issue and made it legal tender. This proved to be the state's last emission, and in the fall session, after the surrender of Cornwallis, the assembly passed an act making state paper no longer legal tender except in payment of taxes, and establishing its value in Spanish dollars at 100 to 1. The outstanding paper money could be exchanged, at the rate of 1,000 to 1, for new loan certificates, bearing 6 percent interest and redeemable in specie on or before December 1, 1791. George Mason was behind this measure, but it also had the support of Patrick Henry. Perhaps Henry realized that the paper currently in circulation was worthless and felt that the loan certificates would be a stable, reasonably permanent substitute.[4] He undoubtedly also subscribed to the general view that paper was to be resorted to only in extreme circumstances.

Whatever Henry anticipated, the result was a rapid deflation. Within a year the amount of paper circulating in Virginia declined from £60 million (in face value) to less than £1 million. Over the next couple years perhaps as much as another £1 million in certificates was issued to pay the state's demobilized soldiers, but in 1782 the assembly permitted holders to exchange these for western lands. A year later it made taxes payable in certificates, even making such payment compulsory for certain levies. Over the next four years it retired £625,000 in paper certificates through tax receipts.[5] While this substantially reduced the state debt, it also contracted the money supply. The extent of this contraction is evident from the report of a legislative committee in 1784, which calculated that

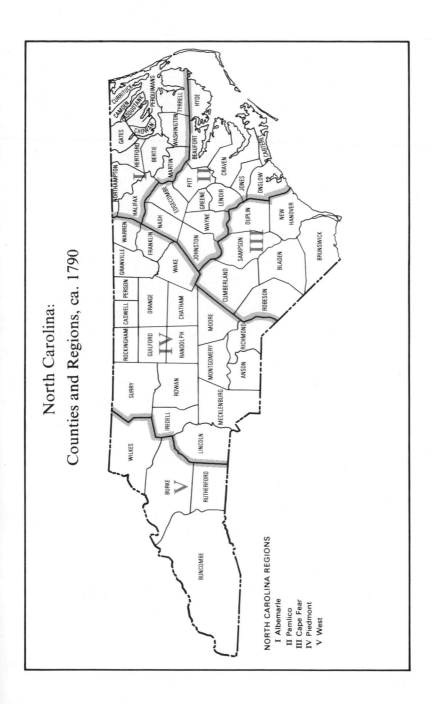

North Carolina:

Counties and Regions, ca. 1790

NORTH CAROLINA REGIONS

I Albemarle
II Pamlico
III Cape Fear
IV Piedmont
V West

the state was retiring its war debt at the rate of £207,700 a year. Since annual expenditures were estimated at only £256,293, this meant that over 80 percent of the annual budget was devoted to debt retirement.[6] Since debt certificates were a major part of the circulating medium, the state's currency was reduced by that much each year, and the dwindling supply of money could not help but aggravate the postwar price depression.

The Maryland assembly indulged in an orgy of paper issues early in the Revolution and then spent the rest of the war renouncing the habit. By 1777 it issued nearly half a million pounds in bills of credit, and the money quickly deteriorated in value, even when the assembly made it legal tender. In 1780 the state followed the advice of Congress and redeemed the money at one-fortieth of its face value. Thereafter the assembly was more circumspect. In 1780 and again in 1781 it authorized some £250,000 in new bills, but this time it tied the money to confiscated Loyalist property. It was to be used in payment of public debts only, and as the state sold the property to private investors it retired the paper money. By 1784, when the sales were virtually completed, the paper money had all but disappeared. Thus Maryland paper was not intended for commerce, and what little the state issued late in the war was rather quickly retired.[7]

North Carolina went through a similar experience. Its credit suffered from British invasion and a legislature in constant flight. Its currency depreciated rapidly, and by the time the British were driven from the state it had virtually ceased to circulate. As early as 1779 the assembly recognized that the state's paper was not the equivalent of specie and because of its uncertain status the money was of little value in trade. Until the assembly authorized a new emission in 1783 money was as scarce in North Carolina as it was in Maryland and Virginia.[8]

The hardship sliced diagonally through Chesapeake society. Middling farmers owed money to wealthy planters, and the wealthy owed large sums to merchants at home and abroad. All suffered alike from the shortage of currency, and cries for relief were heard from all quarters. As a result, the measures undertaken by the assemblies at the end of the war had broad support. The relief debate did not separate rich from poor, nor were political lines firmly drawn.

TAX RELIEF

Tax defaults were the most prominent symptom of the currency malaise. Local debts were often resolved by barter, but taxes had to be paid in currency, even in specie unless the legislature made special provision. The primary source of revenue in all three states was the property tax levied on land and slaves. Though the wealthy paid more, the burden of the tax was felt most acutely by poor farmers. During the war Virginia levied a tax of one shilling per hundred acres, making no distinction between fertile river bottom and barren mountains. Under pressure of western delegates the assembly in 1782 divided the state into four "natural" regions, scaling the levy by region. Like acreage was taxed at ten shillings per pound valuation in the Tidewater, seven shillings sixpence in the Piedmont, five shillings sixpence in the Valley, and three shillings beyond the Alleghenies. Land values were determined by local assessors, usually prominent gentlemen in each parish. North Carolina levied a tax of five shillings per hundred acres until 1786 when it divided the state into three regions and imposed a graduated tax similar to Virginia's.[9] Even with scaling of assessments, the tax caused the greatest difficulty for the poor, who lived on the edge of the cash economy and seldom had the wherewithal to pay.

In Maryland the tax rate was set annually by the assembly, and it occasioned an annual battle. Indeed, the attitude toward the tax level was the main feature that distinguished the political factions at the end of the war. Land valuations also caused intermittent squabbling, along with the question of which officials would make the assessments. Although the adherents of governmental solvency were usually in the majority, the rate per £100 of landed property declined over the decade, from a wartime high of thirty shillings to less than ten by 1787.

The Office of Intendant of Revenue was an additional point of contention in Maryland. Created in 1781, the Intendancy was to supervise the state's finances, including tax collections and the sale of confiscated property. The debtor element, having no interest in making the tax system more efficient, disliked the concept from the beginning, and their suspicions were further aroused when the assembly filled the post with Daniel of St. Thomas Jenifer, a fiscal conservative who had served before the war as the proprietor's agent and receiver general. Early in 1782 the House voted to abolish the office, but when the Senate stood firm the House relented and renewed it for another year.[10] The parties fought over the office for the rest of the decade.

Only landowners paid the property tax; landlords, unless their leases specified otherwise, entered the lists in behalf of their tenants, but all free adult males had to pay the poll tax. Slaveowners paid for each adult slave, though slaves between the ages of 12 and 16 were assessed at a lower rate. Although the poll tax, like the property tax, fell most heavily on the poor, that class also found it most easy to escape payment.

County sheriffs were responsible for tax collection, for which they were rewarded with a portion of the proceeds. But they were also held personally accountable for defaults. Thus the office could be quite lucrative in good times and a disaster in a depression. They could seize property for nonpayment, but in many cases it was not worth the trouble. Edmund Randolph reported in 1783 that sheriffs were unable to sell distrained property for more than a fourth of its real value. One sheriff complained to the governor that when he seized some horses and slaves for back taxes, a band of men came in the night and carried them off.[11] The sheriffs' only other recourse was to the legislature. Throughout the postwar years the assemblies were flooded with petitions for relief from delinquent sheriffs. These were usually granted unless there was some evidence that the officer had been laggard or overly kindhearted in his collections.

In Virginia and North Carolina, where the rate level was not subject to annual assessment, county petitions for relief exceeded even those of sheriffs. The list of excuses had marked similarity—scarcity of money, low prices for tobacco, bad crop yields due to weather, and poor roads that kept farmers from getting to market.[12] The Virginia assembly was the first to respond. In the fall 1781 session the assembly passed an act enabling residents of the western counties to pay their taxes in tobacco, flour, or hemp. The following spring Patrick Henry sponsored a bill to postpone for several months the taxes due to be paid on June 1, and to add deerskins to the list of commodities that could be used for taxes. Neither measure seemed to raise much opposition, though state creditors grumbled privately.[13]

In the spring of 1783 the relief cause won new adherents. George Mason, who usually stood firm on fiscal responsibility, advocated postponing tax collections until the fall. Because money was scarce and trade not yet fully recovered from the war, merchants could depress the price of tobacco by refusing to buy. A planter who had to sell tobacco in order to pay his taxes was at the mercy of the merchants, Mason argued. By autumn a new crop was in, ships would arrive from Europe, competition would prevent merchants from managing prices, and planters would at last reap "the Benefits of Peace." Significantly, he addressed these remarks to Patrick Henry.[14] In the House of Delegates only Richard Henry Lee voiced opposition to postponement of taxes. His argument that it would mean delay in forwarding the state's congressional quota was not calculated to attract wide support, however. By a vote of 53 to 50 the House in committee of the whole approved a postponement until December.[15]

In the fall 1783 session Henry arrived late, as usual, and the tiny band of creditor men, led by Henry Tazewell, attempted to commit the House to the principle of taxation sufficient to meet the needs of government. The idea even received support from Henry's ally John Tyler, and the House approved it by a margin of 30 votes. Then Henry arrived and gave a rousing speech against the measure, whereupon Tyler and some 60 other delegates reversed themselves. The House then approved, by 61 to 23, a bill that enabled eastern Virginians, as well as westerners, to pay their taxes in commodities. The roll call revealed that Tazewell's following was largely confined to delegates from the lower James River Valley, but it was a base on which Madison could build when he entered the assembly the following spring.[16]

Madison was prepared to do battle with Henry, but not on the question of taxation. Petitions for relief poured into Richmond through the spring of 1784, and Henry arrived for the May session "charged high with postponement of the collection of the taxes." So reported John Marshall, one of Madison's new recruits. The assembly postponed tax collections for six months, while Madison grumbled privately about the "strange figure" which the state cut in national affairs. Madison wisely deferred a fight over taxation and concentrated instead on other issues, notably trade regulation and repayment of British debts.[17]

As a result of these constant deferrals, through 1784 Virginia avoided any serious popular disturbances, while retiring most of its paper money and reducing its debt. Though not the result of a conscious political program, tax relief benefited nearly every planter in the state, and only the tiny band of Madison men, committed more by ideology than interest to fiscal responsibility, saw any reason for complaint.

NORTH CAROLINA:
THE CURE FOR THE ILLS OF PAPER IS MORE PAPER

North Carolina accomplished essentially the same result, but by different means. Its property tax rate of three pence per pound valuation was the lowest in the South, and its valuations, fixed by county assizers, were understated. Beginning in 1781, moreover, the assembly permitted certain taxes to be paid in "specifics," such as grain, pork, and beef.[18] Even so, there were continuous cries for relief. Depreciation of the wartime paper led to hoarding of what little hard money there was. Barter was the most common form of exchange. Backwoods farmers and merchant speculators alike complained of the scarcity of money. The catalyst was a list of grievances drawn up by the North Carolina Line, which greeted the assembly when it met in Hillsborough on April 8, 1783. The Continental troops had not been paid in almost four years, and some men were threatened with imprisonment for debt. The plight of the line removed whatever hard-money opposition there was in the assembly; William Blount himself took charge of the bill authorizing a new emission.[19]

Although there was no roll call on the bill, the Commons did engage in lengthy and heated discussion. Conceding defeat on the principle, Archibald Maclaine and his hard-money allies concentrated instead on protecting the new paper from depreciation, and in this they were generally successful. The debtor element wanted the money backed by nothing but the credit of the state and the promise of gradual retirement through a special sinking fund tax. The sinking fund idea was tabled, however, and instead the assembly set aside the proceeds from the sale of confiscated property for the redemption of the currency, a device that had worked well in Maryland. In a further effort to instill faith in the currency the amount was limited to £100,000, and it was made legal tender for all debts public and private. To distinguish it from the discredited wartime issues, which were expressed in dollars, the new currency was put in values of pounds and shillings (one pound equaling 2½ Spanish silver dollars).[20]

The debtor element acquiesced in these provisions, but it showed its muscle in other ways. On the heels of the emission bill the assembly enacted a stay law that suspended for a year all suits for the recovery of debts before May 1, 1783. Then it departed for home without ever adopting legislation to establish a sinking fund out of the proceeds from confiscated estates. As a result the paper was never actually tied to Loyalist property and remained, in effect, fiat money.[21] Even so, the merchant community reacted favorably. A town meeting in Edenton on August 1 adopted resolutions, probably drafted by Iredell, which promised to support this particular emission while denouncing paper in general. Organizations of merchants were formed in Edenton and Wilmington to prevent deliberate depreciation of the money. By the fall of 1783 Governor Alexander Martin could report that faith in the currency was "pretty well established."[22]

The 1783 emission thus held its value reasonably well, especially when compared to the wartime issues. By the end of 1783 it depreciated about 15 percent off its nominal value when exchanged for specie, but thereafter it stabilized and remained steady for the next two years. At no cost to itself, the assembly silenced the war veterans and provided the economy with a credible circulating medium. The total amount of paper emitted was not sufficient to provide much help to debtors, but until the depression struck a year later the cries for relief subsided.[23]

TORY PROPERTY, PAPER MONEY, AND SPECULATORS IN MARYLAND

Tax relief in Virginia and paper money in North Carolina, whatever their practical effects, were at least verbally justified as aid to the poor. Paper money in Maryland had no such cover. Though it originated in the military emergency of 1780–81, it was tied from the outset to confiscated Loyalist property. Insofar as it became a relief measure, it benefited chiefly the public debtors who owed money for this property, men who were among the most enterprising, if not the most wealthy, in the state. Hinterland farmers endorsed paper money, just as their compatriots south of the Potomac did, but the state never issued enough, or gave it sufficient tender, to do them much good.

In November 1777 Congress recommended as a war measure that the states seize the property of Loyalists. The suggestion got a sympathetic response in Maryland, where Loyalists had caused considerable difficulty, especially on the Eastern Shore. Moreover, in the newer counties at the head of the bay, Harford and Cecil, tenant farmers had taken over lands owned by absentee Loyalists, some of them belonging to the Calvert proprietors. Confiscation might give them an opportunity to secure titles. Pressured by these manifold interests, the House of Delegates in December 1779 unanimously approved a confiscation bill. The Senate rejected it as a violation of property rights, and a bitter controversy ensued, the House claiming that the proceeds from the sale of the property were necessary to meet the state's congressional requisitions. The issue soon became entangled in the Chase-Carroll feud, which kept the two houses at loggerheads through the last years of the war.

In 1780 a new element intruded—the state's bank shares in London. This story dated back to 1766 when the colony's proprietor invested £26,800 of public funds in Bank of England stock. Three London merchants held the stock in trust, and dividends were to be used for the benefit of the colony. At the advent of the Revolution the state naturally claimed title, but the claim was contested by several Englishmen with estates in Maryland that had been seized by tenants. Prime among these was Henry Harford, the proprietor's heir, who came into his estate when he attained majority in 1779. This group prevailed upon the London merchants to refuse to transfer the bank stock until their claims were settled.[24]

Pressed by military disasters and eager to retaliate, in June 1780 the assembly issued £30,000 in bills of credit (later called "black money") and authorized the state treasurers to draw bills of exchange on the London trustees to redeem the stock. Its sale would help finance the state's war effort. Should the trustees refuse to honor the bills (either because the state's title to the stock was unclear or because of the use to which the funds were to be put), the assembly authorized holders of state paper money to recover their losses against the trustees' property in Maryland or against the estates of Henry Harford. In this way the House of Delegates wedged open the door to confiscation.

During the fall of 1780, Benjamin Franklin, who served as state agent, among his other duties, informed the assembly that the trustees refused to honor the bills of exchange. Loyalist property was thereafter the only untapped resource, and the Senate had to accept confiscation or see the state's paper money rendered worthless. The act of 1780 authorized the sale of all British property in the state, and it specifically earmarked the proceeds from the sale of the Nottingham Company ironworks (one of whose owners was a stock trustee) for retiring the spring issue of "black money." The best the Senate could do was win an amendment that exempted debts owed by Marylanders to British citizens, but this was a hollow victory since the assembly had already approved a measure permitting Marylanders to discharge their British debts in state paper.[25] The following year the assembly authorized a new issue to finance the war in the Carolinas (designated "red money"), and the proceeds from the sale of other estates were set aside for its retirement.

Three commissioners were appointed to supervise the sale of the confiscated property, though in 1784 the problem was turned over to the Intendant of Revenue. By 1778 most of the lands had been sold. The largest parcels were those belonging to the two companies that had made Maryland the foremost iron-producing colony. The Nottingham Company, owned in partnership by four English merchants, possessed some 12,000 acres in Baltimore County and an ironworks that employed 160 slaves. The 1780 law ordered the property to be subdivided, but the forges and mills, together with about 5,000 acres, were sold intact to a consortium headed by Baltimore merchant Charles Ridgely. A prominent member of this group was House leader Samuel Chase.

The other ironworks, owned by the Principio Company, was even older and larger. It held some 30,000 acres of land in Baltimore and Cecil with four furnaces and two forges. The commissioners succeeded in breaking it up into smaller parcels, but among the largest purchasers were again Charles Ridgely, Samuel Chase, and Sam's cousin, Jeremiah T. Chase. Although Samuel Chase obviously had had an interest in acquiring Loyalist property from the very beginning, the measure was not a legislative pork barrel. Of the 39 individuals listed as sharing in the acquisition of the two estates, Chase was the only member of the assembly at the time the law was passed, and only 7 other purchasers served in the assembly at any time during the decade.[26]

Confiscation nevertheless had important political ramifications, for the purchasers had no more tangible resources than the state did. Few paid for the lands with state paper, and even fewer offered hard money. Most gave the state personal bonds which they hoped ultimately to redeem, just as the state hoped to redeem its bills of credit. Indeed, the promises came to rest on each other, for the ability of the speculators to pay their debts depended to some extent on the availability of currency. This wedded them to paper money, though for the moment they did not ask the legislature to print more. Instead, when they got into payment difficulties they went to the assembly to beg for more lenient terms. Not until the depression of 1784 did they decide that the solution to their problems was currency inflation. Nevertheless, it was widely suspected that private rather than public interests were behind the paper money campaign. The "principle" involved, said one distraught senator, "was a rascally one which often pervades public

Bodies in which too great a Number of Persons are interested to make public Measures bend to their private lives."[27] The storm passed quickly in 1781, but it left clouds of suspicion. Any future requests for relief were certain to brew new thunderheads.

After Senate resistance collapsed in 1781, neither confiscation nor paper money caused much controversy. In the following year the House of Delegates modified the confiscation legislation in minor ways. The result is not always clear from the *Journal,* but Chase and his friends were always in the majority. The Senate approved a bill relating to confiscated property by 7 to 1, and a few days later it passed by 6 to 2 a bill enabling purchasers to use the 1781 "red money" in payment for all types of confiscated property (hitherto it had been tied to particular estates). Both of the Carrolls voted in favor of these measures; James McHenry was the only consistent opponent.[28]

Paper money caused no trouble, either. Although there was no demand for a new emission, the assembly maintained what it had. The assembly followed Virginia's example by paying its discharged soldiers with certificates, and it even made them transferable so that they would circulate. The paper forces also defeated every effort to retire the money by making it acceptable for payment of taxes, as Virginia did.[29]

In the two 1782 sessions there were five votes in the House of Delegates involving paper money. If the record of Samuel Chase is taken as the model, the House generally favored paper. Support for it came from all regions, though it was most prominent among delegates from the upper Potomac and upper bay. Of the two factions that fought over taxes and official salaries, debtors supported paper money and creditors were divided. About half sided with Chase and paper money; the remainder held firm. But there were important differences between Chase and his debtor allies. Chase and his creditor friends sought to maintain the value of the paper money by keeping it on a par with specie, insofar as possible. The debtor element opposed this; their motives were purely inflationist.[30] Most of the debtor group also voted against the bills which eased the terms for purchasers of confiscated property, while Chase and his friends naturally favored leniency toward speculators.[31]

In 1783 the Senate became concerned that the state might not get full value for the confiscated property unless the commissioners were empowered to accept paper money in all sales. A resolution directing the commissioners to accept continental paper, as well as black and red state paper, passed 7 to 1, with only Charles Carroll in opposition. Surprisingly, the Delegates rejected the idea, 20 to 22.[32] Opposed to it was a combination of men who disliked paper money in any form and hinterland debtors, who may have objected to the continental feature. Perhaps they did not want to benefit holders of the national debt. In any case, the vote did not represent opposition to either speculators or paper money. The House had already approved by a substantial 33 to 8 margin a resolution directing the treasurer of the Western Shore to stop issuing executions of court orders against speculators who had failed to pay the required two-thirds of the purchase price for state lands, and by a similar margin it approved a bill permitting all those who owed money to the state to pay in military certificates. The Senate quickly approved both these measures, the only opponents being Charles Carroll and Edward Lloyd.[33]

In summary, neither paper money nor confiscation provoked much controversy in Maryland down through the end of 1783. They won general approval because the poor hoped to benefit, and certain spokesmen for the wealthy actually did benefit from them. Even in the Senate Charles Carroll was a lonely voice of opposition. Backing the speculators in 1783 were such stalwarts as William Hindman, who had bitterly opposed confiscation, and James McHenry, who fought every other type of relief legislation. The consensus was possible partly because the state was in good shape economically. It emerged from the war virtually undamaged, and the assembly managed its money supply in such a way as to avoid the wild fluctuations that tormented Virginia and North Carolina. But the good will depended on prosperity, and it collapsed in the postwar depression.

BRITISH DEBTS: VIRGINIA

While paper money attracted most of the attention in Maryland and North Carolina at the end of the war, Virginians were preoccupied with another feature of debtor relief, their prewar obligations to British merchants. Although only about 500 planters were named in the accounts, it seems likely that indebtedness covered a much broader range. Among the largest debtors, moreover, were some of the most prominent political figures in the state. Because the issue involved both personal integrity and state reputation, it became the most divisive of the postwar years.

Americans, and Virginians more than most, entered the Revolution deeply in debt. Throughout the eighteenth century Virginians were accused of living beyond their means, but more prudent management would only have mitigated their difficulties. They needed to import capital to develop their vast hinterland, and their failure to service their own export trade insured a chronic imbalance of payments.

During the Revolution there were many guesses as to the total indebtedness of Americans, but there was no accurate information until 1791, when a number of British merchants submitted to their government a joint statement of the American account. As of that year, Americans owed a total of £4,930,656, nearly all of which was owed by southerners. Virginians alone accounted for nearly half (£2,305,408), and Marylanders owed another £517,445. These figures included accumulated interest since the beginning of the war, and of course excluded debts that had been paid. It thus appears that the total private indebtedness of Americans at the outset of the Revolution was about £4 million, and Jefferson's estimate that Virginians owed £2 million was not far wrong.[34]

There is no evidence that Virginians or other Americans joined the rebellion in order to escape debt payment, but once they took up arms they saw little point in reimbursing the enemy.[35] George Mason, who personally favored repaying British creditors, reported that he frequently heard it asked: "If we are now to pay the Debts due to British merchants, what have we been fighting for all this while?!"[36] Some of these obligations were owed directly to the great mercantile houses of London, Liverpool, or Glasgow; others were owed to British factors in America.

During the war the assemblies of both Maryland and Virginia, hoping to obtain some cash while relieving their constituents, authorized debtors to discharge their obligations with state paper money. The states would hold the funds in their loan offices and pass them on to British creditors at the end of the war. Before Virginia's law was repealed in 1780, some 500 planters discharged all or part of their obligations in this way, depositing over £250,000 in paper money worth about £12,000 sterling. Marylanders paid off some £144,574, valued at £86,744.[37] However, few actually expected British merchants to accept this arrangement.

In November 1781 the Virginia assembly placed a moratorium on both foreign and domestic debts. The following spring it replaced this with an act closing the state's courts to suits by British citizens. Those who regarded this as permanent were disappointed by the Anglo-American peace agreement, preliminary articles of which were signed in November 1782. Article IV provided that creditors on both sides would meet with no legal impediments to the recovery of debts in sterling. Leading the outcry against this provision was Meriwether Smith, a member of the governor's council and a long-time ally of Patrick Henry's in the assembly. In the course of 1783 he published several pamphlets strongly advocating a continuation of the debt moratorium, at least until Virginia was reimbursed for the damage done by British armies. In addition to the destruction wrought by Arnold's fleet and Tarleton's raiders, Virginians estimated that British armies carried off some 30,000 slaves, though they failed to reckon that a substantial number of these had fled voluntarily to British lines in search of freedom.[38]

Given the residue of hostility from a destructive war and the obvious advantages of procrastination, the marvel is that anyone might be bold enough to advocate repayment. Yet there were some who desired just that, and among them were some of the most prominent debtors. Motives varied, of course, with each individual. Those with a broad perspective recognized that economic development depended for the foreseeable future on British capital, and there was little chance of securing future loans until past debts were settled.[39]

Others had more personal considerations. Many of the wealthier Tidewater planters did a substantial importing business for their neighbors, having long since discovered that trade was more lucrative than growing tobacco. Possessing little fluid capital of their own, they were necessarily dependent on foreign credit, and that meant sustaining a reputation for honest dealing.[40] Others, like Washington, recognised that they could not in justice demand payment from their local debtors while refusing to pay their own international obligations.[41] But the most commonly expressed sentiment was pride. William Grayson thought the assembly ought to repeal the laws impeding recovery of debts "to preserve the honor of the State." Beverley Randolph even borrowed money from a friend in order to repay a debt to a British merchant because he "conceived [his] Honour to be at stake," adding in explanation that "The numberless Reflections which have been thrown on our Country men on this subject renders me the more anxious to avoid a participation of them."[42] Such sentiments were not confined to merchants or to the wealthy. A 1783 petition in behalf of paying British debts drafted by George Mason contained the signatures of 85 freeholders of Fairfax County (see table 4.1). Only three of them resided in the city of Alexandria; the rest were planters. And in terms of slaveholding wealth they represented a fair cross-section of the county (61 could be identified in the Fairfax personalty books for 1782 and 1783).[43]

Paying the interest that had accumulated during the war was another matter, however. Washington pointed out to a Loyalist friend, upon repaying a debt in sterling, that if he had paid it when it became due during the war, he would have had to pay it in paper money, "thereby giving the shadow for the substance of the debt."

TABLE 4.1   FAIRFAX PETITION ON BRITISH DEBTS, 1783: WEALTH OF SIGNATORIES

Slaves Owned	Signatories
0	11
1–4	19
5–12	19
13–24	8
25–49	3
50–99	0
100+	1

Since the creditor himself benefited from the delay, it seemed unreasonable to demand interest. In a similar vein, Jefferson informed a British creditor that he had sold lands in 1776 in order to pay his debts, but all he got for them was paper money that had less value than oak leaves. Even though the British had burned his fields and carried off thirty of his slaves, Jefferson was willing to repay the principal, but he objected to paying the wartime interest because the delay was not his fault, but Britain's for starting the war. Jefferson ultimately agreed to an interest rate of 5 percent for the war years.[44] In the end, the Virginians' own penchant for legalism undermined their resistance. Judge Edmund Pendleton spoke for many when he observed, "A National War, tho' it might suspend, ought not to destroy the contracts or engagements of individuals."[45]

The peace treaty seemed to solidify this creditor sentiment, just as it did the opposition. As soon as the preliminary articles reached the United States by packet in March 1783, George Mason started writing letters to legislative figures, hoping to prevent "more mischief" on the debt problem. If the assembly created further impediments to the collection of debts, he reasoned, it would discourage British merchants from trading in Virginia, and it might give Parliament an excuse to abrogate the peace treaty altogether.[46] In its May session the assembly did approve a bill repealing the acts that had authorized the confiscation of British property, but it showed no disposition to go further. Thomson Mason, George's brother, offered a proposal to open the state courts to British suits but enabling Virginians to pay judgments in five annual installments. The House rejected this compromise by 66 to 23.[47]

In the fall 1783 session the creditor element managed to add to a bill suspending executions for debt a proviso that "nothing in the act contravenes the treaty with Britian," but the proviso was struck out, 47 to 26. The prevailing sentiment, Governor Harrison explained to the state's congressional delegation, was that debt payment ought to be delayed until Britain offered compensation for slaves taken by its armies.[48] By early 1784 Virginians had an additional excuse for procrastination. Britain was violating the treaty in its own right by maintaining garrisons in forts south of the

Great Lakes—at Oswego, Niagara, Detroit, and Michillimacki-
nac—on territory that Virginia had not yet formally ceded to
Congress.[49]

British debts were high on Madison's agenda when he arrived
in the House of Delegates in the spring of 1784. When the matter
came before the House, the Henry-Tyler forces sought to capitalize
on British transgressions with a resolution complaining of the slaves
carried off to New York at the end of the war. The Madison men
countered with a resolution to repeal all legislation that obstructed
the peace treaty. The House turned aside this frontal attack, by 37
to 57, and appointed a committee to look into the Henryite
allegations. The committee returned with a proposal that the state
inform Congress that it would not cooperate in fulfilling the treaty
until Britain reimbursed the slaveowners for their losses. Madison
then suggested a compromise. Debts could be paid in installments.
If Britain failed to comply with her end of the treaty, damages could
be taken out of the second installment. This failed by a similar
margin, 33 to 55.[50] Edmund Randolph felt that a particularly
virulent anti-British pamphlet by Meriwether Smith was responsible for the assembly's continuing intransigence.[51]

During the summer pressure from Congress and other states
strengthened Madison's hand. While investigating investment possibilities in western New York, congressional delegate Monroe
learned that the British were using Virginia's impeding laws as an
excuse to retain Niagara and other posts. Richard Henry Lee
reported that this news increased northern hostility toward the
state. Virginia nationalists felt their worst fears confirmed. The
state's intransigence would give Britain an excuse to abrogate the
treaty, and that would tear the union apart.[52]

In the fall 1784 session Joseph Jones renewed the assault with
a series of resolutions committing the House to a repeal of the laws
closing the courts to British suits. The nationalists' arguments had
taken effect, and the resolutions passed handily, though Madison
feared that any resulting legislation would contain "some improper
ingredients" in regard to slaves and northwest posts. Unable or
unwilling to resist the majority view, Henry and Tyler wavered in
their opposition to the measure, and Henry finally departed alto-

gether. The House then passed "by a very great majority" a bill providing for repayment in seven annual installments but excluding any interest charges for the war years. The Senate added some clauses providing for repayment of debts owed to Loyalists, whether from a desire to repay all obligations or a wish to kill the bill Madison was uncertain. While a conference met to resolve the differences, a few members crossed the James River to Manchester and were detained there several days by bad weather. This deprived the House of a quorum and prevented it from acting finally on the bill. After waiting a few days while attendance dwindled further, it adjourned, and the debts bill was never formally approved by both houses.[53] No one, including the state judges, knew whether the old legislation was still in force or not.[54] But there the matter rested until 1787, when it became embroiled in the contest over the Constitution.

Unfortunately, neither the Jones resolutions nor the bill that finally passed evoked a roll call vote, but there were three such votes in the two previous sessions. Lacking the external pressure that was manifest in the fall of 1784, they may reflect more elementary responses to the issue. In any case, lines were firm and the division, given in table 4.2, is revealing (the table uses only those who voted consistently, 3 out of 3, or 2 of 2).[55] The regional

TABLE 4.2 VIRGINIA HOUSE OF DELEGATES: BRITISH DEBTS, 1783–1784

	Favoring Repayment	Opposing Repayment
Northern Neck	5	2
Middle Tidewater	5	4
Piedmont	2	4
Southside	3	19
West	3	5
	18	34
Federalists, 1788	14	1
Antifederalists, 1788	1	11
Unknown	3	22
	18	34

distribution offers a clue to the nature of the factional lineup that was taking shape in the Virginia assembly by 1784.[56] Madison's creditor-minded following drew its strongest support from the Northern Neck and the lower James (three of the middle Tidewater delegates and one of the Southside delegates lived on the James). Patrick Henry's strength lay in the Southside and the Piedmont. A correlation with later stands on the Federal Constitution demonstrates the persistence of this factional division, but it also indicates that the question of repaying the debts involved national feeling as much as economic self-interest. The one Northern Neck nationalist who deserted Madison on this issue was voting not his own interest but from a mistaken impression of his constituents' desires.[57]

In some respects, the most interesting feature of the table is the split among the western delegates, hitherto consistent allies of Patrick Henry. Chief among those switching to Madison's side was Alexander White, a lawyer from Winchester. Westerners were evidently becoming alarmed at the British presence in the Northwest and the effect this might have on the Ohio Indians. Since they owed no debts to British merchants, it was easy enough for them to deprive the British of their excuse. This reasoning eventually caused a complete shift in the stance of the western delegates. Allying themselves with Madison in 1787, they provided the critical votes that resolved the problem of British debts and secured ratification of the Federal Constitution.

BRITISH DEBTS: MARYLAND

In December 1779, following Virginia's example, the Maryland House of Delegates passed a bill permitting debtors to discharge their obligations to nonresidents by depositing paper currency with one of the state treasurers. Senate objections held up the bill until October 1780, when it finally met with approval along with confiscation and paper money. The act also suspended prosecutions for debt for a limited time, a period which the legislature subsequently extended to January 1, 1784. Marylanders quickly deposited £144,574 in state paper money, a sum representing about a third of their total obligations. Since the state paper was then pegged to sterling at a 40 to 1 ratio, British creditors understandably disregarded the deposits.

At the end of the war British debts never became a source of political controversy in Maryland. No Meriwether Smith surfaced to agitate the issue, and even those who disliked the 1780 law, such as General Otho Holland Williams of Baltimore, thought that "those who complied with it ought to derive all the advantages proposed by it."[58] The assembly permitted the law closing the courts to British suits to expire quietly on New Year's Day, 1784. Agents of British mercantile firms entered the state and opened debt-collection offices. Although they occasionally encountered resistance, it seldom had political repercussions. The most spectacular event occurred in 1786 when a Scots attorney named Alexander Hamilton, who had spent the war in semi-exile in the Shenandoah Valley, filed over a hundred suits on behalf of a Glasgow firm in the Charles County court. A mob began to form, and the three judges, all connected with the creditor faction in the House of Delegates, suggested that Hamilton withdraw the suits lest he fill the county jail with indebted citizens. The attorney obliged and the mob dispersed. Hamilton then protested to Governor William Smallwood, who investigated and exonerated the judges, though he did fine the mob leaders and prohibited such outbursts in the future.[59]

After the war the only feature of the British debt problem that drew the attention of the legislature was the question of wartime interest. Marylanders seemed generally willing to repay the principal, though they managed to delay most of the suits until prosperity returned in the late 1780s, but they objected to paying interest for the war years when it was physically impossible to pay the debts except under the terms of the 1780 law. This matter too was handled without controversy. In 1783 the House of Delegates refused, 13 to 28, even to consider a bill that would have eliminated wartime interest charges.[60] There was no regional pattern to the vote, and the alignment bore no relation to voting on other matters, such as domestic debts and taxation. As a result, the question of interest was left to the courts, and after some conflicting opinions by county judges, the court of appeals finally ruled in 1790 that interest for the war years would be disallowed.[61]

The remaining issue was whether Article IV of the peace treaty, which prevented states from interfering with debt payments, rendered void the 1780 statute and the paper deposits made under it. In 1786 the House agreed, by 30 to 16, to set up a committee to inquire into the amount of paper money deposited in the treasury under that law, but the committee's report was postponed to the next session, 21 to 18.[62] Again there was neither a regional nor a partisan pattern to the voting. Both factions, whose ranks held so firm on other economic issues, were divided. It was clearly a matter of individual interest, or conscience.

One reason, perhaps, that the Maryland assembly remained calm on the subject of British debts was state's hostage bank stock. At the end of the war Samuel Chase went to London as agent for the state, but he returned empty handed. The state did not actually recover the stock until 1804 after the various Loyalist claims were settled. In the meantime, no one was anxious to aggravate British mercantile opinion by parading the subject of British debts. In 1785 one British legal agent reported Samuel Chase to be "very moderate and favourable to Britain" on the subject of planter debts.[63]

In April 1786, Congress, prodded by the British refusal to evacuate the northwest posts until Americans paid their debts, formally asked the states to repeal all laws that were in violation of the peace treaty. The Maryland senate promptly passed the requested act, but the House rejected it, possibly out of fear of its impact on the state's confiscation of Loyalist property. The House measure simply stated that the peace treaty was the supreme law of the state and should be so considered in all courts of law.[64] The creditor element generally favored outright repeal, while Chasites and debtors backed the compromise language. But party lines were not firm, and the voting bore no relation to subsequent stands on the Constitution. As a result, the matter was handled by the courts, and by the early 1790s nearly all Marylanders had come to terms with their British creditors. It was no longer a source of concern to them when John Jay in 1794 signed a treaty subjecting the remaining unpaid debts to international arbitration.

BRITISH DEBTS: NORTH CAROLINA

During the war North Carolina also closed its state courts to British creditors. Although its citizens owed less than other southerners,[65] it amounted to a substantial obligation in a state forever short of hard currency. Archibald Maclaine grumbled about the inhibiting legislation, but he could do little until the peace treaty was signed and its debt provisions became known.[66] In the spring of 1784 the subject was high on the Lawyers' agenda. A joint committee, heavily weighted with Lawyers, reported in favor of bills that would repeal the laws that contravened the treaty. The proposal, Benjamin Hawkins reported, stirred up loud "complaints of hard times and heavy taxes" and "clamours against the refugees and payment of British debts . . . by men who cannot possibly be [benefited] if all bona fide debts are wiped off with a sponge."[67]

In the confusion, Abner Nash and William Blount, both opportunists with pretensions to popular leadership, reversed the support they had given the proposal in committee and joined the outcry. A bill repealing all acts in conflict with the fourth and sixth articles of the treaty (Loyalists' rights as well as British debts) failed on its first reading, 32 to 37. The vote was closer than might have been expected, however, and a few days later the Lawyers worked out a compromise with their opponents. The Commons resolved unanimously that the acts tending to contravene the peace treaty ought to be repealed. The Lawyers thereupon announced their opinion that this was sufficient to open the courts to suits for British debts.[68] Whether the courts would see it this way was up to the judges, and sympathizing with the debtor element, they did nothing. There the matter rested until the end of the decade, when different judges and easier times enabled British agents to collect. The legislature took no further action, and the problem of British debts in North Carolina was resolved in peacemeal fashion, as in Maryland.

DEBTOR RELIEF AND THE EMERGENCE OF PARTIES

In the two-year interval between the end of the fighting at Yorktown and the final ratification of the peace treaty the Chesapeake states coped fairly successfully with the social and economic problems connected with demobilization. War damage and economic dislocation caused some hardship, but the legislatures responded in practical ways, through currency manipulation, court closures, and tax relief. Because these measures had broad impact and brought benefit to a wide variety of social interests, they created few political tensions. Small farmers of the hinterland supported these measures because they expected help, and they did benefit, though perhaps not as much as they had anticipated. The wealthy were divided. Some feared the effects of relief legislation out of self-interest and principle. Others benefited enough so that they were willing to compromise principle for immediate interest. Although the political lines lacked definition, each debate gave rise to small corps of men opposing each other. When the political issues became more hotly contested under the impact of postwar depression, the factions enlarged to the point where they dominated the legislatures.

Some of the controversies even spilled out of the assembly halls and caught the attention of voters. The German tourist Johann Schoepf, traveling from Bladensburg to Baltimore in the fall of 1784, found the public houses flowing with conversation about politics. The main concern at the moment was British debts and the question of wartime interest. The assembly elections were at hand, and voters were apparently extracting commitments from the candidates. When all was over, the general feeling was that only the Baltimore delegates, who had a mercantile constituency, would favor payment of the wartime interest.[69] The prognos ration proved quite correct. And it foretold the end of the politics of personalities. Issue-conscious voters who felt their own interests keenly would become less and less satisfied with a vague promise to guard the common weal offered by some "gentleman of respectability." When candidates felt obliged to commit themselves on the issues at election time, the character of the whole representative system had changed.

Associating the various issues with one another was but a short step, one already made by such perceptive leaders as Madison and Iredell. In this association lay the germ of a political platform. Here

Virginians led the way. In December 1783 Madison's Shenandoah Valley friend Alexander White received a set of resolutions drafted by a citizens meeting in Winchester. The resolutions opposed any further tax postponements, demanded compliance with the requisitions of Congress and a strengthening of its powers, favored the expansion of the state judiciary, and suggested that any person who "obstructed the execution of the [Peace] Treaty in America ought to be considered as an enemy to his country."[70] Thus, by the end of 1783 several ingredients of a party system were present:

—associations of like-minded men in the assemblies acting together out of common interests and attitudes;
—formation of a coherent political program in response to those interests;
—public discussion of the issues and efforts to influence the behavior of representatives, or, alternatively, a review of the legislators' behavior at election time.

The ingredients were there but unformed. Depression was the catalyst.

CHAPTER FIVE

Emergence of State Parties, 1784–1787

THE YEAR 1784 was a critical one for the birth of parties in the Chesapeake states, for in that year political leaders came to realize the interrelationship among various issues and hence recognized the need for organization. Those who first perceived this, Iredell and Madison, built upon nuclei that had formed in the immediate postwar years. Madison took over from Henry Tazewell a tiny band that had favored payment of taxes and British debts; Iredell worked closely with the politically aware lawyer-merchants of coastal North Carolina. But the critical difference in 1784 was the formation of a program that spanned a number of state and national concerns—and a conscious search for allies who could help put the idea into effect.

The outline of this program was similar in all three states, and beneath it lay a common attitude, if not an ideology. The gist of it was resistance to the economic measures that had been instituted by the debtor majority at the end of the war. Those measures had been conceived in piecemeal fashion, isolated responses to new problems created by the war and independence. Because there was common agreement on the solutions proposed and because there was widespread benefit from the relief laws, no one felt the need to rationalize them into a "program" or defend them collectively. Being a majority, the rural debtor element that promulgated these measures felt no need to organize itself or win allies.

As a result, the first genuine party activity came from their opponents, from men who disapproved the relief measures and sought to overturn them. The attitude they shared can best be described as "creditor," though by no means did that mean that all of them were wealthy. It was a matter of a man's world view, not his balance sheet. In a rural society with few banks, Chesapeake planters relied on friends and relatives for credit. Each of them was involved in a complex web of financial relationships. George Washington, who was an enormously wealthy man in terms of land and slaves, often complained that he did not know whether his assets matched his obligations. Among those who owed him money in the postwar years were such prominent planters and merchants as John Francis Mercer, Thomas Newton of Norfolk, Robert Rutherford of Winchester, Robert Alexander, and John Armistead.[1]

Complicating these credit arrangements was the endemic scarcity of money. Specie had always been hard to come by, and what little remained after the European armies departed was driven out of circulation by the flood of paper money. Creditor men objected to paper money because its depreciation complicated their financial arrangements, but its retirement deprived them of the one medium of exchange they had (outside of tobacco warehouse certificates, which were an important colonial currency but which did not seem to enter financial calculations after the war). The very poor had always functioned on a barter economy; as money disappeared altogether after the war, even the rich paid the rich in produce. Cumbersome as this was, creditor men preferred it to paper money. Washington finally agreed to settle John F. Mercer's debt in slaves (three artisans and three ditch diggers), wheat and corn, and military certificates. Of the three forms of payment, Washington was most reluctant to accept the certificates. He had never wanted to possess depreciated securities, he said, because he disliked speculation.[2]

Wealthy planters such as Washington took advantage of the relief legislation, but they did so with many misgivings. When the legislature in 1788 passed a tax-relief measure enabling planters in arrears to pay their back taxes in certain kinds of public securities, Washington threatened to take the securities he possessed and "commit them to the flame." He had accepted them in the discharge of past debts; he had not purchased them for speculative purposes and knew nothing of their market value. Yet he took advantage of the law to pay the state £107 in taxes on his western lands for the years 1785–86. To his friend David Stuart he confided that a combination of an expensive household and poor crops "have occasioned me to run into debt and to feel *more sensibly* the want of money, than I have ever done at any period of my whole life."[3]

Dictating this set of attitudes was a mixture of self-interest and ethics. Washington and others like him equated hard money and debt payment with honesty; it was a matter of pride and integrity. It was equally obvious—though not so often expressed—that those virtues improved one's credit rating. In regard to a debt he owed in New York, which was secured by Governor George Clinton, Washington complained of the comparatively high 7 percent interest charge and observed that he would have tried to secure a reduction in the rate "if my credit was not at stake to comply with the condition of the loan." To retire the remainder of the debt, which he had reduced in a year from £1,069 to £800, he was even prepared to sell land and slaves.[4]

Washington was a farmer who spent part of his time doing the business of a banker. The justice of debt payment concerned him at least as much as the profit involved. Among others, such as merchants with interstate connections, the reliability of money was a matter of survival. Seeking to reassure a wealthy Virginia client that his account in Maryland currency would hold its value, a Baltimore mercantile firm sent him a list of newly elected members of the state senate, "by which you will see," they added, "we have little to fear from a depreciated Paper Currency. Had we not thought we should have had such security to our Government for five years We would have protested your drafts."[5]

This set of attitudes was not, however, confined to the wealthy or the mercantile-minded. Neither Madison nor Iredell was a man of great wealth; nor did they engage in large speculative enterprises. Madison, in particular, virtually ignored his landed estate and lived primarily on the emoluments of public office. There were, in addition, numerous village merchants and lawyers whose business affairs were as tangled as Washington's, though on a much smaller scale. Although less articulate than Washington, they shared many of his attitudes. A 1784 meeting of one hundred citizens in southwestern Botetourt County asked its delegates to secure repeal of the laws inhibiting payment of British debts because such laws were "inconsistent with those principles of honesty and patriotism which we have uniformly avowed."[6]

The debtor mentality was equally complex. Small, penniless farmers were understandably debtor-minded, but so were some of the wealthy. "In North Carolina," observed one traveler, "there are considerable landholders, owning 200–300 Negroes, who yet cannot command enough cash to pay their taxes, and must sell Negroes or horses to get money."[7] Nor was it always a matter of an individual's account books. Patrick Henry and Willie Jones were both wealthy men suffering no observable cash shortage, yet both consistently championed relief measures, possibly from conviction, perhaps because it was the road to popularity. Baltimore merchant Charles Ridgely was the best example of this breed. He favored debtor-relief legislation throughout the 1780s, supporting the principle even before his partner in speculation, Samuel Chase, did. Ridgely was one of the wealthiest men in the state. Baltimore tax records for 1783 credited him with £13,150 in land, mills, and forges, plus 122 slaves. Some of this was Loyalist property for which Ridgely owed money to the state, but his assets almost certainly exceeded his liabilities. He backed paper money and debt postponement in company with Chase and other speculators, but he also voted debtor on occasions when his own interests were not so immediately involved—on taxation, for instance, and officials' salaries. His record made him the most popular political figure in the county. Until his death in 1790, Baltimore freeholders regularly returned him to the lower house, and he often led the poll. Discouraged opponents felt such regularity was a sign of electoral stupidity. One claimed that "if you were to set up a Stone the People of the County would vote for it."[8] The freeholders knew better, for, whatever his motives, Ridgely represented their interests.

It is impossible—and probably unnecessary—to determine whether any of these men were following interest or ideological conviction. In most cases the two were related. What is important to note is that the extension from narrow considerations of self-interest to broad formulations of principle, even principle that was nothing more than interest broadly defined, was another step in the evolution of political parties.

PARTY FORMATION: 1784

The set of resolutions drafted by James Iredell and approved by a popular meeting in Edenton, North Carolina, in August 1783 was the first announcement of a coherent political program in the Chesapeake states. Iredell deftly wove together public and private fiscal responsibility, court reform, the return of Loyalists experienced in mercantile affairs, and a strengthening of congressional powers. Beneath all lay a vision of long-term commercial development for both state and nation through a stable political system that encouraged savings and investment. Whether such a scheme served the immediate needs of North Carolinians was open to question. But the formation of a political creed and the effort to give it legitimacy through the endorsement of an open public meeting were immensely significant. Popular meetings were a common device in the struggle against imperial rule, but during the Revolution they fell into disuse. In the 1780s party leaders found new uses for them.

In the spring elections of 1784 the Lawyers made a conscious effort to increase their strength in the assembly. In midwinter Archibald Maclaine heard a report that both Johnston and Iredell planned to stand for election. The latter evidently did give it some thought and decided against it. Spring legislative sessions, he had complained in a postscript to his manifesto, discouraged participation in political life because they coincided with both the planting season and the sessions of the Superior Court. However, Samuel Johnston, who was wealthy enough to feel fewer obligations, did step forward for a Senate seat. The opposition put up three candidates against him, but if they hoped to split the electorate they failed. Johnston received twice as many votes as the runner-up, even though he was out of town during the entire campaign. Iredell inferred from Johnston's report of the contest that it was a party battle, but it is clear from the outcome that his personal prestige was still an important factor.[9]

In the Senate Johnston joined forces with Allan Jones, elder brother of Willie. Jones lived across the Roanoke River from his brother on a magnificent plantation that boasted over 100 slaves.[10] The careers of the two brothers had diverged during the Revolution when Allan became a brigadier general of militia and opposed the legislature's efforts to avenge itself on the Loyalists. During the last years of the war he alternated between the Senate and Congress. Maclaine considered him sensible on both Loyalists and fiscal policy.[11]

The extent to which the Lawyers exerted themselves to change the complexion of the assembly is indicated by the number of newcomers in the 1784 session. Among them was General Jones's son-in-law, William R. Davie. Though born in England, Davie had joined the Revolution and at the age of 24 attained the rank of commissary general in Nathanael Greene's Southern Department. As early as 1781 he came to the attention of Johnston and Iredell as a man of potential. Iredell found in him "much goodness as well as greatness of soul," phrases that, on such short acquaintance, meant little except an identity of political views.[12] The following spring Davie married a daughter of Allan Jones, moved to Halifax, and opened a law practice. He quickly earned statewide notoriety by conducting the defense of several prominent Loyalists who had been charged with treason. It is likely that he was still living in the house of his father-in-law when he was elected to the Commons from Northampton County. At least he owned no land in the county, so the general probably helped him obtain the seat.[13]

From Warren County, just across the Roanoke River, came Benjamin Hawkins, who had recently returned from a three-year stint in Congress. There he had come under Madison's influence, and after his return to Carolina he kept up a steady correspondence with the Virginia nationalists. He kept them informed of the activities of the North Carolina assembly on such items of mutual concern as the impost, treatment of Loyalists, and British debts.[14] As a result, he was an important link in the exchange of ideas that led to the formation of a creditor-nationalist program. Hawkins, like Madison, was almost a professional public servant, though he possessed a handsome plantation of 2,770 acres and ten slaves.[15] In 1785 Congress employed him to negotiate settlements with the Creeks and Cherokees, and after his return from the Southwest he spent two more years as delegate to Congress. In 1789 he entered the federal Senate, and when the Republican assembly retired him in 1795 President Washington made him federal Indian Agent for the Territory South of the Ohio, a post he held until 1816, two years before his death.

Completing the Lawyers' circle in the lower house was William Hooper, a Harvard-educated son of a Boston clergyman who had moved to Wilmington in 1767 and set up a very successful law practice. An early adherent of the Revolutionary movement, he was disbarred by the colonial legal fraternity for his radical writings. The assembly sent him to the First and Second Continental Congresses, and he was a signer of the Declaration of Independence. His radicalism, however, was confined to the imperial connection; he made it clear that he would have no truck with democracy at home.[16] Then in 1777 he retired from politics, dismayed, perhaps, by the democratic features of the North Carolina constitution, embarrassed, possibly, by the Loyalism of his brother.[17] Sometime thereafter he moved to distant Hillsborough in the north-central Piedmont. The change cost him nothing financially, for he emerged from the war in possession of seven plantations scattered from the Roanoke to Cape Fear, plus a magnificent house in Hillsborough valued at £1,500.

These four joined Maclaine in the 1784 Commons, and though they could not hope to control the house, they certainly infused it with a new spirit. Hooper and Hawkins, old hands in the assembly, managed to obtain seats on the committee to determine a legislative agenda, and there they pushed hard for the program outlined in Iredell's manifesto.[18] Shortly after the session opened Davie was ready with a bill to retire the paper money in circulation through sales of confiscated property and special levies. The bill obtained enough support from paper money adherents, who wanted to see its value maintained, to pass three readings, but it died in the Senate.[19]

Next the Lawyers turned to the newly ratified peace treaty and specifically to the fourth, fifth, and sixth articles, which asked the states to remove the restrictions they had placed on the collection of prewar debts owed to British merchants, recommended the restitution of confiscated Loyalist property, and prohibited the states from making any further confiscations. Few North Carolinians owed money to the British, but feelings on the Loyalist issue still ran high. The Lawyers did prevent the enactment of a new confiscation law, but when they introduced a bill to restore to Loyalists confiscated estates that had not yet been sold, they went down to defeat, 18 to 62. They then introduced a bill almost identical to the one that George Mason had been pushing in Virginia. It sought to repeal all state laws inconsistent with Articles IV and VI of the treaty (i.e., postwar confiscations and British debts). This was rejected on first reading by 32 to 37, but the closeness of the vote indicated that another approach might work.[20] So they offered a vague resolution to the effect that laws inconsistent with the treaty ought to be repealed. This finally won approval by voice vote. The Lawyers hoped this verbal stance would open the state courts to British suits, although debtor-minded judges failed to see it that way.[21]

The Lawyers made more headway on matters of national concern, in which the debtor majority had little immediate interest. The assembly approved Congress's 1783 request for power to levy an impost and an amendment to the Articles of Confederation granting Congress power to regulate trade. Not content with that, the Lawyers managed to get a law granting Congress the power to levy a property tax within the state, proceeds of which would be used to discharge the national debt. It would not take effect unless the other states adopted similar measures (and, as a result, never did), but it was a striking display of nationalist feeling. The Lawyers confessed privately that they had pushed it through the assembly only with great difficulty.[22]

Another nationalist victory was the cession to Congress of the state's territorial claims west of the mountains, following a similar cession earlier that year by Virginia. Finally, before departing for home, the assembly harkened to Iredell's plea and changed its sessions from spring to fall, beginning in the autumn of 1784. Otherwise, the Lawyers' achievements were largely negative. "The political phrenzy ran high, beyond anything I had foreseen," Hooper explained to Iredell. "Those obnoxious men, the lawyers, prevented some mischief being done. But for them, we should have been saddled with some Acts of Assembly, that would have marked the Annals of this country with an infamy that no time or atonement could have wiped away. A Court of Chancery with ———— for a judge; unlimited jurisdiction to County Courts; a law continuing confiscation, and directly violating the treaty of peace. These are a small part of the evils which died abortions."[23]

Unfortunately, the Commons disposed of most of these items without roll call votes, so it is difficult to determine the extent to which the House was polarized by "the political phrenzy." It did hold 11 roll calls, however, nearly all on important issues, including the cession of the West (5 votes, one omitted from the tabulation as repetitious), taxes (2 votes), and one vote each on confiscation, British debts, and a land office. Using the record of Archibald Maclaine and his circle (Hooper, Hawkins, and Sitgreaves agreed with him 100 percent) as a model, the alignment was as shown in table 5.1 (minimum participation 3 votes, agreement threshold of 75 percent).

Only the bare nuclei of parties can be seen in this table; over half of the House voted more or less randomly. But the regional and political pattern established here would persist for the next decade. The Lawyers were still in a minority—perhaps more so even than the figures indicate—but their political success was the result of their cohesion. Among their most prominent men, only

TABLE 5.1 NORTH CAROLINA COMMONS: PARTIES, 1784

	Lawyers	Rural-Debtor	Middle
Albemarle	8	3	11
Pamlico	5	3	10
Cape Fear	4	2	4
Piedmont	4	11	11
West	0	6	6
	21	25	42
Federalists	10	1	11
Antifederalists	1	10	9
Anti- 1788, Fed- 1789*	0	2	0
Unknown	10	12	22
	21	25	42

*This category is made necessary by the state's two ratifying conventions. It seems useful to record here and in subsequent tables the positions of men who voted against the Constitution in 1788 and in favor of it in 1789.

William R. Davie failed to agree 100 percent of the time. William Blount, who usually voted creditor, went his own way on Loyalists and British debts, but the Lawyers never regarded him as an ally anyway. Conversely, among the rural leaders only William Lenoir and Joseph McDowell invariably disagreed with Maclaine. Thomas Person and Timothy Bloodworth unaccountably voted in favor of enforcing the peace treaty, and Matthew Lock voted yea on taxes. The Lawyers doubtless capitalized on this sort of confusion throughout the session.

The Commons conducted no roll calls of importance in the fall session, but the Senate did. And the regional pattern was similar.[24] The upper house held four roll calls—one on the cession of the West, one on a tax measure, and two on paper money amendments to a bill directing the sale of confiscated property. The acknowledged antagonists in the Senate were Allan Jones and Griffith Rutherford. The latter missed this particular session, so the debtor element lacked its usual verve. The most prominent figure in it was General William Lenoir of Wilkes, who had moved over from the Commons in the summer election. In his train was young Nathaniel

Macon of Warren, just embarking on a legislative career that would span the next half century.

Five senators agreed with Jones on all four votes, and another 7 supported him on three of the four. Voting against Jones at least 75 percent of the time were 10 senators. The split was almost perfectly sectional. Jones's followers all lived on the seacoast (Jones's own residence at the rapids of the Roanoke was the farthest west of the group), and they were about evenly distributed among Albemarle, Pamlico, and Cape Fear districts. His opponents all came from the Piedmont and western counties. Most remarkable is the extent of polarization, given the variety of issues on which the senators voted. Of the 31 men who attended the session, 23 identified themselves with one side or the other. Of Jones's followers 4 became Federalists in 1788 and 3 became Antifederalists (one of whom voted for the Constitution in 1789). On the other side, 5 opposed the Constitution, 1 supported it.

When the session ended in June, the Lawyers were fairly pleased with themselves.[25] One might have expected them to redouble their efforts in the fall session; instead, they gave up. Johnston, Davie, and Hooper returned to their law practices, and Hawkins was defeated in the late-summer elections (required, ironically, by the change to fall sessions) after opponents of the Tennessee cession accused him of being an agent for Congress. Maclaine in the Commons and Jones in the Senate were left to carry on almost alone. It is unlikely that more intensive effort would have done the Lawyers much good anyway. As the state slipped into economic depression, the debtor majority recovered its strength and initiative. For the next four years it outnumbered its opponents by a margin of almost two to one. The factional lines drawn in 1784 nevertheless persisted; indeed, they tended to harden under the impact of economic duress.

In Virginia the creditor-nationalist element likewise faced a loose-knit, largely silent, farmer majority that looked to Patrick Henry for such leadership as it required. Desiring change, but finding themselves in a minority, the creditor-nationalists were forced to take the lead in organizing. In Virginia the critical figure was James Madison, who returned home from Congress in December 1783. His congressional experience had reinforced all his political attitudes—a preference for sound, orderly government in place of the feckless drift that seemed to characterize the Confederation; a stable economic system in which debtors would meet their obligations and moneyed men would be encouraged to invest, thereby promoting national development; a society that could hold its head up in the world by meeting its international obligations and by making itself commercially as well as politically independent. Madison never published his political ideas, perhaps because, unlike Mason and Iredell, he did not have a collection of friends and neighbors whom he could muster at a moment's notice.

That he had a coherent program is evident from his actions upon his return to Virginia and the unaccustomed energy he infused into the legislature. The political conception probably matured in discussions with Jefferson, who joined him in Congress in 1783. The two had become friends during Jefferson's term as governor when Madison served on the council. In Congress the friendship ripened into a political and ideological union that lasted the rest of their lives. That the two held long discussions in Philadelphia on political topics and legislative tactics is evident from their later correspondence.[26] Madison returned to Virginia ready to put their midnight thoughts into action.

On his way south from Philadelphia Madison stopped at Gunston Hall and had a long talk with George Mason. He immediately reported the results to Jefferson. Mason was one of those men who could perform great public services—for which he was justly famed—but he was also capable of much mischief. As a political ally he was too independent to be reliable, too doctrinaire to be effective. Despite his immense wealth and broad learning, he was incredibly provincial. Only rarely would he venture as far as Richmond to attend a legislative session. The 180-mile journey to Philadelphia in 1787 was the farthest he ever got from home. Yet his standing in Virginia was such that he could not be ignored. His support for an item of business was a welcome boost; his opposition could wreck any political timetable.

The two men covered the whole ground of issues, from the congressional impost (to which he was "much less opposed . . . than

I had expected," Madison confessed) to the cession of the West. On the state's legislative agenda the two saw eye to eye. "His heterodoxy," Madison concluded, "lay chiefly in being too little impressed with either the necessity or the proper means of preserving the confederacy."[27]

During the spring Jefferson won another recruit to the cause— James Monroe. Recently appointed delegate to Congress, Monroe had journeyed to Philadelphia while Madison was on his way home. Monroe had been under Jefferson's wing since 1780, when he left William and Mary to join the governor's staff in Richmond. In Philadelphia he took up lodgings with Jefferson, who apparently resumed the dialogue that had been broken by Madison's departure. When Jefferson was nominated for a mission to France, he quickly wrote Madison to recommend his protégé. Explaining that Monroe wished to open a correspondence, Jefferson pointed out that he would be in a position to keep Madison informed on congressional politics. Moreover, Madison could trust him with confidential communications. "A better man cannot be," Jefferson summed up.[28]

Madison spent the winter digesting classical treatises on government, and then in April 1784 stood for the House of Delegates. News of his election spread quickly among the creditor element and raised high hopes. "Our friend of Orange," Edmund Randolph predicted to Jefferson, "will step earlier into the heat of battle, than his modesty would otherwise permit. For he is already resorted to, as a general of whom much has been preconceived to his advantage." "They have formed great hopes of Mr. Madison," added William Short. "A Majority of this Assembly are new Members and consequently we may expect new Measures."[29]

Others noted the high turnover in members, even though it was no higher than usual for the House of Delegates.[30] But the spring elections had generated a good deal of popular interest and a spirit of change seemed to be in the air.[31] The creditor element anticipated that the new men would prove tractable, despite the presence of "a few hot spirits." Edmund Randolph thought that Madison might even be able to organize them as a counterbalance to the three prevailing "corps" belonging to Patrick Henry, Richard

H. Lee, and John Tyler.[32] No one mentioned the names of any newcomers, but the high hopes generated suggest that the credentials of some, at least, were known. Among them was a young Richmond attorney, with whom Randolph must have been acquainted, John Marshall. Although in the assembly he represented Fauquier County (where he possessed lands inherited from his father Thomas, who had moved to Kentucky), Marshall had moved to Richmond a year before and married the daughter of Jacquelin Ambler, treasurer of the state and one of the wealthiest planters on the lower James. For the friends of energetic government and fiscal orthodoxy, Marshall was a firm and articulate ally.

Another new face was that of Edward Carrington, Marshall's brother-in-law who had married the other Ambler daughter. Although he possessed several plantations in Cumberland and Powhatan counties across the James from Richmond, Carrington mingled farming with the law and spent a good deal of time in the city. His uncle, Paul Carrington, was Chief Justice of the General Court and a strong nationalist. This social and professional circle[33] formed the heart of Richmond Federalism until Jefferson's presidency.

Three other men of ancient lineage and substantial wealth completed the class of freshmen legislators in 1784—Wilson Cary Nicholas, Richard Bland Lee, and Francis Corbin. Nicholas was a friend and neighbor of Jefferson's from Albemarle. Lee, brother of "Light Horse Harry," was a young, 23-year-old gentleman of leisure, who was in line to inherit extensive lands in the Northern Neck. Corbin was newly returned from England where he had spent the war attending school—Cambridge and the Inns of Court. His father was a Loyalist who remained in England, suffering the seizure of his Virginia estates. Young Francis recovered some of them and through his law practice rebuilt the family fortune.[34] He and Lee both remained lifelong Federalists; Nicholas followed the politics of his friends Jefferson and Madison after 1789.

Madison's first project, when the assembly opened in early May, was to secure the commercial independence of Virginia, from northern as well as British merchants. The Henryites had sought to sever the British connection by closing state courts to British suits and placing restrictions on the return of British factors. Madison felt these moves did more harm than good because they hampered the flow of credit and left the state at the mercy of Yankee merchants. Far better to build up a class of domestic merchants. These would cater to the commercial needs of the planter majority and leave the state less dependent on outsiders. That, in turn, would alleviate the fears of northern domination frequently expressed by such men as George Mason and Richard H. Lee and thereby reduce the opposition to congressional power.[35]

The basic difficulty, ran Madison's diagnosis, was decentralization of Virginia's trade. So long as every planter with a wharf was a tobacco exporter and wholesale importer, Virginia would be in the hands of foreign merchants—whether from London, Glasgow, or Philadelphia—who could coordinate shipments and arrange long-term credit. As evidence, he pointed out that prices for tobacco were 15 to 20 percent higher in Philadelphia than they were on the James River. The differential, Madison felt, ought to be retained by Virginians. Thus, among his first targets at the opening of the 1784 session was the chairmanship of the House commerce committee.[36] The committee quickly drafted a bill to confine Virginia's foreign trade to the ports of Alexandria and Norfolk, a solution that was soundly grounded in mercantilist thought, if not in common sense. Madison explained to Monroe that he hoped to establish "a Phila[delphia] or a Baltimore among ourselves."[37]

Supporters of the measure quickly thought of secondary benefits. Since the act would apply only to vessels owned by non-Virginians, it would give a competitive advantage to resident merchants and stimulate the state's shipbuilding industry. Edward Carrington predicted that the bill would attract merchants and tradesmen to the favored cities, and that in turn would promote manufactures, which "can never flourish but in large & prosperous Towns."[38]

Though well-intentioned, the measure was ill-conceived, and it would have excited resistance and promoted smuggling. Confining the state's trade to two ports was much too restrictive, and in the assembly it quickly ran afoul of local interests. In short order the ports of York, Tappahannock (below the falls at Fredericksburg), and Bermuda Hundred were added to the bill. The logrolling alienated a few, such as John Marshall, who thought the original intent was being undermined, but it also won some new support. On June 17 the House approved the revised bill by 64 to 58.[39] Supporting Madison were nearly all the same members who backed the proposal to open the state's courts to suits for British debts. Restored credit and commercial development went hand in hand.[40]

Indeed, the voting on these two issues is an important clue to the development of Virginia parties. British debts were the subject of three roll calls in the 1783–84 sessions.[41] These votes, combined with the voting on the port bill, are shown in table 5.2 (counting only those who voted at least 3 times and were perfectly consistent). The numbers are small because of electoral turnover; and because two sessions are involved there is no way of measuring the degree of polarity in the House. Nevertheless, the relationship to stands on the Federal Constitution four years later suggests that parties were beginning to form. Madison's geographical strength was in the Northern Neck and the lower James.[42] The opposition was centered in the old Henryite strongholds of the south and west.

Only four delegates who favored repayment of British debts

TABLE 5.2   VIRGINIA HOUSE OF DELEGATES,
1783–1784: BRITISH DEBTS AND PORT BILL

	Favor Both	Oppose Both
Northern Neck	4	2
Middle Tidewater	3	1
Piedmont	0*	3
Southside	3	12
West	2	5
	12	23
Federalists, 1788	9	0
Antifederalists, 1788	0	10
Unknown	3	13
	12	23

*Madison himself was not included in the tabulation, even though he favored paying British debts, because he was not in the 1783 session.

voted against the port bill, evidently because they objected to the alterations made by the assembly. All subsequently voted with the Madison party and became Federalists in 1788.[43] Thus Madison's following, tiny though it was, showed considerable internal cohesion on these two issues. The debtor-antinationalist group had less. Fifteen of those who were opposed to paying British debts supported the port bill, including Patrick Henry himself. All except Henry came from counties in the vicinity of the preferred ports.

Though two groups were present, they hardly amounted to a party system. The creditor group, despite their active search for friends, failed to attract more than a handful of new recruits. Most of the support Madison obtained on the port bill fell away on matters of domestic debts and taxation. The assembly was still debtor-minded. In 1784 Madison commanded no more support than the Lawyers did in North Carolina, but, unlike the Lawyers, Madison continued to build.

THE FIRST PARTY SYSTEM: MARYLAND, 1784

Maryland possessed no political leader with the perception of Iredell and Madison, nor did anyone in Maryland seek to articulate a political platform comparable to Iredell's manifesto. But it did possess rudimentary party blocs as early as 1782, and by 1784 these blossomed into well-formed parties. There is no evidence in the written record of conscious efforts to form party organizations in this period, but there must have been some collaboration, some form of direction, to account for the remarkable cohesion evident in the computer print-out reproduced as table 5.3. A comparison of this cluster bloc matrix with that of 1782 (table 3.1) offers dramatic visual evidence of the crystallization of parties.[44]

The House of Delegates conducted a total of 89 roll calls in the 1784 session, 68 of which are used here to compare agreements. As in earlier sessions a majority involved economic matters—property taxes (17 votes), customs duties (12 votes), salaries and fees (8 votes), and the state debt (3 votes). But there was a wide variety of other issues, ranging from religion (8 votes) to education (5 votes), relations with Congress (3 votes), and internal improvements (2 votes). Given the number of legislative concerns and the lack of evidence that there was an established "party line" on anything, the degree of internal cohesion is really quite remarkable. In the creditor party there was a solid core of pairs who agreed with each other more than 80 percent of the time and very few delegates who failed to agree with every other member of the bloc at least 70 percent of the time. Since voting on educational matters and religion tended to be random, as each delegate followed his own predilections, in order to achieve this sort of unity agreement on the economic issues must have been close to 100 percent. The debtor party has more gaps and only a few isolated pairs exceeding 80 percent agreement. As in earlier sessions, there is no evidence of other clusters of like-minded delegates. It was a two-party system from the beginning.

Twenty-eight legislators were absent or abstaining on at least half the roll calls and were accordingly omitted from the calculations. But every other delegate entered the matrix, that is, agreed with somebody else 70 percent of the time (in 1782, 11 delegates failed to make this threshold). There were 22 in the creditor bloc (ending with Digges of Prince George's), 15 in the debtor bloc (from Cellars of Washington to Stevenson of Baltimore; Worthington, Taney, and Seney are assigned to the middle), and 11 in the middle group. This means that of those who voted on at least half the roll calls, 77 percent sided with one party or the other, a degree of legislative polarization that would not be improved upon until after 1800. The regional split was essentially the same as in 1782, northern and western counties against the southeast and the cities. The creditor party was in the majority primarily because of malapportionment; the Eastern Shore was overrepresented in the House and the upper Potomac was underrepresented.

As in earlier sessions economic issues were the main source of party dispute. The creditor force held out for higher taxes, more substantial salaries for public officials, and retirement of the state debt at face value.[45] Interestingly enough, the mode of taxation did not seem to matter. Only one delegate favored high property taxes

TABLE 5.3   MARYLAND HOUSE OF DELEGATES, 1784: CUSTER-BLOC MATRIX (SHOWING CREDITOR PARTY)

	CHAS ESAN	QUYN NAAN	DASH JOSO	HIND MNTA	DASH JSWO	FRAZ RACA	CHAI LEWO	WATE RSSO	STEE LJDO	CARO LNAA	HARD CSCR	DEBU TSSM
CHASESAN	—	100	100	98	97	94	93	91	90	90	89	88
QUYNNAAN	100	—	97	98	97	91	93	89	91	90	89	85
DASHJOSO	100	97	—	97	94	91	90	91	91	87	90	84
HINDMNTA	98	98	97	—	98	94	95	93	92	92	88	88
DASHJSWO	97	97	94	98	—	90	97	94	91	92	83	86
FRAZRACA	94	91	91	94	90	—	90	88	87	82	83	77
CHAILEWO	93	93	90	95	97	90	—	88	86	88	85	84
WATERSSO	91	89	91	93	94	88	88	—	90	88	88	88
STEELJDO	90	91	91	92	91	87	86	90	—	90	83	83
CAROLNAA	90	90	87	92	92	82	88	88	82	—	86	88
HARDCSCR	89	89	90	88	83	83	83	85	88	83	—	86
DEBUTSSM	88	85	84	88	86	77	84	88	83	88	86	—
GIBSNWTA	88	92	88	92	92	89	89	92	95	82	86	81
JOHNSRPG	86	85	81	85	85	78	87	80	80	80	81	91
ELLZEYSO	84	87	85	86	85	79	80	90	85	77	76	75
TOWNSDWO	83	81	85	84	85	82	83	83	83	81	79	77
MCMECHBT	82	80	76	78	81	75	78		76	74		
DENTGECH	79	78	79	84	77	74	76	74	84	71	71	75
GRAHMJCA	78	75	77	80	71	85	72	74	77		71	73
WAREFRCH	77	78	77	79	76		76	70	75	71	73	73
GANTTEPG	73	78	72	79	79		77	74	81	86	72	80
DIGGESPG	72	73	70	71	70		72					
HARRISTA						70						
BOWIEWPG							71				71	76
PLOWDNSM												
GRAVESKE												
BEATYTFR												
RIDGYWBA												
ROBERTTA												
CRAMPHMO												
CELLARWA												
SWINGLWA												
STULLJWA												
WORTHNAA												
MILLRSCE												
NORRISHA												
JOBXARCE												
LOVEJOHA												

Top header fragments (partially cut off at page top), over the right-hand columns: GECH ← "LENT", MJCA ← "GRNT", FRCH ← "WARL", TEPG ← "GANT", ESPG ← "DIGO", ISTA ← "HARK", EWPG ← "BOWI".

	NWTA	SRPG	EYSO	SDWO	CHBT	GECH	MJCA	FRCH	TEPG	ESPG	ISTA	EWPG
CHASESAN	88	86	84	83	82	79	78	77	73	72		
QUYNNAAN	92	85	87	81	80	78	75	78	78	73		
DASHJOSO	88	81	85	85	76	79	77	77	72	70		
HINDMNTA	92	85	86	84	78	84	80	79	79	71		
DASHJSWO	92	85	85	85	81	77	71	76	79	70		
FRAZRACA	89	78	79	82	75	74	85	76			70	
CHAILEWO	89	87	80	83	78	76	72	76	77	72		71
WATERSSO	92	80	90	83		74	74	70	74			
STEELJDO	95	80	85	83	76	84	77	75	81			
CAROLNAA	82	80	77	81	74	71		71	86			
HARDCSCR	86	81	76	79		71	71	73	72			71
DEBUTSSM	81	91	75	77		75	73	73	80			76
DIBSNWTA	—	81	94	84	71	87	76	76	73			
JOHNSRPG	81	—	70	72	73			70	79			
ELLZEYSO	94	70	—	73		73	79	71	79	73		
TOWNSDWO	84	72	73	—		74						
MCMEGHBT	71	73		74	—					88		
DENTGECH	87		73			—		87				
GRAHMJCA	76	70	79	71			—				79	
WAREFRCH	76	79	79			87	—	—				
GANTTEPG	73	73	79					—	—			
DIGGESPG					88				—	—		
HARRISTA								79		—	—	
BOWIEWPG											—	—
PLOWDNSM		71			79				73	81		
GRAVESKE				74								
BEATYTFR					83					73		
RIDGYWBA					70					71	78	
ROBERTTA							76				77	
CRAMPHMO												
CELLARWA												
SWINGLWA												
STULLJWA												
WORTHNAA												
MILLRSCE												
NORRISHA												
JOBXARCE												
LOVEJOHA												
WHEELRHA												
EDWARDMO												

MARYLAND HOUSE OF DELEGATES, 1784: CLUSTER-BLOC MATRIX (SHOWING DEBTOR PARTY)

	PLOW DNSM	GRAY ESKE	BEAT YTFR	RIDG YWBA	ROBE RTTA	CRAM PHMO	CELL ARWA	SWIN GLWA	STUL LJWA	WORT HNAA	MILL RSCE	NORA ISHA
JOHNSRPG	71											
ELLZEYSO												
TOWNSDWO		74										
MCMECHBT	79		83	70								
DENTGECH												
GRAHMJCA					76							
WAREFRCH												
GANTTEPG	73											
DIGGESPG	81											
HARRISTA			73	71	78	77						
BOWIEWPG												
PLOWDNSM	—											
GRAVESKE		—										
BEATYTFR			—	76								
RIDGYWBA			76	—		70		73	72			
ROBERTTA					—	70	77		72			
CRAMPHMO					70	—				70		
CELLARWA				77			—	98	93		78	76
SWINGLWA				73			98	—	90		77	75
STULLJWA				72			93	90	—		79	75
WORTHNAA						70				—		
MILLRSCE							78	77	79		—	77
NORRISHA							76	75	75		77	—
JOBXARCE							75	78	74		81	90
LOVEJOHA							75	80	77		81	94
WHEELRHA							74	75	77		76	72
EDWARDMO							71	76	75		73	77
OGLEVECE							70	74	73		89	77
BREVADCE								71	72		84	75
ONEALEMO										78		
BONDJAHA										71	72	83
TANEYMCA										71		
SHRIVRFR											78	76
STEVNSBA											71	77
SENYJOQA												

TABLE 5.3 (SHOWING CREDITOR PARTY) CONTINUED

	JOBX ARCE	LOVE JOHA	WHEE LRHA	EDWA RDMO	OGLE VECE	BREV ADCE	ONEA LEMO	BOND JAHA	TANE YMCA	SHRI VRFR	STEV NSBA	SENY JOQA
JOHNSRPG												
ELIZEYSO												
TOWNSDWO												
MCMECHBT												
DENTGECH												
GRAHMJCA												
WAREFRCH												
GANTTEPG												
DIGGESPG												
HARRISTA												
BOWIEWPG												
PLOWDNSM												
GRAVESKE												
BEATYTFR												
RIDGYWBA												
ROBERTTA												
CRAMPHMO												
CELLARWA	75	75	74	71	70							
SWINGLWA	78	80	75	76	74	71						
STULLJWA	74	77	77	75	73	72						
WORTHNAA							78		71			
MILLRSCE	81	81	76	73	89	84		71		78	71	
NORRISHA		90	94	72	77	75		72		76	77	
JOBXARCE	—		70		89	81		83		79		71
LOVEJOHA		—	90	71	74	72		84			85	
WHEELRHA	70	90	—	71	76	71		82		82	81	
EDWARDMO		71	71	—	71	78	76	73				
OGLEVECE	89	74	76	71	—	91	72	72		86	73	
BREVADCE	81	72	71	78	91	—				77		
ONEALEMO				76	72		—	72		78		
BONDJAHA		84	82	73	72		72	—		81	84	76
TANEYMCA									—			
SHRIVRFR	79		82		86	77	78	81		—		
STEVNSBA		85	81		73			84			—	
SENYJOQA	71							76				—

TABLE 5.4   MARYLAND HOUSE OF DELEGATES:
ECONOMIC ISSUES, 1784

	Creditors	Debtors	Middle
Eastern Shore	13	0	6
Upper bay	0	10	1
Western Shore	9	3	4
Upper Potomac	0	6	4
Urban	4	0	0
	26	19	15

and low customs duties; the rest remained consistent throughout. Using the 37 votes on economic issues alone, it is possible to assess the attitudes of some delegates who did not vote enough to gain admission to the computer matrix. Requiring a minimum of 8 votes and an agreement threshold of 75 percent,[46] the results are as given in table 5.4. The basic regional pattern shown in this table persisted, with only minor alterations, throughout the history of the first party system.

The one economic issue where party unity broke down involved the Consolidating Act, which set up a sinking fund to redeem the state debt. The act involved special interests, for Samuel Chase, the most prominent member of the creditor party, and several of his friends were indebted to the state for purchases of confiscated property. They thus voted with the debtor element on this particular issue. Because it generated only three roll calls (only one of which distinguished the Chasites from other creditor supporters of the act), it did not influence the session-wide matrix. Chase's behavior is worth noting, however, because it forecasts the factionalization of Maryland politics in 1786.[47]

The Maryland Senate was not nearly so well organized. It recorded 12 roll calls in 1784, and there was no pattern at all. Indeed, the erstwhile leader of the Senate, Charles Carroll of Carrollton, was in the minority on 7 of them. The members were in broad agreement on the most important matters of state and federal policy, and nearly all were creditor-nationalists. Only one senator, John Smith of Baltimore, voted in favor of paper money and against the congressional impost.[48]

MARYLAND PARTY DIVISIONS, 1785–1787

Mounting economic difficulties in 1785 increased the cries for debtor relief, but the demand did not translate at election time into a larger bloc of debtors in the House of Delegates. The two parties retained about the same relative strength when the assembly opened in 1785. There was a new wrinkle, however. Samel Chase endorsed paper money as a form of relief and in so doing split the creditor party. A combination of Chasites and debtors passed an emission bill, but the Senate halted the venture.

Chase was hardly motivated by humanitarian concern for the poor. He and other speculators still owed substantial sums to the state for Loyalist property, and hard times plus the retirement of wartime paper made payment difficult. A new emission was an easy solution to their problems. Chase's defection, however, did not destroy the party structure that had appeared in 1784. Only a handful of friends and fellow speculators followed his lead. And his apostasy involved only paper money. On such questions as tax relief, private debts, court reform, and the office of Revenue Intendant, Chase and his friends voted creditor.[49] If the paper money ballots distinguish the Chasites from the regular creditors, the geographical distribution of parties was as shown in table 5.5.[50]

Despite the factionalization, House polarity remained about the same as in the previous year—75 percent were associated with one of the thee groups. Only about half the Chasites followed their leader into Antifederalism; the rest supported the Constitution, regardless of the threat it posed to paper money. Chase's following

TABLE 5.5 MARYLAND, HOUSE OF DELEGATES: FACTIONS, 1785

	Creditors	Chasites	Debtors	Middle
Eastern Shore	5	6	0	6
Upper bay	1	0	9	0
Western Shore	7	3	0	7
Upper Potomac	2	1	6	2
Urban	1	3	0	0
	16	13	15	15

thus seems to represent more a conjunction of interests than personal charisma.

Throughout this session the Senate remained the repository of fiscal orthodoxy. It is probable that none of the senators indulged in property speculation, and they were too self-contained (both financially and politically) to be influenced by pressure groups. Creditor bias, rather than personal antipathy to Chase, motivated them, however. When Charles Carroll tried to keep alive his feud with Chase by blocking appropriation of funds to reimburse Chase for his legal costs in Britain, he got the support only of his nephew Daniel Carroll and his friend Edward Lloyd.[51] The Senate continued to function as a collection of individuals; Carroll was in the minority on a third of the roll calls in the session.

Finally, toward the end of the session, after weeks of stalemate, the House circumvented the Senate with a resolution making 1781 "red money" legal tender for all debts owed the state. Previously that money could be given the state only in payment of taxes.[52] Naturally the chief beneficiaries were the speculators in confiscated property. The hinterland poor benefited not at all, and by the summer of 1786 the cries for relief were louder than ever.

Discussion of paper money dominated the autumn elections. It was the first time that a Maryland election centered on one overriding issue. Newspaper contributors attacked the Senate's obstructionism and hinted of a concerted effort to win control of the lower house.[53] By chance, this year offered a rare opportunity because voters were to choose senatorial electors as well as delegates to the lower house. By election eve partisans openly appealed to the voters to elect only candidates who were declared supporters of paper money.[54] In the cities there was even some rudimentary organization. One Baltimore group describing itself as traders and artisans publicly endorsed James McHenry for Senate elector.[55] McHenry, who had just completed a term in the Senate, was a known foe of paper money. In sum, issue orientation, voter awareness, and party organization went hand in hand.

Neither side could claim a victory, but the election did show the extent to which the public debate had hardened attitudes. A total of 40 new men were sent to the House of Delegates (an extraordinary 53 percent turnover), but of these only 17 favored paper money, while 23 opposed it. Opposition to paper hardened on the traditionally creditor Eastern Shore and in the cities.[56] Chase shifted his seat from Annapolis to Anne Arundel County (sensing public opinion?), and town voters replaced him with a vigorous opponent of paper. At the same time, he stood for Senate elector from Annapolis and lost. The new delegate from Baltimore Town was also anti-paper.[57]

In the debtor regions support for paper money firmed. Baltimore in the north and Montgomery in the west, previously divided, returned solidly pro-paper delegations. The one exception to the regional lineup was Frederick County (upper Potomac), where the election of former governor Thomas Johnson moved a divided delegation into the anti-paper camp.[58] Johnson's prestige was such that he could ignore the political outcry.

Despite the pleas of newspaper essayists, the freeholders failed to change the Senate. The electors chosen seemed content with the incumbents: when the electoral college met, it returned every incumbent senator who would agree to serve (9), and all 5 of the new men it chose were creditor-nationalists. The Senate would remain a bastion of fiscal conservatism.

Because the regional pattern held firm, party strength in the House of Delegates remained about the same (see table 5.6).[59] As in the previous year, Chasites agreed with creditors on all questions except paper money and relief for insolvent debtors. The debtor element agreed with Chasites only on the issue of paper money. Most of them opposed granting relief to speculators.[60] Although the Chasites seemed to represent the interests of speculators, there were speculators in both of the other factions. For instance, Charles Ridgely, one of the biggest speculators in the state and a partner of Chase in several ventures, voted debtor on nearly all roll calls.[61] His cousin, Senator Richard Ridgely, attorney from Annapolis, voted against all debtor-relief measures, even though he too owned large amounts of confiscated property. On the other hand, several members of the Chase clan, particularly those from the Eastern Shore, had no known speculative interests. They sided with him out of coincidence, friendship, or mutual interest of another kind.

TABLE 5.6   MARYLAND HOUSE OF DELEGATES: PARTIES, 1786*

	Creditor	Chasite	Debtor	Middle
Eastern Shore	4	5	3	10
Upper bay	3	6	6	3
Western Shore	8	1	2	5
Upper Potomac	1	1	8	1
	16	13	19	19
Federalists, 1788	9	2	3	9
Antifederalists, 1788	3	4	9	1
Middle†	0	3	1	1
Unknown	4	4	6	8
	16	13	19	19

*The table was compiled from 22 roll calls involving economic issues alone. Minimum participation 4 roll calls; agreement threshold of 75%. None of the urban delegates recorded enough votes to be included.

†This group includes William Paca, who was elected to the ratifying convention as an Antifederalist and voted in favor of the Constitution, and four men who voted inconsistently in the assembly.

The Chasites were a "temporary bubble," as Edmund Randolph would have put it. The group had no geographical base, and several of the men who sided with Chase on other issues seemed uncertain what to do on the critical matter of paper money.[62] Nor did the group have much continuity. Only 4 had sided with Chase in the previous year; the rest were new men. In 1788 they split in all directions on the Constitution. It was thus a "faction" in the eighteenth-century sense of that term—a temporary, loose-knit association of interested men. Some may even have agreed with Chase by chance, rather than intent.[63] The party alignment that had formed in 1784 remained essentially intact, and the lineup was essentially the same when the Federal Constitution came before the assembly in 1787.

MADISON ORGANIZES VIRGINIA, 1785–1787

In the course of 1785 Madison's political program gained wider currency. On the eve of the spring elections Edmund Pendleton, a prominent and rather conservative[64] member of the assembly during the war, endorsed the port bill and additional law courts. By the time the assembly opened in October, Washington was an Apostle for the whole creditor-nationalist idea: he approved the Commerce Amendment, then under discussion in Congress, opposed paper money, and favored the port bill, tax collection, the British treaty, and additional law courts, "or any substitute for the speedy administration of justice."[65] Washington, and perhaps others as well, had at last perceived the relationship among issues.

Even so, the politics of personality had not quite died away when the legslature assembled in October 1785. Former governor Benjamin Harrison stood for the House of Delegates, and to his mortification was defeated.[66] Unbowed, Harrison presented himself in Surry County across the James, and won. Some thought his defeat was due to the "machinations" of John Tyler, who feared Harrison might be a rival for the Speaker's chair.[67] It was not a question of party, for Harrison had given public support to debtor relief while corresponding sympathetically with the Madison circle. Like Alexander Martin in North Carolina, he avoided commitment to either party.

When the assembly opened on October 17 there was a "warm & fully argued" contest between Harrison and Tyler for the Speakership. Archibald Stuart, a Shenandoah Valley lawyer who had entered the House in the previous year, wanted to put Madison in nomination but evidently decided against it.[68] Harrison won, but then the Tyler forces counterattacked with a challenge to Harrison's Surry seat on the grounds of nonresidence. The Committee of Privileges and Elections went against Harrison by the deciding vote of the chairman, but the House reversed the committee on a roll call of 57 to 49.[69] Madison and his friends sided with Harrison. As governor, he had endorsed an act granting Congress limited power to regulate foreign trade, and on financial matters he had been reasonably orthodox.[70]

When the House finally settled down to business, Madison picked up where he had stopped the previous year and scored some early victories. The assembly refused to consider paper money, rejected a measure to postpone taxes, gave tentative approval to the commerce amendment, passed most of the elements in the long-delayed revision of the law code begun by Jefferson, Pendleton, and Wythe, and passed the Statute for Religious Freedom. Archibald Stuart crowed that Madison had "by means perfectly constitutional become almost a Dictator upon all subjects."[71] Stuart's confidence was premature. Madison could command only a small minority on any given issue, and even among his friends he never insisted on total unity of action.[72] If he seemed to be in control it was because the rural majority lacked leadership. Patrick Henry was returned to the governor's chair, in place of Harrison, and no one could perform his role in the assembly. Benjamin Harrison, perhaps with an eye on his new Southside constituency, was an early foe of taxes and congressional power, and later John Francis Mercer arrived to add to the "mischief" (as Madison put it).[73]

As in the previous year, the question of British debts was the surest indicator of Madison's strength. Dispatches from John Adams in London resurrected the issue. Adams sent a lengthy report to Congress detailing a discussion he had had with British Foreign Secretary Lord Carmarthen on Virginia's transgressions. The secretary was disappointed that the bill repealing the obstructions to debt collection had failed "by the accidental circumstance of a frost," and he was distressed that the proposed payment failed to include accumulated interest. Adams valiantly defended Virginia, or so he reported to Congress. He pointed out that the Virginians had suffered such property damage during the war that they were unable to pay, and the whole western part of the state continued to suffer from Indian depredations because the British occupied the Great Lakes posts in violation of the peace treaty. The Virginians in Congress promptly sent a full account to Madison, who doubtless circulated it around the assembly.[74]

Adams's capable defense ought to have undermined some of the opposition in Virginia, but how much it strengthened Madison's hand is uncertain. A nationalist-dominated committee headed by Madison drafted a bill opening Virginia courts to British suits, but it quickly ran into a barrage of criticism—against the peace treaty, Congress, New England, and even Adams. The bill survived a motion to postpone by a margin of ten votes, but then the opponents succeeded in adding a proviso that suspended operation of the measure until Britain surrendered the northwest posts. The nationalists felt that this was an unwarranted interference in the nation's foreign affairs and would embarrass Congress. In fact, Madison suspected that suspicion of the North and of Congress were the real motives behind the opposition; debt payment was only an excuse. For the moment, however, there was little the nationalists could do. They accordingly decided it was "best to let it sleep" and left the bill lying on the table until the next session.[75]

Since no roll call was taken on the bill, it is impossible to ascertain the sources of Madison's support, but it is likely that the pattern of previous years held. The temporary majority in behalf of the bill was encouraging, however, and the linkage with the western forts promised new leverage. A year before, James Monroe had returned from a tour of the Niagara frontier with word that the British army intended to remain on American soil until New York (which had seized Loyalist property after the war ended) and Virginia ceased violating the peace treaty.[76] For the moment it mattered little, for the posts were remote and the frontier was relatively peaceful. But should the Ohio Indians take the warpath, supplied with British arms, the frontiersmen, who owed few debts to British merchants, would recognize that they would be carrying the burden for the Henryite debtors. When that happened, there would be a massive realignment in the assembly.

The contest over British debts brought the leaderless debtor element back to life. By the end of the session the House had reversed itself on taxes and postponed collection until March, so decimated the commerce amendment that even Madison voted to postpone it, rejected a bill to establish courts of assize, and postponed a motion to open the state's courts to suits for British debts. In despair, Archibald Stuart, who was even deprived of his seat for nonresidence, denounced the session as "the most stupid, knavish, and designing Assembly that ever sat in this or . . . in any other country." For proof he needed "no other argument . . . but that Madison after the three first weeks lost all weight in the House, & the general Observation was that those who had a favorite scheme ought to get Madison to oppose it, by which means it would certainly be carried."[77]

It is difficult to determine precisely the relative strength of the two parties because the House held few roll calls on important matters. But there were five that involved elements of the creditor-nationalist program—one vote on court reform, two on tax postponement, and two on the commerce amendment. The latter involved some confusion because the assembly limited to thirteen years the grant of power to Congress, and when the nationalists failed, 28 to 79, to win an extension, Madison and several others voted to postpone it altogether. To Washington, Madison explained that a limited grant was worse than nothing because it might "stand in the way of a permanent one."[78] Shifting with him were Charles Simms and David Stuart of Alexandria and James Innes of Williamsburg. Most other nationalists, including Zachariah Johnston and Archibald Stuart, stuck with the amendment. If one allows for this tactical maneuver, Madison's record on those five roll calls can be used to test Stuart's description of the House; the results are given in table 5.7 (minimum participation of 3 votes; agreement threshold 75 percent).

Stuart's disparaging estimate was generally accurate—the rural-debtor interest was as strong in Virginia as it was in North Carolina. The degree of polarity was also about the same as in North Carolina. Slightly more than a third of the Delegates saw no relationship among the issues, or found that their interests varied. Only a few leaders had yet grasped the relationships among the

TABLE 5.7   VIRGINIA HOUSE OF DELEGATES: PARTY VOTING, 1785

	With Madison	Against Madison	Middle
Northern Neck	4	4	6
Middle Tidewater	7	8	8
Southside	8*	18	9
Piedmont	3	3	7
West	4	13	9
	27	46	39
Federalists, 1788	18	7†	6
Antifederalists, 1788	2	11	10
Unknown	7	28	23
	27	46	39

*Six from the lower James.
†Five were westerners.

various political issues facing the assembly, and as yet they had made no effort to disseminate their ideas.[79] Given the lack of organization and planning, it is perhaps most surprising that the patterns are as clear as they are. As in North Carolina, the party alignment that had appeared by 1785 persisted through the contest over ratification. Indeed, in Virginia the partisan division was stronger than the regional one. Madison had less support in the Northern Neck at this point than one might have expected, and more followers in the west. Moreover, the few allies he had in the predominantly debtor areas—Southside, Piedmont, and west— remained Federalists, for the most part. With the exception of the westerners, who turned Federalist on the eve of ratification for reasons of their own, his opponents in 1785 became Antifederalists.

By the following year the creditor party had made good progress. This was evident in the early ballots for various offices. Gone from the Speakership contest was the old, and largely meaningless, Tyler-Harrison rivalry. The new Speaker was a young lawyer from Williamsburg, Joseph Prentis. Prentis's voting record was sufficiently mixed so that he was probably acceptable to all sides, but he defeated Theodorick Bland, a prominent Southside planter who was a personal friend of Patrick Henry's.[80] Among the other ballots Madison was particularly pleased with the "considerable majority" by which Edmund Randolph was elected governor to succeed Patrick Henry. The tabulation in that race was: Randolph 73, Theodorick Bland 28, and Richard H. Lee 22. The state's congressional delegation had always been nationalist, despite the presence of Richard H. Lee, but now it was solid: Madison himself, Edward Carrington, William Grayson, and Joseph Jones. When Lee declined reappointment the assembly named General Henry Lee, cavalry hero of the southern campaigns.[81] The attorney generalship went to James Innis, another Williamsburg lawyer and lifelong Federalist; his only opponent was John Marshall.

The session went quite smoothly for the creditor party. A resolution of George Mason's that paper money was "unjust" and "impolitic" passed by an overwhelming majority, and the recommendation of the Annapolis convention in favor of still another convention to revise the confederation government was approved unanimously.[82] In speeding the news of the House's approval of the Federal Convention to Jefferson, Madison could not resist a measure of self-congratulation. "The unanimous sanction given by the Assembly," he wrote, "marks sufficiently the revolution of sentiment which the experience of one year has effected in this country."[83] At the end of the session Governor Randolph noted with satisfaction that "this state is in perfect tranquillity," a condition that clearly contrasted with the uproar that Shays's rebellion was then causing in Massachusetts.[84]

Despite these victories the Madison circle watched the spring election with their customary apprehension. "Our attention is now entirely turned toward the next elections," wrote John Marshall in March 1787, "—the debtors as usual are endeavoring to come into the Assembly & as usual I fear they will succeed."[85] Madison was absent in Congress, and Patrick Henry was planning to return to the assembly. If he endorsed debtor-relief measures, there was little doubt that he would obtain them. "Paper money or not seems to agitate the generality of the counties," reported Edmund Randolph, and apparently nearly every candidate had to take a stand. A Hanover County delegate, Randolph continued, won reelection only "after a positive and unalterable declaration in public of his affection for paper money." On the other side, former governor Benjamin Harrison "disclaimed paper money in the streets of Richmond on the 2d of this month" and then won reelection to the House by a slim margin of 22 votes.[86]

As in Maryland the previous year, this election marked an important step in the development of Virginia parties. For the first time there was a single overriding issue, and candidates for the legislature felt obliged to declare their positions on it. The issue was not just paper money, however, for that was only one of several debtor palliatives. After a tour of the counties along the North Carolina border, John Dawson, Monroe's law partner from Fredericksburg, reported to Madison on widespread discontent. Debt-ridden farmers were demanding paper money and tax relief. Paper money was particularly popular in that border country because of North Carolina's experience. North Carolina's paper had depreciated 100 percent, Dawson claimed, evidently meaning that its value was halved, and debtors were relieving their burdens with cheap currency. In Patrick Henry's home county the sheriff, having failed to post bond, was unable to collect taxes, "and the people appear happy in this expedient."[87]

When the fall session opened the debtor forces were better organized than ever before, and for the first time they appeared to have a coherent policy. Madison's intelligence network reported that George Nicholas had spun together a program linking British debts, domestic debts, and court reform. Nicholas's solution was debt payment by installments, and he planned to add such a proviso to every piece of relief legislation that appeared. This approval, which at least promised payment of debts, won more support than Patrick Henry's intransigence. On the vital subject of British debts Henry got the support of only a handful of delegates in his opposition to any sort of repayment. Archibald Stuart reported during the session that Henry seemed ineffectual as a leader and even irritated his own followers.[88] Even the mighty Henry had to learn to bend to the needs of party.

The creditor-nationalists were equally busy. By 1787 they were even developing lines of communication at the county level. In June a popular meeting in Prince George County (on the south bank of the James) drafted an address which opposed paper money, demanded reform of the court system, and asked the assembly to revise the laws on British debts "least our national character may be tarnished."[89] Popular meetings of this sort had appeared in the early days of the Revolution, and George Mason occasionally used them to vent his political views. But as an instrument of political pressure the device was comparatively new. They first blossomed in the religious disestablishment controversy of 1785, and Madison had early recognized their potential (see chapter 7). From this point on they became an increasingly important feature of the Virginia party scene.

Even the word "party" was beginning to lose its pejorative connotations. From Paris Jefferson wrote Monroe seeking information on the assembly, "a history of the most remarkable acts passed, the parties and views of the house, etc."[90] Groups of men that differed on matters of principle and policy were becoming an accepted part of the political landscape.

After all the uproar paper money had evaporated as a political issue by the time the assembly opened in the fall of 1787. No one said so openly—indeed, the complaints of the wealthy continued— but the state was evidently experiencing some economic recovery. Prices for the main staple exports remained low throughout the year (see tables 6.1, 6.2, and 6.3), but county tax lists show a substantial increase in farm livestock, especially in the cattle-raising Southside, during 1787. Piedmont counties, moreover, experienced a larger-than-usual increase in population, both white and slave, in 1787, indicating a recovery of social mobility that may have been related to improved economic conditions.[91] Another indication of returning prosperity was state tax receipts, which rose from £349,000 in 1785–86 to over £400,000 in 1786–87.[92] Whatever the reasons, paper money, debtor relief, and tax postponement virtually disappeared from the assembly journals after 1787.

Instead the assembly faced a new and equally important issue in the federal Constitution, completed by the Philadelphia convention in September and sent to the states for ratification. Strengthening the federal government had not been discussed during the spring elections, but political observers thought they knew precisely how the assembly would divide on the issue. Reaction to the Constitution, all agreed, would follow the party pattern established in the debtor-creditor battles of 1785–86. The Virginia party system had taken shape by 1787, and the even balance between the two sides forecast a close contest over the Constitution.

LINES FORM IN NORTH CAROLINA, 1785–1787

In the immediate postwar period most of the factional battles in the North Carolina assembly involved Loyalist legislation and taxation. Items such as debtor relief and paper money won general approval; the tiny creditor element registered its opposition bitterly but privately. The appearance of the Lawyers party in 1784, however, changed matters. Although it was never able to control the assembly, it felt strong enough to join battle. The Lawyers made a political issue of paper money for the first time, demanding four roll calls on the subject in 1785 and two more in succeeding years. Maclaine and Hay, the party's leaders in the Commons, worked for court reform to speed debt-recovery procedures, and they made repeated efforts to increase taxes. In all, there were seventeen roll calls on these and related issues in the 1785–87 sessions.[93] Because the issue at stake is not always clear from the House *Journal,* it is necessary to construct a model Lawyer from the votes of Maclaine, Hay, Davie, and Sitgreaves.[94] The combined record of the debtor party leaders, Person, Philemon Hawkins, Matthew Lock, and Jesse Franklin, was the reverse of the Lawyers on all seventeen roll calls (see table 5.8).[95]

A total of 217 individuals served in the House of Commons during these three sessions.[96] Of these 143 participated in four or more roll calls involving economic issues, and 105 (70 per cent) voted with one part or the other three-fourths of the time. This index of polarization is not far from that of better-organized Maryland, and it would remain essentially the same through the contest over the Constitution and the formation of national parties.

The sectional structure of the party system would remain virtually intact for the next decade also. The Lawyers were strongest in the Albemarle-Roanoke watershed, with the rest of the Tidewater evenly divided.[97] Debtors dominated the rest of the state (except for heavily German Lincoln County in the southwest), and

TABLE 5.8   NORTH CAROLINA COMMONS: PARTY VOTING, 1785–1787

	Lawyers	Rural-Debtor	Middle
Albemarle	20	3	11
Pamlico	11	12	9
Cape Fear	5	5	6
Piedmont	3	36	7
West	1	9	5
	40	65	38
Federalists, 1788	19	3	5
Antifederalists, 1788	1	25	9
Anti- 1788, Fed- 1789	0	1	1
Unknown	20	36	24
	40	65	38

as a result it controlled the assembly. The Lawyers, moreover, failed to develop a legislative leader of Madison's caliber. Johnston and Iredell remained aloof, preoccupied with their law practices, and Benjamin Hawkins was retired by the voters in 1784. Maclaine retired in failing health after the 1786 session.[98] Others appeared only sporadically. The only prominent Lawyers who served in all three sessions were two new acquisitions, Stephen Cabarrus and Richard Dobbs Spaight. Cabarrus, 30 years old when he entered the Commons in 1784, was a French émigré who had built up a sizable fortune as a merchant in Edenton.[99] Though a political newcomer, Cabarrus was widely respected. By the end of the decade he was Speaker, and his shift to the Jeffersonians early in the 1790s was a blow to the Federalists.

Spaight, 29 years old in 1785, was a New Bern lawyer who had served briefly in the House during the Revolution. In 1783 the assembly sent him to Congress, but his record there was so erratic that Jefferson called him a "young fool" whose chief function was to divide the North Carolina delegation.[100] Spaight nevertheless returned from Congress a nationalist, although he remained a political maverick all his life. After sitting silently through the 1785 session, he blossomed in 1786. He was constantly on his feet introducing bills, making committee reports, offering amendments. Some may have considered him Maclaine's successor when the old warhorse retired at the end of the session.[101] But Spaight was not a partisan in the mould of Maclaine. His opposition, for instance, helped blunt a Lawyers' assault on the debtor-minded Superior Court in the 1786 session. Though blessed with much talent, the Lawyers (and later the Federalists as well) were barren of leadership.[102]

Conversely, the rural element seems highly organized, although the absence of surviving correspondence makes it difficult to identify the leaders. Thomas Person departed after the 1785 session, spent the 1787 session in the Senate, and reappeared in the Commons in 1788. Richard Caswell, who had sided with the rural party in his infrequent legislative appearances, was governor from 1785 to 1787. Caswell gave verbal support to relief measures, but he spent most of his time promoting colonizing projects in the west, often in league with the Blounts. It is unlikely that he exerted any decisive political leadership. Nonetheless, the size of the party (65 members in three sessions) and the fact that relatively few of the undecided (middle) delegates came from the Piedmont and west suggest that those who attended regularly voted fairly consistently. Somehow lines of communication were developed so that even semiliterate backbenchers understood the issues at stake.

Parties underwent a similar development in the Senate during these years, although that body never achieved the polarity of the Commons. General Allan Jones failed to attend the 1785 session, and the debtor element under General Griffith Rutherford ruled. The Senate approved a paper money emission by 31 to 7. As evidence of the creditor's disarray, eastern senators who subsequently became Federalists supported paper money by 6 to 4. Jones was still absent from the 1786 session, but there is some evidence of a Lawyers' revival. The Senate rejected a bill to strengthen the state's paper money and turned back an effort by General Rutherford to restrict the activities of attorneys.[103]

The following year, Rutherford retired from politics, and Thomas Person moved over from the House to take his place. But Allan Jones returned and seemed to have the Senate firmly under control. He forestalled an effort by Thomas Person to reject the Federal Constitution, and got his way on paper money, taxation, and attorney's fees. There were eight roll calls on such matters in the 1786–87 sessions, and the sectional pattern was similar to that of the Commons.

By 1787, then, there was at least the outline of a party system in North Carolina. There is less evidence of organization than in her sister states to the north, and relatively little electioneering on the issues. But the Carolina legislators, at least, were well accustomed to voting along partisan lines, and they generally followed the same lines in reacting to the Federal Constitution. The difference in North Carolina was that the rural-debtor element retained a solid majority, even as economic conditions eased in 1788. As a result, the Constitution was in deep trouble in that state, and the Federalist Party that it spawned was never more than a tiny circle of lawyers and merchants.

CHAPTER SIX

Depression Politics, 1784–1787

E CONOMIC QUESTIONS dominated Chesapeake politics throughout the 1780s and provided a catalyst for the first party system. The earliest political associations were in reality interest groups, alliances among men who shared similar financial interests and who hoped to benefit from governmental action or inaction. Such issues as taxation, debt management, and financing the army, of course, were not new. They had dominated the legislative discussion throughout the war. But during the war, and even for some time afterward, the conflicts they produced were muted by the demands of patriotism. Necessitated by the military emergency, and defended as temporary expedients, even the most unorthodox schemes aroused little opposition. Thus, for instance, the paper money which Maryland issued in 1780–81 and North Carolina issued in 1783 raised few objections, even among fiscal conservatives, because it was earmarked for payment to the army. By 1784 the military crisis was long ended and the army discharged. Patriotism faded in financial hard times. Unorthodox fiscal expedients, no longer blessed by consensus or justified as temporary, engendered alarm. Thus, in contrast to the relative harmony of the immediate postwar years, the depression of the mid-1780s intensified the divisions in Chesapeake society and generated some bitter political disputes.

One reason, perhaps, why this depression generated such ill feeling was that it was so little understood. Commodity prices held up reasonably well, with the exception of tobacco. Prices for that held up through the year 1784, when some northern merchants were feeling the pinch,[1] and did not collapse until the last quarter of 1785. Tables 6.1 and 6.2 show prices for tobacco and wheat, the Chesapeake's primary staples, as listed in newspapers and private correspondence.[2] Wheat, and hence flour, held quite firm through-

TABLE 6.1 QUARTERLY TOBACCO PRICES IN THE CHESAPEAKE, 1783–1787
(IN SHILLINGS PER CWT, LOCAL CURRENCY)

		Baltimore	Alexandria	Richmond	Wilmington
1783	1				
	2		30	36	
	3	40	28		
	4				
1784	1				
	2	40		33	56
	3	45	30	38	56
	4	40		40	
1785	1	35	28		
	2	32			
	3	43	30		56
	4	38	22		
1786	1				
	2		20	23	
	3		20	20	40
	4		20	26	
1787	1		21	30	
	2		20	28	
	3				
	4				

TABLE 6.2   QUARTERLY WHEAT PRICES IN THE
CHESAPEAKE, 1783–1788
(IN SHILLINGS PER BUSHEL, LOCAL CURRENCY)

		Baltimore	Alexandria	Richmond
	1	4/6		
1783	2	5/6	5	
	3		4/6	
	4	6/6		
	1			
1784	2			
	3	8	5	
	4			
	1		6	
1785	2		6	
	3		6	
	4			
	1		5/6	5/6
1786	2			
	3		5	5
	4			
	1		4/6	5
1787	2			
	3		4/6	4/6
	4			
	1			
1788	2			
	3	6		
	4			

out the period, though it began sliding in 1787. In the Philadelphia
market, wheat did not reach its depression low until the first quarter
of 1788. Price information on other important exports, such as beef
and pork, is too spotty to be meaningful, but in Philadelphia prices
for these items held up through the decade. Pork was actually at its
lowest in 1783 and rose steadily thereafter until 1788.[3] Except for
tobacco, Chesapeake planters could not complain much about the
prices they received for their products in the depression.

The collapse in tobacco prices was spectacular but should not have been surprising. Prices for tobacco at the end of the war were artificially high, probably because Britain had been deprived of its familiar brands during the fighting. The average prewar price for James River tobacco in Philadelphia was 31 shillings a hundredweight.[4] When allowance is made for transportation costs (about 30 percent), this is not far from the "depressed" price of the mid-1780s. Tobacco prices, moreover, remained at that level for many years. Not until war disrupted markets again in the 1790s did it return to its 1783–84 level (see table 6.3).[5]

Nor was it possible to define the depression in terms of declining sales. Great Britain, the Chesapeake's largest customer, increased its imports dramatically after the war. And, except for some leveling off in 1787 (probably a reflection of the hard times complained of in Virginia in 1786), there is a fairly steady increase (see table 6.4). To be sure, the figures represented less than half the prewar exports to Britain, but new sales in France and the Netherlands more than made up the difference.[6]

What, then, caused the anguished howls of distress? The timing of the depression offers a clue. The business correspondence of the Philadelphia firm of Coxe and Frazier, which did a substantial business in the Chesapeake, contains evidence of hardship more than a year before the collapse of tobacco prices. Beginning in the spring of 1784, Chesapeake firms who imported through Coxe and Frazier began to experience difficulties because they were unable to collect from smaller merchants in the interior. Toward the end of the year, several Baltimore houses went bankrupt. By the spring of 1785 cries of agony could be heard from as far as North Carolina. Explaining why he could not pay his own debts, a New Bern merchant listed half a dozen bankruptcies in North Carolina during the winter that had carried everyone down in the "general ruin."[7]

The depression, it seems clear, resulted from a scarcity of money. In the northern cities there was a drain of specie to Britain in payment for imports, but the critical factor in the Chesapeake was the deflationary policy of the state governments. Following orthodox monetary practice, all three states retired their wartime issues of paper, usually through taxation, without anticipating the

TABLE 6.3   SEMIANNUAL PRICES FOR JAMES RIVER TOBACCO IN PHILADELPHIA, 1784–1801
(IN SHILLINGS PER CWT UNTIL 1791; THEREAFTER IN DOLLARS)

1783	1785	1786	1787	1788	1789
59 67	57 55	52 40	50 45	47/6 47/6	47/6 47/6

1790	1791	1792	1793	1794	1795
47/6 47/6	47/6 35	4.67 4.67	4.67 4.67	4.67 4.92	5.70 6.20

1796	1797	1798	1799	1800	1801
6.34 7.20	8.25 9.50	11.00 12.50	— 13.00	— 5.50	6.25 6.25

SOURCE: Arthur H. Cole, *Wholesale Commodity Prices in the United States, 1700–1861* (Cambridge, Mass., 1938), pp. 78–126.

TABLE 6.4   BRITISH IMPORTS FROM VIRGINIA AND MARYLAND, 1783–1790
(IN OFFICIAL STERLING VALUES)

1783	1784	1785	1786	1787	1788	1789	1790
£105,063	390,251	443,581	451,671	423,335	504,672	539,355	566,774

SOURCE: Jacob Price, "New Time Series for Scotland's and Britain's Trade with the Thirteen Colonies and States, 1740 to 1791," *William and Mary Quarterly*, 3d ser., 32 (1975), 307–25, esp. 323.

impact this drastic reduction in the quantity of currency would have on their economies. Even North Carolina's 1783 emission was apparently not sufficient to counteract the state's other deflationary policies. The demand for tobacco and consequent high prices delayed the pinch for a time. Tobacco sales, reported Madison in the summer of 1784, "brought more specie into the country than it ever before contained at one time."[8] When European demand slackened and northern banks, themselves hard pressed for specie, became reluctant to discount notes, the price was certain to fall.[9] That it fell so precipitously was probably due to deflationary governmental policies. Madison reported early in 1786 that Virginia prices were low simply because no one had any money to buy.[10]

After some dislocation, the merchants seemed to recover, or at least their cries of distress subsided. But the pinch continued to be felt by smaller planters and farmers, whose personal bonds were not widely accepted and who could not find the cash to discharge their obligations. Government taxes only added to their problems. Taxes were collected in specie, except where the assemblies made specific exceptions, and the capitation tax levied by all three states fell disproportionately on the poor. Financial hardship was quickly translated into political turmoil as debtors appealed for tax postponement, laws delaying court suits, and an expansion of the money supply. The uproar continued until 1787 when Robert Morris's tobacco contract with France brought some welcome Philadelphia currency into the region. Although prices remained about the same until the mid-1790s, the cries for relief grew fewer.

Precisely because a money shortage was the most important cause of the depression, relief advocates early focused on new emissions of paper. And in a time of serious deflation, it must be said that there was some justice to their cause. With the military emergency long since past, the new emissions were pure debtor relief. As a result, they created a classic debtor-creditor confrontation, though among the advocates of paper were rich debtors as well as poor ones. Nowhere was the pursuit of self-interest so apparent as in the paper money contest, and no other issue was so bitterly fought. In all three states it was the hottest controversy of the decade. It influenced the debate over ratification of the Federal

Constitution, and it affected the formation of national parties in the 1790s.

The battle lines were similar in all three states, although the results were different. Supporting paper money was a combination of merchants and planters, who found themselves overextended in the economic hard times, and hinterland farmers who were chronically short of cash. Opposing them was a mixed breed of men, middling to wealthy planters, some merchants, and lawyers who from interest and prejudice preferred fiscal orthodoxy to experimentation. Only in North Carolina, where the rural element held sway, were the advocates of paper money successful, but in Maryland and Virginia the contest created more bitterness. Indeed, nowhere south of New England was there more excitement over paper money than in Maryland.

MARYLAND: PAPER MONEY FOR THE AFFLUENT

Maryland's last wartime issues of paper money in 1780 and 1781 were backed, in theory at least, by confiscated Loyalist property. Proceeds from the sale of the property were to be used to redeem the money. It did not quite work out that way, for most of the purchasers were short of specie, as was everyone else. As a result, only those who purchased relatively small amounts of property, usually household goods, actually paid in cash. The rest gave the state personal bonds, hoping to redeem them from the profits of resale. Initially, these were short-term obligations, usually only for three to six months, but when the war ended the state granted longer credit, commonly seven years. By 1785, when most of the property was disposed of, speculators were in debt to the state to the amount of £303,440. So long as the economy remained prosperous and money available, they could manage this debt. But the decline in Maryland currency, together with the restrictive policies of Philadelphia merchant-bankers, left them acutely embarrassed. There were two solutions—either the state could relax the terms of repayment or it could issue more paper money. Both were political dynamite.

Although a substantial proportion of Maryland's gentry were

involved in speculation, there were relatively few speculators in the assembly at any given moment. And those who were present did not always agree among themselves.[11] But there were two men in the House of Delegates who were a host in themselves—Charles Ridgely and Samuel Chase. Ridgely's mercantile firm owed the state some £40,000 for confiscated property. Ridgely had the capital to sustain such a debt, but he voted for debtor relief as a matter of habit, and in this instance his votes coincided with his interests. Chase, on the other hand, was grossly overextended. He participated in Ridgely's debt, as a partner in the consortium, and he had purchased some £6,545 in property on his own (though some involved other partnerships). None of this debt had been redeemed by 1785; indeed, Chase teetered on the edge of bankruptcy, his financial plight so desperate that it was common talk in the newspapers.[12] Monetary inflation seemed his only out.

The speculators were experiencing the first pinch of currency shortage in the fall of 1784 when the legislature unwittingly added to their troubles with the so-called Consolidating Act. Brainchild of the creditor party, the act was supposed to bring order out of the state's chaotic wartime finances. First, the majority tested sentiment in the House with a resolution that the state ought to live up to its obligations, treat its creditors fairly, and make provision for the discharge of its debt. When this passed by a good margin, 31 to 13, a committee set to work on a bill.

The committee's bill proposed to consolidate all the state's nominal assets—confiscated property still unsold, bonds taken for confiscated property, and unpaid back taxes—into a general fund. This fund, in turn, would be devoted to paying the state debt by January 1, 1790. Those who owed the state money were given until that date to pay. Some of the bonds taken for confiscated property, however, were put in a separate fund, which was to be used for redeeming the 1780 emission ("black money"). Speculators who had pledged these bonds were expected to pay immediately. A separate but related measure made state paper receivable at its face value (i.e., the equivalent of specie) for all unpaid back taxes. After a few days' discussion, the Consolidating Act passed by almost the same margin as the original resolution, 34 to 16.[13]

Chase and Ridgely both supported the act, possibly because it gave them six years to redeem their obligations to the state.[14] In the Senate, Charles Carroll, who was apparently alone in his opposition, objected to this very feature. Considering the indulgence already given the speculators, he felt that an additional five years was too long.[15] Everyone else, though, seemed satisfied. The bill met the requirements of fiscal orthodoxy while preserving the interests of the speculators. In good times the arrangement might have worked.

Coinciding with the worsening currency shortage, it was a disaster. Tax collectors were suddenly forced to make up arrearages, and state paper became scarcer than ever. The 1780 "black money" swiftly rose to a par with specie.[16] Some speculators were obliged to pay immediately, and even those with a six-year reprieve now had a deadline to meet. As money grew scarcer, their chances of meeting it grew more remote. What the measure actually consolidated was the interests of disparate groups—hinterland farmers pressed by tax collectors and merchant speculators pinched by a lack of fluid capital. The union rekindled the paper money movement.

The first to recognize the approaching monetary crisis was the state's Intendant of Revenue, Daniel of St. Thomas Jenifer. His office had been created in 1782 to supervise the collection and disbursement of receipts from the two state treasurers, one on the Eastern and one on the Western shore. In its 1784 session the assembly also put him in charge of selling the remaining Loyalist property. Jenifer issued his warning amidst the debate over the Consolidating Act in a pamphlet which publicly endorsed a new emission. Since Jenifer had been a fiscal conservative, his change of heart raised the suspicion that he might be in league with the speculators. It earned him a legislative investigation the following year.[17]

Strangely enough, Jenifer's pamphlet provoked no comment in the press. Throughout the winter and spring months the Maryland newspapers reverberted with controversies over religion and education, but there was not a whisper about paper money. Nor, for that matter, was there much discussion of economic issues. Prices for tobacco and wheat held firm through the summer, and the

Tidewater planter majority, with better access to markets than the hinterland and more prudent in its management than the speculators, got along tolerably well.

The subject of money came up again in July 1785, when William Goddard, printer of the Baltimore *Maryland Journal,* called for a paper emission in a rare editorial. Over the next few weeks a number of contributors echoed Goddard's cry, but the topic failed to arouse much public interest. If anonymous contributions to newspapers are an index, state support for religion was the primary issue in the fall elections. Goddard's effort, like Jenifer's, gave every appearance of being managed by Baltimore speculators.[18]

Despite the public indifference, the paper men in the assembly prepared a resolution declaring an emission of bills of credit necessary to relieve the scarcity of money. The resolution won approval, 39 to 16, and the resulting bill passed without a roll call, after surviving a motion to postpone by 25 to 34.[19] While the Senate pondered this measure, the House sought to bolster the paper money issued in 1781. By 25 to 16 it resolved that "red money" might be used to pay tax arrears or any other debts owed the state. This enabled speculators to pay their debts in depreciated paper. Describing the resolution as an effort to prevent further depreciation was simply a cover. A week later the House conducted three roll calls on a bill granting titles to purchasers of confiscated property, and in each case the pattern was similar to the vote on "red money."[20]

Comparing these roll calls with the earlier vote on paper money makes it possible to distinguish the Chasites from the regular debtor and creditor parties. As noted in the previous chapter, they were a tiny fraction of the House, no more than a dozen delegates. Most of them came from the upper bay and Eastern Shore, regions where most of the confiscated property lay. Opposition to them was centered in the lower Western Shore, which disliked paper money, and the upper Potomac, which distrusted speculators.

Ephemeral though it was, the Chasite faction tipped the balance in the lower house in favor of paper money. But in the Senate there were no debtors of any kind, public or private. The Senate unanimously rejected the paper money bill and then joined an attack on Jenifer.[21] The Intendant's apostasy had evoked cries for an investigation of his office as soon as the session opened. After the paper money bill passed, the creditor party in the House sought revenge. An investigating committee, packed with hostile delegates, issued a report criticizing Jenifer's accounting procedures.[22] It was particularly suspicious of a sum of 200 guineas advanced to Samuel Chase and Thomas Stone (also a speculator) that had not been entered on the books.[23] Racing to Jenifer's rescue, the paper money alliance eliminated critical paragraphs from the report, approved a resolution that he had discharged his office with integrity, and passed a bill extending the Intendancy for another year.[24] They could do nothing to save him from the wrath of the Senate, however. That body declared that the office of Intendant was no longer necessary and rejected the Delegates' bill.[25]

The lower house retaliated by rejecting a Senate-passed bill prohibiting "frivolous appeals" by debtors in court suits. Before anyone fully realized it, the old legislative conflict, dormant since 1781, was blazing again. The Senate replied with a lengthy analysis of the state's sorry condition, which it blamed on the extravagance of the debtor class. The House defended "distressed debtors" and pledged that it would help "extricate their persons and property out of the power of cruel or oppressive creditors."[26] The Senate's intransigence thus enabled speculators to slip under the blanket of populism. The deepening commercial depression soon gave substance to their appeal.

By the summer of 1786 the deflationary effects of the 1784 Consolidating Act were felt across the state. Paper money was almost as good as gold and nearly as scarce. Hinterland farmers resorted to barter and hid from zealous tax men who tramped the roads collecting arrearages. The collapse of tobacco prices brought distress everywhere in the Chesapeake that year, but nowhere was the squeeze felt so acutely as in Maryland. By early summer widespread disorder in the countryside echoed the Shays uprising in Massachusetts. As in New England, county courts were the chief targets of the Maryland poor. In June a mob estimated at a hundred gathered at the Charles County court to protest one lawyer's efforts to collect British debts, and the action forced the court to suspend all civil suits. A few days later Harford County farmers prohibited anyone from making bids on lands which sheriffs had seized for nonpayment of taxes.[27]

Nor was the distress confined to the poor. Tobacco planters found themselves in debt to Annapolis and Georgetown merchants, and these, in turn, were pressed by British creditors. "We do sincerely assure you that we are at present highly distressed for cash," an Annapolis firm wrote plaintively to Captain Charles Ridgely, seeking payment of only £120. "This little Sum will be as nothing to your immense funds, but will be of great Consequence to ours."[28] And this came from the largest mercantile house in the state!

Paper money advocates returned to the newspapers with a barrage of letters arguing that a new emission would benefit debtors, raise land values, and stimulate trade. Opponents countered with the standard prediction that the currency would inevitably depreciate, drive specie out of the state, and further depress trade. The debate continued through the summer and into the fall election.[29] Neither side could claim a victory in the election, as we noted in the previous chapter, but the paper alliance of Chasites and hinterland retained control of the House of Delegates.

Chase himself brought in a bill to print £350,000 when the assembly opened in December 1786. The opposition promptly questioned the role of speculators in the paper crusade, and Chase found himself on the defensive. At one point he offered to bet his reputation against a farthing on the "propriety" of the bill, whereupon Thomas Jenings, who had taken Chase's Annapolis seat, replied that it would be "an equal bet."[30] Written into the bill, possibly as a result of this discussion, was a proviso that the paper money could not be used to discharge debts due the state other than taxes. The Chasites supported it anyway. Perhaps they planned to overcome this limitation with a separate enactment. Only the previous spring they had slipped through a law enabling them to use all previous issues of paper money in the discharge of public debts. The paper alliance defeated an amendment that would have prohibited further issues if the money depreciated and then passed

TABLE 6.5   MARYLAND HOUSE OF
DELEGATES: PAPER MONEY, 1786

	For	Against	Mixed
Eastern Shore	9	8	4
Upper bay	6	2	2
Western Shore	7	7	5
Upper Potomac	9	3	0
	31	20	11
Creditors	1	12	4
Debtors	17	0	1
Chasites	10	0	3
Middle	2	7	3
Unknown	1	1	0
	31	20	11

the bill by 37 to 25.[31] In all, the issue generated three roll calls in the House of Delegates with an alignment similar to that of the previous year (see table 6.5).

The Senate unanimously rejected the paper money bill and assigned a committee to draft a message explaining why. In the propaganda war the Senate was not to be outgunned. Its report, entered in the *Journal* a week later and promptly sent to the newspapers, presented the familiar argument that the money would depreciate and further derange the state's trade. There was actually plenty of money in the state, argued the committee; the difficulty was that it failed to circulate. People would stop hoarding only when they regained confidence in the economy, and that, in turn, depended on "a steady administration of justice, a well-ordered government, [and] a flourishing trade." The House replied by suggesting an adjournment to March 20, presumably to enable delegates to sound out their constituents.[32]

Through the early days of January 1787 the two houses clashed repeatedly on matters involving debts and courts. The Senate rejected a bill modifying the law on imprisonment for debt, a bill repealing the act which established permanent salaries for judges, and several bills for the relief of public debtors.[33] The Senate refused even to reply to the request for adjournment, and on January 15 the Delegates lost patience. They passed a motion deferring the appointment of deputies to the Federal Convention (scheduled to meet in Philadelphia in May) until March 20 so that delegates could consult their constituents on that matter as well.[34] To stimulate discussion, the House issued an "address" summarizing the indebtedness of Marylanders—to each other, to the state, and to the British.[35] "The object of the leaders of the House of Delegates," concluded one nationalist who mourned the failure to name delegates to Philadelphia, "seems to be to throw everything into confusion in order to force the paper Bill upon the Senate."[36]

Shaken into action, the Senate hastily named a committee which brought in a reply on January 20—the day the House had assigned for adjournment. Maryland's failure to appoint deputies to Philadelphia, the Senate complained, would sow suspicion among the other states, especially since Pennsylvania and Virginia had already named some of their "first characters." The Senate then listed all the items of unfinished business, implying broadly that the Delegates were concerned only with demagoguery. If the Delegates were going to resort to popular appeals every time the two houses disagreed, complained the upper house, the legislative balance created by the constitution would be destroyed.[37]

It was a weak start for a public debate, but the creditor force gradually gained momentum. Only days after the Delegates' address reached the newspapers, hard money men in Chase's home county circulated a petition to be signed and mailed by voters.[38] In early February former governor Thomas Johnson presided over a meeting of 200 freeholders at Frederick that instructed the county's delegates to vote against paper money. Over the next six weeks similar meetings were organized in nearly every county in the state.[39]

This was Maryland's first experience with a coordinated political pressure campaign. The idea might have come from either Pennsylvania or Virginia, where such tactics had become common. In any case, it represented a further step in the development of party techniques. The newspaper battle appeared to be a draw, in terms of the volume of contributions, but the arguments of the hard money men seemed more effective. Alexander C. Hanson, a young nationalist who tried his hand at medicine and law before finding his true calling in journalism, entered the lists under the pseudonym "Aristides." Hanson's essay, published in December as a broadside and reprinted in the newspapers during the spring, was a devastating exposé of the speculators. He claimed that there was no popular demand for paper money; the impetus came exclusively from speculators.[40] If not entirely true, the thrust nonetheless deprived the Chasites of their populist mantle.

In the end, however, not rhetoric but cash punctured the paper money balloon. The source, ironically, was Robert Morris, who had signed a contract to supply France with American tobacco. Morris's agents scoured Maryland seeking the least expensive tobacco to unload on the French, and they paid for it with Morris's personal notes. Since Morris's credit was as good as that of any government in America, Maryland planters eagerly accepted the notes and passed them in payment of debts. The notes relieved the currency shortage, and a slight improvement in tobacco prices promised a sunnier future.[41] The paper crusade collapsed. By mid-March Charles Carroll could predict confidently that "a majority of the people will be against an emission on loan."[42]

Chase and his allies evidently reached the same conclusion, for when the assembly returned in April there was no further mention of the subject.[43] Nor did the paper money contest further becloud the federal question, as the House readily agreed to a predominantly nationalist delegation. The paper money role played by Chase and his band was a brief aberration. On other matters, the House was predominantly creditor-nationalist, and it would remain so through the contest over the Constitution.

THE PAPER BOGEY IN VIRGINIA

Echoes of the paper money clash in Maryland reverberated across Virginia through the mid-1780s, sparking rumors and apprehension. Fiscal conservatives, chronic worriers, felt certain that Virginia would succumb to the craze, but the threat was more bogus than real. Having made relatively few confiscations, Virginia lacked the speculative element that gave form to the paper money movement in Maryland. The creditor and debtor parties in the Virginia assembly, moreover, were evenly balanced. As a result, the legislature was more receptive to cries for relief, the creditor element was more willing to compromise, and the relief measures adopted, particularly in the field of taxation, siphoned off some of the pressure for paper money.

In the fall of 1785, as the first calls for paper money were being heard in Maryland, Edmund Randolph thought he could discern three types of paper money advocates in Virginia—holders of the public debt who wanted paper so that the state could pay its obligations, others who felt that the commercial depression was caused by a scarcity of cash and wanted an increase in the circulating medium, and a "numerous class" that wanted to use Virginia paper to repay debts owed British merchants.[44] Archibald Stuart agreed that there was a scarcity of specie in the state, due he felt to the excessive import of luxuries, but he feared that "politicians from mistaking the Ground of our complaints will propose" paper money as a solution.[45]

Actually, there was scarcely a "politician" anywhere in the state willing to advocate paper. There were chronic fears that Patrick Henry would do so, but that spokesman for popular interests never publicly or privately endorsed paper. Nearly every other prominent leader was ardently opposed to it—Washington, Richard Henry Lee, George Mason, and William Grayson.[46] To be sure, all these men lived in the Northern Neck, where specie was somewhat more plentiful,[47] but even in the currency-poor south and west hard-money feeling was prevalent.[48]

Virginia, however, did have its own version of the opportunistic Samuel Chase. When the assembly opened, Carter Braxton led a "party" that wanted to abolish all taxes for the year 1785. Braxton was a merchant and land speculator who had had extensive dealings during the war with Robert Morris of Philadelphia. His speculations left him deeply in debt and hounded by creditors. The Madison circle attributed his tax relief motion to self-interest. They claimed he was currying favor with the assembly in order to win appointment to the governor's council "as an asylum." After initially approving Braxton's motion, the House changed its mind and voted it down 48 to 50.[49]

There was considerable support for the idea of paying taxes in commodities, however. This, it was hoped, would improve the market for farm staples and bolster prices, in addition to relieving the currency shortage. In the end the assembly compromised, postponing half the taxes due for 1786 until the autumn and making them all payable in commodities.[50]

Tobacco prices declined further in the spring of 1786, and currency of all kinds became scarcer as the state continued to retire its wartime emissions. Madison feared that the combination would generate a new demand for paper money in the fall assembly, and he enthusiastically greeted George Mason's selection to the assembly as a "counterpoise . . . against the popular cry."[51] He exaggerated the extent of the outcry, however, for there was relatively little talk of money in the newspapers. While the Maryland press thundered with controversy that summer, only one Virginian was bold enough to advocate publicly "a very *liberal* emission of paper money." This anonymous contributor to the Alexandria *Journal* argued that low prices were the result of a scarcity of currency. Because no one was willing to surrender his money, whether to buy a horse or a cabbage, trade was stagnant and prices were low. His diagnosis made sense, but his remedy was unbelievably naïve. He proposed to put the paper into circulation by loaning it "to certain popular characters" without interest in amounts not exceeding "double the worth of the borrower." In addition, he wanted the paper made legal tender even in foreign exchange, and if foreign merchants refused to accept it, "it will be *their own* faults, not *ours,* if they go unpaid."[52] Such a proposal—evoking memories of the Speaker John Robinson scandal of the 1760s—had little chance of winning political approval, but the wildness of the scheme helps explain the hysteria with which men like Washington and Mason greeted the mention of paper money.

When the fall session opened, the opponents of paper money quickly took control. Even though illness delayed Mason's attendance, the creditor party presented a resolution denouncing paper money as "unjust" and "impolitic." It passed by 85 to 17, a margin that probably reflected the genuine lack of paper money sentiment in the state. Even so, Madison continued to fret. When the act permitting Virginians to pay their taxes in tobacco came up for renewal, Madison told his father that he "was not anxious for its success in any form, but acquiesced in it as it stands as the people may consider it in the light of an easement, and as it may prevent some worse project in the Assembly."[53]

As it turned out, the creditor element was in full control throughout. At the end of the session Madison happily reported that efforts to scale down the state debt and to permit private debts to be paid in installments were "got rid of by large majorities," that all attempts to reduce taxes were "baffled," and some new customs duties were expected to "considerably enhance our revenue."[54] Timely concessions and expert organization kept paper money buried for another year.

Continuing economic hardship brought popular complaints to a crescendo in the spring of 1787. Robert Morris's tobacco purchases brought some relief to the Northern Neck, but money continued scarce south of the Rappahannock.[55] In both King William and Kent the courthouses mysteriously burned down and all records were destroyed just before the quarterly courts were scheduled to meet. In western Greenbriar some 300 farmers formed an association to oppose payment of all debts and taxes. The incipient rebellion, similar to a movement on the Tennessee frontier two years earlier, collapsed when the leader, one Adonijah Mathews, was jailed by the county lieutenant.[56]

Throughout the spring and summer petitions circulated in behalf of paper money, for debt payment by installments, and for enabling property owners to tender land in payment of debts on its assessed valuation rather than its market price.[57] "The debtors as usual are endeavoring to come into the Assembly," John Marshall remarked grimly during the spring elections, "& as usual I fear they will succeed."[58] Paper money was widely discussed during the campaign, and several candidates felt obliged to commit themselves in advance. Patrick Henry's announced determination to stand for a seat in the assembly did nothing to calm the fears of the fiscally orthodox. "I take it for granted we are on the Eve of a Revolution," wailed a Fredericksburg merchant as the assembly began its fall deliberations. Even the new Constitution, he feared, could not "entirely avert our Fate."[59]

As it turned out, Henry was more talk than action. Shortly after the session began, Archibald Stuart reported that "Henry is loud on the distresses of ye people & makes us tremble with ye apprehensions of a Rebellion if they are driven to despair."[60] While Henry thundered, George Mason, capitalizing on Madison's success the previous year, introduced a set of resolutions condemning paper money as "ruinous to Trade and Commerce, and highly injurious to the good People of this Commonwealth." Mason dared the advocates of paper to "come boldly forward & explain their real Motives," and when no one moved, the resolutions passed unanimously.[61] It was the death knell of paper money in Virginia. But it was still necessary to defuse the movement for debtor relief.

Madison was absent during this session, superintending the ratification movement in New York, but Mason proved a worthy successor. He faced a new opponent in George Nicholas, an Albemarle planter-lawyer who was second only to Patrick Henry as an orator and more skilled as a parliamentarian. Nicholas had entered the House the previous year, while Henry was serving as governor, and quickly assumed leadership of the debtor-relief party. Nicholas's pet scheme, which he had initiated in 1786, was a bill permitting debtors to discharge their obligations in three annual installments. Mason disliked the idea but felt he lacked the strength to block it. He concentrated instead on modifying it. In committee of the whole, he succeeded in adding amendments that made the system voluntary and required the consent of the creditor. The latter feature, of course, ruined the whole scheme, and when the relief party failed to eliminate it on a 44 to 55 roll call they lost interest in the whole concept.[62]

Patrick Henry's leadership was ineffectual throughout this session.[63] He offered some verbal support to Nicholas's installment plan, but his own pet scheme was a change in the execution law so as to put a floor on the price of property sold for debt. Instead of introducing a bill to this effect, however, he attached it as an amendment to a bill establishing a system of district courts. Left over from the previous session, the court bill was one of Madison's projects. That Henry felt obliged to hitch his wagon to a creditor horse was perhaps a measure of his weakness. His proposal even received some additional watering down before it won final approval. When all was done, Joseph Jones reported to Madison with some satisfaction that the measure would provide some relief to debtors "without any direct interference with private contracts."[64]

The creditor party proved equally pliable on the matter of taxation. Early in the session George Nicholas brought in a bill permitting taxes to be paid in tobacco. Mason considered it "a foolish and injurious project" but made no effort to block it. Since Virginians had been paying in commodities for several years, the principle was well established. The bill passed by 88 to 27 with only the core of Mason's following in opposition.[65] It was the only important victory for debtor-relief in the session.

Virginia's creditor party was not as strong as Maryland's, but it was less riven by faction. By making some timely concessions—particularly in the area of taxation, where the poor felt the shortage of money most acutely—they avoided much of the anxiety that tensed Maryland politics in the depression years. And by successfully portraying paper money as a fearsome bogey they avoided the monetary experimentation that gave North Carolina a bad name throughout the country.

NORTH CAROLINA'S FISCAL EXPERIMENTS

Paper money never carried the same onus in North Carolina that it did in her more northerly neighbors. The wartime inflation had failed to frighten Carolinians, and as late as 1783 the assembly resorted to a paper emission in order to reimburse its retiring soldiers. When trade slowed and prices fell after the war, another batch of paper money seemed a natural expedient. The 1783 emission had the backing of several merchant speculators—notably the Blounts, who needed ready cash for their land-buying schemes—but as the money depreciated, mercantile opposition to paper rose. Petitions to the assembly from seaboard towns in 1785 complained that the 1783 issue was worth only 75 percent of its face value when exchanged for specie, and they feared that rumors of another issue would depreciate it further. The topic dominated the summer election, and the inflationists seemed to have the best of the argument. As in 1783, they stressed the patriotic principles at stake. The state could not collect taxes since its citizens had no money. The treasury was empty; it lacked even the funds to pay the civil list and had contributed nothing to Congress for years. Both state and national welfare required a new emission.[66]

If debtor relief was the object, public finance was the excuse in North Carolina, and the bill that emerged from the Commons in the fall of 1785 demonstrated just that. To avoid mercantile criticism, the total emission was limited to £100,000, an amount that was judged sufficient to meet the needs of government yet small enough to avoid depreciation. Of the total, £36,000 would be used to buy tobacco, which would be sent to Congress as the state's annual contribution. Tobacco prices would be shored up and nationalists kept happy. Neither nationalists nor merchants were impressed, but they lacked numbers. John Gray Blount tested the sentiment of the House with a motion to postpone. It lost, 26 to 54.[67]

Hugh Williamson then unmasked the inflationists with an amendment that would have permitted juries in suits for debt to take into account depreciation in the currency when making awards. This would have eliminated any benefit to debtors and left the emission little more than a method of financing Congress. The paper majority voted this down by a similar margin and then approved the bill, 52 to 21. In the Senate the opposition confined itself to efforts to reduce the size of the emission, and failing that, succumbed, 31 to 7.[68] The similarity of votes in the Commons suggests that lines were firmly drawn on the issue, and the lopsided majorities indicate broad support for debtor relief. Regionally, it was the familiar alignment of Piedmont and west in favor of paper, the Tidewater evenly divided. The towns, which had been divided in 1783, were now solidly opposed.

Just as tax concessions took the steam out of paper money in Virginia, the paper emission in North Carolina took some of the tension out of taxation. Toward the end of that session Maclaine and Hay presented a resolution that taxes for the succeeding year ought to be increased. That passed and the House then agreed, 51 to 27, to increase taxes by 25 percent. The lawyers evidently hoped to soak up some of the paper money in circulation and cut its inflationary impact while putting the government in sounder condition financially. The surprisingly lopsided majority on the roll call may have included some who wanted to avoid an even bigger increase.[69]

North Carolina's experience proved that paper money was more controversial in theory than in practice. As nearly all had anticipated, the 1785 emission depreciated rapidly. By 1788 it was worth only half its nominal value. But the state fared tolerably well, and pleas for further relief subsided. North Carolina's relative tranquillity through 1786–87 contrasted sharply with the furor to the north. Efforts by village merchants to reject the paper or depreciate it deliberately caused some indignation in the assembly, but efforts to protect the money failed. A 1786 bill that would have prohibited merchants from demanding specie split the paper bloc in the Commons. Apparently some delegates preferred to see the money depreciate.[70] There was no chance of another emission thereafter, nor much need to discuss one. The subject was periodically agitated at election time, but it gradually disappeared from the legislative journals. As elsewhere, paper money, prohibited to the states by the Federal Constitution, died with ratification. In the 1790s bank notes, a form of paper more acceptable to mercantile interests, replaced it.

THE SPEEDY ADMINISTRATION OF JUSTICE

That phrase, repeated with minor variations throughout the correspondence of Chesapeake lawyers and planters, was verbal shorthand for court reform. The courts were the final recourse for moneylenders, and in all three states creditors faced a variety of obstacles in recovering debts. Law suits took time and money and held no assurance of success. After months of waiting, a creditor's plea frequently faced dismissal from a hostile judge appointed by a debtor-minded assembly. Sometimes the judges were laymen, ignorant of the law and anxious only to curry popular favor. In times of economic stress legislatures commonly intervened in the judicial process, suspending suits for debt with stay laws or issuing paper money that might negate debts by inflation. So lengthy were the delays that one Richmond merchant preferred an installment system that would insure him some return. A statute requiring payment over a period of four years, he wrote, "would be much better for the creditors than going to the law, when I could not obtain a judgment in less than seven."[71]

In all three states creditor parties put revision of the judicial system to provide fast, efficient, learned resolution of conflicts high on the legislative agenda. This, of course, would have made the courts agents of the wealthy; hence debtor parties resisted all efforts to tinker with the system. Lineups on this issue were almost identical to these on paper money and taxation.

The Jefferson-Pendleton-Wythe committee that had revised Virginia's law code during the Revolution attempted to set up a system of "assize" courts and failed. Borrowed from the common law, the term meant courts of record where suits involving substantial sums could be heard by trained judges, under standardized procedures, and governed by known precedents. Assize courts would have been an intermediate level between the General Court (a court of appeals) and the county courts (controlled by justices of the peace).[72] When Madison returned to Virginia in 1783 full of plans for reform, he resurrected the idea of assize courts. At the opening of the 1784 session he secured an appointment to the Committee for Courts of Justice, but quickly encountered opposition. There were too many members, explained John Marshall, who were "against every measure which may expedite & facilitate the business of recovering debts & compelling a strict compliance with contracts." Worse yet, the assembly was full of justices of the peace who were jealous of their local authority.[73]

Undiscouraged, Madison returned to the fall session with a bill for establishing courts of assize. His measure arranged the counties in groups and assigned some central location—usually the largest town—where such a court would be held annually. Two members of the General Court would constitute each assize court. Three of the new courts were to be located west of the Blue Ridge, answering one of the westerners' chief grievances, the remoteness of justice. The bill placed no particular limitation on the jurisdiction of such courts; Madison probably hoped they would take over many of the functions of county courts. The bill slipped through the assembly with little open opposition, though with "much secret repugnance." Madison attributed the lack of vocal criticism to the absence of Patrick Henry.[74]

Passage of the act did not end Madison's troubles, however. The assize courts were not due to open until January 1786, and in the meantime he had to return to the assembly for some supplementary legislation (possibly defining their jurisdiction). The opposition was better prepared this time and voted down the supplemental act. On Madison's motion the House then suspended the courts. That at least kept the scheme theoretically alive, and Madison hoped a future assembly might be able to ressurect it.[75]

The assembly did approve a bill reforming the county courts, standardizing their procedures and requiring them to clear their dockets quarterly. "It amounts to nothing," Madison complained to Jefferson, "and is chiefly the result of efforts to render Courts of Assize unnecessary. The one bright spot in the session was the approval, at long last, of the Jefferson-Pendleton-Wythe revision of the law code.[76]

In 1786 Madison tried a new tack. He brought in a bill to establish a stratum of district courts with broad jurisdiction, both original and appellate. Instead of being served by justices of the General Court, the district courts would have their own judges, local men in most cases. This undoubtedly made them more politically palatable to the assembly. Another advantage was that Patrick Henry, who was still "positively opposed to despatch in the administration of justice," occupied the governorship, out of harm's way.[77] George Nicholas proved trouble enough, however. Rather than attack the court bill directly, he attempted to link court reform with debt payment by installments. Otherwise, he argued, debtors would be ruined by the new system.[78]

Madison considered this proposal as "obnoxious" as paper money and resolved to "give up the bill rather than pay such a price for it." He managed to delete the installment feature with a substitute amendment that delayed establishment of the courts for a year, but then the House defeated the plan altogether.[79] The legislature continued to grapple with Jefferson's revision of the law code that winter, but was unable to reach agreement. Some suggested that the bills passed the previous year ought to be suspended so that the entire code could go into effect at once, but Madison persuaded the House not to delay. The next assembly "might possibly be unfriendly to the system altogether," he explained to Jefferson. "There was good reason to suspect Mr. Henry will certainly then be a member."[80]

Patrick Henry did return to the House in 1787, but he proved a less formidable antagonist than Nicholas. Madison was in New York that winter, and Joseph Jones took charge of the district court bill. Henry succeeded in tacking onto it a rider that kept property sold in execution of a debt from going at less than 75 percent of its value. Jones accepted it because it promised some relief to debtors without compromising any important principle. The rider also undercut opposition to court reform, and the bill passed by a handsome margin of 86 to 34.[81]

The act was the culmination of Madison's three-year campaign to reorganize the state courts and a major victory for the creditor party. It created eighteen district courts, each containing three judges, and each with both original and appellate jurisdiction. The old General Court was reorganized as a court of appeals at the apex of the judicial hierarchy.[82] Four judges, all but one associated with the Madison party in the assembly, were added to the reconstituted General Court.[83]

NORTH CAROLINA: LAWYERS VS. JUDGES

There was no chance for a similar overhaul in North Carolina because the rural majority was content with the status quo. The best the Lawyers could hope was to chip away at the system established by the legislature in 1777. Under that system the county courts conducted most of the state's legal business, and planter-judges meted out amateur justice that was unencumbered with legal niceties and comprehensible to the average suitor. The only courts of record, where trained lawyers presided, were the district courts located in Edenton, New Bern, Wilmington, Halifax, Hillsborough, and Salisbury. To preside over these courts, which met twice a year, the legislature elected three judges—James Iredell (later replaced by John Williams), Samuel Ashe, and Samuel Spencer. The latter two, in particular, reflected the interests and prejudices of the rural majority in the assembly, and they clashed repeatedly with the Lawyers on Loyalist suits at the end of the war.

Besides the clash of personalities, there were some fundamental objections to the system. The courts were difficult to reach, particularly for westerners, and with only three judges available judicial processes were slow. Worst of all from the Lawyers' point of view, there was no court of appeals to which they could turn. This left them at the mercy of their judicial enemies, Spencer and Ashe. As early as 1782, William R. Davie, just embarking on a legal career, proposed a comprehensive reform of the system. He particularly recommended an increase in the number of judges and districts to speed court processes, a permanent annual salary for judges to reduce the assembly's influence, and a Supreme Court of Appeals. Not until 1805, the year Davie retired from the law, were all three objects achieved.[84]

In 1785 the Lawyers went on the attack. Their leader was John Hay, a Fayetteville attorney with a personal grudge against the district judges. He first appeared in the assembly in the fall of 1784 and promptly joined the Maclaine circle. By the following year he and Maclaine were ready to move. Governor Caswell unwittingly presented the opportunity in his annual message when he mentioned complaints that North Carolina had no published compendium of statutes. The Commons discussed this subject for several days, and somehow Maclaine and Hay managed to turn the subject to court reform. After further debate the House agreed that changes were necessary and ordered Maclaine and Hay to draft a bill.[85]

The measure which Hay reported would have created a superior court of appeals with six judges. Such an institution would answer the Lawyers' need for an appelate forum, and the additional judges would presumably be able to handle double the business. It did not need to be said that a broadened court would also reduce the influence of the unpopular judges Spencer and Ashe. Not content, Maclaine and Hay then sponsored a bill asking the governor and council to form a court of impeachment. Among their objections to Spencer and Ashe was lack of judicial decorum; evidently they thought they could demonstrate grounds for removal.[86]

While the Commons considered these items, the threatened judges, confident of assembly support, indicted two prominent Loyalists for returning to the state without permission. The impeachment bill went down to defeat when it was pointed out that it was so broad in scope that even justices of the peace could be investigated by the impeachment court. Hay's bill to create a court of appeals slipped through without a roll call, but it was killed in the Senate. Then the rural majority counterattacked with a bill extending the jurisdiction of the county courts to include land suits. This enabled prejudiced and ill-trained justices of the peace to take up such intricate questions as confiscated estates.[87] To protect the justices from overdoses of legalism the bill also limited to two the number of attorneys who could appear before the courts in a single suit. An attempt to eliminate this feature failed by 38 to 40, and the bill went through without further ado. William Hooper, who sat out this session, called it "a bill inflicting pains and penalties on attornies."[88] The Lawyers had simply picked the wrong moment to seek court reform. This was the session that approved paper money by a two to one majority, and the lineup on the two issues was similar.

Undaunted, Hay returned to the attack in 1786. In early December, shortly after the Commons got down to business, he leveled a series of sensational charges against the superior court judges. The critical one was a charge of malpractice—levying excessively high fines and pocketing the proceeds. He also accused them of entertaining illegal prosecutions against Loyalists, dispensing with laws when it suited them, and unreasonably delaying ordinary legal business. Finally, he complained that they were guilty of ill behavior toward attorneys, especially Hay himself. The Commons promptly set up a committee to investigate, headed by Richard D. Spaight. Spaight usually voted with the Lawyers, but he was not a trustworthy partisan. On January 2, Spaight's committee reported that it could find no evidence of judicial malpractice, and the House concurred, 49 to 22.[89]

In the meantime the Lawyers had been put back on the defensive by a new court reform bill evidently intended to codify earlier laws and simplify the system. Spaight sought to eliminate the expanded jurisdiction for county courts which the legislature had approved the previous year, but failed. Maclaine then presented an amendment that would have given the court of appeals power to review the constitutionality of acts of the assembly. Clearly the reconstituted superior court now had the Lawyers' favor, but this was an extraordinary power to give it. James Iredell had discussed the concept of judicial review in a suit at law, but this was the first time anyone in the United States had attempted to write it into statute. Maclaine evidently thought anything was preferable to the untutored prejudice of the rural majority in the assembly. That group promptly dismissed the idea, 24 to 58, and passed the bill. A few days later an act involving the jurisdiction of the county courts generated a succession of similar roll calls, as the Lawyers tried to limit the discretion of justices of the peace in awarding judgments and staying executions for debt.[90] As in the previous year, the alignment closely followed that on economic issues—paper money, debts, and taxation.

When the bill altering the court system reached the Senate, General Griffith Rutherford tried to make it even more hazardous for lawyers. He wanted to require attorneys employed in law suits to file their motions and related papers on the first day of each term. If they failed to do so, the suit was to be dismissed at cost to the plaintiff. The requirement of punctuality would have severely limited the number of county courts a lawyer could attend, and it would have delayed executions by postponing all actions that arose after the first day of a term. The amendment failed by 16 to 17, and the Senate then approved the bill with only minor changes.[91]

MARYLAND: AN INDEPENDENT JUDICIARY

The contest over the judiciary in North Carolina did not involve, as it did in Virginia, efforts to change the structure of the

system. Carolina lawyers were more concerned about the compe-
tence of the sitting judges; the rural majority in the assembly
preferred to maintain an amateur system of justice and usually had
its way, though the quarrel was raucous and often angry. Judicial
matters created less ill temper in Maryland, where there was no
visible dissatisfaction with the system or professional standards.
Maryland creditors were concerned primarily with maintaining the
courts' independence to prevent popular and legislative influence
that might impair judgment. Left to itself, the common law guarded
the interest of the propertied few.

At the opening of the 1785 session the Maryland Senate
decided that the practice of paying the state's judges annually
hampered their independence. It accordingly sent to the House a
bill establishing permanent salaries for the chancellor and all
judges. The creditor majority in the House defeated a rural effort
to delete a life-tenure clause and then passed the bill, 35 to 17.[92]

The next item was Alexander C. Hanson's request for compensation for compiling a digest of the statutes of Maryland. Like
salaried judges, law books were a sign of professionalization, and to
hinterland farmers that meant incomprehensible jargon and mysterious procedures. The House approved the principle of compensat-
ing Hanson by 29 to 24 and then haggled for four more roll calls
over the exact amount.[93]

Evidently encouraged by these early victories, the creditor
party in February 1786 presented a resolution that the governor
ought to appoint only the most fit men as justices of the peace. This
was less a criticism of the governor (a military hero) than a means
for encouraging professionalism in the state's lowest courts. When
this won approval, 28 to 16, they were back with a new measure—a
bill enlarging the powers of the high court of chancery, a court that
functioned under principles of equity rather than common law. Its
intricate procedures made it an attorney's paradise. This passed by a
similar margin.

Despite the variety of matters discussed, party ranks held firm.
The lineup was almost identical to the voting on economic issues,
except that the Chasites returned to the creditor fold (see table 6.6;
minimum participation 3 votes; agreement threshold 75 percent).

TABLE 6.6 MARYLAND HOUSE OF DELEGATES: LEGAL-
JUDICIAL ISSUES, 1785

	Pro-Judges	Anti-Judges	Middle
Eastern Shore	12	0	1
Upper bay	1	5	3
Western Shore	11	0	3
Upper Potomac	1	3	0
	25	8	7
Creditor, 1784–1785	10	0	0
Debtor, 1784–1785	0	5	2
Federalist, 1788	10	0	3
Antifederalist, 1788	6	3	1

The depression breathed new life into the antijudiciary element in 1786. Permanent salaries, it complained, prevented the
assembly from economizing in times of economic distress. It could
cut costs everywhere except in the administration of justice. They
accordingly introduced a bill to repeal the act passed the previous
year and slipped it through by 30 to 27. The Senate came to the
courts' rescue. Permanent salaries were necessary to maintain the
independence of the judiciary, it explained in rejecting the bill, and
the salaries granted were not "profuse."[94]

The economizers then tried a new tack. The delegates
approved, with little opposition, a bill reducing the salaries of the
chancellor, judges, and the governor. While the Senate had this
measure under consideration, the two houses became involved in a
dispute over their own pay allowances. The House had suggested
an allowance of 17s. 6d. per day, but the Senate, pointing to the
empty treasury, suggested 14s. instead. The House replied that
such a low rate prevented the less affluent from serving in the
assembly. It then offered a bargain—it would agree to the lower
allowance if the Senate would approve a reduction in both judicial
salaries and attorneys' fees. Spotting the new wrinkle, the Senate
pointed out that attorneys' fees had nothing to do with the condition of the public treasury. The Senate then offered its own package—a legislative allowance of 14s., reduction in salaries of chan-

TABLE 6.7   MARYLAND HOUSE OF DELEGATES:
JUDGES' SALARIES, 1786

	Pro-Judges	Anti-Judges	Mixed
Creditors	12	3	1
Debtors	0	13	2
Chasites	5	2	4
Middle	5	11	2
	22	29	9

cellor and judges, plus a reduction in pay of clerks and other officers of the assembly. The House agreed, 33 to 11.[95]

Although the creditor forces were on the defensive throughout this session, the voting still followed partisan lines (table 6.7; minimum participation 2 of the 3 roll calls; agreement threshold 100 percent).

By 1787 the friends of the judiciary were firmly back in control. They even felt strong enough to introduce a structural change, evidently borrowed from Virginia. They requested permission to bring in a bill to establish courts of assize. The House approved, 31 to 13, and the resultant bill sailed through without difficulty.[96] The vote showed some interesting variations on earlier patterns (table 6.8). The Antifederalists voting in favor of the new

TABLE 6.8   MARYLAND HOUSE OF
DELEGATES: COURTS OF ASSIZE, 1787

	For	Against
Eastern Shore	11	2
Upper bay	8	0
Western Shore	9	8
Upper Potomac	3	3
	31	13
Federalists	14	3
Antifederalists	7	6
Middle	2	2
Unknown	8	2
	31	13

courts were all Chasites. The three Federalists voting against the bill were debtor members from the upper Potomac. The change in regional positions reflected the decline of the creditor-debtor confrontation with the return of prosperity. The upper bay and upper Potomac were rapidly developing areas with a bright future. Habits of partisan voting continued, but with the end of the money shortage in 1787, economic questions were no longer so clearly defined or so bitterly fought.

CHAPTER SEVEN

Tories, Anglicans, and Slaves

ALTHOUGH Chesapeake legislatures were largely preoccupied with bread-and-butter issues through the 1780s, they also grappled with a number of other matters, social problems of varying import. Some resulted directly from the war and independence, unfinished by-products of revolutionary idealism. Such issues as church disestablishment, publicly financed higher education, and Negro slavery were hotly contested, but they were resolved in a nonpartisan manner—that is to say, the lines which formed on these legislative items bore no relationship to the debtor-creditor contests. The divisions instead were regional; they stemmed from ethnic and religious differences, rather than wealth or occupation. Some social problems, such as the question of returning Loyalists, had economic implications, but reactions were local and personal. The Loyalist question aroused strong passions, but reactions were governed by the head and heart, not the hand and the purse.

During the war the states had confiscated the property of Loyalists who fled and imposed penalties on those who stayed.

When the military emergency ended, many of the disabilities were relaxed, but few were prepared to welcome repentant Tories with open arms. The peace treaty occasioned some new difficulties. Under Article V Congress was obliged to recommend to the states that they restore the property of British subjects who had not borne arms against the United States. It also permitted these individuals to seek recovery of their property by private suit. Article VI prohibited further confiscations or further prosecution of Loyalists. Those imprisoned for wartime activities were to be released. Several of these injunctions ran contrary to state laws, and that raised a new question: to what extent were the states bound by the international obligations of Congress? Fortunately for the Loyalists, the matter of their civil rights was kept separate from the discussion of debts and confiscations. Maryland's Samuel Chase, for instance, was an early advocate of leniency toward Loyalists, even while he busily bought and sold their property.

LOYALISTS AND NONJURORS IN MARYLAND

For reasons that have never been fully explored, the Eastern Shore of Maryland was a hotbed of Tory sentiment early in the war. The bay created a feeling of separateness, as it did in the lower counties belonging to Virginia, and this frequently translated into jealousy or suspicion. Western Shore gentry were in the forefront of the Revolution. Western Shore cities, Baltimore and Annapolis, teemed with "Sons of Liberty." Eastern Shore planters supported the Proprietary before the Revolution and remained reluctant rebels after 1776. In addition, the Eastern Shore was a fertile field for itinerant Methodist evangelists. In 1781, Francis Asbury, John Wesley's American lieutenant, boasted in his journal that it appeared "as if the whole peninsula would be Christianized."[1] It is likely that the ministers of this English-led church reinforced the antirevolutionary feeling in the area.[2]

Actions by Virginia's royal governor Lord Dunmore may have encouraged Eastern Shore resistance. Toward the end of 1775 he issued a proclamation offering freedom to any slave or indentured servant who joined the royal forces. When this action ended what authority he had left among Virginians, he fled to a royal ship in early 1776, ordered incendiary raids along the coastline of the bay, and sent agents to organize Eastern Shore Loyalists. As a result, military recruiters and tax collectors met outright hostility and sporadic resistance when they landed on the Eastern Shore. Although the resistance was never well organized, frustrated county officials began referring to it as an "insurrection," and that was enough to trigger intervention. During the winter of 1776 a combined Maryland-Virginia military force swept through Somerset and Worcester counties, arresting known Loyalists, and criticism subsided.[3]

In October 1777 the assembly passed an "Act for the Better Security of Government," which required every male over 18 to take an oath of fidelity to the state and promise to help defend it. Quakers, Menonites, and Dunkards, whose beliefs forbade oaths, were permitted to make affirmations. Those who refused were burdened with triple taxation, deprived of the right to sue, and prohibited from practicing medicine or engaging in trade. It has been estimated that almost one-third of the people on the Eastern Shore refused to take the oath, though whether from British sympathies or hostility to test oaths is not clear.[4]

In any case, as the twin threats of foreign invasion and domestic uprising evaporated, the assembly eliminated the more severe penalties. By 1781 nonjurors could practice medicine or engage in trade. The decision on whether to permit nonjuring attorneys to practice law was left to the county courts, and several of them excluded Loyalists until 1784 when the General Court ruled in their favor.[5]

Publication of the peace treaty caused little stir in Maryland because most of the restrictions on Loyalists had been either repealed or ignored, and confiscations had ceased. Samuel Chase himself undertook to eliminate the one remaining disability—the law that deprived nonjurors of the right to vote or hold office. In January 1785 the Delegates passed a bill to that effect by 34 to 9, a margin that indicated a general disposition to let bygones be bygones. Surprisingly, the Senate, which had tried to soften Loyalist legislation throughout the war, rejected the bill by 9 to 1. It argued that there was no evidence indicating that Loyalists had repented. It also reminded the Delegates that a number of persons expected to be indemnified for wartime losses out of confiscated property, and that further confiscations would not be practicable if Loyalists were given full political rights. The argument was as disingenuous as it was flimsy. No one envisioned further confiscations, especially since they were prohibited by the peace treaty. If this was an effort to expose and isolate Chase, it was at least none of Charles Carroll's doing. He was the lone opponent of this mischievous move.[6]

The House of Delegates defended its bill on the principle that the maximum number of freeholders ought to have the right to vote. Several delegates also pointed out that many of the nonjurors were not Loyalists, but people who had refused to join the fight for religious reasons. It would be the state's loss if such industrious, law-abiding people emigrated because they lacked political rights.[7] The reply passed the House by a somewhat narrower majority, and it was clear the Senate's stand had caused some second thoughts. A relief bill whisked through silently was one thing; an open conflict with the upper house on such a sensitive matter was quite another. When the Senate adhered to its position, the House agreed by a bare 23 to 22 to a second reply. Although his support had nearly evaporated, Chase boldly produced a three-page address defending the bill. Pride ushered this through the House on a voice vote, but it was clear the bill was dead.[8] The Senate's poisoned barb had done its work. Table 7.1 shows the distribution of support for leniency, the hard-core opposition, and those who changed their minds after the initial vote.

Chase's support held among the Eastern Shore delegates. Representatives from the north and west, where Loyalists were fewer, were the ones that shifted. The party division followed the regional lineup. Delegates who voted in behalf of speculators in that session were evenly split. They apparently felt that restoring Loyalists' rights would not hamper titles to confiscated lands.

The proponents of leniency succeeded at last in 1786. By a strong margin of 35 to 22 the House approved a bill removing the political disabilities on nonjurors. The regional and partisan lineup was virtually the same as in 1785. In order to win Senate approval,

TABLE 7.1 MARYLAND HOUSE OF DELEGATES:
RESTRICTIONS ON LOYALISTS, 1784

	Pro-Tory	Switched from Pro- to Anti-	Anti-Tory
Eastern Shore	10	1	1
Upper bay	2	6	2
Western Shore	8	1	4
Upper Potomac	0	4	2
Urban	3	1	0
	23	13	9
Creditors	15	3	3
Debtors	4	9	4
Middle	4	1	2
	23	13	9

the House agreed to an amendment requiring nonjurors to swear the loyalty oath required of all citizens.[9] One Eastern Shore Loyalist wrote joyfully that the measure "gave the most ample & liberal relief to the whole body of Nonjurors. Upon taking an unexceptionable Oath of Allegiance, they are entitled to all privileges of citizenship. The legal barriers being now removed, I imagine I ought without much difficulty take a part in public affairs."[10] A year later he was sitting in the state ratifying convention prepared to vote for the Federal Constitution. Loyalism was no longer an issue in Maryland.

NORTH CAROLINA: AFTERMATH OF CIVIL WAR

North Carolina was more tolerant of Loyalists during the war and less lenient afterward. The reason for both attitudes was the size of the Loyalist population. North Carolina had more difficulties with Loyalists than any other state. The planter squirarchy was predominantly Patriot, as in Virginia, but town merchants, many of them Scots, and the Highlanders in the Cape Fear Valley remained loyal to the empire. At least a fourth of the white population of the state were British sympathizers, and perhaps another fourth were indifferent to the outcome. The problem would have been much more severe if the Loyalists had not suffered a quick defeat at Moore's Creek Bridge in 1776. Thereafter they remained relatively quiescent until the arrival of British armies four years later.

At the beginning of the war the legislature, operating under the British theory that aliens could not hold property within the realm, confiscated the estates of all those who left the state prior to the Declaration of Independence, unless they returned and became trustworthy citizens. A few officials had fled to New York or Bermuda, but it is unlikely that this action affected very many. Nor was the state able to sell the property because it never knew when the absent might return with professions of allegiance. Instead, it rented the property and spent the proceeds. The assembly did impose a test oath, but it found that most Loyalists were willing to take it. Sectarians who refused on religious grounds were ignored.

In 1779 the assembly sought to tighten the system of confiscation by singling out a large number of prominent Tories, who had presumably escaped retribution hitherto. The measure was severe enough to warrant a public protest by 15 members of the Commons, among them Willie Jones, that it involved "such a Complication of Blunders and betrays such ignorance in Legislation as would disgrace a Set of Drovers."[11] Confiscations certainly increased under this legislation, but how many were carried out before the British invaded the state is uncertain.

In any case, when Lord Cornwallis arrived in the South in 1780, the North Carolina Loyalists were neither cowed nor controlled. The British were able to recruit several regiments of Loyalists in the state, and the operations of these forces turned the Revolution into a civil war. The assembly, hounded from town to town by British raiding parties, appealed frantically for support. It even offered full pardon and relief from confiscation to any Loyalist or neutralist who joined the American army. The humiliation left some bitter memories, and when General Nathanial Greene drove the last British from the state in the fall of 1781, the legislature began screaming for revenge. Confiscations mounted, and in 1782 it started selling the property to merchant speculators for state paper money.[12]

In the latter stages of the war a number of British sympathizers, fearing the wrath of Patriot committees, fled to Charleston. These people presented a particularly difficult problem, for they had not actually taken up arms against the state. To what extent were they liable to confiscation, and under what conditions should they be allowed to return? Archibald Maclaine, a personal friend of one of the Charleston emigrés, George Hooper, made himself the spokesman for their interests. In the spring sesson of 1783 he drafted an amnesty bill but found anti-Tory fever still running too high. "Many well disposed men," he reported to his clients, "very unjudiciously thought it best to give way at present, & let the violent cool by degrees." The assembly did pass a bill pardoning those who had accepted commissions from the crown, but it contained so many exceptions that few actually benefited. The emigrés had to comfort themselves with the thought that at least the assembly had not enacted new restrictions.[13] Those who did return got a hostile reception. The state judges, reflecting the public distemper, ruled that pardons did not give Loyalists the right to sue in court and levied fines on all who returned to the state without permission.[14]

Maclaine was back the following year and undoubtedly expected to get some help from his Lawyer friends. The Lawyer-dominated committee on a legislative agenda reported in favor of codifying the state's confiscation laws, and a bill to that effect was introduced. Tory-baiters quickly spotted a provision for restoring all estates that had not been sold and rejected the bill on first reading, 18 to 62. As might be expected from such a wide margin, hatred for Tories was widely distributed around the state. Only the Cape Fear Valley, where most Loyalists lived, supported the measure. The rural-debtor men were unanimously opposed to the bill; Maclaine's circle of Lawyers was evenly divided.

The House then proceeded to redraft the bill, retaining all names listed in previous confiscation acts and adding a few more. General Griffith Rutherford, to whom had fallen the nasty job of suppressing Loyalists late in the war, added a few choice enemies, but, reported Maclaine, "The old brigadier was quite outdone by Tim. Bloodworth, who (as Rutherford himself expressed it) meant to depopulate N. Hanover county." In the upper house, Samuel Johnston succeeded in adding an amendment granting a pardon to all persons not named in the bill, but then the Senate rejected the measure altogether. Being too prescriptive for some and too lenient for others it no longer had any supporters.[15]

A more indirect attempt to help the Loyalists came closer to success. The agenda committee prepared a bill to repeal the state laws inconsistent with Articles IV and VI of the peace treaty (thereby lumping Loyalists with British debts). The proposal was designedly vague. Since many members of the rural majority were not prepared to admit that any laws were in violation of the treaty, they could hardly object to a harmless statement. Which laws it affected would have to be decided by the courts, and that was probably the Lawyers' intent. The Senate took up the measure first, and Samuel Johnston was pleased to note that his old foe Willie Jones, present in the assembly for the first time in some years, supported him on this particular issue. Debate focused on Article V of the peace treaty and Congress's recommendation that Loyalist property ought to be restored. Everything was proceeding smoothly until General Rutherford made a fiery speech denouncing Loyalists as "Imps of Hell," and when it was over not ten senators could be found to vote their cause. It probably mattered little because the House also rejected the bill, 32 to 37.[16] Because this measure involved British debts as well as Loyalists, party lines held firm on this roll call. Of those whose parties can be identified (and most cannot because there were few roll calls on economic issues in this session) the Lawyers unanimously backed the bill, and their opponents with equal unanimity rejected it.

Tory-baiters did prepare a bill to authorize new confiscations, but the Lawyers managed to quash it without a vote. That marked the end of persecution; thereafter the government was on the defensive as Loyalists began returning to the state looking for means to recover their property.

"Not a word have I heard of tories or toryism," Maclaine reported to his emigré clients shortly after the 1785 session opened. "If there is anything hatching, it must be very secret."[17] Maclaine's new foe on Loyalist affairs was former governor Abner

Nash, who shared Ritherford's bitter wartime memories. Concerned about the effect of the peace treaty, Nash drafted a bill confirming the titles of purchasers of confiscated estates and forbidding the courts from entertaining suits for recovery of the property. Although Nash was "attacked from all quarters," according to Maclaine, the bill somehow slipped through. All Maclaine could do was file a protest denouncing it as unconstitutional and therefore "nugatory."[18]

Nash's statute was pregnant with mischief. Attorney General Alfred Moore publicly expressed his misgivings about it,[19] and an opportunity to test it soon arose. In May 1786 a Mrs. Bayard, who had inherited a house and wharf in New Bern that had been confiscated, brought suit against one Singleton, who had bought the land from the state. The suit directly challenged the confiscation acts and the titles derived from the state. Mrs. Bayard evidently possessed both wealth and influence as well as a promising case, for she was able to hire James Iredell, Samuel Johnston, and William R. Davie to argue her cause. Singleton countered by hiring Abner Nash, who naturally invoked his 1785 law denying the court jurisdiction. Iredell and Johnston replied that the act was unconstitutional because it, in effect, deprived their client of the right to trial by jury. It was a specious argument since it could be applied to any statute limiting the jurisdiction of courts, but, amazingly enough, the judges appeared to accept it. And the judges—Spencer, Williams, and Ashe—had never before viewed sympathetically the legal doctrines of Johnston and Iredell.

Though the judges refused to quash the case, they were equally reluctant to overturn an act of the legislature. Accordingly, they temporized, hoping the assembly would repeal the law. The delay gave the Tory-baiters in the assembly an opportunity to interfere. They demanded a legislative inquiry, and a committee was accordingly appointed in November 1786. Weakening, Justices Spencer and Williams attended the hearings, but Samuel Ashe refused, declaring somewhat confusedly that his judicial character was "righteous and therefore bold." The committee was stacked with Lawyers and returned, as might be expected, with a highly critical report. It accused the judges of errors of law, unnecessary delays in determining suits, pocketing fines levied by themselves, and failing to attend their own courts on a regular basis. The two houses set up a joint committee to investigate the charges. This one quickly exonerated the judges and the House approved its report, 49 to 22.[20] The lineup defined the two parties as well as any roll call did in that session. In the meantime the Lawyers had drafted a bill repealing Nash's statute. It survived a first reading but it was put to rest during the judicial investigation and not brought up again.[21]

Encouraged by the legislative backing, the judges returned to their case with stronger nerves. Their decision in *Bayard* v. *Singleton* (May 1787) accepted the Johnston-Iredell argument, and they ruled the 1785 act unconstitutional. They went on to appease the assembly, however, by upholding the legitimacy of the confiscation laws themselves.[22] The reception of this remarkable decision—one of the earliest American expositions of judicial review—indicated the slackening of tension. In its fall session the assembly formally endorsed the peace treaty, thereby permitting Loyalists to return and make use of the state courts. The judges continued to uphold titles derived from state confiscation, thus denying them recovery, but the public and the assembly had lost interest. There were three roll calls in the Commons in 1787 on matters involving confiscated property, but there was no pattern among them. Nor did the voting bear any relation to subsequent stands on the Federal Constitution.[23] As political targets, the Tories were at last free.

VIRGINIA LOYALISTS: TOO FEW TO CAUSE CONCERN

Virginia, united in revolutionary ardor from the outset of the imperial conflict, had few Loyalists and almost no confiscations. Those who rallied to Lord Dunmore's standard in 1776 discreetly departed for Nova Scotia or Britain after the burning of Norfolk, and few returned. There were a number of Scots merchants who had fled at the beginning of the war and who could be expected back, but they posed no threat to state security. Some interests were certain to be affected by their repatriation, but the overall impact was not clear. Returning Loyalists, especially the merchants, would bring some wealth with them, and they would help speed the reestablishment of the tobacco trade. On the other hand, restoration of the old ties with London and Glasgow would leave the state in colonial vassalage, and the return of merchant-factors demanding repayment of prewar debts would embarrass many planters.[24]

In May 1783 Patrick Henry himself introduced a bill to repeal the laws preventing Loyalists from returning to the state. For once he had the backing of Richard Henry Lee, who felt that the peace treaty prohibited discrimination and the state could benefit by the additional population. Nevertheless, the alliance of these two political giants was not enough to overcome lingering hostility. Even a moderate like Joseph Jones thought that repeal was premature. The House voted to postpone it, 56 to 27.[25] Instead the assembly passed an act which denied citizenship to all "statute staple men" who had left the state since April 1775. Loyalists began trickling in anyway, generally without incident except in Norfolk. In that much-battered city citizens groups took to court and expelled any Loyalists that ventured ashore.[26]

In the fall of 1783 a House committee headed by John Taylor of Caroline reported a bill that opened the way for Loyalists to regain full rights of citizenship. Patrick Henry, sensing that his earlier stand had not had full public endorsement, reversed himself and opposed it vigorously. Reaction to the measure was critical but nonpartisan. Joseph Jones thought a short residence ought to be required of returning Loyalists, and John Page wanted to refuse citizenship to anyone who had voluntarily left the state during the war. Westerner John Breckinridge favored a policy that would encourage immigration but deny political rights to Loyalists.[27]

After some discussion the House compromised on a pair of bills which permitted Loyalists who had not participated in the war to return, but denied them the right to vote or hold office for two years. No one was wholly satisfied with the settlement, but it did end what little controversy there had been.[28] The two assembly sessions generated a total of four roll calls on Loyalist matters, and voting was quite mixed. No one registered as many as three anti-Tory votes, and many split their ballots. There were 15 consistently pro-Tory delegates; all but one represented counties in the neigh borhood of Alexandria, Fredericksburg, Richmond, or Norfolk. Delegates who tended to be anti-Tory came from the Piedmont and west. As in Maryland and North Carolina, those who lived closest to the Loyalists were most inclined to be lenient.

Individual prejudices lingered, and they seemed to flare up whenever the subject of British debts arose. In 1785 an anonymous voice that had all the tones of Meriwether Smith's tried to arouse Virginia merchants to the competitive threat from Loyalists who were "anxious to become citizens, that they may have full license to scrample [sic] more eagerly and openly, for the Loaves and Fishes."[29] In 1786 the assembly completed the structure of citizenship legislation. It continued the ban on those who had actively aided Britain during the war, but all other immigrants or returnees could become naturalized simply by swearing a loyalty oath. The one exception to this open-armed policy was people who entered the state to collect British debts. Each of these was required to register with the governor, who was then obliged to announce the alien's presence, particular business, and place of residence in the Richmond newspaper. The one roll call, involving a Senate amendment to the bill, revealed no particular pattern. Significantly, Madison did not even bother to mention the act to Jefferson in his annual review of assembly activities. Loyalists were all but forgotten.

VIRGINIA'S STATUTE FOR RELIGIOUS FREEDOM

In Virginia, and perhaps in Maryland as well, the most important social issue of the decade was disestablishment of the Church of England. The American Revolution, like all great modern revolutions, was anticlerical in tone because the religious establishment (except in New England) was linked to the old order. From New York south, the Church of England was under attack because it was both a vestige of monarchy and a symbol of Old World debilitation. Since the mid-seventeenth century, when Maryland and Virginia forcefully resisted the Puritanical republicanism of Oliver Cromwell, the Chesapeake had been regarded as the New World home of Anglicanism. But despite the seeming influence of the Church no cleric outside of New England had as much political power as

Commissary James Blair did in Virginia), the Anglican Establishment was a shell that the slightest push could topple. The clergy were few, underpaid, and generally unpopular. In Virginia, moreover, church-state controversies of mid-century—the Pistole Fee, the battle for secular control of William and Mary, and the Parson's Cause—had left the Establishment politically tainted. In Maryland, Governor Robert Eden's proclamation regulating clerical fees had much the same effect, for radicals simply denounced it as taxation by executive fiat.

The appearance of dissenting sects further weakened the Establishment. Scots-Irish and Germans brought the Presbyterian and Lutheran churches into the western counties, plus a variety of pietist sects, Dunkards, Quakers, and Menonites. During the war Methodist itinerants made numerous converts on the Eastern Shore and Virginia's southside. It has been estimated that there were more Methodists in the Chesapeake than anywhere else in America.[30] Baptists were less numerous in Maryland, but in southern Virginia and northern North Carolina their numbers exceeded those of any other denomination.

The one thing these various churches and sects had in common was dislike for the Anglican Establishment. They all wanted the Church of England shorn of its privileged connection with the state so that they could share in the tax revenues that were devoted to religion. Although few wanted total separation of church and state, disestablishment and toleration had broad appeal.

In North Carolina, where dissenters were most numerous of all, disestablishment was no problem. There were only half a dozen Anglican ministers in the state at the outbreak of the war, and most were Loyalists. The state's Constitution of 1776 effected the break by declaring that the government could not favor one church over any other and no citizen could be compelled to contribute financially to any church. Christianity remained a requirement for officeholding, but otherwise religious freedom was complete. By prohibiting taxation for religious purposes, North Carolina also avoided major battles that disrupted and delayed disestablishment in Maryland and Virginia.

Virginia's Declaration of Rights of 1776 offered toleration to religious minorities but did not sever the tie with the Anglican Church. A major step toward that end was taken three years later when the assembly repealed all taxes for the support of religion, but the church was so interwoven with the fabric of Virginia society that total separation took years to accomplish. The vestries, for instance, were vital organs of local government, having charge of poor relief, the care of orphans, even the licensing of taverns. The church also remained in possession of certain public properties, notably the glebe lands which the imperial government had donated to each parish for the support of its minister. Staunch Anglicans, moreover, were inclined to fight back, and the loss of their privileged financial position opened the way for an alliance with other Protestant churches. Because of past frictions it is unlikely that there was any sort of formal agreement, but there were certainly grounds for cooperation.

In the spring legislative session of 1784 the House committee on religion issued a report favoring a general assessment for religious purposes. Such a tax would have benefited almost all denominations, but it also would have reinforced the dominant position of the Anglican church. The suggestion was allowed to rest there for the time being, however, because, said Madison "The friends of the measure did not chuse [sic] to try their strength in the House."[31] In June of that year the Anglican clergy held a convention at Richmond, which drew up a petition for an act incorporating the Protestant Episcopal Church. The Revolution made necessary a formal separation from the Church of England, the clergy pointed out, and even offered opportunity for reform. They wanted the assembly to incorporate them as a separate Protestant denomination. Under their plan the vestries would be chosen by church members only, deprived of all secular duties, and vested with all church property.

Although such reforms seemed both necessary and harmless, there was more than met the eye. The effect would have been to confirm the church's title to the glebe lands, property which gave it a financial advantage over every other denomination, and prevent any future legislative intervention. Quick to spot danger, the Reverend John B. Smith, president of Presbyterian Hampden-Sydney College, declared that confirming the glebes would make the Episcopalian clergy largely independent of both vestries and parishoners and effectively reestablish their preferred position. The assembly was impressed but not prepared to abandon the incorporation project altogether. Instead, Madison reported, the project was "preserved from a dishonorable death by the talents of Mr. Henry. It lies over for another session."[32]

Patrick Henry made himself champion not just of the Anglican establishment but of religion in general. Henry had long been associated with the dissenting churches, and among his best friends was Reverend Smith, whose college was the intellectual center of Henry's home county. Reverend Smith objected to legislative interference in religious matters, but he saw nothing wrong with a taxpayer's being obliged to support the church of his choice. As a result, the assessment bill was still very much alive when the legislature reconvened in November, and Henry was its new champion. To quell Protestant fears that such ecumenical support might have undesirable results, Henry "endeavored to show that Jews, Mahometans, Deists, and pagans professed and practiced such abominations as rendered their persuasions unworthy the sanction of legal support."[33] The religiously dedicated were probably a tiny minority of the assembly, but Henry got substantial support from those who felt that religion did have its social uses. "The experience of all times shows religion to be the guardian of morals," pontificated Richard Henry Lee. "And he must be a very inattentive observer in our Country, who does not see that avarice is accomplishing the destruction of religion, for want of a legal obligation to contribute something to its support."[34]

Religion was thus the first item on the legislative agenda in the fall of 1784. On November 11 the House passed a resolution favoring a general assessment by 47 to 32. The division was primarily regional—all but four Tidewater delegates favored the tax while all but three westerners opposed it. The Piedmont was evenly divided. Madison thought that "The majority was produced by a Coalition between the Episcopal & Presbyterian Sects."[35]

Further evidence of cooperation between these two old institutional rivals came a week later when the House approved by 62 to 23 a resolution favoring the incorporation of all Christian societies in the state. Presbyterians were not opposed to incorporation, explained their commissioners; they had meant to protest only the incorporation of the Anglican church by itself. Standing firm against the alliance of churches was a tiny handful of liberals, led by Madison, Zachariah Johnston, and John Breckinridge.[36] Although the two titans, Madison and Patrick Henry, were on opposite sides on yet another political issue, the division had no connection with parties. Most of Madison's creditor following sided with the religious conservatives.

On December 2, Francis Corbin brought in a bill spelling out the details of religious taxation. It permitted each taxpayer to designate the clergyman his payment would benefit. Those who wished could donate their rates to secular education instead.[37] To that point the churchmen seemed to be in complete control. They then made a tactical error that gave Madison his opening. Although the incorporation resolution had embraced all Christian societies, the only one that had actually requested action was the Anglican church. Carter H. Harrison, assigned to draft a bill under the resolution, accordingly came in with an "act to incorporate the Protestant Episcopal church." This immediately aroused the suspicions of the Presbyterians and confirmed the fears of the Baptists. Although Harrison's bill was introduced more than a week after Corbin's, it somehow got on the agenda first. The House discussed it for three days and passed it on December 22 by 47 to 38. Madison voted for it, he explained to his father, because it "parried for the present the Genl Asses[men]t, which would otherwise have certainly been saddled upon us."[38]

At the cost of incorporation—which did essentially change the status of the Anglican church—Madison hoped to break up the conservative alliance. The strategy worked admirably. The House took up Corbin's bill that same day, discussed it for a time, and then postponed it to the following session. It then ordered both the bill and the roll call published so that popular sentiment on the subject could be ascertained.[39] Because of the tactical voting, only a few delegates registered much consistency, but the pattern was still predominantly sectional. Of the 11 delegates who consistently favored a religious establishment, 9 (Patrick Henry and Carter H. Harrison were the exceptions) came from the Tidewater. Of the 19 who opposed it, 16 were from the Piedmont and west. Known Anglicans seemed about evenly divided; it is likely that their positions were determined largely by the number of dissenters in their constituencies. When the assembly adjourned, Madison looked back on the session with some satisfaction. The only damage resulting from Patrick Henry's religious crusade was the incorporation bill, and Madison thought that would ultimately prove unpopular. In the meantime he considered it "a standing exam[ple] to them of the danger of referring religous niceties to a legislature."[40]

Madison's strategy of delay paid off handsomely. There were so many religious interests in Virginia that any sort of legislative action was certain to create more problems than it solved. The incorporation act, for instance, stirred the wrath even of Washington, a man who seldom committed his religious thoughts to paper. The bill, he told Zachariah Johnston, was "inconsistent with my Ideas of Religious Liberty." Washington feared that the privilege of incorporation would be confined to a few large denominations, and smaller sects would be excluded. He even went to the trouble of drafting a bill of his own, which would have permitted any group to incorporate itself merely by registering with the county clerk and supplying him with a membership list.[41] This proposal clearly fell short of the "Ideas of Religious Liberty" held by Jefferson and Madison, but it did indicate that there was a wide variance in opinion even among religious conservatives. While undertaking a revision of the law code during the war, Jefferson had drafted a bill totally separating church and state in Virginia and permitting complete freedom of belief, including disbelief. Anticipating a controversy, Jefferson had not submitted the bill with his law revision. He and Madison decided to hold it until a more opportune moment. So Madison played for time.

The assembly's appeal for public reaction gave Jefferson's Albemarle County friend, George Nicholas, an idea. Why not flood the legislature with petitions, he suggested to Madison. If it were managed in such a way that the petitions "all hold the same language," thereby revealing "an exact uniformity of sentiment in a majority of the country, it would certainly deter the majority of the Assembly from proceeding."[42] This may well have been the most important political insight of the time. Conceding that the proponents of a religious assessment were in the majority, Nicholas hoped to intimidate them by an outburst of public opinion. He clearly assumed that the legislature would respond to the voice of the people, itself an indication of how contemporaries viewed Virginia's political system. His suggestion that the popular voice could be artificially expanded in volume in order to manipulate the system was a major step in the developing concept of a party system. Petitions were only one device. It would not take long to recognize that mass meetings, widely circulated sets of resolutions, even anonymous contributions to newspapers would all accomplish much the same thing. Once the idea caught hold, the parties would cease to be interest groups confined to the assembly and become instead organizations that both shaped public opinion and translated it into policy.

Nicholas's letter arrived in the midst of the annual assembly elections, and Madison was anxiously looking for some sign that popular feeling was turning against the religious assessment.[43] The assembly's request for information brought forth a number of newpaper contributors, and the issue clearly dominated the campaign.[44] But the electorral results were uncertain; it was time to put Nicholas's scheme into operation. Madison quickly drafted a "Remonstrance" against the assessment, which was printed and circulated around the state by friends.[45] Publication of the "Remonstrance" started a new barrage of antiassessment contributions in the newspapers.

In August the Presbyterians arranged a general convocation at Bethel in western Augusta County. Advertisements in the *Virginia Gazette* asked every congregation in the state to send delegates. After several days the meeting adopted a "remonstrance" that closely resembled Madison's in language and spirit; it denounced any contact whatsoever between church and state. Simultaneously, the general committee of the Baptist Church, meeting in Powhatan across the James from Richmond, adopted a similar resolution and urged local churches to petition the legislature.

The reasons for the change in attitude among the nonconformist churches can only be guessed. It seems most likely that they finally recognized that forced contributions could benefit only the Anglican majority. Historically the Anglican church had embraced the entire citizenry. Dissenting churches received staunch support from their members, but could hardly expect much from anyone else. Thus most of the religiously indifferent, from habit or ignorance, would have turned over their payments to the Anglican vestries. The option of giving the money to schools required a commitment of another kind that would have been rare in practice.

The effect of this alliance between secular and sectarian forces was striking. The House of Delegates received petitions from groups in 48 of the state's 72 counties; 41 were opposed to the assessment. The number of signatures protesting the bill exceeded 10,000, while only about 1,200 endorsed it.[46] Not until the Jay Treaty a decade later would Virginia witness such a vast, well-organized outpouring of popular feeling.

By the time the assembly convened in October 1785, the notion of levying taxes for the support of clergy was dead. The Delegates did not even bother to take up the bill they had postponed the previous winter. Instead, Madison, sensing that the time at last was ripe, introduced Jefferson's statute for religious freedom. It slid quickly through the House without alteration, though Madison noted some "warm opposition" in debate. The only fight involved a last-ditch effort to strike out Jefferson's sweeping declaration of freedom in the preamble and substitute one closer to the temporizing language of Mason's Declaration of Rights. This lost by 38 to 66, and on December 20 the bill passed, 74 to 20. The Senate insisted on modifying the preamble, a Jeffersonian paean to intellectual freedom, and rather than lose the substance of the bill the House eventually agreed.[47] When the battle was over only Pennsylvania among the American states could equal Virginia's commitment to spiritual freedom. And if the methods employed were at times devious, they marked a new level of sophistication in the art of political combat. It was a lesson not to be forgotten.

CHURCH, STATE, AND PUBLIC SCHOOLS
IN MARYLAND

Maryland's Bill of Rights of 1776, like Virginia's, included only a limited grant of religous toleration. It stressed the right of each individual to worship God in any way he chose and declared that no one could be compelled to attend a church other than the one of his choice. But it also permitted the legislature to impose "a general and equal tax for the support of religion." The constitution, to which the bill of rights was appended, permitted each taxpayer to designate the church or minister who was to receive payment, and if he wished he could apply it to the benefit of the poor. The Anglican Church was effectively disestablished, but there was much room for political intervention in religion. In addition, the constitution required a declaration of belief in Christianity for officeholders. Members of pietist sects who refused to swear oaths were restricted in their court appearances. They were allowed to make affirmations in order to bear witness in minor law suits, but they were not permitted to testify in cases involving capital crimes.[48]

In 1779 the legislature moved to complete the disestablishment of the Anglican church. It provided that vestries were to be elected by church members in each parish, and it turned over to them the glebes and other church property. The assembly did not, however, exercise its authority to levy a tax for the benefit of clergy, and as a result each minister was left to make his own bargain with his parishioners. Most were treated harshly. Troubled by their weakened position, the Anglican clergy in 1783 obtained the permission of the assembly to draft a bill to incorporate themselves as the Protestant Episcopal Church. As in Virginia, this move would have enabled the institution to own property and set up schools for the training of ministers. The act easily slipped through the assembly but then ran into a storm of controversy. It seemed to give Episcopalians preferment over other churches; some considered it the opening wedge for reestablishment.[49]

Among the most vocal of the critics was a Presbyterian clergyman, Dr. Patrick Allison, who in the fall of 1784 entered the newspapers under the pseudonym "Vindex." Significantly, Allison was concerned only with the favoritism accorded the Anglican

Church; he had no objection to taxation for the support of religion generally.[50] Like the Virginia Presbyterians, he had much to learn.

The assembly already had the question of religious taxation under consideration. Samuel Chase, son of a minister and the acknowledged spokesman for Episcopalian interests, introduced an assessment bill in the 1784 session after testing House sentiment with some innocuous resolutions on the social utility of religion.[51] After voicing initial approval of the measure, the House divided on the question of whether the tax was to be on property or polls. With the church forces in temporary disarray, opponents of the bill persuaded the House to postpone it so that delegates could consult their constituents. The House then approved an address defending the concept of financial support for religion. Opponents of taxation then suggested publishing the roll calls in the newspapers, but churchmen, not wanting quite that much publicity, voted it down.[52]

The issue occasioned six roll calls in the House of Delegates, and lines were firmly drawn. As in Virginia, the division was fundamentally regional. Tidewater delegates, from both Eastern and Western shores, favored religious taxation by 24 to 1. Delegates from the upper bay and upper Potomac, where dissenting churches predominated, opposed the assessment by 16 to 2. City delegates were evenly divided. The party split reflected the regional distribution.[53]

The assembly contest caused a newspaper controversy that raged into the summer of 1785. Despite the onset of depression and rising interest in paper money, the church-state issue seemed the primary concern in the fall elections. The orthodox argued, as did their counterparts south of the Potomac, that religion was the foundation of morality and hence deserved public support without regard to denomination. Critics replied that the money could be better spent, and they predicted that state support would lead to a new Establishment.[54]

The assembly's request for instructions gave Marylanders their own opportunity to manipulate opinion. An anonymous contributor to the *Maryland Journal* announced that those opposed to the assessment were "signing throughout the State a Piece in the form of Instructions to their Representatives," and he asked the editor to print the petition, leaving blanks for the voters to fill in the names of their delegates. The editor obligingly did so. After the election another religious liberal printed a follow-up notice. Having followed election results, he had concluded that a majority of the House of Delegates were against the religious tax. But, he cautioned, "Care should nevertheless be taken to forward the Instructions circulated and signed against this obnoxious Measure . . . to Annapolis without Delay."[55]

Delegates returned to Annapolis in a nervous mood. Religious liberals offered a weathervane motion to the effect that taxes for the support of ministers would actually damage religion. Then, sensing that this sort of frontal assault might alienate moderates, they hastily withdrew the motion. It was then the Anglicans' turn to err. They asked permission to bring in a bill to levy a tax for the support of ministers. This was denied, and religious taxation was dead.[56]

Demise of the taxation proposal by no means ended the church-state controversy, however. The newspaper discussion had brought out a secondary conflict involving the future of higher education in Maryland, and when the tax question was settled this matter quickly took center stage. It proved to be much more durable. In the newspaper war the opponents of a religious establishment expressed a concern that publicly supported colleges would be used primarily for training clergy. This sort of indirect aid to religion, they feared, would relieve the Anglican church of a pressing burden and pave the way for reestablishment.[57]

There was some justice to the argument, for nearly all American colleges had been founded by religious denominations. Even Benjamin Franklin's secularly endowed College of Philadelphia had fallen under the Anglican influence of its provost, William Smith. Removed from office when the college was rechartered as the University of Pennsylvania in 1776, Smith departed for Maryland. He arrived in Chester Town in 1780 in search of a pastorate, and by the end of the year he was in charge of the Kent County Free School, an elementary school for the poor. He combined that with a private class he was tutoring, hired some additional instructors, and called it an academy. In 1782, with the student population grown to 140, the academy petitioned the legislature for incorporation as a college, to be named after George Washington. The assembly obliged, and Smith was installed as the college's first president.

Washington College was an instant success. Smith successfully appealed to Eastern Shore pride, placed prominent men on the Board of Visitors, and raised an endowment of £14,000 within five months. In 1784 Washington himself visited the college to inscribe his name as one of the governors.[58] Even so, the funding was insufficient, and in the fall of 1784 the visitors went to the legislature for financial support. Their appeal coincided with a petition from Western Shore delegates asking the assembly to elevate King William's school in Annapolis into a college. The assembly approved both requests and added a further provision establishing a convocation to supervise both colleges under the name University of Maryland. Although there had been some early opposition to the Washington request, mostly from upper Potomac delegates, the conjunction of regional interests plus the promise of secular control won quick approval. The bill passed 33 to 18. Table 7.2 indicates

TABLE 7.2   MARYLAND HOUSE OF DELEGATES: COLLEGIATE EDUCATION, 1784

	Favoring Colleges	Anti-Washington & Pro U. of Maryland	Opposing Colleges
Eastern Shore	13	0	0
Upper bay	0	0	11
Western Shore	8	3	2
Upper Potomac	0	0	5
Urban	2	0	1
	23	3	19
Creditors	19	2	1
Debtors	1	0	15
Middle·	2	1	3
Unknown	1	0	0
	23	3	19
Pro-church	20	1	1
Anti-church	0	2	17
Unknown	3	0	1
	23	3	19

the distribution of votes on the three roll calls, involving aid to Washington College alone and aid to the two colleges combined.[59]

The tabulation suggests that all three factors—region, party, and religion—influenced voting. Opposition to state-supported colleges was centered in the northern and western counties most remote from the colleges and least likely to benefit. Placing the two colleges under the University of Maryland did not sway many minds, unless it prevented some Eastern Shore delegates from voting against St. John's College. Creditors favored colleges regardless of where they resided; debtor men opposed colleges. Religious concerns were probably secondary, for the proviso placing the combined colleges under secular control failed to break the hardcore opposition. Debtor men, representing the less affluent parts of the state, apparently considered the colleges a needless extravagance that would benefit only the low-country rich.[60]

That, at least, was the burden of most of the newspaper essays that spring. As soon as the college bill became law, journalistic polemics broke out anew. Opponents objected to being taxed "for gentlemen's children to be educated at the public expense."[61] Although inspired by different motives, the opponents of colleges found the pressure tactics of religious liberals useful. By April 1785 newspapers were circulating blank petitions demanding repeal of the college appropriation. The newspaper subscriber needed only to fill in his county and the names of his delegates.[62]

By the time the legislature reconvened in the fall, the depression was being felt, and college opponents shrewdly linked the appropriation question with debtor relief. By a margin of 32 to 29 they won permission to draft a bill suspending college appropriations and applying the funds instead to "the exigencies of government" in order to ease taxes. The House then became stalemated on the question of whether the previous year's act amounted to a contract with the colleges that could not be annulled. It finally ordered all resolutions and roll calls—15 in all—on the subject published in the newspapers.[63]

Legislative lines held firm throughout. Any shift from the previous year was due to new men, not changed minds. The only important change was in the stance of the Eastern Shore. Previously in favor of colleges, that area now seemed to have misgivings. One explanation may be the establishment of Methodist Cokesbury (the name a combination of its two patrons, Dr. Thomas Coke and Francis Asbury) at Abingdon, Harford County.[64] Construction was only beginning in 1785, but the prospect of an institution of their own may have made Eastern Shore Methodists less friendly toward Washington College. The new Eastern Shore delegates were also debtor men inclined to be frugal with public monies. In fact, the legislative division in general followed partisan lines to a greater extent than in 1784. Creditors favored the colleges by 24 to 2, debtors opposed them by 16 to 0.

St. John's College had carefully tried to avoid sectarian criticism by placing on its Board of Trustees both the Presbyterian divine Patrick Allison and the Reverend John Carroll, a prominent Roman Catholic (he became the nation's first Catholic bishop in 1790). Even so, St. John's also suffered from legislative penny-pinching. Lacking funds to hire faculty, it struggled on for some years under the lone hand of Ralph Higginbotham, former headmaster of King William's school and rector of St. Anne's parish. The university concept fared no better. Both Washington and St. John's were preoccupied with their own troubles, and both depended heavily on local pride. No attempt to hold a convocation, as required by the 1784 act, was made until 1790, and after a few ineffectual meetings, each college went its own way. Their annual request for help brought occasional outbursts in the assembly, but none ever compared to the storm of 1785.

SLAVERY: FALSE DAWN OF HOPE

Chesapeake planters worried throughout the war about the reactions of their slaves. Many of the reports of rural insurrection in Maryland, for instance, were nothing more than the nagging apprehensions of slaveowners. In Virginia and North Carolina, where roving British armies disrupted plantation discipline, slaves dropped their farm tools and fled by the thousands. The British took the fugitives with them when they departed at the end of the war, and after numerous vicissitudes many ended up in the experimental colony of Sierra Leone. Unable to face the truth, Virginians accused the British of capturing slaves for their own uses, and they demanded recompense. Through the 1780s the issue was entangled with the problem of British debts.

While many northern states eliminated or restricted slavery during the Revolution, the Chesapeake legislatures held firm. The only important criticism of slavery in the region came from the Society of Friends, and its petitions—even for such modest change as easing the restrictions on manumission—got nowhere.[65] In the Virginia assembly the annual Quaker memorandum was invariably greeted by a motion to place it under the table, a joke which only high annual turnover kept alive.

In 1785 Maryland's House of Delegates voted 32 to 21 to reject a collection of manumission petitions without even reading them.[66] Both parties were internally divided; such pattern as existed was regional. The Western Shore favored slavery, but Eastern Shore delegates, surprisingly, did not. There were a number of Quakers on the Eastern Shore, and they may have received some support from Methodists. The upper bay favored slavery, and the upper Potomac was evenly divided. In both regions hopes for future development may have canceled ethnic and religious opposition to slavery. Whatever the rationale, it left little hope for blacks.

Only in North Carolina was there any movement on the slavery issue—probably because religious dissidents were more numerous and large slaveholding a rarity. In 1785, Archibald Maclaine introduced a bill permitting owners who were "conscientiously scrupulous" to free their slaves, and it passed with no apparent discussion and without a roll call.[67] The following year the assembly banned the import of slaves from northern states which had undertaken emancipation, but a bill to ease further the restrictions on private manumissions suffered a resounding defeat on its first reading.[68]

In 1788 a bill prohibiting the further import of slaves from Africa passed the Commons, 52 to 40.[69] There was no clear regional pattern to the voting. The Tidewater was evenly divided, the Piedmont favored it by two to one, but the west (especially Tennessee) was opposed. Perhaps, like the western Marylanders, they anticipated future growth. The Federal Constitution provided for the ultimate prohibition of the trade, but this did not affect attitudes toward the North Carolina law. Federalists split 12 to 12; Antifederalists supported the import restriction, 28 to 17. The Senate killed the bill, and that halted discussion for the time being.

Slavery was one of those issues that political leaders detest. Essentially a matter of conscience, it was the sort of legislative business that voters forgot about when one agreed with them and never forgave when one did not. The people most affected had no political rights, and those who spoke for them were a tiny band whose voices were scarcely heard. When a young, eager delegate from Wilmington sought Maclaine's advice, just weeks before the old warhorse died, Maclaine was prepared to be candid. He recognized that his young protege was moved by "religious enthusiasm" in wanting to eliminate the slave traffic, but he pointed out that the idea was unpopular in Wilmington, even among nonslaveowners. If he had informed the voters of his peculiar notions during the summer elections, his majority would have been substantially reduced, if not lost altogether. Maclaine's advice was to let it slide until Congress obtained the constitutional authority to prohibit the slave trade in 1808.[70]

In the absence a strong popular movement for change, political leaders were inclined to ignore or evade embarrassing social issues, such as religion, education, and slavery. In the case of the latter the strong popular voice came eventually from outside the Chesapeake, and that only placed new strains on the political system.

CHAPTER EIGHT

The Western Question

INDEPENDENT VIRGINIA claimed a sizable portion of the American West—not only Kentucky but the entire region between the Ohio River and the Great Lakes. The claims were based on the colony's charter of 1609, which extended Virginia's westward limit to the South Sea. Other states with sea-to-sea grants challenged portions of Virginia's territory, however, as did land companies which had made purchases from the Indians. When in 1776 the assembly sought to erect Kentucky into a county, the Indiana Company, together with other speculative interests, objected on the grounds that they had claims in the area as valid as Virginia's. The assembly compromised by dividing westernmost Fincastle County into two districts, one of which was Kentucky. Any more formal arrangements for Kentucky would have to await settlement of the land.

In December 1778 Maryland injected a further complication by refusing to ratify the Articles of Confederation until the larger states ceded to Congress their western lands. Behind this roadblock were Baltimore land speculators who, in league with some Philadelphia merchants, hoped to loosen Virginia's hold on the West. Congress, they felt, would be more likely to recognize existing claims in the Northwest and make new grants. Holding fast, the Virginia assembly passed a resolution invalidating all unauthorized purchases of land from the Indians, and in 1779 it set up a land office for the sale of its western territory in small parcels. To insure that its soldiers were not left out of the bonanza, it granted 200 acres to each enlisted man, with higher allotments for officers, and set aside a large district in Kentucky for their claims. Kentucky was separated from Fincastle and subdivided into three counties so the new arrivals would have some agencies of local government.

As an olive branch to the land speculators, the assembly offered to validate all claims for which the surveys had been completed prior to the act of 1778. When all such claims were settled, the land office, placed under the supervision of Richmond merchant John Harvie, offered for sale the remaining lands at £40 per hundred acres, with no limitation on the amount that could be purchased by any individual.[1] By helping to retire the state's paper money, and hence its war debt, the West was to make its own contribution to the Revolutionary cause.

The scheme did not work out as well as was hoped. Most of the lands went to large speculators like Robert Morris, and the payments in depreciated currency did little for the state treasury. Frontiersmen who objected to having the West engrossed by absentee landowners unleashed a stream of petitions on the assembly.

On January 2, 1781, the Virginia assembly ceded to Congress its claims to the country north of the Ohio, but only on condition that Maryland approve the Articles of Confederation, that new states ultimately be erected out of the ceded territory, and that the land companies' purchases from the Indians be invalidated. The last proviso was the stickler, and Virginia had hoped to secure Congress's prior agreement to it. But military necessity demanded some political concessions. On that very day Benedict Arnold made an amphibious landing at Hampton Roads, and Lord Cornwallis was moving northward into North Carolina. A month later, Maryland, impelled by similar considerations, ratified the Articles and brought the union into being.

Instead of greeting these moves with patriotic enthusiasm, Congress appointed a committee to reinvestigate the entire matter of western lands, including the claims of the land companies. In June 1781 this committee recommended that the Virginia cession be rejected, together with similar cessions by New York and Connecticut, and that Congress itself assume authority over all lands west of the Appalachians with a view to erecting new states in the region. A second report six months later proposed that the more reasonable claims of the land companies in western Virginia and Kentucky be validated.

Congress did not accept the reports, but it did stall for two years on the Virginia cession. Not until early 1784 was the transaction completed, and only then after Virginia withdrew its demand that unauthorized land titles be invalidated. In the meantime Congress's action gave new hope to the land companies, while encouraging frontiersmen to expect the early creation of states in the West that would enable them to deal with the speculators in their own way. These twin—and somewhat incompatible—expectations gave rise to a number of separatist movements in the West as the war dragged to a close.

ARTHUR CAMPBELL AND SOUTHWEST VIRGINIA

Of the various land companies who were pressing their claims against Virginia territory, the most successful was the Loyal Company, which in 1749 had obtained from the governor and council a grant of 800,000 acres in the region of the upper Tennessee Valley. Partly because the title derived from a colonial grant, rather than from Indian purchase, and partly because the company consisted almost entirely of Virginians, the assembly validated some 200,000 acres of the company's claim in 1778. In the meantime settlers had moved into the area under legislation permitting them to preempt up to 400 acres of land. However, this law did not vitiate any prior claims; hence land companies could still lay claim to all tracts they had surveyed. Since many of the prewar surveys were incomplete and unrecorded, no one was sure who owned what. After the Loyal Company's title was tentatively confirmed in 1778, every squatter in the Southwest lived in fear of company agents who might suddenly appear and demand payment for lands the settlers had cleared and fenced. Frontiersmen flooded the assembly with petitions protesting this situation, and many were directed to Arthur Campbell, delegate and county lieutenant of Washington County, from whom they clearly expected a sympathetic ear.

Campbell's interests were complex. He possessed large tracts of land that overlapped the Loyal Company's claims, and he had political ambitions that could be furthered by making himself the champion of a popular cause. He also carried on a personal feud with the most prominent political and military figure in the region, Colonel (soon General) William Russell. The feud evidently stemmed from efforts to outdo one another in leading expeditions against the Indians. Russell, in turn, was closely allied to Colonel William Preston, a leading figure in the Loyal Company, who was pressuring frontiersmen to submit to company surveys.

The congressional committee report of November 1781 suggesting that Congress assume control of all lands west of the Appalachian divide changed Campbell's protest movement into a secession plot. By anticipating Congress, westerners, Campbell reasoned, could organize their own governments and administer the public lands, keeping Congress satisfied by sending it the proceeds from sales. In the spring of 1782 Campbell even tried to organize a convention to consider the alternatives. Evidently, nothing came of the idea, and instead charges against Campbell were presented to the House of Delegates in its fall session. The House referred the accusations to a committee, which quickly buried them. Governor Benjamin Harrison may have considered the secessionist threat a useful lever against Congress. Campbell remained in possession of his various offices.[2]

Campbell's forays into the Indian country to the southwest convinced him of the strategic and political unity of the Tennessee Valley. In 1781 he constructed a fort at the forks of the Tennessee and wanted Congress to recognize the importance of the site by stationing an Indian agency there. When he began contemplating the establishment of an independent state, it was natural to include the entire valley as far south as the "Great Bend" of the Tennessee (Muscle Shoals, Alabama). This ambition greatly complicated the enterprise, for south of 36° 30' the Tennessee Valley was under the jurisdiction of North Carolina.

NORTH CAROLINA AND THE WEST

The first settlers on the headwaters of the Tennessee River came from Virginia after the French and Indian War. The Cherokees, who had suffered defeat during the war, had the best Indian claim to the land, but successive purchases and leases removed their title from the Holston and Watauga valleys. For a time Virginia speculators led the movement, but then a North Carolina consortium, headed by Judge Richard Henderson, entered the picture. Organized as the Transylvania Company, Henderson and his associates hoped to establish a new colony in the Southwest, paying quitrents to the king if he would recognize them, declaring independence if he would not. In company with Arthur Campbell, then a major of Virginia militia, Henderson and his associates went to the Cherokee settlement at Sycamore Shoals and purchased the land between the Kentucky River and the Cumberland.

Henderson had originally hoped to obtain the Tennessee River, but the Cumberland tract was the most that the Indians would sell. The deal was consummated on March 17, 1775, barely a month before fighting broke out at Lexington and Concord. The war temporarily ended hope for an independent colony, and Virginia's refusal to recognize land titles obtained from the Indians effectively eliminated the Transylvanians from Kentucky. In 1779 Henderson sent an expedition under Colonel John Donelson to found a settlement (Nashville) on the Cumberland River, well within the boundary of North Carolina. In the late years of the war, pioneers trickled across the Cumberland mountains from the older settlements on the Holston and Nolichucky rivers to the fertile, rolling hills of Middle Tennessee. In 1783 the North Carolina assembly rewarded its soldiers with additional grants in the Cumberland Valley.

At the end of the war other speculators took an interest in the region west of the Smoky Mountains. In the spring session of 1783, John Gray Blount steered through the assembly a bill reopening the state land offices, which had been closed since 1781. The act offered for sale all the lands west of the mountains as far as the Mississippi, except for the military grants and a small Indian reservation. The price was set at £10 in North Carolina paper money, but because of depreciation the real price was less than a quarter of that. The act nullified all earlier claims, but Henderson persuaded the assembly to make him a new grant of 100,000 acres in Middle Tennessee.[3]

Blount's act flagrantly violated all treaties with the Indians, confused the land titles of Tennessee settlers, and infringed upon claims that South Carolina and Georgia had in the area. But it enormously benefited the merchant speculators who had been collecting North Carolina paper. The land office was located in Hillsborough for their convenience, and they rushed to convert depreciated paper into wilderness land titles. In all, something like 3 million acres were taken up under the act.[4] To insure a steady supply of paper William Blount engineered a new emission in the fall of 1783. The land act limited individual purchases to 5,000 acres, but by amalgamating claims and purchasing military warrants, companies established by the Blounts and by Richard Caswell were able to obtain title to hundreds of thousands of acres.

The Blounts had their eyes set on the Great Bend of the Tennessee, a strategic location deep in the Indian country. A trading post at the Muscle Shoals would be a connecting point between the two patches of settlement in Tennessee and a short overland hop from New Orleans. The difficulty was that the region was claimed by Georgia and South Carolina, while the Cherokees remained in actual possession. The task of purchasing the lands from the Indians was entrusted to John Donelson and Joseph Martin, Virginia's Indian agents in the Southwest. To secure the proper amount of influence in all quarters the Blounts took into their consortium Senator Griffith Rutherford, Wade Hampton of South Carolina, and John Sevier, a Virginian who had migrated to the Holston country in 1773. In early 1784 William Blount induced the Georgia assembly to appoint commissioners to discuss a grant of land on the Tennessee. He then offered each of the commissioners a share of stock in the company to insure a friendly report and made plans to open a land office in the West. But before Blount could confirm his grant from Georgia or deliver goods to the Cherokee for the land, his scheme became entangled in western secessionism.[5]

In the spring of 1784 Congress accepted Virginia's cession of the territory north of the Ohio River and gave tentative approval to Jefferson's plan for territorial governments in the region. Under Jefferson's resolutions Congress could erect new governments in the West on its own initiative or at the behest of the residents. It was this latter feature that revived the flagging schemes of Arthur Campbell and other secessionists in the unceded lands south of the Ohio. And in this instance their interests coincided with those of eastern land speculators. The Blounts and other speculators welcomed congressional intervention because they felt that Congress had a better chance of negotiating cessions from the Indians and terminating the border warfare, all of which would increase the value of their holdings. As early as 1782 Blount and Hugh Williamson had written from Congress to encourage North Carolina to cede its western claims.[6] Governor Alexander Martin and the antinationalist assembly rejected the proposal, arguing instead that the state needed to get some return from the lands in order to pay off its own debts. These same people therefore enthusiastically supported John Gray Blount's land office bill of 1783 because it promised profit to the state while serving the speculators.

To protect these investments, eastern speculators hoped to turn the West over to Congress. In the spring 1784 assembly session William Blount proposed that the state cede all its claims west of the mountains. It would guarantee current titles in Tennessee, but Congress could sell the remaining lands. Thomas Person objected that the cession would cost the state a source of income and damage its creditors. Person and his rural following claimed that North Carolina speculators were in league with congressional speculators. They accused Benjamin Hawkins, who had recently retired from Congress, of being sent home to negotiate the cession.[7] Blount managed to survive this assault, turned aside several tactical motions, and won passage for the cession by 52 to 43.[8] The roll calls showed both a regional and a partisan alignment. The eastern delegates supported the cession by 30 to 9; the Piedmont and the west opposed it by 27 to 5. All seven of the Tennessee delegates voted against it. Speculators alone did not have strength to win passage of the bill. Easterners generally and Lawyers in particular apparently thought the West was an unnecessary burden. Leading the fight for the bill were Maclaine, Hooper, and Nash, none of whom had any known interests in the West. Voters, however, were not happy with the cession and seemed inclined to believe the accusations against Benjamin Hawkins. In the summer election Hawkins and several other cessionists met defeat. In October the assembly hastily repealed the cession law.[9]

The reversal stirred Tennesseans to action. Many of the settlers west of the mountains wished to be governed by neither North Carolina nor Congress. They wanted statehood. Using a system that Arthur Campbell had devised in 1782, militia companies summoned conventions in each county—Sullivan on the Virginia border, Washington along the Watauga, and Greene, which embraced the newest settlements south of Knoxville. These county conventions, in turn, selected delegates to a general convention held at Jonesboro, seat of Washington County, on August 23.[10] John Sevier and Joseph Martin, partners of the eastern speculators, were both present, though both later denied having initiated the secession movement.[11] Doubtless both hoped to protect their own interests in any political venture that was launched. The leading spirits at the Jonesboro convention were William Cocke, articulate spokesman for western interests, and David Campbell, younger brother of Arthur.[12]

Arthur Campbell himself dashed down from Virginia and was permitted to address the convention. In a fiery speech he predicted that Washington and Montgomery counties in Virginia would join the new state, and he promised to "stand in the front of the battle" if the parent states objected to the separation. The convention agreed to include the Virginia counties in any government set up. It then drew up a memorial asking Congress to accept the North Carolina cession and adjourned until the following December.[13]

Returning home, Campbell sent to Richard Henry Lee, president of Congress, a lengthy description of the convention's activi-

ties. Cocke, who had been delegated to carry the memorial to
Congress, was "a confused, shallow body," Campbell explained, and
he hoped that Congress would not act until spring "when others
better informed" might come northward. No one, seemingly, was
better informed than Campbell himself, for he proceeded to outline plans for two new states in the West—Kentucky and Franklin.
The first would extend from the mouth of the Kanawha to the falls
of the Ohio, bounded east and west by lines of longitude. Franklin
would extend from the point where the New River joined the
Greenbriar southwestward to the Great Bend of the Tennessee.
The Blue Ridge would form Franklin's boundary with Virginia and
North Carolina. Both states, Campbell felt, were authorized by the
congressional resolution of April, even though that was intended to
apply only to the Virginia cession north of the Ohio.[14]

Campbell then turned to his neighbors in southwest Virginia.
Because of inequalities in representation, he told them, the assembly ignored the interests of the West. Westerners bore a heavy
burden of taxes on necessities such as salt, yet they derived no
benefits. The assembly was unable even to afford them protection
from the Indians. The argument was an effective one, and it won a
lot of sympathy, even among people who were suspicious of Campbell's motives. Archibald Stuart and John Breckinridge, Madison's
western allies, felt it necessary to respond to Campbell's allegations
with a printed circular reminding westerners that they seldom paid
taxes anyway, and that the assembly had generously offered to let
them discharge their arrears in hemp.[15]

The Holston settlers, meanwhile, followed their own course. It
seems likely that they rejected Campbell's offer of leadership from
the beginning. That, at least, would explain their choice of Cocke as
emissary to Congress and Campbell's attempt to undermine his
mission. Moreover, they doubtless realized that annexing the
southwest corner of Virginia would only add to their enemies and
alienate Congress.[16] They also ignored the overtures of Governor
Alexander Martin, who had sought to win friends in the West by
elevating Sevier to the rank of brigadier general and making David
Campbell a circuit judge. The second Holston convention met at
Jonesboro on December 14, 1784, and proceeded to organize the

state of Franklin, heedless of the North Carolina assembly's repeal of the western cession some five weeks earlier.

The second convention, however, gave the first indication of a division of opinion in the western country. The August meeting had contained some of the most militant secessionists, and its deliberations seem to have been conducted amid general agreement on the need for action. But only about a third of the members of that body were elected to the second convention in December. Among those conspicuously absent was General Sevier.[17] Among the new delegates were a number of men who opposed secession, though they remained a minority. The critical moment came when William Cocke moved the formation of "a separate and distinct State, independent of North Carolina, *at this time.*" The motion carried, 28 to 15.[18] Leading the opposition was Colonel John Tipton of Washington County, who remained thereafter the leading advocate of the North Carolina connection. Tipton's support came from the older settled counties along the Virginia border; most secessionists came from the Great Bend area. It is not clear what forces were at work, for neither birthplace nor speculative interests were a factor. Virginians actually opposed secession, while delegates born in North Carolina favored it.[19] The newly created borough of Nashville (Davidson County), founded by speculators, did not even participate in the convention.[20]

The Jonesboro convention petitioned Congress for admission to the confederation and drafted a temporary constitution for the new state. It then authorized yet a third convention to establish a permanent one. An assembly, elected under the provisional constitution, met in March 1785 and elected John Sevier governor. Sevier accepted with some reluctance. He later confessed that he had been "dragged with the Franklin measures by a large number of the people of this country."[21] A hero of the border wars, Sevier was easily the most popular man west of the mountains. By accepting the post he satisfied his sense of obligation to his constituency while keeping an eye on his own speculative interests.[22] The legislative records have been lost, but the most prominent leaders in the assembly were the same men that had organized the first Jonesboro convention in August. David Campbell became chief justice of the superior court; William Cocke went to Congress.

Although the Tennesseans made no further overtures toward southwest Virginia, Arthur Campbell intensified his agitation in the spring of 1785. At the March court for Washington County he and several followers told the freeholders not to pay their taxes until the county received what was due to it from the state. Although a justice of the peace himself, Campbell advocated interrupting the proceedings of the county court as a means of pressuring the legislature.[23] The Campbellites took no overt action, however, contenting themselves with meetings and petitions. The affair never amounted to a rebellion or even a conspiracy. Campbell himself had little of the conspirator in his makeup. He freely expressed his discontent to Governor Patrick Henry and openly defended the westerners' desire for secession.[24]

Patrick Henry was unsympathetic. He removed Campbell and several of his friends from their militia posts. He then appointed Campbell's archenemy, William Russell, to command the militia in the district. In July 1785 Russell appeared before the Washington County court, over which Campbell presided, and demanded to be sworn in as commander. Campbell refused and the matter ended in stalemate.[25] Campbell's influence was already on the wane, however, possibly because of his own rhetorical excesses. In March he had persuaded the freeholders not to send delegates to the assembly, but the July court deserted him and elected William Russell. In the fall the assembly approved an "Act for punishing certain offenses," which made it a crime to dismember the state without the consent of the assembly. Madison remarked that it was specifically directed against Campbell's "faction."[26]

In December 1785 Washington County sheriff James Montgomery brought before the Executive Council formal charges against Campbell for misconduct as a justice of the peace. Campbell, he claimed, had even gone so far as to step down from the bench and make a public address advising people to disregard the militia law and refuse to pay taxes. Backing Montgomery's charges was a collection of depositions, all referring to events of the previous spring. The council gave each side until March 15 to take additional depositions and transmit them to the governor. Campbell promptly submitted a host of counterdepositions from friends who claimed to have heard nothing inflammatory. The council took no further action, but the secessionist movement in southwest Virginia was dead.[27]

THE STATE OF FRANKLIN

The Continental Congress did not view the secessionist movements in the Southwest with great enthusiasm. Mindful of the confederation article that permitted subdivision of a state only with its consent, and unwilling to antagonize Virginia and North Carolina, Congress ignored the various petitions of the Holston settlers. But the threat of Indian war forced it to act.

The spread of white settlement in the Tennessee country alarmed both Cherokees and Creeks, and when Creek chieftain Alexander McGillivray (a half-breed whose father was a South Carolina Loyalist) offered to ally himself with the Spanish, an Indian war seemed unavoidable. In the spring of 1785 Congress named a commission of five men, all strong nationalists, to treat with the Indians.[28]

After many delays the commissioners met the Creeks and Cherokee at Hopewell, South Carolina, plantation of commissioner Andrew Pickens. Benjamin Hawkins, a man far ahead of his time in his conception of justice for the red man, dominated the proceedings. The result was a treaty whose generosity forestalled a major Indian war for a generation (until the Creek uprising of 1813) and essentially preserved the lands of the southern tribes until the Treaty of Fort Jackson (1814). By the Treaty of Hopewell, the Indians swore allegiance to the United States, thus bypassing the state governments, and Congress in turn guaranteed the preservation of all their lands. The treaty nullified the claims of the state of Franklin, the sales of the North Carolina land office, and the imperial schemes of William Blount and John Sevier.[29]

The Treaty of Hopewell caused an uproar in the Tennessee settlements. Sevier opened negotiations with Georgia, asking per-

mission to settle the Great Bend in return for Tennessee's participation in expeditions against the Creeks. In the fall of 1786 the
Franklin assembly authorized expeditions against the Indians, and
the following year it opened a land office that was almost certain to
intrude upon Indian claims. The prospect of a general Indian war
sent shivers of apprehension as far as Richmond.[30]

In the meantime Noth Carolina began to have second thoughts
about the value of the connection with the trouble-prone westerners. In the fall of 1786 a Commons committee reported that
separation was desirable but premature. When the "numbers and
wealth of the citizens on the western waters" were sufficient for
self-government, the assembly would gladly oblige them. In an
open letter to westerners Governor Caswell predicted that the
assembly would soon grant separation; privately he assured General
Evan Shelby that he would give his own support to it.[31]

During the summer of 1787 the Franklinites debated among
themselves the best strategy to pursue. Tiptonites wanted to run
candidates in the August elections to insure representation of
western interests in the Carolina assembly. Militants retorted that
this involved a tacit recognition of North Carolina's authority. They
preferred negotiations leading to a formal separation. When Tipton
and his men stood for seats anyway, secessionists disrupted the
elections. The result was a series of contested elections that left the
assembly more confused than ever. The Senate even refused to seat
Tipton, thereby undermining its best friend in the West.[32]

In the fall of 1787 the Senate passed a bill repealing the 1784
act that had repealed the act of cession. Whether this is what the
Franklinites wanted—being ceded to Congress—is unclear. In any
case, the Commons rejected it.[33] Senate roll calls revealed the same
regional division as in 1784. There was no party division, however,
for the lineup bore no relation to votes on the Federal Constitution
in this session.

Chagrined at being unseated by the Carolina Senate, Tipton
returned to the Holston country seeking revenge. Armed with
warrants from the Carolina government naming them county sheriffs, Tipton and his friends began raiding courthouses to take
possession of the county records. Franklinites, led by Sevier,

replied in kind. Jonesboro was captured and recaptured three times. The climax came in February 1788, when Sevier and Tipton fought an open battle resulting in about a dozen casualties. Shortly afterward, General Joseph Martin, commanding the North Carolina forces west of the mountains, reached a truce with Sevier that ended the fighting and silenced Tipton. After Sevier's term as governor expired on March 1, the Franklin regime slowly disintegrated.[34]

During the summer the two sides buried their differences long enough to wage a particularly ferocious campaign against the Indians.[35] Sevier returned a hero and was promptly elected to the North Carolina Senate. His acceptance of the seat ended any pretense of Franklinite independence.

In the meantime the patience of North Carolina wore thin. Alarmed by the reports of civil disorder, on July 29 Governor Samuel Johnston issued an order for Sevier's arrest on a charge of treason, provided there was evidence of the crime. It was a strange and somewhat belated command, reflecting in its own confusion the fundamental problem of communications between East and West. Judge David Campbell refused to obey, but another judge, on temporary duty from the East, issued the order. Colonel Tipton appointed himself to carry it out. He arrested Sevier and spirited him off to North Carolina for trial. Sevier's friends followed the group to Morganton, Burke County. While their hero was being arraigned they created an uproar in the courtroom that enabled Sevier to slip out the door and onto the back of a waiting horse. The state wisely made no further efforts to prosecute him.[36]

Tennesseans, despite some flirtation with Spanish authorities, had never wished to leave the American union.[37] Separation from North Carolina and statehood were the goals of nearly all of them. What they had lacked was some institutional channel that would enable them to achieve it. The appearance of political parties apparently provided just that.

Congress set things in motion. Taking its cue from North Carolina, Congress had made no response to the letters and petitions from Franklin. But then in July 1788 it informed the people of Kentucky, who had also asked for admission to the union, to wait until the new federal government was installed.[38] This news reached the western country along with word that North Carolina had refused to ratify the Federal Constitution. The implications for Tennessee were clear. The new Constitution gave Congress specific power to provide for the western territories and arrange for their admission to the union. Since North Carolina had refused to join the union, it was probable that the new regime in New York might take a friendly view of the admission of Tennessee. At least there was room for bargaining.

Some time during the summer of 1788—exactly when is uncertain—Sevier and his Franklinite friends became supporters of the Constitution.[39] At the North Carolina ratifying convention in July the Tennessee delegates voted against the Constitution by a margin of 19 to 2, and prominent among the Antifederalists was Sevier's enemy John Tipton, together with several of Tipton's antisecessionist friends from Washington County.[40] It was easy for Sevier to enlist on the other side.

An alliance with Sevier likewise presented advantages to North Carolina Federalists, who had long favored separation. "The Western people are very pressing for an Indian war," reported Governor Johnston to Judge Iredell during the fall session of the assembly. That, he continued, "is strongly opposed by the Eastern members, who have introduced a Bill to cede all the country West of the mountains to Congress." The Commons postponed the cession bill, possibly because of the recent violence in Tennessee.[41] Although there was no roll call, there is good reason to think that the western question was becoming a party matter. The Commons approved a bill that fall granting amnesty to Franklinites by 70 to 23. The margin indicates broad support for leniency, but there was still a party slant to the voting. Federalists from both east and west favored the measure; Antifederalists were evenly divided. Three Federalists from Tennessee supported amnesty, while the three Antifederalists voted against it on an early ballot and then reversed themselves.[42]

Whether there was any firm understanding between Federalists and Franklinites can only be conjectured. Perhaps an expressed one was unnecessary. In the second North Carolina ratifying convention of November 1789, Sevier himself headed a Tennessee delegation that favored the Constitution by a margin of 21 to 2.[43] In the assembly, which met simultaneously, Federalists introduced a bill ceding North Carolina's western lands to the federal government. The Commons approved it by 68 to 30 and the Senate by 30 to 13.[44] The regional split was the familiar one—the east nearly unanimous in approval, the west (except for Tennessee) divided. But party voting was more apparent than ever. Of those who can be identified, Federalists supported the measure by 50 to 5; Antifederalists opposed it 22 to 9. The five assemblymen who had switched from Antifederalism in 1788 to Federalism in 1789 also supported the bill.

The alliance between eastern Federalists and western separatists was a tenuous one, nonetheless. Said Archibald Maclaine when it was over: "The cession of the Western Territory is at last completed, so that we are rid of a people who were a pest and a burthen to us."[45] There was no long-term identity of interests, and before long Tennessee would be overwhelmingly Jeffersonian. But its early political history followed a pattern strikingly similar to that of the older states on the Chesapeake. The divisions that appeared in the 1780s affected attitudes toward the Federal Constitution and helped shape the first party system.

THE SECESSION MOVEMENT IN KENTUCKY

The Virginia land act of 1779 caused an enormous boom in Kentucky lands. Settlers streamed down the Ohio from Pittsburgh, braving the Indian raiders along the river. Responding to the influx, the Virginia assembly in May 1780 divided Kentucky into three counties: Jefferson, Lincoln, and Fayette. It naturally filled the new county offices (militia commanders, surveyors, justices of the peace) with the men who had carved the first settlements—George Rogers Clark, Daniel Boone, Benjamin Logan, John Floyd, and George May. As agents of prewar land companies these Virginians possessed claims to large tracts of Kentucky land, claims that took precedence over any sales made under the act of 1779. As a result, newcomers had to search hard for choice parcels, and they had to make sure they were not encroaching upon some earlier title.

It so happened that many of the newcomers after 1780 were non-Virginians. Most were small farmers from Pennsylvania and North Carolina moving west in search of opportunity. Lacking funds, most of them had not even bothered to purchase a claim; they merely "squatted" on empty land in hopes that occupation would eventually establish some sort of title. Others who had made purchases found that they conflicted or overlapped with claims made by the wealthy Virginians who dominated the government. By the end of 1780 this landless element began holding meetings and drafting petitions asking for separation from Virginia. They evidently hoped that Congress would annul the claims derived from prewar land companies and thus open the way for a more equitable distribution. The county elite, naturally opposed to this idea, denounced their critics as "partisans."[46]

There matters stood until the end of the war brought a new wave of Virginia emigrés. This wave included a number of lawyers and merchants who attached themselves to the older, landed Virginia element. Two of these were nephews of William Preston, the Valley grandee who claimed enormous tracts in Kentucky through participation in the colonial land companies. Robert Breckinridge reached Kentucky in 1781, apparently acting as an agent of Preston, and he was soon working as deputy surveyor of Jefferson County. Within a couple years his brothers William and John joined him in the new land. Preston's other nephew was John Brown, who finished his law studies at William and Mary in 1782 and journeyed to Kentucky to open a practice.

A year later Thomas Marshall left a plantaton of 2,000 acres and 22 slaves in Fauquier County and moved to Kentucky. A surveyor by trade and a friend of Washington's, Marshall had been a prominent figure in Fauquier. He served for many years in the House of Burgesses and represented the county in the revolutionary convention of 1775. As a colonel in the Continental Line at the end of the war, he was entitled to some 8,054 acres in bounty lands, and, being surveyor of Fayette County, he was soon possessed of thousands more. As his deputy he appointed his nephew, Humphrey Marshall, a 23-year-old lawyer who had 4,000 acres in bounty lands of his own. The last of this circle was Harry Innes, a Bedford County attorney, whom the assembly, as a reward for his industry in collecting taxes during the war, appointed attorney general for the western district. He moved to Kentucky to take up his new post in the fall of 1784. These lawyers reinforced the stranglehold of what was coming to be called the "court party." When the Virginia assembly created a district court for the three Kentucky counties, Harry Innes was made presiding judge, and Caleb Wallace, John Floyd, and Samuel McDowell became associate justices.

Merchants who established themselves in Kentucky at the end of the war augmented the ranks of the court party, though few of them could claim Virginia ancestry. The first merchant in the newly erected town of Louisville at the falls of the Ohio was Daniel Brodhead, Jr., son of the Pennsylvania colonel who had commanded at Pittsburgh in the last years of the war. Arriving in 1783, Brodhead established commercial contact with George Rogers Clark and his cousin William, who were then surveying the Virginia military district across the river. These men, in turn, had interests in the down-river trade with New Orleans, and they had contacts with New Orleans merchants as a result of Clark's military expeditions. Before long, Brodhead too had mercantile acquaintances in Spanish Louisiana. At the end of 1783, General James Wilkinson, a Maryland physician who had married into the Philadelphia Biddles, arrived in Louisville to open a general store. He was soon deeply involved in land speculation with members of the Virginia clique.

By 1784, the court party began to agree with their opponents that separation best served the interests of Kentucky. They resented the control that Richmond could still exert over ther land policies. And there were other considerations. They hoped to make Kentucky the commercial and manufacturing center of the West, and to achieve that they needed independent powers of taxation and trade regulation. Though Virginia had been reasonably cooperative in expanding county agencies and courts in Kentucky, rule from Richmond was still awkward. It required eight weeks to make the round trip, and in that time much could become dated or irrelevant in a rapidly developing land. The communications lag was especially annoying in matters of defense because permission had to be obtained for all expeditions against the Indians. Discontent became stronger when Spain closed the Mississippi River to American trade in 1784. Separation then offered additional benefits—the possibility of complete independence and special arrangements with Spain for use of the river and the port of New Orleans. Not all members of the court party were swept up in the "Spanish intrigue," but a number of them were, including James Wilkinson and John Brown.[47]

The congressional resolution of April 1784 favoring self-government in the West and the stirrings among the Holston Valley settlers seem to have prompted action in Kentucky. In November, Colonel Benjamin Logan summoned a conference of militia officers in Danville to discuss matters of defense, and the result was a decision to hold elections in the various militia districts for delegates to a general convention. The separation movement was slow in starting, as old political rivals searched for new alliances, and it took two more meetings in 1785 before a firm request was sent off to Virginia. The third convention, meeting in August 1785, finally authorized Harry Innes and George Muter, both members of the House of Delegates, to request a formal separation. No appeal was made to Congress, though the Kentucky leaders intended to join the Confederation. Until they obtained independence, they did not want Congress interfering in the old Virginia land titles.[48]

Nearly every prominent figure in Virginia politics favored separation. Since Kentucky was in the firm hands of Virginians, no one could doubt that the westerners had the capacity for self-government, and as Richard Henry Lee observed, they were "more expense than profit to the rest of the country." It occurred to Madison, however, that separation ought to be made contingent upon Kentucky's entry into the Confederation. Otherwise it might remain independent, either to avoid sharing in the national debt or to avoid paying for the support of the central government. Whether he was concerned about the Spanish connection at this point, Madison did not say.[49]

On January 10, 1786, the House of Delegates approved, without a formal roll call, a separation bill that reflected Madison's ideas. But speculators with claims in Kentucky added some additional provisos that could only anger Kentuckians. The new state had to recognize as valid all Virginia land grants, it could not discriminate in taxation against nonresident landowners, nor could it interfere with the free navigation of the Ohio. The assembly also demanded another Kentucky convention to consider these terms. If it approved and Congress agreed to admit Kentucky to the Confederation, Virginia's authority would end on September 1, 1787.[50] Both parties in Kentucky were dismayed by these conditions. The partisans resented the pretensions of absentee speculators, and the court party saw the commercial restrictions as a hindrance to their plans for development. A convention which met in September 1786, as demanded by Virginia, could not even muster a quorum. It could only schedule yet another convention and request an extension of time, which Virginia granted.[51]

In the interim, attitudes in Kentucky hardened. The example set by the Tennesseans, who had simply declared their independence, drafted a constitution, and asked for admission to the union, appealed to the court party. The partisans would have preferred congressional rule, but their position was undermined when news of Foreign Secretary John Jay's request to abandon the navigation of the Mississippi reached Kentucky at the end of 1786. Jay's thunderbolt caused a merging of interests in Kentucky. Partisans had long been in contact with the Holston secessionists, through the North Carolina element in their ranks and through John Campbell. Court party leaders Harry Innes and Benjamin Logan opened a correspondence with Arthur Campbell early in 1787, and talk spread of the possibility of an independent western republic embracing all the settlements west of the mountains. In June, James Wilkinson departed for New Orleans to discuss with the Spanish governor the possibility of prying open the door for Kentucky products. He returned a year later with a tobacco monopoly and the promise of a Spanish pension.[52] While he was gone the Federal Constitution was drawn up at Philadelphia, but Wilkinson and his Kentucky friends had no use for a stronger central government that might assert its authority over the West.

There were some in Kentucky, however, who shrank from the notion of independence, particularly those who had strong ties with the nationalist element in Virginia. The leader of this group was Thomas Marshall, father of Madison's ally John Marshall. He failed to attract much support among Kentucky leaders, but there is little doubt that he spoke for the vast majority of Kentucky farmers, most of whom had little interest in independence and less in a Spanish connection.

Unfortunately, Marshall's pleas for moderation received little help from Virginia. In February 1787 word arrived that Virginia demanded yet another convention and refused to retract any of its conditions. Once more elections were held, and in September Kentucky's fifth convention approved separation on the terms proposed by Virginia. Then, following the Franklin example, it called for a constitutional convention to meet the following summer.[53]

The drafting of a state constitution was the culmination of the long secessionist movement, and the 1788 convention attracted every important figure in Kentucky. They were obliged to miss the Virginia ratifying convention in Richmond which met simultaneously in June, and Kentucky was represented in the latter body only by second-rate figures. This mattered little, for the secessionists had scant interest in the Federal Constitution. Among their number, only John Brown, who was then a delegate to the Continental Congress and a friend of Madison's, favored the Constitution.[54] Marshall's group were Federalists, but they were able to win only 3 of the 14 seats allotted to Kentucky at the Richmond convention (Humphrey Marshall, Thomas's nephew, and the delegates from Jefferson County, Robert Breckinridge and Rice Bullock).

In July 1788 the New England delegates in the Continental Congress blocked the move to admit Kentucky to the Confederation, and the whole separatist movement was back where it had started. In its fall session the Virginia assembly passed a third enabling act, demanding an eighth convention for the summer of 1789. Besides retaining all the old conditions, it imposed a new one that Kentucky land grants, for a certain period of time, had to be approved by Virginia. In addition, Virginia veterans would have unlimited time to make good their claims to military bounty lands in Kentucky. The court party rejected this intolerable affront to Kentucky sovereignty and boycotted the 1789 convention. That gave Thomas Marshall and his band of loyalists an opportunity to capture the secession movement. They expected support from small farmers, who wanted separation at any price so that they could control their own courts and provide their own military defense.[55]

Kentucky's eighth convention, meeting in July 1789, abandoned the belligerent rhetoric of its predecessors and rejected the notion of total independence. Instead, it sent an address to the Virginia assembly objecting to the terms of separation and asking that they be modified. It also petitioned Congress once more for admission to the union. In December 1789 the Virginia assembly passed its fourth and last act of separation, removing the objectionable conditions but calling for final ratification by yet another Kentucky convention. Again there was no roll call vote, but cooperation between Virginia Federalists and the Marshall faction in Kentucky was apparent.

In the meantime, the independence movement in Kentucky collapsed. Congressman John Brown conducted some desultory negotiations with the Spanish minister Don Diego de Gardoqui in the wake of Congress's initial refusal to admit Kentucky, but when he was elected to the new Federal Congress in early 1789 he abandoned this scheme. In the House of Representatives Brown worked closely with Madison, and Madison's influence in the West was further enhanced when George Nicholas moved to Kentucky later that year. Before long, Brown, Nicholas, and the rest of the court party were firm Republicans.

The Marshall element remained Federalist, but their strength was confined to Louisville and Jefferson County. By the end of 1790 the emerging national party system had absorbed the factional structure in Kentucky. That made Kentucky politics more respectable, and more comprehensible to outsiders. In February 1791 Congress passed an enabling act, and on June 1, 1792, Kentucky was formally admitted to the union. Author of its state constitution was Madison's old enemy-turned-ally, George Nicholas.

BUILDING COMMERCIAL LINKS WITH THE WEST

Before the Revolution Washington and other investors recognized the need for improvement in communications with the West.

Washington candidly admitted that he possessed "Lands in that country the value of which would be enhanced by the adoption of such a scheme"; and the secession movements in Kentucky and Tennessee lent political urgency to the idea.[56]

After the war Jefferson took up the cause, though less from personal interest (his speculative holdings were in the upper James and Roanoke valleys) than from a desire to bind the union together. On his way to Congress in the spring of 1784 he stopped at Mount Vernon to rekindle Washington's interest.[57] Washington approved enthusiastically, and in the autumn he wrote Governor Harrison asking him to recommend assembly action. He suggested that, to avoid regional jealousies, the bill provide for surveys of both the Potomac and James River routes to determine which was better. If the assembly balked at spending public funds on such a project, he suggested it could incorporate companies of private adventurers to raise the capital.[58] These companies could then clear the rivers of rocks and build canals around the falls. News of the scheme spread quickly up the Potomac Valley and was greeted with special enthusiasm by merchants with western connections. Within a month, notices were circulated in newspapers announcing a meeting in Alexandria for all persons interested in forming a company and appealing to the legislatures for incorporation.[59]

With a petition from numerous potential subscribers on its table, the Virginia assembly asked Washington and General Horatio Gates (who had retired to his plantation in the lower Shenandoah Valley) to coordinate matters with Maryland. When Washington and Gates arrived in Annapolis, the Maryland assembly named a committee of ten of its most prominent men, including Chase and Carroll, to treat with the Virginians. All were members of the dominant creditor party.[60]

Meeting on December 22, 1784, the conference recommended establishment of a Potomac Company and asked the two states to subscribe fifty shares apiece. The states should finance surveys of the river, they added, and should ask Pennsylvania for permission to lay out a road from Cumberland, Maryland, to the Yohogania (Youghiogheny) River, a tributary of the Monongahela. Five days later the Maryland assembly briskly approved a bill establishing the Potomac Company, and in a separate action it appropriated £3,333, to be matched by Virginia, for a road from the upper Potomac to the Cheat River. It also agreed to ask Pennsylvania for permission to construct a road to the Yohogania.[61] The only opposition came from delegates of Baltimore and Harford counties, who evidently thought their constituents did not stand to benefit. They were also debtor men who commonly looked askance at public expenditures.

In the meantime, Madison took charge of the internal improvements plan in Richmond. In December the assembly approved a collection of resolutions designed to satisfy all regional interests. It agreed to loan money to the trustees in charge of clearing the James River, and it approved the construction of roads from the Potomac to the Monongahela and from the headwaters of the James to the New River–Kanawha system. A final act appointed commissioners to survey a route for a canal from the Elizabeth River to Albemarle Sound, with the cooperation of North Carolina. Madison apparently found it necessary to include this new project in order to secure the support of Patrick Henry, who had substantial holdings in the border country and expected to profit handsomely from a canal across the Dismal Swamp.[62] All fronts were secured by the time Washington returned with the Maryland act, and the Virginia assembly passed an identical law without opposition.

The act creating the Potomac Company authorized a president and four directors to be elected by the stockholders for three-year terms. After clearing the river, the company was authorized to collect tolls to recover its expenses. State treasurer Jacquelin Ambler would be present at company meetings to represent the state's interest.

Within five months the company raised over £40,000, about two-fifths subscribed by the cities of Winchester, Annapolis, Georgetown, and Frederick. In May 1785 the stockholders held their first meeting in Alexandria and elected Washington president. The Maryland directors were former governors Thomas Johnson and Thomas Sim Lee; Virginia directors were Alexandria merchants, John Fitzgerald and George Gilpin. The opening meeting drew 57 investors; not surprisingly, most lived in Alexandria or

TABLE 8.1 POTOMAC NAVIGATION COMPANY SUBSCRIBERS

Occupation		Political Service	
Planters	11	Assembly or ratifying conv.	23
Merchants	27	City government	4
Lawyers	4		
Physicians	3		
Party, 1787–1789			
Federalists	33		
Antifederalists	0		

neighboring Georgetown. Of the 34 who sent proxies, nearly all lived in Frederick, Maryland, or the Shenandoah Valley. Although only a minority of the 91 stockholders can be identified, it is clear that the company was dominated by merchants and nationalists (see table 8.1).[63]

Alexandria and Georgetown merchants may have been primarily interested in improving their trade, but for others the main purpose of the company was political. Washington felt that the link with the West was the main object. If the tramontane region were not tied commercially to the East, he feared, it would find an outlet through New Orleans. This, in turn, would inspire new demands for western independence. Washington even saw benefit in Spain's refusal to permit American traffic on the lower Mississippi, and he hoped the Potomac passage could be completed before Spain opened the river.[64]

As a gateway to the Ohio Valley, the Potomac project never did live up to Washington's hopes, and the western secessionist movement faded away without commercial inducements. But the Potomac Company's improvements did prove to be of enormous benefit to the western parts of Maryland and Virginia. It immediately began constructing a canal around the Great Falls, using indentured servants from Ireland,[65] and by 1789 the river was open for barge traffic as far as Old Town on the South Branch. In June of that year a flatboat loaded with 24 hogsheads of tobacco made it from Old Town to Berlin, Maryland, a distance of 180 miles, in a day and a half. Up-river traffic was slow and laborious, but some boats made the trip, carrying casks of rum and wine, along with tools and farm implements. In the high-water months the river was capable of carrying vessels of considerable size. Colonel William Darke, the aging Indian fighter, sent a flatboat from Shepherdstown on the Shenandoah to Georgetown with 262 barrels of flour that spring. Such was the amount of traffic that five wagons were kept busy unloading the boats at Georgetown.[66]

The benefits from such improved facilities were incalculable. Farmers with access to water got their flour to market and were ready to start plowing again while those in the hinterland were still hauling theirs around in wagons. With some clearing operations in the tributaries of the Potomac, nearly every farmer and tradesman in the western region could benefit. One farmer in Washington County, Maryland, who wrote to congratulate the Potomac Company in 1789 for its improvements, claimed that most of the tributaries were usable for 40 to 50 miles away from the river. Though he did not say how remote his own establishment was, he reckoned that the reduction in freight costs saved him £250 to £300 a year. By the early 1790s it was commonly estimated that the cost of shipping flour had been cut nearly in half.[67]

In the summer of 1789 Henry Lee toured the upper Potomac and reported universal enthusiasm for the region's prospects. Prosperity and nationalism went hand in hand. "They go now with the persuasion that we shall continue to be one people," he told Madison. The only other favor they could ask was that the federal government locate "the imperial city on the northern banks of the Potomack."[68] When President Washington accomplished this a year later, the political loyalty of the upper Potomac was sealed.

LOGROLLING PROJECTS:
THE JAMES RIVER AND DISMAL SWAMP CANALS

Proponents of the James River route to the West were as active as the Potomac Company in peddling subscriptions in the spring of 1785. Richmond merchants took the lead, but interest extended to the remotest parts of the watershed. Among the more active salesmen were William Cabell, who possessed a number of plantations in the Lynchburg area, and George Clendinen, a Greenbriar rancher and innkeeper. To Washington's embarrassment the assembly voted to give him several shares of stock in the company, which the conscientious hero, not wishing to shake confidence in the project, reluctantly accepted. The stockholders met in August and elected Washington president even though he was unable to attend. On the board of directors were Cabell, Richmond attorneys Edmund Randolph and John Harvie, and a Richmond merchant, David Ross.[69]

By the end of September company commissioners had surveyed the James River from Lynchburg to the mouth of Dunlap's Creek in Botetourt County and found it navigable all the way. From that point, they reported, there was a good road across the North Mountain to the Greenbriar. The report was somewhat optimistic, for there were several points on the James that could be passed only at high water. Where the river broke through the Blue Ridge near the Peaks of Otter was a rocky rapids that hampered boats for years. Not until 1790 was a company agent able to report that with dynamite he had "blowed near all the Rocks in the aforesaid Falls."[70] Nor did the commissioners mention that the Greenbriar River trickled for many miles before it was capable of floating anything more than a canoe.

The western project never materialized, although there were periodic efforts to revive it until almost the eve of the Civil War. Not until the railroads arrived with tunnel engineers at the end of the next century did Virginians conquer the North Mountain. Even so, the limited improvements made by the James River Company did facilitate transportation and improve land values in the Piedmont. The commissioners' report alone returned a substantial profit to several of the stockholders. "In consequence of these Prospects," observed Archibald Stuart in summarizing the report for Jefferson, "Lands on the River and those adjacent have risen fifty percent in their Value." And a Baltimore speculator was driven to ask Washington how much his holdings on the distant Little Kanawha had increased in value as a result of the James River project.[71] The anticipated benefits from improvements were often as important as the real ones.

The same mixture of "booster" pride and profit was behind the Dismal Swamp scheme. That project also dated from before the war when a company was formed to drain the swamp and cut a canal connecting it to Chesapeake Bay. Washington was a member of that company too, and even helped to survey a route. Eventually a seven-mile waterway was built, known still today as "Washington's Ditch." After the war, the inveterate speculator Dr. Thomas Walker tried to revive interest in a canal across the swamp, but nothing happened until it mysteriously appeared in the assembly's internal improvements package of 1785.[72] When the assembly endorsed the project, Patrick Henry acquired additional lands along the canal route and even tried to interest Washington in the venture. Washington declined on grounds that he was short of cash. Henry suffered no such embarrassment, for he paid for his lands with state certificates, which he bought at a rate of half a Spanish dollar per pound Virginia.[73] Most of the Virginians involved in the scheme agreed that the increase in land values was as important as the commercial advantages of the canal.[74]

North Carolinians were not so sure. Many feared that it would channel the state's trade through Virginia and further hamper the development of its own port facilities. All reports from south of 36° 30' indicated that there would be a "powerful opposition" to the project in the Carolina assembly.[75] Undaunted, Governor Henry drafted a bill authorizing the company to proceed with the work, and entrusted it to assembly delegate William Ronald, a Richmond merchant who had helped investigate the route. Unfortunately, Ronald's wife died, he failed to attend the session, and the bill languished. The assembly's only action was to appoint commissioners to treat with North Carolina.[76]

It mattered little, for North Carolina's opposition was firm. When a bill appropriating funds for the canal appeared in the Commons in the 1786 session, Richard D. Spaight moved to postpone it for a year and distribute copies in every county so that the voters could discuss the measure and instruct their representatives. Spaight's motion carried, 56 to 30.[77] Voting with Spaight, who represented New Bern, were the Pamlico and Cape Fear delegates, who feared competition from Virginia, and westerners who saw no advantage at all in the project. The only support from the canal came from the Albemarle-Roanoke watershed.[78]

In 1787 the Virginia assembly reincorporated the Dismal Swamp Company and assigned prominent merchants in every Tidewater city to receive stock subscriptions. North Carolina did nothing until the following year, when the Commons at last approved a canal bill. The Commons must have eliminated any state contribution to the cost, however, for the main opposition this time came from the Albemarle-Roanoke delegates. Their hostility was evidently enough to kill the bill in the Senate.[79] In 1790 a legislative committee drafted a new bill more acceptable to the Albemarle interests. This one passed both houses.[80] Responsible for the change of heart were a handful of delegates from the Cape Fear and the west, who may have had some projects of their own and wanted a quid pro quo. The act authorized the company to raise $80,000 in shares of $250 each, made it responsible for all improvements and maintenance, and prescribed a long list of tolls it could collect. Work at last began in the spring of 1792 when slaves were put to work digging a ditch 16 miles long, 32 feet wide, and 8 feet deep. Work was started simultaneously at both ends, and when the company ran out of money four years later the two crews were still 5 miles apart, with the most difficult part of the swamp yet to go. Lacking funds to proceed further, the company connected the two terminals by a plank road.[81] The waterway was not completed until 1814, far too late to be of much service to its godfather, Patrick Henry, although as late as 1791 he was offering tracts for sale in the area with the forecast that "The proposed canal which is to connect the navigation of the Chesapeak with that of Albemarle Sound, it is supposed must necessarily pass through these lands."[82]

The western question remained on the fringes of Chesapeake politics during the 1780s, flaring only occasionally into violent disputes, but it presented problems of national importance. Indeed, no other issue of the decade—except the question of amending the Articles of Confederation—prompted so much discussion about the nature of the union. Problems posed by land speculators and Indian resistance demanded interstate cooperation; the search for commercial ties with the West brought merchants in contact with nationalists; and the threat of western secession inspired new concern for the future of the Confederation. It was scarcely an accident that a matter involving the West, Potomac navigation, sparked the movement for federal reform.

PART THREE

The Constitution and National Parties, 1788–1792

CHAPTER NINE

The Movement for Federal Reform

ONCE THE DISPUTE over western lands was resolved and Maryland approved the Articles of Confederation, the three Chesapeake states became the mainstays of congressional authority. Throughout the Confederation period they consistently sent nationalist delegations to the Continental Congress, and they prided themselves on their generous response to congressional requests for funds.[1] Here, too, originated the movement to strengthen the powers of the general government. The instigators were the innovative leaders of the creditor parties, and the movement stemmed directly from their concern for the free flow of trade and credit. Just as they opposed artificial burdens on commerce imposed by debtor-relief measures, they favored uniform regulations imposed by national authority. As a result, they enthusiastically endorsed amendments to the Articles of Confederation that would have empowered Congress to levy customs duties and regulate trade.

The attempt to add to the powers of Congress originated in the nationalists' reforms of 1780–81. In the military and fiscal emergency of those years Congress funded its paper currency, established Robert Morris as Secretary of Finance, and chartered the Bank of North America to handle its credit needs thereafter. In order to secure a permanent revenue, in February 1781 Congress sent the states an amendment to the Articles of Confederation that would enable Congress to levy a duty of 5 percent on the value of all goods imported into the United States. The amount of tax to be levied was thus limited, but the power would be of indefinite duration. Eleven states approved the grant; only Rhode Island and Georgia prevented it from going into effect.

Although the Chesapeake states counted themselves as substantial importers, on whom the tax burden would fall rather heavily, they approved the impost amendment in short order. North Carolina and Virginia, whose legislatures were only one step ahead of the British that summer, approved the amendment without formal votes. Maryland ratified in its spring 1782 session, but by a vote of 6 to 4 its Senate tacked on a proviso to the effect that any limitations on Congress's tax power imposed by other states would automatically apply to Maryland. Voting in favor of the limiting amendment were nationalists James McHenry, Daniel Carroll, and George Plater; perhaps they felt a compromise necessary to insure approval in the House of Delegates. The bill then passed the Senate 7 to 3 and the House without a roll call. The three opponents in the Senate—Matthew Tilghman, John Smith, and Charles Carroll, Barrister—then published a dissent objecting to the grant of such an important power for an indefinite period of time.[2]

Then, in the fall of 1782, Virginia unaccountably revoked its approval. Madison and the other congressional delegates were stunned. Governor Benjamin Harrison told them that the revocation had been slipped through the assembly so quietly that he knew nothing of it until it appeared on his desk after the legislators had gone home. Before long, however, he was able to point the finger of suspicion at the Lees. Edmund Randolph seemed to agree. Some delegates, he told Madison, felt the impost act had been passed without sufficient consideration during the war emergency, and others thought that the present system might be sufficient now that the fighting had virtually ended. Randolph wondered if the state's initial agreement might be considered an irrevocable contract, but this was wishful thinking.[3] Congress abandoned plans to pressure Rhode Island, and the impost amendment was dead.

Congressional nationalists went back to work, and in March 1783 a select committee reported a new scheme. Instead of a permanent amendment to the Articles, it proposed a temporary grant of power to levy customs duties for 25 years. The proceeds, moreover, would be applied only to the interest and principal of the public debt. The states would appoint the collectors of revenue, and the income would be applied to each state's annual quota. Congress debated the report for more than a month, added some other features designed to appease special interests, and finally sent it on to the states. Accompanying it was an eloquent appeal drafted by Madison. Washington's support was enlisted, and he responded with a jeremiad that predicted "anarchy and confusion" if Congress were not granted this power.[4]

The new proposal reached Virginia while echoes of the dispute over the first impost were still reverberating. George Mason had not participatd in the assembly's earlier action, but the new congressional request aroused his temperamental suspicion of power. During the spring elections he appeared at a popular meeting in Fairfax County with a set of resolutions instructing the county's delegates on the matter. The congressional request and Madison's plea, he found, "exhibit strong proofs of lust for power." Customs duties were acceptable only if they were levied and collected by the states. "Congress should not even have the appearance of such a power," he warned. "When the same man or set of men, holds both the sword and the purse, there is an end of liberty."[5]

Mason's objections were too abstract to sway many delegates, but Richard Henry Lee's argument was more earthly. He appealed to the state's commercial interests and latent sectional jealousies. Federal customs duties, he argued, would "strangle our infant [commerce] in its birth, make us pay more than our proportion and sacrifice this country [Virginia] to its northern brethren."[6]

Jefferson, discharged from the peace commission after Congress received word of the signing of a provisional treaty, stopped in Richmond during the spring session to lobby for the impost. Its fate depended on the attitude of Patrick Henry, he reported to Madison, and "Henry as usual is involved in mystery: should the popular tide run strongly in either direction, he will fall in with it. Should it not, he will have a struggle between his enmity to the Lees, and his enmity to everything which may give influence to Congs."[7]

On May 14 the House of Delegates approved a resolution favoring the impost and ordered a bill to be drafted. Henry was a member of the committee that drafted the bill, but he wavered in the debate. He eventually gave a grudging support to the impost on the grounds that it would fall most heavily on the wealthy, but this did little for the nationalists' cause.[8] After several close contests in committee of the whole, the bill emerged with some changes which nationalists thought made it "unfit to be enacted into law." Proceeds from the 5 percent duty would go into the state treasury, and the state would continue to pay its quota of Congress's requisitions.[9] This, of course, made it nothing but a state impost. Henry Tazewell then suggested a compromise that would keep the collection of revenue under state control but earmark the proceeds for Congress. Nationalists disliked this idea too because it would set a precedent for other states. As a result, the entire matter was postponed to the following session.[10]

During the summer, sentiment in favor of the impost increased. John Tyler, Henry's close ally, found himself "every day a greater friend" to the idea. Since Congress had the power to borrow money, it could undertake obligations which the states ultimately had to fulfill. Far better, he concluded, to give Congress an independent income that would force upon it some responsibility. When the issue reappeared in the fall session, nationalists cleverly picked up Henry's argument that it amounted to tax relief. John Breckinridge, a 23-year-old lawyer from the Valley already serving his third term in the House, pointed out that the state's current £122,000 annual requisition came out of property taxes. The impost would shift this burden to those actively involved in foreign trade. By voice vote, the assembly approved the congressional request without alteration.[11] Coupling this action with the assembly's agreement to cede its lands north of the Ohio, Joseph Jones called them "sacrifices to the common benefit of the federal Government ... [which] cannot fail to produce harmony and greatly cement the Union."[12]

In the spring of 1784 North Carolina also approved the impost with relative ease. Since the state had little import trade, it was quite willing to shift the burden of financing Congress to the states that did.[13] The Maryland assembly, curiously, did not act on the 1783 impost, but it did reaffirm its ratification of the 1781 amendment.[14] Perhaps its nationalists considered that amendment to be sufficient authority for Congress to proceed with a tax; perhaps they thought the second measure not strong enough. It mattered little, for the opposition of New York killed even the modest 1783 plan. By then, nationalists were seeking alternative means to strengthen the central government.

MADISON'S RETURN

In December 1783 Madison finished his three-year stint in the Continental Congress and returned to Virginia, but he carried with him a fierce nationalism hardened by the vicissitudes of Congress— bankruptcy, homelessness, ridicule, and periodic menace by its own army. He spent the winter at Montpelier immersed in the study of public law, requesting Jefferson to send him from New York "whatever may throw light on the general constitution and droit public of the several confederacies which have existed." In April he was elected to the House of Delegates.

A visit with George Mason, in which the two reached general agreement on a range of issues, was the first step toward organization.[15] Already his cause had a name, for the word "federal" was commonly employed whenever the powers and stature of Congress were discussed. The term was at once a description of the central authority and a shorthand method of describing the program for strengthening it.[16] Before long Madison and his friends would be referring to their opponents as "Antifederal."[17]

Next to the absence of tax power, the main flaw in the Confederation seemed to be the lack of uniform regulation of trade. Congress had no power over interstate or foreign commerce. As a result, each state set up its own regulations, causing conflict and confusion. British actions aggravated the problem. A flood of British goods at the end of the war had drained the nation of specie and helped start a depression. In addition, Britain excluded American vessels from the British West Indies after the war, thereby cutting off an important source of income. Many merchants felt that Congress ought to have the power to retaliate. Some even desired uniform federal regulations that would help create a national market. In the fall of 1783 Maryland suggested an amendment which would give Congress power to restrict foreign ships entering the United States. Virginia urged Congress to prohibit the importation of West Indian products in British vessels.[18]

Prodded by these and other requests, Congress in the spring of 1784 asked the states for power to pass navigation acts to protect American shipping for a period of 15 years. Virginia promptly agreed, but elsewhere the idea was frustrated by local interests.[19] When Monroe took Madison's seat in Congress, he immediately interested himself in the problem. Urging him on was Jefferson, who was then in Europe trying to interest the British government in a trade agreement. If Congress had the capacity to retaliate, Jefferson felt, it would have greater bargaining leverage.[20]

Placed at the head of a committee to reexamine the question, Monroe in March 1785 drafted a new amendment to the Articles of Confederation. Wrapping commerce and the impost together, Monroe's amendment asked for permanent power to regulate interstate and foreign commerce as well as power to levy duties on both exports and imports. Not surprisingly, the proposal caused a verbal storm in Congress. Within the Virginia delegation, only Samuel Hardy sided with Monroe. Grayson was mildly critical, and Richard Henry Lee was adamantly opposed.[21] Ever suspicious of northern merchants, Lee argued that such a power was certain to be abused because "The spirit of Commerce throughout the world is the Spirit of Avarice." Northern merchants, he predicted, would persuade Congress to pass navigation acts that would give them a monopoly of the nation's trade. Madison replied that since southern trade was already in the hands of British merchants, planters could hardly lose by the change, and the amendment would give Congress the leverage to negotiate a more favorable trading relationship with Britain.[22]

The argument was scarcely convincing. Even a nationalist like James McHenry of Maryland feared that the amendment might give the northern states "a monopoly of the carrying trade of the Union." As a compromise, McHenry thought a mild navigation act that promoted the gradual development of shipping in all the states might be the "true policy." But this sort of give and take required a broader framework of federal powers than the Monroe amendment contemplated. Unable to reach agreement, Congress did nothing.[23]

Anticipating that any amendment Congress approved would become ensnared in provincial jealousies, Joseph Jones suggested to Madison that a "Convention of Deputies" might frame trade regulations which could then be enforced by Congress. The idea of using a convention to bypass Congress was not new. Northern nationalists periodically mentioned it whenever one of their projects was thwarted. In 1782, when Virginia revoked its approval of the impost, the New York assembly had approved resolutions drawn up by Alexander Hamilton favoring such a convention.[24] Jones's suggestion, however, was the first time the thought had been expressed in Virginia. Most important, whether Jones was aware of it or not, the opportunity to promote such a convention was already at hand, in a meeting of commissioners from Maryland and Virginia to discuss joint regulation of the Potomac.

THE MOUNT VERNON MEETING

The idea of a conference on Potomac navigation originated in 1784, during the same session of the Virginia assembly that adopted the Port Act. Concerned that its merchants suffered great inconveniences from the lack of uniform regulations on the waterway, the assembly proposed a meeting with delegates from Maryland, and anticipating Maryland's acceptance, it even named four commissioners—George Mason, Edmund Randolph, James Madison, and Alexandria merchant Archibald Henderson. In recounting this action for Jefferson's benefit, Madison gave no hint that he saw any potential in such meetings for expanding the powers of Congress.[25] That notion appeared only in the wake of the discussion of the commerce amendment the following spring.

In its fall session the Maryland assembly accepted the invitation and named commissioners of its own—Thomas Johnson, Daniel of St. Thomas Jenifer, Thomas Stone, and Samuel Chase, all members of the dominant creditor faction. Like Madison, the Maryland delegates did not anticipate going beyond the immediate problem of Potomac navigation.[26] The Marylanders proposed a time and place to Governor Patrick Henry, and, receiving no reply, they assumed Virginia accepted the arrangement. Henry, in fact, communicated with no one, and the Virginia commissioners evidently decided that the whole plan had been abandoned. Washington, however, learned of the arrangements from friends in Maryland, and when the Virginia commissioners failed to appear in Alexandria at the appointed time, he wrote to Edmund Randolph to find out why. Randolph promptly went to Governor Henry, who had a sudden loss of memory. Henry could not remember what he had done with the Maryland proposals but thought he might have sent them to Madison. No one was fooled. It was clear that the governor, who had little interest in trade regulations and even less in secret conclaves of like-minded nationalists, was trying to scuttle the whole project.[27]

In the meantime, the Maryland commissioners appeared in Alexandria and sought out George Mason, who learned of the meeting for the first time. Thinking it a good idea, Mason found Henderson and together the group sat down to await the arrival of Madison and Randolph. When Mason at last received a letter from Randolph, obviously written before Randolph had heard from Washington, containing no reference to the meeting, Mason concluded that "there must have been some Blunder or Neglect in some of the public Offices." Unwilling to let the Marylanders return empty-handed, he and Henderson decided to act on their own. At that point Washington invited the entire group to Mount Vernon, and after enjoying Washington's hospitality for a few days the group signed a pact for the joint regulation of the river.[28]

The Maryland assembly took up the commissioners' report as soon as the fall session opened. The House of Delegates turned it over to a select committee headed by Chase and loaded with creditor-nationalists.[29] Two days later Chase's committee came in with a collection of resolutions that went far beyond Potomac navigation. They proposed joint military defense of Chesapeake Bay, a standardized rate of exchange for their state currencies, uniform export duties, and comity in the drafts of merchants of one state upon merchants of the other. Finally—and most important of all—they adopted the recommendation of the Mount Vernon commissioners that there be annual meetings and suggested that Delaware and Pennsylvania be invited as well. It was a natural extension, for the assembly was already involved in discussions with those states concerning a proposed Chesapeake-Delaware canal.[30] On November 22 the House approved the resolutions by voice vote, and the whole batch was sent on to Virginia.

Later in the session the House shouted approval of a bill granting Congress the power to levy a 5 percent impost.[31] As with the ratification of the Mount Vernon compact, there was no roll call, but it is clear that the rift in the creditor party over paper money did not extend to matters of interstate or congressional relations.[32] Marylanders were solidly behind the nationalist movement, but they had not yet realized the implications of these interstate meetings. That was the contribution of the Virginians.

THE ANNAPOLIS CONVENTION

The Virginia assembly was much more hostile to the nationalists' plans. Throughout the summer Madison was afraid that it would reject the commerce amendment. The hinterland was always hostile to conferring new power on remote authorities, and a sizeable number of merchants were Scots who might well dislike the idea of giving Congress power to retaliate commercially against Britain.[33] The Mount Vernon agreement only gave new ammunition to the Henryites, who could reasonably argue that the commissioners had exceeded their authority. But the deepening commercial depression worked in Madison's favor. During the autumn merchants in various port towns petitioned the assembly to approve the commerce amendment, and they also asked for legislation that would restrict the operations of British vessels and Scottish factors. The House of Delegates took up the petitions early in the session, and after "a pretty full discussion, it was determined by a large majority" to approve the commerce amendment. Although some qualifications were attached, Madison did not think they would be "subversive of the principle." Those opposing the amendment apparently wanted state legislation regulating British merchants and their vessels.[34]

Then, toward the end of November, sentiment in the House changed. On November 30 it adopted drastic amendments to the bill, some apparently suggested by the Senate. The assembly reduced the time limit during which Congress could exercise its powers from 25 years to 13, and it added a proviso that any trade regulation must receive the approval of two-thirds of the state delegations in Congress. The latter was a response to the sectional suspicions of Benjamin Harrison and Carter Braxton, who had denounced Congress and the northern states with unprecedented ferociousness. The nationalists tried, and failed by a margin of 79 to 28, to extend the grant beyond 13 years. The House then approved the much mutilated bill by voice vote, but the following day it rescinded its action. The nationalists themselves were apparently responsible for the change of heart. Madison, who voted with the majority, explained to Washington that the limitations placed on the grant made it worse than useless. Once in effect, it would stand in the way of a more permanent grant of power, and it would encourage British intransigence by demonstrating that Americans were weak and divided.[35]

For the next few days the House discussed the alternative of a state navigation act, the remedy proposed by the Harrison-Braxton coalition. It had given tentative approval to the idea and ordered a bill drafted when the set of Maryland resolutions arrived. These were referred to the commerce committee, headed by Carter Braxton. But they temporarily sidetracked the drive for unilateral state action and gave the nationalists new hope.[36] The commerce committee, which numbered Madison among its members, was evenly divided between the two parties.[37]

At the same time, the Maryland resolutions gave John Tyler an idea. While the House was routing them to committee, he drafted a resolution of his own proposing a general meeting with commissioners from other states to discuss "commercial regulations" of common interest.[38] This too was evdently referred to the commerce committee, as was a letter from George Mason a week later enclosing the recommendations of the Mount Vernon meeting. While the committee deliberated, the House turned to other business.[39]

What impelled Tyler to broaden the Maryland suggestion into a general commercial convention is a mystery. Although the Madison circle considered him an ally of Patrick Henry, Tyler had earlier supported the commerce amendment.[40] Having been ousted from the Speaker's chair that session, he may have been trying to regain his stature in the House by taking a middle path between the aspirations of the nationalists and the apprehensions of the Henryites. His motion, after all, was hardly a radical departure. Interstate agreements of the sort worked out at Mount Vernon actually enhanced state control of commerce. By making the existing system work more smoothly they lessened the need for change. For this reason the nationalists were skeptical of such conferences; they preferred amendments to the Articles.[41]

The commerce committee discussed its various alternatives for several weeks. Finally, on December 27, Chairman Braxton sent to the floor a bill to encourage Virginia's shipping industry and another levying state customs duties. Both represented the views of the localists, but neither generated much enthusiasm. That same day the House passed the bill creating the Potomac Company, and it committed a bill ratifying the Mount Vernon pact to a select committee headed by Madison. Madison quickly put on the finishing touches and the House passed it on December 30.[42]

What happened next is unclear. Summarizing the results for Monroe after the session ended, Madison explained, "This failure of local measures in the commercial line, instead of reviving the propositions for a general plan [i.e., an amendment to the Articles], revived that of Mr. Tyler for the appointment of commiss[ioners] to meet commiss[ioners] from the other states on the subject of general regulations."[43] Unsure of the usefulness of such a meeting, Madison was inclined to play down his own role in the outcome, but his explanation omitted some intricate maneuvers. Because of Madison's reticence, their exact nature can only be guessed.

On January 10 the House took up Braxton's navigation act and discussed it intermittently for several days. The act failed to win much support, probably because it would have meant higher shipping costs for planters. As the session drifted to an end, it became obvious that the House had to do something. Perhaps it was Madison who reminded the commerce committee that it still had the Maryland resolutions before it.[44] At any rate, on January 13, Braxton reported out a set of resolutions that were identical to those sent from Maryland, with one important exception. The invitation to meet with commissioners from Maryland and Virginia the following September was to be extended to all the other states, not just Delaware and Pennsylvania.[45] This was a natural extension because the assembly was in the midst of negotiations with North Carolina on the Dismal Swamp canal.[46] Braxton, like Tyler, failed to see the potential in such meetings. The House quickly approved the resolutions, except for two that dealt with monetary interchangeability (fears lingered that Maryland might yet issue more paper) and sent them to the Senate.

Passage of the resolutions established the principle of a general meeting, and Braxton's acquiescence calmed the fears of the localists. On January 21, the last day of the session, the House retrieved John Tyler's resolution from the table and passed it "by a very great majority," though Meriwether Smith remained opposed to the end.[47] The object of the meeting, according to the resolution, was to draft a new amendment giving Congress power to regulate commerce. This fairly clearly represented a compromise between those who wanted only interstate discussions on commerce and the Madisonians who wanted to add to the powers of Congress. But the limited agenda also helps to explain the lack of opposition.

The House initially named as delegates Madison, Edmund Randolph, and Senator Walter Jones.[48] Then the nationalists, who may have begun to sense opportunity in the convention proposal, procured the addition of St. George Tucker, a Williamsburg lawyer whom Madison considered "sensible federal and skilled in commerce." This seems to have aroused the suspicions of the antinationalists, for someone—Madison was not sure who—insisted on adding Meriwether Smith.[49] The Senate tossed in George Mason, David Ross, and William Ronald.[50] Smith and Mason both spelled trouble, and Madison predicted sourly that the "multitude of associates will stifle the thing in its birth." But in the next breath he decided that the meeting "may probably lead to better consequences than at first occur."[51] It was at last beginning to be realized that such conferences, properly managed, might be put to the advantage of the nationalists.

Within a month several states replied favorably, and the Virginia commissioners decided that the "convention" (as Edmund Randolph began to call it) should meet in Annapolis on the first Monday in September.[52] They rejected New York and Philadelphia as sites to avoid any suspicion that northern merchants might dominate the proceedings. In mid-March William Grayson reported that some members of Congress were discussing the possibility of a general convention to rewrite the Articles of Confederation.[53] The revival of this idea among northern nationalists buoyed Madison's spirits, and his hopes for the Annapolis meeting brightened steadily through the spring. He worked hard to convert Grayson and Monroe, both of whom initially preferred to seek additional amendments. By early May Madison was arguing that Congress ought to suspend further attempts to amend the Articles pending the outcome of the Annapolis meeting.[54] And by that date Washington, in independent communication with northern nationalists, was beginning to regret that the agenda for the meeting had not been phrased in more general terms which would enable the delegates to hold "a General Convention . . . for the purpose of revising & correcting the defects of the federal Government."[55]

Unfortunately, no one thought to communicate the new "line" to the Maryland nationalists, and they almost wrecked the whole scheme. In March the House of Delegates nominated eleven commissioners, all strong nationalists.[56] But the Senate, driven perhaps by the apprehensions of Charles Carroll, refused to cooperate. Among the "weighty objections" that occurred to the Senate was the fear that such state-managed conventions would undermine the authority of Congress. Maryland had already approved the commerce amendment, the upper house pointed out. What the nation needed was federal regulation of trade, not regional agreements. This convention, moreover, might lead to "other meetings, which may have consequences which cannot be foreseen. Innovations in government, when not absolutely necessary, are dangerous."[57] The latter argument betrayed the almost paranoid conservatism of Charles Carroll, who had been wringing his hands for years over the growing power of the "lower orders." The movement to reform the federal government required some taste for innovation, and Carroll was not up to it—either in this year or in the next.

The Senate recommended instead holding two meetings. Maryland would discuss the Potomac navigation with Virginia, as originally planned, and it would appoint other commissioners to discuss the Chesapeake-Delaware canal with Pennsylvania and Delaware. The following day—the last day of the session—the House of Delegates agreed to the consultations with Virginia under the Mount Vernon pact, but it rejected the meeting with Pennsylvania and took exception to the Senate's reasoning about the dangers inherent in multistate conventions.[58] There the matter rested, as the two houses departed for home.

By the time the Virginians learned of the disaster it was too late to do anything. Since Maryland was technically the host for the conference, the Senate's action was a severe blow. Edmund Randolph, ever quick to panic, thought the absence of Maryland delegates left a "dreadful chasm," but the convention movement maintained its momentum.[59]

In May, Congress opened a general debate on the subject of federal reform, but it made little headway other than appointing a new committee to draft amendments to the Articles. Part of its problem was poor attendance, and part of it was the reluctance of some delegates to discuss substantial change without consulting their state legislatures. The notion of what might be accomplished by a separate convention, however, found new favor. Reporting the debate to Madison, Grayson suggested that since Virginia had called the Annapolis meeting, it ought to go further and ask the other states to give their delegates enough power to "comprehend all the grievances of the Union."[60] Fertilized from such diverse sources, the convention idea bloomed by midsummer.

By the end of August, nine states had named delegates, though some of the northerners failed to appear. The North Carolina assembly had broken up that spring before it learned of the Annapolis meeting, but the governor and council took it upon themselves to appoint delegates. All but one of the men they selected were from the Lawyers' party, but only one, Hugh Williamson, was a member of Congress. The rest evidently found it too long a trek. Williamson went down to Annapolis from New York, but he arrived a day after the meeting adjourned.[61]

The commissioners assembled in Annapolis on Monday, September 11, but found only five states represented—Virginia, New York, Pennsylvania, Delaware, and New Jersey. They therefore appointed a committee to consider what should be done. The next day the committee reported that since so few states were represented it was inexpedient to undertake "the business committed to them," and it suggested yet another meeting of commissioners from all the states. After approving this idea, the convention named another committee to prepare an address. Hamilton undertook this task, and he finished it in an evening. The next day the convention adopted Hamilton's draft without substantial change and promptly adjourned. When Hugh Williamson arrived on the fifteenth not a delegate was still in town.

After all the months of preparation, the Annapolis convention acted with unseemly haste to achieve a limited result. Besides Williamson, commissioners from three other states—New Hampshire, Massachusetts, and Rhode Island—were known to have been appointed (they actually left New York for Annapolis on September 10). Since tardiness was a common failing in all assemblies of this period, particularly in continental ones, why did not the commissioners wait patiently a few days for late arrivals? Rhode Island's attendance—a rare sign of cooperation for that state—one might suppose would have been particularly welcome. Surely nine states would have made a significant quorum for the adoption of some proposals for changes in the frame of government.

The convention's reasoning must be reconstructed by guesswork because only the barest record of its proceedings was kept, and the correspondence, even among such prolific letter writers as Randolph and Madison, is mysteriously silent on the subject. What happened, it seems most likely, is that the handful of men who arrived in Annapolis on time found themselves in general agreement on the need for "reform" as Madison later called it. Hamilton, long an advocate of a convention, and Madison, a new convert to the idea, reinforced each other. But the proposal had to be vaguely phrased so as to alarm no one. The report drafted by Hamilton merely pointed out that there were "important defects in the system," and proposed another convention to meet the following May in Philadelphia with power to do whatever "shall appear to them necessary to render the constitution of the Federal Government adequate to the exigencies of the Union." The Philadelphia convention, acting under so ambiguous a mandate, could do anything it wanted. The Annapolis convention then quickly adjourned lest new delegates arrive who wanted to enter some caveats on the record. New Englanders were particularly to be feared because in the spring congressional debate they had expressed the opinion that any change in the Articles ought to be confined to matters of trade regulation.[62]

In sending the convention's address to the Virginia delegates in Congress, St. George Tucker admitted somewhat apologetically that the meeting had exceeded its authority by calling for yet another convention; but he thought it important to keep up the momentum and asked the congressional delegation to support the idea. Henry Lee replied that Congress was divided on the subject. Some agreed with the idea of another convention, others preferred to reform the government through state conventions, and a third group felt that only Congress had power to change the Articles.[63] For the moment Congress's attitude did not matter because the whole governmental reform movement was suddenly threatened by a tempest over the Mississippi River.

THE JAY-GARDOQUI NEGOTIATIONS

Spain viewed the young American republic with a mixture of fear and disdain. Although Spain had followed France into the

Revolutionary War, it neither allied itself with the United States nor recognized its legitimacy. Determined to isolate its empire from Americans and their subversive republican ideas, Spain in 1784 closed the Mississippi River to American traffic. Since the river was the only foreseeable outlet for western products, the newly arrived settlers in Kentucky and Tennessee were understandably aroused. In some alarm, Spain sent over a minister, Don Diego de Gardoqui, with instructions to persuade the United States to surrender its claim to the use of the river. Since the river, in its lower reaches, flowed through Spanish territory, any American claim was tenuous, but Gardoqui was authorized to offer trade concessions if the Americans acquiesced.

John Jay, who became Secretary for Foreign Affairs in 1784, shared the view of many northern merchants that opening the door to the Spanish market was more important than the trickle of trade that floated down the Mississippi. If the West did not make itself independent, the river would ultimately come into American hands anyway. So, in the summer of 1786 Jay asked Congress to alter its instruction to stand firm, and instead to allow him to surrender for a period of twenty or thirty years the American claim to use of the river. After a bitter sectional debate, Congress granted the request, 7 states to 5. Delegates from the 5 southern states opposed it to a man, denouncing the proposal as a sellout that would wreck the union. The unanticipated storm in the South and West ultimately wrecked the negotiations, and it almost destroyed the movement for constitutional reform.

Echoes of the congressional uproar reverberated in Virginia throughout the winter. Nationalists particularly feared the capital that Patrick Henry might make of the issue. Jay's request resurrected the old fears of northern commercial domination and added to the misgivings of lukewarm nationalists, such as Monroe and Edmund Pendleton.[64] Madison was particularly concerned that the Jay negotiations might induce the sectionalists who had opposed the commerce amendment to ally with eastern land speculators and western pioneers who wanted the Mississippi opened. Such an alliance, manipulated by Patrick Henry, would kill the federal reform movement in its infancy. A rumor that Henry planned to resign from the governorship so that he could fight Jay in the assembly heightened nationalists' concern.[65]

With his usual political acumen, Madison forestalled trouble in the assembly by joining the hue and cry.[66] Even though several Virginia nationalists, among them Washington, had earlier expressed indifference to closure of the river, Madison now made sure that there was virtually unanimous support for a strong stand against Jay.[67] Early in December the House of Delegates shouted through a series of resolutions instructing the state's congressional delegation not to yield on the issue.[68] The storm subsided, but Madison continued to worry about its impact. "Many of our most federal leading men are extremely soured with what has already passed," he complained to Washington, and among them he named Monroe and Pendleton, both of whom had voiced suspicion of northern intentions.[69] But no further damage was done, and toward the end of the session the assembly unanimously endorsed the report of the Annapolis convention and named a slate of delegates for the next one at Philadelphia.

THE ROAD TO PHILADELPHIA

Throughout the spring of 1787 Virginia Federalists[70] fussed over the delegation that would represent the state at Philadelphia. The assembly chose a stellar group that included nearly every important figure in the state. Headed by Edmund Randolph, whom the assembly had elected governor earlier in the session, it included Washington, Madison, Mason, Patrick Henry, George Wythe, and John Blair. Though it was widely anticipated that Henry would reject the invitation, the nationalists tried hard to induce him to accept, hoping that his attendance might co-opt him. Henry refused, pleading lack of funds, but he later confided to a friend that he "smelt a rat." Madison suspected that he merely wanted to "leave his conduct unfettered" for the fall assembly, "where the result of the Convention will receive its destiny from his omnipotence."[71]

The council then tried General Thomas Nelson and Richard Henry Lee. There was some suspicion of Lee's "unfederal opinions," but Governor Randolph hoped that participation in the convention might convert him.[72] When both men declined, the council turned to one of its own number, James McClurg, a Richmond physician. The delegation had been weighted with nationalists from the beginning; it was now solid. The one question mark was George Mason. After a talk with him Madison optimistically reported to Jefferson that Mason was "renouncing his errors on the subject of the Confederation, and means to take an active part in the amendment of it."[73]

The Antifederalists' hostility to the convention and the doubts in the executive council concerning Lee's nomination indicate that attitudes on the subject of constitutional revision had hardened well before the convention opened. While delegates were still gathering in Philadelphia in mid-May, Congressmen William Grayson and Richard Henry Lee voiced the suspicion that the New England delegates planned to scrap the Articles altogether and replace them with a "general system" that could be dominated by their merchants and manufacturers.[74] Both sides at last had come to recognize the potential, for good or ill, of conventions. Whatever the delegates at Philadelphia proposed, it was sure to cause a fight.

Party lines were as firmly drawn in Maryland, and there the selection of a delegation occasioned some extraordinary maneuvers. It is fairly evident, however, that Maryland nationalists still did not appreciate the significance of the reform movement. As a result, it was largely through accident that the delegation finally selected was predominantly Federalist.

In the winter of 1786, while Virginia nationalists fretted over the impact of the Jay-Gardoqui negotiations, the federal movement in Maryland stumbled over paper money. The assembly battled the issue throughout the session and finally adjourned to consult the electorate before it got around to choosing delegates for Philadelphia. During the early weeks of 1787 the public debate over paper money drowned out any discussion of federal matters.

But then the whole storm blew over almost as quickly as it had arisen. In a recovering economy, public interest in paper money vanished.[75] As a result, the assembly's spring session was conducted with unaccustomed propriety. The Senate rejected a House bill permitting speculators in confiscated property to pay their debts in paper warrants rather than specie, and the House meekly acceded. The Senate, in turn, came to terms with the House on a bill involving debts owed British merchants, and it approved a House bill providing for payment of other debts in installments. It did make some changes in the installment bill, but when some dissidents tried to provoke a fight over the amendments in the House, they were silenced.[76] The session ended with more gentlemanly decorum than the state had seen for years.

Both Chase and Carroll refused to attend the Philadelphia convention, after being nominated by the assembly, and it has often been suggested that neither could trust the other enough to leave the state.[77] This explanation assumes that both men underestimated the importance of the federal convention, which may well have been the case, but it does not seem adequate in the circumstances. The convention delegation was not finally settled until the very end of the assembly session, on May 24, and once the assembly adjourned neither man had anything to fear until it returned in November. Nor had either so totally dominated his branch of the legislature that his presence was essential; each got his way only when his views coincided with the majority. The Senate was unanimous in its disapproval of paper money; Carroll's vote was not needed. In any case, Philadelphia was not that far away.

The manner in which the assembly went about selecting delegates, however, does render plausible the view that each side was trying to maneuver its opponents out of the state. The House of Delegates nominated ten men, including Carroll. All had been prominent members of the creditor party, but not one could be considered a friend of Chase.[78] The Senate added Chase, William Paca, Thomas Johnson, and Thomas Stone. Paca voted for paper money in 1786 and was considered an ally of Chase. Johnson and Stone were nationalists who had been prominent in the convention movement. Two of the House nominees and three of the Senate's refused to serve, and in joint ballot the assembly chose Robert H. Harrison, Charles Carroll, Thomas Stone, James McHenry, and Thomas Sim Lee.[79]

If all this was only a cynical maneuver to eliminate the opposition by sending it to Philadelphia, why did Carroll agree to serve in the first place? Or, why did Chase withdraw so early? The Philadelphia meeting was still some weeks away (it was scheduled to open on May 14 but the leisurely arrival of other delegates prevented it from beginning formal sessions until May 25). There was plenty of time to pursue any plans he had for the legislative session. It seems more likely that Chase, like Patrick Henry, suspected the purpose of the convention and preferred to retain an independence that would enable him to oppose it in the future. Although he had never voiced much support for the constitutional reform movement, he had consistently given it his ballot. He had favored the various amendments to the Articles of Confederation and cooperated with both the Mount Vernon and Annapolis meetings. Chase loved orderly government and feared the masses as much as Charles Carroll did, but his politics was always dictated by personal interest. Given his straightened circumstances and the number of opponents of paper money that were joining the Federalist cause, a "wait and see" posture probably seemed wise.

A few days later Thomas Stone declined to serve. Since he died later that year, ill health may have been the reason. To replace him the House nominated Daniel of St. Thomas Jenifer, Gabriel Duvall, and Alexander C. Hanson, again all creditor-nationalists.[80] The Senate forebore any nominations of its own. In the balloting Jenifer and Duvall tied, and Duvall won in a runoff. A week later the House discovered that five more ballots had been cast in that contest than there were members attending. It proposed a reballoting. The Senate replied that this was impractical because in the interval new members had arrived and others had departed. It suggested a ballot on new nominees, with Duvall and Jenifer excluded. Pointing out that time was running short, the House proposed instead to send both Duvall and Jenifer without further balloting. The Senate agreed, though it would have preferred its own solution.[81]

At that juncture—May 10—Charles Carroll decided not to attend the convention. Why he waited so long, if he really was apprehensive about leaving Chase alone in Maryland, is a mystery. The session was nearing its end, no mention had been made of paper money, and the two houses were in the process of compromising their differences on debtor relief. A few days later Justice Harrison and Gabriel Duvall also declined to serve. A week later the House of Delegates nominated Luther Martin, John Francis Mercer, and Daniel Carroll. The Senate pointed out that it would save time to send all three to Philadelphia, instead of balloting for two of them. Since decisions of the delegation were to be by majority vote, it would be better to have an odd number. The House agreed.[82]

In this casual way Maryland sifted through its leadership elite to find five men who were willing to ride eighty miles to attend a convention. If the creditor-nationalists got a firm majority of the delegation, it was purely by accident. Luther Martin was the only member on whom Chase could count. Mercer ultimately opposed the Constitution, but his position at this point was uncertain. He was newly arrived from Virginia, where his political role had been chiefly distinguished by a family feud with the Lees. Though not a member of the Maryland assembly, he had sided with the Senate in the paper money conflict.[83] The other three—Carroll, McHenry, and Jenifer—were all personal friends of Washington who had participated in the reform movement from the beginning.

Both houses seemingly made their nominations without regard to political affiliation. The nomination of Mercer, Martin, the two Carrolls, and McHenry, for instance, all emanated from the House of Delegates. This, together with the haphazard way in which nominations were declined, suggests that none of the legislative factions—creditor, Chasite, or debtor—fully appreciated the importance of the Philadelphia meeting. Or, more likely, they were so uncertain of its impact on their interests that they did not want to be committed in advance. This was true even for a nationalist like Charles Carroll, who had expressed his misgivings about such meetings the previous year.

The same casual uncertainty prevailed throughout the summer. Despite its proximity to Philadelphia, Maryland had one of the worst attendance records of any state. McHenry, the first to arrive, stayed only three days and did not return until August 6. The illness of his brother was the reason for his absence, but if he fully appreciated the importance of the convention it is unlikely that he would have stayed away so long. Jenifer, who appeared on June 2, was the only one who remained all summer, and much of the time he divided Maryland's vote with Luther Martin, who finally left in disgust on September 4. Daniel Carroll, the strongest nationalist on the delegation, did not appear until July 9. Mercer finally arrived in town on August 6, complained mightily about the trend of events, and departed abruptly on August 17.[84] None of this suggests much awareness of the issues at stake.

Nor do the discussions that took place within the delegation. When McHenry returned on August 4, he found the delegation deeply divided. He promptly organized a meeting at Daniel Carroll's lodgings to secure unity. His reasoning was that "unless we could appear in the convention with some degree of unanimity it would be unnecessary to remain in it, sacrificing time and money." His suggestion for compromise was that the delegation ought to work to strengthen the existing Articles "without altering the sovereignty of suffrage." This, of course, was the policy the Maryland Senate had been pursuing for years, but at this point it seems a bit unrealistic. The Constitution had already emerged in near-final shape from the Committee of Detail. Incredibly, only two members of the delegation openly disagreed with McHenry's suggestion—Carroll liked the way things were going in the convention, and Mercer objected to any change in the Articles at all.[85] McHenry, it must be admitted, was a particularly obtuse individual largely dependent on others for ideas. But the irrelevance of his approach itself suggests the uncertainty that prevailed among Maryland nationalists. Not only was there no conspiracy in the selection of the Maryland delegation; there was not even much collaboration. The Virginians, who were themselves late to recognize the potential in such meetings, would have done well to communicate some of their newborn enthusiasm across the Potomac.

By the end of the summer most Marylanders realized their error, however. In mid-August, as soon as it became clear that the Constitution was going to prohibit state monetary and debtor-relief experiments, Luther Martin raced home to spread the alarm among the Chasites. By the time the convention finished its work the lines had formed. As in Virginia, they followed the factional pattern that had developed over the previous three years under the pressure of economic hard times. As lines hardened most of the Chasites drifted back to the Federalist camp, leaving Chase in virtual isolation and the opponents of the Constitution in a small minority. Perhaps Chase's biggest mistake—like Patrick Henry's—was in failing to attend the convention in the first place.

Willie Jones in North Carolina committed the same error. He was nominated by the assembly but refused to go. Though not as vocal as Henry nor as secretive as Chase, Jones probably also felt that there was no point in attending. If he disagreed with the outcome, which was almost certain, he would be in a better position to oppose it by remaining aloof.

The antinational North Carolina assembly viewed the problem with similar indifference. Indeed, it was only after much prodding from the Lawyers' party that it undertook to name anyone at all. Then it found that it had to include Lawyers because they were the only ones willing to go. Thomas Person and Timothy Bloodworth would surely have been named had they evinced any desire to attend. The assembly did name Governor Caswell, who had allied himself with the Jones forces on debtor-relief measures, but he also declined to serve, pleading a lack of funds. He later cooperated in the naming of nationalists to the delegation, as he had in forming the Annapolis delegation the year before. He does not seem to have felt very strongly about the convention movement, if indeed he understood it at all. Caswell had been a competent military commander in the war and he was an expert dealer in western lands, but he gave little evidence of political perception.

Along with Jones and Caswell, the assembly's original list contained William R. Davie, Richard D. Spaight, and Alexander Martin. When Jones and Caswell decided not to go, the governor searched for replacements, and his chief criteria seem to have been convenience and cost. Hugh Williamson and William Blount were already serving in Congress, and friends assured the governor that they were willing to make the short trip from New York to Philadelphia. Caswell accordingly made the nomination and the council approved.[86]

The North Carolina delegation, then, was packed with Lawyers. Alexander Martin was the only one whose politics were in doubt. As governor he had vacillated between the legislative parties, and he continued to waver at Philadelphia. Objecting to the ultranationalism of the convention, he left before it was over, but then reversed himself and backed the Constitution in the ratifying convention. Had Jones and Caswell consented to serve, they could have reinforced Martin's misgivings and given the antinationalists a three to two majority. Since the North Carolina delegation voted with the Virginia nationalists from the outset, a consistently different posture by that state might well have altered the events at Philadelphia.[87]

Even though Willie Jones followed the same pattern as Henry and Chase, it did not spell disaster for his cause. The division of opinion on the Constitution in North Carolina also followed the factional lines that had emerged in the legislature. But this is the one state where the debtor party was in firm control, and it is the one state where the Antifederalists were victorious.

CHAPTER TEN

Ratification with or without Amendments

ON SEPTEMBER 17, 1787, members of the federal convention signed the final draft of the Constitution and sent it to the states for approval. The document itself specified that the states were to elect special conventions to consider it, and it would go into effect when nine states ratified. Several delegates had left Philadelphia in the course of the summer, distressed with the nationalist trend of the convention. At the last minute, three other delegates—George Mason and Edmund Randolph of Virginia and Elbridge Gerry of Massachusetts—refused to lend their signatures because the document lacked a bill of rights. Their action assured the Constitution a stormy reception in the Chesapeake states.

Nearly everyone assumed that the reaction to the Constitution would follow partisan lines. In all three states parties had been forged out of the clash of interests on such issues as debts and taxation, paper money, Loyalist property, and judicial reform. The Constitution affected every one of these in one way or another. By granting Congress power to tax, it reduced the sources of state revenue and thus the potential for state action. This, in turn,

resurrected the old suspicions of national power wielded by merce-
nary Yankees. The power to regulate commerce and impose navigation acts only enhanced these suspicions. The Constitution's
protection of contracts and injunction against paper money effectively prohibited any future debtor-relief legislation, and the establishment of a federal judiciary promised a new set of courts manned
by trained judges and claiming superior powers. Antifederalists
might well be excused if they assumed that their old enemies had
sneaked in their whole economic program under the guise of
federal reform.

Although the party lines were familiar, the campaign for ratification was by its very nature a new type of election. Candidates
were chosen for a single purpose—to consider the Constitution.
And, although the issues were complex, the ultimate choice was
simple, "the single question of union or no union," in Edmund
Randolph's words.[1] As a result, voters looked at candidates in terms
of their stands on the Constitution, and in most districts candidates
felt obliged to pledge themselves in advance. For some years the
politics of personalities had been yielding to the politics of issues.
In 1785 religious questions had dominated assembly elections in
both Maryland and Virginia, and paper money had been the preem-
inent topic of discussion in all three states in 1786–87. These
controversies had also pioneered some new devices of propaganda
and persuasion. The Constitution presented a new opportunity to
practice these arts.

It also inspired some experiments in party organization.
Because every vote was critical, parties organized tickets in some
counties to avoid splitting their supporters. Party planners also
moved candidates from one constituency to another, sometimes to
secure a marginal victory in a divided county, sometimes to insure
the election of a respected leader. Though not yet fully respectable,
political parties were becoming established institutions, and for the
first time they divided on an issue of national importance. This, in
turn, opened the way for interstate alliances and the formation of a
national party system. The contest over ratification brought giant
strides in party organization and in the active participation of the
electorate.

MARYLAND: EARLY SKIRMISHES

"Baltimore resounds with friendship for the new constitution," Edmund Randolph reported to Madison on his way back from Philadelphia. Madison may have been puzzled by the Federalist tone of the communication, given Randolph's behavior at the end of the convention, but the news was nontheless welcome. Given the recent contest over paper money and the divisions within the Maryland delegation at Philadelphia, there was good reason to suppose that the state was evenly divided. The attitude of Baltimore was thus critical, and in Baltimore much depended on the stand of Samuel Chase.

Assuming Madison knew this, Randolph quickly launched into a résumé of his own interview with Chase. The night before he arrived in town, Chase had given a rousing speech at Fell's Point, which apparently shed more heat than light. Asked when he had finished whether he supported the Constitution or not, Chase enigmatically took out a copy of the Maryland constitution and said, "Here gentlemen is a form of government under which we have lived happily for more than ten years. Shall we make a new experiment precipitately?" Refusing to answer his own question, he simply declared that he had not made up his own mind. If Chase confused the Baltimore populace, he got his reward the next day when he called on Randolph. Suspecting that Chase was looking for ammunition, Randolph avoided any discussion of what had transpired at Philadelphia. Chase no doubt departed as puzzled as he was empty-handed.[2]

Samuel Chase never did undertake a thorough critique of the Constitution. He may have done so in one of his lengthy speeches in the Maryland ratifying convention, but the records of that convention are scanty and there is no surviving record of what was said. Some weeks after the Maryland convention ended Chase wrote to a New York Antifederalist to push the idea of amendments, but instead of listing the flaws in the Constitution that needed correcting, he contented himself with the observation that "The government is not a government of the people." Congressional districts, he felt, would be so extensive that the electorate would lack effective control over their representatives.[3] This was the only time in his life that Chase expressed any concern for the people, and it was the only time he sought to explain his opposition to the Constitution. The tardiness of the effort and its lack of depth suggest that Chase's real objections were personal, not philosophical. It seems likely that his own financial position was the primary consideration.

The role played by Luther Martin at Philadelphia was probably symptomatic of the reaction of the Chasites. Martin resisted the nationalists every step of the way and did his best to hold the Maryland delegation in the small-state camp. Finally, when he saw the form the Constitution was taking, he raced down to Baltimore to spread the alarm. Because convention delegates were sworn to secrecy, Martin could not publish his criticism, but he almost certainly confided in Chase. The misgivings of Mercer, who also left the convention early, and Chase's friend William Paca reinforced Martin's shrill accusations. The Chasites were firm in opposition before the great debate even began. The Constitution's prohibition of paper money was probably only one consideration. A national judiciary, with powers to entertain suits by citizens of other states and other countries, together with a firm power to make and enforce treaties, all spelled trouble for insolvent speculators.

Outside his immediate circle, however, Chase had little influence. Edmund Randolph's observation was accurate; the Constitution was generally popular in the state. That Chase himself recognized this was evident in his equivocation at Fell's Point. Given time, Chase might have chipped away at public support for the Constitution, but the fall election was at hand and the composition of the assembly was critical. The giants of Federalism, Thomas Johnson, Thomas Sim Lee, and Richard Potts, who had not appeared in the assembly for some years, stood for seats in the House "with a view principally of preventing mischief and forwarding this great object."[4] In order to secure his own election Chase let it be known that he favored the summoning of a convention to consider the Constitution. Immediately after the poll was taken he entered the newspapers under the pseudonym "Caution" to urge a delay in ratification until the Constitution could be amended.[5] One of the earliest pleas for conditional ratification, Chase's essay was a forecast of Antifederalist strategy in all three Chesapeake states.

Shortly after the assembly opened a resolution was introduced to invite the state's delegation at Philadelphia to give an explanation of the convention's proceedings. Federalists outside the assembly immediately assumed that this was an Antifederalist maneuver. "They want the Attorney General to harangue on the *mischievous intrigues & plots* of the Convention," said one.[6] Maneuver or no, the House agreed to the motion by 28 to 22.[7] Federalists, if they suspected a plot, evidently felt they could not oppose the motion without seeming to stifle discussion. As anticipated, the invitation gave Luther Martin a forum for a two-day diatribe, which he later elaborated upon in a pamphlet, *The Genuine Information.* In somewhat briefer appearances Mercer and Jenifer reinforced Martin's accusations. McHenry attempted to defend the Convention's action, but only intimate friends were impressed with his address.[8]

There followed a series of maneuvers that left everyone more confused than ever. The House agreed to a resolution calling for an election to be held early in April for a convention which was to meet on the twenty-first of that month. Senate Federalists quickly objected to the relatively late date. A committee headed by the two Carrolls recommended January elections and a March convention. It also wanted to impose a £500 property qualification on convention delegates and to limit the scope of their decisions to the mere "assent and ratification" of the Constitution. The Senate hoped to avoid a clause by clause discussion of the document, which would provide a forum for its critics. The Senate approved these resolutions unanimously, but the House, by a vote of 24 to 23, adhered to its stand. Again Federalists were divided, embarrassed perhaps by the illiberal partisanship of the Carrolls. The House then imposed a year's residence requirement on convention delegates and gave the convention broad powers to ratify, reject, or adjourn. Each of these resolutions passed by substantial margins. Unwilling to permit further delay that would only prolong the debate over the Constitution, the Senate acceded to the House resolutions.[9]

From the moment the lower house approved the resolution

summoning the convention delegates to appear before it the Federalists seemed in disarray, and the Senate's evident disdain for the rules of fair play only added to their embarrassment. Many apparently feared that the Senate's attempt to muzzle the convention would alienate moderates and the undecided. The result was a good deal of tactical voting that makes it impossible to determine party allegiances from these roll calls. However, it is possible to ascertain the eventual stand on the Constitution among those who served in 1788, either in the ratifying convention or the assembly. These results are given in table 10.1. Assuming that attitudes toward the Constitution were formed as early as the fall of 1787 and that few changed their minds (the evidence indicates that this was the case in all three states), the table suggests that the 1787 House of Delegates was evenly divided. That alone would explain the moderation, even the tactical uncertainty, among Federalists.

The basic party division of the mid-1780s persisted, but there were some changes in the regional alignment. The upper Potomac, an area that had been solidly debtor a few years before, was now evenly divided. By 1790 it would be solidly Federalist—the result of increased population, improvements in the Potomac, and the prospect of settling the national capital in the Potomac Valley. On the other hand, Federalist strength on the upper bay was only

TABLE 10.1   MARYLAND HOUSE OF DELEGATES: PARTIES IN 1787

	Federalists	Antifederalists	Middle
Eastern Shore	9	1	5
Upper bay	4	5	2
Western Shore	7	9	4
Upper Potomac	6	6	0
Urban	1	3	0
	27	24	11
Creditors, 1786	8	1	1
Debtors, 1786	1	5	1
Chasites, 1786	0	3	1
Unknown	18	15	8
	27	24	11

temporary, the anomalous attitudes of a few short-term delegates. In the spring 1788 election it went Antifederalist and remained so thereafter.

It is tempting to infer that the strong Antifederalist showing in this session was due to Samuel Chase and his speculator allies. The Chasites did account for the shift of the cities (Chase and McMechen in Baltimore, Allan Quynn in Annapolis) from creditor to Antifederalist, but otherwise they had little effect. They persuaded the House to grant speculators another year to discharge their obligations to the state, but the voting bore no relation to attitudes toward the Constitution.[10] Federalists backed the speculators by 14 to 9; Antifederalists divided evenly, 9 to 9. Among the Antifederalists were four Chasites, but the remainder were either new men or old debtors. Indebtedness to the state for confiscated property was a minor factor in shaping attitudes toward the Federal Constitution.[11]

What then were the main issues in Maryland's debate over ratification? Contemporaries all agreed that economic interests were the key. Federalists felt that debtors of all kinds were at the heart of opposition to the Constitution.[12] Baltimore merchant Samuel Smith, for instance, thought most of the opponents were men who owed debts to British merchants and therefore "dislike the Complexion of the Federal Courts."[13] Antifederalist writers, adopting a tone reminiscent of the paper money rhetoric of previous years, argued that the Constitution was an aristocratic plot to perpetuate rule by the rich.[14]

After the election, analysts were more inclined to point to the influence of speculators. "Baltimore and Harford counties alone are clearly Antifederal," wrote a correspondent of the *Pennsylvania Gazette*. In that area, he continued, "are many powerful and popular men who have speculated deeply in British confiscated property and for that reason are alarmed at shutting the door against state paper money. The same men . . . are more violently Anti-Federal because they paid considerable sums into the treasury in depreciated continental currency and are scared . . . about a due execution of the treaty between Great Britain and America."[15]

The conflict of interests had shaped the state's parties, and men naturally looked at the Constitution in the same light. How did it affect state relief legislation, tax policies, paper money, judicial reform? The same questions were asked in Virginia and North Carolina, and the results were essentially the same. The voting on the Constitution followed roughly the regional pattern that characterized the postwar parties.

The upper Potomac, traditionally debtor in outlook and pro—paper money, was the one region to shift its allegiance. A gradual shift had been under way for some years. Frederick County delegates were voting creditor as early as 1786; Washington County followed suit in 1787, leaving only Montgomery in the debtor camp. Change in political complexion was related to population and economic growth. This was true of the entire watershed, for a similar reversal took place in the Potomac–Shenandoah–South Branch counties of Virginia. It was not simply the kind of agriculture, for Potomac products did not differ markedly from those of other parts of Maryland.[16] It was instead a matter of development. The Potomac watershed was a land of enormous agricultural potential; it needed only to be opened. After the Revolution population flowed into the area, coming mostly from the older, creditor-oriented counties to the east. As the wilderness retreated, so did the debtor psychology of remote and isolated farmers. Improvements in the Potomac riverbed opened the interior to interstate and international trade and raised land prices, while bringing the up-country farmers into direct contact with Federalist merchants in Georgetown and Alexandria. Periodic rumors that the valley might be blessed with the location of the national capital enhanced the hopes of enterprising "boosters" and stimulated interest in federal affairs.[17]

MARYLAND'S DISCIPLINED PHALANX OF FEDERALISTS

The great debate waxed hotter as the April election date approached. Issues dominated from the outset. Personal influence—even from so prominent a personage as Charles Carroll—was almost completely submerged. Nearly every candidate felt obliged to declare his sentiments in advance, and when the dust settled observers were able to predict the outcome of the convention to the last vote. The Burkean concept of independent representation was fading. Voters chose representatives who would reflect their views.

The lower Eastern Shore was the most solidly Federalist part of the state. Like the adjacent parts of Delaware, it was a land of "steady habits," heavily influenced by Methodism, conservative in outlook.[18] In several counties Antifederalists did not even put up candidates. Antifederal opinions became more common toward the head of the bay. In northern Kent County the leading Federalist candidate thought that the election was in doubt up to the last moment. He was pleasantly surprised when the Antifederalist slate received less than a fourth of the votes.[19]

The situation was similar on the lower Western Shore. In the few counties where the Antifederalists posted candidates they were swamped, with the exception of Anne Arundel. That divided county was the scene of a ferocious party battle. Federalists put up a strong slate of Charles and James Carroll, Brice T. B. Worthington, and Annapolis lawyer John Hall, all prominent members of the assembly. Since Charles Carroll could easily have won election in his home county of Prince George's, his switch to Anne Arundel was undoubtedly an effort to lend his personal prestige to the cause.

The Antifederalist ticket was of nearly equal stature—Jeremiah Townley Chase, Annapolis lawyer, speculator, and cousin to Samuel; John Francis Mercer, who had attended the Philadelphia convention; and Benjamin Harrison, a member of the Governor's Council. Searching for a fourth candidate, Antifederalists approached Governor Smallwood and were turned down; they then put up Samuel Chase, even though Chase had moved to Baltimore a year before. Learning of his nomination, Chase raced down to Annapolis four days before the election and organized a campaign. He "harangued" in one part of the county while Mercer and J. T. Chase covered another part. Federalists, who had a nonresident candidate of their own, could hardly object to Chase's dubious qualifications, but they were annoyed at a Mercer handbill which portrayed the Constitution as a product of Robert Morris's financial schemes. The Federalist ticket lost the election by about 50 votes. With some justice, they blamed the Antifederalists' whirlwind campaign of rumor and innuendo.[20]

The Baltimore Town election was even wilder. For a time the only announced candidates were Samuel Sterett and David McMechen. The former was a newcomer to politics, but McMechen was a city attorney who had long represented the interests of the prominent Ridgely family and who invariably sided with Chase in the assembly.[21] Federalists relaxed when both candidates declared on their "honor as gentlemen" that they favored ratification without prior amendments. But then on the eve of the election Samuel Chase departed for Annapolis, while his friends William Paca and Luther Martin journeyed to Harford County. This alarmed Federalists, who wondered why the Antifederalists were giving up Baltimore without a contest. A hastily formed delegation waited upon the candidates once more. Under questioning, McMechen admitted he favored prior amendments, but Sterett merely resorted to a "petulant speech" (Samuel Smith's description) that enlightened no one. Federalists then quickly called a popular meeting which nominated James McHenry and Dr. John Coulter. The election was already under way at that point, but such were Federalists' resources of communication that they won by more than 500 votes. Both sides manipulated the poll shamelessly. Antifederalists admitted inserting some 250 fraudulent votes but claimed that Federalists cast almost 800 illegal votes. When it was over the Federalists organized a victory procession of several thousand citizens, led by the shipbuilders and merchants.[22]

Baltimore County, along with the rest of the upper bay, was Antifederalist country. County society was dominated by two prominent families, Ridgelys and Deyes. Captain Charles Ridgely and his cousin Charles Ridgely (son) "of William," had been perennials in the county delegation in the lower house since the end of the war. Captain Charles owned numerous plantations, forges, and mills in the county with over a hundred slaves, but he also owed the state some £11,000 for Loyalist property he had purchased. His cousin Charles of William was a man of more modest means and even more embarrassing debts. He owed British merchants £3,273, and when he was finally forced to pay (in 1790) it nearly bankrupted him.[23] Both men voted debtor in the assembly, and if their votes reflected their interests they also coincided with the wishes of their constituents. Otherwise the Deyes would have been more politically successful than they were.

Thomas Cockey Deye was also a perennial member of the Baltimore delegation, and the House of Delegates regularly elected him Speaker. Family wealth and personal prestige probably won him the honor,[24] but his politics were obviously also acceptable to the creditor majority. In 1787 Deye extended creditor influence in the Baltimore delegation by recruiting a popular young lawyer, Harry Dorsey Gough.[25] Gough defeated Ridgely of William for an assembly seat, and in the spring of 1788 he led the Federalist ticket for the ratifying convention. With him were "three more known Federalists," although their names were little known to the voters.[26]

One of these, George Lux, set out to make himself better known while educating voters in the process. Not only did he tell the electorate exactly how he planned to vote if elected, but he assessed the viewpoints of all the other candidates. He even discussed the relative strength of the parties in each section of the county with all the intimate knowledge of a twentieth-century precinct captain.[27] Federalist essayists warned voters against "a rich intriguing antifederal character" whose "embarrassed circumstances" dictated his votes, but they were unable to break Ridgely's hold on the county.[28] At the last minute they dropped Lux in favor of a better-known personality, Colonel John E. Howard, a hero of the Carolina campaigns, but it did them little good.[29] The Federalist ticket received less than 20 percent of the vote.[30]

Neighboring Harford County at the head of the bay was the most Antifederal of all. No Federalist candidate even stepped forward, and Chase treated it like a pocket borough. His young protégés Luther Martin and William Pinkney, neither of whom had held elective office before, journeyed up there from Baltimore to stand the poll, and William Paca slipped over from Federalist-dominated Queen Anne's. Pinkney, at least, had practiced law in the county; the other two had no better claim to residence than the possession of some Loyalist property. Together with the Baltimore and Anne Arundel delegations, Harford brought the total number of Antifederalists in the convention to 12, though from the outset there was some doubt about Paca, who had said he would vote for the Constitution if amendments were promised.[31]

The most interesting contests were in the upper Potomac counties. Outside of Baltimore these were the only places in the state where both parties put up slates of candidates and where newspapers kept careful record of the poll. The ferocity of the contest may have been the result of the political realignment the region was undergoing. The exception was Frederick County, which had sent creditors to the assembly since 1786 and where former governor Thomas Johnson's weighty voice assured a decision for the Constitution. Newspaper correspondents claimed that there was only one Antifederalist in the entire county.[32]

Montgomery was another story. Its assembly delegation, led for the past decade by Laurence Oneale, was solidly debtor, and all four delegates declared themselves candidates for the ratifying convention. Of the Federalist candidates, two were new to politics; the others had been politically inactive for some years. Two were wealthy planters; the others were Georgetown merchants (one a member of the Potomac Company). Reputation probably meant little, for the poll, together with the labels conferred by the newspapers, indicated that voting was exclusively by party (see table 10.2). Despite the substantial Federalist margin, the county was still in the process of realignment. In the assembly election later that summer the electorate sent two Federalists and two Antifederalists (including Oneale) to the lower house. Old ties were hard to break.

TABLE 10.2   MONTGOMERY COUNTY, MARYLAND:
ELECTION FOR RATIFYING CONVENTION

Thomas Cramphin	896	Edward Burgess	313
Richard Thomas	895	Lawrence Oneale	312
William Deakins, jr.	894	William Holmes	312
Benjamin Edwards, Esq.	891	Henry Griffith	311
"(These four gentlemen are Federal)"			"(Antifederal)"

SOURCE: *Maryland Journal* [Baltimore], Apr. 15, 1788. The party labels were given by the newspaper.

The story of Washington County was much the same. Its assembly delegation was also old debtor, and three of the four offered for the ratifying convention. Declaring for the Constitution were Colonel Thomas Sprigg, reputed to be the wealthiest man in the county, John Stull, a convert from the debtor party, and two political newcomers.[33] Two of the Federalists and one Antifederalist were of German extraction. Germans were an important ethnic element in all the western counties, but no one was sure where they stood politically. Stull, himself a German, thought most favored the Constitution, and by 1789 with the first congressional elections, they do seem to have been predominantly Federalist (see chapter 11). At this point, both sides were anxious not to alienate them. In neighboring Frederick County, Federalists placed a German, Abraham Faw, on their ticket, even though Faw was a Chasite with a mixed record in the assembly. One Federalist who was unhappy with the choice rationalized it thus. Faw, he wrote, was "a German and as this kind of people forms a very numerous & industrious part of the Community; it is well enough I think & not inconsistent with policy that they should be indulged in having one of their own class for to represent them."[34] Antifederalists also placed a German on their ticket in each of the western counties, so the effect of ethnicity in this election is difficult to gauge. More important factors, probably, in the realignment of the west were the opening of the Potomac and contacts with the solidly Federalist Shenandoah and South Branch valleys of Virginia. Western Virginia was undergoing a similar realignment under the stimulus of border warfare. By the spring of 1788 Indian raiding parties were penetrating deep into Harrison County (Clarksburg), only a few miles from the Maryland settlements on the upper Potomac. Whatever their motives, Washington County voters were solidly Federalist. The four Federalist candidates each received 657 ballots; Antifederalists varied from a high of 25 to a low of 14. The results sent to newspapers again labeled each candidate by party.[35]

The sweep of the west gave Federalists a total of 64 delegates, and no one expected last-minute switches. With the exception of Paca, all delegates were publicly committed.[36] Maryland Federalists hastily posted the results to friends in Virginia, hoping to bolster the cause south of the Potomac.[37] Their only remaining concern was that the convention might utilize the power given it by the assembly to adjourn from day to day until the results of the Virginia convention were known. Washington and Madison issued repeated warnings against this tactic, lest it boost the morale of Virginia Antifederalists and give them "a fatal advantage." They also wanted Maryland to keep up the momentum. If both Maryland and South Carolina ratified, Virginia could be the critical ninth state. "The pride of the State is already touched upon this string," said Washington, "and will be raised much higher if there is fresh cause."[38]

The Virginians need not have worried. The ranks of Maryland Federalism were trimmed with quarterdeck efficiency. The convention assembled in Annapolis on Monday, April 21, elected George Plater president, and adjourned. The Federalists, with all but two of their members present,[39] held a caucus that evening, the first ever recorded in Maryland. The conclave agreed to a resolution that the Constitution ought to be approved quickly since it was unlikely that, after seven months of discussion, "any new lights could be thrown on the subject" and because "each delegate was under a sacred obligation to vote conformably to the sentiments of his constituents."[40] In practice it meant that the Federalist majority would not waste time with words, nor would it tolerate any changes in the Constitution. Next to an inconclusive adjournment, the Federalists feared amendments, which might induce other states to reconsider or perhaps even force a second federal convention. Edmund Randolph and George Mason had introduced the subject at Philadelphia, and other states, notably Massachusetts and Virginia, had discussed the possibility throughout the winter. Maryland newspapers even reprinted some northern essays on the subject. At least one Maryland election turned on the question of amendments (Baltimore Town), and it was widely assumed that political trimmer William Paca was coming to Annapolis with a pocketful.

To record its actions, the convention appointed Dr. Thomas Lloyd, a Philadelphian who had taken notes at the Pennsylvania convention. Fortunately for the Federalists, their opponents never discovered that Lloyd had originally been employed to spy on the Maryland convention by Philadelphia merchant Tench Coxe.[41]

Samuel Chase would have made a feast of such a juicy morsel. Lloyd's journal, if he kept one, has since been lost, and as a result the only testimony as to what transpired is in two letters published shortly before the convention ended. The first was an Antifederalist exposé entitled "A Fragment of Facts Disclosing the Conduct of the Maryland Convention . . . ," and the other a Federalist reply written by Alexander Contee Hanson.[42] It matters little, for there was no genuine debate such as Virginia witnessed. The Federalists, secure in their overwhelming majority, moved with silent precision; the Antifederalists were verbose, peevish, and disorganized. Their most important leaders, Chase, Paca, and Martin, did not even appear until the fourth day when the convention was ready to vote.

On Tuesday the convention adopted rules and examined credentials. Significantly, the Federalists did not even bother to challenge the legitimacy of Chase, Paca, Martin, and Pinkney, who did not reside in the counties they represented, in violation of the rules laid down by the assembly. It would have taken additional time, especially since three of the four had not yet appeared (perhaps for that same reason the Antifederalists were deliberately tardy). The parties were so lopsided that their votes did not matter much, in any case. Then on Wednesday the Constitution was read and the convention resolved against debating it clause by clause. This forestalled a tedious discussion of details and confined the debate to generalities.

On Thursday Chase at last appeared, obtained the floor, and spoke for two and a half hours. When he sat down "a profound silence ensued," and after some time Thomas Johnson observed that as there was nothing before the House they should adjourn for dinner. It was unaccustomed treatment for a man who had been at the vortex of controversy for so long, and all the more humiliating when his own friends failed to pick up the cue. Luther Martin, it turned out, had a sore throat, a disability which smug Federalists felt "saved a great deal of time and money to the state."[43]

During the recess William Paca arrived in the city, and when the convention reassembled late in the afternoon he took the floor. He had a number of objections to the Constitution, he explained, and desired amendments. But the amendments need not be a condition of ratification, he said, seeking to quiet Federalist fears. It would be sufficient if the amendments simply accompanied the ratification as a guide for future congressional action. He had not, however, had time to draft the amendments and asked the convention to adjourn until morning. His tone was moderate and his request reasonable; Thomas Johnson accordingly moved the adjournment. Like a number of Virginians, including Jefferson, Johnson felt that some legal guarantees for the rights of citizens could be added to the Constitution without jeopardizing the fundamental powers of the new government. Moreover, the unseemly haste with which the Federalist phalanx was moving made him uncomfortable. He recognized that they would only injure their own cause by stifling discussion.[44] Paca had great influence in the upper Eastern Shore and deserved to be heard. Some Federalists were concerned over Johnson's conciliatory gesture, which left them exposed on the flanks, but they covered their discomfiture by agreeing to the motion.

During the night Paca prepared his amendments, and the Federalists regrouped. The next morning, as soon as Paca arose to offer his amendments he was interrupted. One by one delegates arose, one from each of the Federalist counties, and solemnly declared that they had been elected for the sole purpose of ratifying the Constitution and were not authorized by their constituents to consider amendments. When Paca stood up again, Federalist George Gale called him to order, protesting that the question of amendments could not be taken up while the main question of ratification was before the House. Speaker Plater sustained the point, and Paca was not allowed even to read his proposals. Antifederalists thundered for the rest of the day and into Saturday morning against the ruling, but their opponents simply sat "inflexibly silent." When the Antifederalists had talked themselves out, the majority called for the question and carried it, 63 to 11. The lineup followed the election results exactly, with the exception of Paca.

As soon as the tally was in, Paca was on his feet to explain that he had voted for the Constitution "under the firm persuasion" that it would be amended. A resolution to set up a committee of thirteen headed by Paca (together with nine Federalists and three

Antifederalists) then passed by 66 to 7, and the committee was instructed to consider Paca's amendments, as well as others. Meeting on Sunday, April 27, the committee approved 13 amendments, "most of them by a very great majority." All were procedural guarantees, designed to protect trial by jury, prohibit unwarranted searches and seizures, and protect freedom of speech and press. Another 15 amendments were then submitted and rejected. These would have involved more substantive changes—restricting the powers of Congress over taxation and trade and limiting the President's treaty-making power and authority over the army. Afraid that individual Antifederalists might submit the 15 amendments to the convention anyway, Alexander C. Hanson sought guarantees that only the committee's report would be considered. He also wanted to issue an address to the people stipulating that the amendments were intended only to quell the fears of the opposition and did not imply that there were flaws in the Constitution. This, he later told Madison, was designed to prevent the Maryland amendments from being used as ammunition by Virginia Antifederalists.[45]

Chase refused but offered to compromise. He would not push for additional amendments on the floor if Federalists on the committee would accept 3. The amendments demanded by Chase (and the choice demonstrates his limited grasp of the issues at stake) would have (1) prevented militia from serving beyhond the limits of an adjoining state without legislative consent, (2) prevented Congress from altering the time of elections, and (3) suspended any direct tax imposed by Congress if the state furnished the sum to the federal government first. This proposition was quickly voted down, although Thomas Johnson again broke Federalist ranks to support it. Chase then threatened to bring before the convention any amendment "he might deem proper," whereupon the committee rescinded its support even for the original 13.

Committee Federalists spread the word of what was afoot, and when the convention met Monday morning it quickly passed a resolution stating that it would consider no propositions except those formally submitted by the committee of thirteen. Paca then rose to describe what had passed in the committee, read the 13 amendments originally agreed to, and explained why the committee had no formal report. A motion to agree to the 13 amendments as well as Chase's 3 was shouted down, and a motion to adjourn passed, 47 to 26.[46] Voting against adjournment were 14 Federalists, who presumably wished to stay and discuss amendments. Of those who had served in the assembly earlier, 4 had been creditors, 2 Chasites, and 2 had mixed records. In 1789 one would vote Antifederalist in the assembly and one agree to serve on an Antifederalist ticket for Presidential electors. These two became Republicans; the rest remained Federalists. Like Thomas Johnson, who was among their number, they seem to have shared some disposition to amend the Constitution in minor ways. But the division in Federalist ranks was neither serious nor permanent.

When the convention quit, the enraged Antifederalists took to the press and to the streets. At first they sought to arouse public sympathy by exposing the Federalists' lack of fair play, and when that failed they turned their attention to the fall assembly elections. If anything, those were even more furiously fought than the convention contests. Strangely, though, the Antifederalists made no effort to influence the Virginia convention, due to meet only a few weeks later in Richmond. Federalists worried mightily about the effect that Maryland's proposed amendments (which were printed in the newspapers) might have on the wavering in Virginia. A widely circulated address or an agent at the assembly door in Richmond might have given Patrick Henry the ammunition he needed. But the Marylanders never made the effort. It was their ultimate failure.

BRITISH DEBTS AND THE REALIGNMENT
OF WESTERN VIRGINIA

When the battle over ratification in Virginia was all over, Madison summarized the results for Jefferson. "The articles relative to Treaties, to paper money, and to contracts," he wrote, "created more enemies than all the errors in the System positive and negative put together."[47] Aware of Jefferson's equivocal attitude toward the Constitution, Madison was anxious to assure him that they were battling the same enemies they had fought since the end of the war—and that the issues were essentially the same. To a large extent that was true, and for that reason the contest in Virginia over ratification was extremely close. Indeed, the Constitution would surely have been rejected in Virginia, had westerners not shifted to the Madison camp, after years of voting with the Henryites.

The reason was frontier warfare, sparked by a senseless raid of George Rogers Clark, who burned the Shawnee settlements at Chillicothe and Old Piqua in 1786. Clark's invasion united the Ohio tribes, who retaliated against the white settlements in Kentucky, Virginia, and Pennsylvania.[48] Begging for help, westerners told the authorities in Richmond that if they lacked the resources to defend the frontier, they ought to seek aid from "the United States."[49] The Constitution promised even more effective federal aid;[50] the people of western Virginia gave it solid support.

The border warfare also demonstrated at last the price they were paying for easterners' debts. So long as the Ohio forests were relatively tranquil, westerners cared little about British occupation of the Great Lakes forts. But Indian raids invariably fostered rumors of British meddling. Never willing to admit that the Indian wars were a product of their own land hunger and sharp trading, frontiersmen found a convenient scapegoat in the British presence. And it required no great expenditure of intellectual energy to transfer the blame from the British to eastern planters.

Throughout 1786, as frontier tension heightened, the triangular connection between British merchants, the London foreign office, and the Ohio wilderness became increasingly clear. In May of that year John Adams sent new dispatches outlining further conversations with British Foreign Secretary Lord Carmarthen. In response to a request that Britain evacuate the Great Lakes posts, the secretary had refused on grounds that several states were violating the peace treaty on the question of prerevolutionary debts. He added, according to Adams, "That whenever the States shew a disposition to fulfill the treaty on their part, the King will perform his engagements according to good faith." Virginians in Congress quickly transmitted the word, and Virginia newspapers carried excerpts from the dispatches during the summer.[51] For westerners, huddling fearfully in their wilderness cabins, the solution was obvious: eliminate the restrictions on debt collection and reinforce the military strength of the central government.

Eastern Virginians made a similar connection. They were less concerned about who possessed the Great Lakes, but they did recognize the effect the Federal Constitution would have on their financial obligations. Edmund Randolph, after surveying Virginia opinion, decided that the likelihood "of every defendant being hurried sooner or later to the seat of the federal government" to face British law suits was "the most vulnerable and odious part of the constitution." As members of the legislature gathered in Richmond that fall, the governor predicted that the votes on British debts would be a good indication of the fate of the Constitution.[52] Madison, in New York for the congressional session, thought the same. He was still uncertain of Virginia's reaction, he told Philadelphia Federalist Tench Coxe a month after the Constitution was published. However, the legislature was assembling, and in a few days he expected to be able "to form a tolerable estimate of opinions there."[53]

On November 14, 1787, only ten days after his triumph over paper money, George Mason brought before the House of Delegates a resolution to repeal all the laws that were in conflict with the treaty of peace. After "three days of warm debate" Mason concluded that he needed to compromise in order to undermine Patrick Henry's support. He agreed to a clause suspending the act until other states passed similar laws. That move split the debtor party, and when Patrick Henry moved to suspend Virginia's action until Britain complied with the peace treaty first, he went down to defeat, 42 to 75. Mason also turned aside a proposal to pay British debts by installments, and his resolution then passed, 72 to 42.[54] A tabulation of these roll calls (table 10.3) shows the split in the debtor party between moderates (led, according to Mason, by George Nicholas) and Henryites. It also reveals the shift in western opinion, and the effect this would have on ratification.

AMENDMENT POLITICS

Kept informed of these legislative battles, Madison by early December felt he could see three "parties" in Virginia. Some

TABLE 10.3   VIRGINIA HOUSE OF DELEGATES: BRITISH
DEBTS, 1787

	Creditors	Moderate Debtors	Henryites
Northern Neck	9	1	0
Middle Tidewater	5	6	0
Southside	6	15	8
Piedmont	1	6	1
West	21	0	0
	42	28	9
Federalists	20	4	0
Antifederalists	1 (Mason)	17	7
Middle	2	0	0
Unknown	19	7	2
	42	28	9

favored approving the Constitution as it stood. A second group, led
by George Mason and Edmund Randolph, approved the substance
of the Constitution but desired "a few additional guards in favor of
the Rights of the States and of the People." Then there was a "third
Class, at the head of which is Mr. Henry. This class concurs at
present with the patrons of amendments, but will probably contend
for such as strike at the essence of the System." Support for the
Constitution, he thought, was centered in the Northern Neck and
the west; the Southside was opposed and the remainder of the state
divided.[55]

Madison's analysis was reasonably accurate. The Antifederalists were internally divided. Patrick Henry led the extremists who
opposed any change in the Articles of Confederation, any extension
of federal power. He had considerable support in the region south
of the James, but, except for some old friends like Theodorick
Bland and the Cabells, few prominent Antifederalists agreed with
him. At the other end of the Antifederalist spectrum was George
Mason, who had shared in the constitution-making until the last
minute when he objected to the lack of a bill of rights. Even then, as
he confided to Washington, "a little moderation & Temper in the
latter end of the Convention might have removed" his objections.

He would have been satisfied with a few amendments dealing with civil rights and judicial procedures.[56]

Edmund Randolph, who joined Mason in refusing to sign the Constitution, also worried about national powers and popular rights. But Randolph was never able to pursue an independent path for long, and after agitating for several months in favor of a conditional ratification he joined the Federalist camp.[57] Mason, temperamentally more doctrinaire and philosophically more committed to individual rights, stayed with the Antifederalists, and by midwinter he was campaigning actively against the Constitution. "I would think he might have been satisfied with the publication of his objections," grumbled David Stuart, "without taking the pains to lodge them at every house."[58] When the ratifying convention opened in June, Mason entered the door arm in arm with Patrick Henry, a gesture that caused a number of raised eyebrows in Richmond.[59]

Richard Henry Lee was yet another type of Antifederalist. Lee had sided with Madison on paper money and British debts, and he favored some strengthening of the Articles of Confederation. He was prepared to grant Congress the power to tax, and he felt that state laws in conflict with congressional acts ought to be "*ipso facto* void."[60] On his way to the congressional session in the summer of 1787 he stopped in Philadelphia to learn what he could of the convention proceedings. He concluded that the delegates were creating "a Government not unlike the B. Constitution—that is an Executive with 2 branches composing a federal Legislature and possessing adequate Tone." Added Lee: "This departure from simple Democracy seems indispensably necessary, if any government at all is to exist in N. America."[61] George Mason had not, at that point, raised the question of excessive power, but there is no indication that Lee was concerned about civil freedoms anyway. What concerned Lee was not the extent of power but who would wield it. If Mason pointed out that northern merchants were likely to have an important voice in the new regime and thus make use of federal powers to dominate southern trade, Lee would turn against the whole scheme.[62] Benjamin Harrison, who shared Lee's fears, flatly predicted that under the Constitution "the States south of the

Potomac will be little more than appendages to those to the north-ward of it."[63]

Other Madison allies, William Grayson and James Monroe, straddled the fence for months before coming down on the Anti-federalist side. What finally moved them is not clear. Grayson, like Lee, had long voiced suspicions of northern merchants, of Robert Morris in particular. Monroe seems to have been swept along by a mixture of pride and friendship. As a member of Congress, he felt entitled to a place on Virginia's delegation to the federal convention. He blamed Madison for the omission, but did not interrupt his correspondence with Madison. Privately he told Madison he favored the Constitution; in public he remained a cipher. His uncertainty was evident from a pamphlet he wrote during the spring of 1788. Three-fourths of it was a critique of the Articles of the Confederation and a plea for stronger government. His objections to the Constitution were unpersuasive. He disliked the federal judiciary, for instance, even though a congressional committee he chaired had recommended precisely that only a year before. His friends Grayson and Joseph Jones persuaded him to stand for a seat in the ratifying convention. When the lost the election in King George, Spotsylvania Antifederalists added him to their ticket. After winning, he continued to profess neutrality on the Constitution, though he finally voted against it.[64]

Shortly after returning from Philadelphia, Edmund Randolph suggested that the Virginia assembly circulate a list of desired changes in the Constitution. If other states responded favorably to the list, Virginia could ratify on the condition that the changes be incorporated into the Constitution. Antifederalists scooped up the plan because it was the one common ground they had. Those who wished for guarantees of civil rights and those who wanted to emasculate federal powers could both agree on the need for amendments. A conditional ratification, moreover, would throw everything into confusion. It might even force a second federal convention. Best of all, the call for amendments masked Patrick Henry's extremism and enabled Antifederalists to attract the undecided. Federalists found that friends of the Constitution who desired minor changes were "drawn into steps favouring the antifederal scheme."[65]

On the federal side there were similar divisions of opinion. Those who had fought the debtor-relief battles of past years knew precisely what they wanted in the new system. But their aim was not so much private advantage as public good, though the two often coincided. Advising Washington to hold on to his military pay certificates, a Federalist friend wrote: "If the proposed constitution be agreed to, . . . the public securities will appreciate and in a few years perhaps be of considerable value."[66] Instead Washington cashed his certificates and used the proceeds to pay his state taxes. To him honor was more important than cash flow.[67] National honor was a common theme of Federalist addresses, and it meant both domestic stability and international pride. General Adam Stephen, aging veteran of the Indian wars, hoped that a strengthened government could curb some of the "wild men" of the West who were cheating Indians and inciting warfare. Internationally, he predicted that "Congress will have as many Ambassadors as Augustus Caesar had when he first came to the Imperial throne. . . . Few states in Europe will command equal respect."[68]

Few Federalists, however, were as unflinching in their devotion to the Constitution as Washington, Madison, or John Marshall. A number were attracted by the idea of amendments. In Paris, Jefferson, who had generally approved Madison's blueprint, found many a "bitter pill" in the final draft. He particularly objected to the perpetual eligibility of the President for reelection and the lack of a bill of rights. In February 1788 he sent to Richmond merchant Alexander Donald his own plan for conditional ratification. After the Constitution was approved by the requisite nine states, he suggested, the remaining four ought to hold out for amendments. Patrick Henry somehow obtained a copy of this letter and used it in the ratifying convention as evidence of Jefferson's support for conditional ratification. By then, however, Jefferson had decided that the only amendments really necessary were procedural guarantees for the rights of citizens, and he felt these could be added after the Constitution went into effect.[69]

"I am for it and against it," exclaimed John Breckinridge, who had recently moved across the mountains to Albemarle County. "I sufficiently despise the present [system] and the one proposed has some Fundamental Objections." At the same time, Breckinridge feared that a second convention might aggravate state jealousies and endanger the entire movement. Other waverers followed the same path. John Page of Rosewell on the York River, whose enormous wealth barely matched his illustrious lineage, favored amendments and a second convention until he found that critics of the Constitution could not agree on the kind of amendments they wanted. Without an agenda a second convention could prove a disaster. Far better, suggested Joseph Jones, who had his own reservations about the Constitution, to rely on "the wisdom and moderation of the legislature rather than impede putting the new plan in motion."[70] Prominent justices of the Court of Appeals, whose early criticism had worried the Federalists, also shifted in the course of the winter, apparently on the same line of reasoning.[71] By the time of the April elections Federalists were generally agreed on a strategy. The convention would ratify unconditionally but recommend changes for future action. This compromise brought the political chameleon Edmund Randolph back into the fold, though he waited until the convention opened to announce his conversion.[72]

VIRGINIA APPROVES, WITH RESERVATIONS

In the fall 1787 session of the assembly the motion to summon a convention to consider the Constitution produced "a great ferment," Governor Randolph reported, with Patrick Henry, William Cabell, French Strother, and Theodorick Bland "among the heroes of the opposition." But then the resolution authorizing a convention "freely to discuss and deliberate on the constitution" passed unanimously. Randolph felt that the addition of this phrase appeased the Antifederalists because it would enable them to talk it to death. Perhaps a better explanation of the unanimous vote is that neither side was as yet willing to test its strength. The two sides also agreed on dating the convention as late as possible in order to see how other states acted. Federalists hoped to profit from the psychological effect of ratification elsewhere; their opponents needed time to organize interstate alliances. If the other states proved to be divided, Virginia could "mediate," as Monroe put it, "& lead the way to an union more palatable to all."[73] The assembly accordingly set the convention for June 1788. Whether from design or accident, its meeting would coincide with conventions in the two other predominantly Antifederal states, New York and North Carolina.

Monroe claimed that he was elected to the convention without publicly committing himself on the Constitution, but he was almost the only one who was.[74] For several years elections in Virginia, as in Maryland, had increasingly focused on issues. Only the previous spring Virginians had been entertained by the novel sight of assembly candidates "declaiming" their views on paper money in village streets. The fight over the Constitution was the culmination of this process.

As in the paper money contest, it was widely assumed that victorious candidates would stand by their pledges and reflect the wishes of the voters, and the citizenry was quick to make its opinions known. Shortly after the Constitution was published, an informant told Madison that "The freeholders of Fairfax have, in the most pointed terms directed Col. Mason to vote for a convention [in the assembly], and have as pointedly assured him he shall not be in it."[75] Judge James Mercer, an Antifederalist, felt that the people of Fairfax were so solidly Federalist that Mason was the only opponent of the Constitution who even had a chance of winning there.[76] Mason himself declined to test his popularity and prudently moved over to neighboring Stafford County, where he possessed other property, to stand for his seat. On the other hand, George Nicholas, who often pursued an independent path in the assembly, evidently sampled opinion in Albemarle and decided to support the Constitution "however contrary it may be to his own opinions."[77]

Voters in the Antifederal Piedmont and Southside were equally determined. In Amherst County, where the Cabells won with ease, even those who were not eligible to vote "loudly and openly declared themselves in favor of the gentlemen elected."[78] In Powhatan, across the James from Richmond, Edward Carrington reported that the Constitution was so popular that one of the candidates, even though he privately opposed it, felt obliged to declare himself a Federalist. That and his standing as a member of the assembly enabled him to win by seven votes over Carrington, who had never held elective office.[79] In the ratifying convention, however, the delegate, Thomas Turpin, crossed the electorate and voted against the Constitution. The following year he was turned out of the assembly, even though the county itself had become Antifederalist, and he never again served in elected office.

Heightened voter awareness, in turn, forced political candidates to organize more elaborate campaigns. Monroe may have been able to maintain an air of detached statesmanship, but his supporters went to extraordinary lengths in his Fredericksburg district. Federalists facetiously worried that Justice James Mercer would "injure his lungs . . . haranguing" against the Constitution, but they showed real concern about Antifederalists' ability to "poison and prejudice the lower orders of People."[80]

In Orange County, Madison's opponents derived most of their support from the Baptists, who were apparently disappointed at the Constitution's failure to guarantee religious freedom. Madison's lieutenants moved through the Baptist settlements reminding all who would listen of Madison's role in securing disestablishment in Virginia, but opinion in this Piedmont county remained evenly divided.[81] So close was the contest that Madison raced home from New York in order to be present at the poll. On the morning of the election he stood on the courthouse steps and spoke for an hour and three-quarters before the polls opened. Observers thought he won his majority there on the spot.[82]

In early April, Alexandria Federalist Charles Lee informed Washington that "Except from Kentucky, the conventioners are known, and the sentiments of almost all of them have been declared which furnishes some ground for ascertaining the decision of Virginia with respect to the constitution. . . . The majority is in favor of the constitution [but] only [by] about ten or twelve votes." Before long newspapers were circulating an "accurate list" of the victorious candidates and their stands on the Constitution.[83] All this was small comfort to the Federalists, however, for a tie in the east meant that the outcome in Virigina would depend on the ballots of the Kentucky delegates. And it was widely suspected that Kentucky was opposed to the Constitution.

Throughout the 1780s Kentuckians had been given no reason to respect federal authority. Congress had offered no aid in their Indian troubles; it had kept a "hands off" attitude toward their dispute with Virginia; and it had ignored their repeated pleas for statehood. When Congress did act, it was often to their injury. John Jay's request for authority to negotiate a closure of the Mississippi demonstrated that northern merchants would abandon them if it suited their purses, and Kentuckians feared that the same interests might dominate the new government.[84] Kentuckians also seemed better able to handle their problems than the people of western Virginia. They kept the Indians at bay by sending raids deep into Ohio, and they opened negotiations with Spanish officials in New Orleans for trade concessions in the event of independence.[85]

Although most Kentuckians could see no advantages in the Constitution, there were some differences of opinion; and, not surprisingly, the variations followed party lines. The court party, made up of Virginia emigrés, many of whom wanted total independence, disliked every feature of the Constitution. They resented having to pay taxes to a distant and not very responsive authority, and they feared that congressional power over tariffs would prevent them from enacting their own duties to encourage western commerce and manufacturing. The judiciary features were even more alarming. Since the federal courts would certainly be in the East, Kentuckians would have to cross the mountains to try their claims against speculators before unfriendly juries. Their past experience with Congress, moreover, gave them good reasons to expect that eastern speculators would have a large voice in the new government and its courts. Harry Innes, attorney general for the western district, was the leading spokesman for this viewpoint. Virginia Federalists sought repeatedly to reassure him on these matters, but he remained unconvinced until Madison in 1789 arranged for a federal district court for Kentucky and President Washington named Innes to it.[86]

The partisans, mostly landless migrants from Pennsylvania and North Carolina, floundered in confusion. They had earlier supported independence from Virginia, with the stipulation that the state enter the union with representation in Congress. The Jay-Gardoqui interchange eliminated that plan for the time being and left the partisans without a program. Most of them remained silent on the subject of the Constitution. As a result, the only friends the Constitution had in Kentucky were in the tiny "country party"—Virginians, such as Thomas Marshall and James Breckinridge, who went to Kentucky as surveyors and speculators. They favored political separation from Virginia but wanted to maintain the commercial ties. The most articulate exponent of this point of view was young Humphrey Marshall, a nephew of Thomas, who combined the developmental mentality of the court party with the unionism of the partisans. He would remain the central figure in Kentucky Federalism for the next quarter century. Then—and later—his problem was numbers. In the election to the ratifying convention, Marshall and Robert Breckinridge won seats, but otherwise the Antifederal court party swept the field. The one ray of hope for Federalism was that nearly all the court party leaders refused to become candidates. They were much more interested in the separation convention scheduled for June 1788. The one exception was John Brown, who was elected to the ratifying convention while serving in Congress. Unlike other court party leaders, Brown supported the Constitution from the beginning. Evidently his congressional experience broadened his horizons.[87] Even so, the Kentucky delegation stood 11 to 3 against the Constitution as the conventioners gathered in Richmond early in June 1788.[88]

Aside from the Kentuckians, each side went to great pains to field its first team. Every prominent man in the state, except Washington and Richard Henry Lee, secured a seat. The oratory was brilliant and prolonged as the convention took literally its mandate "freely to discuss and deliberate." Public interest was at a fever pitch. So many persons wanted to attend the debates that the convention had to adjourn from the assembly chamber to the Play House. In Fredericksburg crowds greeted the thrice-weekly stage that brought news from Richmond, and partisan spirits rose and fell with every point scored on the convention floor.[89]

The performance was splendidly staged, but it failed to sway many minds. Nearly all the delegates were committed in advance, and they followed the wishes of their constituents. "We have 82 members unmovably fixed for it," announced Archibald Stuart after two weeks of debate, "12 doubtful & ye balance [74] against us as unmovable."[90] Since 86 was the necessary majority, neither side could relax until the final ballot was taken. The uncommitted, though few, were crucial. Most were moderate critics of the Constitution who could be swayed by the promise of amendments. Federalists could not accept prior amendments, for that would imply that Virginia's ratification was conditional. And that, in turn, would foster "a spirit of innovation," as Washington put it, which could "overturn the whole system." Suggestions for change made after ratification, however, could do no harm, and Federalists let it be known that they could accept "a few declaratory truths not affecting its validity." That was apparently sufficient to stall Patrick Henry's drive for conditional ratification.[91]

On June 25, the convention rejected, 88 to 80, a resolution to circulate amendments to other states and then ratified the Constitution, 89 to 79.[92] It then named a committee to draft amendments. On June 27 the committee returned with two sets of amendments. One was a list of procedural guarantees for the rights of citizens. Federalists raised no objection, and the convention agreed to it without a division. The other set of amendments was directed at federal powers. One would have denied federal courts jurisdiction over cases that had arisen prior to ratification—a blanket that would have covered British debts, Loyalist claims, and Kentucky land suits. Another amendment would have forced Congress to levy internal taxes by assigning quotas to each state. The scheme was administratively awkward but not deadly. Since customs duties were not affected, the new government would have had sufficient revenue to survive. It was evidence only of the Antifederalists' dilemma. They could not afford to stand pat on the Articles of Confederation but could not concoct a suitable alternative.

The convention agreed to the substantive amendments by voice vote. Then a motion to strike out the tax amendment failed by 65 to 85.[93] Although a number of members abstained, the roll call was still the most interesting of the convention. Voting to retain the tax amendment were 16 Federalists, among them Edmund

Randolph and the appellate court justices (Pendleton, Fleming, and Carrington) who had wavered throughout the winter. These men may still have been "undecided," but among others the vote was probably tactical.[94]

Antifederalists had failed to win agreement on prior amendments, but Federalists could not prevent substantive amendments from being considered at some point.[95] It may even be that some of them voted in favor of the relatively harmless tax amendment as a method of silencing criticism. Half of those who supported this idea, it is interesting to note, remained Federalists through the party battles of the 1790s. The remainder were from counties that were either predominantly Antifederalist or evenly divided.[96]

Whatever the intent, the vote on amendments restored a gentlemanly comraderie, and the convention broke up "in friendship & Amity." Even Patrick Henry announced that he was willing to give the new government a chance. A month later Joseph Jones surveyed public reaction and reported that "A general acquiescence under the decision of our convention seems to prevail through the country."[97]

THE CHESAPEAKE AND THE CONSTITUTION: A MULTIVARIANT ANALYSIS

Even though there is abundant evidence that the delegates to the ratifying conventions committed themselves in advance and felt they were representing the views of their constituents, it still seems useful to search out the personal factors that entered into their behavior. Lacking modern opinion polls, it is not possible to assay the attitudinal preferences of the eighteenth-century electorate.[98] The historian is necessarily confined to the governing elite. Yet the county delegate at least represents the lowest echelon of that elite; he is as close as we can get to the elusive "common man."

A multivariant analysis of Virginia Federalists and Antifederalists was published some years ago.[99] The technique has since been applied to Marylanders, and a comparison of the two states yields some interesting results. Briefly, the method was this. A list of known Federalists and Antifederalists was compiled for each state.

In order to make the sample as large as possible, those who served in the assembly were added to those who served only in the ratifying conventions. The combination was possible because, among those who served in both convention and assembly, voting was quite consistent. Not a single Virginian voted one way in the convention and another way in the assembly, and only five Marylanders did so (these were accordingly omitted from the analysis). The result was a total of 316 Virginians (161 Federalists and 155 Antifederalists) and 167 Marylanders (121 Federalists and 46 Antifederalists), whose political allegiance could be ascertained.

Each of these men was then traced in the available tax lists, census figures, biographical encyclopedias, county histories, and genealogies.[100] A set of attributes was established for each legislator, and the resulting data was submitted to a multiple classification computer program.[101] This program utilizes a dichotomous dependent variable (Federalist or Antifederalist) and measures the correlation between it and each of the independent variables (or personal attributes). The question asked of the computer was this: what is the effect of x characteristic in disposing delegates toward Federalism (a negative response being its influence toward Antifederalism)? The results come on two levels, shown in tables 10.4 and 10.5. Gross effects are simple percentages, calculated within each category and expressed as deviations from the mean. The grand mean for Virginians is 0.5095 (i.e., 51 percent were Federalists) and for Marylanders is 0.7365 (74 percent were Federalists). Thus the first figure in table 10.4 says that 57 percent of those who held from 0 to 5 slaves were Federalists, and 43 percent were Antifederalists.

The net effect of each variable is ascertained by holding constant the influence of every other variable. The mathematical process, in effect, nullifies, or makes random, the effect of other variables so as to isolate and measure the effect of one. These results are also expressed as deviations from the mean. Although they are not actually percentages (in a few instances in the Maryland table they even exceed 100), they are recorded as such to permit a comparison with gross effects. When the net effect is the same as or larger than a gross effect, it means that the variable exerts an independent influence on party choice and is not affected by the

TABLE 10.4 VIRGINIANS ON THE CONSTITUTION, 1787–1788 (TOTAL N: 316, GRAND MEAN: 5095)

	N	Gross Effects		Net_a Effects		Net_b Effects	
		Deviation	Adjusted Mean (%)	Deviation	Adjusted Mean (%)	Deviation	Adjusted Mean (%)
Slaveholding							
0–5	53	.057	57	.062	57	-.004	51
6–12	60	-.093	42	-.076	43	-.059	45
13–24	64	-.072	44	-.059	45	.003	51
25–49	64	-.088	42	-.089	42	-.057	45
50–99	22	.218	73	.202	71	.260	77
100+	13	.260	77	.334	84	.207	72
Unknown	40	.116	63	.050	56	-.030	48
Occupation							
Planter	186	-.074	44	-.063	45	-.037	47
Lawyer	54	.065	57	.021	53	.011	52
Merchant/Professional	42	.157	67	.150	66	.155	66
Unknown	34	.108	62	.126	64	-.008	50
Age							
20–29	18	.102	61	.051	56	.068	58
30–39	49	.082	59	.089	60	.074	58
40–49	48	.011	52	-.067	44	-.061	45
50–59	34	.079	59	-.048	46	-.006	50
60–79	14	-.009	50	-.131	38	-.161	35
Unknown	153	-.059	45	.009	52	.004	51

	N						
Family							
Pre-1715 Eng., born in Va.	149	−.026	48	−.005	50	−.007	50
Other	106	.122	63	.086	60	.070	58
Unknown	61	−.149	36	−.138	37	−.103	41
Education							
None	9	.157	67	.033	54	−.033	48
Tutor/Academy	30	−.176	33	−.259	25	−.265	25
William and Mary	49	.164	67	.097	61	.077	59
Elsewhere in America	6	.157	67	.106	62	.120	63
Britain	22	.172	68	.100	61	.050	56
Unknown	200	−.044	47	−.000	51	.013	52
Military Service							
Gen., Col., Militia	66	.051	56	.105	61	.096	61
Gen., Col., Cont. Line	32	.116	63	.152	66	.088	60
Lower grade officer, Militia	60	−.109	40	−.124	39	−.156	35
Lower Grade officer, Cont. Line	35	.005	51	−.069	44	−.024	49
Noncom, Militia	9	.046	56	−.040	47	−.031	48
Noncom., Cont. Line	6	−.343	17	−.418	9	−.308	20
Did not serve	77	.023	53	.015	52	.023	53
Unknown	31	−.026	48	−.008	50	.043	55
Region							
Tidewater	124	.135	65			.113	62
Piedmont	104	−.298	21			−.289	22
West	88	.136	65			.182	69

SOURCE: Reprinted, by permission, from *The William and Mary Quarterly*, 3d ser., 31, no. 4 (1974), 613–32. The *N* figures are the actual number of delegates possessing each attribute. These add up to 317 among Virginians and 167 among Marylanders.

TABLE 10.5 MARYLANDERS ON THE CONSTITUTION, 1787–1788 (TOTAL N: 167; GRAND MEAN: .7365)

	N	Gross Effects		Net_a Effects		Net_b Effects	
		Deviation	Adjusted Mean	Deviation	Adjusted Mean	Deviation	Adjusted Mean
Slaveholding							
0–5	13	−.198	.54	−.082	.65	−.113	.62
6–12	27	−.107	.63	−.123	.61	−.082	.65
13–24	32	−.080	.66	−.041	.69	−.059	.68
25–49	33	.051	.79	.008	.74	.058	.79
50–99	22	.127	.86	.060	.79	.015	.75
100+	11	.172	.91	−.065	.67	.046	.78
Unknown	29	.056	.79	.167	.90	.098	.83
Confiscated Property							
None	124	−.003	.73	.016	.75	−.002	.73
£1–199	12	−.070	.67	.034	.77	.061	.80
£200–999	6	.263	1.00	.142	.88	.203	.94
£1000 +	25	−.017	.72	−.134	.60	−.067	.67
Occupation							
Planter	81	−.033	.70	.026	.76	.007	.74
Lawyer	35	.092	.83	−.067	.68	−.036	.70
Merchant/Professional	31	.102	.84	.162	.90	.117	.85
Unknown	20	−.186	.55	−.250	.49	−.149	.59
Age							
20–29	9	−.070	.67	.173	.91	.091	.83
30–39	36	.069	.80	−.092	.64	−.070	.67
40–49	32	.107	.84	.040	.78	.009	.74

	N						
50–59	20	.013	.75	-.070	.67	-.056	.68
60 +	7	.120	.86	.103	.84	.141	.87
Unknown	63	-.102	.63	.018	.75	.024	.76
Family							
Pre-1715, English, born in Md.	75	.050	.79	—*		.030	.77
Other	49	-.061	.68	—*		-.046	.69
Unknown	43	-.109	.63	—*		-.112	.63
Education							
None	0	—	—	—	—	—	—
Tutor/Academy	27	.078	.81	.133	.87	.110	.85
Amer. College	11	.081	.82	-.066	.67	.059	.79
Europe	15	.234	1.00	.512	1.25	.368	1.10
Unknown	114	-.070	.67	-.092	.64	-.080	.66
Military Service							
Gen., Col., militia	20	-.036	.70	-.021	.71	-.021	.71
Gen., Col., Cont. Line	12	.098	.83	.133	.87	.089	.83
Officer, militia	31	-.123	.61	-.127	.61	-.117	.62
Officer, Cont. Line	11	.081	.82	.231	.97	.151	.89
Noncom., militia	1	.234	1.00	.104	.84	.158	.89
Noncom., Cont. Line	0	—	—	—	—	—	—
Did not serve	26	.033	.77	-.192	.54	-.146	.59
Unknown	66	.021	.76	.077	.81	.078	.81

*This particular model was subdivided for experimental purposes to ascertain the relative importance of ethnicity, time of migration, and birthplace. Hence combined figures are not available. Because of the small deviation from Gross to Net$_b$ it was not deemed worthwhile to run another model.

presence of other factors. A decline in net effect indicates that other influences are also at work among the group of legislators who share the initial attribute. The program calculates the correlation between each variable and every other, and it places the resulting coefficients in a matrix. Thus when the net effect of one variable, or attribute, changes significantly, the matrix reveals which attributes are closely associated with it and are thus responsible for the change, as well as those that have little or no relation to it.

In determining net effects, two models were used—one that included the regional origin of each delegate as a variable (Net_b) and one that did not (Net_a).[102] This method helps to account for regional variations in the sample, and it offers some indication of the extent to which delegates were responding to the perceived interests of their constituents rather than to their own perceptions and interests.

Slaveholding was used as the index of wealth.[103] The information was obtained from Virginia tax lists and from the Maryland census of 1790 (Maryland tax lists are spotty).[104] In both states there is a definite relationship between wealth and Federalism. In Maryland there was almost a linear correlation—the wealthier one was, the more likely he was to be a Federalist. In Virginia the situation was a little more confused because of the Federalist slant among those who possessed the fewest slaves (a group that included a number of western farmers and eastern merchants). Otherwise, region was not a factor—men voted their purses regardless of where they lived. But wealth, it should be noted, was not the most important factor. Occupation and military service were more influential in both states.

The category of "unknowns" is treated in the program like any other independent variable. It is of concern only when the delegates in that category show a decided preference for one party, an indication that there might be bias in the evidence. In the Virginia table (10.4), for instance, the "unknowns" include Kentuckians for whom no tax information was available. Since nearly all the Kentucky delegates were Antifederalists, the category leans in that direction. The Maryland "unknowns" (10.5), in contrast, tend toward Federalism. Most came from the Eastern Shore (a Federalist area), where some of the census data has been lost.

Except for government securities, which Forrest McDonald has determined were not a factor in either state,[105] there is no good index to holdings of investment capital. In Maryland, however, the records of purchasers of confiscated Loyalists property are complete and available. It is thus necessary to consider this factor, especially since the common view is that Maryland Antifederalists were speculators indebted to the state, who disliked the Federal Constitution's injunction against paper money.[106] The critical flaw in this interpretation is that it rests on the assumption that all (or most) of those who gave personal bonds for British property were still indebted to the state in 1788. Actually, all but a tiny handful (Chase, Ridgely, and perhaps half a dozen others) had paid off their debts by that time.[107] Since this is clearly a negligible figure, there is no point in submitting it to a mathematical test.

The calculations in table 10.5, therefore, are an attempt to ascertain the influence of confiscated property in general. Most significant is the finding that the vast majority of delegates in both parties purchased no British property at all. Those who purchased small amounts leaned slightly toward Antifederalism, while all 6 of the "middling" purchasers were Federalists. The 25 major purchasers (£1,000+) divided politically very close to the mean; 18 were Federalists, 7 were Antifederalists. Only among this handful of Antifederalists was confiscated property an important factor. The dramatic change in the Net_a effect in this category suggests that, but for their speculative investments, they might have been Federalists.[108]

In terms of occupation, there was a slightly higher proportion of lawyers and merchants among the Maryland delegates, but planters were in the majority in both states. Since nearly everyone in the Chesapeake owned land, the distinction made here is between full- and part-time farming. In the tables the nonplanting occupational categories include everybody who had some employment besides farming. An effort to determine the primary occupational interest of each individual would have involved a good deal of guesswork.

Instead, it seemed more useful to separate those with any sort of entrepreneurial interest from those who were farmers only. The merchant/professional category therefore includes, in addition to town-dwelling merchants, ministers, and physicians, planters who owned iron furnaces, taverns, or stores.

Farmers tended to be Antifederalist in both states, though not as heavily as one might have supposed.[109] Lawyers leaned slightly toward Federalism in Virginia and toward Antifederalism in Maryland, and in both states men with entrepreneurial interests were decidedly Federalist. Among personal attributes, only high military rank was as important as mercantile or professional endeavor in the making of a Federalist.

It has sometimes been suggested that Federalists were relatively young men.[110] The Virginia figures seem to bear this out, but the Maryland record is mixed. Because of the sizable number of "unknowns"[111] it seems likely that the Virginia results are an accidental peculiarity of the sample. Age was probably not much of a factor.

Family background, on the other hand, was an important influence in both states, though in different directions. In fact, this is the only instance where the two states differed markedly. Three elements were considered: ethnic origins, birthplace of the delegate, and the date that his ancestors arrived in the state. Test models indicated that the three were related—those of more recent arrival were more likely to have been born out of state or of non-English stock. To avoid colinearity the three elements were combined. Those who were born in Virginia or Maryland, of English stock, and whose ancestors arrived before 1715 were compared with all others, i.e., those who deviated on any or all attributes. Those of old family split almost evenly in Virginia and were decidedly Federalist in Maryland. One is tempted to explain that in Maryland the areas settled earlier, such as the Eastern Shore, were predominantly Federalist, but that family influence held regardless of region (Net_b effect). In Virginia delegates of more recent arrival or of non-English stock were decidedly Federalist, while in Maryland this element was Antifederal.

The explanation for the influence of family in Virginia is a fairly simple one. Those who were subject to some sort of external influence, by virtue of non-Virginia birth or family, were more likely to be Federalists, while those whose roots were provincial were more likely to be Antifederalists. Federalists were generally more cosmopolitan; Antifederalists were more locally oriented. And this conclusion is substantiated by the impact of education and military service in both states. The variance of the family factor in Maryland is a curiosity. Perhaps because of the state's small size, its proximity to highly mobile Pennsylvania, and the large number of delegates born out of state, the entire Maryland sample was more cosmopolitan in attitude than the Virginians. The large number of "unknowns," in any case, make the Maryland figures suspect. These were obscure men, disproportionately Antifederalist, who failed to make the genealogies. Their surnames indicate that most were of English stock. If so, they would virtually neutralize the other categories, were they added. Family background was probably not of much importance in Maryland.

Education and military service were important in both states. Any sort of education was a Federalist influence, and the farther the delegate ventured from home the more likely he was to be a Federalist.[112] The net effect of education, however, is slightly lower because many educated men were also lawyers, physicians, or ministers. The large number of "unknowns" in this case is significant. Since the records of college attendance are quite complete, nearly all the "unknowns" can be presumed to have had little or no formal training. In both states this group is heavily Antifederalist. It was not, in all likelihood, the amount of formal training that was important, but the broadening of intellectual horizons. Education was a source of interstate or foreign contact.

Military service had a similar effect. In Virginia military rank had a larger net effect on attitudes toward the Constitution than did any other personal attribute. In Maryland, the type of service, whether in the Continental Line or the militia, was the important factor. But in both states military service was enormously important. Among Federalist influences, only wealth and mercantile interest approached high rank in the Continental service. Lesser rank and militia service were Antifederal to about the same degree.

Military service, moreover, was independent of other influences. One might expect, for instance, rank to be associated with wealth. But in both states the net effect of military service actually increases when other factors, including wealth, are held constant. Perhaps important military responsibilities, especially away from home, instilled a breadth of view, a concern for national problems and policies, as well as a desire for a strong, orderly political system. Like education, foreign birth, or mercantile activity, military authority fostered a cosmopolitan outlook. A stint in Congress or a post in the Confederation government may have had a similar effect, but the number of these in each state was too small for mathematical analysis.

The common denominator among these influences was perspective—whether a man's viewpoint was predominantly cosmopolitan or provincial.[113] Federalists in general were men with some sort of out-of-state contact, interest, or allegiance. In both states they tended to be well-to-do and educated, were often born or educated out-of-state, had entrepreneurial interests instead of or in addition to agriculture, and held positions of high rank in the Continental service during the Revolution. Antifederalists, with some exceptions, of course, were more typical of the society that elected them. They were "middling" planters, born locally and of English stock, and possessed little formal education or other broadening experience.

At the same time, it should be remembered that all these factors combined account for only a tiny portion of a delegate's voting behavior. The biggest single factor in political affiliation was residence.[114] Voting, in short, followed regional patterns, and those patterns, with some variations, were essentially those that had persisted since the crystalization of parties at the end of the war. The importance of the Constitution is that it brought together all the ingredients for a national party system: (1) local interests had become merged in national issues; (2) voters perceived the issues and felt they understood the impact on their interests, for they demanded and received pledges at election time; (3) rudimentary organizations (evident from the speed with which parades and mass rallies were arranged) were being formed to perpetuate voter allegiance.

NORTH CAROLINA: ANTIFEDERALISTS IN COMMAND[115]

Four of the five North Carolinians who attended the Philadelphia convention were associated with the Lawyers party, and the delegation actively cooperated with the nationalists at the meeting. But as soon as the general outline of the Constitution became apparent they began worrying about reaction back home. Expecting that it would follow familiar partisan lines, they anxiously scanned the midsummer elections to determine how many friends the Constitution would have in the assembly.[116]

They had good reason to worry. As soon as the Constitution was published, the rural majority found fault with it, though characteristically they did not publish their objections. As in Virginia, the Federal judiciary and the tax power bore the brunt of the assault. Willie Jones, reported William R. Davie from Halifax, was "continually haranguing the people on the terrors of the Judicial power, and the certainty of their ruin if they are *obliged now* to pay their debts." Not surprisingly, the judges of the general court lined up solidly against the Constitution.[117]

The tax power caused even more concern because of the scarcity of currency. No paper had been issued since 1785, and the depreciation of that emission had virtually eliminated hard coin. "Money is so scarce this way," complained one Pamlico merchant, "that I can't Collect a single shilling that is due me in this Neighborhood."[118] In commerce, barter arrangements could supplant money, and state taxes could be paid in kind. But Congress, in all likelihood, would demand specie.

The assembly was hostile to the Constitution, as Federalists had anticipated, but critics were unwilling to kill it without consulting their constituents. As a result, the resolution calling for election of a ratifying convention slipped through the Commons without visible opposition. In the Senate, Thomas Person's effort to limit the powers of the convention were voted down, with members of both parties joining against him. The two sides also agreed to delay the meeting as long as possible, evidently in the hope of getting outside help. Washington's correspondents told him that the convention was delayed "for the purpose of taking the tone from Virginia."[119] The convention was scheduled for early July, by which time every other state except Rhode Island would have acted.[120]

In a sudden afterthought the assembly instructed the convention also to fix a permanent seat of government for the state. The job involved so many sensitive interests that the assembly was unwilling to do it. Whether intentionally or not, the assignment sealed the fate of the Constitution. The ratification question became entangled in the web of regional interests. A number of electoral contests that spring hinged on the capital fight rather than on the Constitution.

Federalists did emerge with one small concession. The resolution authorizing elections did not contain the normal residence requirement for candidates. The main beneficiary was James Iredell, the Federalists' most articulate spokesman. Party leaders persuaded Stephen Cabarrus to switch to Chowan County so Iredell could run unopposed in Edenton. The rearrangement also demonstrated some rudimentary campaign organization.[121]

Reporting on the election to Madison, Benjamin Hawkins thought it "certain that the honest part of the community whether merchants or planters are for it. People in debt, and of dishonesty and cunning in their transactions are against it. This will apply universally to those of this class who have been members of the legislature."[122] Hawkins was anticipating that the state would divide along the debtor-creditor lines that defined the politics of the assembly. And, in general, he was right. Federalists carried every town and most of the counties around Albemarle Sound, but Antifederalists controlled the rest of the state.

As elsewhere in the Chesapeake, the election turned on issues, not personalities. Some of the most prominent men in the state— Allan Jones, William Blount, and William Hooper—failed of election. The voters even proscribed Alexander Martin, who, like Edmund Randolph, had departed from Philadelphia without signing the Constitution and then reversed himself during the winter. Samuel Johnston, recently elected governor, Iredell, Maclaine, Spaight, and Davie were left to carry the federal torch. To lead the opposition Willie Jones and Griffith Rutherford emerged from retirement, joining Thomas Person and his band of stalwarts from the assembly.

When the convention gathered in the Presbyterian church in Hillsborough on July 21, 1788, Federalists were momentarily heartened by news of Virginia's approval. A few days earlier New Hampshire had become the ninth state to ratify, and Virginia's approval (nevertheless crucial because of its size) meant there would be a new government no matter what North Carolina did. Willie Jones refused to yield, however, and neatly shifted the focus of debate to the question of amendments. One Federalist observed, "Mr. Jones says his object will now be to get the Constitution rejected in order to give weight to the proposed amendments, and talks in high commendation of those made by Virginia."[123] After discussing the Constitution for ten days, the convention adopted, by 184 to 84, a resolution calling for a bill of rights and changes in "the most ambiguous and exceptionable" parts of the Constitution. Turning to the question of a capital, it settled upon a site in Wake County, to be known as Raleigh.[124]

North Carolina had not exactly rejected the new federal union; it had merely set up conditions for joining. Within a year most of those conditions were met by Madison's adroit handling of amendments. The Bill of Rights, approved by Congress in the summer of 1789, offered North Carolina a second chance.

CHAPTER ELEVEN

Federalists Triumphant

IT HAS OFTEN been remarked that while the framers of the Constitution made no provision for political parties, the governmental structure they set up was so awkward that it could not have functioned without them. Whatever truth there be in this assessment, the Constitution did provide the structure for the development of national parties. By imposing severe restrictions on the states in such fields as debtor relief, where local partisanship had been most intense, and by adding new powers to the federal legislature the Constitution virtually required the state parties to expand their horizons.

The first federal election presented instant opportunity. The election of congressmen, senators, and Presidential electors was a continuation of the battle over the Constitution because both sides recognized the importance of controlling the new government. And because of its importance, the election encouraged new organizational efforts and interstate collaboration. It was an important step in the transition from local partisan groups to a national party system.

From the beginning the Antifederalists were less organized and more uncertain of their objectives, but they made considerable progress during the ratification debate. The idea of amendments, or even a second convention, held them together and enabled even the most extreme among them to mask their designs with the cloth of reasonableness. New York governor George Clinton's circular suggesting concerted action to amend the Constitution presented a unique opportunity. Even though it arrived too late to influence the Virginia and North Carolina conventions, it opened the possibility of an interstate alliance devoted to altering the Constitution.

The possibility was enough to unnerve the Federalists. Learning of Patrick Henry's declaration that he would accept the Constitution but work to change it, James McHenry wrote to Madison to find out what the latest Antifederalist "plan" was. If Henry's declaration signaled a shift in Antifederalist tactics, McHenry fretted, it was echoed by the opinion of some in Maryland that "the distinction of fed. and antifed should be done away, which should it gain ground will ensure Mr. Chase his election." Except for his paper money aberrations, Chase, after all, had been a member in good standing of the creditor-nationalist majority in Maryland. Washington likewise feared "that a considerable effort will be made to procure the election of Antifederalists to the first Congress, in order to bring the subject [of amendments] before the State legislators, to open an extensive correspondence between the minorities for obtaining alterations, and in short to undo all that has been done."[1]

The Federalists worried unnecessarily. Their opponents proved to be too local-minded to organize an effective interstate coalition. Writing to congratulate Richard Henry Lee on his election to the federal Senate, Patrick Henry made it clear that he had had no intention of entering national politics. He had no interest in any place outside Virginia, he said, "unless in North Carolina from which I am not very distant & to whose politics I wish to be attentive." He pointed out that in the twenty counties south of the James "at least 19/20th are antifederal & this great Extent of Country in Virginia lays adjoining to No. Carolina & with her forms a great Mass of Opposition not easy to surmount."[2] An

Antifederal coalition extending from the James River to Cape Fear may have been among the Federalists' nightmares, but Patrick Henry never bothered. There is no evidence that he made any contact with the Antifederal leaders of North Carolina.

Since Maryland was relatively safe, from the Federalist point of view, and North Carolina was hopeless, attention centered on evenly divided Virginia. Because of its size and history of leadership, the state had a disproportionate influence on national affairs. Federalists feared that the majority which endorsed the Constitution was a fragile one. On the basis of past experience they could not count on a majority in the legislature, which was authorized to set the conditions for the federal election. "To be shipwrecked in sight of the port," moaned Washington, "would be the severest of all possible aggravations to our Misery and I assure you I am under painful apprehensions from the single circumstance of Mr. H. having the whole game to play in the assembly of this State."[3]

VIRGINIA: THE BATTLE RESUMED

"The parties feds and anti have in most transactions been pretty distinguishable," Joseph Jones reported to Madison shortly after the 1788 session opened. John Beckley, perennial clerk of the House of Delegates, agreed. After counting noses he announced that the Antifederalists had a majority of about fifteen votes.[4] The House was no more polarized than it had been in the previous year, but now, as a result of the contest over ratification, each side had a name. By conferring enduring identity, names, in turn, lent a degree of respectability. Jones's use of the term "party," applying it to friends as well as enemies, suggests that even that label was losing its pejorative connotations.

Party distinctions remained apparent, if for no other reason than that the Constitution continued to be an issue, kept alive by Governor George Clinton's convention. Governor Randolph, who ordered Clinton's circular published in August 1788, was, as usual, on the fence. From the moment he left Philadelphia he had desired changes in the Constitution, but he now recognized that another convention might open a Pandora's box of changes.[5] He resolved the dilemma by resigning his post and taking a seat in the assembly. The Antifederalists' candidate for a replacement was Benjamin Harrison, but under the state constitution he was not eligible for the post until December (three years after his last term expired). They accordingly left the place empty for three months (a measure of its administrative importance) before holding the election. Harrison's opponent was Beverley Randolph, former lieutenant governor, who, though not a member of the ratifying convention, was known to be an opponent of the Constitution.[6] Harrison won by four votes; Federalists evidently backed Randolph as the lesser evil.[7]

In late October, as expected, Patrick Henry introduced resolutions calling for a second convention. Federalists countered with a substitute proposal, which, while endorsing the idea of amendments, suggested they be added through the process outlined in the Constitution. This went down to ignominious defeat, 38 to 85. Evidently a few Federalists failed to get the message and voted against any sort of amendments. With Madison absent in New York, assembly Federalists were still trying to organize themselves.[8]

The Antifederalists, by contrast, showed that they had learned from past mistakes and delegated leadership tasks with smooth efficiency. The delay in the gubernatorial election suggests that Harrison was earmarked for that position from the outset; Richard Henry Lee and William Grayson were slated for the U.S. Senate. Theodorick Bland undertook to write the unpredictable Lee to insure that he would be available for a concerted effort to "render that government secure and harmless."[9] When Patrick Henry publicly endorsed Lee his election was a foregone conclusion. The Federalists' only hope was that Madison might have enough personal influence in the assembly to slip in ahead of Grayson. Party lines held firm, however. After turning aside the Federalists' amendments proposal the assembly took up the subject of congressional elections. On November 10 the two houses conducted a joint ballot for senators, and the tally was Richard H. Lee 98, Grayson, 86, Madison 77, Patrick Henry (who was not a candidate) 26, and the rest scattered.[10] Writing to congratulate Lee, Theodorick Bland could not resist some self-congratulation on his party's new-found cohesion: "The gentlemen on the federal side, . . . finding themselves stript of the Lion's skin, with great dexterity put on the Fox's tail, but neither art or strength would avail them."[11]

Arrangements for the congressional election occasioned even more maneuvering. In the past year, each side had scored one election victory; both were still wary of testing their strength on a statewide basis. It was quickly agreed that the state ought to be divided into districts, each to select a member of the federal House of Representatives. That virtually insured that each would win some representation in Congress. How much was the critical question. When the districting bill emerged from House committee, it contained a provision requiring candidates to be residents of their districts for twelve months prior to the election. Edward Carrington, who was beginning to assert himself as Federalist leader, suspected that this provision was directed against Madison, who had already announced his intention to stand for Congress.[12] Since the northern Piedmont was heavily Antifederal, Madison stood a better chance in a safer region. Carrington moved to delete the residence requirement, but the motion proved a tactical error. Representation without residence smacked of British imperial theory. The motion lost, 32 to 80, with several Federalists breaking ranks.[13]

Carrington was beginning to learn, however. When the House returned to the question of a second convention, he was ready with another substitute. Designed for broader appeal, this one called on Congress to approve the amendments adopted by the Virginia ratifying convention. Antifederalists were not fooled, but the margin was closer, 50 to 71.[14] Such tactics required discipline and Carrington was encouraged. "It has hithertoo been unfortunate that the federalists in the House have not acted in proper concert," he told Madison. "We are however getting Martialed and I hope we shall, at least, upon every occasion be able to show a respectable Minority."[15] Four days later an Antifederalist measure prohibiting officials of the federal government from holding office under the state passed by an almost identical margin, 71 to 52. Having "Martialed" his ranks, Carrington was ready to appeal to the voters. He demanded a published roll call so the taxpayers would know whom to blame when they found themselves supporting large numbers of redundant officials.[16]

Between them, the two issues—a second federal convention and the congressional election—generated four roll calls in the House of Delegates. Despite some tactical voting, they give a fair indication of relative party strength. Madison, apparently relying on them for information, concluded that the Antifederalists had a two-thirds majority in the assembly, and his estimate was not far off the mark.[17] The delegates who participated in at least three divided as shown in table 11.1 (threshhold of 3 votes and 75 percent agreement). The polarization was nearly complete—91 percent sided with one party or the other, and the figure would have been higher if the Federalists had been organized from the outset. Most of those classified as "middle" were western Federalists who strayed on the two early ballots. It is possible that they were reluctant to submit to the leadership of easterners, Carrington, Corbin, and Page, but more likely it was a matter of communication. The eastern creditor leaders needed time to open contacts with their new allies.

Party unity extended only to these clear-cut national issues, however. On matters involving regional economic interests delegates went their separate ways, but such voting did not eradicate party identities. After a losing battle against a tax reduction bill, Carrington admitted that "Fed and Antifed united to a great major-

TABLE 11.1   VIRGINIA HOUSE OF DELEGATES: PARTIES, 1788

	Federalists	Antifederalists	Middle
Northern Neck	8	2	0
Middle Tidewater	5	11	3
Piedmont	4	13	1
Southside	3	27	0
Valley & West Va.*	13	8	6
Kentucky*	3	5	2
	36	66	10

*In earlier tables these two were lumped together as "west," but beginning with the votes on British debts in 1787 they diverge, and it seems useful to examine them separately, especially since the Kentucky delegates depart in 1791.

ity" in favor of the measure. It was a regional question—Tidewater versus the rest of the state.[18]

TRANSITION TO NATIONAL PARTIES: VIRGINIA

"It is probable that each party will fix on one man," wrote Henry Lee of the congressional election, "& that the election will decide the will of the people, provided the districts have not been artfully designated."[19] Federalists worried throughout the autumn session that their opponents might make use of their majority in arranging the congressional districts, but their concern proved unnecessary. The districts were made nearly equal in population, and this served the interests of the Federalists, whose western wing was underrepresented in the assembly. After carefully weighing these factors, Madison confidently predicted that the Federalists would win a majority and might even take as many as 7 of the 10 seats alloted to the state.[20]

The Federalists were mainly concerned about Madison's district, which had been almost evenly divided in the contest over ratification. But there is no evidence of Antifederalist tinkering. The district created by the assembly was a fairly symmetrical group of counties in the central Piedmont, extending from the Rappahannock to the James. Under any other arrangement—attaching neighboring counties from the Tidewater or Northern Neck, for instance—the Antifederalists could reasonably have complained that the district was "artfully" arranged to insure Madison's election. In the ratifying convention five of the counties had been Antifederal, two Federal, and one divided. Madison's difficulty was that he was an anomaly in the predominantly Antifederalist Piedmont.

To add to his troubles, his friend Monroe decided to run against him, ostensibly to initiate amendments in Congress. Madison privately suspected that "the party" had put him up to it.[21] Monroe claimed Spotsylvania County for a home, though he actually resided in Fredericksburg, and in neighboring Culpeper he had the backing of the powerful old debtor leader, French Strother. Madison could count on Orange and Albemarle, the two largest in the district, but the counties along the James were hopelessly

Antifederal. Friends warned him that the contest turned on Spotsyl-vania and Culpeper; they recommended that he "visit the counties previous to the election and attend the Culpeper election" in person.[22]

The idea of riding circuit through the district addressing the voters was certainly a revolutionary one, and there is no evidence that either candidate was prepared to go to such lengths. Madison did hurry home from New York to put his "political Machine into activity," and he allowed his friends to print an appeal in the Fredericksburg newspaper to the religious minorities of the district, reminding them of his role in securing the statute for religious freedom.[23] All this "electioneering," as Madison had earlier described it to Jefferson, had its effect, for he won the election by a firm margin of over 300 votes.[24]

This one contest contained all the ingredients of the new politics—concentration on issues, extensive analysis of voter senti-ment, the use of prominent figures with local influence, candid appeals to minority interests. Madison's victory in counties that had previously been Antifederalist—and before that predominantly debtor—suggests that the new techniques had some effect. But there is also evidence that many voters followed old habits. One election poll survives from this contest—in Amherst County, taken on February 2–4, 1789. Written down by the county clerk as each voter came forward to state his choice, the poll lists each freeholder by name and ballot. Monroe won the county by 236 to 145. Approximately 84 percent of Madison's voters and 79 percent of Monroe were found in the county tax lists. Table 11.2 shows the distribution of wealth among the voters.[25]

As might be expected, the wealthy were more inclined to appear at the polls than the small property owners, but the lesser people by sheer weight of numbers determined the election. Those with fewer than five slaves (or less than £150 in land) cast more ballots for Monroe than Madison received altogether. Expressed differently, a poor man was twice as likely to vote for Monroe, while a wealthy man was twice as likely to vote for Madison. Since neither candidate lived in or near the county, and neither appeared in person, party allegiance undoubtedly dictated voter preference.

TABLE 11.2   AMHERST COUNTY ELECTION, 1789: HOUSE OF REPRESENTATIVES

A. *Distribution of Voters by Land Valuation (expressed in pounds Virginia currency)*

Wealth	Madison Voters	% of Madison's Total	Monroe Voters	% of Monroe's Total	All County Taxpayers	% of County Total
£0–24	8	7	22	12	157	19
£25–74	24	22	70	36.5	280	35
£75–149	19	17	37	19	128	15
£150–399	39	35	45	23	185	23
£400–799	14	13	12	6	44	5
£800–1,499	4	4	3	1.5	10	1.5
£1,500+	2	2	4	2	10	1.5
	110	100	193	100	814	100

B. *Distribution of Voters by Slave Ownership*

Slaves	Madison Voters	% of Madison's Total	Monroe Voters	% of Monroe's Total	All County Taxpayers	% of County Total
0	28	27	63	31.5	617	50
1–4	22	21	59	30	293	24.5
5–12	24	22	56	29	202	18
13–24	18	18	14	7	63	5
25–49	9	9	3	1.5	23	2
50+	3	3	2	1	7	0.5
	104	100	195	100	1,205	100

SOURCES: Amherst County Deed Book F, 1787–90, pp. 296–98, and Amherst County Personalty Books, 1787, 1788, VaSL.

Although there is no earlier poll list available for this county, it is a reasonable guess that the less affluent voters favored debtor candidates earlier in the 1780s. It is an equally reasonable inference that many voters perceived the Federalist-Antifederalist clash as a continuation of earlier party battles, just as most of the political leaders did.

In other congressional districts one party or the other was dominant, and the main problem was to narrow the list of candidates to avoid dividing the vote. Henry Lee's early prediction "that each party will fix on one man" anticipated some rudimentary nominating procedures. Before the assembly broke up in December the Antifederalists drew up a slate of ten candidates for Congress and twelve Presidential electors, which they then circulated around the state.[26]

The Antifederalists' nominations quickly eliminated one potential candidate, Arthur Lee. In the district comprising the eastern Northern Neck and Middle Tidewater, Lee early announced his candidacy in a printed handbill. The Antifederalist slate listed for that district Thomas Roane, a King and Queen County planter who had served in the convention, and Lee quickly withdrew from the race.[27] Federalist Henry Lee also had aspirations, but when he learned that John Page was offering himself in opposition to Roane, he too withdrew.[28] Page won the election with ease.

The lower Tidewater was also Federalist country. Samuel Griffin, a Williamsburg lawyer with limited political experience, won in that district, apparently with no opposition. Across the James in Norfolk, Federalists backed Thomas Mathews, who had been selected Speaker of the House of Delegates in the fall session. The Eastern Shore was tacked on to the district, and Isaac Avery, Episcopal minister of Northampton, long-time senator and opponent of debtor relief, hoped to obtain some local backing for his own candidacy, but friends persuaded him to withdraw rather than divide the "federal interest."[29]

It was important that the Federalists maintain a united front because the district contained some Southside counties that were evenly divided on the Constitution. Evidently hoping to split the Norfolk vote, the Antifederalists chose Josiah Parker, who had served as naval officer of the port since the end of the war. Parker had failed in election to the ratifying convention, but his strength in the city combined with the Antifederalist votes from the interior (he had a large estate in Isle of Wight County) was enough to carry the election. Federalists, at first unsure of his politics, soon discovered that he was a flaming critic of the Washington administration.[30]

The rest of the Southside was a "Mass of Antifederalism," according to Edward Carrington; Isaac Coles stood for one collection of counties and Theodorick Bland for the other. Carrington, who saw no point in his own candidacy, did set out to find "a less obstinate anti than Bland," but failed in even that. His estimate proved correct, for when the results of only 5 of the 11 counties were in, Bland reported a lead of 619 to 27.[31] Those were the only bright spots for the Antifederalists, however. The west returned three more Federalists, Alexander White and Andrew Moore from the Valley and John Brown of Kentucky. When all was done, Madison's initial estimate of 7 Federalists and 3 Antifederalists was right on the nose.

The Presidential election produced similar results—9 Federalist and 3 Antifederalist electors.[32] Although the Antifederalists had named a slate of candidates, there was little disagreement concerning the top office. "The voice of this State runs pretty unanimously for Genl. Washington as Presid," reported Carrington during the fall legislative session, but "Mr. H. is putting in agitation the name of Clinton for vice Presidt which takes well with the Anti's."[33] John Adams, generally considered the Federalist choice for Vice President, was not popular in Virginia. New Englanders seldom were. But Virginians were also critical of his political writings, which seemed aristocratic in tone, and many felt that he had not sufficiently promoted American (and Virginian) interests during his service in London.[34] As a result, Federalist ranks broke in the balloting. All 10 electors voted for Washington (2 Federalists failed to attend the meeting), but only 5 voted for Adams. The 3 Antifederalists went for Clinton, but 2 Federalist votes were thrown to John Hancock and John Jay.[35]

TRANSITION TO NATIONAL PARTIES: MARYLAND

Maryland's Antifederalists were also better organized and noisier after the ratifying convention than before. For one thing, Federalist tactics in the convention, by seeming to violate the rules of fair play, gave them a rallying point. Throughout the summer they bombarded the newspapers with demands that the convention proceedings be published so that the electorate could see for itself the ruthlessness of its servants.[36] The late-summer assembly elections also kept the political pot boiling. Federalists, their chronic fears rekindled by rumors that the opponents of the Constitution were forming a nationwide organization, resolved to be particularly on guard "against attempts of the antifederals to get into our assembly." As in Virginia, the composition of the assembly was critical, for it was expected to set the ground rules for the congressional election.[37]

As usual, the most exciting contest—and the one best reported in the press—was in bitterly divided Baltimore. "That Arch Fiend of Hell," exclaimed a city merchant, "—Satan's Premier (& our Judge) Sam. Chase *Esq,* is playing the Devil in Town with his D——d Anti nightly meetings & keeps us all in Hott waters."[38] Chase and his friend David McMechen campaigned on the promise to seek amendments. The Federalist nominees, McHenry and Dr. John Coulter, claimed that it was absurd to turn the job of amending the Constitution over to its enemies; it would be as reasonable to "trust their lives to a physician who thirsted to drink their blood."[39] Not to be outdone in popular appeals, the Federalists organized meetings of their own. When one of these was broken up by a gang of toughs, they retaliated by disrupting an Antifederalist rally and then went on to "demolish" the windows in Chase's house.[40] On the first day of balloting the Federalists even organized a parade—a miniature ship representing the union was carried through town, colors flying, accompanied by fifes and drums.[41] Though obviously inspired by the parades that had attended the ratification celebrations, this was the first time any one attempted to stage a "band wagon" in an election campaign. The Federalist slate won by about 120 votes, a substantial decline from their 600 vote margin of the previous spring. Despite the electoral ballyhoo, voter turnout was also lower than in the spring, by about 100 votes.[42] The losers promptly appealed to the House of Delegates, alleging that the Federalists intimidated voters and that one (probably McHenry) spent a large amount of money on the election. The House conducted a perfunctory investigation, but the Federalist majority refused to take action.[43]

The Antifederalists improved over their spring performance in other parts of the state as well. They swept Baltimore, Harford, and Ann Arundel as they had in the spring, and they made new inroads into the lower Western Shore. St. Mary's, Calvert, Charles, and Prince George's all returned split delegations. Antifederalists elected only two delegates in the upper Potomac, however, and the Eastern Shore was likewise firmly Federalist. Table 11.3 shows the

TABLE 11.3   MARYLAND HOUSE OF DELEGATES: PARTIES,
1788

	Federalists	Antifederalists	Middle
Eastern Shore	17	3	5
Upper Bay	2	7	2
Western Shore	4	14	3
Upper Potomac	10	2	0
Urban	3	1	0
	36	27	10
Party, 1785–1786			
Creditors	11	2	1
Debtors	1	8	2
Chasites	2	6	1
Middle	4	1	0
Unknown	18	10	4
	36	27	10

regional distribution of parties on the basis of twelve party-determining roll calls.[44]

Federalists were aware that they had lost ground in the election,[45] but they had no intention of mending their ways. They
buried the Baltimore election protest as quickly as they could, and
then set the rules of the federal election to their own advantage.
The state was alloted 6 congressmen, and a House committee
suggested dividing the state into districts. But that meant Antifederalists would carry one, perhaps two districts at the head of the
bay. So the Federalist majority rejected that. The system finally
adopted, after much maneuvering, was the strangest in the nation.
They divided the state into districts and required each candidate to
be a resident of his district. But candidates were to be elected at
large; in effect, every voter was permitted to cast up to six ballots.
The Federalists thereby insured that their statewide majority would
return a uniform congressional delegation.[46] The election was
scheduled for the first Monday in January; thereafter elections
would be held in October.

Antifederalists doubtless felt this was more dirty politics, but
they had no time to mount a complaint. The campaign was already

under way. By December 19 the Federalists had a party ticket ready for the newspapers. The concept of a ticket itself was a novel one in the Chesapeake, though the term had been in use for some time in neighboring Pennsylvania. Pleading a lack of time to sound public sentiment in each district, the notice merely declared that the men chosen were "believed to be most acceptable in their respective districts" and they would give the state "a genuine federal representation."[47]

The committee of assembly Federalists who arranged the slate ran into only one minor problem. Nathaniel Ramsey, a lawyer from Charles Town in Cecil County, expressed a desire early in the fall to be a candidate. Ramsey had served in the House for one session (1785) and had made a brief appearance in the Continental Congress. The legislative committee initially obliged Ramsey and placed him on the ticket, but then it changed its mind and substituted Joshua Seney, a lawyer from Queen Anne's.[48] Seney had served several terms in the assembly, as well as the Continental Congress; he was undoubtedly better known in the area and came from a more populous county. Besides, he was already on the Antifederalist ticket. The Federalists obviously knew their man and probably felt that any opposition votes he pulled were all to the good.[49] Ramsey contemplated standing a poll anyway but finally decided to acquiesce lest he give "general offense" to the party.[50] The committee made a shrewd choice, for Seney led the Federalist ticket, both in his own district and statewide.

Rather than renew their cries of foul play, the Antifederalists produced some tricks of their own. By the end of December they had ready a slate of candidates for both Congress and the electoral college, which they put before the public as "Friends to Amendments."[51] In areas where they were particularly weak—the Eastern Shore and upper Potomac—they tried to enlist prominent men who were publicly uncommitted, but the Seney affair indicated that they were still a step behind the Federalists. Their other choice for Eastern Shore congressman was William Vans Murray, a newcomer who had voted consistently Federalist in the fall assembly session. When the Antifederalists realized their error (or Murray declined to serve), they replaced him with John Done, another Federalist but one who at least had favored amendments in the ratifying convention.[52] Among their Presidential electors from the Eastern Shore they included William Tilghman, a Chester Town lawyer who was already on the Federalist ticket. Tilghman had no previous political service, having been excluded by his refusal to take the state's loyalty oath, but a cursory investigation would have revealed him to be a staunch Federalist.[53]

The Antifederalists ran into even greater difficulties in the upper Potomac. Their leading adherent in that area was Abraham Faw, a Chasite who had deserted his mentor to vote for the Constitution in the ratifying convention, probably because of electoral commitments.[54] For the electoral college the Antifederalists had no difficulty recruiting Lawrence Oneale of Montgomery, for years the debtor party leader in the upper Potomac, but they made a mistake when they also named Moses Rawlings, a war hero who was popular in Washington County. Rawlings was offended, with some reason since he had voted for the Constitution in the ratifying convention (his only venture into public service). Privately he blamed Faw for deliberately trying to confuse the voters; publicly he embarrassed the Antifederalists by ostentatiously withdrawing from the ticket.[55]

Western Federalists, by contrast, organized a smooth-running political machine. Early in January they held a meeting in Hagerstown and, according to the local physician (who had never held public office) "pledged ourselves to one another that every exertion shall be made to bring in voters & . . . to counteract the Dark & Villainous designs of the Antis." Among the "designs" of the Antifederalists was the German vote. Both sides apparently agreed that westerners of English ancestry were Federalist, but no one was certain of the Germans. Lacking resident spokesmen in the west, the Antifederalists sent a Baltimore physician into the area to make an appeal to the Germans. Federalists ran him out of the county with a threat of tar and feathers. Even so, they were immensely relieved on polling day when "150 men in one body" with two Germans at their head came over to Hagerstown from Williamsport on the Potomac to vote Federalist.[56]

Assured of victory from the outset, western Federalists seemed most concerned with voter turnout. Militia companies furnished them a rudimentary "grassroots" organization. One Federalist leader in Frederick wrote to all the *"Big Captains"* to enlist their help, and on election day a colonel in Washington County sent "about 15 Light boys Equal to myself [out] to Scower the County" for voters. As a result, public interest hit a fever pitch. By the time the polling contest ended, wrote John Stull, militia colonel, assemblyman, and justice of the peace, "There could not have been less than 2 or 3 thousand persons, men women children & negroes" jammed into Hagerstown. The crowd doubtless had a chilling affect on minority sentiments, for not a single Antifederalist vote was cast in Washington County. The Federalists obtained an astounding 1,167 ballots (about 50 percent of all the white adult males), and then celebrated their victory by roasting "a large one on the spit with his horns on."[57] Between parades in Baltimore and barbecues in the mountains, Maryland was rapidly acquiring all the trappings of democracy.

The Antifederalists did not fare much better in the eastern counties, where creditor-nationalists had long held sway. Weak candidates and a growing popular disposition to give the new government a chance also worked to their disadvantage. Their only congressional candidate of any note was John Francis Mercer. Samuel Chase might have won in Baltimore, since the Federalists put up a novice who had never held office, but instead he backed his old friend Samuel Sterett, who had lost three city elections in a row. The Federalists outpolled their opponents in the statewide congressional balloting by two to one. Only three records of the popular vote survive—for Baltimore and Harford counties, both Antifederal, and for Baltimore Town, which went Federalist by a narrow margin.[58] A total of 444 voters attended the Harford poll, as indicated by the total for Seney, who was listed on both tickets (see table 11.4; the polltaker, evidently with inside information, recorded him as a Federalist). Since no candidate was a resident of the county, there were no "native sons" to confuse the issue. Party lines held firm; not more than one or two voters deviated in any

TABLE 11.4 CONGRESSIONAL ELECTION, 1789:
HARFORD COUNTY, MARYLAND

A. District	Federalists	Harford	Statewide
1	M. J. Stone	203	5,154
2	Joshua Seney	444	7,616
3	Benjamin Contee	205	5,476
4	William Smith	204	5,415
5	George Gale	205	5,456
6	Daniel Carroll	206	5,819
B. District	Antifederalists	Harford	Statewide
1	George Dent	241	2,731
2	———		
3	J. F. Mercer	239	2,339
4	Samuel Sterett	240	2,424
5	John Done	238	1,832
6	Abraham Faw	236	1,964

SOURCE: Harford County Congressional Poll List, 1789. Harford
County Papers, MdHS.

contest. The polling for Presidential electors followed exactly the
same pattern, except where the shortage of Antifederalist candidates gave the Federalists a double vote.[59]

The Baltimore poll shows a similar adherence to party, even
though two of the candidates, Samuel Sterett and William Smith,
were residents of the city. Sterett led the Antifederalist slate by
about 25 votes, but Smith was low man on the Federalist ticket. The
party dropped him in the next election. In Baltimore Town Seney
got 212 Federalist votes and 176 Antifederalist votes, which was
approximately the margin of the Federalist victory. The fact that the
votes were not added together (as in Harford) suggest that most
voters cast single-ticket ballots. Perhaps the ballots were even
printed beforehand (such ballots had already come into use in
neighboring states to the north).

Exulting over the Federalist victory, one Baltimore merchant
felt the margin would have been even larger "had the other ticket
been avowedly antifederal." He thought that the inclusion of Federalists on the opposition ticket had confused the voters.[60] This seems

unlikely. The rigid adherence to party lines indicates that the electorate followed tickets, not charismatic leaders. If that was true generally, the statewide results were a fair measure of party strength. Daniel Carroll, the leading Federalist, won by 5,819 to 1,964 over his opponent, and the Federalist with the fewest votes, Michael Jenifer Stone, won by 5,154 to 2,731. The Federalist majority was close to two to one across the state.

Victorious Federalists were still not ready to relax. Rumors that northerners might ease one of their own into the Presidential spot in place of Washington caused new concern. The Constitution provided that the person who placed second in the electoral college would be Vice President, but if northern ranks closed around a Yankee, such as John Adams, he might win the first place. As a result, when the 8 Maryland electors met in Annapolis in early February, they cast their second ballots for Chief Justice Robert Hanson Harrison. "Had we given our vote to Adams," explained one, "he might have been thrown too far forward. I hope we have made the General's election altogether safe."[61] Within the national parties there would still be some sectional tensions.

NORTH CAROLINA'S CHANGE OF HEART

Federalists were then on the verge of success even in North Carolina. Shortly after the Hillsborough delegates reached home, Governor Johnston, Iredell, and William R. Davie mounted a campaign to persuade the legislature to arrange another election. They drafted petitions for presentation to popular meetings in the coastal towns, taking care to alter the wording slightly in each to make it look like a spontaneous outburst of opinion. Well-organized meetings approved the petitions, and some denounced debtor-relief laws and paper money for good measure.[62]

The fall assembly elections turned on the question of a second convention, and Federalists were overjoyed at the result. Some of the most influential Antifederalists, such as Griffith Rutherford and Matthew Lock, went down to defeat. Willie Jones moved to the Senate. The biggest change was in the far western Piedmont, where Surry, Rowan, Lincoln, and Mecklenburg counties voted Federalist.

All lay on waters (the Broad-Catawba system) that flowed through South Carolina to the sea. Although there is no written evidence to substantiate the idea, farmers in this area may have worried about having to trade through "foreign" territory if North Carolina remained outside the union.[63] The German vote may also have been a factor, although the evidence (as in western Maryland) is indirect. Lincoln County, the most heavily German of all, voted in favor of the Constitution in the first convention and remained Federalist through much of the next decade. The other counties also had sizable German populations.

When the legislature gathered in Fayetteville early in November 1788, the Federalists circulated a notice of a secret meeting on the eve of the opening session. Attendance at this gathering, the first party caucus held in North Carolina, convinced them they had a majority, though a slim one, in both houses.[64] When assembly housekeeping arrangements were completed, Federalists secured appointment of a Commons committee to consider the expediency of a second convention. The committee surprised them by reporting against the idea. But the Senate came to the rescue, adopting by 30 to 15 resolutions for a second convention to meet in Fayetteville a year hence. This action reopened discussion in the Commons. Federalists won an early test when an amendment giving Fayetteville representation passed, 46 to 43 (the town was a center of Federalism). Thereafter opposition collapsed, and the Senate resolutions were shouted through. When Thomas Person attempted to have them reconsidered, the House refused. 32 to 50.[65]

A tabulation (table 11.5) of the four roll calls on the convention resolutions shows a sizable group of delegates who voted inconsistently. These were no doubt Antifederalists at heart who only reluctantly agreed to a second convention. Even so, the regional distribution is a familiar one, except for the shift to Federalism in parts of the Piedmont. The high electoral turnover makes comparison with the parties of 1785–86 tenuous, but it is interesting to note that most of those listed as "unknown" are men new to politics. As in Maryland and Virginia, counties that shifted their political stance ousted old delegates and elected new ones.

TABLE 11.5   NORTH CAROLINA HOUSE OF COMMONS:
PARTIES, 1788

	Federalist	Antifederalist	Middle
Albemarle	13	2	6
Pamlico	3	5	3
Cape Fear	5	0	5
Piedmont	9	14	10
West	2	2	9
	32	23	33
Lawyers, 1785–1786	6	0	1
Debtors, 1785–1786	3	7	2
Middle	3	2	0
Unknown	20	14	30
	32	23	33

The assembly resolutions called for new elections to be held in August at the same time as the regular state elections, and the second convention would meet simultaneously with the assembly in November. Federalists tried to move up the election date, evidently in an effort to maintain their momentum, but failed. They need not have worried, for the Antifederalist position deteriorated steadily through the spring of 1789. A sign of the times was the steady retirement of the state's paper money by means of a sinking fund created in 1787. By June 1789 there was only £150,000 in circulation, and the value had risen dramatically. Rumors circulated that General Person wanted a new emission but that Willie Jones himself had stopped him.[66] Antifederalist ranks, once a silent phalanx, seemed suddenly in disarray.

Actions by the new federal government gave additional ammunition to North Carolina Federalists. In midsummer Congress enacted a tariff law containing a provision, actually inserted by Madison, for discriminatory tonnage duties on foreign vessels. Shipping interests in the Albemarle area feared that the duties might be applied to them so long as the state remained outside the union. They asked Congress to exempt the state from the duties, and when that failed they let it be known that if the Constitution was rejected a second time they would "divide this State leaving the Gentlemen who care nothing for Commerce to shift for themselves."[67]

The constitutional amendments approved by Congress that summer were the final blow to North Carolina Antifederalism. Willie Jones had never advocated scrapping the Constitution; he only demanded changes in it. At Hillsborough he had argued successfully that rejection of the Constitution would increase the chance of amendments. When the Constitution went into effect anyway, Antifederalists predicted confidently that the entire subject would be forgotten. Thus, Madison's announcement to the House of Representatives on May 4, 1789, that he intended to introduce amendments sliced the ground from under their feet. "Nothing ever gave me so much pleasure," trumpeted William R. Davie, "and this, coming from a Federalist, has confounded the Antis exceedingly."[68] Madison candidly admitted the political design when he sent a copy of his amendments to Samuel Johnston: "It aims at the twofold object of removing the fears of the discontented and of avoiding all such alterations as would either displease the adverse side or endanger the success of the measure."[69]

Thomas Person, "the bell weather of Opposition in this State" according to Hugh Williamson, remained "indefatigable in his Endeavors to preserve the Spirit of Antifederalism," despite the amendments, but only the judges Spencer and Ashe remained by his side. Willie Jones fell silent and refused even to serve in the second convention.[70] Archibald Maclaine heard of at least one Antifederalist who renounced the faith in order to get elected to the Fayetteville convention, but the amount of switching was small.[71] Most Antifederalists simply stayed home, and many of those who did go voted against the Constitution a second time. The Fayetteville convention approved the Constitution by 195 to 77. A majority on both sides (70 percent of the Federalists and 55 percent of the Antifederalists) were new men. Only 22 of the Hillsborough Antifederalists switched and voted for the Constitution at the second convention.[72]

The regional division at Fayetteville was similar to the split in the assembly. Only the central Piedmont remained hostile to the

Constitution. Besides the western Piedmont, the most dramatic change was in Tennessee. In 1788 the Tennesseans, led by the Tiptons, voted 19 to 2 against the Constitution. In 1789 John Sevier headed a delegation that voted 21 to 2 in favor of the Constitution. Apparently they felt that the Constitution improved the prospects for statehood.[73]

Congressional elections were held a few weeks after the convention adjourned. They attracted little attention,[74] and most candidates were probably elected without opposition. The only Antifederalist sent to New York was Timothy Bloodworth of Wilmington. Except for Sevier of Tennessee, the remainder—Hugh Williamson, John B. Ashe, and John Steele[75]—were relics of the old Lawyers party. It was evident that most Carolinians were disposed to give the new government a chance. But by that time the Federalists' efforts to flesh out the Constitution had stirred up a host of new controversies.

CHAPTER TWELVE

The Death of Antifederalism

THE ANTIFEDERALISTS fared badly in the congressional election, but those who survived set out for the nation's capital prepared for trouble. "The President and vice president are not yet arrived," Theodorick Bland caustically reported six weeks after the congressional session began. "But couriers have been dispatched north & south for them—great preparations are made for their reception which will be with much furor and something approaching *royal* Solemnity."[1] As if to justify Bland's sarcasm, the Senate shortly stumbled into a discussion of what title should be used to address the President. Among the suggestions were such absurdities as "His Elective Highness," which proved a fat target for Antifederal humor. Virginians, proud of their republican simplicity, were particularly upset by the discussion. Only staunch friends of the President such as Henry Lee considered the matter "insignificant"; moderate Federalists, especially those who had expressed misgivings about the Constitution, worried about the remnants of monarchism they saw in Congress.[2]

Washington's arrival in New York did nothing to calm their apprehensions. Conscious that he was establishing precedents, Washington sought a pattern of dignity and decorum that would command respect for the office. Unfortunately, his aloofness and formality were widely misunderstood, and before long there were new whispers of monarchical tendencies in the administration. Before departing for New York, Washington had asked his old friend David Stuart to keep him informed on Virginia opinion, on the creditable notion that no leader could afford to be divorced from the populace. After a midsummer tour of the "lower parts" of the state, Stuart reported that Virginians were seriously disturbed by the administration's practices, more so even than the newspapers had indicated. Besides the controversy over titles, they were concerned about the formality with which Washington conducted himself and the aristocratic bearing of the ever-unpopular Vice President, rumored to be dashing around New York in a coach-and-four.

"Pained" at Virginia's "sour" disposition, Washington undertook a lengthy defense of his conduct. He assured Stuart that the title dispute was none of his doing, and he hoped the subject would never arise again. His formal receptions on Tuesdays and Fridays, as well as the policy of not returning visits, were dictated by necessity, he explained. He would otherwise be swamped by casual visitors, unable to get any work done at all. Nor did he see anything untoward about the Vice President's conduct. Mr. Adams was a model of republican purity; Washington, in fact, had never seen his coach pulled by more than *two* horses.[3] Persuasive as the President's arguments were, he would have a hard time convincing provincial Virginians so long as their government remained in the distant and corruptive surroundings of a northern city. Washington never entirely overcame the imputation of monarchism. The amount of truth in the allegation never really mattered; its importance lay in its symbolic value. It was the first good weapon that his opponents claimed, and they never put it down. Before another year was gone the opposition was calling itself "republican," a choice of names that was a standing rebuke to the President.

No sooner had the inauguration furor subsided than Congress ran into a swarm of partisan and sectional rivalries on the question of revenue. Even before he was acquainted with the dimensions of the administration's program, Congressman Bland was prepared for the worst. Though not sure yet who would head the Treasury, Bland predicted "that whoever plays the Music the Southern States will pay the piper. A General and complete System of revenue is on the [agenda] and a great number of Enumerated articles under the Idea of promoting manufactures and suppressing Luxury are contended to be highly taxed—you will easily perceive where this will fall." There was, moreover, little the South could do about it, for "Seven will always be more than four."[4]

Madison, assuming from the outset the role of administration spokesman, brought in a bill to levy a 5 percent ad valorum duty on imported goods, with protective duties of up to 50 percent on some items. As special interests clamored for preferment, Antifederalists, both in and out of Congress, voiced objections to the principle.

Arthur Lee apprehended that a regular income of any sort would put the government in the hands of Robert Morris and his fellow financiers, who would afford the Treasury its immediate needs "provided the entire administration of the Revenue in future is secured to them or their friends."[5] Less hysterical critics were concerned about the protective features of the bill. Revenue was the principal object, but the measure did provide duties of up to 50 percent on some manufactured goods, such as steel and cordage. That southern staples, such as tobacco and indigo, also received protection meant little, since these items were not imported. Samuel Chase doubted that Congress had power to levy duties for the protection of manufactures—the first breath of strict construction. But it was William Grayson who gave vent to the sectional fears behind such arguments. "You would be astonished at the progress of manufactures in the seven Eastern States," he wrote Patrick Henry from New York. "If they go on in the same proportion for seven years they will pay very little on imports, while the South will continue to labor under pressure. This added to the advantage of carrying for the productive states will place them in the most desirable situation whatever." Henry Lee, less concerned with northern intentions, thought that the solution was to build up southern manufactures. His only objection to the tariff bill was that it did not provide enough protection for some of Virginia's products, such as bar iron.[6] Federalists put the best face on it they could, but when all was done Madison himself had to admit that the items subject to a high duty "were pretty generally taxed for the benefit of the manufacturing part of the northern community."[7] The bill passed both houses without a roll call, although Theodorick Bland, who objected to the bill in debate, probably stood against it to the end.[8]

Tonnage duties stirred up even more controversy. By levying a tax on foreign ships entering American harbors Madison hoped to encourage a domestic merchant fleet. No one objected to this since shipbuilding was a widely diffused industry in both the North and the South, and it offered Chesapeake planters a chance to break the British stranglehold. But Madison went on to suggest that additional discriminatory duties be levied against the ships belonging to nations which had no commercial treaties with the United States. His particular target was Britain, who had refused to open even regular diplomatic intercourse since the end of the war.[9]

Madison's suggestion caused the first fissure in the ranks of the Federalists. Northerners, aware of their dependence on British credit, were reluctant to undertake punitive measures that might invite retaliation. In Congress Madison defended his proposal in terms of the national welfare, dwelling on the advantages of mutual interdependence at home and freedom from interference by foreigners. But the immediate advantages lay with his home base, the Chesapeake. James Monroe, whose correspondence with Madison had suffered only brief interruption during the election contest, saw this instantly. Discrimination, he told Madison, would give the United States a lever to pry open the British West Indies. Edward Carrington agreed. A trade agreement with Britain that cracked open the empire would be of great benefit to the South since the West Indies were a good market for lumber and cattle.[10] Wilmington might expect to profit from such a trade as much as Norfolk or

Baltimore, but Senator Johnston was inclined to accept the northern view that the loss of British capital and credit would outweigh the disadvantages.[11]

The House approved Madison's tonnage bill without a roll call, but then the Senate struck out the discriminatory feature. Madison demanded that the House adhere to its position, even though the Senate action had been nearly unanimous. The House receded anyway, 31 to 19.[12] The Chesapeake backed Madison by 8 to 5, but there was no pattern to the voting. Supporting Madison were Antifederalist Isaac Coles and two middle-of-the-road men, Seney and Parker, while Federalists divided evenly. So did the delegates with important seaports in their districts. Daniel Carroll (Georgetown) and Josiah Parker (Norfolk) favored discrimination; William Smith (Baltimore) and Richard B. Lee (Alexandria) opposed it. Controversial though the matter was, it was apparently a conflict of special interests, not party principles.

The judiciary was another matter. It had been a prime target of Antifederalist criticism and seemed certain to inspire a new public controversy. Federalists in the Senate, anxious to placate the opponents of federal courts, sought a compromise in drafting the bill. While they created a federal hierarchy consisting of a Supreme Court, two circuit courts, and thirteen federal district courts, they confined the jurisdiction of all federal courts to cases arising under the Constitution and acts of the federal government. All ordinary civil and criminal matters were left to the state tribunals. Even this compromise did not satisfy the Virginians. As soon as the Senate took up the bill on June 22, Lee and Grayson proposed that the federal courts be confined to maritime and admiralty jurisdiction. The debate was not recorded, but diarists indicated that the tone was often bitter. Opponents pointed out, rightly enough, that such a limitation would render the new courts virtually useless; it would, in fact, have unraveled the whole judiciary article of the Constitution. Lee's motion was turned down, and on July 17, after nearly a month of discussion, the bill passed by 14 to 6 (the Senate's first and only roll call of the session). In the minority were Lee and Grayson.[13]

In the House the judiciary bill was subjected to a prolonged debate, which, undertaken in committee of the whole, unfortunately went unreported. After nearly three weeks of discussion, it passed on September 17 without a roll call. In the published debate the main opponents were South Carolina Antifederalists Thomas Sumter and Aedanus Burke, along with James Jackson of Georgia, a political newcomer. The only Federalist critical of the measure was Michael Jenifer Stone of Maryland, who resurrected the familiar argument that the federal courts would either preempt or clash with the state courts.[14] Within a year Stone counted himself a Republican.

DISTRIBUTION OF FEDERALIST PATRONAGE

The contests over the revenue system and the federal judiciary in the summer of 1789 revealed some important differences within the party that wrote and ratified the Constitution, and they gave Antifederalists the grim satisfaction of seeing their jeremiads fulfilled. But the two measures also created a host of federal offices, and Washington shrewdly filled them with political allies. It was a giant step in the evolution of a national party system.

In filling the highest offices in his command—the cabinet and the Supreme Court—Washington was primarily concerned with organizing a government that was both representative and respected. He earnestly sought the most prominent men in every state, and he tried to insure that each region got its share of positions. In filling the major offices he was not particularly concerned with political philosophies. If he was aware, for instance, of the different reactions that Jefferson and Hamilton each had toward the Constitution, it did not seem to concern him. At the same time, he never considered an important Antifederalist for any of these positions.

In regard to the lesser offices, he was more open in outlining the criteria he considered important. "In every nomination to office," he wrote Joseph Jones concerning a district judgeship, "I have endeavored, as far as my own knowledge extended, or information could be obtained, to make fitness of character my primary object." Others sensed this as well. Edmund Randolph began a

recommendation in behalf of a local tax collector: "As I am convinced that a knowledge of character is all which you will require in
the disposal of offices. . . ."[15] Once the nominee's virtue was established, other qualities were considered. The judicial posts, Washington felt, needed to be filled with prominent lawyers. Mere ability
was not enough. He rejected Robert Smith, a fast-rising Baltimore
attorney, for the Maryland district judgeship because he was young
and untested. "The world will look for a character and reputation
founded on service and experience," he wrote Smith's patron. On
the other hand, where character and experience were equal, Washington was prepared to consider the "peculiar necessities of the
Candidate." In giving preference to Cyrus Griffin for the Virginia
judgeship he noted that Griffin was "*out* of office and in *want* of the
emoluments of one."[16] The line between patronage and spoils was
ever a fine one.

Although character was Washington's main criterion, he often
defined the quality in political terms. His explanation for Rhode
Island's refusal to join the union, for instance, was that her "People
bid adieu long since to every principle of honor, common sense,
and honesty."[17] He considered only Federalists for office, not in a
conscious effort to reward loyalty but because he felt that political
rectitude was an indication of intelligence and character. His friends
seemed to agree with this. In recommending young Robert Smith,
General Williams listed among his attributes the fact that he was
"respected particularly by the friends of the present government, in
the support of which his exertions have been sensibly felt by its
adversaries." Washington's friends shared his concern for the
needy. James McHenry, though not at the moment in need of an
office for himself, was happy to recommend "some honest but poor
federals" from Baltimore.[18]

Perhaps it was natural for men who had just emerged from an
intense political controversy to mention partisan contributions in
their recommendations. Yet there is some evidence that even the
lowliest aspirants felt that their party loyalties might be a consideration. An examination of applications for office received by Washington during 1789 shows that about 10 percent mentioned their
adherence to the Federalist cause. And not one admitted to a
connection with Antifederalism.[19]

Maryland presented Washington with a plethora of able Federalists, though there was a distressing tendency among them to refuse national service. The state's chief justice, Robert Hanson Harrison, was Washington's first choice for one of the southern slots on the Supreme Court, and when he declined the place went to James Iredell.[20] For district judge the President first tried Thomas Johnson, and when he declined turned to William Paca. It was a shrewd choice. Samuel Chase would undoubtedly have accepted the position, but Washington could not quite bring himself to that.[21] Paca's appointment honored a distinguished lawyer, appeased the Chasites, and rewarded a timely convert.[22] The appointment of Richard Potts as district attorney and Nathaniel Ramsay as U.S. marshall compensated two prominent Federalists who had been overlooked by the state committee that had nominated Federalists for Congress.

Virginia was even easier. John Blair, a distinguished justice on the state court of chancery and member of the Philadelphia convention, was a natural choice for a seat on the Supreme Court. The district judgeship was offered first to Edmund Pendleton and then to Cyrus Griffin. John Marshall declined the post of district attorney, probably because he had higher ambitions, and the place instead went to William Nelson, Jr. Son of General Thomas Nelson, William, like Paca, was a marginal Federalist with considerable political influence.[23] Edward Carrington accepted the post of U.S. marshall.

North Carolina caused more difficulties. Federalists were scarcer, and Washington had little direct knowledge of the state. Before making his judicial selections he asked Jefferson to sound the state's congressional delegation. Jefferson did, and received a collection of nonpartisan character references. Washington sifted through them and probably weighed his own recollections of the state's politics, for he came up with a phalanx of Lawyers: William R. Davie for Judge, John Sitgreaves as attorney, and John Skinner, marshall.[24] That Washington should turn to lawyers for judicial posts is perhaps not surprising, but he pointedly ignored the three Antifederal state judges. In Maryland and Virginia state judges received first consideration.

The judicial appointments were clearly Washington's. Treasury nominations were up to Alexander Hamilton, but he undoubt-edly relied on Washington's experience among southerners. There is no indication in Hamilton's correspondence that he solicited opinions from anyone else. The key officials, collectors of customs at Baltimore, General Otho H. Williams, and at Alexandria, Charles Lee, were both well known to the President. In some respects the most revealing choice of officials was in North Caro-lina. Jefferson's memorandum of early 1790 did not extend to Treasury appointments, but Washington and Hamilton must have obtained information somewhere.[25] The state's seacoast was divided into six customs districts, each with its own collector, naval officer, and surveyor. Of the 18 men appointed, 10 can be identi-fied through service in the assembly or ratifying conventions, and every single one was a Federalist.[26] Partisan criteria evidently extended even to the most minor offices.

Whether Washington intended to act in a partisan way or not, his distribution of the federal patronage served to reward the faithful and to create a core of administration supporters in influen-tial positions of local government. In at least one case—Samuel Chase—the availability of government offices assisted in the con-version of a prominent Antifederalist. Chase's party shift, for all practical purposes, brought an end to Antifederalism in Maryland.

THE RECONVERSION OF SAMUEL CHASE

Chase might have returned to the fold anyway. His venture into paper money and Antifederalism was an aberration in his career, dictated apparently by financial embarrassment. At least, there is nothing in it to indicate that he had any broad conception of the public welfare. His public declarations on the Constitution—what few of them survive—consisted mostly of slogans. He never offered a systematic analysis of its shortcomings, nor did he betray any philosophical concern for excessive power on the one hand or human rights on the other. In early 1789 he was relieved of the particular difficulties caused by his excessive speculations when the assembly permitted him to declare bankruptcy, with the proviso that he convey certain lands to his creditors. Though no longer in need of legislative relief, he was nearly destitute and pressed by the needs of a large family. For years Chase had subsisted primarily on the emoluments of public office. The vast array of new positions in the federal government presented an opportunity too good to pass up. That it required a political change of heart seemed not to bother him at all.

Chase's reconversion can be traced through his correspondence in the summer of 1789. On May 16 he wrote, evidently in reply to an overture from Richard Henry Lee, to complain about Congress's lack of activity on the subject of amendments. He feared that there would be no "substantial alterations" in the Constitution. At that point his Antifederalism seemed firm enough, but his analysis of the local situation revealed more of himself than of Maryland politics. "In this state we are prepared to submit to any government," he wrote. "The spirits of our people are broke. They are bore down to the earth with their debts."[27] On July 2 he again wrote Lee assuring him that he still adhered to his "Republican principles," but he then went on to discuss the Senate's judiciary bill. Chase thought it was "ably drawn" and proposed only minor changes.[28] Correspondence between the two ceased thereafter.

A scant two weeks later he was writing to Washington: "I have, for some time, wished to be employed by the national government." The office Chase had in mind was that "lately held by General Williams"—naval officer of the port of Baltimore. Chase did not come cheap. The office was once described by Baltimore merchant Samuel Smith as the "handsomest appointment in this state," worth a thousand guineas a year.[29] Since Washington and Hamilton had not yet announced the Treasury appointments, the offer to take the place of the most prominent Federalist in Baltimore was presumptuous, to say the least. Anticipating some administration skepticism, Chase promised "to support the present Government" if given an office.[30]

His application was greeted with frosty silence. Undaunted, Chase wrote on September 3 to congratulate Washington on his election to the Presidency, offering no apology for being six months late. In the interval he had raised his sights. This time he asked for a place on the Supreme Court, even though the size and authority of the court was still being discussed by the House of Representatives. Should the President reject the application, Chase asked that it be kept "within your own Breast, for I do not wish to afford my political Enemies (for I never had any private ones) an Opportunity to Mortify and insult Me." He then sought again to remove the most obvious cause for rejection. He assured the President that he was personally loyal to him and would "support the present Government, agreeably to any late solemn Engagements."[31]

Four days later Matthew Ridley wrote to John Jay of New York, the man who seemed to be the leading candidate for the post of Chief Justice. A Pennsylvanian himself, Ridley assured Jay that Pennsylvania's leading jurist preferred to remain on the state court; hence Chase from neighboring Maryland was a logical nominee. Although Ridley claimed he had not consulted Chase, the timing of his letter was too perfect. Besides, the two had been writing letters of recommendation for each other for years. When Jay wrote back expressing doubts—or perhaps surprise—Ridley assured him that he had "since seen" Chase and "he would be very glad to serve." Aware that Chase's sudden conversion lacked credibility, Ridley assured Jay that "Like an old wounded weather-beaten soldier, he wishes for repose." Nor was his ambition unbounded. He would even, Ridley assured Jay, be willing to accept the newly created office of Attorney General.[32]

Washington ignored this finely orchestrated campaign. In 1789 he had plenty of candidates for the Supreme Court and no need to appease political opponents. Six years later, toward the end of his administration, he found himself in greater need of friends and opened simultaneous contacts with Chase and Patrick Henry. In the meantime Washington undoubtedly kept Chase's appeal within his breast, as requested. Even so, a reversal of this sort could not be kept secret for long, and Maryland Federalists probably welcomed such an important acquisition. In 1791 the assembly gratified his need for office by giving him a place on the state Supreme Court. By that time his desire for repose had evidently passed, for he brought to his new position all the partisan zeal of the convert.

Maryland Antifederalists had been a tiny minority from the beginning. Chase was almost their only prominent spokesman, and his defection was a mortal blow. When Luther Martin and William Pinkney followed Chase into Federalism, the only leader left was John Francis Mercer. Elected to Congress in 1791, he quickly moved into the ranks of House Republicans. Antifederalism in Virginia and North Carolina, on the other hand, had a broader popular base, and it lingered on in those strongholds until the controversy over constitutional amendment was ended.

THE BILL OF RIGHTS AND THE END
OF ANTIFEDERALISM

Madison's stunning declaration on the floor of the Virginia convention that he would personally work for amendments once the Constitution was approved met considerable skepticism among Antifederalists. They accused him of making false promises to secure a few needed votes and predicted flatly that nothing would come of it. Madison's motives were indeed political, but not entirely so. His initial reaction to Mason's call for a bill of rights at Philadelphia was that popular rights were adequately protected by the various state declarations. On reflection he saw that this was not necessarily so. Might not Congress, for instance, in pursuit of its power to raise armies, order troops quartered in private homes? At the Virginia convention he was not quite ready to retract his original view. He would support amendments, he told the delegates, "not because they are necessary, but because they can produce no possible danger, and may gratify some gentlemen's wishes."[33]

By the fall of 1788 he had decided that "some additional safeguards for liberty" would be acceptable, even useful, provided the essential powers of government were left intact. It was essential, he felt, to distinguish between amendments that offered procedural guarantees of rights and substantive changes that emasculated the Constitution. This very distinction, moreover, spelled the differences among Antifederalists. Some, Madison thought, were basically "friends to an effective government," but simply felt the Constitution went too far. Others had demanded a second convention to consider amendments "with the insidious hope of throwing all things into Confusion." Procedural guarantees, therefore, would have the effect of "separating the well meaning from the designing opponents."[34] The political implications of amendments were simply too obvious to be ignored. Nor was Madison alone. A Maryland Federalist declared in the midst of the federal election, "The Congress I am in hopes will quickly make some general declaration of rights & take away all claims on the Subject of Jury Trials. This will make the people easy & disarm the Enemies of the Government of their strongest Weapons."[35]

During the spring of 1789 Madison collected the 200-odd amendments recommended by the ratifying conventions and condensed them into a list of propositions which he planned to insert into the text of the Constitution. On May 25 he interrupted a House debate on the tariff bill to announce his intention of introducing amendments. At the time the move seemed hasty, since Congress would not be prepared to discuss the subject for another six weeks, but it was calculated to forestall Antifederalist moves for a second convention. On the very next day Theodorick Bland presented the resolution of the Virginia legislature, but the House quickly buried it, along with a similar proposal from New York. When the tariff debate finally ended in July, the House took up Madison's recommendations. After considerable discussion it voted to append the amendments separately, rather than insert them into the text. Though seemingly a minor point, it had important consequences. Listed separately, the amendments immediatey became a formal Bill of Rights, thereby attracting public attention and enhancing their political impact. The House sent a total of 17 amendments to the Senate; the upper house condensed them to 12. The states ultimately ratified 10.[36]

As Madison anticipated, the amendments splintered the ranks of the Antifederalists. In the House prominent Antifederalists approved the amendments and helped slip them through against the arguments of stout Federalists who still considered them unnecessary. Others, realizing Madison's political motives, fought them bitterly. When Madison arose on May 25 to announce his intent, Richard Henry Lee was instantly skeptical. "I apprehend that his ideas, and those of our convention, on this subject, are not similar," he wrote to Patrick Henry. As soon as he got a look at Madison's specific proposals Grayson complained that they were too much preoccupied with personal liberty and ignored such flaws in the Constitution as the judiciary and the tax power.[37] In the Senate Lee and Grayson tried to add some of the substantive changes recommended by the Virginia convention, but failed. The changes that the Senate did make, they felt, actually "mutilated and enfeebled" the amendments so that they were worse than ever.[38] Even George Mason, who might have been expected to greet enthusiastically Madison's body of liberties, expressed disappointment at the lack of "material Amendments."[39]

On September 28, after the two houses had compromised their differences on the amendments, Lee and Grayson sent copies to the governor and assembly with cover letters designed to give ammunition to Virginia Antifederalists. Warning that the republic was in danger of becoming a "consolidated Empire," they argued that only the adoption of substantive amendments such as those suggested by Virginia would prevent "the annihilation of the State Governments." So extreme was the language that Madison was surprised his old ally Grayson had signed it.[40] Although some Antifederalists, in their concern for the rights of states, overlooked the genuine protection that Madison's amendments afforded individuals, others did not. After he returned to Montpelier that autumn, Madison reported to Washington on local opinion: "One of the principal leaders of the Baptists lately sent me word that the amendments had entirely satisfied the disaffected of his sect, and that it would appear in their subsequent conduct."[41] Extreme Antifederalists might rage against the Bill of Rights for months to come, but politically they were dead.

The political impact of the amendments was soon evident in the assembly. When the session opened, Patrick Henry presented a resolution of thanks to Virginia's senators for their vigilance in behalf of popular liberties, but the motion was coldly received and Henry dropped it. When a House committee brought the amendments to the floor, Henry suggested postponing them to the next session in order to ascertain popular feelings on the subject. House reaction to this was no warmer, so Henry tabled his resolution and departed for home without even calling for a vote. Carrington felt that the entire session betrayed "much less intemperance than prevailed last year."[42]

The first ten of the congressional amendments were approved with only slight opposition. Edmund Randolph then registered an objection to the eleventh and twelfth (the present ninth and tenth), both of which sought to express the limited nature of the government by reserving to the states and to the people all powers not delegated. Randolph thought the phrasing too general, since it did not specify which rights were retained. He wanted to add a restriction that would specifically confine Congress to its enumerated powers. Randolph's distinction between restriction of powers and retention of rights was abstruse enough to confuse everyone, and the House rejected both amendments. Madison, furious at such a "fanciful" distinction, accused Randolph of "furnishing a handle to the disaffected" and giving North Carolina (whose convention was then meeting) a pretext "to prolong her exile."[43]

Encouraged by the disorder in Federalist ranks, the Antifederalists presented a resolution demanding that Congress approve the other amendments recommended by the Virginia convention. The proposal was twice rejected, but then on a public roll call (the only one of the session involving the Constitution) the House deadlocked at 62 to 62. Speaker Thomas Mathews cast the deciding vote against the resolution. Federalists then closed ranks; the House reversed its earlier stand and adopted the two disputed amendments "by a pretty good majority." Carrington, with considerable relief, wrote, "Had Mr. Henry conceived that such would have been the temper in the latter stages of the Session, he would not have left us."[44]

It was then the Senate's turn to stir up trouble. That body rejected the eleventh and twelfth amendments and two others for good measure. In an unprecedented move, it then ordered its objections to the amendments published in the newspapers. Its argument followed Edmund Randolph's—the retention of unspecified rights was simply not enough to prevent the abuse of national power. Madison's friends suspected that the real purpose was to pressure the House into approving some substantive amendments, especially on the matter of taxation, which had drawn some Federalist support in the ratifying convention.[45] This time House Federalists stood firm. A conference committee failed to resolve the issue, each house adhered to its stand, and Virginia's ratification of the Bill of Rights was postponed to another year.[46]

The effect, ironically, was to give Virginia an opportunity to cast the decisive vote in favor of ratification. By December 1791, when the amendments were submitted to the assembly, ten states had given them their approval; only one more was needed. They swept through without a roll call in either house. Only one voice was raised in opposition—that of Patrick Henry, who registered his dissent and promptly left town. It was the last echo of Antifederalism in Virginia. By then Patrick Henry stood alone. Moderate Antifederalists, such as James Monroe, hastened to restore good relations with the administration as soon as the first election ended.[47] The death of William Grayson in 1790 and George Mason in 1792 removed two of their most respected leaders. The day after Mason died, Richard Henry Lee resigned from the Senate and retired to his Westmoreland plantation. Younger Antifederalists drifted into the ranks of the Republican party.

NORTH CAROLINA:
THE RURAL MAJORITY ON THE DEFENSIVE

As the assembly gathered in Fayetteville in the fall of 1789, crusty old Archibald Maclaine noted with rare satisfaction that it was "said to be the most moderate one since the Revolution, and that there are nearly one-half new members."[48] The assembly met simultaneously with the second ratifying convention, and while Federalists remained in the minority, they seemed to have the initiative throughout the session. At the outset Samuel Johnston was reelected governor, but after the Constitution was approved, the assembly decided to send him to the U.S. Senate. Antifederalists supported the move, to Johnston's surprise—perhaps they wanted him out of the state.[49] The new choice for governor was the political trimmer Alexander Martin, who soon distinguished himself for opposition to the Washington administration. In 1793 the assembly rewarded him with Johnston's Senate seat. The loser in the contest for governor was William Blount, whose Federalism was somewhat firmer than Martin's but who was weak on almost every other ground. Federalists suspected him of favoring paper money, and the rural element criticized him for speculating in the public debt.[50] His ambitions frustrated, Blount moved to Tennessee to carve a new political career. A year later President Washington obliged by naming him governor of the Territory South of the River Ohio. The other federal senator named during the fall session was mild-mannered Benjamin Hawkins, who had left his Indians and returned to politics to serve in the second ratifying convention.

The state debt—and the bearing which ratification might have upon it—was the main issue before the assembly that fall. Among the arguments the Antifederalists had used at the Hillsborough convention was that the constitutional provision concerning the obligations of contracts would force the state to redeem its paper money at face value. They also predicted that the federal government would take over the debts of the states, thereby enriching speculators and contributing to the tax burden on the people. During the campaign for a second convention Federalists sought to answer these arguments with a simple proposal. If the state itself bought up continental debt certificates, just as northern speculators were doing, it would make a tidy profit when Congress funded the federal debt, and the proceeds would enable it to retire its own paper money.[51]

The idea was basically impractical, since few continental certificates were floating in North Carolina, and even assembly Federalists failed to give it serious consideration. Instead they sought to set aside specific funds for the redemption of all the state's postwar paper issues. The most the assembly would agree to was a renewal of the option to use paper money in the payment of taxes. While rejecting Federalist proposals, the rural majority did feel obliged to do something about the state's enormous debt. The old expedients for retiring the money through the sale of confiscated property or western lands were no longer available. So they tried a new approach that retained paper money while satisfying its critics. The debtors' compromise bill required all certificates to be brought to the treasury by January 1, 1791, where they would be exchanged for new certificates. The new notes would be backed by a sinking fund, created by revenue from land taxes and import duties. Old notes would be exchanged for new ones at a ratio of four to three, thereby devaluing the old money by 25 percent. Thus paper money would continue to circulate; indeed, there would even be a new emission. But the tax revenue pledged to the ultimate redemption of the new certificates meant that they would hold their value. This was enough to satisfy fiscally orthodox Federalists.[52] The bill slipped through the Commons with no visible opposition, and passed the Senate by 28 to 10. Among those who can be identified by party, Federalists backed the bill by 14 to 3, Antifederalists split evenly, 6 and 6. A few days after the Senate gave its approval, 8 of the opponents entered their objections into the record. The argument reflected the party mixture that drafted it. In an engaging appeal to the poor, they pointed out that devaluing the old money in the exchange would injure not the wealthy (many of whom had already exchanged it for western lands) but the little people who still held it. They then adopted the old creditor argument that repudiation undermined confidence in the government and violated the sanctity of contracts.[53] Given the assembly's past record on the subject of money, the Federalists had reason to congratulate themselves over this final resolution of the issue.

The solution did mean, however, that the proposals for funding the national debt, given to Congress by Alexander Hamilton only a month later, were of particular importance to North Carolina. Federal assumption of state debts could mean a splendid windfall or a crushing burden of taxes—depending on how the state's debt was calculated. The proposal was the bridge from paper money–Antifederalism to anti-Hamiltonian Republicanism.

FIGHT OVER RALEIGH

By making provision for the removal of the state's capital, the Hillsborough convention had unnecessarily complicated the question of ratification. Ironically, the Constitution gained approval long before the capital question was resolved. Despite the fortuitous link at Hillsborough, the two issues remained separate. The state's capital involved regional, rather than partisan interests. The shifting regional alliances, however, ultimately affected the geographical bases of the political parties.

The Hillsborough convention proposed a site in Wake County, on the eastern edge of the Piedmont, for the new capital. Though more centrally located than any of the places where the legislature had been meeting, the new site was not far enough west to suit the Piedmont and too far north to satisfy Cape Fear delegates. As a result, the assembly wrestled with the issue for four years, from 1788 to 1791. Whenever one house achieved a compromise that won a temporary majority, the other would reject it.[54] Finally, on January 4, 1792, a bill establishing a permanent seat of government squeaked through the Commons by two votes. The next day the Senate approved it by a margin of three votes after a violent scene in which the losers complained that "the interest of the most valuable part of the state [was being] sacrificed by the tyranny of an accidental and most trifling majority."[55]

Providing the "trifling majority" were the Albemarle and Pamlico delegates, who supported the Raleigh site to a man, and the Piedmont delegates from the vicinity of Wake County. Cape Fear delegates, evidently still holding out for Fayetteville, were solidly opposed, as were westerners. The most curious development was the changed attitude of easterners, who had resisted for years any westward movement of the capital.[56] Behind the shift may have been a bargain concerning the creation of new counties. During the war and for some years after a number of new counties were erected, mostly in the west. As a result of the additions, Albemarle, the politically dominant region throughout the colonial period, yielded to the Piedmont. After Rowan County was subdivided in 1788, easterners dug in their heels, and for the next two years the assembly rejected every county subdivision bill.[57]

Then, within a week after the capital bill passed in January 1792, the assembly created two new counties, one on the seaboard and one in the Piedmont, while rejecting a bill creating a new county in the far west.[58] Albemarle-Pamlico delegates supported not only the eastern county but the new one in the Piedmont.

Clearly a bargain had been struck preventing the erection of yet another western county. Yet it was not simply a county trade-off, for the Cape Fear delegates voted against all the new counties, even though the eastern one (Dobbs) was in their vicinity. The bargain must have included the capital relocation. Thus, Albemarle-Pamlico delegates won an east-central location for the capital and a new eastern county. The eastern Piedmont won both the capital and a new county. The Cape Fear won a new county, while losing the capital, and the west was left out in the cold.

It was a regional bargain; political parties were not involved. They were eventually affected, however, The following year westerners seeking revenge joined with Cape Fear delegates in a vote keeping the capital at Fayetteville for another year. That contest, as we shall see in a later chapter, resulted in another compromise that brought the state its first Republican U.S. senator, Alexander Martin.

ANTIFEDERALISM: DEATH AND RESURRECTION

Surveying the state of the union at the end of 1790, one rather ordinary, semiliterate farmer from the upper Cape Fear Valley was inclined to be pessimistic. Though finally reconciled to the Constitution, he was apprehensive for the future of the South because the northern and middle states, "being more Similar in their Interests, manners, customs, and Trade, will be more united, and by being more numerous and powerful will form the laws of the general Government to their own advantage and convenience." Among the threats to the South, he felt, were Congress' willingness to discuss emancipation of slaves, a federal treaty with the Creeks, and the administration's proposed excise on whisky.[59] Although the dangers were more apprehended than real, the list betrayed a deep-seated, if rudimentary, sectional consciousness.

The parts of the Chesapeake that had been most hostile to national authority and most suspicious of northern designs—the head of the bay, the Virginia Piedmont and Southside, and central North Carolina—retained their localist frame of mind. And all their suspicions were soon confirmed by Alexander Hamilton's proposals for funding the national debt. So patently northern was Hamilton's scheme in conception and mercantile in effect that it seemed to vindicate all the dire prophecies of the southern Antifederalists.

Hamilton's system thus resurrected the party warfare. Because the Constitution was no longer an issue, a party label for the opposition had to be found, and the rebirth occasioned some shifts among political leaders. But the new parties that emerged—Federalist and Republican—drew their main strength from the old regional and political alignments.

CHAPTER THIRTEEN

The Chesapeake Wins the Capital

"THERE HAS not yet been much debating in the Senate," reported North Carolina's newly appointed senator, Samuel Johnston, early in 1790. "In some few instances where there has, it would appear that the sentiments of the Northern or Eastern and Southern members constantly clash, even when local interests are out of the question. This is a thing I cannot account for; even the lawyers from these different quarters cannot agree on the principles and construction of law, though they agree among themselves."[1] If Alexander Hamilton's Report on the Public Credit had been dropped into a Congress free from sectional tensions, it would, in all likelihood, have precipitated nothing more than an arid debate on government finance, similar to the annual report of Britain's Board of Treasury. But the conflict among regional interests was never far from the surface during the first session of 1789, in tariff levels, trade policy, the judiciary, or the unending controversy over the location of the nation's capital. It was with visible relief that Congress turned the thorny problem of credit over to the Secretary of the Treasury as it departed for home in October 1789.

The question of the public debt had always aroused sectional jealousies. Through the 1780s Virginians prided themselves on their ability to maintain the state's annual subsidy to Congress, and they frequently complained of the laggard New England states. In 1784 one of the state's delegates claimed that Virginia's contribution was the only thing that kept Congress functioning.[2] The tendency among New England states to ease their domestic difficulties with paper money (Rhode Island tainted the entire region), while defaulting on the continental obligations, was an important factor in the sectional hostility voiced by men such as William Grayson and Richard Henry Lee.[3] The debt question was an exposed nerve; almost any solution was certain to evoke screams of pain from Virginians. Hamilton unfortunately did nothing to ease the shock.

Hamilton consulted congressional and state leaders before drafting his report. Madison's response was typical. He wanted the debt paid off as speedily as possible, he told Hamilton. Though not exactly sure how, he thought the revenue from the sale of public lands might be the most painless way. High land prices, moreover, would prevent "licentious settlements, by which the value of the property will not only be lost, but the authority of the laws impaired."[4] This was the voice that had combatted Arthur Campbell and Patrick Henry; nowhere was there a hint of evading debts. Hamilton could well be pardoned for assuming he had an ally in any scheme designed to restore the nation's credit by discharging its past obligations at their face value.

It was the magnitude of Hamilton's proposals that antagonized Virginians. The report, which he sent to Congress in January 1790, proposed to combine the various monetary obligations of the government, amounting to some 52 million dollars, together with the arrears of interest (approximately 15 million) into a single fund, and issue new bonds to the entire amount. Securities which had depreciated badly under the old Congress would be accepted at their face value. The new debt certificates would maintain their value because a certain part of the government's revenue would be pledged to discharge both interest and principal. In addition, Hamilton boldly proposed that the federal government assume the war debts of the states (about $19 million more). These obligations had been incurred in the common defense, he argued; it was only fair that they be discharged by all. Besides, by eliminating most of the state debts, he eliminated their need for revenue. As the federal government's purse grew larger, so would its powers.

Virginians favored paying debts, but they were not prepared for this. Reimbursing the present holders of government securities, with no effort to find the original holders, meant an enormous windfall to speculators, most of them northern merchants. A debt of such enormous size, moreover, could not be discharged quickly. The nation would labor under it for years, and Congress would be forced to levy new taxes to pay it off. Assumption of state debts was the cruelest blow of all. By devoting 80 percent of its revenue to debt retirement, Virginia had managed to reduce its state debt from over £4 million in 1784 to less than £1 million in 1790.[5] Now it appeared that Virginians would be taxed all over again to pay the debts of other states. Far from being rewarded for her fiscal orthodoxy and disinterested patriotism, Virginia had to continue paying, and most of the proceeds would end in the pockets of the very men who had failed in time of crisis—the northern merchants.

MADISON'S PLAN OF DISCRIMINATION

When the funding idea came before the House of Representatives in mid-February, Madison was instantly on his feet with a counterproposal. Cashing the government's securities at their face value, he told the House, would give an undeserved profit to speculators and neglect the interests of original holders who had been forced to sell out during the depression. He suggested instead that the treasury discriminate among the various classes of security holders, giving present owners the current market value (then about 50 percent of face value) and the remainder to original holders insofar as they could be found. Finding them was the flaw in the plan, for the securities had changed hands like paper money, and in most cases the original purchasers were not recorded. The House rejected the idea, 31 to 13. Only the numbers were recorded, but a Federalist congressman later asserted that 9 of the minority were Virginians.[6]

Reaction to Madison's proposal followed familiar partisan lines. Maryland Federalists generally approved of Hamilton's report. Given advance word by friends in New York, some were busy themselves buying state and federal paper. "Send me your money," General O. H. Williams wrote a friend. "I'll make what I can on't. There's no danger of loss."[7] In Congress, only Michael J. Stone sided with Madison, and he lost his seat in the fall election.

Most Virginia Federalists felt the same. "The Commercial and most noisy part of [the state] is against" Madison, David Stuart informed the President. Discrimination was "such a deviation from the plain and beaten track as must make every Creditor of the Public tremble." Stuart himself worried that Madison's scheme amounted to a legislative interference in private contracts, something the Constitution was designed to prevent.[8] Valley Federalists were equally critical. General Adam Stephen summed up western sentiment: "Twas said let Hamilton be, and all was right."[9] Edmund Randolph and Joseph Jones, chronic trimmers, considered discrimination just but impractical. George Mason, on the other hand "strenuously" backed the idea, and Madison received a stream of reports that his stand was popular in the Antifederal parts of the state.[10]

ASSUMPTION OF STATE DEBTS

Assumption was another matter. "The people of Virginia," reported Edmund Randolph, "are, I believe, almost unanimous against the assumption of state debts. Some of the strongest antifederalists here are high in their eulogiums on all of you who have opposed the measure."[11] Virginians objected not only because they had virtually discharged much of their own debt, but because assumption might shortchange various other claims that the state had. Maryland and North Carolina shared this concern. Maryland congressmen, reported William Smith in February, had not yet heard from their constituents on the subject of assumption, but he thought they would all vote against it.[12] All three states had been slow in establishing their claims against the central government for their contributions to the war effort. Because the South had been the main theater of fighting in the latter stages of the war, the Chesapeake states had sizable claims. But the claims were difficult to assemble because government had been disrupted and records destroyed. They feared that an immediate assumption of state debts, as proposed by Hamilton, would leave them short.[13]

At the very least, they wanted the ultimate balance of payments worked out first, so they would know how they stood. The method by which the federal claims commissioners worked, after all, was crucial. In the past, they had been extremely cautious, accepting only claims against the central government that had full documentary support. If such rigid criteria were applied to the state claims as well, the southerners would be losers. A more liberal attitude, on the other hand, would turn them from debtors to creditors. Assumption under those conditions could be a blessing. Such considerations, however, were confined to congressmen. The public saw nothing but federal encroachment.

Popular suspicions were further aroused, David Stuart informed the President, by "the number of Speculators who have been traversing the State purchasing up State Securities."[14] Antifederalists reminded all who would listen of their dire prediction that the South would fall into the hands of northern merchants under the Constitution. Patrick Henry, who had left the legislature in midsession the previous December for lack of support, found himself once again the center of attention. "Henry already is considered as a prophet," observed Henry Lee. When assumption suffered an initial defeat in the House, Edward Carrington expressed deep relief, for the scheme posed many problems for the "supporters of the Government" in the Virginia assembly. It was certain to "add to the Enemies of the Govt many of its friends as a discontented party."[15] Already outnumbered two to one, administration Federalists scarcely needed more enemies.

In North Carolina, only Judge Iredell gave wholehearted support to Hamilton's plan. Samuel Johnston feared that assumption might so enlarge the debt that the government would have to either default on its obligations or increase taxes. The first was as much anathema to him as the second was to his constituents. Benjamin Hawkins, the state's other senator, was rumored to favor it. That was untrue and he publicly denied it, but the allegation ended his legislative career. The assembly replaced him in 1792.[16]

On March 8, 1790, the Hamiltonians won an initial test on assumption by 31 to 26 in committee of the whole. Such a margin was too close for comfort, given the uncertainties of congressional attendance. Nor were the Hamiltonians reassured when, toward the end of the month, assumption survived another test by an even narrower margin of 29 to 27. Among the absentees were the North Carolina delegation, except for Hugh Williamson. As the state's agent for the settlement of claims, Williamson understood what was at stake and fought the measure furiously on the floor. In the course of the month Ashe and Bloodworth took their seats. Both were "decidedly opposed," and it was predicted that assumption would be rejected the next time it came to a vote.[17] It was, on April 12, by 29 to 31. North Carolinians later boasted that it was they who "gave a turn to the business," but there were some switches as well, probably among Pennsylvanians.[18]

In the House debate only Daniel Carroll and Theodorick Bland, among Chesapeake congressmen, voiced approval for assumption. Bland told his colleagues privately that his reason for doing so was to demonstrate to the world what the Antifederalists had been saying all along, that the Constitution would lead to a consolidated national government.[19] The reasoning was a bit specious. Perhaps better reasons for his curious behavior were personal interest (he owned over £5,000 in securities) and antipathy to Madison.[20] Stone and Seney of Maryland, as well as Page and Moore of Virginia, all of whom would soon be calling themselves Republicans, backed Madison in the House discussion.[21]

Richard Bland Lee and Alexander White, both of whom would remain Federalists, temporized. Lee thought assumption might be palatable if the final accounts were equitable and Virginia ultimately got what she considered due her. He would have preferred to make all payments out of the income from land sales, however, and he backed a motion by White to ask the Secretary of the Treasury what taxes, if any, he planned to levy in order to pay the debt. The House approved White's motion on March 2, but nothing more was heard of it. White himself was more critical of assumption, but he was willing to compromise. One solution, he suggested, was for the government to assume only the difference between what a state owed its creditors and what the central government owed it.[22] Nothing further was heard of this suggestion either, but it was clear that the administration could expect little help from the Chesapeake states until there was some movement on the question of who should settle the state accounts and how.

On April 16, four days after the assumption was rejected, Thomas FitzSimons, a Philadelphia merchant-banker and one of Hamilton's ablest supporters, moved to appoint a committee to draft a bill for the "speedy" settlement of state accounts. FitzSimons apparently had been in contact with Hugh Williamson, the chief spokesman for the states with laggard accounts. Williamson took credit for FitzSimon's motion in a private note to Governor Martin and predicted that the resulting bill would "suit our State." With proper management, he felt, North Carolina would end up a creditor state to the amount of $2 million. He even planned to charge the federal government for Indian depredations and unused coastal fortifications.[23]

A week after the FitzSimons-Williamson committee began its deliberations—April 26—FitzSimons moved to discharge the assumption question from committee of the whole, in effect postponing further consideration of it for the time being. The motion passed by an astonishing 32 to 18. Only New England and South Carolina Federalists held out against it. Chesapeake congressmen unanimously favored it (with the exception again of Theodorick Bland), and so, significantly, did the Pennsylvanians, including several besides FitzSimons who had backed assumption in debate.[24] Clearly, a bargain was in the air. For the next month the House marked time with other matters, mostly the details of the funding system. Then on May 27 FitzSimons sprang another surprise—a motion that Congress move to Philadelphia for its next session. Through the succeeding ballots it was evident that there was a firm understanding among Pennsylvanians, Marylanders (except for Smith of Baltimore), and Virginians.[25]

A Pennsylvania-Chesapeake alliance concerning the location of the nation's capital was not new. A double removal, first to

Philadelphia and then to the Potomac, had been discussed for several years, but advocates of New York had managed to keep it from fruition. In the previous session, 1789, the alliance had fallen apart, owing to the cynical movements of Robert Morris. Assumption of state debts, it seems, was the cement that put it back together. It was a natural linkage, for the very states that were most bitterly opposed to assumption were the states who seemed most eager to obtain the permanent seat of the federal government.

THE RESIDENCE CONTROVERSY

For nearly a decade the political leaders of Maryland and Virginia had been conspiring to win the seat of government. Throughout the war they had grumbled about the chill winters of Philadelphia, but there was little that could be done until the military contest ended. In the spring of 1783, as soon as terms of the preliminary peace articles were announced, New York suggested that Congress make Kingston on the Hudson River its permanent seat. Anticipating offers from other states as well, Congress postponed debate on the question until October. A few days later a mutiny in the Pennsylvania Line forced Congress to flee to Princeton and made the choice of a permanent location urgent. There was general support for settling in some place "where the Laws are pure & the Citizens are good Whigs," as one Virginian put it.[26] In the fall of 1783, Madison drew up a list of advantages which the Potomac offered.

The Potomac did have impressive assets. It lay close to the center of the nation, north and south. It was easily defended, yet open to Atlantic commerce, and it offered access to the interior of the continent. Jefferson approached the Maryland delegation with a proposal that they jointly offer Congress a district straddling the Potomac near Georgetown. The joint offer would have more force than one from a single state, he thought, and the central location ought to prove "generally agreeable" to all.[27] The idea met a cold reception in the Maryland assembly, however. Development of the Potomac might well come at the expense of Baltimore's trade, it feared. Instead, it unanimously resolved to invite Congress to make

Annapolis its permanent home.[28] This idea became lost in the welter of invitations from other states. In the fall of 1783 Congress sought to appease all regional interests by constructing two capitals, one on the Delaware near Trenton and one on the Potomac. While facilities were being built on these locations, Congress would reside half the year in Trenton and half at Annapolis.[29] This compromise was clearly impractical, however. It involved huge, unnecessary expenses at a time when Congress was having difficulty paying its foreign creditors and its army. When Congress convened at Trenton in the fall of 1784 it settled on the Delaware River location and appropriated £100,000 for the construction of buildings. Maryland's defection temporarily doomed the Potomac site. Congress then adjourned to New York while its permanent residence was being constructed.[30]

Advocates of the Potomac refused to give up. Among the reasons for establishing the Potomac Company to improve the river was the hope that Congress might be induced to change its mind.[31] In Congress, William Grayson, a resident of the Northern Neck, undermined the Delaware River project with the help of delegates who wanted to remain in New York. They got the appropriation for the new city reduced from £100,000 to £30,000 and finally eliminated altogether.[32]

Congress continued to sit in New York until the Constitution reopened the residence question by authorizing a ten-mile-square district for the new government. Behind this provision undoubtedly was an understanding among the Pennsylvania and Virginia delegates in the convention. No one else stood to gain by it. Marylanders might have caused difficulty had they been in constant attendance, but the only one who stayed all summer was Daniel Carroll, a resident of the Potomac. The provision for a federal district evoked some discussion during the ratification campaign, and several states followed up their approval with offers of land cessions to Congress.

In the summer of 1788 the old Congress was confronted with the residence question once more, for it had to assign a place for "commencing proceedings" under the Constitution. On July 28 a motion in favor of Philadelphia received the vote of 6 states to 4 (2 divided) but failed for lack of a majority (7 states).[33] Whether or not the Pennsylvania and Virginia delegates had reached an understanding at the federal convention, they had certainly done so by the summer of 1788. In fact, even Maryland momentarily overcame its misgivings. Every delegate from the three Chesapeake states voted in favor of Philadelphia. The alliance with Pennsylvania held firm through dozens of roll calls over the next six weeks.

A few days after the initial roll call Madison explained to Washington the rationale behind the Virginia-Pennsylvania alliance. There were four sites in contention, he felt—New York, Philadelphia, Baltimore, and the Potomac. Assuming that the ultimate object of Virginians was to secure a permanent seat on the Potomac, the question was which of the other three made the best temporary location. New York, he felt, was inconvenient for the South and West, and so far to the north that the ultimate compromise was certain to lie north of the Potomac, probably somewhere in New Jersey. Baltimore, on the other hand, was too far south. A majority of states lay to the north of it, and delegates dissatisfied with the city would produce a coalition favoring a permanent seat to the northward. Philadelphia was so centrally located that there was an even balance of states on either side. This made it more acceptable to all but also easier to escape. The key was the Pennsylvanians themselves, and they, Madison hinted, might be offered a sweetener—the promise of a fairly lengthy stay in the temporary seat. "The only chance the Potomac has is to get things in such a train . . . that the final seat may be undecided for two or three years, within which period the Western and Southern population will enter more into the estimate."[34] He did not need to say it because Washington well knew that the admission of Kentucky and Tennessee would tip the balance.

What prompted the Marylanders to join thePennsylvania-Virginia axis at this point is unclear. Perhaps, having failed with the Annapolis project in 1784, they recognized that the only chance for a southern capital lay in a joint appeal with Virginia. That, at least, was the feeling of General O. H. Williams, one of the most prominent figures in Baltimore.[35] North Carolina's adherence to the coalition was largely due to the influence of Hugh Williamson, a native of Pennsylvania who had taught for a time at the College of Philadelphia. After the initial ballot, northern delegates pointed out the impropriety of North Carolina's participation in the choice of capital since it had not yet ratified the Constitution, and Williamson accordingly departed for home.

New York from the outset had the best chance of winning that summer because it had the backing of the New England states, plus New Jersey and South Carolina. The South Carolinians, it was whispered, had mistresses in New York and were unwilling to venture into new social pastures. The Pennsylvania-Maryland-Virginia coalition, once Philadelphia was defeated, accordingly backed a succession of other sites—Lancaster; Wilmington, Delaware; and Baltimore. Each failed to win the necessary majority.

In early September Tench Coxe, a prominent merchant of Philadelphia who had lent freely of his purse and pen in the cause of ratification, wrote Madison to express concern at the delay. Better, he thought, to settle on New York as a temporary meeting place than to hazard the new government. Madison had already reached a similar conclusion. The Pennsylvania delegates agreed, but the Marylanders left for home rather than publicly yield.[36] On September 12 Madison and Carrington made a final effort to secure approval of a more central location without naming a site, and when this failed they capitulated. A resolution making "the present seat of Congress the place for commencing proceedings under the said Consitution" passed with only Delaware voting nay.[37]

Madison worried some that the surrender might mean a lengthy stay in New York, and northerners probably felt the same. But there was too much at stake to let the prize go by default. As soon as the First Congress settled down to business in the spring of 1789, members of the Maryland contingent began sounding Pennsylvanians about the possibility of removal.[38] By the end of August talks had proceeded to the point where the residence question could be reopened as soon as the Congress completed action on the executive and judiciary. "The plan now projected," Arthur Lee wrote home on August 29, "is to unite the southern & middle voices by establishing the permanent Seat on Potowmac & the temporary residence in Philadelphia."[39] Two days earlier a Pennsylvania congressman had presented a motion in favor of a more central location for the capital.[40]

The Pennsylvanians, however, had been playing a double game. While some conversed with the southerners, Robert Morris and others had been making an arrangement with the New England congressmen. The Pennsylvanians, in essence, agreed to support whatever spot in Pennsylvania the New Englanders named. Morris evidently expected them to point to the falls of the Delaware, the place that he himself most desired. It was an incredibly naïve assumption, for the New Englanders could have had no other motive than to break up the suspected Pennsylvania-Virginia alliance.[41]

The Virginians soon got wind of the double-dealing. On the evening of September 1, Morris called a meeting of the Pennsylvanians at the lodgings of Thomas FitzSimons, who seemed to be the strongest personality in the delegation. Attending the meeting, evidently on Morris's invitation, were Rufus King of New York and Benjamin Goodhue of Massachusetts. While these agents were presenting their proposals, Madison appeared, evidently armed with proposals of his own. The result was that the meeting broke up in disorder, with several Pennsylvanians declaring themselves no longer bound by any agreement.[42]

Then it was New England's turn to play a double game. When the House took up the removal motion on September 3, Goodhue offered a substitute resolution naming the Susquehanna as the site for a permanent seat. Their intent, it seemed, was mainly to embarrass Morris. Morris nevertheless adhered to the bargain, probably in the hopes of substituting the falls of the Delaware in the upper house.[43] The Virginians tried unsuccessfully to secure an adjournment and then offered a motion to substitute the Potomac for the Susquehanna. This was defeated without a roll call; neither side was yet willing to test its strength or its allies. Infuriated at the cynical double-dealing among northerners, Madison twice took the floor to complain of an overbearing northern majority. In defense of southern interests he turned almost instinctively to states' rights. Contradicting arguments he had expressed as lately as *The Federalist* essays, he urged the importance of local authority in a republic; it was, he thought, the best defense of minority rights.[44] It was the beginning of the transition from Madison-the-Federalist to Madison-the-Republican.

On September 5 Thomas FitzSimons presented an additional resolution authorizing the President to appoint commissioners to ascertain the best location on the Susquehanna for a capital city and to begin purchasing land. Perhaps the Pennsylvanians felt that their state stood to benefit regardless of the outcome. In any case, their alliance with New York and New England was firmly reestablished.[45] When Richard Bland Lee again moved the Potomac, he went down to defeat by 21 to 29. All the Pennsylvanians voted against the Potomac, and with them two Marylanders, Smith and Seney, whose districts bordered on the Susquehanna. The northern alliance held firm through a succession of votes as the Virginians proposed first Wilmington as an alternative and then a broad choice of Potomac, Susquehanna, or Delaware, and finally made a motion to keep the Susquehanna but permit the commissioners to choose a site in either Maryland or Pennsylvania. In all the votes the only change was in the stance of a couple of Maryland congressman, seeking advantage for their homeland. The Virginians did get some new-found support from the South Carolinians, who evidently considered the Susquehanna a social desert, but it was not enough. The northern coalition held a majority that averaged about six votes.[46]

Giving up on the permanent seat, the Virginians sought to split their opponents on the temporary capital. They first tried to substitute Wilmington for New York as the temporary seat, and when that failed they suggested Philadelphia. This was the supreme test for the northern alliance, but the Pennsylvanians adhered. All but one voted to stay in New York.[47] FitzSimons's resolution then passed by 28 to 21 and a committee was ordered to draft a bill. The Susquehanna bill occasioned a few more days of debate toward the end of September before being approved 31 to 17.[48] At the end the Marylanders, except for Daniel Carroll, yielded and endorsed the bill.

When the bill reached the Senate, Robert Morris showed his colors. Deserting his New England allies (who could hardly have been surprised), he moved to substitute Germantown for the Susquehanna, with the additional proviso that the move would not be undertaken until the state of Pennsylvania voted £100,000 for the construction of the capital. The Senate divided equally on this, 9 and 9, and the Vice President startled everyone by casting the decisive vote in favor. Adams's rationale was that Congress ought to accept Pennsylvania's offer of money.[49] In the House, Thomas FitzSimons repaired the northern alliance by promising that Pennsylvania would support New York as the temporary capital for three years. The House accordingly passed the Germantown bill (without a recorded vote), but it attached a minor amendment that forced the Senate to reconsider it. On the last day of the session the Senate instead decided to postpone the entire matter. Robert Morris, in a final act of perfidy, voted for postponement.[50] Doubtless he decided that Germantown was too implausible a capital; once settled in New York, the government would probably stay there. His own interests demanded that the government be moved immediately to Philadelphia, even if the price was ultimate relocation on the Potomac.

On his way home Madison stopped off in Philadelphia to see Morris. In his conversation, Madison informed Washington, the Pennsylvania senator "betrayed his dislike of the upshot of the business at N. York and his desire to keep alive the Southern project of an arrangement with Pennsylvania." Madison, still bitter, reminded Morris of the conduct of the Pennsylvania delegation and demanded assurances of future loyalty. Morris agreed to keep his cohorts in line, and the two mapped strategy for the next session. They decided to ignore the postponed Germantown bill and make a fresh start, possibly with a motion to move the government to Philadelphia. Anticipating that such a motion would resurrect the New England offer to relocate on the Susquehanna, they decided to delay the matter until midway through the 1790 session. They would bide their time in the hope that events would present some favorable opportunity.[51] During the winter the Virginia assembly attempted to smooth the way by passing resolutions offering to cede land for a capital city and providing the federal government with information on the navigability of the Potomac. The only opposition to the idea, reported Madison's assembly informant John Dawson, came from the counties south of the James, which were "under an apprehension that it would not be advantageous to that part of the State; and from some of the Antis who considered it as a favour to Congress."[52]

THE COMPROMISE OF 1790

True to plan, the residence issue was absent from congressional debate during the early part of the 1790 session, but it was discussed continually among the delegations and at social gatherings. Among the Pennsylvanians, who dined together every Monday evening, it was early evident that Robert Morris had been at work. As soon as Senator William Maclay arrived in town, he was bombarded by arguments in favor of a Philadelphia-Potomac bargain.[53] Everyone seemed to be awaiting the proper moment to reopen the question. The defeat of assumption on April 12 apparently presented the opportunity.

By the end of March the assumption and residence questions were being linked in the private meetings of the Pennsylvania delegation. Whenever one subject came up, the other seemed to follow.[54] The initial defeat of assumption on March 29 brought the first discussions of a deal. A few days later the Pennsylvanians' boarding house entertained a mysterious guest for dinner, a Mr. Jackson, whom Senator Maclay described as a member "of the President's family."[55] This individual was undoubtedly Major William Jackson, an old friend of Hamilton's. At Hamilton's behest, Jackson served as secretary of the Constitutional Convention, and he subsequently became a partner of William Bingam, Thomas Willing's son-in-law.[56] What he represented in New York was a combination of the Philadelphians' interests and Hamilton's.

The result of the meeting was a suggestion that Pennsylvania switch some votes to favor assumption of exchange for votes from South Carolina and Massachusetts in favor of relocating the capital in Philadelphia. The scheme got a cold reception from the opponents of assumption, Speaker Frederick A. C. Muhlenburg and Senator Maclay, but three days later the Hamiltonians were back.

On April 7, FitzSimons and Clymer extolled the virtues of Massachusetts and South Carolina and hinted that Pennsylvania could have the capital if it would back assumption. This time Maclay flatly refused, suggesting instead that assumption be postponed and that they push the residence question "while both parties feared and both courted the Pennsylvania vote."[57]

This scheme was doomed from the start—and not just from Maclay's intransigence. The Pennsylvanians had no reason to trust Massachusetts; they had been burned by the Yankees on the capital question the previous fall. Southerners were better allies on the capital issue, and they could be made to swallow assumption—if they could be satisfied on the matter of final settlement. In addition, southerners soon learned of the talks involving a capital-assumption bargain between Pennsylvania and Massachusetts and threatened to abandon all support for Philadelphia.[58] The Pennsylvanians really had little choice but to adhere to the bargain struck by Morris and Madison the previous autumn.

On the day of the crucial vote on assumption, April 12, FitzSimons and Clymer both stated in debate that they hoped the system would be arranged so there was equitability in the balance of payments between federal and state governments. This was an open bid for Chesapeake support. When assumption failed anyway by two votes, 29 to 31, FitzSimons rose again to express the hope that it would ultimately be approved "under proper modifications."[59] The Chesapeake delegates apparently accepted this invitation to negotiate, and within a week there was general agreement on the framework of a bargain. On April 20, FitzSimons and Williamson secured the appointment of a committee to draft a new law on the settlement of accounts. When the Pennsylvanians met for their weekly social hour that evening, the two Philadelphians, Clymer and FitzSimons, argued in favor of a "Potomac contract."[60] Maclay again threw cold water on the idea of a bargain, but he succeeded only in getting himself ostracized. When Maclay called on FitzSimons on the April 26, seeking an explanation for his unexpected motion to discharge the House from further consideration of assumption, the Philadelphian refused even to discuss it.[61] Until the bargain was consummated Maclay was nothing but trouble.

On May 13, Hugh Williamson informed Governor Martin that the settlement bill was nearly completed, and its main purpose was to make it easier for the states to justify their claims. He anticipated that North Carolina "must gain a Million of Dollars by the difference of Systems."[62] That same day FitzSimons began lining up support for the new measure. Falling in with Maclay on the street—and thereby ending the senator's brief isolation—he launched into a plea for help. According to Maclay, he argued that "These Southern people have a matter much at heart, and it is *my* [i.e., Maclay's] *power to oblige them.* They fear settlement; they cannot bear it; they have been negligent of their accounts, and the Eastern people have kept exact amounts of everything."[63] At that point the conversation was interrupted, and Maclay was left puzzled at what it was all about. Given Maclay's aversion to bargains, FitzSimons may have simply changed his mind. But it is evident that the settlement bill was part of the backstairs negotiations.

Besides, it was time to bring things into the open, and there, at least, Senator Maclay's candor could be utilized. The plan, at this point, was to offer a simple motion in the Senate to open the next session in Philadelphia. Maclay readily agreed to support this, even though he was aware that there was some sort of understanding in regard to the Potomac. He and Robert Morris spent the weekend of May 15–16 lining up support. The initial plan was to ask Richard Henry Lee to make the motion, but Morris decided to do it himself.[64] A thin house kept Morris from introducing the resolution until May 24, and he occupied the interval with further talks with Major Jackson and the New Englanders.[65] Morris was still keeping his options open, though he risked everything in doing so.

When Morris at last made his motion, Schuyler of New York obtained a one-day postponement. New Yorkers wanted the capital as badly as anyone, but until Morris broached the subject they had seen no need to discuss it—publicly, at any rate. But once it was in the open, they swung into action. In the course of one evening they pressured Johnston and Hawkins of North Carolina while simultaneously offering a deal to Virginia. They would back a permanent seat on the Potomac if the Virginians would permit the capital to remain temporarily in New York. Virginians probably doubted the sincerity of this last-minute appeal, and in any case, their negotiations with the Pennsylvanians had proceeded too far to turn back.

The North Carolinians were another matter, however. They were equally avid for a southern location for the capital, but more inclined to distrust Philadelphia. "Once they get us there," wrote John B. Ashe, "adieu to the Potomack."[66] Nor do they appear to have been fully apprised of the Pennsylvania-Virginia arrangements.[67] The Virginians apparently took them for granted on the Potomac capital and the settlement bill, and regarded them as hopeless on the matter of assumption. On May 26 Morris's motion in favor of holding the next session in Philadelphia was postponed by 13 to 11, with Johnston and Hawkins casting the decisive votes against removal. Carroll, Henry, Lee, and Walker sided with the Pennsylvanians.[68]

The next day Morris withdrew his motion, and Thomas Fitz-Simons brought it before the House of Representatives. The Pennsylvania-Chesapeake coalition had a better chance in the House, where population gave them greater representation. Proponents of New York offered amendment after amendment, but the alliance held firm through a succession of roll calls. On May 31 the House approved the resolution by the surprisingly strong margin of 38 to 22. About half the Massachusetts delegation deserted the New Yorkers, probably as a result of an understanding with Robert Morris.[69]

Proponents of New York were far from finished. That same day Pierce Butler of South Carolina rose in the Senate with a bill providing for both a permanent and a temporary capital. The locations were left blank, but it was clearly a move to erase the effect of the House action. The Pennsylvanians tried to get it postponed, but failed when the Senate tied 12 to 12 and Adams voted nay. The bill was then referred to a select committee by the same margin, Adams this time voting yea. On each vote adherents of the Delaware-Potomac scheme involved New Hampshire, New Jersey, Pennsylvania, Delaware, Maryland, and Virginia.[70] New Hampshire's accession to the coalition is no surprise. The two New Hampshire senators, John Langdon and Paine Wingate, had backed Philadelphia from the outset; indeed, Langdon had seconded Morris's May 24 motion. Langdon was the New Hampshire agent for Morris's mercantile firm, and he owned over £27,000 in securities, both state and federal.[71] On May 20, when the coalition was formed, Senator Maclay noticed that Langdon was closeted much of the day with Morris and Major Jackson.[72] He was undoubtedly part of Morris's residence-for-assumption negotiations.

More curious was Robert Morris's absence from the Senate during these crucial votes. He later offered the rather lame explanation to Maclay that he was too busy with his accounts. Maclay was particularly chagrined because Morris's influence was needed in constituting the committee. As it was, the committee appointed, apparently by John Adams, was "rather unfavorable." In fact, it contained a three-to-two margin against the Delaware-Potomac coalition.[73] The House resolution in favor of Philadelphia was then referred to the same committee. The reason for doing this, Secretary of State Jefferson explained to his former private secretary, William Short, was to "try to draw out time" until the arrival of Rhode Island's senators. That state had finally acceded to the Constitution and her senators were expected in ten days or so. They were expected to favor keeping the capital in New York; hence by referring all residence motions to committee the New York–New England alliance hoped to delay action.[74]

While the Senate dallied over the capital issue, the House on June 1 took up Williamson's bill for the settlement of state accounts. So far as the Chesapeake was concerned, this was the necessary sweetener on the funding system pill. And Williamson had done his work well. Virginia's commissioner for accounts, Colonel William Davies, had experienced the same difficulty Williamson had in locating and validating his state's claims. But late in May, with the substance of Williamson's bill before them, Davies and Madison spent two days reexamining the accounts in various federal offices, and they were "happy to find" that Virginia would be as well off as "her more immediate antagonists, Massachusetts and South Carolina, should the business of assumption be brought up again."[75] Williamson's bill loosened the standards for accepting state claims, but the critical matter—as with any legislation—was the way in which it would be interpreted and enforced. Williamson had even seen to that—he included a provision that expanded the federal examining commission from three men to five. Virginia, given its size and population, would have a good claim on one of the appointments. New Englanders also realized this, and from the outset, this provision was the most controversial feature of the bill.

On Sunday June 6, Jefferson sent a hastily scribbled dinner invitation to Tench Coxe by way of Madison, graciously seeking Coxe's pardon for "asking him to so unceremonious a one."[76] The occasion was clearly political—otherwise Jefferson would have sent the message by a servant. In all likelihood, Madison conveyed the exact purposes orally. The obvious agenda was the final settlement bill before the House, the residence bill before the Senate, and the entire question of assumption of state debts. It was time to draw the threads together.

Jefferson and Coxe were both comparatively new to the bargaining table. Coxe had arrived in New York on May 7 to take up his duties as Assistant Secretary of the Treasury. He immediately established contact with the Pennsylvanians in Congress, who kept him informed of the residence schemes. A prominent Philadelphian with great influence at the Treasury, Coxe was a natural link in any capital-assumption arrangement. He undoubtedly joined Major Jackson as Hamilton's spokesman in the various negotiations.[77] Jefferson was even newer to the political scene. He arrived in New York on March 21 to take up his duties at the State Department and was immediately flattened with a migraine headache that lasted until the end of May. He moved into permanent quarters at 57 Maiden Lane on June 2, and this was probably his first effort to entertain. Once involved, however, Jefferson became an integral part of the negotiations.[78]

The next day, June 7, the House resumed discussion of the settlement bill, accepted an amendment by Madison (the nature of which was, unfortunately, not put on the record). On the ninth they sent the bill to a select committee for further amendment, and a week later FitzSimons reported it back to the floor. At that point northern congressmen tried to delete the provision for extra commissioners but failed, and the bill slipped through the House on June 22 with little debate and no roll calls.[79]

In the meantime the Senate had been wrestling with the residence question. On Monday June 7 the Butler committee came in with its report. It went to the nub of the problem but failed to resolve it. It agreed that the permanent seat ought to be on the Potomac (few objected to that because no one, except the Chesapeake people, thought it would ever come about), but it confessed that it could not agree on a temporary location. That evening the Pennsylvania delegation met for its weekly social hour, and it decided to invite all the senators who were part of the Delaware-Potomac residence alliance. There was general agreement that the Butler report, which left blank the temporary seat, was another effort to split the alliance. They therefore agreed to vote against every place named by their opponents, whether the Potomac, the Delaware, or Germantown. Richard Henry Lee would then reintroduce the simple House resolution to move to Philadelphia. If that failed, the whole subject could be taken up anew in the House of Representatives.[80]

The next morning Lee moved to postpone the Butler report so that the House resolution could be taken up. This failed, 11 to 13, with precisely the same lineup by which Morris's motion had been postponed two weeks before. The Senate then turned to filling in the blank in the Butler bill, but the Delaware-Potomac alliance rejected, with scattered assistance from their opponents, every location that was mentioned—the Potomac, Baltimore, and Wilmington. The Senate then adjourned amid furious uproar.[81]

The Senate then returned to the questions of funding and assumption while the House took up the residence question. Seeking to arouse the pride of the House, Virginians expressed indignation at the Senate's treatment of their resolution. Josiah Parker demanded that the House adhere to its stand, but on June 11 the House surprisingly moved to substitute Baltimore for Philadelphia by a vote of 31 to 28. Amid much confusion, it then passed a bill naming Baltimore as the capital by 53 to 6. No one thought that represented the true sense of the House, however, and the Senate was certain to reject it.[82] Further negotiations were in order.

That evening a group of congressmen met at the lodgings of the Philadelphians Clymer and FitzSimons. Maclay, smelling a bargain, refused to attend. Coxe and Major Jackson were both present, ostensibly representing Hamilton. Their offer was a straight swap—Pennsylvania would get the permanent residence in return for enough votes to pass assumption. The next morning Morris arranged a meeting with Hamilton in order to ascertain the exact price. As Morris later related the story to Maclay, Hamilton "wanted one vote in the Senate and five in the House of Representatives; that he was willing and would agree to place the permanent residence of Congress at Germantown or the Falls of the Delaware, if he would procure him these votes." Morris agreed to consult with the Pennsylvania delegation, but the price he demanded was the permanent seat in Philadelphia, not elsewhere in the state.[83]

It is questionable whether either man could deliver.[84] Hamilton was forced to tell Morris the next day that he could not negotiate the residence because "his friends will not hear of it."[85] New York and New England would not move the capital for any price. The best Hamilton could offer on that score was an agreement not to interfere with Morris's alliance with New Hampshire, but it is unlikely he could match Morris's influence with John Langdon anyway. The Virginians were another matter, and it may well have been at this point that Jefferson encountered Hamilton in front of the President's house, looking "sombre, haggard, and dejected beyond description." As Jefferson later recounted the story, he arranged a dinner at which Hamilton agreed to the Potomac seat in return for the switched votes on assumption of two Virginians, Richard Bland Lee and Alexander White.[86]

Morris had equal difficulty persuading his colleagues. Senator Maclay proved intractable, even when Tench Coxe dangled the possibility of moving to the Susquehanna (instead of Philadelphia) in front of him. Morris did win some promises of support from George Read of Delaware, but the Senate was not the crucial battleground on assumption.[87] The advent of the Rhode Islanders gave Hamilton a firm majority.[88] The House was another matter, and there the five Pennsylvanians who objected to assumption held firm. Evidently they felt they would get the capital, permanently or temporarily, whatever happened. The most intriguing possibility of all is that Morris as well as Hamilton turned to the Virginians in order to live up to his end of the bargain.

The Virginians were certainly talking to somebody. Madison's correspondence at this juncture is frustratingly vague, but on June 13 Jefferson wrote a revealing letter to George Mason. After informing him of the House vote in favor of Baltimore, Jefferson went on to predict that the capital would ultimately be located in Georgetown after a temporary stay in Philadelphia. Switching quickly to the subject of assumption, he hinted of the possibility of compromise. The opponents, he suggested, might have to agree to a partial assumption. The details he was not yet sure of, since his official duties prevented him from "mingling in these questions," but he warned Mason: "In general I think it necessary to give as well as take in a government like ours."[89] Knowing Mason's influence and his penchant for doctrinaire stands, Jefferson seemed primarily concerned with preparing the aging statesman for a bargain. His denial of personal involvement was a hedge against Mason's anger and a means of preserving his own reputation.

Two days later, on June 15, Robert Morris called a special meeting of the Pennsylvania delegation at 6:00 in the evening. He told them of Hamilton's offer "to give the permanent residence to Pennsylvania at Germantown or the Falls of the Delaware, on condition of their voting for the assumption." He then mentioned a new communication from Jefferson suggesting a "temporary residence of fifteen years in Philadelphia and the permanent residence at Georgetown."[90] In some respects, the most curious feature of this proposal is the length of time that the government would remain in Philadelphia. Previously all suggestions as to the temporary seat had involved something like three years, and it was generally agreed that even a short stopover would enable the advocates of that location "to fortify and entrench themselves with such systematic arrangements that we should never get away."[91] Did the Virginians have assurances from Washington that he could insure an ultimate relocation through administrative direction?[92] Jefferson did not demand a trade on assumption as Hamilton had, because he did not need to. The Pennsylvanians were firm on that subject; if any votes were to be switched they would be Virginians'.[93]

By June 20 the negotiations had proceeded to the point where Jefferson could write Monroe fairly confidently that the capital would move to the Potomac after a temporary sojourn in Philadelphia. "If this plan of compromise does not take place," he continued, "I fear one infinitely worse, an unqualified assumption and the perpetual residence on the Delaware." Assumption and the residence were inseparable, he seemed to be saying, and his chief concern was that Monore be prepared for a bargain. First he enlarged on the need for some sort of debt-payment program in order to restore the nation's credit abroad, using essentially the same arguments that he later claimed Hamilton had used on him. Then he pointed out that most of the "injustice" of assumption could be eliminated if it were so arranged that each state received from the general government exactly as much as it paid. Like the letter he wrote to Mason a week earlier, Jefferson's note to Monroe had about it the air of preparing Virginians for a compromise.[94] It certainly would have been a shame, after all the bargaining and intrigue, to see the settlement destroyed by uninformed reaction from home. And it was Antifederalists such as Mason and Monroe who were likely to be most critical.

By June 24, two days after the House approved the final settlement bill, the arrangements were firm enough so that Pennsylvania's inflexible gadfly, Senator Maclay, could be informed and brought into the deal. Virginia's John Walker, a courtly soft-spoken gentleman, was given the task. He told Maclay "that the Pennsylvania delegation had, in a general meeting, agreed to place the permanent residence on the Potomac and the temporary residence to remain ten years in Philadelphia." In the intervening week the Virginians had whittled the temporary stay down from fifteen years to ten. Hurrying to Morris for confirmation of the "contract," Maclay was surprised when Morris blamed him for the retreat. Had he been more tractable earlier, Morris declared, Philadelphia could have kept the capital for fifteen years. Morris was clearly concerned about the fragility of his Senate coalition, but Virginia's only leverage lay in the House. Conceivably the price of New Hampshire's (or perhaps South Carolina's)[95] votes on residence was a switch in the House stand on assumption. In any case, Morris showed more anger than relief when Maclay, with surprising ease, agreed to go along with the bargain for the sake of Pennsylvania unity.[96]

Whatever the exact nature of Morris's arrangements, they must have been exceedingly fragile, a careful balance of honor and interest that had to hold through a succession of votes that might go on for weeks. "We have a plan which is ripe for execution tomorrow," Richard Bland Lee informed his brother on June 26. "Its success depends on new movements and therefore not so certain as I could wish—but very probable. This week will decide the fate of the Potowmack forever. If we are successful the place to be selected will be left to the discretion of the President. Georgetown as is probable should be the fortunate spot."[97] While Morris and Hamilton worked upon the greed of northern speculators, the Virginians relied on Washington's sense of provincial loyalty.

The Senate took up the residence bill again on June 28. A motion to follow the earlier House action by filling the blank with Baltimore failed by 10 to 15. The surprisingly firm margin was due to switches by South Carolina's senators and Hawkins of North Carolina. The former betrays the hand of Morris, or perhaps Hamilton; the latter was probably Madison's doing. The Potomac was then approved by 16 to 9; the new convert was Samuel Johnston. The fragility of Morris's web of intrigue then showed itself when, after a brief argument about the date of removal to the Potomac, the Senate by 13 to 12 selected New York as the temporary capital. The South Carolinians, torn, apparently, by conflicting desires, deserted the coalition, as did Samuel Johnston.[98]

The evening witnessed more furious negotiations. Hamilton attended a meeting of the Massachusetts delegation to persuade them to abandon their New York allies. His argument, as reported by Rufus King, ran thus: "The project of Philadelphia and Potomack is bad, but it will ensure the funding System and the assumption: agreement to remain in N. Yk and Baltimore will defeat it, so that in the present state of things nothing but Philad. or Phila and Potomack will ensure it."[99] King, who had recently moved from Massachusetts to New York, was furious at the betrayal. He even threatened that if the capital left New York he would vote against assumption in the Senate, but Hamilton quickly countered this by securing a commitment from Charles Carroll, who had been wavering, that he would support the assumption bill.[100] Assumption needed only one vote in the Senate, but it needed several in the House, and Hamilton's argument clearly implied that he could secure some southern switches in return for Massachusetts' support on the residence.[101]

Massachusetts was more interested in the assumption bill than any other state, and Hamilton's pitch was at least partially effective. On June 29 the Senate reversed itself and rejected New York as the temporary seat by 16 to 9. Besides the two Massachusetts senators, Pierce Butler of South Carolina and William Few of Georgia changed their votes. The New Englanders could not quite bring themselves actually to endorse Philadelphia (they might have had to answer at home for that), but the coalition retained Butler and the two Georgians and carried Philadelphia, 14 to 12. The entire Philadelphia-Potomac package then passed to a third reading by 16 to 10. On July 1 it survived two more efforts at amendment and won final passage without formal roll call.[102] The next day Speaker Muhlenburg dined with the President and returned to inform his colleagues that assumption would pass the House.[103]

The House was not yet ready to reconsider assumption, but it did take up the Senate's residence bill on July 6. Here the difficulties for the coalition were a bit different. They could count on a core of 24 votes, 33 if New Jersey and North Carolina adhered. With reasonable attendence this would be sufficient, and no deals with New Englanders were necessary. The problem, however, was to keep Maryland in line. They had helped blast the coalition in the previous year, and during the spring the Marylanders had shown a distressing tendency to advance the prospects of Baltimore. From early June the Virginians had sought to appease Maryland opinion by talking of a capital at Georgetown on the north bank of the Potomac, and when the bargain was consumated some time around the twentieth there was a specific understanding that the public buildings would be erected in Maryland.[104] Marylanders emphasized this advantage when they wrote home to explain the outcome.[105] They probably recognized also that Baltimore was never seriously in contention. The temporary endorsements it won in the House were the result of tactical voting, and Madison scarcely needed to remind the Marylanders that the city had been "repeatedly rejected" by the Senate.[106]

New Yorkers moved to substitute Baltimore anyway, and this motion occasioned a brief debate. Smith and Seney of Maryland voiced support for Baltimore, but the rest of the state's delegation held firm with the Potomac alliance. Richard Bland Lee made an extensive plea in behalf of national unity, which the recorder saw fit merely to summarize, but by extolling the advantages of compromise he seemed to be hinting that his own flexibility deserved some response. The House in committee of the whole then rejected Baltimore by 23 to 37, a decisive margin that signaled the firmness of the Potomac coalition.[107] The debate then subsided quickly. Michael J. Stone probably expressed a general feeling when he pronounced himself sick of the entire subject and "wished to have the business finally and unalterably fixed." On July 9, the House finally approved the Philadelphia-Potomac move by 32 to 29.[108] Except for Smith and Seney, the coalition held firm, including all the North Carolinians and two of the four New Jerseyites. But it also gained critical support from the four Georgians, who, because of late arrivals, were an uncertain factor, and from Thomas Sumter of South Carolina. The remaining South Carolinians, as well as every congressman from New Jersey northwards, voted against the bill.

THE PAY-OFF:
FUNDING AND ASSUMPTION APPROVED

The compromise on the federal capital rested on the promise of Virginia's switched votes on assumption of state debts, but the Virginians, in turn, demanded that assumption be made more palatable. That part of the compromise was achieved by the Senate, which wrestled once more with the funding system while the House completed work on the residence. On July 2, Ellsworth of Connecticut surprised the anti-Hamiltonians by suddenly moving to take up a committee report on assumption that had lain dormant for two weeks. At that point Morris and Hamilton evidently felt secure about their majority. The Senate margin all along had been one vote. The convert, Senator Maclay claimed, was George Read of Delaware, although Charles Carroll also came down firmly in favor of assumption after some earlier hesitation.[109]

In early June the House of Representatives had adopted a funding bill with no provision for assumption of state debts; a Senate committee subsequently recommended that assumption be tacked on to the House bill as an amendment. It was this proposal that Ellsworth brought up on July 2 and succeeded in referring to yet another committee. Headed by Charles Carroll, this group was obviously charged with the task of finding some means of sweetening the assumption pill. It succeeded simply by increasing the amount of sugar. During the spring the figure agreed upon for the total amount of state debt to be assumed by the federal government was $19,300,000. Of this sum, each state had a certain allocation, varying from $4,000,000 for Massachusetts down to $200,000 for Delaware and Rhode Island. Carroll's committee simply raised the total federal obligation to $21,000,000 and credited two-thirds of the increase to Virginia and North Carolina. New England and South Carolina got none; the other states received token increases.[110]

While Carroll's committee deliberated, the Senate took up the other feature of the assumption package, the bill for the settlement of accounts. The House amendment providing for extra commissioners quickly came under the fire of New Englanders, who feared "that one of the additional commissioners will be taken from Virginia." They got some support, probably from northerners in Morris's coalition who were averse to giving everything to Virginia, and the provision was deleted. The Senate retained, however, two other key provisions. One outlined the anticipated quotas for each state (thereby insuring that no one would be a big loser); the other delayed the final reckoning until July 1, 1791, thus granting ample time for southerners to get their accounts in order. Senator Maclay almost upset the applecart by drafting an amendment designed to defeat assumption altogether by giving additional benefits to the debtor states. He took his proposal to Richard Henry Lee, who in turn, consulted Madison. Madison "spoiled" it, in Maclay's view, by making it much more obscure. Maclay introduced it anyway; Lee seconded it in perfunctory fashion and then "saw it perish with the indifference of a stranger." Maclay felt betrayed, but the Virginians were holding to a bargain. The Senate approved the bill on July 12.[111]

It took up Carroll's report the next day. The increased allotments, which Carroll recommended, attracted little attention; the need for a sweetener was obviously felt.[112] But another of Carroll's proposals struck closer to home. He suggested that the interest paid on the assumed debts be 4 percent, instead of the 6 percent borne by the remainder of the federal debt.[113] The opposition throughout the spring had been demanding a reduction in the proposed interest rate, both to make the debt more manageable and to ease the tax burden. Carroll's proposal was another important concession. But it quickly brought the big speculators, Morris and King, to their feet. Unless he got the full 6 percent, Morris declared, he would vote against the assumption plan altogether. Carroll calmly replied that if the rate went above 4 percent he would vote to defeat the assumption plan. His hard-won majority disintegrating, Hamilton stepped in quickly. On the evening of July 13 he arranged a new settlement under which the principal of the old federal debt would be funded at 6 percent; the arrears of interest (about a third of the total obligation) would be funded at 3 percent. The amount assumed from the states would carry the same ratio—two-thirds at 6 percent and one-third at 3 percent. The compromise restored Hamilton's thin majority, and the Senate approved the funding-assumption bill on July 21 by 14 to 12.[114] Among Chesapeake senators, only Charles Carroll voted for the measure. But that was enough. The true test of the Senate compromises would be in the House.

The Senate's concessions improved the prospects for assumption in the lower house. The crucial test came on July 25 when James Jackson of Georgia, the most vociferous opponent of Hamilton in Congress, moved to reject the entire bill. This failed by 29 to 32. The next day the House adopted several amendments which increased the interest scales (the Senate agreed to about half of them) and then approved the assumption provision by the surprisingly large margin of 34 to 28.[115] The two additional votes came from Huger and Sumter of South Carolina.

It is tempting to compare the 31 to 29 margin by which the bill survived on July 24 with the 29 to 32 vote that defeated assumption on April 12 and argue that the switches by Lee and White of Virginia made the difference. But as Jacob E. Cooke has pointed out, this cannot be done because the composition of the House was not the same.[116] Two North Carolinians, Sevier and Steele, both opposed to assumption, arrived after the April vote, and Theodorick Bland, a supporter, died on June 1. Thus, at least three votes were needed in addition to switches by Lee and White. But it is equally unfair to conclude, as Cooke does, that there was no assumption-residence bargain. Although Hamilton admitted in mid-June that he needed five votes, neither he nor any other architect of the compromise (Morris, FitzSimons, Jefferson, Madison) had any way of knowing how close the final vote would be. Thus every vote—especially every switch, which involved a subtraction as well as an addition—was crucial. Hamilton and Morris might well have offered a lot for those two Virginia votes, and the testimony of every contemporary involved was that they did. The other votes probably stemmed from the concessions on assumption made in the Senate. The most likely possibilities are George Gale of Maryland and the two South Carolinians who sat on the fence until the very end, Huger and Sumter.[117]

From the point of view of the Virginians, it was a satisfactory arrangement. They had won the residence, and whatever the expectations of the Philadelphians Washington would see to it that the bargain was consumated. The price they paid, acceptance of the funding system, could be justified. Both Jefferson and Madison were sufficiently concerned with the nation's credit to rationalize it in their own minds,[118] and Virginians retained their public purity by voting against it to the bitter end. Lee and White, whose constituents were heavily Federalist anyway, could argue that the concessions they won on assumption were actually of great benefit, and they could congratulate themseles on their own consistency since they had advocated just those changes from the very beginning.[119] Jefferson used the same arguments until the contract was sealed and there was no longer any danger from home.

They were disappointed when the Senate struck out the provision for extra commissioners on the board that settled accounts. In early August, after the compromise was completed, Madison drafted a separate bill naming two more commissioners to the board, but the Senate again vetoed the idea. In the end, it mattered little, for the existing board proved extremely generous in accepting state claims without detailed examination. Both Virginia and North Carolina profited substantially from the assumption of state debts.[120]

Not all were convinced, of course, and Patrick Henry had no difficulty securing a majority for a resolution denouncing assumption in the fall session of the assembly. The controversy did mark the beginnings of a new opposition party, and the remainder of Hamilton's program—bank and excises—would bring it into the open. It bore a new name (Republican was in common use by the end of 1791), but its initial strength was in the Henryite country of the Piedmont and Southside. The Northern Neck and the Valley, dazzled by the prospects for the Potomac watershed, remained for the moment more tolerant of the administration's growing reliance on northern merchants.

The affect of the compromise on Maryland was similar. Removal of the capital confirmed the Federalism of the Potomac counties and the lower Eastern Shore. But the upper bay, after losing on both of its seemingly excellent sites, Baltimore and the Susquehanna, reacted bitterly. In addition, the Maryland populace seemed to be far less content with Hamilton's measures than the congressional delegation had been. Five of its six congressmen lost their seats in the fall election. Because of the rumors of a congressional bargain, those who were least happy with the residence outcome were also inclined to be most critical of the Treasury program. The result in Maryland was a regional and political realignment. It appeared first in the congressional elections of 1790 and soon merged into the national party system.

CHAPTER FOURTEEN

Rise of the Republicans

THE COMPROMISE of 1790 had a profound impact on the politics of the Chesapeake. The Potomac watershed, which anticipated substantial advantages from the federal residence, was overjoyed at the result. The nationalist leanings already evident in the contest over the Constitution were reinforced, and the region remained wedded to the Federalist party for the remainder of the decade. Elsewhere, the reaction was quite the opposite. Baltimore and the Susquehanna Valley felt cheated by their loss and feared the competitive position of the Potomac. Southern Virginia and North Carolina saw little direct benefit in the capital's relocation, and if the price was surrender to Hamilton and his mercantile friends, it was too high.[1] Both regions had been debtor-Antifederalist, by the end of 1790 the only thing their anti-administration politics needed was a label.

ASSUMPTION IS "REPUGNANT TO THE CONSTITUTION"

The death of William Grayson left one of Virginia's Senate seats vacant, and Virginia Antifederalists naturally explored Patrick

Henry's desires. Henry declined the honor because the government was founded on "subversive" principles and engaged in practices which were "at variance with republican sentiments."[2] Hamilton's policies seemed to bear out the Antifederalist contention that
the Constitution would place the southern states in the pockets of
northern merchants. If the Bill of Rights killed the Antifederalists
politically, the funding system resurrected them. But in the interval
there had been a metamorphosis. Their objections were not to the
system itself, but to the people who ran it. "Henry already is
considered as a prophet," exclaimed Henry Lee. "His predictions
are daily verifi[ed]. His declaration with respect to the division of
interest which would exist under the constitution & predominate in
all the doings of the govt already has been undeniably proved."[3] Lee
himself was openly critical of Hamilton's proposals, but he
remained a staunch Federalist. Friendship for Washington was
doubtless a factor, but Lee was also speculating in lands in the
vicinity of the new capital.[4]

Henry was prepared to exploit Hamilton's unpopularity when
the assembly convened in the fall of 1790. He arrived with a set of
resolutions that denounced federal assumption of state debts as
"repugnant to the Constitution." The irony in his switch from critic
to interpreter of the Constitution apparently escaped him. Edward
Carrington, who was rapidly becoming the administration's chief
spokesman in Virginia, objected to Henry's resolutions not in
principle but because of their "intemperance." Federalists put up
only feeble resistance, and the resolutions whisked through the
House by 78 to 52. The Senate approved them without a roll call.[5]
The distribution of the vote shows a familiar regional pattern, but it
also reveals the erosion of Federalist strength. (table 14.1).

Although Hamilton had cost the Federalists some support,
party lines remained quite firm. Henry Lee and Francis Corbin
broke ranks to vote against the administration, but they were
almost the only ones. In general when voters abandoned the administration they elected new men. Most Federalist losses were in the
Tidewater and southwest. The Potomac-Shenandoah watershed
remained solid, and the arrival of the capital seems to be the best
explanation. The federal city offered a potential market for farm
products and boosted land prices throughout the region.[6]

TABLE 14.1 VIRGINIA HOUSE OF
DELEGATES: RESOLUTION
DENOUNCING ASUMPTION OF
STATE DEBTS, 1790

	Yea	Nay
Northern Neck	10	5
Middle Tidewater	16	8
Piedmont	5	5
Southside	29	7
West	18	26
Urban	0	2
	78	52
Federalists, 1788	6	24
Antifederalists, 1788	38	4
Unknown	34	24
	78	52

"POTOMAC" VS. "CHESAPEAKE" PARTIES IN MARYLAND

Arrival of the capital had a similar impact on Maryland. The Potomac counties, who had begun to shift their political stance in the contest over the Constitution, became wedded to Federalism, and remained fast in the faith for the rest of the decade. The Baltimore-Annapolis interests, on the other hand, together with the counties on the northern fringe of the bay, felt they had lost by the capital compromise. Already Antifederalist and suspicious of Hamilton, they now faced the prospect of commercial competition from the Potomac. The Eastern Shore, whose interests were not directly affected either way, remained predominantly Federalist, and their votes enabled the Federalists to control the state for the rest of the decade.

Some individuals had to change sides as the regional lines hardened, and the shift took place under the cover of new—but temporary—party labels.[7] As early as June 1790 a newspaper contributor suggested an alliance of Chesapeake counties—Baltimore, Harford, and Anne Arundel—to counteract the Potomac interest.[8] The key, as always, was Samuel Chase. Even Alexander C. Hanson, his old enemy, admitted that Chase had been "the mover of almost everything this state has to boast of." The admission was part of a memorandum of July 25, 1790, which was clearly a reaction to the capital compromise. A staunch defender of Annapolis interests, Hanson was dismayed by the victory of the Potomac and began looking around for allies. Baltimore—and hence Chase—were natural ones. He may even have been aware of Chase's overtures toward the administration. The memorandum, in any case, was clearly intended to heal old wounds. With firm hand and straight face Hanson continued: "Without him how very seldom would anything good have passed the legislature. . . . I have viewed him with admiration and with . . . kindness." The memo duly found its way into Chase's hands,[9] and the political wedding was consumated in short order. As a gift Federalists dropped their long-standing opposition to reimbursing Chase for his services in England in connection with the state's impounded bank stock. That autumn the House of Delegates passed by a wide margin a resolution paying Chase £350 for his services as state agent. Remnant Carrollites in the Senate objected but gave way when the House insisted.[10]

Fruits of the marriage were evident in little more than a month. In mid-September a popular meeting in Baltimore put forth a slate of candidates for the fall congressional election. The assembly had divided the state into districts the previous December, and the meeting boldly named a candidate for each district. The list—Philip Key, Joshua Seney, William Pinkney, Samuel Sterett, William Vans Murray, and Upton Sheredine—revealed the elements in the new coalition.[11] Pinckney and Sterett were Chasites who had opposed the Constitution. Seney was an incumbent congressman from the head of the bay, who had supported Baltimore in the capital fight. Murray was an ambitious lawyer of uncertain politics from the lower Eastern Shore. Elected to the House of Delegates in 1788, he supported the Constitution on every roll call, but the Antifederalists placed him on their congressional ticket that winter and he never declined the nomination. Sheredine, a novice who had never held elected office, may have been the only willing candidate the

Chesapeake people could find in the upper Potomac. Key, who represented the lower Potomac, had served intermittently in the assembly since the war, but his voting record was mixed.[12] His cousin, Philip Barton Key, an Annapolis lawyer, was a friend of Hanson's.

Potomac people quickly countered with a popular meeting of their own, in Annapolis, probably to give the impression of strength outside the river valley.[13] Their ticket included Daniel Carroll, Michael J. Stone, Benjamin Contee, and George Gale, all of whom had backed the Potomac compromise in Congress. They also picked James Tilghman, an Eastern Shore attorney and a strong Federalist, and, surprisingly, Samuel Sterett. In naming Sterett, who was already on the Chesapeake ticket, they may have been courting the Chasites. They could hardly lose, for they had no support in Baltimore anyway. In the election the city cast 3,036 votes for the Chesapeake's ticket and only 12 for the Potomac's.

Although the candidates were required to be residents of the districts they represented, they were elected at large, as in 1789. Not surprisingly, Sterett led the poll, and the Chesapeake faction won the election, resulting in a complete turnover in the congressional delegation. The Potomac counties loyally supported their nominees, but they were outvoted statewide by the powerful alliance of Western Shore and upper bay. The Eastern Shore, as might be expected, was evenly divided. The Chesapeake ticket was also extraordinarily successful in turning out the vote. In Baltimore and Harford Counties over 50 percent of the eligible voters appeared at the polls, and in Baltimore Town it was an astounding 99 percent.[14]

It then developed that Pinkney, a resident of Baltimore, had violated the residence requirement by standing for the Anne Arundel–Prince George's district. Challenged by Governor Howard, Pinkney was forced to resign. He was replaced by John Francis Mercer, another former Antifederalist. With the exception of Murray and Sterett, whose records were mixed, the entire delegation sided with Madison and the Virginia Republicans in the Second Congress.[15]

The voting muscle exhibited by the Baltimore area in the

congressional election threw a fright into the rest of the state. The Potomac counties had pioneered the technique of mobilizing voters during the ratification contest, but when Baltimore used the same methods—and even more successfully—they became alarmed. In the fall session, the assembly hastily revised the election law, managing to do so without a single roll call vote. Under the new law electors voted only for candidates in their own districts. Moreover, each candidate had to be a resident of his district—a provision designed to interrupt the old Chasite practice of sending popular votegetters, such as William Pinkney, to stand in marginal counties or using counties where they had firm control, such as Harford, to elect needed lieutenants like Luther Martin.[16]

The lack of a public roll call suggests a certain acquiescence in the measure by the Chesapeake forces. They had some reason for it because they could not always count on the phenomenal turnout that enabled them to control this election, and the way in which the districts were arranged virtually assured them three of the state's six congressmen.[17] Baltimore Town and County alone formed one district. Neighboring Harford and Cecil shared a district only with Eastern Shore Kent, enabling them to dictate that choice. To the south Anne Arundel was attached to evenly divided Prince George's. The Potomac and Eastern Shore were left with the other three districts.

In the course of the following year the terms "Chesapeake" and "Potomac" gave way to national party labels, and the Chesapeake alliance itself fell apart when resentment over the capital bargain subsided. Chase, lured by the promise of office, shifted to the Federalists, taking with him his friends Luther Martin and William Pinkney. Hanson and Key also returned to the Federalist fold, as did the counties on the lower Western Shore. Other Chesapeake leaders, the Smiths of Baltimore and Seneys of Queen Anne's, eventually became Republicans. The regional alignment, however, remained essentially that outlined in 1790. The Baltimore-Susquehanna basin became the heart of the Republican party, and as it gained strength it spread outward from that base—eastward into Queen Anne's and Kent, westward into Prince

George's and Frederick. By 1800 only the Eastern shore and the lower Potomac—the old bastions of the creditor party—were still Federalist.

SQUABBLE OVER ASSUMPTION

The only thing really new about the "Chesapeake" and "Potomac" tickets in 1790 was the use of the terms. They revealed a conscious search for party labels. The alignment in the House of Delegates that autumn was essentially what it had been, although Hamilton's system cost the Federalists some support, as it did in Virginia. On December 16, the critics of assumption brought three resolutions to the House of Delegates. The idea may have stemmed from Patrick Henry's resolutions in Virginia, but the Marylanders formed their own phrases. The first declared assumption a threat to state sovereignty, the second declared it "particularly injurious to this State," and the third proclaimed it "unconstitutional." Predictably, support tapered off as the denunciation became more extreme. The first passed by 32 to 26, the second by 30 to 28, and the third was rejected, 26 to 33. A week later, toward the end of the session, a motion was made to rescind the action on the first two. A tie of 26 to 26 was broken by Speaker George Dent in favor of rescinding.[18]

It is tempting to look for the hidden hands of Maryland's speculators behind the House's strange reversal. The debate was not reported, and the queries of newspaper contributors were never answered.[19] But if speculators in state certificates were dismayed by the initial resolutions, there is no evidence that they exerted any influence. Uriah Forrest, Georgetown merchant and one of the largest speculators in the state, voted in favor of the resolutions and against rescinding them. In fact, not a single member of the House reversed his early stand.[20] The changed stance of the House can be attributed solely to the fortuitous departure, late in the session, of a few members.[21] Federalists apparently saw their opportunity and quickly drafted the rescinding resolution.

The remarkable feature of the voting was not the seeming reversal but the rigidity of party lines. Taken together, the four votes provide an index of the party balance in 1790 (table 14.2;

TABLE 14.2 MARYLAND HOUSE OF DELEGATES:
ASSUMPTION OF STATE DEBTS, 1790

	For	Against	Middle
Eastern Shore	12	5	0
Upper bay	0	9	2
Western Shore	6	8	3
Upper Potomac	7	5	0
	25	27	5
Federalists, 1788	9	3	3
Antifederalists, 1788	1	13	0
Middle	1	0	1
Unknown	14	11	1
	25	27	5

threshhold of 3 votes and 75 percent agreement). Despite the use of new labels in the congressional elections, the regional and partisan alignment of the assembly remained essentially what it had been. Reflecting on the actions taken by the Chesapeake states on assumption, James McHenry concluded that "the old leaven is by no means exhausted, and that it will be used on every promising occasion to ferment" opposition to the administration.[22]

NATIONAL POLITICS HIT NORTH CAROLINA

Hamilton's critics were equally well prepared in North Carolina. At the opening of the legislative session the House of Commons named a committee to consider the funding system. It quickly returned with a set of resolutions denouncing assumption and instructing the state's congressmen to work for repeal. Federalists, whose principal spokesmen had been siphoned into national service, dared not contest them openly.[23] One of the resolutions was postponed (it would have had a committee investigate whether any of the House members themselves were holders of securities); the rest were shouted through.[24]

Federalists would have done well to leave it at that, but in early December they tempted fate with a resolution of their own requiring members of the assembly to take an oath, administered by the governor, swearing to support the Federal Constitution. It was a shrewd attempt to embarrass the opposition. The majority had to either submit to a humiliating and unnecessary oath or confess that they were still resisting the Constitution. The Federalist contention that opposition to the administration was only a guise for undermining the Constitution would thereby be vindicated. It was clever, but it backfired. The confident majority simply voted it down, and when Federalists demanded a roll call to expose the anti-Constitutionalists, they succeeded only in exposing their own weakness. The resolution lost, 26 to 55.[25]

The opposition got its revenge a week later with a resolution commending the state judges for provoking a confrontation with the federal courts. The issue involved a contested will of which James Iredell was one of the executors. Among the contestants were British citizens and northern merchants. At their request, the Federal Circuit Court (Justices Blair, Wilson, and Rutledge) took jurisdiction in the case, evidently on the basis of diversity of citizenship, and issued a writ of certiorari to the North Carolina Court of Equity. The state judges refused to surrender jurisdiction, and it was this action that the House approved, 46 to 29.[26] State pride and hostility to British merchants combined to smother the Federalists once again. Taken together, the two votes provide a fair index of the relative strength of the two parties in 1790 (table 14.3).

TABLE 14.3   NORTH CAROLINA HOUSE OF COMMONS: PARTY
VOTING, 1790

	Federalists	Opponents	Middle
Albemarle	6	2	5
Pamlico	3	6	4
Cape Fear	2	4	1
Piedmont	0	5	3
West	0	1	1
	13	31	19
Federalists, 1788–1789	10	7	8
Antifederalists, 1788–1789	0	15	1
Anti- 1788, Fed- 1789	0	1	0
Unknown	3	8	10
	13	31	19

The state's approval of the Constitution had been dictated by necessity; once that battle was over, the old lines reestablished themselves. The rural forces, boosted by Hamilton's unpopularity, recovered their old two-to-one majority.

Federalists fared somewhat better in the state Senate in 1790, primarily because they were a cohesive bloc, while their opponents were slack in attendance and erratic in voting. The Federalists also avoided a trial of strength where their ground was weakest. The Antifederalists also seemed willing to delay a confrontation, perhaps because several of their number were late in arriving. As a result, the Commons resolutions on assumption of state debts sailed through with little discussion and no roll calls.[27]

Midway through the session the Antifederalists apparently felt strong enough to take the offensive. They introduced a seemingly innocuous resolution asking the state's U.S. senators to persuade the federal commissioner for loans to establish his office at Hillsborough so that he might have free access to the records of the state treasurer. The hidden barb was the location: there was contention over the temporary state capital while Raleigh was being readied. Establishment of a federal office would have strengthened the pretensions of Antifederalist Hillsborough over Federalist Fayetteville (where the legislature was then sitting). Federalists from the Roanoke Valley deserted ranks, and the resolution passed, 24 to 10.[28] That quick slash seemed to release pent-up party feeling, and in the last three days of the session every matter that remotely bore on state-federal relations was subjected to a public roll call—even such trivial items as reimbursing a county clerk £15 for expenses incurred in the congressional election and the appropriation of £60 for office and supplies for the state's agent in the settlement of accounts.[29]

In all, there were five roll calls on matters that seemed to involve party allegiance. Defenders of the administration numbered 14, their opponents 10, and another 10 senators failed to side with either 75 percent of the time. The regional alignment and relationship to attitudes toward the Constitution were similar to the House of Commons.[30]

The apparent Federalist majority was due to confusion and absenteeism on the other side. Where issues were more important and better defined, opponents of the federal administration controlled the upper house as well as the lower. This was apparent in the most important act of the session, a congressional districting act. It passed both houses without a roll call; but Federalists complained privately that the measure placed them at a disadvantage.[31] Their fears, as usual, were exaggerated, for in the winter election they did as well as could be hoped. In the Cape Fear Valley Fayetteville attorney William Barry Grove ousted old Timothy Bloodworth. This Federalist victory was matched by the election of Nathaniel Macon (young Antifederalist protégé of Willie Jones) from a new district in the eastern Piedmont. Elsewhere, incumbents were returned—Hugh Williamson, John B. Ashe, and John Steele. All were Federalists who had been critical of the fiscal system. Steele remained a Federalist; the other two sided with Madison and the Virginia Republicans in the Second Congress.

ROUNDING OUT THE FISCAL SYSTEM:
THE BANK AND THE EXCISE

By the time Congress returned to work in December 1790 Hamilton was ready with two more reports. His Second Report on the Public Credit advocated internal taxes to help finance the debt he had amassed, and the Report on a Bank outlined a financial institution that would serve as agent of the Treasury in servicing the debt and making new loans to the government. The bank would be a partnership of business and government, in which the Treasury would own one-fifth of the shares and the President would name one-fifth of the board of directors. Private subscriptions for stock could be tendered in either gold or government securities, thereby creating a new market for the securities holders.

In Virginia and North Carolina the bank was viewed as the consumate union between the administration and northern merchant speculators. In Congress, Madison preferred to rest his objections on the question of constitutionality, a tactic that permitted him to evade the sectional and economic issues at stake, but others were more candid. Joseph Jones, a confidant of Madison throughout the 1780s, openly expressed his hostility to northern merchants. Giving a wry twist to the old paper money argument, he claimed that Hamilton was flooding the country with inflationary paper, from which only speculators would benefit, and posterity would be left saddled with the debt. It was an argument that John Taylor of Caroline would soon elaborate in pamphlet form. Jones and others worried also that locating the bank in Philadelphia would strengthen that city's claim to the capital and undermine the Potomac bargain.[32] Thus, when the bill incorporating the Bank of the United States passed the House of Representatives on February 8, 1791, the only congressmen from districts south of the Potomac in the "yea" column were North Carolina's Federalists, Sevier and Steele. Virginia's Federalists, Richard B. Lee and Alexander White, voted against it.[33]

The Marylanders were another story. The bank aroused little discussion in the newspapers, and there is no evidence that the Maryland electorate took much interest in it. The political elite gauged its interests carefully. The state had recently chartered a bank of its own, in which several leading political figures had invested. It was expected that the federal bank would "swallow up all the State Banks," as Congressman William Smith put it, and this provoked some opposition. On the other hand, Daniel Carroll felt that the paper money men (an evident reference to the Chasites) approved the federal bank in anticipation that it would enlarge the money supply.[34] In the House vote it was every Marylander for himself. Stone and Gale opposed the bill, as might be expected, but so did staunch Federalists, Carroll and Contee. Smith, who decided to trade his state stock for federal stock, supported the bill, and so did Joshua Seney of the Eastern Shore.[35]

Senate voting was almost as confused. When the bill passed to a third reading, only Charles Carroll, Monroe, and Gunn of Georgia opposed it. Even though the bank was modeled on Robert Morris's old Bank of North America, Richard Henry Lee favored it, as did Hawkins and Johnston of North Carolina. The two North Carolinians did join in various efforts to limit the duration of the charter and eliminate the monopoly granted the bank, but the only consistent opponent of the bank in the Senate was James Monroe.[36]

Congressional reaction to Hamilton's excise proposal followed more closely along party lines. Congress had considered an excise bill of its own in the previous year. Southerners had then objected to a tax on whisky because most of the small-scale distilling operations were in their neighborhood, and they succeeded in excusing from the tax all stills under 35 gallons' capacity.[37] A tax on distilled spirits was a major feature of Hamilton's scheme as well, and it was again criticized as a burden on the South.[38] This time, however, Madison refused to join the opposition, declaring that, much as he disliked excises, the government needed revenue and a tax on spirits was the "least exceptionable method."[39] Madison had long favored taxing luxuries. On final passage (35 to 21) Carroll, Griffin, Lee, and White—all Federalists—joined Madison in support of the bill. The opponents were all those who regularly opposed Hamiltonian measures (with the exception of Steele of North Carolina and the unpredictable Seney and Smith of Maryland).[40]

Compared to the uproar over assumption, public reaction to the bank and the excise was hesitant. When Edward Carrington reported that Virginians were indifferent to both, Jefferson and Madison discounted his opinion as Federalist bias. Their correspondence with him was soon dropped.[41] Francis Corbin offered to raise the bank question in the Virginia assembly, but Madison, perhaps suspecting his motives, ignored him. Corbin too broke off personal contact.[42] In fact, none of the three legislatures discussed national politics in the autumn sessions of 1791, a sign, perhaps, that fiscal policy was losing its sting. From the West came rumbles of discontent with the excise, but the political reaction was delayed.[43] For the moment, the electorate got a brief, and probably deserved, moment of repose.

APPEARANCE OF NATIONAL PARTY ORGANIZATIONS

Not so the leaders. Secretary of State Jefferson, who was as alarmed as Madison was about the implications of Hamilton's bank, took an even more active role. During the congressional debate on the bank he began sounding the views of political leaders across the nation, intimating his growing misgivings about the direction of the administration and suggesting that men of similar views should present themselves for Congress. It was the first step toward creating an interstate Republican organization.[44]

Monroe, who had long since mended his differences with Madison, was evidently given the task of approaching Virginia Antifederalists. He got a predictable chorus of fulfilled prophecies from Patrick Henry, Richard Henry Lee, and St. George Tucker.[45] Jefferson himself undertook to contact George Mason, but the aged republican died before he could take up the sword in one last crusade against governmental power.[46] By the spring of 1792 Monroe had added two new correspondents to his list, Henry Tazewell and John Breckinridge, both old allies of Madison who had voiced reservations about the Constitution. In writing Breckinridge, Monroe referred casually to the "republican party," an indication that the name was becoming common and that the term "party" had virtually lost its pejorative connotations.[47]

The Federalists were equally active but less inclined to define themselves. The Virginia assembly chose Henry Lee governor in the fall of 1791. Lee was still denouncing Hamilton's policies to anyone who would listen, and the assembly majority doubtless thought to reward a new ally.[48] But the old war hero was not a partisan by nature, and the thought of deserting the administration never crossed his mind. He promptly wrote the President to renew the friendship, and expressed the intent to govern Virginia in the same way that Washington ran the country.[49] He endorsed John Adams for the Vice Presidency in 1792, to the surprise and dismay of Republicans,[50] but the tone of his administration was otherwise nonpartisan. The assembly reelected him in each of the next two years.

Edward Carrington was a better party man, and when Hamilton undertook to counter some of the propaganda being disseminated by Republicans, he turned naturally to his treasury agent.[51] The Carrington-Marshall people in Richmond were thereafter the leaders of Virginia Federalism—symbolically, if not in fact. They actually had little scope for leadership because Federalism withered rapidly in eastern Virginia.

Federalism held fast in the western part of the state, however.

Part of it was simply a matter of sectional rivalry. The west had always been underrepresented in the assembly, and it had frequently accused the eastern-dominated government of ignoring its interests, particularly in regard to frontier defense. Beginning in the late 1780s it looked more to the national government for protection. President Washington's announcement, in his second Annual Message, that he intended to pacify the frontier had considerable impact west of the mountains.[52] The Ohio expeditions of Harmar and St. Clair, though unsuccessful, displayed the President's willingness to fulfill his promise.

Location of the capital on the Potomac and the improvements made in the river also benefited the west. Land prices on the upper Potomac and Shenandoah rivers rose dramatically in the 1790s.[53] Boosters predicted that the Potomac-Monongahela route would become the gateway to the West; and to provide westerners' need for manufactured goods, cities would soon appear.[54] All of these blessings—both real and imagined—were traceable to federal policies. Federalists received the credit.

The congressional election of 1792 was the first test of strength for the two parties. After the census of 1790 Congress increased Virginia's allotment from 10 to 21. The Republican-dominated assembly did not bother to rearrange the districts created by the Antifederalists in 1788; it simply subdivided them.[55] In the ensuing election, Federalists retained only 3 seats, all in the west. The best indication of party strength in the assembly that year was the balloting for a U.S. senator to replace Richard Henry Lee. John Taylor of Caroline received some "90 odd" votes, Arthur Lee 39, and Francis Corbin 33.[56] Taylor and Corbin were no doubt party nominees; Lee's support probably came from the nonaligned.

Jefferson and Madison were willing to accept Antifederalist support, but they had no desire to share leadership with old enemies, such as French Strother or Patrick Henry. Toward the end of 1791, Henry let it be known that he wished to open a correspondence with Madison. Transmitting the news, Madison's brother William thought the offer ought to be accepted because Henry could provide "more information of the disposition of the different parts of the State than perhaps any other man in it." Madison's reply was revealing. He appreciated any "friendly sentiments" Henry might have, but since he had never written to Henry in his life, he feared that the "abrupt commencement" of a correspondence might seem odd.[57] Henry, in short, would have to write the first letter, and, given this frigid response, it is not surprising that he never bothered. Madison had no cause for regret. Henry was an unpredictable ally and a potential liability. His presence at the front of Republican ranks would only seem to confirm what administration supporters were saying—that the opposition was Antifederalism in disguise.

Republicans had the advantage in Virginia from the outset. They could play to a predominantly Antifederal audience full of provincial pride, and their national leaders, Jefferson and Madison, were Virginians. They overcame the fact that Washington was also a Virginian by emphasizing Hamilton's role in the administration.

In Maryland the party situation was the reverse. Hamilton's policies aroused little opposition; some of the more prominent leaders even benefited from them. Location of the federal seat eliminated any doubts that might have lingered in the debtor counties of the upper Potomac. The "Potomac Ticket" of 1790 slid easily into the Federalist party. The "Chesapeake Ticket" split after 1790 as some of the Baltimore merchants who helped organize it returned to the Federalist fold. Thus Republican strength in the state was confined to the counties at the head of the bay. Republicans were also short of leadership until the Smiths of Baltimore switched sides toward the middle of the 1790s.[58]

The Federalists had a solid organization in Maryland from the beginning. The key figure was James McHenry, who helped dispense administration patronage, just as Carrington did in Virginia. So confident was he of his position that he even scolded Hamilton when his advice was not followed.[59] On the eve of the congressional election of 1792 McHenry cautioned his friends not to be fooled by the name changes that had occurred two years earlier. He expected of "the Antifederals" that "their whole force . . . under different forms and names will be everywhere brought forward." Whatever the guise, he declared, the basic issue was still "whether they or we are to govern."[60] Actually the anti-administration forces were not organized enough to have a label; Federalists ran as "friends to government."

The census results increased Maryland's congressional allotment from 6 to 8. Each side picked up one of the new seats, and the party balance in the Third Congress was four Federalists, three Republicans, and one maverick.[61] The defection of James Tilghman to the Republicans almost cost the Federalists one of the Eastern Shore districts. When the election was over, McHenry wrote to Hamilton asking him to find a spot in the Treasury for one of the men who had helped the party retain the seat. To propose a government office as a specific reward for political services was something new. Recognizing that he was on dangerous ground, McHenry asked Hamilton to burn the request when done with it.[62]

Congress doubled North Carolina's delegation as a result of the census (from 5 to 10), and the arrangement of the new districts occasioned a ferocious contest in the assembly. A Republican-dominated Commons committee brought in one plan; Federalists suggested several alternatives, each of which was voted down.[63] The four roll calls provide an index of the relative strength of parties on the eve of the second presidential election (table 14.4).[64]

Polarization was about what it had been in the 1780s—75 percent of those who voted enough to be identified lined up with one of the two parties. The regional nature of the parties was more pronounced than ever. Two-thirds of those who supported the

TABLE 14.4   NORTH CAROLINA COMMONS: PARTY VOTING, 1792

	Federalists	Republicans	Middle
Albemarle	18	0	1
Pamlico	10	1	7
Cape Fear	0	10	1
Piedmont	2	26	11
West	1	3	4
	31	40	24
Federalists, 1788–1789	11	5	2
Antifederalists, 1788–1789	1	12	5
Anti- 1788, Fed- 1789	0	3	1
Unknown	19	20	16
	31	40	24

Constitution were still Federalists; one-third had become Republicans. As in Virginia, the majority of Republicans were former Antifederalists. But unlike Virginia, North Carolina had most of its Federalist strength in the east.

The real battle of the 1792 session was a behind-the-scenes contest for governor and U.S. senator. Samuel Johnston retired from the Senate that year, and Republicans nominated Governor Alexander Martin for his seat. Martin, a lukewarm supporter of the Constitution, was considered a critic of the Washington administration. Thomas Blount became the candidate of the Federalists. The contest became so heated that fistfights broke out on the assembly floor, and in mid-December the assembly adjourned to let tempers cool. In the interval a compromise was worked out. Martin went to the Senate, and Fayetteville was chosen as the site for the next assembly meeting, the move to Raleigh being postponed. Fayetteville and neighboring Cumberland County, formerly Federalist strongholds, sent Republicans to the assembly that year. The Federalist end of the bargain was the choice of New Bern lawyer Richard Dobbs Spaight as governor.[65] Spaight was a political maverick like Martin, but at this point he was considered a Federalist. North Carolina's governor, like Virginia's, was only a figurehead, but the apparent involvement of the office in a party contest was a significant development. By the end of the decade parties would seek to monopolize all government offices.

The congressional election, set for February 1793, showed why the Federalists had fought so fiercely against the assembly's redistricting plan. Of the five new districts created, Federalists carried only one, in the Pamlico Sound region.[66] Federalists did manage to replace the unreliable Hugh Williamson, who had moved to Philadelphia, with a more regular partisan, William Dawson. William Barry Grove of Fayetteville also won reelection, making a total of 3 North Carolina Federalists in the Third Congress. Opposing them were 7 Republicans, all, except for Nathaniel Macon, new men. Well, not exactly new. At least three were familiar names. Matthew Lock, Alexander Mebane, and James Gillespie were all leaders of the 1780s debtor party and opponents of the constitution in both conventions. Antifederalism was back in style.[67]

PRESIDENTIAL POLITICS: 1792

Until mid-1791 party organization was largely what it had been in the 1780s. There were identifiable parties in every legislature, and state leaders exchanged information and opinions by mail. In the summer of 1791, Jefferson and Madison, distressed by the administration bias of the Philadelphia press, set out to establish a newspaper that would reflect the views of the opposition. It was an important step in party development, for a newspaper would focus party views, disseminate tactical information to state leaders, and propagandize the electorate.[68]

After some searching for a publisher, the two agreed on Philip Freneau, a farmer-poet from New Jersey whom Madison had known at Princeton. Since an opposition sheet was certain to be excluded from government printing contracts, Jefferson afforded Freneau a part-time clerical position in the State Department for subsistence income. Republican leaders actively solicited subscriptions in Maryland and Virginia, and the first issue of the *National Gazette* was peeled off the press on October 31, 1791.

Madison took advantage of this new vehicle to become an essayist, a congenial pastime that he had not indulged in since the *Publius* venture of 1787–88. His initial foray was a philosophical excursion into the problems of overpopulation, in which he anticipated many of the points raised seven years later in England by Thomas Malthus. But as politics heated in the approaching Presidential contest his contributions became more partism. In January, 1792, he warned his readers that political parties, though evil, were inevitable.[69] This was the first public exploration of this concept in America, and it reflected Madison's own changing views on the nature of party. Among Madison's correspondents the term "party" was coming to be used ever more casually. The changed attitude no doubt stemmed from his experience and Jefferson's in organizing an opposition in Congress; Madison may have felt it was time to educate the public.[70] In April Madison undertook to delineate the views of the opposition. The real friends to the union, he told *Gazette* readers, were those who relied on the authority of the people, who resisted all tendencies toward monarchy, and who considered a national debt injurious.[71] Simultaneously, Jefferson undertook to explain to the President that the "republican party" wished to preserve the government in its present form, while the "corrupt squadron of paper dealers" who dominated Congress planned to do away with the Constitution. A few weeks later Jefferson complained of Hamilton's base tactics in "daring to call the republican party a *faction*."[72]

Hamilton was equally active in establishing interstate party connections. His primary contact in Maryland was James McHenry. In the fall of 1791, McHenry entered the state senate at Hamilton's urging, though there was little need for him since the Senate was solidly Federalist.[73] As the election approached, McHenry kept Hamilton informed on the congressional contests and inserted Hamilton's essays in Maryland newspapers.[74]

In Virginia, Hamilton was less sure of himself, since several leading Federalists, such as Henry Lee, had been openly critical of his policies.[75] Treasury officials were his best bet, and in May 1792, he addressed a lengthy note to Edward Carrington. Knowing that Carrington was an old friend of Madison's, he argued that Madison had deserted the principles on which they had founded the federal government and was now "head of a faction" hostile to the administration. He then detailed the partisan movements of Madison and Jefferson, culminating in the enlistment of Philip Freneau.[76]

Establishment of the *National Gazette* rankled more than anything, because by the spring of 1792 Freneau was engaged in a full-scale assault on the funding system and the bank, while leveling accusations against the speculators and stockholders in Congress. In July Hamilton counterattacked with a series of letters under various pseudonyms (the change in names evidently intended to suggest that his views were widely held) questioning Freneau's connection with the State Department. It was a legitimate complaint and seriously embarrassed Republican leaders until Hamilton, in his efforts to expose Jefferson as the hidden hand behind the opposition, published excerpts from a previously secret government document. Republicans pounced on this indiscretion and forced Hamilton into retreat, evasion, and eventually silence.[77]

At a meeting of the Virginia triumvirate at Monticello it was decided that Madison and Monroe would assume the burden of replying to Hamilton. While Monroe rushed to the defense of Freneau, Madison resumed his spring essay series. "A Candid State of Parties," which appeared in Freneau's paper in September, was a biased description of the split that had arisen in Congress and the administration. Rather than a straight discussion of the implications of Hamilton's policies, Madison indulged in hyperbole and symbolism. On one side were the defenders of the people's liberties; on the other were those who condemned the people as stupid and licentious and disregarded their liberties. It was not very enlightening, but it did not have to be, since the intricacies of Hamiltonian finance were beyond the grasp of most voters anyway. Political shorthand, in the form of easily recognized symbols, was far more effective in swaying voters, and Madison, a veteran of the newspaper wars of the 1780s, was keenly aware of this. Such symbolic terms as "monarchy," "tyranny," "anarchy," and such smooth catchwords as "Keepers of the People's Liberties," served as lenses that brought complex political issues into popular focus.

Whatever might be said of its polemical quality, Madison's essay did acquaint the public with "The Republican party, as it may be termed." The phrase (itself a symbolic criticism of the administration) had been common in private correspondence for a year, but this was the party's first public christening. With a lower-case r "republican" was an attitude of mind; by capitalizing it Madison made it an institution.[78]

The approaching Presidential contest enhanced the need for an identifiable party label. There was no thought, of course, of replacing Washington. During the spring both Madison and Jefferson had visited the President to induce him to stay on in office. His departure would precipitate open party warfare and might even endanger the government. But Republicans had no such qualms about the Vice Presidency. John Adams, they feared, had too many monarchical tendencies. He had argued in numerous essays the need for a strong executive, as well as an upper house to defend the interests of the wealthy, and his actions as president of the Senate, particularly in the titles controversy, seemed to confirm their suspicions.

How and when the Republicans settled on New York Governor George Clinton remains a mystery. In the spring of 1791

Jefferson and Madison made a tour of New York State, examining the countryside and collecting floral specimens. They spent one night in Albany, and if they saw Governor Clinton at all it must have been the briefest of visits. When the 128-mile trip ended in June, Jefferson hurried home, but Madison lingered on in New York City for some weeks. He undoubtedly talked to Chancellor Robert R. Livingston (who was piqued over Hamilton's support of Rufus King for the New York Senate seat) and with Aaron Burr. What sort of arrangements were made can only be guessed. Neither Jefferson nor Madison gave any hint that their New York trip involved politics, though this is hardly surprising. It would have been foolish to commit such delicate negotiations to the mails. Jefferson, as a member of the administration, probably did not involve himself, in any case.[79] At this point nothing more was needed than mutual expressions of respect. Tactical details could be worked out in congressional boardinghouses.

However the understanding was reached, it was clear by early 1792 that Republicans had agreed to back Clinton. It was an uncomfortable alliance. Clinton had an unsavory reputation as a politician, and his strong opposition to the Constitution left the Republicans vulnerable to the Federalist accusation that they were only Antifederalists in disguise. But the Virginians needed northern allies if they were to achieve a party of national scope.

In the New York spring elections Clinton was reelected governor over Federalist John Jay by the narrowest of margins. Jay appeared to have won the contest until the Republicans challenged the returns from Otsego County. The state election board (which Clinton controlled) promptly threw out the disputed ballots and awarded the election to Clinton. Virginians were shocked. Jefferson thought that Clinton, in good conscience, ought to resign or at least seek a new election. But what really concerned him—Jefferson, after all, was familiar with New York politics—was that Clinton's actions would reflect on the party. "I really apprehend that the cause of republicanism will suffer," he told Madison, "and its votaries be thrown into schism by embarking it in support of this man." Party unity during an election was his main concern. Monroe agreed, but felt the party had no choice. Some aspects of Clinton's character were "highly exceptionable" and his conduct on this occasion was particularly "vicious," but he was nonetheless "a center of union to the republican party in that State." They had to adhere to the alliance.[80]

In October 1792 the alliance was threatened again when Burr promoted his own candidacy. It was a nicely orchestrated campaign. New York and Philadelphia Republicans wrote simultaneous letters to the Virginia leaders suggesting Burr be substituted for Clinton. There was no question of disrupting the New York–Virginia axis; it was merely a question of personalities. The Virginians disliked the idea. Burr was a newcomer in politics, comparatively unknown, and of uncertain "principles."[81] Rather than reject the idea outright, they waited a week while they ostensibly sounded Virginia opinion. Then on October 19 Madison and Monroe drafted a joint reply. Avoiding any direct criticism of Burr, they simply pointed out that Clinton, being better known, had the best chance of garnering electoral votes. "The object of the Republican interest, so far as the voice of this State may be estimated, requires that things should be kept to the course which they have in a manner spontaneously taken."[82]

However spontaneous the alliance was, it was certainly well organized by the fall of 1792. John Beckley, former clerk of the Virginia House of Delegates and now clerk to the House of Representatives, used his office to coordinate party activities. Lists of electoral candidates were printed and distributed throughout Pennsylvania, and letters were sent to South Carolina and Georgia to communicate the party line. Beckley happened to be in New York when Burr made his move, and it is likely that he communicated the initial reaction of Virginians. On October 16, three days before Madison and Monroe sent their formal reply, Beckley attended a meeting of New York Republicans where it was decided "to exert every endeavor for Mr. Clinton, and to drop all thoughts of Mr. Burr." To make double sure, Beckley paid a visit to Burr and got his assurance "that he would cheerfully support the measure of removing Mr. A[dams] and lend every aid in his power to C[linton]'s electon."[83]

The result showed the fruits of organization. When the Presidential electors chosen by Virginia (21) and North Carolina (12) met that winter, they unanimously gave their first ballots to Washington, and their second to Clinton.[84] Maryland remained firmly Federalist. In desperation Republicans put out anonymously the suggestion that Charles Carroll be given second place on the ballot instead of Adams. Carroll promptly announced that he would not serve if elected, and the scheme fell apart.[85] Eight of the state's ten electors met in Annapolis on December 5 and cast their ballots for Washington and Adams.[86] Illness cost Adams two electoral votes, but this time they were not crucial.

The election marked a further step in party development. Each side now had an official label; each was developing the rhetorical symbolism to give it a ready identity among the voters. Federalists had been the first to achieve a rudimentary organization, building upon the patronage at the disposal of Washington and Hamilton. By the end of 1792 Republicans had built an organization of their own, utilizing the methods of communication developed in the party battles of the 1780s.

All that remained was to polarize the electorate, so that each potential voter felt a more or less permanent affinity for one party or the other. The war in Europe and problems of American neutrality achieved that.

PART FOUR

The Party System Matures, 1793–1800

CHAPTER FIFTEEN

The Politics of Neutrality, 1793–1794

SEVENTEEN NINETY-THREE was a banner year in the evolution of the first party system. The execution of Louis XVI and the outbreak of war between the French republic and a coalition of monarchies organized by Great Britain injected a new and highly emotional issue into American politics. Americans generally agreed that they had to maintain an official neutrality, but privately they quickly chose sides. The European contest set a newborn republic and old friend, France, against a collection of staid monarchies, most of whom had sneered at the American experiment. Republicanism and Monarchy, the political symbols to which Americans most readily responded, were engaged in a death struggle.

When radical Jacobins seized power in the summer of 1793 and began a "reign of terror," the struggle took on a new meaning. To many Americans the disdainful monarchies became symbols of law and order, stability, and responsible government. Such symbols were already commonplace in American rhetoric; the European war merely enhanced their dramatic value. The new associations lent warmth to old accusations. No one wanted to enter the conflict, but Republicans backed the French, Federalists cheered the British.

The war also created some sticky diplomatic problems, for the nation was still tied to France by the treaty of 1778. This agreement, which had brought France into the American Revolution, did not require the U.S. to enter the current war, but it did oblige America to aid in the defense of the French colonies in the West Indies. The obligations of this alliance occasioned an intense debate, first in the President's cabinet and then in Congress. Because the issues were so easily distilled into symbols, the discussion soon overflowed Congress and the administration, and spilled into newspapers, village taverns, and country farmhouses. The public chose sides, just as the politicians did, and the stakes seemed so clear that few could remain uncommitted.

Political leaders quickly took advantage of this new spirit of partisanship. The familiar devices for manipulating opinion—mass rallies, addresses, and cleverly circulated resolutions—hitherto used primarily at election time became virtually permanent features of the political landscape. By the end of the year the outline of a national party system could be clearly discerned. In Congress and the state assemblies moderates and waverers were being eliminated; at the "grass roots" voters were forming habits of association that would be hard to break.

THE GILES RESOLUTIONS

Had they paused to reflect on the matter, Republicans might have welcomed the French Revolution as a political deliverance. For three years they had raised one issue after another—aristocratic titles, funding, assumption, excises, the Bank—without noticeable impact on the electorate. After a brief flurry in the newspapers each controversy seemed to die away. Fiscal policy, perhaps, was too complex a subject to serve as a text for popular appeals. Opposition to the whisky excise still simmered in parts of North Carolina and Pennsylvania, but when the Bank of the United States opened a branch in Richmond, not a whisper of protest was heard. As the Second Congress drew to a close early in 1793, the "Republican interest" was no larger than it had been in 1790—fifteen or twenty representatives (when all were present) clustered around Madison.[1]

During the fall election in Maryland, John Francis Mercer made several speeches accusing Hamilton of having twisted the law. The Secretary of the Treasury, Mercer claimed, had leaked information to speculator friends, enabling them to make huge profits in the public debt, and he had manipulated debt payments to the advantage of certain creditors at the expense of others. Republicans had been voicing these suspicions privately for years; Mercer was the first to try to make electoral capital out of them. He succeeded only in drawing Federalist wrath. His opponents reported the charges to Hamilton, who promptly demanded an explanation. The result was an angry exchange of letters, numerous affidavits, and a series of accusations that could only have left the public (when Mercer moved the whole controversy into the newspapers) bewildered.[2]

In the meantime Maryland Federalists trained all their guns on Mercer. Newspapers accused him of damaging the state's reputation, and broadsides reminded voters that he was "a *Virginian* in his connexions and politics." James McHenry even tried to prevail on Bishop John Carroll to swing the Catholic vote to Mercer's election opponent. Mercer won in his previously Antifederal district, but by a mere 400 votes.[3] Attacking the Secretary of the Treasury had gained him little, if any, support.[4]

The last salvo in this three-year Republican war against the funding system—and in some respects the most futile shot of all—came early in 1793. Mercer's accusations probably inspired the move, but it was Virginians who led the way. Toward the end of December 1792 the House of Representatives approved a resolution asking the executive branch to provide Congress with information on the foreign debt, together with interest payments and balances due. Madison was probably behind this, his suspicions aroused by Hamilton's reluctance to make debt payments to revolutionary France.[5] Had Hamilton played favorites with the foreign debt, as he was rumored to have done at home? This, at least, was an accusation that would be relatively easy to prove, though the amount of political mileage in it was doubtful.

Hamilton's reply proved unsatisfactory. In 1790, he admitted, he had borrowed from Dutch bankers, without authority from Congress, money to repay the debt to France. Then later that year, when Congress authorized such loans, Hamilton transferred some of the funds to the U.S. Treasury instead of giving them to France. The Secretary explained that such procedure, though technically without legislative authority, was not actually illegal, and it had benefited the Treasury.[6] Professing himself still unsatisfied, William Branch Giles drew up a more detailed set of resolutions. Giles was a 30-year-old lawyer from Petersburg, who had taken Theodorick Bland's vacated seat in 1790. Federalists considered him Madison's political axman, and the reputation was probably deserved. He had a taste for controversy and a penchant for intrigue that kept his surroundings in turmoil throughout his forty-year public career.[7]

Giles's resolutions asked the President to furnish copies of the 1790 laws and instructions under which Hamilton had acted. He also wanted an accounting of all payments made to foreign creditors, as well as a semimonthly statement of the government's account with the Bank of the United States. Giles asked for the government's bank statement because, he said, when all of Hamilton's sums were calculated a million and a half dollars remained unaccounted for.[8] Although Giles admitted that several of his accusations were based partly on conjecture (and Hamilton quickly refuted his sums), it was a shrewdly timed maneuver. Only with extraordinary effort could Hamilton answer all queries before the session ended. There was good prospect that the accusations would stand, and in time allegations often became truth.

Hamilton understood this and put forth the effort. He gave his principal report to the House, totaling some 12,000 words, on February 13, 1793, and the final documents went in on the February 25. Republicans scanned the reports eagerly and were disappointed to find no evidence of wrongdoing other than the transfers of 1790. Putting the best face on it, Madison wrote to Edmund Pendleton that the documents indicated "there has been at least a very blameable irregularity and secrecy in some particulars of it, and many appearances which at least require explanation."[9]

Prudence might have left it at that, but party spirit was now running high. Besides, Hamilton had neatly turned the trap they had laid. If the House adjourned without further action, Hamilton would have the last word. And his defense was shrewdly conceived. He pointed out to a tax-conscious people that as a result of his manipulations he had reduced the interest on the federal debt from 5½ percent to slightly less than 4½ percent, and the nation's credit was now as sound as any in the world.[10] On February 27, Giles brought in a new series of resolutions boldly censuring the secretary's conduct. He accused Hamilton of violating an act of Congress, making unauthorized financial arrangements, and refusing to provide information on his transactions. So extreme were the resolutions that they had no chance of passage. Committed Republicans were still a tiny minority of the House. To have any chance of success they had to attract support among moderates and waverers, most of whom were at least nominal Federalists. The House rejected the third resolution—concerning the shift in funds—by 40 to 12, and the others lost by even more lopsided margins.[11]

It was a humiliating revelation of Republican weakness, but Giles's effort cannot be dismissed as the isolated act of a rash partisan. He acted in concert with Republican leadership. Indeed, there is a draft of Giles's resolutions in Jefferson's handwriting, a draft that is even more shrill in its condemnation of the Secretary of the Treasury.[12] In all likelihood the resolutions were drawn up to influence opinion in Virginia; the House vote was probably secondary. Virginia was then in the throes of a congressional election (the last of the 1792 series), and it was a critical one because the census had nearly doubled the state's representation.

Hamilton probably suspected as much. In early February he sent Edward Carrington several copies of his defense, with a request that they be circulated as widely as possible.[13] Carrington inserted the defense, together with the House roll calls, in the Norfolk, Petersburg, Alexandria, and Winchester newspapers. As usual, he misjudged Virginia opinion; in fact, publicity may have been precisely what the Republicans wanted. Carrington later admitted that Samuel Griffin's votes in support of Hamilton were a liability, though the Williamsburg attorney was reelected anyway.[14]

Actually the assault on the Treasury probably had little to do with the outcome of the election. The campaign was at fever heat long before Giles took the floor. The number of popular meetings and the number of pseudonymous contributors to newspapers indicated a level of partisan activity not seen since the campaigns of 1788–89. Much of the discussion involved efforts to clarify the shift from Federalist-Antifederalist to Federalist-Republican conflict. For years Federalists had accused their opponents of being Antifederalists in disguise, and Republicans spent much time trying to rid themselves of the stigma. Several of the contests, especially in the newly created districts, pitted Republican against Republican, the only difference between the two being their earlier stance on the Constitution. One such contest in the central Piedmont (formerly part of Madison's district) caused a spirited newspaper exchange. "Gracchus" finally had the last word when he suggested that voters forget the old distinction between Federal and Antifederal. The problem was not the frame of government, he argued, but the way it was managed. "Let us endeavor to correct this error," he pled, "not by opposing the Constitution, but by correcting the administration of it."[15]

When the dust settled, Madison was generally satisfied with the result. All who had opposed the administration in the previous Congress were reelected, he told Jefferson, and the one that had most consistently supported it (Alexander White) was defeated.[16] The victor in that contest was Robert Rutherford, a wealthy merchant from Winchester and former Federalist.[17] Madison did not know his current politics; he was content with the turnover. Actually Rutherford courted Federalist support in the election, but he usually voted with the Republicans once he reached Philadelphia.[18]

Madison did note that Richard Bland Lee was reelected without opposition, but he ignored the victory of Samuel Griffin, and he was probably uninformed about the politics of two new westerners, Joseph Neville and George Hancock.[19] Even so, he had cause for optimism. In addition to retaining all their old seats, Republicans captured all but two of the new ones and outnumbered their opponents in the coming Congress, 15 to 4. Madison would need this enlargement of his "solid column of disciplined Prussians," as northern Federalists called it.[20] The war in Europe was already causing a new problem with political ramifications.

ARRIVAL OF CITIZEN EDMOND GENET

Americans were delighted with the outbreak of revolution in France. The fall of the Bastille in the summer of 1789 and the summoning of an assembly, President Washington felt, were events of "so wonderful a nature that the mind can hardly realize the fact." He predicted that the French "nation will be the most powerful and happy in Europe," although he expected more "paroxysms . . . before matters are finally settled."[21] For some time even the "paroxysms" that shook France were welcome. It experimented for a time with constitutional monarchy, and then in the fall of 1792, after Austria and Prussia declared war, it deposed Louis XVI, proclaimed itself a republic, and announced a "war of all peoples against all Kings." Even after Louis was executed and Britain entered the war, opinion in the Chesapeake was still pro-French. "Light Horse Harry" Lee, governor of Virginia since 1791, even contemplated journeying to France to offer his services until Washington pointed out the problems that might create in view of his position.[22]

Britain's entry into the war, news of which arrived in early April, presented some diplomatic complications. America's treaty commitment to help defend the French West Indies was worrisome in itself, for Britain customarily attacked the French Empire whenever the two nations went to war. The parallel Treaty of Commerce, moreover, permitted French vessels to enter American ports freely, a privilege no other nation had. Whatever the administration decided to do about the French treaties, the spread of fighting to the high seas was certain to affect American shipping. Some kind of official posture was necessary, and it had to be taken quickly. A new French emissary representing the Girondist Republicans, Edmond Charles Genet, was expected at any time. On April 5, Hamilton sent word of the expanded war to Washington, who was resting at Mount Vernon, and three days later Genet landed at Charleston, South Carolina.

On April 9, Hamilton wrote Chief Justice John Jay (who combined legal expertise with diplomatic experience) asking him to draft a proclamation of neutrality for the President.[23] It was clear that Hamilton hoped to bypass the Secretary of State, whom he doubtless suspected of harboring pro-French sympathies. Washington hurried back to Philadelphia and summoned a cabinet meeting on the nineteenth. Hamilton prepared the agenda and arrived with a draft of a proclamation drawn up by Jay.

Hamilton opened the discussion with an argument that the removal and execution of the king abrogated the treaties. He also felt that the military obligations were incompatible with a strict neutrality, and he was afraid that the privileges accorded French vessels in American ports might invite British retaliation. Jefferson replied that there was no need to worry about the military obligations until the West Indies were actually threatened and France requested aid. And as to the commercial privileges, Britain had no cause for complaint since she had refused even to discuss a commercial agreement with America. Washington sided with Jefferson. The treaties would be considered in effect and Genet would be received, a de facto recognition of the new French regime.

The question then was, what kind of declaration ought to be issued? Hamilton demanded an immediate proclamation of neutrality so that neither belligerent would mistake the U.S. position and American merchants might freely trade with both. Jefferson objected to an official neutrality because it narrowed the country's options. Britain might well expect the United States to side with France, for instance; so a perfect neutrality was to her advantage. She might even be willing to bargain for it with trade concessions. He also objected that any such proclamation was beyond Presidential authority. Since Congress alone had power to declare war, he reasoned, it also had the power to declare "no war," or neutrality. This seemed to everyone else legal hairsplitting, and Washington this time sided with Hamilton, though the word "neutrality" was deleted from the proclamation in deference to Jefferson's feelings.[24]

The President's proclamation of impartial conduct appeared on April 22. By then Genet had started triumphantly northward. He had chosen Charleston for embarkation in hope of a friendly reception, and the gamble paid off. The citizenry welcomed him joyously, and local officials (including some prominent Federalists) organized banquets in his honor. The French government had instructed him to commission privateers and organize an expedition against Spanish colonies, if the Washington administration proved agreeable. Assuming that his enthusiastic reception in Charleston reflected the attitude of the government, Genet saw no reason to delay implementing his instructions until he was officially received. So with the blessing of Governor William Moultrie, he issued letters of marque to four privateers and made the initial arrangements for an attack on Spanish Florida. On April 18 he started north in a carriage purchased from General Thomas Pinckney. He proceeded in leisurely fashion, savoring his welcome, until he reached Richmond, where he saw, for the first time, a copy of Washington's proclamation. Sensing a coolness in the administration, he declined a public dinner and hurried on to Philadelphia.[25]

It is difficult to determine the extent to which the public reception of Genet was deliberately organized by Republicans for party purposes. Jefferson and Madison both expressed the hope that Genet's arrival would, as Jefferson put it, "furnish the occasion for the people to testify their affections without the cold caution of the government."[26] But there is no evidence that either sought to mobilize that "affection." Genet's reception in South Carolina was clearly nonpartisan, reflecting the general sympathy for France that existed before the implications of the European conflict became clear. As he wound his way northward, the public reaction began to follow party lines. In Salisbury, North Carolina, Federalist John Steele viewed Genet with a critical eye, though the citizenry had given him a cordial welcome. Steele even suspected his good humor and easy familiarity, fearing that the Frenchman would try to "laugh us into war, if he can."[27]

Even in the absence of directives from above, local party leaders seemed to sense the capital that could be wrung from the occasion. In mid-May Madison learned that the Federalists who controlled Alexandria saw to it that Genet was virtually ignored, but that the Republicans in Georgetown "repaired the omission."[28] By the time the minister reached Philadelphia, Republicans were fully alive to the opportunity. They arranged a highly partisan affair, drawing out over a thousand residents for the occasion (Jefferson's estimate; Hamilton thought it closer to 500), all calculated to impress the President with the amount of pro-French sympathy in the country.[29]

Suspicious of the fanfare, Washington sent Edmund Randolph to Virginia to ascertain the true state of public opinion. Randolph toured the Federalist strongholds Alexandria, Richmond, and Williamsburg and concluded, not surprisingly, that the administration had broad support. The only opposition seemed to be of a personal nature.[30] By the time Randolph returned in late June Genet's own indiscretions had created an explosive political situation.

When Genet arrived in Philadelphia, he found Secretary of State Jefferson cordial but firm on the subject of neutrality. The privateers which Genet had dispatched from Charleston were a clear violation of American neutrality, and Britain had rightfully protested. The problem became all the more embarrassing when one privateer brought a prize right into Philadelphia. When the President ordered this and other prizes seized and returned to the British, Genet became infuriated. An acrimonious exchange of letters ensued, and the controversy came to a head in early July when Genet dispatched another privateer (which he commissioned *La Petite Democrat*) from the capital city. To Alexander James Dallas, Pennsylvania's Secretary of State, who made a special trip to plea for delay, Genet announced his intention of defending the rights of France by moving his "appeal from the President to the people."

Genet had obviously misinterpreted the outpouring of sympathy that attended his arrival, and the Republicans' stage-managing now threatened to backfire. If Genet did attack the President openly, the people were certain to regard it as foreign interference. They would rally to the President, his policies, and his party. "Never in my opinion, was so calamitous an appointment made as that of the present minister of France here," Jefferson exploded to Madison.[31] He was even more distressed when Genet made good his threat and gave copies of his correspondence with the Secretary of State to the newspapers. In August the cabinet agreed to send to Paris a summary of its exchanges with Genet, together with copies of his letters and even newspaper clippings, on the assumption that the French government would voluntarily recall its envoy once it learned of his indiscretions. It eventually did (though Genet remained in America and became a citizen), but in the meantime the political damage was done.

Federalists were quick to take advantage of Genet's misconduct. Improving somewhat on the Republicans' stage management, they organized a series of popular protest meetings. The first was held in Boston in July, and the idea quickly spread southward. On August 16 a meeting in Richmond adopted resolutions approving the administration's adherence to strict neutrality and denouncing Genet for lack of respect to American institutions. Such meddling, the resolves concluded, "might, too probably, lead to the introduction of foreign gold and foreign armies." Presiding over the meeting was much respected George Wythe; the secretary was Andrew Dunscomb, a Richmond merchant and securities speculator. John Marshall headed the committee that drafted the resolutions. Over the next month similar meetings were held in the neighboring counties; each adopted resolutions similar in tone to Marshall's, though they differed somewhat in wording. Prominent Federalists chaired each meeting, but the committees that drafted the resolutions sometimes contained men who were voting Republican in the assembly. The King William committee even contained four former Antifederalists.[32] Genet's antics caused widespread indignation, and Federalists made the most of it.

Stung by the Federalist initiative, Madison suggested that the Republicans counter its effect "by setting on foot expressions of the public mind in important Counties, and under the auspices of respectable names." He hastily penned some sample resolutions, which he hoped would be considered "an authentic specimen of the Country temper," and sent them to Jefferson, Monroe, Pendleton, John Taylor, and Archibald Stuart. Madison was an old hand at creating "authentic specimens" of popular opinion, ever since the religious assessment fight of 1784. The irony was that this time his chief foe was the man he had taught so much about manipulating opinion, John Marshall. When Monroe carried Madison's resolutions across the Blue Ridge to Staunton, he found that Marshall had already contacted a prominent Valley Federalist, Judge Gabriel Jones, who was circulating the Richmond address. Monroe claimed that his arrival "effectually changed the current and gave it a direction against the antirepublican faction," but then he had to make the ride seem worthwhile.[33]

Alerted by Jefferson that Genet was "incorrigible" and had to be abandoned, Madison toned down his resolutions and eliminated any reference to the French minister. He would have done better to have dropped the idea altogether, for the end product was vague and defensive. He began with the conventional statement of affection for the President and approval of neutrality. Without mentioning the proclamation, the timing of which he had criticized earlier, he denounced all efforts to drive a wedge between the United States and France, predicting that a rupture with the French republic would lead to a more intimate connection with Britain and thus the danger of assimilating the "form and spirit of the British monarchy."[34] To suggest that only by leaning on France could the nation retain the purity of its institutions was hardly a vote of confidence in his countrymen.

John Taylor edited the resolutions Madison sent him before submitting them to a Caroline County meeting "to avoid a suspicion of their being coined in the same mint." Taylor's additions strengthened the resolutions, but they probably also embarrassed the Republican leadership. The authors of the Neutrality Proclamation, he cried, were aiding those insidious persons who "desire a closer union with Britain and desire to alter the government of the United States to a monarchy." This was the strongest criticism of the President yet published in Virginia. Nor was Taylor prepared to abandon Genet by ignoring him. Instead, he blamed the Federalist press for distorting the facts on his conduct.[35]

NEUTRALITY AFFIRMED

If Federalists got the better of this propaganda exchange, they hardly seemed aware of it. As the summer wore on, their fears, never fully suppressed, intensified. In France the radical Jacobins seized power and began to hunt down their enemies. In America secretive clubs calling themselves Democratic Societies appeared in the course of the summer, and Federalists, associating them with

Genet and fearing French subversion, labeled them "Jacobin Clubs." The societies were pro-French and Jeffersonian, but Genet was associated with only two of them.[36] Most were located in the North. Only one appeared in the Chesapeake before the end of 1793, and that was in Norfolk.[37]

If the Norfolk society was typical, Federalist apprehensions were exaggerated as usual. It was founded in late May, shortly after Genet left the state, and was undoubtedly a by-product of his tour. But the declaration of the association, drafted by its "Standing Committee," was so bland that only the paranoid could take alarm. Its main thrust was the need for constant vigilance in a republic—a point with which Federalists readily agreed—and the only reference to France was in terms of sympathy for a fellow republic. The reason for the society was to guard against those "whose principles and sentiments are opposed to all free governments," but the declaration made no effort to connect these with the Washington administration. To such generalities many a Federalist could have subscribed in good conscience.[38] President of the standing committee was Thomas Newton, Jr., a prominent merchant, landowner, and canal-promoter.[39] Newton specialized in the flour trade,[40] probably with the West Indies, and Genet's promise of increased trade was doubtless an attractive prospect. As one Richmond merchant told Genet when he passed through Virginia, France's struggle against the league of European tyrants presented "opportunities for enterprise" for Americans, "opportunities which combine the most powerful springs of action, by uniting to exertion in the Cause of Freedom, the prospect of accumulating wealth."[41]

This was not the stuff with which to overthrow a government. Indeed, the most radical pronouncement to come out of Republican ranks that entire summer was John Taylor's Caroline resolutions, and even these affirmed loyalty to the President. Federalists nevertheless pressed on—for once, their apprehensions blended with shrewd politics. Republicans were on the defensive, and a public defense of administration policy would keep them there. "Everybody seems engaged in interested pursuits, and pay little regard to Politicks," commented a newly elected Federalist from Shepherd's Town, a small, predominantly German, Shenandoah

Valley community. "They Generally Rest Contented in placing all Confidence in the Government & will I hope continue to do as long as the Good old Man is at the Head of the Busyness—He is taking every Just Step to prevent our being involved in the troubles of Europe, especially as we are unable to assist our Friends and old Allies the French."[42] This was the sort of attitude—a mixture of confidence in Washington and an apathetic unwillingness to consider alternatives to his policies—that Federalists needed to tap.

On the eve of the legislative session Governor Henry Lee expressed his fears to Washington that Genet had succeeded in forming a party to "draw America into the views of France," though he had some hope that Genet's excesses had "stopped the further efforts of the conspirators." Lee wondered if the assembly might strike a blow against "the malignant combination."[43] The President was receptive to the idea. In August he had visited Jefferson at his summer retreat outside Philadelphia to plead with his Secretary of State to remain in office a few months longer. He feared that Jefferson's departure would open the government to partisan attack. Jefferson used the occasion to repeat the assurances he had made a year earlier, that "what is called the Republican Party" was not attempting to undermine the government. From his acquaintance with congressional Republicans, he told the President, he expected nothing more than efforts to render Congress more independent of the executive. Washington agreed that the motives of the "Republican Party were perfectly pure," the first, and probably the only, time he ever conceded the legitimacy of the opposition. But, he warned Jefferson, "when men put a machine in motion it is impossible for them to stop it exactly where they would chuse."[44]

The machine the President had in mind was party organization, particularly the mobilization of what he considered "lower orders" in the Democratic Societies. For some weeks Hamilton had been telling him that the societies represented a threat to the security of the government.[45] Governor Lee's offer thus seemed a good opportunity to expose them. He too, he informed the governor, had evidence that certain groups intended "nothing short of the subversion of the General Government and that they would do it at the expense of plunging the Country into the horrors of a disastrous war." How the Virginia assembly might prevent this the President did not say, but he gave Lee the go-ahead.[46]

When the assembly convened in Richmond toward the end of October, Lee in his opening message asked it to endorse the administration's neutrality policy. It was an extraordinary request, for no governor had asked the assembly to comment on national affairs since the end of the war. And the topic was political dynamite.

In the House of Delegates the governor's request was referred to a select committee dominated by Republicans. The request placed them in a dilemma. To approve the President's policy, even in general terms, was to approve the proclamation. Refusal, on the other hand, implied a rejection of neutrality itself, a confession of French bias, and an oblique criticism of the President. The committee evaded the dilemma with a resolution stating that the President's policies were a federal matter with which the state had no concern. Pressing their advantage, Federalists offered a substitute that approved the Proclamation and applauded the President's efforts to preserve peace. This snared the waverers and passed 77 to 48.[47] The governor had won, for the moment.

A week later the Republicans counterattacked with a resolution thanking the state's congressmen for initiating an investigation of the Treasury Department. This time Federalists were in a dilemma. The investigation, after all, exonerated the secretary, and Hamilton himself had made sure that the results were disseminated in Virginia. They resolved their difficulty with a substitute motion commending Congress for requiring an accounting of all public monies. This was rejected, 24 to 99, and the Republican motion passed, 111 to 13.[48] Each side had drawn blood.

Some days later the old Henryite element entered the fray with their familiar resolution (not heard since 1791) asking the state's congressmen to push for further amendments to the Constitution. Republican leaders were anxious to sweep this one under the rug, and it was quickly postponed, 63 to 54. The narrow margin nonetheless revealed the amount of Antifederalist feeling there still was in the party.[49] In the course of debate on this question Francis

Corbin sought to tar the Republicans with the brush of Antifederalism. When someone pointed out that the state's senators, Monroe and Taylor, had advised the assembly to draft new amendments, Corbin leaped to his feet. "It is a well known fact," he reminded the House, "that those two gentlemen were opposed to the Constitution tooth and nail and therefore I do suspect that they mean to destroy that Constitution—I like not the advice—I like not the Advisers." John Dawson, Monroe's law partner, heard the speech from the gallery, called Corbin out of the House, and told him that he planned to inform the senator of Corbin's reflections on his character. Dawson's action violated the privileges of the House and became the subject of a new debate. By 59 to 51 the House passed a resolution pronouncing Dawson guilty and then departed for home.[50]

The four roll calls on partisan issues[51] touched on a wide variety of questions—foreign policy, Hamilton's management of the Treasury, the Constitution itself, and a personal clash between two party leaders. Yet party lines were clear. Of the 110 delegates who voted enough to be identified (three times), only 25 failed to side with one or the other 75 percent of the time (see table 15.1). The sectional division was essentially what it had been, although

TABLE 15.1   VIRGINIA HOUSE OF DELEGATES: PARTIES, 1793

	Federalists	Republicans
Northern Neck	5	4
Middle Tidewater	7	7
Southside	6	19
Piedmont	1	8
West	20	6
Urban	2	0
	41	44
Federalists, 1788–1791	9	2
Antifederalists, 1788–1791	5	8
New since 1792	22	20
Unknown, 1788–1791	5	14
	41	44

Federalists had lost some strength in the Northern Neck. Given the Republicans' dominance of the state's congressional delegation, the Federalists remained surprisingly strong in the assembly.

The French imbroglio had a similar impact in Maryland and North Carolina, though in neither state was there the uproar that Governor Lee precipitated in Virginia. In North Carolina there were sporadic efforts to organize public meetings in support of the administration's policies.[52] On the eve of the fall assembly session John Steele wrote Hamilton to ask whether "expressions of the public sentiment" on the President's policies were desired. Defeated in his bid for reelection to Congress, Steele evidently planned to take charge of the Federalists in the assembly. Failing to get a reply, he went ahead anyway. He used the Richmond resolutions as a model but altered them substantially because he felt they had too much the appearance of "intermeddling" in federal affairs. Steele evidently favored a simple declaration of support. The Senate approved his address unanimously, "but in the House of Commons," Steele reported to Tench Coxe, "the opposition was violent and noisy." Republicans faced the same dilemma as in Virginia. They resolved their problem by denouncing the resolutions on the floor and voting for them on the public roll call. Steele's address passed, 120 to 5.[53]

Maryland Federalists, secure in their assembly majority, could afford to be bolder. The President's proclamation was well received in the state, particularly because it promised a continuance of the profitable West Indies trade. "It assured & confirmed the mercantile interest in Baltimore which was wavering and timid," William Vans Murray reported to Tench Coxe, adding "Wheat rose immediately from 7/6 to 9/."[54] It may have been the first instance of a Presidential announcement affecting a futures market. Having learned of the proclamation before he reached the state, Genet hurried through Maryland, and Baltimore Republicans had no chance to arrange a celebration, even if they had wanted to.[55] They may have been too wary, or too weak, to do much anyway. A pro–French Fourth of July celebration in Annapolis toasted the republic, the National Convention, and its armies, but it made no mention of the French emissary or the President's proclamation.[56]

When news of Genet's clash with the administration reached the state in mid-August, Federalists took the offensive. "Be assured that this state is right," Samuel Smith wrote Hamilton, "& except for half a dozen fools of no Consequence at Chester will act right."[57] At least one popular meeting was held before the Richmond resolutions arrived, and publication of John Marshall's resolutions stimulated more.[58] Marylanders read them with "great Pleasure," Samuel Smith reported, "as well from the Words as from the Persons who appear to have drawn them."[59] While Federalists congratulated themselves on the unanimity of sentiment in behalf of the administration, especially among the "most respectable," Republicans maintained a discreet silence. Even when the newspapers dutifully printed John Taylor's Caroline County resolutions, they failed to pick up the cue.[60] Federalists pressed their advantage at the winter meeting of the assembly. Resolutions praising the President as well as the timing and tone of his proclamation passed the Senate unanimously and the House of Delegates by a large margin. Federalists quickly shot them to Philadelphia to boost morale in the administration.[61]

BRITISH DEPREDATIONS AND REPUBLICAN RECOVERY

Republican embarrassment over the antics of the French envoy did not last long. In mid-December 1793, while the Chesapeake assemblies wrestled with the Federalist resolutions, Jefferson opened a counterattack. He sent to Congress a report on British treatment of American commerce, a document that had been two years in the making. Jefferson and Madison had long felt that Britain's refusal to enter into a commercial agreement hurt American trade. The two gathered evidence showing that, while American commerce was fairly well treated in most parts of the world, it was subject to severe British restrictions. The report was substantially completed by the spring of 1792, but Jefferson withheld it, probably awaiting an effective moment.[62]

There was no better time than the opening of Congress in the winter of 1793. Republicans desperately needed something that would deflect national attention from French affairs. A well-documented summary of British transgressions was the ideal weapon. Supporting the report, in early January Madison introduced a series of "Commercial Propositions," resolutions calling for discriminatory tonnage duties against nations having no commercial treaty with the United States, retaliation for port restrictions on American vessels, and reparations for American citizens who sustained losses from foreign regulations that contravened the law of nations.[63] It was the same sort of mercantilist nationalism he had proposed in 1789, but this time it also served a party purpose.

For once, the curious twists of European affairs favored the Republicans. While Congress discussed Madison's propositions, word arrived of a British order in council issued in December. It authorized British warships to seize any neutral vessel found trading among the French West Indies. Since Americans dominated this trade, the order was directed primarily at them. Over the next few months some 250 unarmed American ships were confiscated. Word of the seizures trickled into Philadelphia during the spring. Mounting American outrage measurably strengthened Madison's hand. Virginians, many of them still nursing old grievances against the British, felt that Madison's proposals did not go far enough. "A pretty strong Expedition into Canada," growled Spencer Roane, "paid with money due british Creditors, could scarcely fail."[64]

Congressional reaction to Madison's proposals followed party lines. New Englanders, led by Fisher Ames of Massachusetts, denounced him for trying to provoke a war with our most important trading partner. Maryland Federalists William Vans Murray and Samuel Smith joined in the cry. On February 3, before the extent of British depredations was fully known, Federalists moved to strike out the first resolution. The House rejected the motion by 51 to 46.[65] This was the first head count (unfortunately the names were not recorded) that reflected party strength in the new Congress. The two sides were about evenly matched; a handful of uncommitted members would hold the balance.[66]

A furious propaganda battle ensued, as both sides took to the press, but the critical element was the building evidence of British seizures.[67] Impressed by the public outcry, Samuel Smith concluded that some sort of retaliation, such as an embargo, was the only way to prevent war.[68] Federalists tried to relieve some of the pressure by calling for increases in the army and navy. The only effect was to negate their earlier criticism that Madison's resolutions were excessively belligerent and likely to provoke war. Toward the end of March 1794 Republicans stepped up the pressure with a resolution for a thirty-day embargo. Federalists at first defeated it, 46 to 38, but then the House reversed itself and approved it by a large majority. The Federalist-dominated Senate concurred the next day. Madison felt the reversal was due to the popular uproar, but the public mood was already evident.[69] More likely, the Federalists awoke to the fact that a blanket interdiction of trade would harm the French more than the British.

Republicans seem to have reached the same conclusion, for on April 7 they brought in a resolution to suspend commercial intercourse with Britian alone. This survived a test vote, was quickly shaped into a bill, and passed the House on April 25 by 58 to 34.[70] The Senate managed to kill this measure, and after some wrangling the two houses compromised on a one-month extension of the embargo. The Federalists' dwindling minority reflected both the pressure of public opinion and the fear that unless something were done there might be war. In all the question of commercial retaliation stimulated seven House roll calls (some repetitive) during the spring. The stance of the 36 congressmen from the Chesapeake states reveals both the importance of party and the erosion of Federalist strength. Table 15.2 was constructed from five roll calls, arranged in order of the amount of support in favor of retaliation (the reverse of the chronological order). Except for the very first roll call, when two members defected, Republican support for retaliation was firm throughout. Federalist ranks broke on the first roll call, when Grove of North Carolina voted for Madison's resolution. Smith and Griffin deserted on the next one, and William Vans Murray went over on the last two. Within a year Samuel Smith was a Republican; Griffin, Murray, and Grove remained moderate Federalists.

This string of votes was the first Federalist defeat on an important issue since the government began, and they took it hard.

TABLE 15.2 CONGRESSIONAL VOTES ON RETALIATION AGAINST BRITAIN, 1794

Roll Calls*		5	4	3	2	1	5	4	3	2	1
Blount	(R, NC)	y	y	y	y	y					
Christie	(R, Md)	y	y	y	y	y					
Coles	(R, Va.)	y	y	y	y	y					
Dent	(R, Md)	y	y	y	y	y					
Giles	(R, Va)	y	y	y	y	y					
Harrison	(R, Va)	y	y	y	y	y					
Heath	(R, Va)	y	y	y	y	y					
Lock	(R, NC)	y	y	y	y	y					
Macon	(R, NC)	y	y	y	y	y					
Madison	(R, Va)	y	y	y	y	y					
Mebane	(R, NC)	y	y	y	y	y					
Moore	(R, Va)	y	y	y	y	y					
New	(R, Va)	y	y	y	y	y					
Nicholas	(R, Va)	y	y	y	y	y					
Parker	(R, Va)	y	y	y	y	y					
Preston	(R, Va)	y	y	y	y	y					
Venable	(R, Va)	y	y	y	y	y					
Walker	(R, Va)	y	y	y	y	y					
Williams	(R, NC)	y	y	y	y	y					
Winston	(R, NC)	y	y	y	y	y					
Hancock	(U,† Va)	y	y	y	y	y					
Neville	(U, Va)	y	y	y	y	y					
Rutherford	(U, Va)	y	y	y	y	y					
Sprigg	(U, Md)	y	y	y	y	y					
Grove	(F, NC)	y	y	y	y	y					
Gillespie	(R, NC)	y	y	y		y					
Page	(R, Va)	y	y	y	y						
Dawson	(R, NC)	y	y								
Claiborne	(R, Va)	y	y	y	y						n
McDowell	(R, NC)	y	y	y	y						n
Griffin	(F, Va)	y	y	y	y						n
Smith	(F, Md)	y	y	y	y						n
Murray	(F, Md)	y	y						n	n	n
Forrest	(F, Md)						n	n	n	n	n
Hindman	(F, Md)						n	n	n	n	n
Lee	(F, Va)						n	n	n	n	n

Jonathan Dayton of New Jersey tried to expose the Virginians by going them one step further. He suggested that the government sequester the prewar debts owed British merchants and hold the funds as security for American property captured by British cruisers. Coming from a prominent Anglophile, this was nothing but a cynical move to force southerners to pay the rest of their debts, with northern merchants mockingly pocketing the proceeds.[71] When the balloting was over, New York's Senator Rufus King told John Taylor of Caroline that the union ought to be dissolved since North and South "never had and never would think alike."[72] After examining the early roll calls, Taylor wrote a pamphlet entitled *A Definition of Parties,* in which he pointed out that "the existence of two parties in Congress" was evident from the division on every important question. "Whether the subject be foreign or domestic— relative to war or peace—navigation or commerce—the magnetism of opposite views draws them wide as the poles asunder."[73]

Nor was hot-tempered party loyalty confined to Congress. Baltimore, which was heavily involved in the West Indian trade, was particularly hard hit by the British seizures. Republicans were already experiencing a swift recovery from the Genet debacle, their ranks swelled by Germans and Irish, who had never held any love for the British, and French refugees from the strife-torn island of

---

*The roll calls from the *Annals of Congress,* 3d Cong., 1st sess., were:
1 Motion to postpone Madison resolutions for one month, 51 to 47 (pp. 431–32, Feb. 5).
2 Call for previous question on nonintercourse resolution, 53 to 44 (p. 596 Apr. 15).
3 Question of whether to take up the nonintercourse resolution, 57 to 42 (pp. 600-1, Apr. 18).
4 Nonintercourse resolution passed, 58 to 38 (p. 602, Apr. 21).
5 Nonintercourse bill passed, 58 to 34 (p. 606, Apr. 25).
Two other roll calls on procedure (pp. 604-6) were deleted because they were virtually identical to the final vote.
†The "unknowns" are westerners about whom there is little information. Most, perhaps all, were elected as Federalists. By 1795 Sprigg and Rutherford were voting with Republicans, but it is not known whether they had shifted at this point or not. Neville (who served only one term) did not vote enough to ascertain his party. Dauer, *Adams Federalists,* p. 292, calls Hancock a Federalist without supplying evidence. In 1796 he voted for the Jay Treaty, but more than half his votes were Republican.

Santo Domingo.[74] The British depredations brought over a number of merchants, including, eventually, the Smith brothers, and the lower elements became more unruly than ever.

When the government allowed the embargo to expire, some Fell's Point Republicans expressed their displeasure by lowering the flag to half-mast. Federalists objected and a riot ensued. The perpetrators were arrested and brought before the Baltimore criminal court, Judge Samuel Chase presiding. Chase showed his Federalist colors by instructing the jury to convict them. The jury instead censured Chase for his intemperance and set the Republicans free. Chase thereupon rushed a defense of his conduct into the newspapers and appealed to the governor for protection. Since Baltimore troops were unable or unwilling to uphold the law, he pleaded, he needed the help of the state militia.[75] Chase's antics did the Federalist cause little good, but they did confirm to party leaders his latest political posture and, as a result, ultimately earned him a post in the federal government, something he had sought for nearly five years.

In the midst of the congressional battle, the President moved to ease tensions by naming a special emissary to reach an agreement with Britain. Although Federalist leaders expected that Hamilton would be given the task, Washington considered him too controversial and named Chief Justice John Jay instead. From the Federalist point of view it was an excellent choice. Jay's earlier position as Secretary of Foreign Affairs in the Confederation underscored the importance the administration attached to the mission. As Chief Justice he had held aloof from partisan controversy, and his position on foreign affairs, Washington had every reason to suppose, was that of genuine neutrality.

Among Republicans, however, and particularly among Virginians, Jay's appointment was less popular. His request for authority to enter into an agreement with Spain that would close the Mississippi in exchange for commercial concessions was still a scarlet memory. Jay had been oblivious to southern interests before, and he might be again. Among Virginia interests at stake was the old problem of British debts, together with the twin concerns that had been tied to British debts in the past—wartime runaway slaves and British outposts south of the Great Lakes. When the Senate took up the nomination, Virginia's duo, Monroe and John Taylor, tried to block it. In a lengthy speech Monroe reviewed the Gardoqui negotiations and accused Jay of being pro-British. Taylor then offered a resolution declaring it contrary to the spirit of the Constitution for a justice to hold any other office. This was voted down, 17 to 4, and the nomination approved, 18 to 8.[76] But a party alert had been sounded.

From the outset public reaction followed party lines. "I am really sorry the appointment of Mr. Jay is disapproved of," wrote Alexander White from Frederick; ". . . I confess I was pleased with it." Edward Carrington complained to Hamilton that "our good democrats" were denouncing the mission before Jay even had a chance to do anything.[77] Madison was quick to see the potential for an orchestrated campaign. "If animadversions are undertaken by skillful hands," he told Jefferson, "there is no measure of the Ex[ecutive] administration perhaps that will be found more severely vulnerable."[78]

What Madison had in mind was soon evident. In June, shortly after Jay sailed for London, an anonymous contributor to the Alexandria papers criticized Jay for being *"very friendly* to the British interest."[79] Democratic Societies quickly picked up the cry. The Pennsylvania society passed resolutions objecting to the appointment because of the dual officeholding. Holding additional offices made judges subservient and biased, it pointed out, and a member of the Supreme Court could hardly be a fair judge of a treaty he himself had made.[80] In July, the newly organized Democratic Society in Wytheville, Virginia, echoed the Philadelphia complaint, adding that not much could be expected from the negotiations since the administration "uniformly *crouched* to Britain." Federalists at the other end of the Valley (Winchester) replied with an address of their own, accusing Republicans of trying to drag the nation into the European war.[81] It was clear that whatever Jay managed in London it would be the subject of partisan controversy. It was equally clear that if he slighted southern interests, the Republicans would capitalize on it.

There is no evidence that Madison or other national leaders inspired this outpouring of criticism. Such a connection would signify the beginnings of interstate organization. Whether such an apparatus existed by that time cannot be determined. But in any case the spontaneous local response (since Senate debates were still secret, it is unlikely that the stance of Monroe and Taylor was widely known) suggests the existence of local organizations headed by men with strong feelings on public affairs. New controversy would generate further efforts at organization. The Atlantic crossing and Jay's lengthy discussions with the British foreign ministry created a communications lag of several months. The icy silence took some of the heat out of the Republican protests. Fortunately for them, an uprising in western Pennsylvania against the Whisky Excise of 1791 kept the political pot simmering, until Jay's return set it frothing again.

CHAPTER SIXTEEN

The Politics of Taxes and Treaties, 1794–1795

IN HIS Report on the Public Credit Hamilton had proposed a variety of new taxes to finance the national debt, and he repeated the request when Congress resumed in December 1790. Hamilton considered a tax on distilled liquor particularly appropriate, since hard drink was a luxury and a socially harmful one at that. Madison, who had voiced loud criticism of other features of Hamilton's program, offered no opposition to this one. Some years earlier he had presented the same arguments for a whisky tax in the Virginia assembly. A few southern congressmen grumbled, but the excise slipped through the House with comparative ease.[1]

What no one recognized at the time was the peculiar incidence of the tax. The large commercial distilleries of New England simply passed on the levy to their customers. From Pennsylvania southward, distilling was on a small scale. Like feed mills, there was one in every neighborhood. The tax on output could not be easily absorbed, and an additional levy on stills hit directly. As early as the summer of 1792, Benjamin Hawkins reported to the Treasury from the Roanoke region of North Carolina that the tax was quite unpopular, especially when a good fruit harvest made it a prime brandy year. "Literal compliance" with the law, he warned, was "impracticable."[2]

The excise posed an even bigger problem for farmers living west of the mountains, especially in regions that specialized in cereal grains, such as the Monongahela Valley. With the western rivers stoppered by Spaniards and Indians, tramontane settlers had to send their products east to market. But the only feasible way to get wheat or rye across the mountains by packhorse was to convert it to whisky. A single horse could carry two eight-gallon kegs, worth about a dollar a gallon in Philadelphia, and on the return journey it brought the few items, chiefly ironware and salt, that a farmer could not produce himself. A still was thus a necessary appendage to every farm, and those who could not afford one depended on their wealthier neighbors. The excise of 1791 hit these people directly, and from the beginning it rankled the poor more than the rich. Westerners with fairly large operations even approved the law because it threatened to demolish the competition.[3]

Reaction to the tax was also partisan, almost from the beginning. Opposition was centered in the four counties of southwestern Pennsylvania, staunchly Antifederalist in 1787 and solidly Republican in 1794.[4] Despite administration fears, the discontent failed to spread to the neighboring parts of Maryland and Virginia—the upper Potomac, South Branch, or even the Virginia end of the Monongahela Valley (Morgantown and Clarksburg), where grain and whisky were equally important. All these valleys had supported the Constitution,[5] and in 1794 their assembly delegations were still predominantly Federalist. Interstate rivalries probably also played a role. The Virginians' resistance to overtures from Pennsylvania seems to have stemmed, at least in part, from a suspicion of meddling outsiders. At one point during the uprising about thirty men in blackface besieged the house of the excise collector in Morgantown. The official promptly resigned and left town. But when a body of Pennsylvanians appeared a few days later to win support for their movement "they were in a few minutes driven out of town."[6]

Trouble began in the summer of 1794 when the administration decided to enforce the law and collect the tax. A U.S. marshall appeared in western Pennsylvania armed with warrants for the arrest of tax evaders. He met armed resistance, and the spirit of revolt spread rapidly. A mob attacked the house of the local excise inspector (Joseph Neville, one of the richest men in the west), and desperados robbed the Pittsburgh mail, hoping to intercept any appeals for federal help. They found enough to enrage them further, and on August 1 a mass meeting at Braddock's Field, site of the 1755 massacre, voted to attack Pittsburgh. Bloodshed was averted only when the townspeople voted to join the uprising.

On August 7 Washington issued a proclamation calling on the insurgents to disperse, while offering amnesty to all who would pledge obedience to the law in the future. At the suggestion of Edmund Randolph, new Secretary of State, he also named a commission to talk to western leaders. To strengthen the government's hand, he called on the governors of Pennsylvania, New Jersey, Maryland, and Virginia to furnish some 12,900 militiamen for federal service. When the commissioners failed to reach a settlement, the President on September 25 issued another proclamation declaring the four Pennsylvania counties in a state of insurrection and ordering the militia to march. Washington himself accompanied the army as far west as Bedford and then returned to the capital, leaving Hamilton behind to represent his wishes (though without military command). Formal command devolved upon Virginia's Governor Henry Lee, who assembled the Virginia and Maryland contingents at Cumberland, Maryland.

On August 27, Governor Lee issued a proclamation of his own. Announcing that "banditti" from Pennsylvania had entered the state and forced a United States marshall at Morgantown to flee his home, he asked all Virginians to uphold the law and ordered state officials to arrest any offenders. He specifically demanded that all Pennsylvanians entering the state be closely watched.[7] Lee did not mention the President's proclamation; instead he made it a matter of preserving the state's tranquillity. It was a shrewd bid for broad support.

Popular response nevertheless followed party lines. Augustine

Davis, publisher of Richmond's Federalist newspaper, printed the Pittsburgh resolves allegedly drafted by Albert Gallatin. Then, in a rare editorial, he suggested that Virginians remember at the next election which of their congressmen sided most often with Gallatin. "Birds of a feather flock together, so do men of the same views and opinions," he warned. On the chance that some readers had not been watching congressional roll calls, he pointed out that Samuel Griffin and Richard Bland Lee (Virginia's only Federalists) were consistent "opponents to these conspircuous [sic] Pennsylvanians."[8] Federalist counties in the Potomac-Shenandoah watershed quickly mustered their militia regiments, and westerners made up a good majority of Virginia's quota of 3,300 men.[9]

Republicans, anxious to avoid the early mistakes they had made with Genet, publicly denounced those who openly resisted the law, but privately they viewed the crisis as manufactured by the administration. Congressman/Colonel John Page was willing to lead his regiment to the fray, but he was not sure who the true enemy was. If he got shot in the back because he was facing the wrong direction, he remarked, he would simply claim it was vertigo.[10] Military commanders recognized the need to follow orders, but they sometimes had difficulty with their men. General Joseph Jones, commanding the region south of the James, had great difficulty mustering his regiments. There were no mutinies, but periodic refusals to parade delayed the organization of his force, and it failed to arrive at Winchester in time to join the governor's march into Pennsylvania. The Governor's Council was alarmed enough to threaten legal proceedings against the delinquents.[11]

Federalist Maryland filled its 2,350-man quota with alacrity. Eastern Shore militia battalions met promptly on Washington's call, and each produced 20 or 30 volunteers for action. "A firm federal tone is the characteristic of the whole shore," beamed William Vans Murray, adding "you may put down this state versus those sweet Irishmen of Washington & Alegany." The state's militia were ill-equipped, but officers reported morale high and expected the men to give a good account of themselves in battle.[12]

Eastern Republicans, still struggling for survival, ran for cover. The Republican Society of Balitmore quickly adopted resolutions approving the administration's firm stand, and in the House of Delegates Republicans voiced no opposition to a set of Federalist resolutions approving the use of the state's troops in suppressing the rebellion.[13] Only one instance of rebel sympathies was recorded in the entire state, but it portended much. On September 1 a Hagerstown crowd raised a liberty pole and drank a toast to the Pennsylvanians. Congressman/General Thomas Sprigg hastily put in an appearance and cut down the pole. After several tense moments the crowd dispersed, hurling insults at the general. Sprigg subsequently took action to "bring those insurgents to justice," but it cost him politically. In the October election Republicans fielded a candidate against him, even though he had sided with Madison on British policy that spring.[14] Sprigg won anyway, but he got the message. Thereafter he voted Republican.

The incident suggests that there was some sympathy for the Pennsylvania dissidents in the western parts of Maryland and Virginia, even if there was no disposition to join. The administration's heavy-handed treatment of the insurrection, while it certainly demonstrated federal authority, probably caused additional dissatisfaction. Even though the uproar on the Monongahela had subsided by the time the army arrived, over 100 persons were arrested and 20 paraded back to Philadelphia for trial. Maryland's far western Allegany County began drifting to the Republican camp after 1794, as did neighboring Hampshire and Harrison counties in Virginia.[15]

Virginia Republicans seemed determined to capitalize on this sentiment in the fall session of the assembly. Some openly accused the President of abusing his powers by calling out the militia of neighboring states before Pennsylvania even had a chance to quell the uprising.[16] Federalists were not prepared for a trial of strength on the issue. The House of Delegates approved unanimously a resolution praising the state's militia for its role but criticizing the intervention of federal troops in the affairs of Pennsylvania.[17] Not satisfied, the Republican majority turned its wrath on Governor Lee. Though a Federalist and a friend of Washington's, Lee had been reelected annually since he entered the office in 1791. The post was largely honorary, so few were its powers, and it had never been a source of party rivalry. Even in the 1780s factional contests more often revolved around the Speakership. Moreover, Lee's open criticism of Hamilton's Treasury policies doubtless made him acceptable to Republicans. But his role in suppressing the insurrection made him a ready target.

Shortly after the assembly opened, Republicans brought in a resolution removing Lee from office under the 1788 statute that prohibited state officials from accepting federal appointments. Federalists argued that Lee had served only as commander of the state militia, and his command of an interstate force was only temporary and unofficial. To no avail; the resolution passed by a party vote of 73 to 52. The Senate, feeling perhaps that the motion was unduly harsh, rejected it, but the House declared the office vacant anyway. Meeting in joint session, the two houses then elected Robert Brooke over Federalist James Wood (who had been Lieutenant Governor) by a margin of 90 to 60.[18] The action was a giant step in the evolution of parties. Hitherto confined to the legislature, the parties now saw the importance of controlling other branches of the government.[19] Before long other officials would be chosen—and even dismissed—on grounds of party ties.

John Taylor's resignation from the U.S. Senate gave assembly Republicans another office to fill that fall. There had never been any doubt that that post was a party one. Antifederalists had seized the Senate seats in 1788, and persons with Antifederalist credentials had occupied them ever since. Learning of Taylor's intent, Patrick Henry's son-in-law Spencer Roane wrote to Senator Monroe to express the hope that Taylor and Monroe would both "remain in office till our affairs are put upon a proper footing." With a broad hint as to what a proper footing might be, he asked if Monroe expected Congress to draft any further amendments to the Constitution.

Taylor, who easily grew impatient with the mundane duties of political office, resigned anyway. The two senators then jointly urged Henry Tazewell to offer himself as a candidate. An ally of Madison's in the 1780s, Tazewell was a critic of the Constitution but did not serve in the ratifying convention. He was currently a member of the newly formed Supreme Court of Appeals. Tazewell protested that he was not eager to serve, but he would do so lest "a person of very different political sentiments . . . become his Successor."[20] In the end, Monroe also vacated his seat, accepting a mission to France. The assembly first offered it to Patrick Henry and when he declined chose Stevens Thomson Mason, nephew of George and another former Antifederalist. For neither seat did assembly Federalists even put up a candidate. Francis Corbin, who had emerged as the Federalist leader in the assembly, informed Tench Coxe that not a "federal man amongst us" had a chance of winning; "we have determined therefore not to have any of our names put up."[21]

The growing unpopularity of the Washington administration cost the Federalists heavily in the spring 1795 congressional election, despite Corbin's hopes that a strong party effort in the assembly might sway the electorate "in favor of federal principles."[22] Samuel Griffin, whose district embraced the lower James, was in trouble early. In March 1794 several of Richmond's militia companies met and adopted resolutions approving Madison's scheme of commercial retaliation. Since Richmond was the main stronghold of Federalism in the district, the warning was clear. "If his *city* friends forsake him," wrote one Republican, "he may as well hang up his fiddle." The administration's handling of the Pennsylvania uprising did not help, and in December Madison noted with satisfaction that "Mr. Griffin resigns his pretensions" to reelection.[23] Federalists did field a candidate in Burwell Bassett,[24] recent heir to an immense estate in New Kent, and the party made a strong showing despite its handicaps. Republican John Clopton, a country lawyer of modest means,[25] won the election, but the contest was close enough to induce Bassett to appeal (unsuccessfully) to the House of Representatives.

In the Northern Neck, Richard Bland Lee lost his seat to Republican Richard Brent, a Prince William attorney. In the lower Valley, Federalists unhappy with Robert Rutherford's apostasy put up the old warhorse General Dan Morgan, but Rutherford kept his seat after another close contest.[26] Also reelected was George Hancock, whose mixed voting record reflected his politically mixed district (a combination of Republican Piedmont counties and Federalist Valley counties) in the upper James/Roanoke watersheds. But Hancock was the only question mark in the Virginia delegation; the rest of it was now solidly Republican.

Even in distant North Carolina the Whisky Rebellion cost the administration some support. The President had not involved the state in his militia call-up, but Federalists nevertheless introduced an assembly bill authorizing a militia muster should the President need more troops. It was a grievous error, for the whisky tax was unpopular everywhere in the state. Federalists would have done better to maintain a discreet silence. The pace of their decline is hard to measure because the assembly conducted no roll calls of party significance in 1794 or in 1795, but a "Protest" against the militia bill affords one clue. The document was drafted by John Hay, Fayetteville attorney and long-time Federalist, and it was signed by fourteen members of the assembly. Hay argued that suppression of the rebellion was a problem for the federal government to handle, not the state, and a mobilization of the state's militia would place undue stress on the treasury.[27] Six of the fourteen signers had been supporters of the Constitution and the Washington administration, among them such prominent leaders as Stephen Cabarrus and David Stone. Both were firm Republicans thereafter. More ominous still was the fact that all but one of the Federalists came from counties around Albemarle Sound, the one part of the state that had been solid in support of the President. In the congressional election that autumn Albemarle Federalist William J. Dawson lost his seat to Nathan Bryan, an Antifederalist-become-Republican. The defection of Albemarle virtually eliminated Federalism from eastern North Carolina. The Jay Treaty finished the job.

JAY'S TREATY

Unhappy from the outset with the nomination of John Jay to treat with the British, Republicans expected the worst from his mission, wringing their hands over every rumor that floated across the Atlantic. When word arrived early in the summer that Jay had been hospitably received in London, a Northern Neck Republican growled, "It is to be feared that if the business is to be settled at convivial entertainments, that some of our poor countrymen will be choused out of their rights."[28] Jay's every report was scanned with a critical eye. Fredericksburg attorney Joseph Jones, who was heavily involved in a suit before the federal Supreme Court on British debts, objected to the "supplicating" tone of Jay's description of his preliminary talks and wished the envoy would adopt a firmer stand.[29] The treaty was signed in November, but it took all winter to get across the Atlantic. In mid-February, Madison, who had heard only rumors of the contents, admitted "it is wrong to prejudge" and proceeded to do just that. "I suspect that Jay has been betrayed by his anxiety to couple us with England," he told Jefferson, "and to avoid returning with his finger in his mouth."[30] The Jay Treaty did not make political parties;[31] parties made the Jay Treaty a political issue.

The treaty, it must be said, was a weak one from the American point of view, but this was not entirely Jay's fault. His mission was ill timed from the beginning. Britain seemed to be winning the war in Europe in the fall of 1794, at the head of a strong coalition of monarchies, and Jay lacked the leverage to extract concessions. He did secure evacuation of the forts south of the Great Lakes and commercial privileges in British colonies in the Far East that proved of lasting value (concessions in the British West Indies were so burdened with restrictions that the Senate deleted the article). But in order to win even these limited concessions, Jay had to abandon any effort to define American rights, the central issue that had prompted his mission. The omission, in effect, amounted to an acquiescence in the British definition of blockades, contraband, even the terms of neutral trade with enemy colonies. Worst of all—especially from the Republican point of view—the United States promised not to levy discriminatory customs or tonnage duties against British ships and products for a period of ten years. Thus, with one stroke of a pen the entire foreign policy Madison had been pushing since the government began was eliminated. Not only did the treaty allow Britain to establish any maritime regulations she saw fit, Jefferson and Madison felt, but it deprived America of her only feasible weapon if those regulations proved oppressive.[32]

At the same time, these flaws do not explain the burst of outrage that emanated from Virginia. To object on the basis of broad national interests, such as the promotion of maritime rights, required a breadth of view and a fund of information that was beyond the average voter. With time, and some coaching, he might have come to see the point. But in the meantime, something else must have stirred him, for the Virginia reaction was instant and apparently spontaneous. The remaining article—and the one that most immediately affected Virginians—concerned British debts. And so far as Virginians could see it was all to their disadvantage.

The controversy over British debts had, if anything, intensified since the Constitution was drafted. George Mason's 1787 resolution opened the state's courts to British creditors, and the erection of federal courts gave them a new avenue for litigation. British merchants hastened to take advantage. In the Order Book of the United States Circuit Court for Virginia, three-fourths of the cases that appeared between 1790 and 1795 involved contracts between British merchants and American debtors.[33] The issues had been narrowed essentially to three:

—Did British infractions of the peace treaty, such as retention of northwest posts, invalidate American obligations under the treaty, notably debt payment?
—Did payments into the state treasury under the act of 1777 discharge the debtor's obligation and bar further recovery?
—Were debtors obliged to pay interest for the war years when the military situation prevented them from paying either principal or interest?

The first of the debt cases to arise under the Constitution was called by the federal Circuit Court at Richmond on November 23, 1791. It involved a suit by Jones and Farrell, merchants of Bristol, against Dr. Thomas Walker of Albemarle, Kentucky pioneer and one of the largest landowners in the state. The sum involved was £2,151, a debt which Walker claimed to have discharged by payments into the Virginia loan office in 1779. At stake, then, was the very principle of such payments, which had amounted to a total of £272,000. Each side received financial support from interested parties, and the courtroom was spangled with the stars of the

Virginia bar. At Walker's table alone were Patrick Henry, James Innis, John Marshall, and Alexander Campbell. On the bench were Justices Thomas Johnson and John Blair of the federal Supreme Court and Virginia District Judge Cyrus Griffin. Two Virginians and a Marylander forming the rules ought to have been of some comfort to debtors, but all three were Federalists who had long favored repayment.

The assembly, which was meeting simultaneously, demonstrated its concern by entertaining resolutions against debt payment until Britain evacuated the northwest posts and paid for slaves carried away in the war. It was the old Henryite alternative, and Federalists managed to substitute milder resolutions asking Virginia's senators to induce Congress to come to the relief of the state. The assembly then decamped to the courtroom; for six days the Speaker could not even muster a quorum. Oratory flowed in torrents. Henry alone entertained the assemblage for three days, moving Jefferson to the rare compliment that he "really distinguished himself." But the session ended in anticlimax. Justices Johnson and Griffin were in doubt on the key question, whether payments into the state loan office discharged the debt, and when the death of a son called Justice Blair home, the court adjourned without coming to a decision.[34]

The British merchants tried again, this time instituting suit against Daniel L. Hylton and Company, Richmond merchants.[35] Hylton again hired Patrick Henry, assuring him that "Your countrymen look up to you as the rock of their salvation."[36] The case came before the circuit court in the spring term of 1793. Presiding this time, along with Griffin, were Chief Justice John Jay and James Iredell. Henry was again at his best. Iredell confessed to being swept off his feet by Henry's rhetoric, though he was not persuaded by it "in the slightest degree." Iredell and Jay both rejected the argument that British infractions of the peace treaty eliminated American obligations. But Iredell agreed with Griffin that payments into the Virginia loan office were legitimate under the state law and barred the plaintiffs from further recovery. Jay dissented, and Virginians marked down another grievance against the Chief Justice. The decision gave Virginia debtors only a temporary reprieve. The plaintiffs appealed to the Supreme Court, and, with the views of the Chief Justice known, prospects for debtors were bleak. The Court in 1796 did, in fact, reverse the decision of the lower court, but by then the Jay Treaty had made it a new game.[37]

The treaty removed the entire issue from the courts, turning it over instead to an international commission made up of two British, two Americans, and a fifth member chosen by the commissioners themselves (they chose an Englishman who subsequently voted against the Americans). Establishment of the commission amounted to an *ipso facto* recognition of the legitimacy of the debts. Indeed, when the commission finally met, the only question left to settle was the matter of wartime interest. When that decision went against the debtors, the American members withdrew and the commission never met again.[38]

Virginia debtors could not entirely foresee this result, but they could read another clause in the treaty article which authorized the commission to admit creditors' account books as evidence of debt, a kind of evidence that was not normally admissible under the common law. British creditors thus had a better standing before the commission than they would have had in a court of law.[39] Nor had the Virginians won anything in return. Easterners were not much interested in the northwest posts, and the treaty failed to mention compensation for slaves. The slaves had never been a serious negotiating point, but for a decade debtor politicians had wrung a lot of mileage from it. Patrick Henry's courtroom oratory in 1793 kept alive the hopes of many. The treaty was a crushing blow, even if it came as no surprise.

The administration worsened the treaty's chances of popular acceptance by grossly mishandling the ratification. Instead of pointing out that the settlement was the best that realistically could be expected, it dawdled in embarrassed confusion for weeks and then decided to keep the treaty provisions secret from all but the Senate. The Senate discussed it behind closed doors, approved it by a party vote, and then voted to maintain the secrecy.[40] All this shamefaced mystery merely confirmed the suspicions of Republicans. When Stevens T. Mason leaked a copy to the press, the reaction was predictable. "The first impression was universally & simultaneously against it," Madison wrote in retrospect. "Addresses to the P[resident] agst his ratification swarmed from all quarters, and without a possibility of preconcert or party influence."[41]

The last was the important point, for Madison's correspondent Monroe, then in France, well knew that the 1793 uproar over administration foreign policy had been carefully orchestrated. Madison took it as a sign of public outrage, and no doubt it was. There is no evidence in his correspondence, or in Jefferson's, that the Republican leaders initiated this petition campaign. Yet there were a large number of well-staged meetings in Virginia that summer, suggesting that local leaders themselves took the initiative. They simply activated communications networks which, in most cases, were already in existence.

The first protest meeting was held in Philadelphia, where the treaty was initially published, but Richmond Republicans were not far behind. A meeting there on July 30, chaired by George Wythe, sent an address to the President objecting to the treaty. The location of the meeting was a slap at the Federalists, who had initiated their campaign against Genet in Richmond, and the use of Wythe was a touch that Madison particularly savored, since it was the Federalists who had first exploited the aging statesman.[42] His public switch was a political coup.

Norfolk Republicans organized a meeting a week later, and by the end of August seven counties and the towns of Petersburg and Fredericksburg addressed protests to the President. In each the remonstrance was drafted by a local committee, which probably represented the party leadership in the county.[43] There was no apparent collusion among them; each betrays freshness and spontaneity. Amelia Republicans excitedly blamed the treaty on a conspiracy of Anglophiles and monarchists; Culpeper calmly but critically analyzed the document clause by clause. In divided Gloucester a meeting could not agree on a position and adjourned without doing anything. Only two counties sent addresses to the President favorable to the treaty—Westmoreland in the Northern Neck, home of Henry Lee and numerous Washingtons, and Frederick in the Valley, where General Daniel Morgan himself chaired a meeting.[44] Eastern Federalists evidently found it better to maintain a discreet silence. Senator Mason claimed that the only open supporters of the treaty in Alexandria were "British merchants & Agents."[45]

North Carolina Federalists were equally cautious. A New Bern meeting avoided any discussion of the document and concentrated its fire instead on the "riotous and tumultuous meetings" of the Republicans. New Bern Federalists were particularly distressed about one in their own town that was not only "riotous and tumultuary," but had been "neither proposed, conducted or countenanced by any person of reflection or respectability."[46] British debts were of less concern in North Carolina, but there was some apprehension that the treaty would enable Lord Granville's heirs to win compensation for the proprietary which the state had seized.[47]

Maryland had fewer debts and less concern about the pretensions of its former proprietor, Henry Harford, but even in that state Federalists were strangely silent. The only popular meeting in the state was a Republican gathering in Baltimore on July 27 which denounced the treaty. The Federalist press ignored it, but that was apparently the best the party could do.[48]

Only in the western parts of Virginia did there seem to be much sentiment in favor of the treaty. Even there the Federalists failed to mount a petitioning counterattack, however, probably because they lacked the local apparatus. Congressman Joseph Neville, who had supported Madison's 1794 resolutions, told Madison frankly that he was content with the treaty. A veteran of the Indian wars himself, he was sure that the frontier would have taken "a damnable beating" in the event of war. He cared little that the treaty failed to define maritime rights. American merchants were doing well enough, and some of them probably were trading in illicit goods. The talk of rights was a mere cover for other interests. Virginians who opposed the treaty, he was sure, "are influenced by British gold. That is, the British Debts." In the southwest, Arthur Campbell, who felt that "The Treaty may be the best that could be obtained," fretted that the clamor against it might induce Britain to renege on the promise to surrender the Great Lakes forts. He even considered asking the President for permission to occupy the forts in advance of the treaty deadline.[49]

Neither Campbell nor Neville were strong party men; they were reflecting western interests, not Federalist propaganda. Westerners were remote from the maritime conflict, suspicious of eastern debtors, and considered the surrender of the posts and the assurance of peace a tangible benefit. Such sentiments, of course, were not universal, and Federalism continued to decline, even in the west. But it held on there longer than in eastern Virginia. Jay's treaty was at least partially responsible.

THE VIRGINIA AMENDMENTS OF 1795

The petition campaign against the Jay Treaty was spontaneous and locally organized. By the time the assembly met in the fall of 1795, Republican leaders had prepared a more organized attack. Questioning the constitutionality of the treaty, they felt, would broaden the grounds of opposition, perhaps generate enough concern in other states to force the Senate to reconsider.[50] During the Senate debate on the treaty, Henry Tazewell had raised the constitutional question by accusing the executive of usurping power. Clauses in the treaty that promised restitution of Loyalist property violated the rights of states, and the commercial articles interfered with Congress' power over interstate and foreign commerce.[51] It was an argument full of legal niceties that, not surprisingly, failed to sway the Senate. But Virginia leaders took the cue.

As soon as the assembly settled down to business they came in with a resolution commending Tazewell and Mason for voting against ratification. John Marshall and Charles Lee countered with a resolution declaring that the House had no authority to comment on foreign affairs. The issue was hotly debated for two days, with Republicans focusing on the question of constitutionality. Marshall was concerned enough over the effect of their arguments to devote three hours to a reply. The Federalist substitute then went down, 52 to 98, and the original motion passed, 100 to 50. In the course of the debate Federalists pointed out that the Republican resolution was an implied criticism of the President. To parry this thrust, Republicans, the day after their motion passed, brought in a new resolution stating that the assembly held the highest regard for

Washington's integrity and patriotism and did not intend to "censure the motives" which induced him to sign the treaty. Federalists countered with another substitute stating broadly that the President possessed "the undiminished confidence of this House." This too failed, 59 to 79, and the Republican version passed, 89 to 56.[52] The Senate passed the resolution praising Tazewell and Mason by 16 to 2. The vote was unusually lopsided because three Federalist senators had not yet put in an appearance.[53]

House Republicans were still searching for ways to excite discussion of the treaty in other states. In early December 1795 they brought in a resolution asking Virginia's congressmen to seek amendments to the Constitution. The four changes they proposed were designed more to provoke controversy than to repair flaws. They would have

—required any treaty that involved powers delegated to Congress (i.e., the commerce power, in this case) to be ratified by the House of Representatives, as well as the Senate;
—created a special tribunal for impeachment, removing the process from the Senate (where Federalists, because of extended terms, still had a majority);
—reduced the terms of senators to three years; and
—prohibited federal judges from holding any other offices.

The discussion was extended and often bitter. In the end, a Federalist motion to postpone was rejected, 59 to 70. The first proposition then passed by 88 to 32, and Federalists let the rest go through without a roll call.[54]

In the Senate, Federalists again moved to postpone the resolves, arguing that the people needed time to consider such "radical" changes in the Constitution. This was defeated by a party vote, 6 to 11; the proposed amendments then passed, 9 to 8. The two who shifted had earlier sided with the Federalists in support of the President.[55]

The conflict over the Jay Treaty generated 6 of the 22 roll calls held in the 1795 House of Delegates, a measure of the extent to which party conflict dominated the session (there had been only one party roll call in the previous year). Perhaps because of the

TABLE 16.1   VIRGINIA HOUSE OF DELEGATES: PARTIES,
1795

	Federalists	Republicans	Middle
Northern Neck	10	6	3
Middle Tidewater	11	9	3
Piedmont	5	14	1
Southside	1	48	1
West	26	14	2
Urban*	2	0	0
	55	91	10

*Norfolk borough was not represented in this session.

tense conflict, attendance was higher than usual, and a total of 156 members (out of the 176 elected) cast enough ballots to be identified.[56] The regional breakdown is a familiar one (table 16.1).

The House was elected before the provisions of the treaty were known, and the balance betwen the two parties was essentially the same as in 1793. Despite the uproar over the treaty, there were few, if any, conversions among legislators. The main increase in Republican strength was due to the Southside delegates, previously lackadaisical in attendance, who now made their numbers felt. The main effect of the treaty was to harden party lines and decimate the middle. Among Federalists, 91 percent sided with their party 100 percent of the time; 81 percent of the Republicans had perfect scores. Given the complex procedural moves and the subtle variations among alternative resolutions, it seems obvious that both parties had a communications network for spreading the "line" among backbenchers. Party organization in the assembly was complete.[57]

The contest also left some lasting scars. Some months later the Winchester *Centinel* carried a notice of a public meeting to consider a petition to Congress "praying that a new State may be laid off, to be composed of the northern neck and the territory west of the Blue Ridge to the boundary line [of North Carolina]." The reasons for splitting the state were "The hardship and inconvenience which the people of the western parts of Virginia lay under from the want of a State constitution and equal representation; and also from the great contrarieties of sentiment respecting the measures of the general government."[58] The inclusion of the Northern Neck in the scheme suggests that this was more than western separatism. Though ungainly in a territorial sense, the new state would have embraced the most Federalist parts of Virginia. Someone had been following the assembly roll calls.[59]

JAY'S TREATY IN MARYLAND AND NORTH CAROLINA

Madison, who had kept careful watch on the Virginia assembly's handling of the treaty, observed when the session ended, "Virginia has indeed set a firm example, but Maryland, North Carolina & New Hampshire have counteracted it."[60] From the Republicans' view, the response of Virginia's neighbors left much to be desired. Maryland's Federalists, though mysteriously quiet during the petition campaign, had no intention of letting Republicans use their assembly as a vehicle for antitreaty propaganda. They had resolutions in hand when the fall session opened, and their choice for master of ceremonies was a shrewd one—William Pinkney, whose return to politics as a Federalist signaled Samuel Chase's full turnabout.[61] Drawn in terms to which no one could object, Pinkney's resolution simply praised Washington and denounced his critics without specifically mentioning the treaty. It was shouted through without dissent, and effectively forestalled any Republican move.[62]

Virginia's amendments arrived too late in the session to be considered, but they were taken up in the following year. Charles Carroll drafted a reply, which both Houses approved without recorded votes. To the Virginians' demand that the House of Representatives ought to participate in treaty ratification, Carroll shrewdly pointed out that this would be a disadvantage to the small states, who had equal representation in the Senate. He demolished the Virginians' proposal for changing the impeachment process by reminding them that the present system had never even been tested. How could anyone say it was flawed? Shorter terms for federal senators met the Adams-like response that the upper house was a tempering influence, removed from popular passions. This was less convincing, and after his strong start Carroll finished with a limp. The final amendment, prohibiting federal judges from holding other offices, he dismissed with the irrelevant comment that it was directed solely at one man and did not belong in the Constitution.[63] All in all, it was hardly the public controversy the Virginians had desired.

The North Carolina assembly was no bigger help. Except for a couple meetings in New Bern and Edenton, the treaty had not excited much interest in the state.[64] Its citizens were not much involved with neutral rights, British debts, or Ohio Indians. With one exception: General Thomas Person owed large sums to British creditors, and the treaty threatened ruin.[65] Person was thus ready to cause trouble for the treaty in the fall meeting of the assembly, but with characteristic lack of political sense he waited until the very end of the session to make his move. The Commons postponed his resolutions, 81 to 15, without even discussing them. Because of its lopsided character and the absence of other party roll calls, the vote is not very instructive.[66] Perhaps delegates were in a hurry to get home; perhaps they felt Person's motives were suspect. Either way, it was no comfort to the Virginians.

There is some indication, however, that the war, and hence the treaty, did have some influence on the North Carolina electorate. As in Virginia, the treaty decimated eastern Federalism. By 1798, when the assembly for the first time in years held roll calls on some politically significant issues, the only Federalist footholds in the state were Fayetteville and the far western Piedmont (Mecklenburg, Anson, Lincoln counties), an area that had been debtor, Antifederalist, and Republican. Heavy delegate turnover in the western counties during the mid-1790s suggests that voters were realigning themselves. Reactions to the European contest seem to be the reason. Fayetteville had a large Scottish population, and travelers commonly observed that these people were pro-British and hence Federalist.[67] The western counties had a sizable German element, and this group was naturally anti-French. The Jay Treaty and the subsequent policies of Washington and Adams apparently convinced them that the Federalists were too (see chapter 20 for a further discussion of this phenomenon).

JAY'S TREATY IN THE HOUSE OF REPRESENTATIVES

The last echo of the treaty fight came in the spring of 1796. An appropriation was needed to finance the various commissions set up under the agreement, and the President duly sent a request for funds to the House of Representatives. Republicans replied with a resolution asking the President to provide the House with all the documents relative to the treaty. The motion was clearly a fishing expedition, intended to find grounds for reopening the controversy, and Madison himself had some doubts about it. Since it was a new Congress, he was not yet sure of his party's strength. To his surprise, the motion passed by the substantial margin of 62 to 37. Seemingly harmless, it attracted support from waverers such as Dent and Smith of Maryland, Hancock of Virginia, and Grove of North Carolina.

The President then played into the hands of Republicans by refusing the request on grounds that the papers were not relevant to anything Congress had before it (implying that Congress's purpose was purely partisan). House Republicans then held a policy caucus, apparently the first such meeting to be held in Congress. They decided upon new resolutions asserting the power of the House to withhold appropriations for a treaty and thereby substantiating the need for information. Federalists evidently decided not to fight the battle on this ground, and these resolutions also passed by a surprisingly large margin, 57 to 35.[68] Among Chesapeake congressmen, only hard-core Federalists William Hindman and William Vans Murray opposed them.

After three more weeks of debate, the House at last brought itself to a vote. On April 29, voting in committee of the whole (hence the names were not recorded) the House tied 49 to 49 on the resolution saying that, while the treaty was "highly objectionable and may prove injurious to the United States," provision should be made for carrying it out anyway. Samuel Smith, who was among the waverers Republicans needed, still thought the phrasing too strong and succeeded in getting all except the word "objectionable" deleted. The temporizing won a few friends, but to Madison's chagrin, it also alienated some of the more extreme antitreaty Republicans. "Before some were ripe for arrangements, others were rotten," he grumbled to Jefferson. The clerk erroneously recorded the vote as a tie (although in fact it was 49–50), so Speaker Muhlenburg gave it the *coup de grace*.[69]

The House then reafirmed its halfhearted endorsement of the treaty by 51 to 48.[70] This time party ranks held firm, except for three Marylanders—Christie, Dent, and Smith—who gave the Federalists the winning margin.[71] In the earlier committee vote a conscience-stricken Christie had risen to inform the House that, although he considered the treaty "a bad bargain," he felt bound by the wishes of his constituents, who wanted it carried into effect. Evidently the wheat-growing farmers of the Susquehanna bottoms hoped the treaty would end British interference with their flour ships. He voted against the compromise amendment (a stance that satisfied both conscience and constituents) and then in favor of the treaty. The fickle electorate retired him anyway at the next election.

Dent and Smith were both nominal Federalists in the process of becoming Republicans, and both wavered with every breath of public opinion. Smith criticized the treaty at an early stage of the debate, but then Baltimore Federalists, led by James McHenry, organized an intense pressure campaign. McHenry himself drafted a petition which was circulated by hand, winning signatures. When Republicans tried to organize a mass meeting of "Manufacturers and Mechanics," only a couple of hundred people appeared, and most of those, so Federalists chortled, were indifferent spectators. The simple fact was that the treaty was generally popular in Maryland. On April 22 Smith made another emotional speech criticizing the treaty; a week later he voted in favor of it. In the end, Federalists were the losers, for their pressure tactics cost them one of the most powerful politicians in the state. Despite Smith's last-minute bid for rectitude, the city's merchants continued to suspect him. Isolated and in need of allies, he turned to the mechanic's societies. Within a year he had built a strong political organization capable of controlling the city. Baltimore was firmly Republican thereafter.[72]

FEDERALISTS GO A-COURTIN'

Even before the defections occasioned by the Jay Treaty, Federalists recognized the need for greater popular support. It was evident by early 1794 that the parties were evenly balanced in Congress, and Federalists could no longer count on the huge majorities that had sustained their policies ever since the first election. In the Chesapeake there were no bigger prizes than Samuel Chase and Patrick Henry. Each was the most widely known man in his state. Because of their prominence in the Revolution, each had a symbolic importance that went far beyond their political abilities. A public conversion—acceptance of a post in the government would do—would have a profound impact.

Chase had made known his availability within weeks after Washington was inaugurated. Only the President's sense of delicacy prevented him from joining the administration (see chapter 12). It was not long before Washington was also made aware of the availability of Patrick Henry. Jefferson and Madison had gathered up Henry's antifederalist following while ignoring the old war-horse.[73]

By the end of 1792 Washington had reason to suspect Henry was disenchanted with the Republican leaders, for he asked Governor Henry Lee about the possibility of bringing Henry into the government. Lee was skeptical. He was not certain of Henry's attitude, and if Henry should decline an offer the administration would be embarrassed; or worse, the President could be accused of trying to bribe his enemies with federal patronage. By 1794 Lee had changed his mind; he now had evidence that Henry might accept a post. Washington was delighted, feeling "strong inducements on public & private grounds to invite Mr. Henry into any employment . . . to which his inclination might lead."[74] Two days later Secretary of State Randolph wrote Henry to offer him the post of envoy to Madrid. The Mississippi question was still in a stalemate, he explained, but the government anticipated that Spain might be ready to yield.[75] It was a shrewd nomination, for Henry had been the most vocal critic of Jay's negotiations eight years earlier; almost anything he agreed to would be accepted in Virginia and the Southwest. Perhaps Henry smelled a trap; nothing came of the idea and Thomas Pinckney went to Madrid instead.

The administration had better luck with Samuel Chase, who had been waiting in the wings since 1789. It was McHenry who reminded the President of Chase's availability. Impressed by Chase's partisan handling of the Fell's Point rioters in 1794, McHenry wrote to suggest the elevation of Chase to the federal Supreme Court. "Chase and I are on neither good nor bad terms, neither friends nor enemies," he assured the President, then hinted: "To profound knowledge he adds a valuable stock of political science and information." Late in 1795 William Vans Murray added his own endorsement. Not only did Chase seem politically reliable, he felt, but so was Luther Martin. A single overture could win a bagful of support. The resignation of John Blair gave Washington the opportunity, and in January 1796 Washington named Chase to the Supreme Court. "Chase will accept," wrote a delighted McHenry; "you have made an old veteran very proud and happy."[76] Chase responded with partisan gratitude. His very first opinion turned aside a Virginia challenge to the federal carriage tax, one of Hamilton's excises. He rejected the Virginians' argument that the tax was a levy directly on the people and therefore a "direct tax" that had to be apportioned among the states. And by finding the statute constitutional he indirectly affirmed the principle of judicial review.[77]

Cabinet resignations in 1795 brought a renewal of the courtship of Patrick Henry. Henry Lee was again the intermediary, writing Henry to inquire if he was interested in any sort of federal office. Henry replied directly to Washington, explaining that "deranged finances" and poor health prevented him from taking public office. This, of course, did not completely close the door, and he did go to some length to assure the President of his support.

He had, he said, "bid adieu to the distinction of federal and antifederal ever since the commencement of the present Government."[78]

The departure of Henry Knox from the War Department and the dismissal of Edmund Randolph created new vacancies that fall. Henry's encouraging attitude apparently induced Washington to resume the courtship. In October he offered Henry his choice of the State Department or the attorney generalship. By midwinter he had upped the ante. In January he wrote anxiously to Henry Lee: "Your letter of the 28th Ult. has been received, but nothing from you since; which is embarrassing in the extreme; for not only the nomination of the Ch[ie]f J[ustice] but of As[socia]te J[ustice] and Se[cretary] of W[ar] have been suspended on the answer you were to receive from ———."[79] The President had to be cautious because word of such indiscriminate solicitation would have been ruinous; but, in view of the earlier correspondence, there is no doubt that he referred to Patrick Henry.

Nothing came of it, and Washington turned to his other apostate Chase for the court post. The failure was probably due to Henry's lingering suspicious of the administration. The appointment of New Englanders like Pickering and Wolcott to cabinet posts scarcely reassured him. Later that spring John Marshall was sent to sound Henry anew, and he returned with the impression that Henry was still apprehensive about those who "fill high executive offices."[80] "As to the Reports you have heard of my changing sides in politics," Henry wrote his daughter some months later, "I can only say they are not true. I am too old to exchange my former opinions which have grown up into fixed habits of thinking." He thought the Jay Treaty "a very bad one indeed," but Republican opposition, he felt, was politically motivated. Except for "a transcient effort," if he were desperately needed, he planned to remain in retirement.[81]

Henry's rejection of Federalist overtures soon reached Republican ears. Jefferson thought that the Federalists' "assiduous court" might have made "some impression" on him, but he doubted if Henry had undergone any "radical" change.[82] Republicans evidently decided to reply in kind. When the fall 1796 session of the assembly opened, they elected Henry governor (Federalists backed their own candidate, James Wood). Wilson Cary Nicholas quickly sent word of this honor, but Henry again declined, citing his advanced age.[83] Thereafter both sides seemed to give up. Henry remained in retirement until the French crisis of 1799. Evidently he felt this was time for a last transient effort. He stood for the assembly as a Federalist. The voters went along with him and granted his final wish, but he died before he could take his seat. It mattered little. By then there was nothing that could save the Federalist Party in Virginia.

CHAPTER SEVENTEEN

Prosperity Solves Many Problems

THE PARTY CONTESTS of the 1780s and the struggle over the Federal Constitution involved substantive economic issues, and because bread-and-butter interests were at stake the conflict was intense. Economic recovery after 1789 muted these tensions, and the national parties that appeared during Washington's first term found new issues to contest (notably in foreign policy) and developed new symbols. The question is, did the parties of the 1790s, descendants of the debtor-creditor conflict, reflect the old economic division? Did the national parties, preoccupied with questions of national policy, represent a debtor-creditor conflict as well?

The answer for the Chesapeake states depends on when. In the early part of the decade, when the contests of the Confederation were still a vivid memory, the parties reflected their interest-group origins. But by the mid-1790s, when the national party system was fully developed, there was little difference between them on matters of economic principle. Any generalization is hazardous, however, because there were few roll calls involving economic interests,

468

especially in the formative years, 1788–1792. The issues that did appear were not sharply defined, and voting was often random. The lessened importance of pocketbook issues was itself a manifestation of better times. Yet certain questions—particularly in regard to court reform—refused to go away, and on these items the national parties showed traces of their debtor-creditor origins. On the other hand, social questions such as church-state relations, education, and slavery, remained as nonpartisan as they were in the 1780s. Although there is some evidence that religious and ethnic biases affected party affiliation,[1] they did not appear in legislative roll calls. Social questions remained a matter of each delegate's conscience, or his perception of his constituents' desires.

DEBTOR RELIEF AND THE COURTS, 1788–1792

In Maryland court reform had not been a particularly divisive issue during the 1780s. The most articulate among the state's debtors were propertied speculators, who, despite temporary financial embarrassment, respected the law and its judgments. As a result, there was little demand for change in the judicial structure set up by the state constitution; party conflict centered on peripheral matters, such as judicial salaries and attorneys' fees. The one structural alteration, the establishment of courts of assize in 1787, sailed through the assembly with only token opposition. The upper bay counties supported it, and the Potomac was divided (see table 6.7).

A somewhat more controversial change was undertaken in 1789 when court reformers introduced a bill intended to make judicial procedures more uniform across the state. It divided the state into five districts. Each district possessed a chief justice appointed by the governor. Each county court consisted of a three-judge panel: the chief justice and two county justices. The latter had to be residents of the county over which they presided but were also appointed by the governor. The roving district judge would thus provide continuity and perhaps improve legal standards. The law also gave the courts more flexibility in applying procedures for debt collection. Every feature reflected long-standing creditor desires. Unable to defeat the measure, the outmanned debtor element concentrated on amendments. In the end, they succeeded in making enough changes in the bill to discourage its supporters. The House finally postponed it to the next session.[2]

The court reformers were back the following year, though with a somewhat weaker measure. This squeaked through the House, but the Senate stirred up trouble when it tried to strengthen the bill. Among other changes, the Senate wanted to eliminate the residence requirement for district chief justices so that the governor would have wide latitude in securing the best lawyers. The Delegates thereupon rejected the entire package. The Senate then offered to recede from its amendments, and the House agreed, approving the bill on a final vote by 27 to 23.[3] There were in all six roll calls in the House on the issue, and the alignment was a familiar one. Despite the confusion of party labels (the appearance of "Chesapeake" and "Potomac" tickets in the congressional races that fall), the emerging national parties reflected their debtor-creditor backgrounds (table 17.1).

In Virginia and North Carolina, although there was no marked

TABLE 17.1   MARYLAND HOUSE OF DELEGATES: COURT REFORM, 1790

	Creditor	Debtor	Middle
Eastern Shore	10	1	7
Upper bay	3	1	5
Western Shore	6	9	6
Upper Potomac	2	7	4
	21	18	22
Federalist	13	6	8
Federalist/Republican*	3	1	0
Antifederalist/Republican*	1	5	6
Unknown/Republican*	2	4	4
Middle in 1788	1	1	3
Unknown	1	1	1
	21	18	22

*Those designated Republicans are delegates who voted against the administration in criticizing assumption of state debts in this session.

improvement in staple prices and talk of hard times continued to be heard,[4] the old debtor-creditor tensions largely vanished after 1788. Or, if they were present, they did not show up in assembly debates. Paper money, stay laws, sheriff's delinquencies scarcely made the record. In the five years after 1788 Virginia's House of Delegates held only seven roll calls on financial issues, all involving taxation. The voting was largely regional. The south and west favored tax relief as they had in the past. Party leaders on each side evidenced no particular voting pattern.[5]

In 1792 the Virginia assembly finally completed action on the revision of the law code and slightly altered the district court system. In the accompanying roll calls the division was primarily regional, as it had been in the 1780s. The Potomac Valley favored revision, while southern and southwest counties opposed it. Because of the sectional voting, more Federalists supported law reform than Republicans, but party leaders again followed no pattern.[6]

North Carolina was much the same. Each house of the assembly held only five roll calls in the five sessions from 1788 to 1792 on questions of debts and taxation, and there was neither a regional or partisan pattern to the voting.[7] Even the judiciary failed to excite any controversy. In 1790 the Lawyers planned a major effort at court reform, taking advantage, no doubt, of the improved climate following the second ratification campaign. They wanted additional circuits and lengthened terms of sitting, but above all they wanted judges put on a regular salary under the civil list, instead of being paid by the court appearance. Only in this way, Lawyers felt, could some professionalism be introduced into the judiciary. They had to make some compromises to get the revision through the assembly, but they were generally satisfied with the result. The Commons approved the measure by a substantial margin of 46 to 22.[8] Clearly, tempers had cooled since the blowup of 1786. The bill won a majority in every region of the state; Federalists favored it by 22 to 7, Antifederalists by 10 to 7.[9]

Even paper money failed to cause much of a stir in North Carolina. The old sectional split was still there, but parties did not become involved. The issue arose in 1794 with a bill providing for the retirement of the remaining certificate debt of the state. The federal government's assumption of the state's war debt had relieved the state of much of its burden, and hard-money people apparently felt it was time to eliminate the rest. The bill passed 52 to 28; in the minority, presumably, were only hard-core inflationists.[10] The minority was centered in the Cape Fear counties and the far west. The party lineup followed the regional division. Albemarle-Pamlico Republicans were as solidly anti-paper as the Federalists.

In Maryland, the question of officials' salaries was as much a touchstone of regional and partisan loyalties in the 1780s as paper money was in North Carolina. By the mid-1790s it was almost the only bread-and-butter issue that still generated roll calls. In 1796 the House of Delegates got into a salaries squabble that affords a rare peek at its alignment. The House was proceeding through a routine civil list when someone offered an amendment adding an unspecified percentage increase to all executive salaries to keep up with the rising cost of living. After rejecting increases of 15 percent and 12 percent, the House approved 10 percent, but then it refused on a tie vote to add the amendment to the bill. Tempers rose, and thereafter the salary of every office in the state was subjected to a roll call vote.[11] There were ten of these in all, and the regional pattern was a familiar one. The Eastern and Western shores favored higher salaries; upper bay and upper Potomac favored lower ones. As in Virginia and North Carolina, the party division reflected the regional one. Tidewater Republicans were as creditor-minded as Federalists; western Federalists were as debtor-minded as western Republicans.

Prosperity, it seems, solved many problems. The hard times of the 1780s had given rise to the first state parties, but when tensions eased economic questions no longer the occasioned party conflict. Indeed, economic issues appeared on the legislative agenda with less and less frequency during the 1790s. And when they did appear, they were less likely to generate public roll calls. The lack of interest in establishing a public record itself suggests that such matters were becoming less controversial. As party organizations developed in the 1790s, however, a few issues—notably banking and the law courts—were caught up in the partisan warfare.

OF BANKS, FEDERAL AND STATE

Local interests, rather than party mandates, dictated the initial reaction to a federal bank. Hamilton's proposed Bank of the United States encountered considerable opposition from Republican leaders, but no one outside the capital city seemed much interested. Once the congressional controversy died away the only opposition to the federal bank came from local banking interests who feared the competition. In Baltimore the Bank of Maryland, formed in 1790, was controlled by prominent Federalists, including William and Samuel Smith and General O. H. Williams. In Congress, William Smith and several other Maryland Federalists voted against chartering the federal bank in 1791. When the Bank of the United States undertook to set up a branch in Baltimore in 1792, Hamilton calmed the fears of Maryland Federalists with a promise that his own "forbearance" would prevent the federal branch from endangering the state bank.[12] This was sufficient for Maryland Federalists, and if the state's Republicans harbored suspicions, they were too weak in 1792 to make an issue of it.

Virginia Republicans were stronger, but divided. They did not want a branch of Hamilton's corporation, but they were not sure whether the tactical alternative ought to be state banks or no banks. In June 1791 a meeting in Alexandria drafted a request for the establishment of a branch of the Bank of the United States. The city had no bank of its own (nor was there one anywhere in Virginia), so there was no opposition within the mercantile community. Of the five Alexandrians who signed the petition, four were prominent merchants, one a lawyer, and all were Federalists. Sixty-five residents of the Potomac-Shenandoah watershed, including a sizable number from Maryland, were appointed to seek subscriptions. Of those who can be politically identified, all but one were also Federalists.[13]

Seeing a tentacle of Hamilton's monster insinuating itself into the state, with help from Northern Neck Federalists, the assembly moved quickly. It would not dare a direct attack on the Bank of the United States, Edmund Randolph predicted when the fall 1792 session began, but it would do what it could to hamper it. Among the possibilities was a limitation on the interest rate (say, 5 percent) that the federal bank could charge, or the formation of a state bank to compete with it.[14] The assembly finally settled on the second alternative, issuing a charter to the Bank of Alexandria. The new bank was "warmly opposed" in the House of Delegates, reported Madison's informant, John Dawson, but "I was surprised to find some who had always reprobated the national Bank, and the *principle* of banking," were in favor of it.[15] Some Republicans evidently considered the state bank a means of forestalling a federal branch, but there remained an undercurrent of agrarian opposition to all banks.

A year later John Taylor of Caroline voiced the Republican antipathy to banking enterprise in a lengthy pamphlet. Paper profiteering, he felt, was at the root of the Federalist system. Speculators, bankers, and money changers, said Taylor, making no effort to distinguish among the three, were leeches on society, drawing fortunes in paper profits by manipulating the money supply. The losers were those who produced the only true wealth, the tillers of the soil.[16] Sending Madison a copy for comment, Taylor expressed the hope that it would "produce in the Virga. Assembly a repeal of the bank laws, and an Expulsion of bank paper."[17]

Taylor's writings never lived up to his expectations, but many Republicans remained suspicious of banks. In 1795 the House of Delegates approved, by 92 to 38, a measure authorizing the Bank of the United States to establish branches in the state. The margin alone suggests considerable Republican support. A year later the House rejected, 57 to 83, a bill to charter a state bank in Norfolk.[18] Whether this represented antibank feeling or an effort to reserve Norfolk for a branch of the federal bank one cannot say.[19] General attitudes toward banking enterprise, however, can be discerned from the two votes. John Marshall, for instance, voted in favor of both the federal branch and the Norfolk bank. Agreeing with him were 19 Federalists (11 eastern, 8 western) and 8 Republicans. Voting against both banks were 14 Republicans and 4 Federalists (2 easterners, 2 westerners).

On the subject of banks in general, Republican attitudes were ambiguous, but Federalist banks were another matter. From the beginning the Bank of Alexandria had been a Federalist enterprise. In 1799 the state's only bank went to the assembly for an extension of its charter, and the House of Delegates turned it down. No roll call was taken, but the city's Federalist delegate thought it was a party vote, with the leading Republicans—Taylor, Giles, Barbour, and Madison—lined up against the bank.[20] That was the final shot of the bank war in Virginia, however. The following year the Bank of the United States finally established a branch in the state, in Norfolk, with little apparent opposition, and as soon as the Jeffersonians won the presidency they asked for, and obtained, a branch in the nation's capital.[21]

The federal bank never sought to establish a branch in North Carolina, nor, apparently, was one ever requested. In fact, there seem to have been no banking facilities in the state at all until the Second Bank of the United States opened a branch in Fayetteville in 1817.[22] Had the issue arisen, it would probably have found Carolina Republicans even more hostile to banks than Virginians. Maryland Republicans, on the other hand, were more commercial. In 1795 the Bank of Maryland requested an expansion of its authorized capital. The assembly instead decided to charter another facility, called the Bank of Baltimore.[23] The reasons, apparently, were not political, even though the Bank of Maryland was controlled by Federalists.[24] Federalists opposed the bill, 19 to 15, while Republicans favored it, 15 to 2, but the lineup was regional. The main support came from the environs of Baltimore, a Republican stronghold; the main opposition came from the Federalist-dominated Eastern Shore and Potomac.

Once the bank started operating, however, it became more involved in party rivalry. Perhaps Samuel Smith, who became one of its directors, gave it a Republican flavor. The following year the bank went to the state for financial aid, and the House of Delegates tentatively approved a resolution authorizing the state treasurer to purchase 220 shares of bank stock. It then seemed to change its mind, and a second resolution authorizing the payment of $33,000 for the stock was rejected 26 to 35. On the combined roll calls, Republicans appeared to favor the bank by 10 to 7, while Federalists continued to oppose it, 20 to 11. This time the lineup was both regional and partisan. Every single Federalist from the Western Shore and the Potomac opposed the bank. The bank got only three votes in those areas; all were Republican. Both Federalists and Republicans on the Eastern Shore, however, favored the bank. Any expansion in the facilities of the Baltimore Branch of the Bank of the United States, however, was another matter. The legislature turned a deaf ear to the branch in 1796, and one Baltimore merchant, who supported the federal bank, felt that this was due to opposition from the two state banks.[25] Because each party had a bank, there was no one to defend the interests of the Bank of the United States.

In 1799 the Bank of Baltimore was back again.[26] The House of Delegates entertained a resolution on the general principle that the state ought to become a stockholder in the bank. A motion to postpone the subject to the following year failed, and then a few days later passed by 33 to 31.[27] Parties' attitudes had hardened, as they did on most other matters by the end of the decade. Republicans supported the bank by 16 to 2; Federalists opposed it, 15 to 6. Nowhere in all this maneuvering is there a hint of ideology. Despite the fulminations of John Taylor of Caroline, there was little opposition to banking in principle among Republicans of Maryland and Virginia. Nor were Federalists particularly committed to banks. It all depended, it seems, on who controlled the bank in question.

JUDICIARY POLITICS IN MARYLAND, 1796–1801

After Virginia and North Carolina completed their court reorganization in the early 1790s, legal-judicial matters virtually disappeared from the legislative agenda. Maryland also altered its court system in 1790, but the legislature continued to tinker with it until it finally became a party issue. It was not a matter of debtor-creditor attitudes, for in Maryland both parties were creditor-oriented. Rather, the judiciary system became a political playground, as each side tried to establish rules that would work to its advantage.

In 1790 the Maryland assembly replaced the traditional county courts with five district courts, each staffed by a three-judge commission. The chief justice moved around the district, constituting a court in each county in company with two residents of the county.

Antifederalists resisted the change in 1790, but Republicans manifested no objections to the system. In 1796 the House of Delegates revised it slightly and extended it for another four years by a vote of 47 to 6.[28]

The new courts retained most of the regulatory powers of the old justices of the peace, among them the authority to supervise elections. As Federalists slowly lost their grip on the state in the late 1790s they apparently abused this power. As a result, the courts were a prime target when Republicans finally won control of the assembly in 1801. The very first roll call of the session involved a request to bring in a bill on the administration of justice, and it passed by a strict party vote of 42 to 27. The Republican measure retained the district system (while repealing the acts of 1790 and 1796), but it deprived the courts of their authority to supervise elections. It also reduced the size of the state Court of Appeals from four to three by prohibiting the governor from replacing a judge who resigned or died. Modeled, no doubt, on the Federalist Judiciary Act passed by Congress earlier that year, the measure was clearly intended to freeze the state's highest court until Republicans could win control of the executive.[29]

When the bill reached the House floor in mid-December, Federalists moved to postpone it and lost, 29 to 41. They then sought to make it unpalatable by proposing increases in judges' salaries and charging attorneys fees to practice in the county courts. Republicans turned back both amendments, though both parties split on the question of attorneys' fees. The House then approved the bill, 39 to 33. The upper house (which Republicans captured with the election of the Sixth Senate in 1801) had further suggestions. Among other things, it conferred the power of appointing election judges on the levy courts (county tax courts consisting of local justices of the peace). Republicans rammed these changes through the lower house, even suspending the rules so that the bill could be given two readings on the same day.[30] In all, the bill generated seven roll calls in the House, and party lines were tight. Republicans favored it by 37 to 1; Federalists opposed it by 27 to 1 (minimum participation of 3 votes; agreement threshhold of 75 percent). The only delegates who seemed uncertain about it were the three who were also in the middle on party. But, then, court reform itself was no longer the issue.

INTERNAL IMPROVEMENTS

In all three of the Cheapeake states road construction continued to be a completely local matter. Whenever the legislatures dealt with roads—usually authorizing the counties to undertake construction—roll calls showed no regional or party pattern. Canals were another matter. Canal facilities affected the commerce of entire regions, and the cost of construction often involved the state treasuries. Canal building thus caused some intense legislative battles and created intricate alliances. Party loyalties were not involved, however. Neither party seems to have been philosophically committed to or opposed to public support for internal improvements.

Maryland witnessed the most prolonged fight. So divided was the state in its commercial needs that it seemed almost impossible to reconcile the three great regional interests—the Eastern Shore (which desired a link with the Delaware River), the Susquehanna watershed, and the Potomac. In 1795, the Potomac Company, having completed its works on the upper part of the river, went looking for funds to complete the canal around the Great Falls. It asked the legislature for permission to sell an additional 100 shares of stock, and it wanted the state to purchase as many as it could. A House committee, headed by a delegate from far western Allegany County, reported favorably on the petition, but the House rejected it. Immediately thereafter a motion was made for leave to bring a bill establishing a company to cut a canal between Chesapeake Bay and the Delaware River. This was granted, 36 to 21. A few days later the House reversed itself and approved the committee report on the Potomac Company. The bill enlarging the state's investment in the company swept through, 40 to 30, but then, by a nearly identical margin, the House postponed the Chesapeake-Delaware canal bill.[31]

The two interests evidently regarded each other as rivals.

Nearly all who supported one voted against the other. Nine delegates (most from the Susquehanna region) voted against both. The Eastern Shore gave no support to the Potomac Company, but nine Potomac delegates did back the Delaware canal project. That at least laid the basis for a future alliance, but it was a long time in coming. Neither interest attended the 1796 assembly, but the following year both were back. At the opening of the 1797 session the House agreed to entertain a bill to charter a company to dig the Chesapeake-Delaware Canal. But then the bill itself was rejected by a sizable margin, and when a committee reported favorably on a new request for funds from the Potomac Company that too was rejected.[32]

At that juncture the proprietors of a Susquehanna canal came to the assembly with a request for support. At last someone thought of an alliance. In mid-December the House took up a bill calling for an initial investment in the Susquehanna venture and enlarging the state's share of the Potomac Company. The House insisted on separating the two, but it agreed to the Susquehanna charter and loaned $72,000 to the Potomac Company. Potomac delegates then swung behind the Eastern Shore canal and that bill passed handsomely, 33 to 19.[33] The Senate frustrated that project, but the interests had learned the value of alliances. Throughout the eight roll calls delegates from the Susquehanna counties at the head of the bay backed the Potomac subsidy almost to a man. The Eastern Shore, previously wedded only to its own project, now split evenly, five supporting the Delaware Canal, five backing all three canals. The Potomac delegates divided in the same fashion. Only the Western Shore (Anne Arundel) and the cities continued to oppose any sort of investment in transportation. As in 1795, the parties were evenly divided.

The canal interests returned with palms out in each of the following years, and the voting in 1799 showed how firm the alliance was. Resolutions favoring the incorporation of a Chesapeake-Delaware Canal company, providing additional funds to the Potomac, and purchasing stock in the Susquehanna company were introduced simultaneously, taken up on the same day, and passed by healthy margins.[34] The lineup suggests that "logrolling" had

TABLE 17.2   MARYLAND HOUSE OF DELEGATES: INTERNAL IMPROVEMENTS, 1799

	Potomac Only	Delaware Only	Susquehanna Only	All 3	None
Eastern Shore	0	12	0	5	7
Upper bay	0	1	0	4	1
Western Shore	2	1	0	9	2
Upper Potomac	2	0	0	10	0
Urban	0	0	0	4	0
	4	14	0	33	10
Federalists	4	4	0	10	5
Republicans	0	7	0	4	4
Middle	0	0	0	2	1
Unknown	0	3	0	17	0
	4	14	0	33	10

reached maturity (table 17.2). At least among the Potomac and Susquehanna supporters, it was all or nothing. The alliance also resolved the controversy. For the time being, internal improvements disappeared from the legislative record.

In Virginia there had been a vague alliance among canal interests from the beginning. In the 1780s north-south rivalry was avoided by issuing simultaneous charters to the Potomac Company and the James River–Kanawha Canal Company. In the 1790s the assembly compromised sectional interests in similar fashion. In 1795 the Potomac Company went to the Virginia assembly for help at the same time that it appealed for funds from Maryland. By that date the company had largely completed its original mission, and the river was clear of obstacles from the Great Falls (ten miles above Alexandria) to the South Branch and some sixty miles up the Shenandoah. Its benefits to northern Virginia were the subject of frequent comment, and the company was generally popular. The 1795 request was for funds to complete the canal around the Great Falls, thus opening the river all the way to the sea. The House of Delegates approved the appropriation by a solid margin, 65 to 25.[35] Even the Piedmont and Southside, regions that would not benefit directly, supported the project. Since these delegates were normally inclined to vote their local interests, it is likely that they had a project of their own at hand.

They came in with it the following year—a bill creating a company to improve navigation on the Appomatox River. The improvement would give the central Southside access to the sea by way of the James River. The critical feature was a clause authorizing the state treasurer to purchase 100 shares of company stock. An effort to delete this failed, 55 to 79, and the bill passed by voice vote. Joining the Southside were twenty-four delegates from the Northern Neck and the west, evidently returning the previous year's favor.[36]

As in Maryland, the party division reflected the regional one. Federalists supported the Appomatox improvement by 24 to 20, Republicans backed it 45 to 21. Ideologically, two important principles were involved—state support for public works and state subsidies to private corporations. In this period, the political parties were not committed on either one.

In North Carolina also the internal improvements question was a regional and not a partisan one. The issue arose periodically in the 1790s as various interests asked for aid—the Dismal Swamp Canal, fish passageways in the Tar River, and improvements in the Roanoke River.[37] Each project won support from delegates in its vicinity; otherwise there was no pattern to the voting.

The general principle of internal improvements, never really discussed in Maryland and Virginia, did arise, however. In 1795 Federalist John Steele presented a set of resolutions calling for improvements in inland navigation everywhere in the state. Although individual projects were not specified, coastal counties could expect to benefit less than the west, and the wealthier eastern counties would also bear the brunt of the cost. Their delegates defeated the motion.[38] The only support came from the Piedmont and the west. Federalists opposed Steele's resolutions by 16 to 6, Republicans opposed them by 9 to 8 (among those that could be identified by party).

Of all the political issues in this period, internal improvements was the most local, in interest and effect. The general principle of public investment in transportation facilities was never questioned;

the relationship between the government and private enterprise was never seriously discussed. Individual projects won support whenever enough local interests were wedded to form a majority.

In short, neither party in the 1790s was tied to an economic interest. Despite the private homilies of Jefferson and the public outbursts of John Taylor, neither party in the Chesapeake states was particularly pro- or anti-mercantile. The relationship between economic endeavor and public policy, though widely discussed elsewhere, did not affect Chesapeake politics in the 1790s.

CHAPTER EIGHTEEN

Reform with Restraint

IT HAS OFTEN been pointed out that there was very little that was truly democratic about Jeffersonian Democracy. Jefferson talked much, but did little for the "common man." It should be remembered, nevertheless, that such questions as suffrage and representation were the province of the states. However much Jefferson might have wished for change, he did not feel it was his place, as President, to interfere. In regard to other social concerns, moreover, the federal government in this period had no power whatsoever. National politics was largely confined to taxes, trade, and treaties. Such important questions as separation of church and state, advancement of public education, and eradication of slavery had to be fought on the state level.

The question, then, is how democratic-minded were the Jeffersonians without Jefferson? Did the party represent an independent force for reform? Conversely, were the Federalists as elitist as statements made by some of their national leaders seemed to indicate?

There is no clear answer. Early in the decade neither party

evidenced any interest in social questions. But toward the end of the period, when the party system was fully matured, a few leaders seemed to recognize the political advantages in reform. This was particularly true, of course, in regard to the suffrage, where a liberal policy promised immediate political dividends. On those questions where there was any party difference at all, Republicans were the reformers, but Chesapeake Federalists were not far behind.

THE POLITICS OF CHURCH AND STATE

North Carolina remained almost totally free of religious controversy in the 1790s, as it had in the previous decade. The state's constitution not only disestablished the Church of England but it prohibited any sort of tax support for religion. North Carolina thus escaped the battle between religious conservatives and liberals that engrossed her northern neighbors in the 1780s. In the succeeding decade the only religious questions that came before the assembly were occasional requests for church incorporation. None of these was controversial enough to generate a public roll call.

The Maryland assembly periodically encountered religious questions during the 1790s, but there were no serious conflicts. The last echo of the postwar controversy over incorporation was heard in 1788 when the assembly took up a general incorporation law. Any Christian church or congregation in the state, regardless of denomination, would have been permitted to incorporate for the purpose of owning property. The act seemed innocuous enough, but the assembly was evidently still shaken by the earlier uproar. The House of Delegates approved the bill by a wide margin, 39 to 19, but then had a change of heart. Informing the Senate that it was too late in the session to give the bill adequate consideration, the Delegates recommended that it be published and taken up anew at the next session. Both houses took the unusual step of displaying the provisions of the bill in their journals, but that was the last anyone heard of it.[1]

Thereafter the assembly handled requests from religious societies on an individual basis, and by avoiding general principles it escaped controversy. In 1792, for instance, the Roman Catholic

Church requested permission to set aside certain properties for the support of its clergy. The move evidently required legislative action but no public expenditures. The House of Delegates approved the bill by 47 to 24, and since the treasury was not involved, the division probably reflected individual attitudes toward Roman Catholicism.[2] Not surprisingly, support was firmest on the Western Shore and the cities, where Roman Catholics were most numerous. But there was no clear-cut opposition. The Eastern Shore, where Methodists were numerous, was evenly divided. The upper bay and Potomac, each of which had sizable populations of German Lutherans, generally favored the bill. Both political parties were similarly divided. Three years later a bill incorporating a Roman Catholic Church in Baltimore created an almost identical lineup.[3] The incorporation of Protestant churches during the 1790s rarely rated even a roll call.[4]

In 1797 the House of Delegates engaged in a brief squabble over official prayers, which, if nothing else, revealed some fundamental attitudes toward religion. The customary motion that daily sessions be opened by a prayer from the Reverend Ralph Higginbotham, Anglican minister in Annapolis, was amended to include occasional services by the Reverend Wyeth as well. The dash of ecumenicism may have been intended to silence criticism, but then the whole notion of morning prayers was approved by a slim 22 to 20.[5] Most of the opposition came from the Western Shore and the towns (Roman Catholics, perhaps?). The predominantly evangelical counties on the Eastern Shore and upper bay supported morning prayers, while the Potomac was divided. Federalists leaned slightly against legislative worship; Republicans unanimously endorsed it (not a very meaningful figure since fewer than half of the Republicans were yet in attendance).

The remaining religious question with which the Maryland assembly grappled in the 1790s involved the test oaths. The state constitution required two oaths as conditions for voting and officeholding—one a loyalty oath, the other a declaration of belief in Christianity (with a separate affirmation that permitted Jews to participate in politics). In the 1780s the loyalty oath was made to apply only to future behavior (thereby enfranchising former

Tories), but it remained an obstacle to Quakers and other pietists who objected to oaths in principle. In 1794 a bill eliminating this part of the constitution passed the House by 35 to 15 and the Senate by voice vote.[6] Support for the change was strongest on the Eastern Shore and upper bay, where Quakers were most numerous, and in the upper Potomac with its German pietist population. Opposition centered on the predominantly Anglican Western Shore. The parties split evenly. The following year a bill confirming this action passed by a similar division.[7] In 1797 the principle of simple affirmation was extended to all other civil activities (of which court appearances were probably the most important).[8] The lineup was much the same.

The question of oaths versus affirmations was not a diverse issue. The stands of most legislators were influenced most by the composition of their constituencies. Neither party found it of interest. The religious test was another question, particularly after the storm of accusations against Jefferson that issued from New England pulpits during the campaign of 1800. When Republicans won control of the assembly in 1801, they mounted an assault on the remaining constitutional test, the requirement of a declaration of belief in Christianity (or Judaism) as a condition for voting or holding office. The move failed when a motion to postpone passed by 35 to 24, but this time the lineup was more partisan than regional.[9] By 23 to 2 Federalists favored retaining the religious test; Republicans by 22 to 9 favored abolishing it. The two Federalists on the liberal side came from cities. All the Republicans who voted on the conservative side came from the predominantly evangelical Eastern Shore or upper Potomac. The reason for the Republican stance is unclear. It is possible that they sought political support among voters disfranchised by the religious test. More likely, the religious accusations that dominated the Presidential election of 1800 made both parties more aware of the relationship between politics and religion.

Maryland's religious test, it must be said, was not strictly a spiritual matter. The test itself injected religion into politics; hence it is scarcely surprising that it eventually became the center of party strife. In Virginia, on the other hand, the parties injected themselves into a conflict that was initially confined to the churches.

The Statute for Religious Freedom committed Virginia to total separation of church and state, but there remained one nagging remnant of the Anglican Establishment—the glebe lands granted by the colonial government to each parish for the maintenance of the clergy. Since the lands represented a public investment in the church, they were a lingering vestige of Establishment and a dismay to liberals. By supplementing clerical incomes, moreover, they gave the Episcopal Church an edge over other denominations. In August 1787 the General Committee of the Baptist Church asked the state to recover them. Presbyterian petitions sent to the assembly endorsed the idea. In the fall legislative session a Southside Antifederalist introduced a resolution for the sale of glebes in parishes where there was no resident minister. The plan stopped well short of confiscation, but the House rejected it.[10]

Another Baptist memorial triggered a new barrage of petitions in 1789. This time it was suggested that the proceeds from the glebes would help relieve the county tax burden. The House of Delegates referred the petitions to its Committee on Religion, which was dominated by eastern Anglicans. Reporting for the committee, William Norvel, Federalist from James City, moved that the petitions be rejected. Turning the libertarian argument around, Norvel pointed out that the glebes were the private possession of a religious corporation. Hence confiscation would constitute an interference with religion in violation of the Statute for Religious Freedom. The House postponed further consideration of the Baptist memorial.[11]

The Baptists were back the following year, and this time their memorial was supported by petitions from eight counties. The prospect of a financial windfall was attracting some secular support. The Committee on Religion, though still dominated by conservatives, evidently decided to meet the issue squarely. This time it presented a resolution favoring the sale of the glebes, but the House rejected it. Finally in 1792 a compromise resolution favoring the sale of glebes in those parishes where a majority of communicants desired it passed on a tie vote broken by the Speaker.[12]

Throwing the question back to the parishes relieved the legislature for a time, but in 1794 and again in 1795 the Baptists were back with their familiar memorial demanding confiscation.[13] They failed by a mere seven votes in 1795, but, even so, the result was stalemate. In the eleven votes taken over the decade (1787–1795) there was no hint of party interest; the alignment was regional— Tidewater (including the eastern counties in the Southside) versus the Piedmont and the west. The stance of each delegate seemed to be determined largely by the number of non-Anglicans in his constituency.

The issue of glebe lands was of more symbolic than financial importance, but as the party conflict intensified, religion itself became part of the political symbolism. Northern Federalists belabored Jefferson for his alleged atheism and implied that the decline of religion was partly responsible for the violence and lawlessness of the times. On the other side, the French Revolution may have inspired some anticlericism among Republicans.[14] By 1797 the glebe issue was becoming caught up in the political contest. During the spring elections it was the only issue publicly discussed in the Alexandria area, and in Fairfax County the candidate who promised to vote for the sale of the glebes won the election.[15]

In the fall of 1797 the House of Delegates approved a broadly stated resolution that the various colonial statutes granting land to the Episcopal Church ought to be repealed as inconsistent with religious freedom and the state constitution. A bill to that effect passed on a voice vote, but the Senate added an amendment referring the glebe question to the courts. Since this negated the purpose of the bill, the House rejected it, and the bill died in the disagreement. When the session ended, Madison, who had found the Baptists a useful ally since the beginning of the decade, lamented that the Republicans had not given more support to their crusade against the glebes.[16]

By 1798 that support was forthcoming. The Senate retreated, and the bill swept through both houses. The only recorded vote involved an effort to resurrect the Senate's earlier plan of referring the matter to the courts. Offered in the House as an amendment, it was defeated, 56 to 85.[17] A comparison of this vote with that of the previous year shows how partisan the subject had become. Federalists were almost evenly divided in 1797 (opposing the glebes by 27 to 22); in 1798 they sided with the Anglicans by 34 to 18. Even western Federalists sided with the church by 15 to 11. Republicans were antichurch even in 1797, opposing the glebes by a margin of 44 to 24 (mostly because of their strength in the Piedmont and southwest). In 1798 the margin rose to 63 to 21. Even Tidewater Republicans voted against the Anglican clergy.[18] It seems probable that the use of religious symbols in the national party dialogue affected attitudes toward the churches. Party lines on religion never attained the rigidity they did on national issues, such as foreign policy, but the Anglican Church had become embroiled in party rivalries. Fortunately, perhaps, for it, this statute ended the matter. The glebes were gradually sold in the next few years, and the explosive mixture of religion and politics evaporated.

THE POLITICS OF EDUCATION

Virginians quarreled noisily over matters of religion, but they ignored the field of public education altogether. In the 1780s the legislature shelved Jefferson's scheme for a coordinated statewide system, and in the succeeding decade no one seems to have given any thought to the possibility of public support for the College of William and Mary or the establishment of a secular university. Virginia's neighbors, in contrast, were pioneers in the founding of state universities, and they took the first steps toward statewide systems of publicly supported elementary and secondary schools. But each of these caused political contests.

Maryland's colleges were political footballs from the beginning. To forestall sectional jealousy in 1784 the assembly united Washington College on the Eastern Shore with St. John's in Annapolis to form the University of Maryland. But an effort to provide public funds for the system in 1785 became entangled in depression politics and a violent controversy over state support for religion. Creditor and debtor party lines firmed, and though the colleges won their appropriations, the contest left lasting scars. The debtor element felt that the colleges served only the wealthy, and the argument was heard periodically for years thereafter. After some hesitant efforts to hold joint convocations, as required by the 1784 law, each college went its own way. By the early 1790s they were graduating a few dozen students annually, but neither could be said to be flourishing.

Ironically enough, it was a well-meaning effort to improve elementary education that reawakened the foes of the colleges. Early in the 1792 session a bill was placed on the docket appropriating funds for the erection of new schools on the Eastern Shore. Why the entire state was not included is unclear, but, possibly for that reason, the bill was in trouble from the beginning. A roll call was demanded on the mere assignment of a day for discussing the bill, and the measure was placed on the calendar only with the tie-breaking vote of the Speaker. On the assigned day the bill was preceded by a resolution obviously designed to win it friends. Accusing Washington College of misusing funds given it by the state for the erection of buildings, the resolution declared that the money would be better spent in promoting education generally on the Eastern Shore. The House agreed to the accusation, but it rejected the proposal to reassign the funds. A motion to recover the college donation and put it in the treasury's general fund was likewise rejected. The trouble-making Eastern Shore education bill was then postponed indefinitely.[19]

The college survived the attack, but it clearly had few friends. Indeed, analysis of the balloting indicates that its worst enemies were its Eastern Shore neighbors, doubtless because it still competed with Methodist Cokesbury. Perversely, Western Shore delegates backed Washington College, while opposing Eastern Shore elementary schools. The upper bay and upper Potomac rejected any sort of public aid to education. Both political parties were evenly divided.[20] Strangely, no one thought to support both forms of education. The elementary schools could have gained only at the expense of the college.

Why Western Shore delegates went to the rescue of Washington College is a mystery, unless they feared that St. John's might be the next target. If so, they were right. The following year opponents of the colleges arrived in Annapolis with a bill to withdraw public funds from both schools and give the money to the counties. The bill got a sympathetic reception. The House would not even let the governors of St. John's College present their case. After earmarking the county funds for poor relief, the House passed the bill by 36 to 26.[21]

The Senate then came to the colleges' rescue. It pointed out that the institutions had not misused the funds; depriving them was an unjustified punishment. To the Delegates' argument that the colleges served only the wealthy, the Senate replied that depriving them of public funds would make them even more dependent on the rich.[22] It was a skillful argument, and it temporarily parried the thrust. College foes drafted a new bill simply depriving the institutions of public aid. The Senate blocked this too, and the bill died in the disagreement.[23] For the next three years the Senate remained the protector of the colleges, but in 1797 its resistance weakened. A committee to investigate college funding concluded that the state needed only one institution of higher education and proposed to discontinue the appropriation for Washington. It suggested spending the money instead to develop academies on the Eastern Shore. The Senate concurred.[24]

The House of Delegates also zeroed in on Washington College that year, passing a bill to deprive it of funding while rejecting a similar slap at St. John's. Friendless in its own neighborhood and deprived of its ally across the bay, Washington College was in deep trouble, until once again the Senate came to the rescue. Bills passed by the two houses differed in the disposition of the funds. The Senate wanted to devote the money to Eastern Shore education, while the House simply returned it to the treasury. The Senate insisted that the funds be spent on some sort of education; the House adhered to its stand. And Washington College got another reprieve.[25]

In 1798 the question of support for colleges was once again linked to the broader issue of public education. And this time the two sides reached a compromise that temporarily ended the controversy. Support for publicly financed education had been increasing, despite the vicissitudes of Washington College. In 1796 the Delegates awarded grants to a number of academies, and it rejected by only a narrow margin a bill to establish and finance a uniform statewide system. In 1798 it made even more generous donations, $200 for the founding of an Allegany County school, $600 for an academy in Caroline.[26] This session's bill for the general advancement of learning included appropriations for the two colleges in addition to funds for county schools. Washington suffered its usual setback when $2,000 of its stipend was given to local schools, but the college was allowed to keep $1,300. The House also rejected an effort to reallocate the appropriation for St. John's and then passed the bill by a decisive 49 to 13.[27]

For the first time a substantial portion of the House supported both levels of education, collegiate and elementary, without placing them in rivalry. Voting in favor of appropriations (including that for Washington College) at least three-fourths of the time were 27 delegates; only 16 delegates opposed all forms of education. Washington College was battered but not wrecked, and education everywhere received an important boost. The party lineup is also interesting. Federalists supported the appropriations by 22 to 6, Republicans opposed them, 6 to 4. The upper bay, traditionally opposed to funding, accounted for most of the Republican vote, but Potomac Federalists split evenly. To some slight degree, then, Federalists were more favorably disposed toward education than Republicans.

In North Carolina there was even more evidence of party bias, although education did not become the political issue that it did in Maryland. The university chartered in 1789 was the first publicly endowed state university in the country. Its most ardent supporter was William R. Davie, Federalist lawyer from Halifax. He drafted the charter, brought it before the assembly, and asked Governor Alexander Martin to lend his support, "as a man who knows the importance of education in a country just forming its manners and its Government."[28] Martin evidently agreed, for the bill passed without difficulty.

The chartering act of 1789 endowed the university with all property that escheated to the state through debt, death, or nonpayment of taxes. In 1795 the assembly added further funds to the endowment. In the Commons, Federalists supported the bill by 19 to 4; Republicans opposed it, 11 to 9. Eastern legislators backed the institution; Piedmont and west were divided. Five years later the rural element managed to repeal the endowment altogether.

Although there was no roll call on the motion, Federalists protested in assembly debate and in the press. By then Federalists, possibly because of Davie's influence, also dominated university affairs. In 1798 the Board of Trustees contained only one Republican, Willie Jones. The other seven members were Federalists.[29]

Federalists also promoted elementary education, but with less success. In 1796 Fayetteville attorney William Barry Grove distributed a pamphlet on public education written by Tench Coxe. "The subject of Neighborhood Schools established & Supported by Law," he told Coxe in thanking him for the piece, "I consider one of the most important objects of the State." He promised he would recommend to the legislature "a plan for the Education of all classes of the Youth of the Country," not only "to make good Citizens," but to "cultivate the *true principles of National Equality* among a People whose Republican form of Government demands a *knowledge* and adherence to *those principles.*"[30] The legislature failed to act on the plan, but the seed had been planted.

SLAVERY: MANUMISSION OR ABOLITION

Virginia likewise failed to consider seriously the issue of slavery during the 1790s. In the previous decade Quaker-inspired petitions against the institution were invariably tabled. In the 1790s even these do not appear on the House *Journal.* The only slavery issue which the Virginia assembly did consider during the decade was the question of public compensation to owners of slaves executed for crimes. Through the decade there were periodic efforts by westerners to relieve the treasury of this burden. They were unsuccessful until the very end of the period when a minor change was effected.[31] The issue really had little to do with slavery. It was a question of public favor to slaveowners, and the assembly division was exclusively sectional, east versus west.

North Carolina was a bit more liberal. At least, its assembly was prepared to discuss the possibility of limiting slavery. During the war, Virginia and Maryland, along with the northern states, banned the further import of slaves from Africa. North Carolina started to follow suit in 1788, but its Senate rejected the bill. Not

TABLE 18.1 NORTH
CAROLINA COMMONS:
PROHIBITION OF SLAVE
IMPORTS, 1794

	Yes	No
Albemarle	13	5
Pamlico	19	2
Cape Fear	9	6
Piedmont	35	7
West	7	1
	83	21
Federalists	13	2
Republicans	15	4
Middle	7	1
Unknown	48	14
	83	21

until 1794 did North Carolina act on imports; it was the last state to do so. The 1794 law passed the Commons by a healthy margin, 83 to 21.[32] It has often been suggested that the prohibition on imports was motivated less by humanitarianism than a desire to protect the domestic price of slaves. The broad favor given the bill (and the concomitant failure to ease manumission requirements) lends some support to this view. The breakdown of the vote, however, shows that both supporters and opponents were evenly distributed around the state (table 18.1). Had much thought been given to the question of price, particularly if the point had been made in debate, one might have expected the areas of relatively high slave concentration to be more favorable to the ban, and the slave-importing regions (Piedmont and west) more critical. Since this was not the case, it seems most likely that a desire to limit the number of black slaves in the state was the predominant motive.

This attitude, of course, had less to do with slavery than with color. Aside from Quakers and other pietists, there was not much opposition to slavery in North Carolina. In 1796 the Commons rejected on first reading a bill to permit individual emancipation of slaves. Under previous practice, each manumission required a separate legislative act. A similar bill was rejected the following year.

The two roll calls indicate a better than two-to-one opposition to easing manumission.[33] The only important sentiment in favor of emancipation lay in the western Piedmont and the mountains. Slavery was less entrenched in that cereal-growing region, and there were ethnic and religious prejudices against it. As on the import bill, party persuasion was not a factor.

Maryland was equally resistant to change, but there was enough antislavery feeling to force the assembly at least to grapple with fundamental issues. Maryland Quakers, encouraged no doubt by their brethren in Delaware and Pennsylvania, came forth annually with a petition against slavery, which the assembly discarded by lopsided votes. But it took more seriously a representation from an abolition society founded in Baltimore in 1791. This was a secular organization, the first one, it would seem, to appear in the South. Not content with tabling the society's petition, one ardent slavery defender offered a motion denouncing the organization itself for its "unjustifiable and oppressive" memorial. This passed, 48 to 15, and by a similar vote the House approved a resolution automatically tabling all individual petitions for freedom until the potential costs to slaveowners were established. Encouraged, the proslavery element then introduced a resolution that the Baltimore abolition society itself was unnecessary, and its principles were "repugnant to the laws and constitution of the state." This counterthrust was turned aside, 31 to 33, and the subject was dropped. The three roll calls displayed a spectrum of attitudes on slavery (table 18.2).[34]

Not surprisingly, proslavery sentiment was strongest in the long-settled regions where the proportion of blacks was highest; it was weakest in the newly occupied regions. As in North Carolina, there is no correlation with political persuasion. Thomas Jefferson's views on slavery have received much attention through the years, but even his modest liberalism got no support among his fellow planters of the Chesapeake.

DEMOCRACY: HESITANT STEPS

Suffrage and representation were another set of issues that involved reasonably clear choice of reaction or reform. The Mary-

TABLE 18.2   MARYLAND HOUSE OF DELEGATES:
PROSLAVERY ATTITUDES, 1791

	Extreme	Moderate	Antislavery
Eastern Shore	10	2	3
Upper Bay	2	5	5
Western Shore	10	6	0
Upper Potomac	5	3	2
Urban	1	0	2
	28	16	12
Federalists	10	3	2
Feds/Republicans	2	1	4
Antifeds/Federalists	2	3	1
Antifeds/Republicans	6	2	0
	28	16	12

land assembly wrestled with a variety of demands for suffrage changes, including even black voting and the secret ballot, while Virginia and North Carolina considered only the broader question of whether to summon another constitutional convention. Apportionment of representation was a matter of erecting new counties, and in all three states the division was sectional, east versus west. Except for Maryland, where the parties eventually chose sides on the question of suffrage, democracy was not an issue in the party conflict.

Maryland's constitution was one of the most imaginative of all the Revolutionary instruments of government, but most of its unique features were intended to preserve the wealth and power of the gentry. High property qualifications for officeholding, an upper house chosen at five-year intervals by specially elected electors, and a council chosen by the assembly at staggered intervals were all hedges against popular influence in the government. The variations from governmental practice in other states probably gave ammunition to critics of the Maryland constitution. During the 1780s there were periodic efforts to amend it, and pressure increased through the succeeding decade.

In 1790 a committee of the House of Delegates proposed a number of modest changes in the constitution, among them voter registration to prevent cheating at the polls, biennial, instead of annual, elections, and an increase in the size of the Senate. None went to the heart of the issue, but they were postponed anyway, 34 to 15.[35] The Eastern Shore was adamantly opposed to change, and the Western Shore was evenly divided. Most surprisingly, both the upper bay and the western Potomac also opposed the report. Federalists were against it by 18 to 10, Antifederalists by 8 to 3.

Proponents of reform were back in each of the next two sessions. In 1791 a House committee recommended a dossier of changes in the state constitution. One bill would have allowed persons conscientiously scrupulous of swearing oaths to sit in the assembly, and another sought to repeal constitutional test oaths altogether. There were a variety of proposals for democratizing the government by reducing the property qualifications for members of the lower house, eliminating property qualifications for executive offices, and changing the method of selecting the Senate. Although there was no specific proposal for expanding the suffrage, one bill refined the definition of residence and another would have required all newly erected counties to contain a specified number of voters. Finally, the report included a variety of proposed changes in the court system, the purpose of which is not entirely clear.

The assault on the constitution had a broad front, and its implications were radical enough. The House could accept only one of the recommendations—a previously approved bill prohibiting members of Congress from sitting in the assembly. The rest it postponed to the following year, with a request that they be published in the newspapers.[36]

The scant record kept by the clerk of the House does not disclose the names of the reformers, but, evidently encouraged by the assembly's willingness to submit their ideas to public discussion, they were back the following year. Again their hopes were dashed when the House refused, 30 to 36, to schedule their bills for debate. It then resolved without a roll call not to consider the bills at all. And, for the moment, constitutional reform was dead. James McHenry, who prided himself on his knowledge of assembly affairs, boasted to Hamilton: "We have scattered in air the long string of amendments that had been proposed to be incorporated into our constitution by those who were no friends to the U.S.'s constitution, so we remain a free people and a tolerably virtuous people."[37] A handful of Antifederalists may have been behind the reform movement, but, if so, they had no support even within their own ranks. Former Antifederalists voted 7 to 4 against changes in the state Constitution. Republicans split evenly on the question. On the other hand, McHenry's implication that Federalists were strongly opposed to reform was quite exact. His fellow partisans voted 15 to 5 against any changes. Nor was there any regional pattern to the voting. Delegates apparently followed their own predilections. For the next few years, while the Federalists remained in solid control of the assembly, there were no serious efforts at constitutional reform.[38]

When the assembly did return to the problem toward the end of the 1790s, the question at issue was the suffrage. It is tempting to suggest, as some have done, that expansion of the suffrage was the result of party competition, as each party sought the favor of voters.[39] If this was the case—and there is no direct evidence to substantiate it in Maryland—it was only partially so. Party rhetoric and the involvement of voters in political meetings may have generated a demand for suffrage reform, but both parties were slow to realize the political potential in it. And Federalists never did give wholehearted support to the idea.

In 1797, Michael Taney, a Western Shore Federalist who had supported paper money and debtor relief in the 1780s, introduced a bill reducing the property qualifications for voting. An amendment enfranchising all free adult males, without regard to property, passed by the surprising margin of 32 to 13, and the bill itself swept through, 30 to 21. The House evidently failed to realize that the amendment would have given the vote to free black men. The Senate may have caught the oversight; in any case, it rejected the bill.[40] House voting (exempting those who switched) appears random. Federalists supported the change by 17 to 9, Republicans by 7 to 6. All regions endorsed reform except, surprisingly, the west and the cities.

The failure of Federalists to rally to Taney's cause suggests that he was acting on his own. He was absent the following session, and his reform languished for another year. The most the assembly was willing to consider in 1798, a year of intense party conflict over national policies, was the reform of Maryland elections. The House of Delegates passed a bill that sought to standardize election procedures and prevent unfair influences. After several procedural moves and minor amendments, the bill passed by 47 to 21. The Senate objected to several provisions, but the House held firm, threatening that if the Senate did not yield, "We must let the subject sleep in silence until awakened by our constituents." The Senate was willing to let it sleep.[41] In all, there were five House roll calls on the measure, and voting this time was essentially regional. The upper bay and Potomac unanimously favored the reform, the Eastern Shore opposed it, and the Western Shore was divided. Federalists favored it by 25 to 17, Republicans by 15 to 5. The two Republicans from Baltimore favored regulation, while the two Federalists from Annapolis opposed it, but this was the only hint of a party stance.

In 1799 the Jeffersonians at last made the cause of reform their own, and an impressive series of alterations cleared the assembly. The election bill swept through the House by 48 to 19 and passed the Senate without dissent.[42] Michael Taney had left the assembly (replaced by his son, Roger Brooke, the future Chief Justice), but his bill repealing the property qualifications for voting was back. It went through the House by a healthy margin of 48 to 13 and through the Senate without a roll call. If Senate Federalists had misgivings, they apparently felt it wisest to keep silent. A further test of reform sentiment in the lower house came in regard to legislative pay. No one had seriously challenged legislative pay scales since the mid-1780s, but this year the per diem law received a resounding defense anyway. The Delegates approved a resolution that elimination of per diem allowances would exclude from the assembly all persons who were not wealthy, and that result would "place the poorer classes of the community entirely in the power of the rich."[43] The one reform the House was unwilling to countenance was the secret ballot. A request in late December for permission to bring in a bill altering the parts of the constitution relating to viva voce voting was denied, 14 to 39.[44] Perhaps the Delegates felt it was too late in the session to face new controversies.

The lopsided vote on the suffrage bill suggests that white

manhood suffrage had become generally accepted—or, at least, that it could no longer be resisted. All regions and both parties supported the change, the Federalists by 16 to 7 (with 8 mixed), Republicans by 20 to 0. Eastern Shore Federalists were the principal opponents; Eastern Shore Republicans supported reform.

Republicans were also somewhat more progressive on the matter of election regulations, favoring reform by 11 to 3, while Federalists split 12 to 8. Curiously, few Delegates saw the connection between clean elections and broadened suffrage. Young Federalist Roger B. Taney, for instance, supported his father's suffrage bill, but he voted consistently against election regulations. On the whole spectrum of issues related to popular voting (7 roll calls),[45] Republicans favored greater democracy by 12 to 1, with 8 mixing their votes; Federalists divided 8 to 5, with 14 mixed.

Maryland was the first state in the South to abolish property qualifications for voting, and it was clearly a Republican victory. When Republicans finally won control of the assembly in 1801, they picked up the last thread of electoral reform—oral voting. By a party-line vote of 34 to 28 the House inserted a provision for written ballots into a general elections bill.[46] Republicans favored the move by 31 to 5, Federalists, even westerners, unanimously opposed it. Nonetheless, there were clear limits to the Jeffersonian reform impulse. In 1800 a motion to strike the word "white" from a routine suffrage bill, thereby permitting black voting, was rejected, 16 to 51. Favoring the change were 7 Republicans, 7 Federalists, and 2 "middlers." Most came from the Eastern Shore, probably men with a substantial Quaker element in their constituencies.[47]

The Republicans' support for suffrage reform in Maryland was probably the result of their minority position in the 1790s. In Virginia and North Carolina, where they were in firm control, they showed no such interest. Jefferson and Madison, to be sure, favored a revision of Virginia's constitution, but they made no effort to stamp their views on the party. Moreover, neither was openly committed to democracy. Jefferson felt a propertied stake in society was a prerequisite to responsible voting, though he did favor a generous distribution of public lands to provide effective manhood suffrage. Madison was more concerned with the distribution of power than with the degree of popular influence. His main objection to the Virginia constitution was that it failed to separate the branches of the government, leaving both the executive and the judiciary dependent on the legislature. He also felt the upper house ought to be given more powers. Suffrage and representation he recognized as problems, but he had no reforms to suggest.[48]

In Virginia the main agitation for change came from the underrepresented west, and as a result it was voiced by Federalists more often than Republicans. Shortly after the war ended Madison's friend Archibald Stuart brought to the assembly a series of proposed changes in the Constitution, which Madison endorsed. Patrick Henry was violently opposed, however, and the resolutions were voted down by a large majority.[49] Adoption of the Federal Constitution revived discussion of the state instrument. After the ratifying convention departed for home, Valley Federalist Alexander White openly wondered whether the time was not ripe for a convention on the state constitution, but he abandoned the notion because Patrick Henry was still in charge of the assembly.[50] In 1790 Edmund Randolph boldly set before the assembly a comprehensive revision of the state constitution, but he confessed privately that it was not well received. In the House someone suggested it be treated in the same way as antislavery petitions by throwing it under the table, but instead it was postponed indefinitely.[51]

Through the 1790s scattered voices called for expansion of the suffrage, but there seemed to be no broad movement. In 1792, Henry Banks, a wealthy Richmond merchant whose western speculations (over a half million acres) entitled him to represent Greenbriar in the assembly, publicly demanded both suffrage reform and reapportionment. Since all white adult males were required to serve in the militia, he argued, they ought to have the right to vote.[52] Five years later his brother Gerrard, a Republican, won a seat in the House from Piedmont Culpeper on the promise of supporting universal white male suffrage.[53]

As in Maryland, party rivalry ultimately stimulated demands for change. In 1796, in the wake of the uproar over the Jay Treaty, the Winchester *Centinel* openly advocated a division of the state on the grounds that the north and west were underrepresented in the assembly. The Federalist *Columbian Mirror* of Alexandria quickly picked up the idea, pointing out that the northern counties had repeatedly petitioned for a constitutional convention without success. The boundary line the paper suggested was the Rappahonnock, the headwaters of the Shenandoah, the Greenbriar, and the Kanawha. The editor did not point out—he probably did not need to—that most of the 29 counties in his new state were Federalist.[54]

However motivated, the scheme at least revived discussion of the constitution. The fall assembly approved a resolution urging the people to reexamine the constitution and instruct the next legislature to summon a convention if there were deficiencies in it.[55] Leaving the question to voter initiative might seem a convenient way of burying it, but public discussion continued through the winter. One Federalist contributer to the Alexandria paper tried openly to make it a party issue. Republicans talked much of "aristocracy" in the federal government, he pointed out, but they tolerated an "oligarchical" regime at home. They opposed the central administration not from principle, but out of jealousy for local power.[56] Federalists reverted to this theme again and again during the Adams administration.

In 1797 westerners put the issue squarely before the assembly with a resolution declaring the constitution defective and summoning a convention to revise it. It was no longer possible to evade or rationalize, and the House voted it down, 63 to 84.[57] Faced with a clear choice, a number of eastern delegates backed down (table 18.3). The split was exclusively regional; despite Federalist newspaper jibes, neither party was involved. In 1797, for instance, Tidewater Federalists opposed reform, 17 to 0, Republicans were against it, 20 to 4. Western Federalists favored revision by 24 to 7, western Republicans by 6 to 2. For the next few years Federalists verbally backed constitutional revision in assembly debate, thereby maintaining their popularity in the west, but the reform, for the time being, was dead.

In North Carolina, the question of constitutional revision came up only once during the 1790s, and then in rather oblique fashion. In 1795 the House of Commons went into committee of the whole on the question of summoning a convention, and after

TABLE 18.3 VIRGINIA HOUSE OF
DELEGATES: CONSTITUTIONAL REVISION,
1796–1797

	Favoring		Opposed	
	1796	*1797*	*1796*	*1797*
Tidewater	23	4	31	40
Piedmont	23	27	16	33
West	30	30	9	10
	86	61	56	83
Federalists	35	30	15	27
Republicans	36	28	30	49
Middle	4	3	6	5
Unknown	11	0	5	2
	86	61	56	83

discussing it for some minutes adopted, 69 to 40, a resolution that it was not expedient. The division, as elsewhere, was regional. The eastern counties voted 47 to 12 against a convention, the Piedmont supported the idea, 22 to 18, and the west by 5 to 3. Among the few who can be identified by party (there were no party votes in this session), Federalists opposed a convention by 12 to 5, Republicans by 7 to 3.[58]

In all three states the assemblies represented places, not people; hence the solution to malapportionment was the erection of new counties. Western demands had centered on this since early in the Revolution, and all three states created a large number of new counties during and after the war. After 1790 the impulse slowed. After creating Allegany County in 1790 the Maryland assembly made no further gestures. Virginia created nearly as many eastern counties as western during the decade, and the whole business was done in routine fashion with little discussion and no roll calls.

Only in North Carolina did county subdivision create much controversy, but again the division was regional. Neither party saw fit to take up the cause of the West. In the years 1797–99, for instance, the Commons held six roll calls on the question, all involving the subdivision of Wilkes County on the edge of the mountains. Except for a few Cape Fear delegates who voted with the west, the lineup was exclusively a matter of low country versus the Piedmont and the west. In 1799 the assembly finally compromised by dividing both Wilkes and Tyrrell (in Albemarle).[59] Both counties were Republican.

THE PARTIES AND REFORM

The 1790s was not a decade of great reform impulses. Politically the nation's attention was focused on foreign affairs and the developing contest for the Presidency. If there were social ills crying for treatment, they seldom caught the attention of pamphleteers and polemicists. Yet, in the Chesapeake states a number of unresolved problems lingered from the Revolution; whether willing or not, the legislatures had to face them in the 1790s. When they did grapple with them, party politics were usually not a factor. Legislative stands on such social questions as public education and the amelioration of slavery were determined by individual predilections, not party views. Nor, apparently, did the parties see enough political potential in such issues to take a stand.

Religion, on the other hand, was more susceptible to party uses. In Maryland the Republicans led the attack on the religious test imposed by the state constitution, apparently in an effort to broaden the base of their support. Federalists in this instance stuck with the Establishment. In Virginia a dispute over the glebe lands belonging to Episcopal ministers simmered for years without becoming involved in party politics, but toward the end of the 1790s Republicans joined the anti-Episcopal forces, while Federalists sided with the church. Search for electoral advantage may have been a factor, but it is equally possible that each side was reflecting attitudes formed by the New England assault on Jefferson's religious views. Whatever the reason, the Republicans in both Virginia and Maryland sided with the liberals, Federalists with religious conservatives.

On the question of electoral reform—possibly the most important criterion of all in determining whether a party was "democratic"—the record was more mixed. Maryland Republicans solidly, if somewhat belatedly, endorsed both white manhood suffrage and the secret ballot. But it should be remembered that a majority of assembly Federalists also endorsed the principle of an unpropertied electorate. They fought the secret ballot, but they may have done so because that particular measure was couched in terms that caused them to react in a partisan manner, rather than from philosophical principle. Virginia Federalists gave some lip service to the cause of electoral reform, though they were voicing western interests more than party. The Republican majority in that state nevertheless showed no disposition to usher the "common man" into the government. In North Carolina, where all male taxpayers had the vote, conservatives like Archibald Maclaine felt that commoners had run the state from the beginning. And if the untutored simplicity of Thomas Person at the beginning of the period and Nathaniel Macon at the end are any indication, he was right.

CHAPTER NINETEEN

A Yankee President

For NEARLY a decade George Washington had been the trump in the Federalist deck. Time and again the aging warrior had been used for party purposes—first to lend dignity to the movement for federal reform, then to boost ratification of the Constitution, and finally to help a political party, oriented in its favors toward northern merchants, hold on to the reins of power. Federalists everywhere found Washington a useful symbol, but nowhere was he more used, and abused, than in the Chesapeake, where he was best known and most admired. Time and again Federalists tried to smother opposition to their policies by appealing for unity behind the President. Time and again Republicans had to overcome the imputation of assaulting the nation's father. Endlessly they worked on the distinction between Washington the man, virtuous, public-spirited, patriotic, and Washington the administrator, misguided, ill-advised, and intemperate.

The Federalists lost ground steadily in the Chesapeake during the early 1790s, and what popularity they retained was largely traceable to the President himself. Washington's retirement in 1796 was thus a terrible blow, made worse by the fact that his chosen successor was John Adams. Southerners, particularly Virginians, had never liked or trusted Adams, thinking him a secret monarchist, a bulwark of aristocratic privilege. So unfair were these accusations that one suspects deeper biases, among them the southern distrust of Yankees, voiced so often in the 1780s. It did not matter that Adams himself had no mercantile interests; he represented the insidious connection between the federal regime and northern merchant speculators that southerners had feared ever since Hamilton unveiled his funding proposals. Nor did it matter that Adams was a man of integrity and independent mind, bound to special interests of no sort. Even Jefferson, who should have known better, could not escape the southern bias, though he clothed his feelings in irrelevant gossip about monarchy and aristocrats. Adams's tragic flaw, among the Chesapeake gentry, was simply that he was a Yankee, in speech, in manners, and in thought.

Although Adams's character was the central factor in Chesapeake attitudes, the election did not turn exclusively on personalities. Foreign policy remained the issue, though it was seldom actually discussed. Instead, the parties used, to a greater extent than ever before, the shorthand symbolism of British monarchists versus French Jacobins. In November 1796, at the height of the balloting, French minister Pierre Adet made the symbolism seem real when he published four proclamations announcing the suspension of diplomatic intercourse with the United States and blaming the breakdown on Federalist policies. It was a transparent effort to promote the election of Jefferson, and like all French meddling, it backfired, for it presented Federalists with an opportunity to denounce foreign intervention in American politics. It was just the sort of thing Washington had warned about in his Farewell Address.

Despite some shrinkage in Federalist support, the election followed familiar party and regional patterns throughout the Chesapeake. It even produced some new developments in the evolving party system. Presidential electors were chosen by popular ballot in all three states (there were only six states in all where this was the case), and candidates went to great lengths to make their preferences clear in advance. The original concept of the electoral college—that electors would be chosen for their knowledge of affairs and good judgment, and they in turn would apply those talents to the choice of a President—was completely forgotten. Electoral candidates considered themselves proxies for party choice. The one latitude they permitted themselves was in the choice of a Vice President. Here votes were sometimes wasted, primarily to prevent a tie for the top office.

THE ELECTION OF 1796

So unpopular was Adams in Virginia that Federalist candidates for Presidential elector did not dare mention him by name. In Alexandria, a Federalist stronghold while Washington was in office, lawyer Charles Simms, a candidate for the electoral college, refused publicly to endorse either candidate. He promised only to vote for the best man available.[1] Leven Powell, retail merchant from Middleburg in neighboring Loudoun County, was bold enough to undertake a public defense of Adams's career and a critical review of Jefferson's, but he hedged by announcing his intention to vote for Patrick Henry if he would agree to serve. If Henry declined, Powell would take the "least exceptionable" among the remaining possibilities.[2] Farther to the south Federalists adopted similar nonpartisan stances.[3]

Federalist essayists tried to divert attention from Adams by demanding a substantive discussion of the foreign and domestic policies of the Washington administration.[4] Republicans would have none of that. They refused even to talk about the Jay Treaty. Instead they quoted Adams's published works at great length to demonstrate that he was a monarchist at heart, and they predicted that the New Englander's first move would be to take the nation's capital back to the North.[5]

When the polling was over, the only Federalist winner was Leven Powell, who had used his mercantile connections to build a strong political organization in the northern Piedmont.[6] Loudoun, moreover, along with neighboring (and equally Federalist) Berkeley benefited more from the improvements of the Potomac Company and relocation of the capital than any other county in the valley.[7] Elsewhere Republicans swept the state, for the most part without opposition.[8]

The Republican congressional caucus had sought northern support by placing Aaron Burr on the party's ticket as Vice President. Virginians had never liked Burr; it was they who had killed his aspirations in 1792. In 1796 their dislike was again manifested when the electoral college met. All of Virginia's Republicans cast their first ballot for Jefferson, but only one of them voted for Burr. The rest scattered their Vice Presidential ballots among Samuel Adams (15), George Clinton (3), and even Washington (1). Federalist Powell, despite his early Henryite smoke screen, voted loyally for Adams and Pinckney.

In Maryland, where Federalists were strong enough that they did not have to hide their preferences, opposition to Adams took a different turn. Those who disliked Adams fell in with Hamilton's scheme to dump the New Englander in favor of Thomas Pinckney of South Carolina. The former Treasury Secretary also disliked Adams (because, it is generally supposed, he was too independent, too unwilling to solicit Hamilton's advice); so he concocted a plan that took advantage of the Constitution's method of choosing a Vice President. Each Presidential elector cast two ballots. The candidate with a majority was declared President; whoever came in second was Vice President. Under Hamilton's scheme each Federalist elector would cast a ballot for Pinckney (the party's candidate for Vice President), but a few would waste ballots, rather than vote for Adams. Pinckney would thus become President, assuming Federalists won the election.

Although Hamilton's schemes rarely won sympathy in the South, there was some attraction to this one because Pinckney was a southerner. It apparently had the backing, anyway, of Hamilton's chief lieutenant in Maryland, James McHenry.[9] Charles Carroll of Carrollton, himself a candidate for the electoral college, also favored Pinckney. "Some think . . . his administration would be less opposed than that of Mr. Adams," he informed McHenry in a pointed reference to Adams's supposed monarchism.[10] How extensive such suspicions were in Maryland is not certain, but during the fall campaign several anonymous Federalists joined in the Republican newspaper assault on Adams's writings.

Adams's chief defender in Maryland was Eastern Shore congressman William Vans Murray. Familiar enough with national politics to realize how impractical Hamilton's scheme was, Murray entered the lists under a variety of pseudonyms. Pointing out that a schism might cost Federalists the Presidency, he begged Marylanders to support Adams. When the polls closed, he reported jubilantly that the Eastern Shore had selected not only Federalists, but Adams men. "In this county," he boasted to McHenry, "I think I never knew an election so much of *principles*. . . . Our choice is a party question—not a personal matter."[11]

As in Virginia, Maryland Republicans focused attention on Adams's publications, branding him a British sympathizer and a monarchist.[12] So effective were their accusations that Murray saw fit to write a *Vindication* of Adams's 1787 *Defense of American Constitutions,* which was serialized by the Philadelphia *Gazette of the United States* during December. Midway through the election he feared that the Republicans might win as many as half the state's electoral votes, as a result of their abuse of Adams.[13]

In the end, though, Maryland voters followed old habits. The Eastern Shore and Potomac were solidly Federalist; Republicans carried Baltimore and the upper bay. The main battleground, as usual, was the lower Western Shore. Republicans won Anne Arundel, to the mortification of Charles Carroll, who was the losing candidate, and appeared to win the lower counties (St. Mary's, Charles, and Calvert) by electing George Plater, Jr., son of the former governor.[14]

The voters proved more regular than their representatives. In the electoral college, Plater, rebelling, apparently, against party pretensions, canceled himself by casting one vote for Jefferson and one for Adams. The other three Republicans held to the ticket and voted for Jefferson and Aaron Burr. But William Vans Murray had the final laugh. All six of the Federalists voted for Adams, but two of them, rather than vote for Pinckney, wasted their second ballots on Senator John Henry.[15] It did not make a crucial difference because Adams's friends in New England threw away other Pinckney ballots (enough, in fact, to make Jefferson Vice President), but Murray was rewarded for his party loyalty. The outgoing President, as one of his final appointments, named him minister to the Netherlands.

In the congressional election, held simultaneously, Federalists increased their hold on the state delegation. Murray decided not to run, but he was replaced by another Eastern Shore Federalist, John Dennis, and elsewhere Federalist incumbents were reelected. In the upper Potomac, General Thomas Sprigg, who began voting with the Republicans after the Jay Treaty, declined to run. In the election Federalist George Baer, Jr., defeated a self-proclaimed nonpartisan, Samuel Ringold.[16] Even in the upper bay counties, Republican territory since 1790, Federalists won a notable victory when Gabriel Christie succumbed to a rival he had defeated twice before, William Matthews. Only two Republicans survived the holocaust, Samuel Smith in Baltimore and Richard Sprigg, a political novice from Anne Arundel, both elected without opposition. The result was a delegation of 5 Federalists, 2 Republicans, and 1 undefinable maverick—George Dent of the lower Western Shore, whose record in the Fifth Congress can best be described as utterly random. Given this popular support for Federalists, a result, one supposes of the French crisis, the closeness of the Presidential election is a measure of Marylanders' distaste for John Adams.

North Carolina, as usual, escaped the hysteria and the intrigue that distracted her northern neighbors. The election did call forth some newspaper tracts, the first, it would seem, to appear in the state since the contest over the Constitution.[17] But even these were phrased in general terms—liberty versus tyranny—and never approached the personal vilification of northern papers. Candidates for the electoral college made clear their preferences between Adams and Jefferson.[18] They held to these commitments when the college met in February, but they felt more latitude in the choice of Vice President. The lone Federalist elected adhered to the Adams-Pinckney ticket, but the 11 Republicans split. Only 6 voted for Aaron Burr; the rest, following Virginia's example, scattered their second ballots (giving them, oddly enough, to Federalists—3 to Iredell, 1 to Washington, and 1 to Charles C. Pinckney).

Although Adams's alleged monarchism was not a subject of newspaper polemics in North Carolina, his unpopularity in the state probably contributed to the ultimate demise of Tidewater Federalism. Albemarle and Pamlico completed their drift into the Republican party in this election. The state's lone Adams elector came from the upper Cape Fear, whose Scottish population remained loyal to the Federalists. Albemarle and Pamlico had elected Republicans to Congress in 1794, and they returned them in 1796. In the Pamlico district, Richard Dobbs Spaight, former Federalist and newly retired governor, decided to contest the seat of Republican Nathan Bryan. His candidacy stirred a few Federalists to life. One tried to play on state pride by accusing Bryan of mindlessly following the lead of Virginians in Congress. "The people of Virginia may be better judges of the rules of fighting cocks, or racing horses than we are in North Carolina," he observed sarcastically, but Virginians were not the best judges of North Carolina's interests. The Jay Treaty in particular, he felt, was a boon to North Carolina because Britain took the greater part of the state's trade. Other writers rushed to the congressman's defense, and the whole tempest passed quickly. How much was really at stake is unclear. After losing the election, Spaight sought and won a spot on the Republican ticket of Presidential electors. The lone Federalist left on North Carolina's congressional delegation was William Barry Grove of Fayetteville.[19]

VIRGINIA POLITICS, 1796–1797

The heightened party awareness that attended the Presidential election stimulated new efforts to extend party influence into every branch of the government. The first political parties began as legislative clusters, at both state and national levels; only after they were well formed did they begin to extend their influence beyond the legislative halls. Among the Chesapeake states this did not become a conscious effort until the late 1790s. By 1799 the process was virtually complete—it was the final step to a mature party system.

Virginia's governorship was politicized when Henry Lee was removed for his role in the Whisky Rebellion in 1794. In 1796 both parties tried to use it to further their own interests, while maintaining a facade of nonpartisanship. There was no need to install a strong party man in the office anyway, since it had few powers. The assembly's first choice was Patrick Henry, who for a year had been the subject of an ardent courtship by both sides.

When he declined, the assembly chose former lieutenant governor James Wood over Thomas Madison by 115 to 56.[20] Although no roll call was recorded, the margin was suspiciously close to the relative strength of the two parties. Wood was clearly the Republican candidate. Although a man not given to strong political stands (his last recorded party position was Presidential elector in 1789), he had served on the council, besides as lieutenant governor, to the apparent satisfaction of the majority. He was, moreover, one of the most prominent residents of the lower Valley; his father had founded the city of Winchester and left him an extensive estate. Honoring such a man was certain to benefit Republican fortunes in a previously Federalist region.[21]

Federalists probably had similar motives in backing Madison. He too was a resident of the Valley (Botetourt County) and possessed some symbolic importance, being a cousin of James Madison and a brother-in-law of Patrick Henry. His record in the assembly since 1793 was mixed (7 Republican and 4 Federalist votes), but Federalists were apparently satisfied with him. Two years later he appeared on a list of men deemed loyal enough by Washington to warrant military commissions.[22]

That the gubernatorial vote reflected the party balance was clear from a ballot taken the previous day for U.S. senator. There had never been any pretense that this office was nonpartisan, and the role of the incumbent, Stevens Thomson Mason, in the fight over the Jay Treaty made his reelection a sensitive issue. Federalists put up against him one of their most prominent men, James Breckinridge, a neighbor of Thomas Madison's from Botetourt. Mason won by 114 to 60.[23]

For the first time party feelings began to dictate choices for lesser executive offices in 1796. For the position of Attorney General, Robert Brooke defeated Bushrod Washington by 89 to 71. The closeness of the margin indicates that the Washington name still had some magic, but it was still basically a party choice. Grumbled one Federalist, "Talents, knowledge, & assiduity were on the side of Mr. W., but on the side of Mr. B. were violent party principles & these elected him." Brooke, it will be recalled, had been the Republicans' choice to succeed Henry Lee as governor in

1794. Even the governor's council was not exempt. An innocuous body with only housekeeping authority, the council was appointed by the assembly for indefinite terms (James Wood had been serving on it since 1784). The assembly annually removed certain members and replaced them with others; hitherto it seems to have been little more than a popularity contest. But in 1796 it purged two Federalists (Robert Goode and John Steele) and replaced them with firm Republicans. "This was a disagreeable business," complained the same Federalist that had commented on the earlier election, "& Steele, the most unexceptional character in the whole Council was displaced, because his principles were those of Federalism & moderation."[24] Steele himself probably had little reason to complain. John Adams soon thereafter gave him a federal office.

Virginia's congressional election took place the following February, while the electoral college was meeting to designate formally the new President. As in Maryland the Federalists did fairly well. Adams's unpopularity had not yet carried over to the party. Thomas Evans from the Eastern Shore managed to unseat John Page in the middle Tidewater district. The far northwest was captured by James Machir, a Scots farmer from the South Branch Valley. And, most important of all, the old warhorse Daniel Morgan recovered the lower Shenandoah Valley seat from the renegade Federalist, Robert Rutherford. In the upper valley, George Hancock, the lone Federalist in the previous Congress, decided to retire because of "domestic matters." His district was divided between some Federalist mountain counties and a couple of Republican counties in the southwestern Piedmont. He asked his neighbor James Breckinridge to stand for the seat because there were "three Candidates below the mountain," but Breckinridge apparently refused. The seat was taken by Piedmont Republican (and former Antifederalist), John Trigg.[25] Republicans swept the rest of the state, mostly without opposition, but even so, Vice President Jefferson was dissatisfied. He badly wanted the votes of Virginia's "three renegades" in the evenly divided House of Representatives.[26]

John Marshall was even gloomier. He complained about the Federalists' lack of coordination during the Presidential contest, and he anticipated disaster in the assembly elections later that spring. The Republican "party has laid such fast hold of the public mind in this part of Virginia," he wrote from Richmond, "that an attempt to oppose sinks at once the person who makes it. The elections for the State legislature go entirely against the federalists who are madly & foolishly as well as wickedly styled a british party. Tinsly in Hanover is dropped & a mad jacobin elected in his place. May in Chesterfield has shared the same fate. Baytop of gloster [Gloucester] could not wash out the stain of having voted federally & in York one or both the old members are to be turned out as I am told for voting against Page."[27] Marshall was unnecessarily pessimistic, especially in view of the Federalist congressional victories, but his assessment is the first indication of national party symbols (British monarchist versus French Jacobin) affecting contests for the House of Delegates. The anticipated elimination of Federalist delegates who had helped defeat Congressman John Page also marks a new height in party retribution. Even so, the result was not as bad as Marshall feared. Federalists made up eastern losses with new gains in the west. They were still outnumbered by nearly two to one, but for the moment they had arrested their decline.

After all the electioneering—Presidential, then congressional, then assembly—the populace may have longed for calm normality, but a dispute among national party leaders kept the state in turmoil for the rest of the year. During the congressional contest, Samuel Jordan Cabell sent a circular to his constituents denouncing the administration's foreign policy, particularly its failure to reach an accommodation with France. To Supreme Court Justice James Iredell, who was passing through the state on circuit, this sort of criticism hampered the administration's conduct of diplomacy and verged on sedition. While presiding over a Richmond grand jury in May he publicly criticized officials who subverted the government. The jury, evidently composed of Federalists, took the cue and issued a presentment denouncing the actions of Cabell and other congressmen who "disseminate unfounded calumnies against the happy government of the United States." No crime was alleged (though Iredell might have invoked the common-law crime of seditious libel, as the Pennsylvania circuit did a year later to jail

Benjamin Franklin Bache), but the presentment did seem to threaten the right of congressmen to criticize administration policy. It was, moreover, a novel usage of the grand jury, changing it, as Jefferson noted, "from a legal to a political engine."[28]

Cabell replied with another circular to his constituents condemning the judiciary for meddling in the affairs of Congress, but Jefferson was still not satisfied.[29] Returning to Virginia after the congressional session ended in July, he drafted a petition in behalf of Cabell's constituents protesting the encroachment on free speech and judicial interference in a congressional election. After consulting with Madison and Monroe, he decided to forward it to the assembly at its fall session.[30] Jefferson's initiative and his decision to use the assembly as a vehicle for the dissemination of Republican views were important precedents for the Virginia Resolutions of 1798.

When the anonymous memorial from Amherst County (Cabell's home) reached the House floor in December 1797, knowledgeable Republicans moved to publish it at state expense. Federalists, afraid to defend the grand jury but unwilling to give Republicans a propaganda coup, struggled to escape. First they suggested that Virginia's congressmen ought to initiate a law prescribing the duties of federal grand juries and confining them to the investigation of statutory crimes. Though clearly a worthwhile idea, it was voted down 56 to 94. Federalists then proposed that the assembly ignore the Amherst petition since Congress was competent to protect the rights of its members. This too was rejected, 54 to 93, and a third motion to leave the entire affair to the courts was shouted down. The House then approved the resolution to print a thousand copies of the memorial, 92 to 53.[31]

Although the Republican majority was firm, Madison felt it was not as large as it might have been. He complained that the memorial "was the only test of party strength [in the session], and so far deceptive as it confounds scrupulous Republicans with their adversaries."[32] The Federalists had certainly tried to obscure the issue, but no one was confounded. Not a single assemblyman switched, even when, as on the first Federalist resolution, the motion had some intrinsic merit. Variations in the roll calls were due to abstensions or absences.[33] Moreover, the Republicans' ability to hold together through a series of confusing, even superficially attractive, motions suggests well-developed lines of communication between leadership and backbenchers.

MARYLAND POLITICS, 1796–1797

The fever of Presidential politics also carried over into the Maryland assembly in the fall of 1796. In his annual message Governor John H. Stone, entering his third year in office, commented freely on national affairs, complementing Washington on his administration and expressing sorrow at his impending retirement. The Federalist majority in the assembly drafted an even more partisan reply. It denounced the spirit of party abroad in the country and singled out for special condemnation "the intrigues of foreign emissaries." The latter was a reference to Adet's heavy-handed intervention. Embarrassed Republicans might well have let the innuendo pass, since there was little to be gained by defending France; instead they moved to delete the clause. The House rejected the motion, 20 to 42, and then passed the original draft by voice vote.[34]

Toward the end of the session the assembly received the constitutional amendments proposed by Virginia during the dispute over the Jay Treaty. The Federalists' inclination was to reject them out of hand; Republicans, though hopelessly outnumbered, wanted to soften the rebuff. They brought in a resolution asking the governor to inform Virginia that pressing business prevented adequate consideration of the amendments, but the assembly hoped to give them serious attention the following year. Federalists turned this down, 24 to 35, and refused even to discuss the amendments. Nothing further was heard of them.[35]

Although on unrelated questions, the two roll calls seem to provide an index of party strength on the eve of the Presidential election. Federalists retained the two-to-one majority (44 to 22) they had possessed since the beginning of the decade. There were small but significant changes in regional strength, however. Republicans were beginning to make inroads into the upper part of the

Eastern Shore (Queen Anne's and Talbot counties). Federalists temporarily balanced this by capturing Baltimore Town and County, but Republicans soon recovered both. Republicans had also gained possession of far western Allegany County, which had been moving in their direction since the Whisky Rebellion. If such trends continued, party strength would soon be equal.

There is also evidence of growing voter awareness of parties. In 1797, newspapers began recording, for the first time since 1790, the popular vote in assembly contests. A Frederick County election is particularly instructive, both because it affords a rare peek at western politics and because Frederick was a Federalist county where Republicans were rapidly gaining ground. The fall 1797 election was preceded by intense controversy in the Frederick Town paper, with a dozen different contributors discussing national parties and policies. Possession of the county's four seats turned on national party affiliation, and each side put up a ticket. The procedure for naming a ticket was essentially the same for both. Notices were inserted in the newspaper giving the time and place for a meeting "for the purpose of nominating four Delegates." Party labels were not used; the place of meeting, usually a tavern, was apparently the signal for its tone. The Federalist meeting, after pledging support to incumbent delegates who had backed Adams's policies in the previous session, also enjoined them to oppose all legislative efforts to divide the county or build any new roads through it—the first indication of concern for a platform of local issues.[36]

The election showed that the electorate had become almost totally polarized:[37]

Warfield	1,617	Kuhn	1,341
Thomas	1,575	Quynn	1,318
Bruce	1,555	Shriver	1,298
Gist	1,551	Jamison	1,198

The newspaper did not label the tickets by party, but it did not have to. The winning ticket was firmly Federalist in its assembly voting, with the exception of Joshua Gist, who cast one Republican vote in 1797 and was retired the following year. Among the losers, only

Shriver and Jamison had enough prior legislative service to be identifiable. Jamison had leaned toward the Republicans in a 1793–94 tour of duty, while Shriver was an old debtor-Antifederalist, who had returned to the assembly in 1794 a Federalist. When he finally won election to the House again, in 1799, he was a staunch Republican; his place on the ticket suggests that he made the switch by 1797.

The figures indicate that nearly all voters simply voted the ticket and did not worry about personalities. Unless a large number of voters cast ballots for only two or three men (in the extant Maryland and Virginia poll lists such behavior was rare), the total number of participants was about 2,500 (obtained by averaging the sums of leader and lowest on each side). The federal census of 1800 credits Frederick County and Town with 5,614 heads of households. If two-thirds of those could meet the £30 property qualification (and the land ownership statistics given in chapter 1 indicate that this was the case), turnout among eligibles was close to 70 percent. This is about the same as the Frederick County turnout in the Presidential election of 1800.[38] The voters must have felt there was as much at stake in 1797. And they certainly knew what they wanted. The variation within the Federalist ticket was 66 voters, and on the other side 143. Even if all 66 of those missing from the lower end of the Federalist ticket switched to the other side, the number of voters splitting their ballots was only 2 percent of the total.[39] Frederick voters were backing parties, not individuals, and the newspaper discussion suggests that they perceived in the parties set principles (or at least symbols) and expected those principles to be fashioned into policies. That the House of Delegates had very little, if any, influence on national policies was not the question; it was a matter of organizational loyalty.

THE MATURE PARTY SYSTEM:
CHANGE AND CONTINUITY

The origin and nature of the first party system has been, over the years, a durable source of historical debate. In 1916, Charles A. Beard disagreed violently with earlier scholars who had suggested that the first national parties did not appear until the mid- or late 1790s. In *The Economic Origins of Jeffersonian Democracy* Beard argued that the financial system set up by the Washington administration was, in a sense, a payoff for those who had drafted the Constitution. The Constitution makers expected to profit by their handiwork, and did so. Their opponents, first the Antifederalists and later the Republicans, were people who did not have investments in government securities and thus failed to profit from Hamilton's funding system. They represented instead the broad majority of rural taxpayers who had to pay the bill. Thus, Beard insisted, the first parties were only an extension of the fight over the Constitution.

Recent scholars have rejected this interpretation, pointing out that not all of those who wrote the Constitution possessed securities (Madison), not all securities holders supported the Constitution (George Mason), and not all Constitutionalists remained Federalists. The dispute over fiscal policy, moreover, was confined largely to Congress; the general public did not become much involved in party politics until foreign affairs intruded in 1793. And not until the fight over the Jay Treaty was there even a semblance of a modern party system, with local organizations and a chain of command. The issues were new and by that time so were most of the men; hence, argue Beard's critics, there is no connection between the first party system and the contest over the Constitution.[40]

It is possible, of course, that both are right, at least in part. It is apparent that Hamilton's policies did arouse many of the same passions that had flared in the fight over the Constitution, and, except for Madison and a few others, the lines were essentially the same. Tabulations of votes in the Chesapeake states, produced in earlier chapters, tend to support Beard's position. Although his notion of the importance of government securities is grossly oversimplified, there was in the Chesapeake a clear continuity between the factions of the 1780s, the contest over the Constitution, and the early divisions over Federalist policy. But it is still possible that the revisionists are correct, that true parties, with national organizations and "grass roots" support, originated only after 1793, stimulated by the war in Europe and the symbolic duality it presented, British

monarchy versus French Jacobinism. To test this possibility is the
remaining task. Let us treat the mature party system, 1793–1800 as
a unit, and ask, how many of its adherents were new to politics in
1793? Of those who had served previously in some political capacity—in the assembly, in Congress, in the executive, or as Presidential elector—what stands had they taken in the factionalism of the
1780s and the contest over the Constitution?

The primary means of identifying these people, as it has been
throughout this book, is by their legislative voting behavior,
together with contemporary literary evidence. Although fewer than
half of the men who were politically active in the years 1793 to
1800 can be identified, because of the scant number of party-
determining roll calls, it is possible to tabulate a fairly sizable cross-
section of the governing elite. In the following tables those who
failed to side with one party or the other 75 percent of the time or
who switched sides more than once were placed in the middle. Few
individuals actually switched parties after 1793, but those who did
are classified with their last-known association. Thus, Patrick Henry
and Samuel Chase are considered Federalists, Samuel Smith and
Edmund Randolph Republicans. A total of 261 Marylanders can be
identified, and the breakdown is recorded in table 19.1. The number of new men (about 60 percent of the total) reflects the rather
high turnover due to annual elections. But it also shows that the
parties recruited new members with about equal facility, approximately two additional members for each carryover. Although Federalists lost ground to Republicans over the decade, they retained
their freshness and vitality. Put another way, Federalists were not
an aging elite clinging to power.

Among those with experience prior to 1793 there is a strong
continuity with the party divisions of the 1780s. The one exception
is the large number of Antifederalists who ultimately became Federalists. Most of these, of course, were Samuel Chase's friends. Of
interest also is the high turnover among those in the middle. Only a
few of those who had mixed records in the 1780s lasted politically
into the 1790s. Only two of those who failed to choose between the
parties after 1793 could boast prior political service. Men who
lacked commitment, it would seem, did not last long in politics.

TABLE 19.1   MARYLAND PARTIES, 1793–1800: A SUMMARY

| | Affiliation, 1793–1800 | | |
	Federalists	Republicans	Middle
Affiliation before 1793			
Federalists, 1788–1791	37	9	1
Antifederalists, 1788–1791	12	11	0
Middle	2	2	1
Unknown	9	7	0
	60	29	2
Creditor, 1785–1787	23	1	2
Debtor, 1785–1787	0	7	0
Chasite	8	2	0
Mixed	4	0	0
Unknown	25	19	0
	60	29	2
New after 1792	93	56	21
Total	153	85	23

In Virginia the two sides were a little more evenly balanced, but the results were quite similar. In the absence of the Chasite aberration, the continuity over the two decades was even stronger (table 19.2). The percentage of new men after 1792 is about the same as in Maryland, suggesting again the ability of both parties to recruit regardless of their comparative strength. Among older men, Federalists drew almost exclusively from the ranks of those who had favored the Constitution and opposed relief legislation in the 1780s. About two-thirds of the Republicans were former Antifederalists; one-third were, like Madison, supporters of the Constitution and creditor-minded on debts, taxes, and paper money. As in Maryland, those with mixed records were short-lived politically.

In North Carolina the party ratio was the opposite of Maryland—Republicans had the two-to-one majority (table 19.3). North Carolina had approximately as many politically active men as Virginia (some 600 over the seven-year period, as against about 300 in Maryland), but fewer could be identified because of the paucity of roll calls. The results, however, are similar. The percentage of new

TABLE 19.2 VIRGINIA PARTIES, 1793–1800: A SUMMARY

	Affiliation, 1793–1800		
	Federalists	Republicans	Middle
Affiliation before 1793			
Federalists, 1788–1791	42	28	3
Antifederalists, 1788–1791	4	42	3
Middle	0	0	0
Unknown	21	37	3
	67	107	9
Creditor, 1785–1787	17	11	0
Debtor, 1785–1787	1	16	1
Middle	1	2	0
Unknown	48	78	8
	67	107	9
New after 1792	141	205	28
Total	208	312	37

TABLE 19.3 NORTH CAROLINA PARTIES, 1793–1800: A SUMMARY

	Affiliation, 1793–1800		
	Federalists	Republicans	Middle
Affiliation before 1793			
Federalists, 1788–91	22	25	0
Antifederalists-88/Fed-89	1	3	0
Antifederalists	0	36	0
Mixed	0	1	0
Unknown	3	5	0
	26	70	0
Creditor, 1785–87	7	6	0
Debtor, 1785–87	1	11	0
Mixed, 1785–87	0	2	0
Unknown	18	51	0
	26	70	0
New after 1792	26	50	9
Total	52	120	9

men is about the same as in Maryland and Virginia, and the political death rate among the wavering is even higher. Despite major shifts in regional affinities (the Republican capture of Albemarle and Federalist gains in the western Piedmont), there is the familiar relationship between the national parties and 1780s factions. It has been noted before, but it bears repeating, that relatively few leaders switched parties. When the sympathies of the electorate changed, it turned to new men. In some cases—indeed, a surprising number— shifting voters resurrected men who had been put in political limbo some years earlier. Political consistency clearly was considered a virtue. Perhaps this is why the first national party system was a direct outgrowth of the factional divisions of the 1780s—at least, in the Chesapeake.

In all three states polarization was virtually complete after 1793. Those who voted enough to be identified at all sided with a party 95 percent of the time in North Carolina, 93 percent in Virginia, and 91 percent in Maryland. By the time John Adams entered office, parties had spread their influence into every phase of state government, and rudimentary organizations existed in nearly every county courthouse. The fierce passions aroused by Adams's policies, both foreign and domestic, over the next three years brought those organizations to full mobilization.

THE FRENCH CRISIS

John Adams could not have picked a worse time to become President. The rise of a party press had fostered a particularly vicious brand of editorial journalism. Washington himself was not immune to its sting, and Adams, lacking the hero's mantle, was even more defenseless. The new executive also had the misfortune to inherit a foreign crisis that was none of his making. The crisis dominated his four years in office and eventually contributed to his downfall. It all started with the Jay Treaty.

France, like much of the rest of Europe, assumed that the treaty amounted to an alliance between Britain and the United States; but France, unlike the rest of Europe, felt strong enough to do something about it. The end to the Reign of Terror and the installation of a somewhat more efficient, if also more corrupt, administration called the Directory coincided with a succession of French military triumphs. By 1796 Britain's coalition of monarchies was crumbling, and France was actively subverting the governments of her neighbors in the low countries and western Germany. By the time Adams entered office, France sat secure and powerful within a growing circle of satellite republics. Success also bred an overbearing self-confidence, exemplified by minister Adet's intervention in the Presidential contest of 1796.

Washington and his Secretary of State Timothy Pickering did nothing to alleviate French suspicions. Disliking the French and mistrustful even of their own representative in Paris, James Monroe, they refused to disclose the terms of the treaty until after it was ratified. Monroe was not even given enough information to provide the French with vague excuses, and when he protested, the administration recalled him. The French retaliated by refusing to accept Monroe's replacement, Charles C. Pinckney, a South Carolina Federalist. In a decree of March 1797, timed to coincide with Adams's inauguration, the Directory authorized the seizure of American vessels found carrying British goods. By June the French had seized some 316 American vessels, and the two nations were on the brink of war. Or at least Secretary of State Pickering (whom Adams had retained along with the rest of Washington's cabinet) thought the seizures a cause for war. Adams instead decided to make a final attempt at negotiation. To reinforce Pinckney, who had been expelled from Paris and was waiting nervously in the Netherlands for further instructions, the President nominated John Marshall and an old Massachusetts friend, Elbridge Gerry.

The three envoys assembled in Paris in the fall of 1797 but found Foreign Minister Talleyrand unyielding. His agents (whom President Adams designated X, Y, and Z when he published the correspondence) demanded a bribe as a condition of serious negotiations and a sizable government loan that would have damaged American neutrality and broken the entente with Britain. In December, Marshall and Pinckney sent word of these humiliating demands to the President. For a time Talleyrand seemed more tractable, but in March 1798 Marshall and Pinckney lost patience and returned home, leaving a slightly more optimistic Gerry behind.

The XYZ dispatches, delayed by winter storms, did not arrive in Philadelphia until March. The new Congress met in December, but found itself marking time while it awaited word from abroad. From his seat at the head of the Senate the new Vice President relieved the tedium by counting noses. Federalists had a majority of 22 to 10 in the Senate, he reported to Madison in mid-February, but in the House of Representatives their majority was only two or three, depending on the question. A few roll calls in early March confirmed this estimate. Federalists, who were doing their own counting, reached the same conclusion. The House was almost evenly divided. "Wavering characters," as Jefferson called them, had been virtually eliminated.[41]

On March 5, Adams informed Congress that the mission to France had failed and promised to transmit the dispatches as soon as they were deciphered. On the nineteenth he changed his mind. Publication of the dispatches, he told Congress, might endanger the envoys, who were still in France. So he had decided to withhold them and recommend that Congress take steps to defend the nation's commerce. To Republicans this seemed a flimsy excuse; some wondered openly if the President were not deliberately fomenting a war scare. They called for publication, as they had with the Jay Treaty. Federalists initially backed the President, but as word of the humiliating treatment accorded the emissaries leaked out, they began to realize the political potential in the dispatches. Thus, by a bipartisan margin of 65 to 27 the House on April 2 demanded the release of the XYZ correspondence.[42]

For once, the Federalists correctly forecast the popular temper. Publication of the dispatches caused a storm of indignation. Talleyrand's attitude bruised the nation's pride and provoked an urge to retaliate. "Millions for defense, but not one cent for tribute!" trumpeted the press. Riding the wave, Secretary of War James McHenry on April 9 sent Congress a collection of recommendations for strengthening the army and navy and building coastal fortifications. Federalists quickly went to work, and within a few days the docket was filled with defense measures. Jefferson, whose ceremonial duties left him plenty of time to fret, groaned that, in addition to the public furor, the dispatches "have also carried over to the war party most of the waverers in the H. of R. This circumstance with the departure of 4 Southern members, & others going, have given a strong majority to the other party."[43]

The four deserters were all Virginians—Giles, Clopton, Samuel J. Cabell, and John Nicholas.[44] Giles, who was chronically ill, had arrived late for the session; the others probably had personal business to transact. Clopton was back on the job within a few days; Nicholas returned before the end of the session.[45] Their departure was a blow to Republican leadership. After the retirement of Madison, Albert Gallatin of Pennsylvania had moved to the front of the party, but there were few beside him with a gift for expression. He felt keenly the departure of Giles and Nicholas, both outstanding orators. But otherwise Jefferson was unduly pessimistic. Republican numbers held up quite well, and Gallatin conducted a spirited fight against Federalist war measures. Whatever their impact on public opinion, the XYZ dispatches had no discernable effect on Congress. Party lines were already drawn tight, and they remained so. Even the waverers continued to waver. Among Chesapeake congressmen there were three of these—George Dent of Maryland, Josiah Parker of Virginia, and William Barry Grove of North Carolina. Dent voted Republican once and Federalist 7 times prior to publication of the dispatches, Republican 10 and Federalist 8 times afterward. Parker was 2 and 2 before the XYZ explosion, 6 and 7 afterwards. Grove was 4 Federalist, 3 Republican before April 3, 14 and 6 afterward.[46]

Jefferson had an opportunity to reassess his pessimism the very next day, April 20, when the House took up the naval appropriations bill. A Republican motion reducing the number of vessels to be built or purchased from 16 to 12 passed by 45 to 37. Encouraged, Gallatin sought to weaken the bill further by prohibiting public warships from convoying merchant vessels, evidently fearing that such activity might cause seafights. This amendment failed, 32 to 50.[47] Neither motion involved intense feeling, however, and there was considerable shifting in both directions. Among Chesapeake congressmen, party lines held firm, except for the chronic switchers, who were joined on this occasion by Samuel Smith of Maryland. A better index of party strength came five days later when the House approved, 47 to 41, a bill creating a Department of the Navy with a secretary of cabinet rank. Republicans bitterly fought this move, arguing that such an institution would only encourage wars.[48] Again Smith sided with the Federalists, but Dent canceled him by switching to the Republicans. Chesapeake lines otherwise held steady.

In May the debate waxed ever more fierce. Accusations of foreign influence and sedition flew thick across the House chamber. With the navy problem out of the way attention focused on the administration's call for a provisional army of 50,000 to meet a possible attack. Pointing out that France lacked the navy to mount an invasion, Republicans wondered openly whether the purpose of the army was not to quell domestic opposition. With the support of moderate Federalists they succeeded in reducing the army to 10,-000, but an effort to substitute the militia failed by a party vote of 39 to 51. Moderate Federalists also cooperated in a move to limit the army's duration to one year, but the bill itself passed, 51 to 40.[49] Joining the Republican efforts to weaken the bill were three moderate Federalists from Maryland, two from Virginia (Machir and Evans) and Grove of North Carolina. Two Maryland Federalists (Baer and Hindman) and one Virginian (Morgan) favored the army throughout.

Toward the end of May the division in Federalist ranks became even more apparent. The split originated in the administration. Adams preferred a policy of simple military preparation, while continuing the search for means of negotiation. Secretary of State Timothy Pickering wanted an outright declaration of war and alliance with Great Britain.[50] Extremists became known as High Federalists, the Adams men as moderate Federalists. In Congress, the High Federalists, not strong enough to force a declaration of war, did what they could to provoke an accidental fight. On May 26 the House agreed, 50 to 40, to permit the navy to capture French privateers, and four days later it suspended commercial intercourse with France by 55 to 25. Republican ranks broke on this one. Commercial retaliation was old Republican doctrine, and there was the possibility that it might forestall war. Three North Carolina Republicans and a Virginian sided with the Federalists; four other Virginians simply abstained.[51]

Then, on June 8, came the most critical vote of the session. A bill authorizing the issuance of letters of marque and reprisal to privately owned warships failed by 41 to 42.[52] Commissioning privateers to prey on French commerce was tantamount to an act of war. Had it passed, a formal declaration would surely have followed. The roll call clearly distinguished the High Federalists from the Adams men, and Chesapeake Federalism was on the High side. Only one Maryland Federalist, the westerner George Baer, voted against the motion (joining the waverer Dent and Republican Robert Sprigg). Grove of North Carolina favored privateers (and voted consistently Federalist thereafter); all three Virginia Federalists, who had sided with the militants earlier, abstained.

With the war question temporarily shelved, the Federalist majority, shaky though it was, turned on its domestic enemies. In April a New England Federalist had asked the House Committee for the Protection of Commerce and Defense of the Country to look into the possibility of regulating aliens. Behind this lay the Federalist fear that newly arrived French and Irish refugees, together with some English Radicals such as Jefferson's friend, Joseph Priestley, were a subversive influence. On May 1 the committee recommended an extension of the naturalization waiting period, a system for registering aliens, and a statute authorizing the deportation of aliens from a country with which the United States was at war. Out of this report came the laws, three in all, concerning aliens.[53]

First came the Naturalization Act, which extended the time in which a foreigner must reside in the United States before he was entitled to citizenship from five years to fourteen. The purpose was plainly to prevent, or at least delay, immigrants' participation in politics, since Federalists assumed that most newcomers were Jeffersonians. Republicans put up only token opposition to this measure. The bill was modified and passed without a single public roll call. The one head-count taken (a 41 to 40 approval of the fourteen-year provision) was done without listing names. It is true, however, that by the time this measure came to a vote there were more drastic proposals on the way. Perhaps Republicans thought to reserve their strength for the main event.

Republicans, moreover, had no objection to a well-conceived bill regulating aliens who were potential threats. Indeed, they even participated in the passage of the Alien Enemies Act, which authorized the apprehension of aliens who were citizens of a nation with which the United States was at war. Samuel Smith reported the bill from committee, and Gallatin defended it on the floor. It passed on June 26 with bipartisan support. Since it required a formal declaration of war, the act never went into effect during the French crisis. But it was considered a permanent regulation. The Jeffersonians let it stand after 1801, and it remains on the statute books today.

If Republicans backed the alien enemies bill in hopes of forestalling something worse, they were deceived. By the time it passed on June 26 Federalists had pushed through a more general Act Concerning Aliens (labeled the Alien Friends Act to distinguish it from the earlier law) enforceable in either peace or war. This one originated in the Senate, where the Federalist majority was more secure. Reported by an all-Federalist committee on May 4, the bill authorized the President to detain or deport any alien whom he judged dangerous to the peace and safety of the nation. The Senate softened the bill to some extent, removing among other things a national registration system for aliens, and sent it to the House in early June. The House already had under consideration a bill of its own, one that included more safeguards for innocent aliens. The climax of the XYZ affair caused the House to abandon its own measure, however. On June 13, Dr. George Logan, prominent Philadelphia Republican, departed for France on a peace mission of his own. Federalists were outraged at this intrusion of a private citizen into affairs of state. Three days later the Philadelphia *Aurora,* the most influential of Republican newspapers, published a message Talleyrand had sent to the American government before the State Department released its copy of the text. Federalists seized upon this as clear evidence that there was a direct connection between the Jeffersonians and the French. Two days later President Adams released the final dispatch from Marshall and Pinckney, and Congress ordered 10,000 copies of the whole XYZ correspondence printed for public consumption. That same day, John Marshall arrived in Philadelphia to a hero's welcome.

Patriotism mingled with xenophobia; the House promptly substituted the Senate's bill, debated it for two days, and on June 21 passed it by 46 to 40.[54] The margin was the same that had separated the two parties since the beginning of the session. Both parties had closed ranks. Not a single Republican favored the bill; not a single Federalist opposed it.[55] Among Chesapeake waverers Dent of Maryland opposed the measure, but Grove struck with the Federalists. Virginia's Eastern Shore Federalist Thomas Evans approved the bill; and the two westerners, Machir and Morgan, had already departed for home. If they were unhappy with their northern brethren, they gave no sign of it.[56]

The other piece of Federalist repression, the Sedition Act, passed by an almost identical margin. This "Act for the Punishment of Certain Crimes," as it was innocuously titled, also originated in the Senate. Like the Alien Friends law, it was considered temporary; both were to expire after two years. But that also made them more partisan, for they were transparent efforts to muzzle the opposition party during a Presidential election. Federalists confessed as much when they accepted an amendment extending the act to March 3, 1801, the date that Adams's term ended. From that point on the act no longer had anything to do with a diplomatic crisis.

The Sedition law stemmed from the Federalists' archaic view of politics—their failure to distinguish between partisan criticism and subversion, between opposition to current policy and opposition to the governmental framework itself. Iredell's charge to the Richmond grand jury in 1797 reflected this impatience with criticism, and it initiated a nationwide effort to silence the Federalists' enemies through the common law doctrine of seditious libel. The bill that emerged from the Senate modified that doctrine to some extent by permitting juries to determine the fact of libel and allowing truth as a defense, but it was still a political weapon aimed at Republican newspapers.

The author of the act was James Lloyd of Maryland, who had been sent to the Senate only the previous year in place of John Henry, who had become governor. Aside from his Eastern Shore pedigree, Lloyd's only recommendation appears to have been an ultra-Federalism. "He is as strictly government as it is possible," former Senator Uriah Forrest assured McHenry when the assembly made the appointment, "a man of nice honor and pretty good judgment, slow, and heavy."[57] Lloyd confided to Washington that the Logan mission and the *Aurora's* publication of the Talleyrand letter were what induced him to draft the bill. Not content with refining the definition of seditious libel, Lloyd also sought to define treason. Designating the government and people of France as enemies of the United States, he declared that any effort to give them aid and comfort was treason, punishable by death. Even High Federalists realized that this was of dubious legality, since treason was already carefully defined by the Constitution, and a Senate committee deleted the article. The Senate then passed it on the fourth of July by a straight party vote.[58]

Federalists in the House of Representatives were openly receptive. The idea had been suggested some weeks before by the Committee on Defense, and a sedition bill reached the House floor in early June. During the debates on the Alien Friends Act, Federalists occasionally shifted the argument from enemies abroad to "domestic traitors." But they deferred to the Senate, and after passing the alien laws the House marked time until the Senate completed action on the sedition bill. Then on July 5 Harrison Gray Otis moved to give the bill its first two readings on the same day, Carter Harrison of Virginia responded with a request to read the Bill of Rights, and the fight was on.[59]

The debate lasted five days and covered the whole ground, from the meaning of the First Amendment to the definition of liberty itself. But it is unlikely that any votes were swayed. On July 10 the House approved the bill by 44 to 41.[60] It was another party vote, though not quite so rigid as on the Alien Act. Two Federalists broke ranks to vote against the Sedition Act, Stephen Bullock of Massachusetts and William Matthews of Maryland.[61] Two other Maryland Federalists, Craik and Dennis, abstained, but that was the only indication of moderation among Chesapeake Federalists. Republicans, bolstered by the return of John Nicholas, stood firm. They had made telling points in debate and could carry their struggle against "the three-vote majority," as the *Aurora* called it, back to the states.

Indeed, Chesapeake Federalists would have done well to show more moderation. The repressive legislation was precisely what Republicans had anticipated from the administration of John Adams. By adhering so closely to the unpopular New Englander, Chesapeake Federalists signed their own political death warrant.

CHAPTER TWENTY

Mobilizing the Electorate: 1800

REPUBLICANS were on the defensive in Congress through the spring of 1798, but they had fought a brilliant rearguard action. By holding their ranks together they had modified a number of Federalist military proposals and subjected every measure to critical scrutiny. Federalists, by matching Republicans' discipline, forced through every one of the measures, but they had little cause for exultation. Despite popular indignation over the behavior of France, Congress had not been stampeded. Military preparedness measures, which should have slid through in the atmosphere of crisis, remained in doubt until the final roll call. The Sedition Act, which required general acquiescence if it were to be regarded as anything but partisan repression, passed by the narrowest of margins—a "three-vote majority," sneered the *Aurora*. Though unable to halt the Federalists' drive, Republicans had compiled an impressive public record, one that could serve as a basis for election appeals. What they needed was a forum to initiate the public debate. Not surprisingly they turned to their home base, the Virginia assembly. Madison sensed this need when he stood for a seat in the assembly in the spring 1798 election. As in his earlier moments of political crisis, 1784 and 1788, he fled the national scene to the state to regroup his forces.

The Virginia assembly was well prepared to comment on matters of national interest. In the spring elections candidates for the House of Delegates publicly pronounced themselves either supporters or opponents of the administration, just as the Marylanders had done in the previous year.[1] Although the XYZ dispatches were released to Congress on the eve of the election, there was not time for them to influence the results. Republicans retained the two-to-one majority they had held throughout the decade. When the diplomatic correspondence was published, Federalists capitalized as best they could. On June 1 they sponsored a huge popular meeting in Richmond; resolutions friendly to the President obtained the signature of over 300 persons. During the summer Norfolk Federalists organized a fund-raising drive that accumulated over $16,000 to build and equip warships to be loaned to the government.[2] John Marshall's return in June, and his journey through the state on the way to the nation's capital, afforded Federalists further opportunity for political celebrations. Fevers ran high by the time the assembly met in December.

The need to fill a U.S. Senate seat focused attention on national politics from the outset. In the 1780s Henry Tazewell had masked his partisanship with a veneer of genial gentility, but the federal Senate seemed to toughen him. Federalists detested him for his strenuous opposition to the Jay Treaty and active espousal of the amendments of 1795. Congressman Thomas Evans gave them the ammunition they needed. During the spring uproar over military preparation, Evans reported, Tazewell had declared that he would join the French army if one landed in the United States. Assembly Federalists broadcast the report and demanded an investigation. They did not have the strength to defeat Tazewell openly, theorized Edmund Randolph (now a firm Republican); so they hoped at least "to leave a temporary stigma on Mr. T's character." The effort collapsed when a Federalist motion to postpone the election until the allegations could be investigated lost, 53 to 98. Several Federalists then nominated Madison for the seat, evidently in the hope of dividing the Republican vote. That was too cynical a move for the orthodox, and in the end the Federalists simply confused themselves. The final tally was Tazewell 117, Madison 28, John Marshall 13, and James Breckinridge 10.[3]

The Federalists soon had cause to regroup. On the day before the vote, December 10, John Taylor of Caroline, returning briefly to service in the political emergency, introduced a set of resolutions on the Alien and Sedition laws. The resolutions resulted from a midsummer conference at Monticello involving Jefferson, Madison, and Wilson Cary Nicholas. The question was how to publicize their opposition to the Federalist measures, so as to stimulate a national debate. Legislative resolutions, circularized among the states, were a natural solution. The Virginia resolves of 1795 had sparked considerable discussion north of the Potomac. The technique was certain to work again. Madison went home from the meeting and drew up the resolutions which Taylor carried to the Virginia assembly. Jefferson drafted another set which, under the original plan, Nicholas was to take to North Carolina.[4]

In September, John Breckinridge, who had moved to Kentucky in 1793, paid one of his periodic visits to his old home in Albemarle. Stopping at Nicholas's, he learned of the resolutions and persuaded Nicholas to let him present them to the Kentucky legislature instead. On Breckinridge's assertion, doubtless correct, that the Kentucky assembly was overwhelmingly Republican, Nicholas agreed. He then informed Jefferson, who approved of the change. Referring to the recent congressional election in North Carolina, Jefferson wrote, "Perhaps the late changes in their representation may indicate some doubts whether they would have passed."[5]

North Carolina's late-summer election was indeed a disaster for the Republicans. The congressionally published correspondence had been distributed in the south; public indignation was at its height. The electorate rallied to the President; even Republican candidates for Congress found it necessary to pledge their support for the administration during the crisis.[6] When the election was over, Maryland's William Hindman, the northern Federalists' chief source on southern politics, reported that seven of North Carolina's ten Representatives were Federalists.[7] The report was unduly optimistic, for several of the new members voted Republican once they reached Congress. But there were three new Federalists, besides William B. Grove, and the fact that Republicans felt obliged to cover their allegiance during the election campaign is testimony to the state of public opinion.

The Republicans retained their solid majority in the North Carolina House of Commons, but they lacked the assurance of previous years. While Richmond resounded with the Virginia debate over the Alien and Sedition laws, Republicans in Raleigh remained strangely silent. Encouraged by this, perhaps, and by their gains in the congressional contests, Federalists, on the last day of the session, brought in an address to President Adams expressing approval of his foreign policy and pledging that the state would not tolerate foreign interference in its domestic politics. The address was phrased in terms general enough to satisfy a number of Republicans, and it passed, 51 to 38. Republican leaders then retaliated with a resolution declaring that the Commons "view with pain" the Alien and Sedition laws and asking the state's congressmen to secure their repeal. This motion sorted out the two sides; it passed, 58 to 21.[8]

Assuming that the second roll call was an accurate index of party strength, and that Republicans who voted in favor of both motions represented a moderate, or at least uncertain, element in the party, the breakdown was as shown in table 20.1 (counting only those who participated in both). The French crisis completed the shift of North Carolina Federalism from the Albemarle region to the western Piedmont.[9] Western Federalism was apparently an ethnic phenomenon. The German population of the area became increasingly anti-French in the late 1790s, probably in reaction to French incursions on German soil in Europe. And they translated their foreign prejudices to domestic politics, switching to the Federalist side—an ironic twist to Washington's farewell plea that Americans keep foreign policy and domestic politics separate. Lincoln County, the most heavily German of all, began sending Federalists to the assembly shortly after the Jay Treaty. In the congressional election of 1798 Federalist candidate Joseph Dickson

TABLE 20.1   NORTH CAROLINA PARTIES, 1798

	Federalists	Moderate Republicans	Hard-Core Republicans
Albemarle	3	2	12
Pamlico	1	3	7
Cape Fear	0	4	1
Eastern Piedmont	5	8	9
Western Piedmont	7	3	0
West	2	2	1
	18	22	30

accused his Republican opponent, James Holland, of being pro-French. Holland won a slim majority of 475 votes in four counties of the district, but he lost Lincoln by 1,010 votes, and with it the election.

Republicans still had a majority in the Commons, but with substantial German and Scots elements in their constituencies they were understandably shy about statements on administration foreign policy. The Senate was even more timid. On motion of an Albemarle Federalist, Joseph Riddick, the upper house shelved both resolutions, 31 to 9.[10] Jefferson's decision not to use the North Carolina assembly as a vehicle for his resolutions, though based on only partial information, thus seems a prudent one. Carolina Republicans would almost certainly have tempered his language and perhaps rejected the resolutions altogether.[11]

The resolutions which Taylor presented to the Virginia assembly defined the Constitution as a compact among the states under which certain powers were delegated to the central government. When the federal authorities violated the compact by a "deliberate, palpable, and dangerous exercise of power," the states were "in duty bound to interpose for arresting the progress of the evil." In a final resolution Madison demonstrated that the Alien and Sedition laws were just such a violation.[12]

What exactly Madison meant by having the state "interpose" itself was never very clear. In practice the state did nothing, except to permit its attorney general to appear as defense counsel in the one sedition trial that took place in Virginia. The concept was vague enough to avoid an open challenge to the federal government, while offering some hope that the state might go to the aid of its citizens. Jefferson, with whom Madison consulted at least once during the fall, was not altogether satisfied with it. The resolves he sent to Kentucky used the phrase "null and void" to describe an unconstitutional federal law, and in an apparent attempt to strengthen Madison's language he sent John Taylor an additional resolution declaring the Federalist statutes "utterly void, and of no force or effect." Taylor, recognizing the implications, readily agreed. The modification would place the state and federal governments "at issue," he told the Vice President, and thus might result in another federal convention to institute changes in the Constitution.[13] In Taylor's mind, at least, the new "compact theory" of the Constitution was a logical extension of Antifederalism.

The House of Delegates debated Taylor's resolutions for a week. The novel idea that the Constitution was a "compact" among sovereign states received most of the attention. Federalists argued that the national government derived its existence, and hence its powers, directly from the people. Each government, being sovereign, was its own judge of the extent of its powers. Western Federalists, still smarting from the defeat of constitutional revision in 1796, pointed to the undemocratic nature of the compact theory. It rested power on locality, rather than numbers. Tiny Delaware, under the concept of state sovereignty, had as much influence as mighty Virginia. Turning around the old Antifederalist argument that localized power was more responsive to popular wishes, they pointed out that the Federal government was more popularly based than Virginia's. Congressional districts were apportioned by population, whereas representation in the assembly was by county, regardless of size.[14]

The Federalists concentrated their fire on the final resolution, drafted by Jefferson. On this one they at least had a chance of attracting moderate Republicans who feared that nullification by a single state might lead to anarchy. It worked, and on December 21 the House deleted that resolution. Unfortunately, no roll call was taken, making it impossible to identify the Republican defectors. Perhaps there was an agreement to that effect; Republican moderates may have demanded anonymity as a price for breaking ranks. On every other ballot that day the names were recorded in the *Journal.*

Federalists then focused on some of Madison's more extreme phrases. But a motion to delete a statement that the federal laws subverted the Constitution and transformed the republic "into an absolute, or at best, a mixed monarchy," failed by 68 to 96. Shifting direction, Federalists moved a substitute resolution affirming the right of the people to petition for redress of grievances whenever the government unconstitutionally invaded their rights. This side-stepped the state government and made the question of rights a matter between citizens and federal government, and, phrased as a general principle, it left open the question of the legitimacy of the Alien and Sedition Acts. Republican ranks firmed, and it went down, 60 to 104. The House then approved Taylor's resolutions, 100 to 63.[15] The Republicans who cooperated with the effort to soften Madison's language all came from Tidewater or Valley counties that had substantial Federalist minorities.

In early January Republicans resumed the attack with another set of resolutions, this time criticizing the administration's foreign policy. Responding indirectly to the allegations against Tazewell, they also denied that there were "french sympathizers" in the state who would not fight against France if attacked. The Federalists countered with a declaration of support for the President. This was rejected, 68 to 97, and the Republican set passed, 103 to 58.[16] Six delegates voted in favor of both sets—three were Federalists, two Republicans, and one in the middle. Among the five party adherents, this was their only departure from form. Neither party, in short, could be said to have a consistently "moderate" or "extreme" wing. Deviations were few and random. As in the earlier balloting, the deviants came from politically divided counties.[17]

Routine business occupied the next two weeks, and then on January 22, as the session came to an end, the House took up a lengthy "Address of the General Assembly to the People of the Commonwealth of Virginia." Drafted by Madison, and evidently intended as the opening salvo in the campaign of 1800, the "Address" rehearsed the story of federal encroachment on liberty from Hamilton's fiscal policies to the Sedition law. Not to be outdone, Federalists countered with an "Address from the Minority," which was probably the work of John Marshall. It was an equally lengthy defense of Federalist policies over the decade, including the 1798 legislation.[18] Marshall had privately expressed misgivings about the Alien and Sedition laws, but he had never doubted their legitimacy.[19] Now in the heat of battle he was willing to defend them openly as part of the government's fight against "French influence." In order to retain the confidence of the people, he felt, a government had to protect itself from "falsehood and malicious slander."[20]

The Federalists never asked for a vote on their own report; instead, they moved to postpone the Republican document until March 16. Republicans defeated this, 62 to 79, and then pushed through their own address, 80 to 58. They then proposed that the state print 5,000 copies of the address, together with the resolutions on foreign affairs, the Declaration of Independence, and the Constitution. The governor would be asked to distribute copies in every county court. Federalists tried to eliminate this last provision and failed in a dwindling House, 43 to 81; publication was then agreed to without a roll call.[21]

From the initial fight over Taylor's resolutions to the last squabble over publication, there were ten party roll calls in this session, and all but two delegates voted enough to be identified (table 20.2; agreement threshhold of 75 percent). A comparison with the 1795 tabulation shows the continued erosion of Federalist

TABLE 20.2   VIRGINIA HOUSE OF DELEGATES: PARTIES, 1798

	Federalist	Republican	Middle
Northern Neck	7	12	0
Middle Tidewater	10	21	1
Southside	14	37	2
Piedmont	0	20	0
West	33	16	1
Urban	1	2	0
	65	108	4

strength in the Northern Neck and middle Tidewater. For the first time, Republicans possessed a majority in both regions. Party balance remained essentially unchanged, however, because of Federalist gains in the southwest (and western Southside).[22]

Like the Shenandoah Valley to the north, these counties had a substantial German population. Although the evidence is not as clear as in North Carolina, it seems likely that Virginia Germans were also unhappy with the French and hence with Jeffersonians. Pinckney's treaty with Spain, which helped to pacify the southern frontier, may also have been a factor, though there is no direct evidence for this either. Federalist gains in the western Piedmont and mountains of Virginia and North Carolina were only temporary. After 1800—a year that brought peace with France and the election of Jefferson—Federalist strength evaporated quickly. In the meantime, though, the phenomenon of Mountain Federalism enabled them to survive a while longer.

MARYLAND: "PARTY SPIRIT RAGES"

Maryland's off-year election, like North Carolina's, came on the heels of the congressionl session. But Maryland was closer to the center of action. By the time its electorate went to the polls, patriotic indignation had yielded to concern over Federalist repression. Newspapers that autumn were filled with argument on the Alien and Sedition laws.[23] William Hindman, the most partisan of Federalist congressmen, admitted privately that the Sedition Act, which Republicans in his district labeled "the Gag-law," was extremely unpopular, and he forecast (correctly) his own defeat.[24]

Maryland Republicans had also succeeded in blackening their opponents with the tar of "aristocracy." "At elections of this kind," observed one of McHenry's friends after a tour of the state, "the vote of the Worthless is equal to the most respectable and great pains have been taken to work on them—wherever I went, the Man of Wealth, of information and of good morals, was the supporter of Government and approved its measures."[25] William Hindman, as usual, had the saddest story of all. While dancing with a young lady, he moaned to McHenry, "I trod upon her fan, which has made me very lame ever since & has unfortunately deprived me of the Power of moving among my Constituents, which it seems is essential." His opponent, he noted ruefully, seemed to be "in perpetual motion."[26]

With emotions running high, issues clearly defined, and Republicans appealing to class differences, the contest was the most ferocious in many a year. "Wherever I went," wrote McHenry's roving informant, "the ensuing election for Representatives to Congress seemed to take up the entire thoughts of the People, and party spirit rages every where with great violence."[27] The Baltimore contest was the most bitterly fought of all, not least because it pitted two political opportunists against each other. The incumbent, Samuel Smith, was now firmly in the Republican camp, though he remained on good terms with Maryland Federalists.[28] His opponent, James Winchester, had entered politics as a Republican, but three years in the House of Delegates converted him into a Federalist. "In the Day of *Democratic* Societies," complained one of the party regulars, "Mr. Winchester was not only a member, but a violent one. And when Electors were last chosen to elect a President, he voted and declared himself for Mr. Jefferson, and now he is to be the Supporter of the administration. Let no such man be trusted."[29] Whatever misgivings Federalist stalwarts had, they felt obliged to go with the most popular candidate, for Smith had a strong backing among "the Mechanics and Militia." His organization, complained another Federalist, would "neither Spare pains or Expense to carry their point."[30] Baltimore, moreover, was Republican territory. In 1797 Republicans took from Chasites the city's seats in the assembly, and the county had never been Federalminded.[31] Out of a total of 2,224 votes cast in the district, Smith won by 400.[32]

The Baltimore contest turned on allegations against Smith that he was too pro-French; his valiant struggle against the Sedition Act did not get much publicity.[33] But elsewhere the Federalist legislation apparently had some effect. William Hindman admitted it was the main factor in his defeat, and George Baer, the only other Marylander to favor the Sedition law, had a difficult time getting reelected, despite the predominant Federalism of his upper Potomac district.[34] The upper bay returned to its Republican ways by restoring Gabriel Christie to his seat. In the neighboring district on the upper Eastern Shore Hindman lost to his old rival, Joshua Seney, whom Federalists considered "Gallatin, the Second."[35] When Seney died, just weeks after the election, the voters turned to Joseph H. Nicholson, who had led a solidly Republican Queen Anne's delegation to the assembly the previous year. That Nicholson was related by marriage to Albert Gallatin merely added insult to the Federalists' injury. Federalists Craik and Dennis, both of whom had abstained on the Sedition law, were reelected. Waverer George Dent, who had opposed the Sedition law, was also reelected. The one Republican loss was in the lower Western Shore, where Anne Arundel attorney John Chew Thomas, a perennial Federalist candidate for office, defeated Richard Sprigg. Even so, the Jeffersonians could claim victory. Federalists outnumbered them in the Sixth Congress by only four to three. Dent continued to waver, finally commited himself to Jefferson in 1800, and then moved to Georgia.

Federalists retained their dominant position in the assembly, however, and they seemed determined to capitalize on it. Early in the session (November 26, 1798), they brought forth an address to the President praising him for his conduct of foreign policy. Republicans objected that the motion was out of order, were overruled by the Speaker, appealed to the House, and lost, 23 to 41. Various attempts to soften some of the Federalists' criticism of France failed by similar margins, and the House approved the address, 46 to 20.[36] The following day's agenda included a pair of amendments to the Federal Constitution proposed by the Massachusetts assembly. A reflection of the Federalist xenophobia that had produced the Alien Act, the amendments were designed to erect constitutional barriers against foreign influence. One required Presidents and Vice Presidents to have been residents in the United States at the time of the Declaration of Independence; the other required congressmen to be American citizens for fourteen years prior to their election. Although the latter was clearly directed against Gallatin, the voting did not follow party lines. The 54 to 15 roll call by which the House approved the two revealed more about Maryland's nativism than about its parties.[37]

In December the resolutions written by Jefferson and circulated by the Kentucky legislature reached Annapolis and were referred to a Federalist-dominated committee. The committee decided that the resolutions were "highly improper" and the House agreed, 48 to 14. Republicans suggested that the assembly might at least agree with Kentucky that the Alien and Sedition laws ought to be repealed. This lost, 19 to 46. Republicans then tried to get the House to concede that it at least had the power to comment on the constitutionality of federal statutes. Federalists denied themselves even that.[38]

Then in January the Virginia resolutions arrived, and Federalists apparently decided to meet them head on. A House committee declared that no state government was competent to review federal laws, and it felt that it would be "unwise and impolitic" for Congress to repeal the Alien and Sedition laws during "the present crisis of affairs." The recommendation was approved by 42 to 25—and that was the most strength the Republicans showed in the entire session.[39]

There were eleven of these partisan roll calls during the session, and all but three members voted enough to be identified (table 20.3). Not only was the House almost totally polarized between the parties (96 percent), but over half of the members sided with their party 100 percent of the time. Only one roll call created any significant deviation, and that revealed some division between moderate and extreme Federalists. Before it unanimously approved the address to President Adams, the Senate added some language of its own. One of its amendments accused "the faction opposed to the government of our choice" of being in league with

TABLE 20.3   MARYLAND HOUSE OF DELEGATES:
PARTIES, 1798

	Federalist	Republican	Middle
Eastern Shore	18	7	0
Upper bay	2	8	2
Western Shore	15	3	1
Upper Potomac	12	4	0
Urban	2	2	0
	49	24	3

French agents; another denounced "The destruction of religion and encouragement of loose principles" in the country. By 33 to 35 the House rejected the Senate's belligerence.[40] Voting with the Republicans on this occasion were ten Federalists, all from divided counties. Most of those who sided with the Senate came from the lower Eastern Shore or the upper Potomac.

THE MATURE PARTY SYSTEM: GIRDING FOR BATTLE

"Returns of all the elections have been received," John Marshall wrote the aged ex-President in May 1799. "The Failure of Colo. Hancock & of Major Haymond was unexpected & has reduced us to eight in the legislature of the Union."[41] Marshall loved understatement. What he failed to tell Washington—because Washington well knew—was that the Federalists had actually gained three seats in the House of Representatives. Virginia's total of 6, as against 12 Republicans, was the best they had done since the districts were rearranged in 1793.[42] It does not appear that the XYZ affair had anything to do with the revival, however. Even at the height of the uproar Federalists did not benefit in Maryland and North Carolina, and by the time Virginia held its election in 1799 popular indignation against France had largely subsided. Federalists won seats because they fielded their most prominent leaders— Marshall himself, Henry Lee, and Leven Powell. All ran in closely divided districts (Richmond and the Northern Neck) where their personal prestige was sufficient to attract the few votes needed for victory. Federalists did win one district in the Southside, due perhaps to Patrick Henry's conversion, but this was counterbalanced by the loss of the northwest (Machir retired, and Clarksburg Republican George Jackson recovered the seat he had held in the Fourth Congress). Indeed, with Hancock's failure to recover the seat he had lost to a Republican two years before, Federalists were left with only one western district. The personal triumph of Marshall and Henry Lee only obscured the continued erosion of Federalist strength.

"In the state elections," Marshall continued in a more candid vein, "very considerable changes have been made. There are from fifty to sixty new members. Unfortunately the strength of parties is not materially varied. The opposition maintains its majority in the house of Delegates. The consequence must be an antifederal Senator & Governor." Although Marshall exaggerated the amount of change (there were actually 82 "new" members, 46 percent of the House, about average for the decade),[43] this was the first time anyone sought to gauge the effect of electoral turnover, and Marshall was correct in his conclusion that relative party strength was unchanged. The accuracy of Marshall's summary indicates that electoral contests in nearly every county turned on party, that candidates felt obliged to commit themselves on matters of national policy.

Partly accounting for the turnover was the effort of both parties to pack the assembly with prominent personages. The cream of Federalist leadership stood for Congress, but they did persuade aging Patrick Henry to emerge from retirement. He did so by publicly endorsing Marshall for Congress and standing a poll for the House of Delegates himself. He won, after a memorable forensic duel with a brash young Republican candidate for Congress, John Randolph of Roanoke, but then died in June before he could take his seat.[44] Republicans were more fortunate, placing Madison, Giles, and John Taylor in the assembly. Madison even got some unsolicited support from his old enemy French Strother. Parties were moving into battle formation.

The assembly elections of 1799 summoned prodigious efforts in Maryland and North Carolina, as well. In Frederick, Maryland, a town with a history of political innovations, the newspaper carried a notice signed "Hundreds" which advocated a ticket of "Federal characters" for the House of Delegates. Not since 1790 had assembly candidates associated with each other on "tickets" with newspapers publicizing party labels. The notice pointed out that it was important to prevent an "antifederal" victory in the assembly because of the approaching Presidential election. Next to the name of each candidate was listed his town of residence. Only one lived in Frederick Town; the rest came from other parts of the county.[45] Frederick Federalists overlooked nothing.

Frederick Republicans had a ticket of their own, the same one essentially that they had been nominating since 1797. In a transparent bid for more popular support, the minority party concentrated on the suffrage reform law, which had failed in the previous session. One newspaper contributor astutely pointed out that the county's Federalist delegation had voted in favor of the law on the final roll call only to keep its record respectable. In reality, it had resisted change throughout the debate. Another writer recommended that voters select men committed to reform—the Republican ticket.[46] Republicans lost again, but they had found a hot issue. The following year they captured the county—and kept it—with the same slate of men.

In North Carolina, where newspapers were scarcer, other devices for securing proper assemblymen were used. In western Rowan, militia companies met to nominate candidates for both Senate and House of Commons. The avowed purpose was "to promote unity," and since their slate was Republican it was obviously party unity they had in mind.[47] This may have been a response to John Steele's success in finding Federalist votes in the Salisbury area; organizational efforts were often most intense in divided counties.

Halifax in the Roanoke Valley, home of Willie Jones, had been Federalist in recent years, due, no doubt, to the influence of William R. Davie, but Republicans were determined to recover it in 1799. Wood Jones Hamlin, a political novice, had "run" for the seat the previous year. But the fact that he used that word, instead of the more traditional, and more gentlemanly, concept of "standing," suggested that a new day was at hand. A friend even offered to come over from neighboring Warren County to help in his "electioneering," but Jones lost anyway. In 1799 he was back and won, with the help of Thomas Person himself. Wrote the aging general, "If you know of any Genl. meeting of the people in the upper part of Halifax County in the Course of the Latter part of this week, Inform me, I'll try to attend it. I wish you success in your election."[48] The rural majority in North Carolina still lacked election machinery, but at least it was beginning to cooperate across county lines. And, like the Virginians, it was rolling out the big guns.

Since the mid-1780s party leaders had scanned electoral results and estimated the numbers they could count on in the assembly. By the end of the 1790s, the candidates' commitments at election time gave leaders more reliable information, and there is good reason to think that they used it to hold their ranks in line on House roll calls. If the parties had not yet adopted the English usage of "whips," they had all the apparatus for the office. In the papers of Samuel Chase, for instance, there is a list of men under the heading "House of Delegates, 1798," and they are divided into "Federal" (51 names) and "Democratic" (30 names).[49] Every single member of the House was included; no one was set down as "unknown" or "irregular." And the list must have been drafted on the basis of electoral commitments because it included three men who did not participate enough to be identified on the basis of voting and three men who did not show up at all. The list, moreover, was extremely accurate in its party assignments. The only error was in the Anne Arundel delegation (a county whose representatives in the past were notorious for saying one thing and doing another), where it listed two Federalists (one of them new) as Republicans.[50] The delegates were listed not alphabetically or geographically but in the order in which they voted in House roll calls.[51] It was clearly intended as a check on behavior. Whether it was actually used by someone responsible for party discipline, or whether the rigidity of party lines in Maryland was the result of electoral commitments, is impossible to say. Perhaps it was some of both.

Samuel Chase's memorandum was not the only list being drawn up for party purposes that winter. In Washington's papers are various lists of applicants seeking commissions in the army. Though undated, they were obviously drafted in late 1798 or early 1799 when Washington, having been brought out of retirement, was trying to fill the ranks of the provisional army authorized by Congress. The lists were apparently part of the screening process, for they contained comments concerning the capabilities of various applicants as well as recommendations from congressmen and government officials. On the list of Marylanders and Virginians Washington himself made notations about persons with whom he was acquainted. His comment on John B. Armistead of Loudoun is

"Fed." Of William Armistead he wrote "doubt his politics." James Baytop of Gloucester came "recommended by Evans, Carrington, & Heth," and William Bentley of Powhatan was considered "a friend of order & Constitution." Concerning the Maryland applicant Bradley Beans, Washington wrote, "his brother is a Fed," and Ninian Pinkney was listed as "brother of the commissioner," a reference to Chasite Federalist William Pinkney. Washington did not personally assess applicants from other states, but the informants from whom he solicited recommendations—usually Federalist congressmen—did not hesitate to do so.[52]

Washington's lists, in short, were not quality screens at all. It was a political purge—the only such in the history of the American armed forces. Washington wanted only loyal Federalists behind him in the field if the French ever did attack. Washington, to be sure, had always made a habit of appointing only Federalists to office (his only known departure was sending Monroe to France), but never before had he been this systematic. Behind it, of course, was the diplomatic crisis, the rising tensions between the parties, and the Federalist suspicion that Republicans were French agents. "None but decidedly federal men ought to be appointed to office in the present critical & alarming state of our affairs," wrote Congressman Hindman to McHenry. The Marylander thought that opponents of the administration ought to be proscribed, as the Loyalists were in the Revolution.[53]

Republicans were equally willing to proscribe their opponents, and, at least in private, they were a bit more candid about the reasons. "It really seems to me," John Taylor of Caroline confessed, "that no possible mode exists for obtaining and retaining the presidency, but by becoming the creature of party."[54] Deprived of influence in federal affairs, Republican leaders concentrated on the one strategic political base they did have—Virginia. The first target was the governorship, a post hitherto ignored by the parties, and held since 1796 by a nonpartisan, General James Wood. Previously scorned for its weakness, the position took on new significance when congressional repression and assembly defiance created a confrontation between state and federal governments. "A decided character at the head of the government," Taylor wrote Jefferson, "is of immense importance by the influence it will have upon public opinion. Even Wood has done great service to one side and inflicted correspondent injury to the other. To this influence is also attached many essential powers, . . . besides the important one of commanding the militia. I have therefore always thought that the republicans have been too inattentive to the consequences of having a tory first magistrate & military commander of the state."[55] A Republican senator put it more bluntly when he asked James Monroe to make himself available because a "truely Republican Executive" would provide "a sure foundation for the Election of the next President."[56]

By the time the session opened plans for a party purge extended far beyond the governorship. The first victim was John Stuart, Clerk of the House of Delegates. A year earlier Stuart had helped to found a new Richmond paper, the *Virginia Federalist,* intended as a party oracle after Augustine Davis's *Virginia Gazette and General Advertiser* switched to the Republicans.[57] William Wirt, a young lawyer from Charlottesville, replaced Stuart, and Republicans then turned on the Speaker, John Wise, a respected Federalist from the Eastern Shore who had held the office since 1794. Not since the Harrison-Tyler contests of the early 1780s had the Speakership been an object of concern. In fact, the Republican majority had named a Federalist to the post every year since 1789. Conceivably, this might have been a cynical means of depriving the Federalists of a vote, but more likely it was done in a spirit of gentlemanly bipartisanship. The spirit began to evaporate in 1798 when some Republicans put up Wilson Cary Nicholas for the post. Wise was reelected anyway, to the dismay of Jefferson, who "roundly abused those of his followers who had forgotten their party allegiance at such a time."[58]

Prodded by Jefferson, Republicans were ready to make a fight of it in 1799. They nominated Larkin Smith to oppose Wise, and when Federalists pointed out that Wise had served long and well, Republicans reminded them that the national administration never tolerated its opponents in office. Smith won by 83 to 55, a margin that reflected relative party strength, though, as usual in such elections, the roll call was not recorded.[59]

The next item of business was to fill the Senate seat of Henry Tazewell, who had died in Philadelphia the previous winter. This post had always been the province of the majority, and when

Republicans nominated Wilson Cary Nicholas, Federalists did not bother to contest him. The governorship was another matter, however, and when Republicans, after considerable preparation, nominated Monroe, Federalists reacted angrily. Monroe had the reputation of being an intense partisan, and after Washington recalled him from Paris, he was suspected of being a French agent. Resurrecting the tactic they had used against Tazewell the year before, Federalists asked that the election be postponed until the assembly could investigate allegations concerning Monroe's conduct while ambassador to France. This was denied, and Monroe then swamped the Federalist candidate, James Breckinridge, by a two-to-one majority.[60]

By this time party feelings were running so high that Republicans even deserted tradition and made a partisan issue out of a disputed election. Ohio County in the far northwest had long been closely divided between the parties, and in 1799 it sent a split delegation to the House, with two losing Republicans contesting the results. The committee on privileges and elections, after investigating, recommended seating the two Federalist candidates. Committee reports of this sort normally received routine acceptance, but this time a motion to reject the recommendation and seat the two Republicans passed by 82 to 48.[61]

The approaching Presidential contest forced a tightening of party discipline in all three states, but no one went to the lengths of the Virginians. By 1800 their state government had been turned into a party fortress, its innards purified for a lengthy siege, its parapets manned. The remaining task was to win friends abroad. Republican leaders recognized that a simple critique of the Alien and Sedition laws was not sufficient. They had to mount an attack on the entire Federalist system. In so doing, they created what amounted to the first national party platform.

THE MATURE PARTY SYSTEM:
REPUBLICAN PLATFORM OF 1800

When the purge of offices was done, Madison rose in the House of Delegates to move the appointment of a committee to consider the replies from other states to the 1798 resolutions on the Alien and Sedition laws. Speaker Smith loaded it with Republicans, headed by Giles and Taylor. "We have but two representatives out of the seven," complained one Federalist.[62] In early January the committee brought forth a report and a series of resolutions. The *Virginia Report,* actually written by Madison, has been accurately described as "the most careful and knowledgeable analysis of federal-state relations to appear up to that time."[63] Madison clarified his theory of constitutional compact and sought to answer Federalist criticism that state interposition would create confrontation and anarchy. Specially elected popular assemblies, Madison explained, and not state legislatures, were the proper bodies to review federal laws. Such agencies represented the constituent power of the people, the sovereign power that the people had exercised in creating government itself. The resolutions of 1798, though justified, were mere expressions of opinion by the assembly, not acts of nullification. They were intended only to excite reflection and evoke opinions.

Thus Madison sought to convert what some had considered a challenge to Federalist usurpation into a mere device for mobilizing opinion. The resolutions of 1798 were an ideological platform, Madison was now saying, not a sword of battle. Federalists, recognizing that the *Report* would blunt northern criticism of the resolutions and provide Republicans with a common theoretical ground, sought to bury it. Since the *Report* itself admitted that the assembly was not the proper agency for protest, they moved that it was inexpedient to consider any more resolutions. Republicans countered with a general statement supporting the committee's stand and reaffirming the resolutions of 1798. The Federalist motion failed, 57 to 98, the Republican one passed, 100 to 60, and the *Report* was then adopted by a voice vote.[64]

The House then turned to the committee's resolutions, which, in some respects, were even more important. These appear to have originated with John Beckley, the Virginian who was clerk of the federal House of Representatives and primary link in the national party organization. Early in the session Beckley sent from Philadelphia a list of recommendations. In addition to reaffirming its opposition to the Alien and Sedition laws, he wanted the assembly to protest the increases in the standing army and the taxes they necessitated, and to resist any notion that the common law of England was operative in the United States.[65] It was clearly an effort to broaden the basis of the assault on Federalism. Standing armies were an ancient bogey, and the accusation of militarism was one of the most effective propaganda weapons the Republicans had. If any exceeded its potential, it was the charge that the Federalists were ruining the people with an intolerable tax burden. The question of the common law, a sore point in Virginia since Iredell's misuse of a grand jury, also involved national pride and Anglophobia. The resolutions of the Giles committee, which the House took up on January 10, stressed precisely the same points. They amounted to a party platform in everything but name.[66]

Hopelessly outmanned, the Federalists fought a rearguard action. On the resolution favoring a reduction in the army, they suggested a proviso that it be delayed until the French crisis was ended. The resolution favoring a reduction in the navy carried a promise that the money saved would permit a reduction in taxes. This golden benefit Federalists sought to delete. Each effort lost by nearly identical votes, and Giles's resolutions, formulated as instructions to Virginia's congressmen, were approved, 102 to 49.[67]

In a curious switch, Federalists voiced approval of the resolution on the common law, a signal of defeat that Republicans rubbed in by demanding that the names be recorded in the 149 to 0 roll call. The Senate, which Madison had earlier feared might be evenly divided, decided that if the Federalists could support the resolution, Giles's language was too vague. It rectified the error, making it clear that the federal courts were not to apply common law principles, and passed the resolutions by 15 to 6. The Senate modification went through the House by a party vote, 82 to 40.[68]

SHOWDOWN: SETTING THE RULES

When the propaganda barrage subsided, Republicans turned to the mundane but possibly more important task of setting the election rules to their advantage. Despite their preponderance in the state, Republicans were not certain they could sweep all the state's electoral districts. Federalists, though a minority statewide, were concentrated in certain areas, a circumstance that enabled them to maintain a foothold in the state's congressional delegation. In 1796 the Northern Neck had returned a Federalist Presidential elector, who combined with North Carolina's lone Federalist to give the election to Adams over Jefferson. If the 1800 contest were equally close, it was critical that Republicans insure themselves all of Virginia's electoral votes. This meant shifting from a system of choosing electors by districts to a winner-take-all system under which the candidate with a majority of the popular votes received all 21 of the state's electoral votes.[69]

Republicans brought in their rules change as soon as Giles's recommendations were approved in mid-January. Federalists, objecting that the change was so "radical" that the electorate needed time to consider it, moved to postpone the bill to the next session. The proposal seemed reasonable, even to a number of Republicans, and the party ranks broke. The motion was voted down by a narrow 72 to 79. Republicans were obviously embarrassed, especially since the new scheme so clearly ran counter to the ringing defense of popular rights and regional minorities in the Madison *Report*. Federalists quickly pointed out that the change effectively disfranchised a third of the state's voters. With 5 embarrassed Republicans abstaining and 15 siding with the Federalists, the electoral bill squeaked through, 78 to 73.[70] Nearly all the Republican mavericks were from counties with substantial Federalist minorities. "The plan of a Genl. Ticket," Madison explained to Jefferson, "was so novel that a great no. who wished it shrunk from the vote, and others apprehending that their Const[ituents] would be still more startled at it voted agst. it." But, he added hopefully, "As the avowed object of it is to give Virga. *fair play,* I think . . . it will . . . become popular."[71]

"Fair play" was hardly the issue, as Maryland Republicans would have been the first to testify. Maryland's Federalists, rapidly losing their grip on the state, expected to lose several electoral districts, but they were afraid to switch to a statewide system lest Republicans sweep it all. So they used Virginia's example as an excuse to put selection of electors in the hands of the assembly.[72] This would have required summoning a special session of the legislature in the spring of 1800 to change the law, and Governor Benjamin Ogle, never a strong party man,[73] refused to issue so transparent a summons. Taking to the newspapers, Federalists sniped away at the state's electoral law through the summer, but it did no good.[74] Republicans even captured the lower house in the next assembly, though the old Senate (elected in 1796) still had another year to run.[75]

PARTY TRIUMPH: 1800

On January 21, 1800, the day on which Virginia's general ticket became law, 93 Republicans from the assembly met with party leaders in Richmond to arrange an electoral slate. Recognizing the importance of statewide appeal, they headed it with the most respected names they could find—George Wythe, Edmund Pendleton, and Madison. The rest were men with substantial prestige in their own localities, including Archibald Stuart, William H. Cabell, William Branch Giles, Joseph Jones, John Page, and Thomas Newton.[76] Two days later, with the assembly still in session, Republicans met again to choose a standing committee to head the party organization throughout the state. Its chief function was to correspond with county committees and to see to the distribution of the ticket. The committee was headed by Richmond attorney Philip Norborne Nicholas, and the members all lived in the vicinity of the capital, where they could readily communicate with one another. Over the years the group earned the nickname "Richmond Junto," a respectful salute to their organizational skill.[77]

Federalists met in early February, shortly after the legislative session ended, and appointed a committee to draw up their ticket. Headed by William Austin, a political unknown,[78] the committee labored through the spring to find suitable candidates for the electoral college. At last in May, after the spring assembly elections had run their course (with big losses for the Federalists), the committee came up with a collection of names disingenuously styled "The American Republican Ticket."[79] The disguise itself was testimony to the distance the party had sunk in popular repute. Virginia's Federalist party was dead. What survived the election of 1800 was an unorganized handful of assemblymen, whose Federalist voting habits originated more from western sectionalism and ethnic interests than party ideals.

The roster of names on the ticket also revealed Federalist weakness. John Marshall, the only party leader of statewide repute, had been summoned to Philadelphia earlier in May to serve as Secretary of State. John Wise, James Breckinridge, and George K. Taylor had been prominent in assembly debates and were respected in their localities, but the rest of the ticket consisted of comparative unknowns. Criticizing the Republicans for loading their ticket with "imposing names," Austin sought to make a virtue of the Federalists' obscurity. Since his candidates did not hold positions in the state government, he pled, they would be less likely to "regard the rival authorities of the union with a jealousy." The argument was as weak as his ticket.

Even so, Republicans were taking no chances. Employing the newly founded Republican sheet, the *Virginia Argus,* the Richmond committee published at regular intervals a declaration reminding voters that the electoral slates were only party proxies— the real contest was between Jefferson and Adams. Afraid that voters might be confused by the new electoral system, committee chairman Nicholas in August sent a directive to the county committees asking them to print and circulate sample tickets among the freeholders. In September Governor Monroe demonstrated the value of a partisan executive by naming commissioners in each county to supervise the election; in most cases the supervisors were the same men who staffed the Republican county committees.[80] No stone was left unturned. Congressman John Dawson even wrote to Philadelphia for German newspapers of Republican complexion, explaining to Tench Coxe, "In the upper part of this district there are some Germans, & I think it doubtful how they will vote. I will therefore thank you to lend me some newspapers in that language . . . —they may do some good."[81]

Republicans also seemed to have the initiative in Maryland. Federalist motions to have the choice of Presidential elector given to the legislature was an admission of their failing popularity, and Republicans were quick to capitalize. Signing themselves with such democratic pseudonyms as "Practical Mechanic," they excoriated the Federalists for trying to deprive the people of a voice in the government, linking it with the Federalists' suppression of free speech and failure to back suffrage reform.[82] When former House Speaker James Carroll indiscreetly declared that he would willingly risk his seat for a chance to change the electoral law, Robert Smith tried to track down the remark and obtain witnesses. Publication, he thought, would not only prevent Carroll's reelection, but "will no doubt secure the Election of the whole Republican Ticket in Balt[imore]. Nay more, it will greatly influence the Election of every County in the State."[83]

The Presidential election quickly became entangled with the Maryland assembly contests because the two elections were held only a month apart.[84] Candidates for the electoral college made clear their preferences as they had in 1796, but this time so did aspirants for the assembly. Because there was still a possibility that a Federalist assembly could overturn the election results in its winter session before the electoral college met, Republicans focused on the election law in assembly contests. Some Federalist candidates admitted that they wished for a change in the electoral law to improve Adams's chances, while others pledged to resist any change.[85] When the contest ended, newspapers for the first time ever printed the results of assembly contests under party labels.[86]

In New York, Hamilton revived his 1796 plot to substitute a Pinckney (Charles C. this time, rather than Thomas) for Adams at the head of the Federalist ticket, but the intrigue won little support in the Chesapeake and had no apparent effect on the election. McHenry, summarily dismissed by Adams from the War Department in May, felt the party had no choice but to adhere to "the chief," and he berated Hamilton for making public the split in the party.[87] Only Charles Carroll and Robert Goodloe Harper (a fierce Federalist newly moved from South Carolina and soon to become Carroll's son-in-law) endorsed Hamilton's scheme; the rest of the party stuck with Adams.[88] Across the Potomac, Virginia leaders also begged for party unity.[89] There is no evidence that the split between Hamilton and Adams had any effect on the outcome of the election in Maryland. Federalists worked as hard for their candidate as ever, and, except for McHenry, a chronic pessimist, they expected to win.[90] Luther Martin confidently predicted that they would carry 6 of the state's 10 electoral districts, and in Philadelphia Republican manager John Beckley was inclined to agree.[91]

Everyone was a bit surprised, then, when the state split evenly, 5 to 5. The reason is that the Republicans finally consolidated gains that they had been making piecemeal for some years. They swept Anne Arundel,[92] recovered Baltimore, which had gone Federalist in 1799, and held the two districts near the top of the bay. Republicans also captured the western district by winning in Frederick and Washington counties, leaving only Allegany in Federalist hands.[93] Federalists retained control of the lower Potomac, the lower Western Shore, and the Eastern Shore south of Queen Anne's.

The most dramatic Republican successes, in Baltimore and in the upper Potomac, probably stemmed from opposition to the alien laws among German and Irish voters. Republican backing for suffrage reform and open appeals to mechanics and artisans also had some effect. This was most apparent in Baltimore where newspapers for the first time reported the vote by wards. The candidates for Presidential elector there were Gabriel Duvall and Jeremiah Townley Chase. Both were men of means; neither was a resident of the city. Republican Duvall swept every ward in the city. Chase made a showing (losing by 285 to 148) only in the central first ward, where most of the city's merchants resided. The Republican did best in the remote wards (winning by margins of five or ten to one) where the mechanics and artisans lived.[94] The results in Georgetown, long regarded as a Federalist stronghold, were similar. In the assembly contest (the only one for which results were reported), the Federalist slate carried the city by a mere twenty votes (their candidates ranged from 178 to 182 votes, as against 158 to 164 for the Republicans). Federalists kept their stranglehold on the county (1,171 for their leading vote-getter versus 565 for the leading

Republican).[95] Republican gains in the city, whose merchants were notoriously Federalist, appear to reflect a political awakening among the artisans.

No such awakening was evident in Virginia, where neither party had shown much interest in reform. The three boroughs[96] were evenly divided, as they had been for years. Jefferson carried Williamsburg by one vote, Richmond by seven, and lost Norfolk by seven. In the three together Jefferson won by 215 to 214. The light turnout itself suggests that substantial numbers of artisans were disfranchised by Virginia's property requirements. On the other hand, Federalist complaints, voiced during the debates on the resolutions of 1798, that the west was underrepresented were not substantiated by the election. There were some Tidewater counties with few voters (Warwick with 59 and York with 101, both Republican), but the smallest turnouts were in the west, possibly because of large distances and poor facilities. In the far southwest Russell County mustered only 51 voters and Lee a mere 35. These two were Republican, as was the most populous county west of the Blue Ridge, Frederick (738 voters).

The switch to a statewide system meant that every vote was important, and for the first time the popular vote was carefully recorded for every county in the state.[97] This permits an analysis of Virginia voting behavior not possible for earlier elections. The use of party tickets, moreover, virtually eliminated the role of electoral candidates. The results were simply recorded as votes for Jefferson or Adams. Jefferson won the state by 21,311 votes to 6,024 for Adams. The margin was somewhat larger than the two-to-one ratio by which Republicans controlled the assembly, but it reflected the rapid decline in Federalist fortunes. In the spring 1801 elections Federalists were reduced to fewer than 30 in the House of Delegates, and they remained at about that level until the party disappeared altogether after the War of 1812.

Despite Federalist losses, the regional pattern of voting was very similar to the patterns that had persisted in the assembly since the 1780s.[98] The core of Jefferson's strength was in the central Piedmont, the central Southside, and the far southwest. Six counties in this area cast no votes at all for Adams, and in all but five

Jefferson's margin was better than ten to one.[99] The others he won by about three to one. This was precisely the area that had been debtor and Antifederalist in the 1780s. As if to remind Madison of that fact, the aged rebel Arthur Campbell sent his congratulations from the Holston country: "I mean the joy is general among the Farmers and Laborers of all Classes—Some Merchants and the monied interest with the Bigots and fanatics in religious matters may have their fears."[100]

Adams led in only five counties—the Eastern Shore (Accomac and Northampton), which gave him his largest margin, 427 to 50, Leven Powell's Loudoun and Henry Lee's Westmoreland in the Northern Neck, Augusta in the Valley, and Hampshire and Hardy on the South Branch of the Potomac. The South Branch was the only regional entity that Adams carried (501 to 493), and his strength there dwindled in the remote parts of the watershed around the warm springs. Similarly, Federalist strength in the Northern Neck was concentrated around the nation's capital; the more remote lower counties had long since swung Republican. In the region as a whole Jefferson's majority was 1,437 to 802. Except for Augusta, the Shenandoah Valley had also gone into the Republican camp. Jefferson's margin there was 3,107 to 1,589. Compared to the rest of the state, Federalist minorities in those areas were quite substantial; they were the remnants of a sometime majority.

In the remainder of the state the two parties had been evenly balanced in the early 1790s; in 1800 they were Republican by three or four to one:

	Jefferson	Adams
Middle Tidewater (Rappahannock to York rivers)	1,741	432
Middle Tidewater (York to James rivers)	829	222
Southeast (Norfolk vicinity)	1,094	352
Northeast (Monongahela and Ohio valleys)	832	364
Northern Piedmont (Fauquier-Culpeper)	680	231

Federalist strength had withered over the decade, but it did so evenly. Federalists had lost the decade-long propaganda war; they were out-generaled and less organized. But the regional variations that had given rise to the first parties still had meaning.

The one state in the union where the Federalists did better than they had any right to expect was North Carolina. Tarheel Republicans had good cause to regret that they did not follow Virginia's example in changing the district law. The state that had given only one electoral vote to John Adams in three previous elections now gave him four, with Jefferson and Burr winning the other eight. One of the Federalist votes came from the Pamlico region; the other three represented the far western Piedmont. Popular votes are not available for the Presidential contest, but the congressional election earlier in the summer produced almost the same result—four Federalists and six Republicans. All four of the Federalists were town lawyers—Grove of Fayetteville, William H. Hill of Wilmington, John Stanly of New Bern, and Archibald Henderson of Salisbury.[101] The Federalist victories apparently stemmed from a fortuitous combination of circumstances, rather than a party revival. All four lasted only one term, and from 1802 on the state's congressional delegation was solidly Republican.[102]

John Stanly defeated Richard D. Spaight in a contest that resulted in a duel and Spaight's death. But the most interesting contest was in the western Piedmont, the Yadkin and Catawba river valleys. There Federalist Henderson opposed the old debtor leader, Matthew Lock, who had held the seat since 1793. A third candidate, Mussendine Matthews, was a political cipher. In his last appearance in the assembly he voted Republican, but though reelected annually, he had not put in an appearance since 1795. Incumbent Lock came in third, winning only one county, Carbarrus, the smallest in the district. Matthews took his home county, Iredell, and Henderson won the rest. Henderson's victory margin (1,922 votes to 845 for Lock) came mostly from the counties in the Yadkin Valley, Rowan and Montgomery. The Catawba Valley to the west (Iredell, Cabarrus, and Mecklenburg counties) was about evenly divided.[103] Anti-French feeling among Germans and Scots, mixed perhaps with some western sectionalism, continued to benefit the Federalists. Unfortunately, population statistics are not precise enough to account for the variation between the Catawba and Yadkin valleys. Perhaps the Federalists' military measures distressed the pietist element, Dunkards and Quakers. In any case, the

Yadkin Valley remained a pocket of Federalism until the European war ended (Federalist Joseph Pearson represented the district in Congress from 1809 to 1815).

EPILOGUE: REPUBLICANS CAPTURE MARYLAND, 1801

In 1800 Maryland Republicans at last drew even with their opponents. The 5 to 5 split in the state's electoral vote paralleled the even balance of parties in the House of Delegates that winter. Federalists held fast in the Senate, however, until a new set of Senate electors was chosen in 1801. Charles Carroll retired from politics that year, prophesying anarchy and atheism from Jefferson's rule, and his departure was symbolic. Electors for the Sixth Senate swept the upper house clean, giving the Republicans a two-to-one majority. The 1801 election also gave the Republicans firm control of the House of Delegates, and when the assembly met in November the new majority was prepared to extend its grip over the entire governmental apparatus, just as the Virginians had done three years before.

The first order of business was the governorship, long a Federalist province. Republicans offered it to one of the earliest of their leaders, John F. Mercer. After a brief retirement following his congressional service, Mercer had returned to the assembly in 1800 and instantly became embroiled in a newspaper controversy with Robert Goodloe Harper. Challenged to a duel, he fled to his Stafford, Virginia, estate. Republican leaders interceded in his behalf, and after a lengthy exchange of letters Mercer issued an apology that enabled him to return to Annapolis to take his seat in the House.[104] Mercer's conduct was anything but noble, but the Republican majority could afford to be generous. It even reelected him the following year.

The next item was the Senate seat held by William Hindman. When James Lloyd resigned from the Senate the previous year, Hindman had been chosen to fill the final three months of his term. Federalists wanted to elect Hindman to the full six-year term that began in March 1801, but Republicans blocked it, obviously expecting to win control of the assembly later in the year. The most they would concede was a temporary appointment of Hindman until the assembly could agree on a successor.[105] The stratagem was novel, but it worked. The seat was vacant when the Republican majority gathered in Annapolis in November. The Republicans' candidate was Robert Wright, who had been elected to Congress from the upper counties in 1799; Federalists named William Winder of Somerset. With the two houses balloting jointly, Wright won by 60 to 26, a measure of the new order.[106]

Shortly thereafter a Republican-dominated House committee brought in a proposal to change public printers. The committee felt that the *Maryland Gazette,* which had been printing official proclamations and assembly proceedings for a decade, did not have adequate circulation. The committee proposed to shift the public business to another paper, *The American,* and pay an additional subsidy to printer Frederick Green to publish assembly proceedings in pamphlet form. There was no need to mention the fact that the proposal involved a shift from a Federalist paper to a Republican one. That was completely understood, and the reference to declining circulation was just salt in the wound. After wrangling for a week over the amount of the subsidy to be paid the new favorites, the House passed the resolution, 39 to 31. A few weeks later, the battle was rejoined when the civil list came before the House. The exact amount to be paid the public printer occasioned another series of ballots before the sum of $1,000 was agreed upon and the bill passed, 50 to 20.[107] In all, the controversy generated eleven roll call ballots, a number of them on tactical motions of uncertain import.[108] Party ranks held firm through every procedural twist, a good indication that there were well-developed lines of communication between leaders and rear benches. Only 5 delegates failed to side with a party at least 75 percent of the time, and 60 of the 80 in attendance voted their party 100 percent of the time. The regional distribution, given in table 20.4, shows the Republicans extending their hold on the northern Eastern Shore and upper Potomac.

With the governmental machinery safely under control, Republicans returned to their long-promised goal of electoral reform. In 1799 the assembly had approved a law abolishing the

TABLE 20.4   MARYLAND HOUSE OF DELEGATES:
PARTIES, 1801

	Federalists	Republicans	Middle
Eastern Shore	10	13	2
Upper bay	0	12	0
Western Shore	10	8	3
Upper Potomac	6	10	0
Urban	2	2	0
	28	45	5

property qualification for voting, but such changes in the Constitution required the approval of two successive legislatures. The following year Federalists, stung by Republican jibes in the Presidential campaign, joined in a vote reaffirming the amendment to the Constitution. But this time the Senate balked. In a message that might well have been drafted by Charles Carroll, the Senate adopted the classic argument that voting was a privilege, not a right, a privilege to be exercised only by those who possessed a stake in society. Those without property lacked responsibility and were more susceptible to the promises of demagogues.[109]

The Senate's intransigence, which reflected more the conservatism of the upper house than Federalist policy, forced the assembly to start over in 1801. Even with the wholesale turnover in the Senate, House Republicans were not confident. The upper house was inherently a more conservative body, and Republicans, in any case, did not have firm control. Several of them failed to appear for the session, and early in the session Federalists were able to cause difficulties about the change in official printers. Taking no chances, House Republicans preceded their assault on the property qualification with a bill providing for popular election of the Senate. This passed by a party vote of 42 to 27. Faced with this threat, the Senate collapsed and shouted through the suffrage reform. The House, after inserting a provision for secret ballots by party vote, approved the constitutional change, 48 to 14.[110] The following year both houses finally confirmed the amendment, the Senate this time unanimously.

Republicans were far from finished. They still had a host of

TABLE 20.5 MARYLAND HOUSE OF DELEGATES, 1801: CLUSTER-BLOC MATRIX (SHOWING REPUBLICAN PARTY)

	MART NNTA	ORRE LLCR	THOM ASKE	MOFF ITCE	DOUG SJCR	WOOD PRPG	MILL RWCE	LOVE THBA	LEMM ONBA	LYTL EJHA	MASO NTCR	DICK SNBT
MARTNNTA	—	100	96	96	93	93	93	92	92	92	92	89
ORRELLCR	100	—	94	98	85		82	86	82	92	84	82
THOMASKE	98	94	—	94	83	88	94	92	92	81	81	89
MOFFITCE	98	98	94	—			88	86	90		84	84
DOUGSJCR	93	95	83		—						84	
WOODPRPG	93		86			—	85	94			87	
MILLRWCE	93	82	94	88		85	—	81	81		80	80
LOVETHBA	92	86	92	86		84	81	—	85	95	92	81
LEMMONBA	92	92	92	90			81		—	91	91	91
LYTLEJHA	92	92	81				84	95	91	—		88
MASONTCR	92	84	91	84	84	87	80	92	91		—	
DICKSNBT	88	82	89	84			80	89	91	89	82	—
MONTGYHA	89	82	91	90				91	89	89	83	93
FORWODHA	88		88	85		86	83	97	98	93	82	90
TELLOTCR	88	86	88	80			82	97		90	83	
ROSEWMTA	88	81			83						83	
TOMLNBAL	85	87	83	86				81	89		80	83
SMITHRWA	85	82	88	91				86	82			85
LOWREYQA	85		80	82		82		82			85	80
VNHORNPG	85	80	84	84		83	80	82	84	80	83	81
SHRIVRFR	85	82	84			80	80	89			82	84
HOLLNDQA	84		82	83		85	87	80	81		88	81
BURGSSQA	83		85			81	81	82	85			84
CELLARWA	81		83	83			84	99	98			88
STURTAKE		92	100	93	89	89	83	99	92	85	96	92
STNSBYBA		85	94	87		82	90	95	98	82	87	86
DAVISEHA		84	92	84	81	81	83	94				
HANSNBKE		82	84								82	
ANGIERKE		81									88	
MOORENBA			93	85			92	95	97	84		95
BOWIERPG			89	86		87		85	80	80		81
HAWKNTFR			88	82		82	85	87	87		87	85
SCOTTJBT			86	85								
CARRSLPG			81									
KEMPHYFR						81						
CHAPMNCH												
HOLBRKSO												
JONESSCH												
HYLNDJSO												
MPHERWCH												
QUYNNAAN												
ANDERSDO												

TABLE 20.5 MARYLAND 1801 MATRIX (REPUBLICAN PARTY) *continued*

	MONT GYHA	FORW ODHA	TILL OTCR	ROSE WMTA	TOML NBAL	SMIT HRWA	LOWR BYQA	VNHO RNPG	SHRI VRFR	HOLL NDQA	BURG SSQA	CELL ARWA
MARTNNTA	89		88	88	85	85	85	85	85	84	83	81
ORRELLCR	82	89	86	81	87	82	80	80	82	82	85	
THOMASKE	91	86	88		83	86	82	84	84	83		83
MOFFITCE	90	85	80		86	91		84				88
DOUGSJCR												
WOODPRPG		86		83			88	83	80			84
MILLRWCE	97	83	82					82	80	85	81	82
LOVETHBA	88	97			81	86	82	82	89	87	81	85
LEMMONBA		90				80	82		84		80	
LYTLEJHA		90					80				91	
MASONTCR	93	82						83	82		89	84
DICKSNBT	93	90	83	83	80	85	85	81	84		81	83
MONTGYHA	—	97			83	91	80	82	81			85
FORWODHA	97	—			86	85	84		85	82		
TELLOTCR			—	87	82		84		81	84	88	
ROSEWMTA	86		87	—			82				88	
TOMLNBAL	81		82	88	—	87	80	89			81	
SMITHRWA	84	85	82	85	87	—					88	
LOWREYQA	82	82			80		—	85				
VNHORNPG	81		81				85	—				
SHRIVRFR			84						—		93	
HOLLINDQA	83	85	88		81		82	93	81	—	85	80
BURGSSQA	89	82					88				—	
CELLARWA	92	85				84	85		81			—
STURTAKE	89	89	89			88		89	89		81	85
STNSBYBA		92	91		89	85		90	90			86
DAVISEHA	89	94			83	86		83	82	83		82
HANSNBKE			92						88			
ANGIERKE			81			85			82			
MOORENBA	86	92					87	83	92			
BOWIERPG		85						82		82	83	89
HAWKNTFR		84				84						
SCOTTJBT	80						84					
CARRSLPG												
KEMPHYFR												
CHAPMNCH												
HOLBRKSO												
JONESSCH												
HYLNDJSO												
MPHERWCH												
QUYNNAAN												
ANDERSDO												

TABLE 20.5 MARYLAND 1801 MATRIX (REPUBLICAN PARTY) *continued*

	STUR TAKE	STNS BYBA	DAVI SEHA	HANS NBKE	ANGI ERKE	MOOR ENBA	BOWI ERPG	HAWK NTFR	SCOT TJBT	CARR SLPG	KEMP HYFR
MARTNNTA											
ORRELLCR	82	85	84	82	81						
THOMASKE	100	84	82	84		93	88	88	86	81	
MOFFITCE	83	87	84			88	85	82	85		
DOUGSJCR	89		81								
WOODPRPG	88	82	81				87	88		81	
MILLRWCE	83	90	83			82		85			
LOVETHBA	98	95	94			95	85	87			
LEMMONBA	98	92	88			87	88	87			
LYTLEJHA	85	82				84	80				
MASONTCR	88	87	86	82	88			87			
DICKSNBT	89	92	89			85	81	85			
MONTGYHA	89	92	94			89	86		80		
FORWODHA	89	92				92	85	84			
TELLOTCR	89	81		92	81						
ROSEWMTA	85										
TOMLNBAL	89		83								
SMITHRWA	86	85	85			85			84		
LOWREYQA	85	88	83			83	87			84	
VNHORNPG	89	90	82		88	82	82				84
SHRIVRFR	89		83					92			
HOLLNDQA		81						82			
BURGSSQA		86						83			
CELLARWA	85	96	82	89				89			
STURTAKE	—	100	100					88	93	83	
STNSBYBA	86	—				91	82	92			
DAVISEHA			—			89		83			
HANSNBKE	88			—	81						
ANGIERKE				81	—						
MOORENBA		91	89			—		82			
BOWIERPG		82					—				
HAWKNTFR	98	92	83			82		—			82
SCOTTJBT	83								—	90	
CARRSLPG	83								90	—	
KEMPHYFR								82			—
CHAPMNCH											
HOLBRKSO											
JONESSCH											
HYLNDJSO											
MPHERWCH											
QUYNNAAN											
ANDERSDO											

MARYLAND HOUSE OF DELEGATES, 1801: CLUSTER-BLOC MATRIX (SHOWING FEDERALIST PARTY)

	STUR TAKE	STNS BYBA	DAVI SEHA	HANS NBKE	ANGI ERKE	MOOR ENBA	BOWI ERPG	HAWK NTFR	SCOT TJBT	CARR SLPG	KEMP HYFR	CHAP MNCH
STURTAKE	—	96						88	93	83		
STNSBYBA	86	—	100			91	82	92				
DAVISEHA		100	—	89		89		83				
HANSNBKE	88			—	81							
ANGIERKE				81	—							
MOORENBA		91	89			—		82				
BOWIERPG		82					—					
HAWKNTFR	98	92	83			82		—			82	
SCOTTJBT	83								—	90		
CARRSLPG	83								90	—		
KEMPHYFR								82			—	
CHAPMNCH												—
HOLBRKSO												100
JONESSCH												100
HYLNDJSO												97
MPHERWCH												97
QUYNNAAN												97
ANDERSDO												97
DAVISTMO												96
SWERGNMO												93
STEELTDO												93
VEATCHMO												93
QUINTNWO												93
DASHLWSO												92
NEALERSM												90
TOMLNJAL												90
KEENEMDO												90
GOLDSCDO												89
RIDGYRAN												89
MGUDRRMO												88
SIMKNSAL												85
HRWDRHAA												85
PURNLSWO												
CRSPJOAL												
LOWESTSO												
HEBBWMSM												
MERRIKAA												

TABLE 20.5   MARYLAND 1801 MATRIX (FEDERALIST PARTY) *continued*

	HOLB RKSO	JONE SSCH	HYLN DJSO	MPHE RWCH	QUYN NAAN	ANDE RSDO	DAVI STMO	SWER GNMO	STEE LIDO	VEAT CHMO	QUIN TNWO	DASH LWSO
STURTAKE												
STNSBYBA												
DAVISEHA												
HANSNBKE												
ANGIERKE												
MOORENBA												
BOWIERPG												
HAWKNTFR												
SCOTTJBT												
CARR												
KEMPHYFR												
CHAPMNCH	100	100	97	97	97	97	96	93	93	93	93	92
HOLBRKSO	—	98	95	93	88	85	95	82	88	95	90	92
JONESSCH	98	—	88	88	88	93	90	85	93	95	88	97
HYLNDJSO	85	98	—	93	88	95	88	93	93	92	86	92
MPHERWCH	93	88	83	—	88	90	88	88	90	92	85	92
QUYNNAAN	88	88	88	88	—	92	80		85	84	80	83
ANDERSDO	95	83	85	90	92	—	90	84	85	89	92	88
DAVISTMO	95	90	88	88	80	90	—	87		90	90	89
SWERGNMO	82	85	83	88		84	87	—		89	84	82
STEELTDO	88	93	93	90	85	90	85		—	87	83	95
VEATCHMO	95	95	92	92	84	89	80	89	87	—	87	81
QUINTNWO	90	90	86	85	80	92	90	84	83	87	—	92
DASHLWSO	92	97	92	92	83	88	89	82	95	91	92	—
NEALERSM	84	91	85	87		90	84	83	88	82	86	85
TOMLNJAL	90	88	86	86	80	90	88	80	83	87	92	86
KEENEMDO	96	89	92	84	90	94	94		86	88	96	84
GOLDSCDO	82	89	92	86	84	84	84	83	83	85	92	83
RIDGYRAN	82	82			87	81	81				83	80
MGUDRRMO	88	84	85	88	84	88	96		83	84	83	
SIMKNSAL	82	82		82		86	89	81	86	86	87	81
HRWDRHAA		80			82	81	82				84	82
PURNLSWO	84	90	88	91		90	87	81	87	83	87	83
CRSPJOAL	86	83	81	84	82	82	83		90	87	89	90
LOWESTSO		100	100	100			88		96	92	92	
HEBBWMSM		83							80			89
MERRIKAA											83	

TABLE 20.5   MARYLAND 1801 MATRIX (FEDERALIST PARTY) *continued*

	NEAL ERSM	TOML NJAL	KEEN EMDO	GOLD SCDO	RIDO YRAN	MGUD RRMO	SIMK NSAL	HRWD RHAA	PURN LSWO	CRSP JOAL	LOWE STSO	HEBB WMSM	MERR IKAA
STURTAKE													
STNSBYBA													
DAVISEHA													
HANSNBKE													
ANGIERKE													
MOORENBA													
BOWIERPG													
HAWKNTFR													
SCOTTJBT													
CARRSLPG													
KEMPHYFR													
CHAPMNCH	90	90	90	88	89	88	85	85	94	85			
HOLBRKSO	84	90	95	92	82	88	82		90	83	100	83	
JONESSCH	81	88	89	89	82	84	82	80	88	81	100		
HYLNDJSO	85	86	92	92		85			91	84	100		
MPHERWCH	87	86	84	86	87	88	82			82			
QUYNNAAN		90	90	84	81	84	85	82	90	82			
ANDERSDO	90	90	94	94	81	88	89	81	87	82	88		
DAVISTMO	84	88	94	94		96	81	82	81	83	88		
SWERGNMO	83	80		83			86						
STEELTDO	88	83	86	84		83	86	82	87	90	96	80	
VEATCHMO	82	87	88	85		84	87		93	87	92		
QUINTNWO	86	92	86	92	83	83	81	84	87	88	92	89	83
DASHLWSO	95	86	84	83	80	81	82	82	83	90		89	82
NEALERSM	—									81			
TOMLNJAL		—	83	89		81	87	82	87	87	96		
KEENEMDO			—	97					86	88	96		
GOLDSCDO		89	97	—	83			89	89				
RIDGYRAN				83	—								89
MGUDRRMO	81	81	83	82	89	—	82						
SIMKNSAL	82	87		82		80	—	81		92			
HRWDRHAA		82		89				—				80	97
PURNLSWO									—				
CRSPJOAL	81	87								—		80	
LOWESTSO	88	96									—	88	
HEBBWMSM	89		88									—	
MERRIKAA	82		88								88		—

changes they wanted to make in the electoral system and the county courts. They particularly disliked the law that gave the county courts power to appoint election judges, evidently because the Federalist oligarchy had abused this in the past. These changes too were passed by party votes.[111] Taken together, the questions on which the parties felt an interest—patronage, suffrage reform, and changes in the electoral system—constituted a majority of the roll calls taken in this session.[112] So firm were the party lines on these votes that even when voting on other issues (private debts, education, slavery, and internal improvements) was random, there was sufficient agreement to construct a computer matrix (table 20.5; cluster blocs at 80 percent agreement).

Even with the agreement threshold set at 80 percent, only 6 legislators failed to enter the matrix; another 12 failed to make the 50 percent participation threshold. The 35 Republicans and 26 Federalists are identical to the groups identified on the eleven patronage roll calls. A level of 80 percent agreement is a degree of cohesion that political scientists commonly expect of modern political parties. That amount requires strong lines of communication and a high level of organizational loyalty, if not some form of overt discipline. In Maryland it marks the ultimate maturity of the first party system.

APPENDIX

Computerized Sorting Program
for the Maryland House of Delegates

THE MATRICES used in chapters 3, 5, and 20 were constructed by a computer sorting operation that compared the record of each delegate with that of every other over the course of the legislative session. The House of Delegates annually recorded about 100 roll calls, but not all were used. Particularly lopsided votes were eliminated because there was no substantial area of disagreement (the threshhold ratio used was 5 to 1). Roll calls that were purely personal or local in nature were also eliminated. So were votes that seemed to duplicate one another, such as procedural moves or slight changes in wording.

Among the legislators themselves two requirements were imposed. The first was a pair-wise voting threshhold of 50 percent. The program considered only those pairs of legislators who participated in at least half the roll calls and thus had an opportunity of agreeing or disagreeing a significant number of times. The second was the agreement threshhold required for placement in the matrix. Two threshholds were used 70 and 80 percent. The latter, which is the score commonly expected of modern parties, demands an enormous amount of cohesion, even organizational discipline. Few legislators agreed with one another 80 percent of the time in the 1780s; thus the less stringent requirement of 70 percent was the one used for the matrices exhibited in the text.

The computer constructed the matrix in such a way as to eliminate subjective choice. It began with the pair of delegates who had the highest level of agreement. It then listed all the delegates who agreed with the first one more than 70 percent of the time. When that list was exhausted, it took the second delegate's pairings and followed the same procedure. When it ran out of delegates who fit into this cluster, it picked at random the first pair of delegates who met the 70 percent requirement. If no one agreed with them 70 percent of the time (as in table 3.1), it worked through pairings until it found a pair who did agree with others and thus could start a new cluster.

Notes

Abbreviations

DLC   Library of Congress, Washington, D.C.

MdHR   Hall of Records, Annapolis, Maryland

MdHS   Maryland Historical Society, Baltimore

Md, *JHD*   *Votes and Proceedings of the House of Delegates of the State of Maryland.* Microfilm edition, Early State Records Series.

Md, *SJ*   *Votes and Proceedings of the Senate of the State of Maryland.* Microfilm edition, Early State Records Series.

NCDH   North Carolina Department of Archives and History, Raleigh

NCDu   Duke University, Durham, North Carolina

NC, JHC   Journal of the North Carolina House of Commons, published in Walter Clark, ed., *The State Records of North Carolina,* 30 vols. (Winston and Goldsboro, N.C., 1896–1917), especially vols. 16 to 21. The manuscript journal, 1790–1800 is in the microfilm edition of the Early State Records Series.

NC, SJ   Journal of the Senate of North Carolina. Publication same as above.

NCU   University of North Carolina, Chapel Hill

NYPL   New York Public Library, New York City

PaHS   Historical Society of Pennsylvania, Philadelphia

VaHS   Virginia Historical Society, Richmond

Va, *JHD*   *Journal of the House of Delegates of the Commonwealth of Virginia* (Richmond, 1828)

Va, *SJ*   *Journal of the Senate of the Commonwealth of Virginia* (Richmond, 1827)

VaSL   Virginia State Library, Richmond

VaU   University of Virginia, Charlottesville

VaWM   College of William and Mary, Williamsburg, Virginia

CHAPTER ONE   THE LANDSCAPE AND THE PEOPLE,
FROM THE SUSQUEHANNA TO THE RAPPAHANNOCK

1. For more extensive discussion of the Chesapeake economy and the lack of urban centers see: Lewis C. Gray, *History of Agriculture in the Southern States to 1860,* 2 vols. (Gloucester, Mass., 1958), I, 443. Two more specialized studies of value are: James H. Soltow, *The Economic Role of Williamsburg* (Williamsburg, 1965), and Edward C. Papenfuse, *In Pursuit of Profit: The Annapolis Merchants in the Era of the American Revolution, 1763–1805* (Baltimore and London, 1975).

2. American Council of Learned Societies, "Report of Committee on Linguistic and National Stocks in the Population of the United States [by the census of 1790]," *Annual Report of the American Historical Association for 1931* (Washington, 1932), I, 124.

3. George Johnston, *History of Cecil County, Maryland* (Elkton, 1881), p. 349.

4. Fred Shelley, ed., "Ebenezer Hazard's Travels Through Maryland in 1777," *Maryland Historical Magazine,* 46 (1951), 44–54; Johnston, *Cecil,* p. 349.

5. Johnston, *Cecil,* pp. 46–47; Robert Hunter, Jr., *Quebec to Carolina in 1785–1786: The Journal of Robert Hunter, Jr.,* ed. by Louis B. Wright (San Marino, 1943), p. 178; Francois A. Frederic, duc de La Rochefoucauld-Liancourt, *Travels Through the United States . . . in 1795, 1796, and 1797 . . . ,* 2 vols. (London, 1799), II, 351–52. Oak and white ash is the predominant forest cover of Harford and Cecil today. I assume that when fields were abandoned they reverted to their original cover. Johann D. Schoepf, *Travels in the Confederation, 1783–1784* (Philadelphia, 1911), pp. 372–73, speaks of "a tedious uniformity of pine-forest and sand," but it seems likely that he confused this road with the country to the south of Baltimore.

6. Shelley, ed., "Hazard's Travels," pp. 46–47; Schoepf, *Travels,* pp. 372–73.

7. Johnston, *Cecil,* p. 349.

8. Shelley, ed., "Hazard's Travels," p. 53; see also *Maryland Historical Magazine,* 39 (1944), 282.

9. The census of 1776 for Harford is printed in Gaius Marcus Brumbaugh, *Maryland Records, Colonial, Revolutionary, County and Church,* 2 vols. (Lancaster, Pa., 1928), II, 113–94. In table 1.2 I have included only the heads of households, so as to make it comparable to the assessment of 1783 and census of 1790. The tax list of 1783 is on microfilm, Maryland Historical Society, Baltimore. Although both land and slaves were assessed, I counted only slaveholding, so as to permit comparisons with the other two lists. "Paupers," who possessed less than £10 property and hence were not taxed, were listed as possessing zero slaves. Single men, who were taxed at a flat rate of 15 shillings, regardless of property, were omitted so as to make the results comparable to the census of 1790. For the U.S. Bureau of the Census, *Heads of Families at the First Census of the United States taken in the year 1790: Maryland* (Washington, 1907) all heads of household were counted, including those who were females or free blacks, because these two groups, though small, were included on earlier lists.

10. Karl W. Butzer, *Geomorphology from the Earth* (New York, 1976), pp. 60–64, outlines the basic elements of soil fertility. The most important factor is the presence of organic matter called humus. It helps retain water in the soil, and by

linking with metallic ions (potassium, calcium, magnesium, and nitrogen) it helps to prevent these nutrients from leeching into the subsoil.

11. La Rochefoucauld-Liancourt, *Travels*, II, 276, 278, 286.

12. David Klingaman, "The Significance of Grain in the Development of the Tobacco Colonies," *Journal of Economic History*, 29 (1969), 268–78, esp. 276, suggests that the decline in the price of tobacco relative to wheat is largely responsible for the shift. For a discussion of soil exhaustion see chapter 2.

13. Arthur P. Middleton, *Tobacco Coast: A Maritime History of Chesapeake Bay in the Colonial Era* (Newport News, 1953), p. 33; La Rochefoucauld-Liancourt, *Travels*, I, 550–51, 561.

14. William Hemsley to Tench Coxe, Queen Anne's, June 17, 24, July 25, 29, 1781, Mar. 7, 1782; Jan. 26, Feb. 2, 1783; Forman and Chambers to Coxe, Chester Town, Dec. 2, 29, 1782, Mar. 24, 1783, Coxe Papers, PaHS.

15. La Rochefoucauld-Liancourt, *Travels*, II, 291–92.

16. The 1776 returns are in Brumbaugh, *Maryland Records*, II, 197–230. The 1790 figures are from *U.S. Census, 1790, Maryland*. As in the earlier Harford figures, only heads of families were tallied to provide comparability.

17. The census taker's figures for 1790 do not add up. He reported a total population of 13,084 for the county, yet the sum of his count for whites (8,665), free nonwhites (1,076) and slaves (4,777) is 14,518. The error is probably in the count of free nonwhites: 1,076 would represent about 10 percent of the total free population, yet out of a total of 1,428 heads of families there are only 92 free blacks, or 6.5 percent. Even so, this represents a substantial increase in the free black population, which was only 2 percent of the total in 1776.

18. Hulbert Footner, *Rivers of the Eastern Shore* (New York, 1944), passim; Middleton, *Tobacco Coast*, p. 33; John Dorsey to Tench Coxe, Baltimore, May 11, 1784, Coxe Papers, PaHS.

19. Somerset has complete returns from the tax of 1783, but its schedules for the census of 1790 have been lost. Dorchester has 1790 schedules, but returns from only two districts in 1783. Worcester has complete 1790 schedules and returns from ten hundreds in 1783, representing all parts of the county.

20. The list is obviously incomplete, and there is good reason to think that the omitted hundreds lay in the north and west (see explanation in text). Hence any tabulation of wealth distribution by individuals, such as was done for Harford and Worcester, would have been deceptive.

21. Only four counties—Caroline, Calvert, Somerset, and Talbot—have complete records of the 1783 tax. The regional bias of the Baltimore omissions is inferred from the fact that the county was wedge-shaped, with a relatively small seacoast. It thus seems likely that the lower hundreds included—Middle, Back River, and Patapsco—were the only ones on the coast. Of the 9 other hundreds listed, 5 were in or near the city. Because the 4 interior hundreds listed were not much larger in area than the coastal ones, large parts of the north and west remain unaccounted for.

22. Philip A. Crowl, *Maryland During and After the Revolution* (Baltimore, 1943), p. 66; Papenfuse, *Annapolis Merchants*, p. 178.

23. Samuel & John Smith, Circular Letter, Baltimore, Apr. 15, 1784, Samuel

Smith Papers, DLC; Rhoda M. Dorsey, "The Pattern of Baltimore Commerce During the Confederation Period," *Maryland Historical Magazine,* 52 (1967), 119–34; *Maryland Journal* [Baltimore], Aug. 16, 1785.

24. Hamilton Owens, *Baltimore on the Chesapeake* (Garden City, N.Y., 1941), p. 127; Schoepf, *Travels,* p. 326; Hunter, *Quebec to Carolina,* pp. 179–80.

25. Helen G. Huttenhauer and G. Alfred Helwig, *Baltimore County in the State and Nation* (Baltimore, 1958), p. 40.

26. Ferdinand M. Bayard, *Travels of a Frenchman in Maryland and Virginia with a Description of Philadelphia and Baltimore in 1791,* trans. by Ben C. McCary (Williamsburg, 1950), p. 3.

27. Shelley, ed., "Hazard's Travels," p. 48; Schoepf, *Travels,* p. 349.

28. I am indebted to the U.S. Soil Conservation Service, Baltimore office, for providing me with a soil map of Anne Arundel surveyed in 1929. The 1929–30 surveys of both Maryland and Virginia are especially valuable because the level of population and development had not changed substantially since the Revolutionary period. The land between Baltimore and Annapolis today is largely covered with asphalt and shopping centers. On the other hand, the SCS informs me that the 1929 series of maps for the rest of Maryland's counties has been destroyed. This is a major historical loss, especially for such heavily developed counties as Montgomery and Prince George's.

29. Papenfuse, *Annapolis Merchants,* ch. 3, passim.

30. Ibid., p. 137.

31. Shelley, ed., "Hazard's Travels," p. 48; Schoepf, *Travels,* pp. 363–64; La Rochefoucauld-Liancourt, *Travels,* I, 596.

32. Carville V. Earle, *The Evolution of a Tidewater Settlement System: All Hallows Parish, Maryland, 1650–1783* (Chicago, 1976), passim, argues persuasively that Maryland planters were better horticulturalists and tobacco was less destructive of soil than previously thought. Papenfuse, *Annapolis Merchants,* pp. 219–22, presents the intriguing thesis that wheat rather than tobacco was responsible for whatever soil exhaustion there was. The culture of tobacco and its effect on the soil will be discussed more fully in chapter 2.

33. Charles Francis Stein, *A History of Calvert County, Maryland* (Baltimore, 1960), pp. 1–3.

34. The Calvert tax list of 1782 is reproduced in Stein, *Calvert,* pp. 339–74. The Calvert schedules for the *U.S. Census, 1790* have been destroyed. The Anne Arundel figures are taken from the census of 1790 because there is no extant tax list for the county. There is no reason to expect that the time differential made much difference. The population of both counties remained stable for many years: see Arthur Eli Karinen, "Numerical and Distributional Aspects of Maryland Population, 1631–1840" (Ph.D. diss., University of Maryland, 1958), p. 208. On the Anne Arundel census schedules the number of slaves is illegible for 228 whites; these accordingly were omitted from the tally. It is hoped that the omissions are random, although they include some prominent individuals, such as Charles Ridgely and Philip Key. The census credited Anne Arundel with 2,147 heads of households.

35. Anne Arundel's most electable delegates were Nicholas Worthington (1782–93, 9 slaves), Brice T. B. Worthington (1782–90, 52 slaves), Nicholas Carroll (1783–85, 30 slaves), and John Hall (1782–85, 38 slaves). All but Carroll

voted debtor in the 1780s, though all also became Federalists. Calvert's most chronic servants were John Grahame (1783–87; credited with one slave in 1782, but his father had 328 acres and 15 slaves) Alexander Frazier (1784–85, 1788–89, 740 acres and 17 slaves), Michael Taney (1784–87, 728 acres and 10 slaves), Thomas Gantt (1785–91, 893 acres and 19 slaves), and William Fitzhugh, Jr. (1782, 1786–88, 2,910 acres and 20 slaves). The voting records of Taney and Gantt were mixed, but nearly all the shorter-term delegates from Calvert were creditor-Federalists.

36. Hunter, *Quebec to Carolina,* pp. 187–88; Schoepf, *Travels,* pp. 363–64; LaRochefoucauld-Liancourt, *Travels,* II, 340.

37. Roger B. Farquhar, *Old Homes and History of Montgomery County, Maryland* (Silver Spring, 1962), p. 10; Schoepf, *Travels,* p. 357.

38. Hunter, *Quebec to Carolina,* p. 188; Papenfuse, *Annapolis Merchants,* pp. 184–85.

39. Schoepf, *Travels,* p. 28.

40. Hunter, *Quebec to Carolina,* p. 199.

41. Ethel Roby Hayden, "Port Tobacco, Lost Town of Maryland," *Maryland Historical Magazine,* 40 (1945), 261–76.

42. Ibid., pp. 273–75; Carter to Carroll, Apr., May 1777, quoted in Kate Mason Rowland, *Charles Carroll of Carrollton,* 2 vols. (New York, 1898), I, 203.

43. In this and in succeeding Virginia tax lists multiple holdings belonging to a single individual (or for which he paid the taxes) were added together to obtain an estimate of his total wealth. Thus the figures do not necessarily represent the size of individual farms and plantations. Particularly is that true among the larger holdings.

44. The 30 percent figure was obtained by subtracting the number of persons who paid a land tax in 1782 (358) from the number paying the capitation tax in 1783 (511). Two different tax years were used because of variations in the legibility of the tax books, but it is assumed that there was no substantial change between the two. Only landowners paid the land tax, whereas all free adult males (black and white) plus single or widowed adult females paid the capitation tax. Wives and other adults living within a household were not counted as taxpayers, though the tax collectors counted them in the total polls. Hence there is a difference between my totals and those listed in the tax books. Counting errors would probably cause some differences, in any case. The acreage figure for Richmond County is from the U.S. Bureau of the Census, *1969 Census of Agriculture, part 24 Virginia* (Washington, 1972), Section 2, p. 609.

45. Chapters 3 and 4 will analyze in more detail the political situation at the end of the war. But this view is in substantial agreement with Jackson T. Main, *Political Parties Before the Constitution* (Chapel Hill, 1974), pp. 248–49, and Main, "Sections and Politics in Virginia, 1781–1787," *William and Mary Quarterly,* 3d ser., 12 (1955), 96–112.

46. U.S. Department of Agriculture, Soil Conservation Service, *Soil Survey: Northumberland and Lancaster Counties, Virginia* (Washington, 1963). There is no soil survey available for Richmond County, but no reason to suppose that it differed much from its neighbors. I am indebted to the Richmond Office of SCS for providing me with soil survey booklets and/or maps for the 1929–30 series and the 1959 series for about a fourth of the counties in Virginia. Soil information in the remainder of this chapter and the next is derived from these surveys. I am also

indebted to members of the Department of Landscape Architecture, University of Wisconsin, Madison, for helping me interpret the maps and to project from them the kinds of problems farmers faced.

47. The Virginia schedules for the U.S. census of 1790 have been lost. Thus, what is published in the 1790 census for Fairfax County is actually a personal property tax of 1782, which is used here. The size of the county intimidated me from making an interval count (using, say, the personalty books for 1790), but the similarity of results suggests steady progress without important distributional shifts.

48. Washington to James Maury, Mount Vernon, Feb. 24, 1787, George Lee to Washington [Poplar Hill], Apr. 28, 1787, and Leven Powell to Washington, Apr. 8, 1787, Washington Papers, DLC.

49. David Stuart to Washington, Nov. 18, 1791, ibid.

50. Soil types and descriptions of fertility are taken from, U.S. Soil Conservation Service, *Soil Survey, Fairfax County, Virginia* (Washington, 1963). There are no extant surveys for Fairfax's neighbors, Stafford, Prince William, and Loudoun.

51. Hunter, *Quebec to Carolina,* pp. 189–90; Schoepf, *Travels,* pp. 359–60; Jedidiah Morse, *The American Geography* (London, 1794), pp. 490–91; Fairfax Harrison, *Landmarks of Old Prince William: A Study of Origins in Northern Virginia* (Berryville, Va., 1964), pp. 408–10.

52. Alexandria Land Books, 1787–1800, VaSL; 1787 is the earliest extant record. The sums are those reached by the tax assessors, except for 1796, where I had to do the calculating.

53. Mason to Zachariah Johnston, Gunston Hall, Nov. 3, 1790, and "Fairfax County Petition Protesting Delays in Selecting a Courthouse Site" [Nov. 11, 1790] in Robert A. Rutland, ed., *The Papers of George Mason, 1725–1792,* 3 vols. (Chapel Hill, 1970), III, 1208–15.

54. Stuart to Washington, Nov. 18, 1791, Washington Papers, DLC.

55. Germans came to Loudoun in the 1730s, as part of the migration southward from Pennsylvania to the Shenandoah Valley. They settled in the northwest corner of the county near the Blue Ridge. Quakers came shortly after and chose the rich land in the center of the county between the Catocin Hills and the Blue Ridge. Both communities retained their religious and ethnic identity through the nineteenth century. Opposed to slavery, they sided with the North in the Civil War: Harrison Williams, *Legends of Loudoun* (Richmond, 1938), pp. 46–48. It is also likely that they were responsible for Loudoun's Federalist posture from the mid-1790s to the War of 1812.

56. Diane Lindstrom, *Economic Change in the Philadelphia Region, 1810–1850* (New York, 1977), passim, demonstrates the growth potential in the symbiotic relationship between an urban core and a rural hinterland.

57. Thomas Johnson to Washington, Nov. 10, 1791, Washington Papers, DLC. Johnson thought Montgomery's farmers weaker in soil management than neighboring Frederick's. Although he did not explain why, the reason may be ethnic. Frederick had a heavy German population, while the names in Montgomery tax lists are mostly English and Scots-Irish.

58. There is a 1776 census for Montgomery in Brumbaugh, *Maryland Records,* I, 180–223, but the schedules for only 6 of the county's 11 hundreds survive, and 2 of those have gross figures only. Those 2 are in the Georgetown vicinity, while the other 4 are in the interior. The regional bias thus prevents comparison with the figures for 1783 and 1790. The 1783 tax list for Montgomery contains

figures from all 11 hundreds, so it is unlikely that the anomaly in the table is the result of faulty data.

59. Schoepf, *Travels,* pp. 314–15, 324; Bayard, *Travels of a Frenchman,* pp. 3, 16; Johnson to Washington, Nov. 10, 1791, Washington Papers, DLC.

60. Bayard, *Travels of a Frenchman,* pp. 31–32. How widespread this attitude was among westerners is impossible to say, but it is generally agreed that Germans (especially pietists) and Quakers objected to slavery: Herrmann Schuricht, *History of the German Element in Virginia,* 2 vols. (Baltimore, 1898), I, 97, and John W. Wayland, *Twenty-five Chapters on the Shenandoah Valley* (Strasburg, Va., 1957), p. 83.

61. Herbert C. Bell, *History of the Leitersburg District, Washington County, Maryland* (Leitersburg, 1898), pp. 16, 68–69; Schoepf, *Travels,* pp. 312–13.

62. Bayard, *Travels of a Frenchman,* pp. 27–28.

63. Harry Toulmin, *The Western Country in 1793: Reports on Kentucky and Virginia,* ed. by Marion Tinling and Godfrey Davies (San Marino, Calif., 1948), pp. 51–54; Thomas J. C. Williams, *A History of Washington County, Maryland,* 2 vols. (Baltimore, 1968), I, 163–64; Bayard, *Travels of a Frenchman,* pp. 157–58.

64. John T. Scharf, *History of Western Maryland,* 2 vols. (Philadelphia, 1882), I, 37, 134, 145; James W. Thomas and Judge T. C. Williams, *History of Allegany County Maryland* (Baltimore, 1969: reprint of 1929 ed.), pp. 93 ff.; Frank W. Porter, "From Back Country to County: the Delayed Settlement of Western Maryland," *Maryland Historical Magazine,* 70 (1975), 329–49.

65. Robert D. Mitchell, *Commercialism and Frontier: Perspectives on the Early Shenandoah Valley* (Charlottesville, 1977), 36–58; Mabel Henshaw Gardiner and Ann Henshaw Gardiner, *Chronicles of Old Berkeley* (Durham, 1938), pp. 35–37, 56–59; Schuricht, *German Element in Virginia,* pp. 85–87; LaRochefoucauld-Liancourt, *Travels,* II, 106–7.

66. Samuel P. Kercheval, *The Shenandoah Valley* (Strasburg, Va., 1925), pp. 157–58; Bayard, *Travels of a Frenchman,* p. 92.

67. Stephen B. Weeks, *Southern Quakers and Slavery* (Baltimore, 1896), pp. 98–99; Wayland, *Twenty-Five Chapters,* p. 89.

68. Klaus Wust, *The Virginia Germans* (Charlottesville, 1969), p. 104; Toulmin, *Western Country,* p. 57.

69. Stuart to Washington, Nov. 18, 1791, Washington Papers, DLC; LaRochefoucauld-Liancourt, *Travels,* II, 101–8.

70. Of those who held town lots with little or no farm land, I counted 136 in 1782, 38 in 1790, and 271 in 1800. The wide variance in these figures makes them suspect, and they were accordingly omitted from the table. They do not affect farm size, in any case. Because of the size of the county in 1790 and 1800 I took a 50 percent sample by counting only one of the two personalty books. In each case, the book not counted contained a slightly larger number of slaves; so the percentages given are probably understated. The reader should compare these results with Freeman Hart's discussion of average farm sizes in the Shenandoah Valley in the 1780s: *The Valley of Virginia in the American Revolution, 1763–1789* (Chapel Hill, 1942), p. 163. See Mitchell, *Commercialism and Frontier,* pp. 135–36, for average amount of cleared land.

71. LaRochefoucauld-Liancourt, *Travels,* II, 93–94; John W. Wayland, *History of Rockingham County, Virginia* (Dayton, Va., 1912), pp. 106–7.

72. LaRochefoucauld-Liancourt, *Travels,* II, 97–102.

73. Toulmin, *Western Country,* pp. 48–50.

74. Kentucky's settlement pattern will be discussed in chapter 8.

75. Henry Haymond, *History of Harrison County* (Morgantown, 1910), pp. 251–52.

76. Otis K. Rice, *The Allegheny Frontier: West Virginia Beginnings, 1730–1830* (Lexington, Ky., 1970), p. 159.

77. The land books for West Virginia counties are deposited in the West Virginia Department of Archives and History, Charleston. They did not seem worth a special trip to examine because in this sort of ranching economy, with large amounts of mountainous land unused, farm size does not seem a promising index.

78. Hu Maxwell, *History of Hampshire County, West Virginia* (Morgantown, 1897), p. 319.

79. Greenbriar Personalty Book, 1783, VaSL. Part of the book is illegible; so the results must be considered a sample of unknown reliability.

80. Although the Virginia schedules for the census of 1790 have been lost, Jedidiah Morse, *American Geography* (1794 ed.) published aggregates for each county. Comparison with the tax list suggests the census was undercounted, but it still indicates lack of substantial growth.

CHAPTER TWO   THE LANDSCAPE AND THE PEOPLE,
FROM THE RAPPAHANNOCK TO CAPE FEAR

1. A Fredericksburg merchant complained in the spring of 1783 that tobacco was selling for 22 shillings a hundredweight, but planters would not part with it. They apparently hoped for an even better price when trade with Britain was fully restored. Samuel Paine to Tench Coxe, Fredericksburg, May 20, 1783, Coxe Papers, PaHS.

2. The federal treasury in 1790 recorded only quantities and total value. Hence prices and values for individual products had to be estimated. If the price of tobacco held up while that of other commodities declined, its role was even more important than the table indicates.

3. Avery O. Craven, *Soil Exhaustion as a Factor in the History of Maryland and Virginia* (Urbana, 1925) is the classic indictment of tobacco, but the Craven thesis is no longer acceptable. For more recent views, see: Ben Franklin Lemert, "Geographic Influences in the History of North Carolina," *North Carolina Historical Review,* 12, no. 4 (1935), 297–319, esp. 308–10, and Carville V. Earle, *The Evolution of a Tidewater Settlement System,* 216–17. The price for land clearances is given by Joseph Burr to Tench Coxe, Rutherford County, Apr. 15, 1796, Coxe Papers, PaHS. This is the only figure I have seen, and though it referred to western North Carolina it was probably characteristic.

4. A Caroline County, Va., tax list, which distinguished between "improved" and "unimproved" land, indicates that only a third of the county was under cultivation in 1783, and a mere 66 acres was in meadow. Western North Carolina had extensive grasslands brought about by Indian burnings. German immigrants and Moravians sometimes cleared meadow land.

5. Howard R. Marraro, "Count Luigi Castiglione, an Early Traveler to Virginia (1785–1786)," *Virginia Magazine of History and Biography,* 58 (1950), 473–91, esp. 485; John Joyce to Rev. Robert Dickson, Caroline County, Mar. 24, 1785, 23 (1915), 407–14.

6. Joyce to Dickson, Mar. 24, 1785, *Virginia Magazine of History and Biography*, 23 (1915), 407–14; Johann D. Schoepf, *Travels in the Confederation, 1783–1784* (Philadelphia, 1911), pp. 71–72; Robert Hunter, Jr., *Quebec to Carolina in 1785–1786; The Journal of Robert Hunter, Jr.*, ed. by Louis B. Wright (San Marino, 1943), pp. 233–34; J. F. D. Smyth, *A Tour in the United States of America,* 2 vols. (London, 1784; reprint, New York, 1968), I, 15–16.

7. Elizabeth City County tax lists, VaSL; Gloucester census, 1782–83, *Virginia Magazine of History and Biography*, 12 (1904–5), 14–16, 185–87, 269–71, 414–16. Other counties in the region had similar black-white ratios.

8. Schoepf, *Travels,* pp. 46–47; Hunter, *Quebec to Carolina,* pp. 226–27.

9. William Ronald Cocke III, *Hanover County Taxpayers, St. Paul's Parish, 1782–1815* (Columbia, Va., 1956). My count of his list was done with the following ground rules: *(a)* Only those planters who appeared in more than one year were counted. *(b)* The first and last recordings were used unless these were clearly contrary to the general picture. *(c)* Only those within the 1782–1800 period were counted. *(d)* Possession of horses was used as corroborative evidence where the changes in the tax age for slaves left uncertainty (all slaves were taxed from 1782–87; those over 12 from 1788 onward).

10. Hanover County tax lists, VaSL. These figures also suggest that the growth indices used in chapter 1 need to be supplemented with studies of individual mobility. Unfortunately, no enterprising genealogist has paved the way.

11. Hanover County Tax Lists, VaSL.

12. Charles William Jansen, *The Stranger in America, 1793–1806* (London, 1807; reprint, New York, 1935), p. 399: Schoepf, *Travels,* pp. 48–51: Craven, *Soil Exhaustion,* pp. 33–34; John H. Moore, *Albemarle: Jefferson's County,* (Charlottesville, 1976), p. 32.

13. S. Edward Ayers, "Albemarle County, Virginia, 1714–1770: An Economic, Political, and Social Analysis" (M.A. thesis, University of Virginia, 1968); Abemarle County Tax Lists, 1782–90, VaSL.

14. Moore, *Albemarle,* pp. 78–79.

15. John Breckinridge to Lettice Breckinridge, Williamsburg, Aug. 17, 1783, Breckinridge Family Papers, DLC.

16. Robert Gamble to Johnston, Richmond, June 10, 1794, Zachariah Johnston Papers, NCDu.

17. Klaus Wust, *The Virginia Germans* (Charlottesville, 1969), pp. 96–102.

18. Russell County Tax Lists, VaSL. Russell was formed from Washington in 1786.

19. Netti Schreiner-Yantis, *Montgomery County, Virginia—Circa 1790* (Springfield, Va., 1972).

20. Isaac Weld, *Travels Through the States of North America, and the Provinces of Upper and Lower Canada, During the Years 1795, 1796, and 1797,* 2 vols. (London, 1807), I, 214.

21. Archibald Henderson, *Washington's Southern Tour, 1791* (Boston and New York, 1923), pp. 324–30. The reader can share Washington's impression by comparing the drive on U.S. 250 from Charlottesville to Richmond with the dreary trip on U.S. 60 from Lynchburg to Richmond.

22. R. H. Early, *Campbell Chronicles and Family Sketches* (Lynchburg, 1927), pp. 138–39; Herbert C. Bradshaw, *History of Prince Edward County, Virginia* (Richmond, 1955), p. 298.

23. Bradshaw, *Prince Edward,* pp. 289–91.

24. Maud Carter Clement, *The History of Pittsylvania County Virginia* (Lynchburg, 1929), p. 108: Schoepf, *Travels,* p. 120.

25. Judith P. A. Hill, *A History of Henry County Virginia* (Martinsville, Va., 1925), p. 16.

26. Schoepf, *Travels,* pp. 67–68.

27. Ibid., p. 49; Hunter, *Quebec to Carolina,* pp. 236–37; R. Bennett Bean, *The Peopling of Virginia* (Boston, 1938), p. 72; Arthur G. Peterson, "The Commerce of Virginia, 1789–1791," *William and Mary Quarterly,* 2d. ser, 10 (1939), 302–9.

28. Schoepf, *Travels,* pp. 72–76; Hunter, *Quebec to Carolina,* pp. 259–60.

29. Schoepf, *Travels,* pp. 88–91; Hunter, *Quebec to Carolina,* p. 261; La Rochefoucauld-Liancourt, *Travels Through the United States . . . in 1795, 1776, and 1797 . . . ,* 2 vols. (London, 1799), II, 54–55, 57–58.

30. Smyth, *Tour,* II, 104–5; Hunter, *Quebec to Carolina,* pp. 262–63.

31. Smyth, *Tour,* I, 10–11; Thomas J. Wertenbaker, *Norfolk, Historic Southern Port* (Durham, 1962), p. 76.

32. The Princess Anne Tax Lists are published in *The Lower Norfolk County Virginia Antiquary* 5 vols. (Richmond & Baltimore, 1897–1906), III, 152–54, IV, 146. A Princess Anne census for 1783 (which probably overlooked some poor whites) indicates a slaveholding population of 60 percent, with 10 percent owning more than 12. See U.S. Bureau of the Census, *Heads of Families at the First Census of the United States taken in the Year 1790* (Washington, 1908), pp. 60–62.

33. The poll tax on white males was lowered from age 21 to 16 in 1788. As a result, the collector's count (1,204 whites in 1790, 1,308 in 1800) is considerably higher than mine. The differential is probably young whites over the age of 16 who were not heads of household (i.e., someone else paid their taxes). They were not included in the calculations concerning the number of landless persons in those years. Adult females were not taxed unless they were heads of households.

34. Douglas S. Brown, *Sketches of Greensville County Virginia, 1650–1967* (Richmond, 1968), p. 226; Bradshaw, *Prince Edward,* pp. 135–36, 241; Landon C. Cabell, *The Old Free State,* 2 vols. (Richmond, 1927), I, 363.

35. Malcolm Harris, *A History of Louisa County, Virginia* (Richmond, 1936), pp. 153–77; Helene B. Agee, *Facets of Goochland (Virginia) County's History* (Richmond, 1962), p. 120.

36. W. W. Scott, *A History of Orange County, Virginia* (Richmond, 1907), 44.

37. Harry Toulmin, *The Western Country in 1793: Reports on Kentucky and Virginia,* ed. by Marion Tinling and Godfrey Davies (San Marino, Calif., 1948), p. 19. According to Toulmin there were still only two churches there in 1793

38. Laura C. Cochrane, et al., *History of Caroline County, Maryland, from Its Beginning* (Baltimore, 1971), pp. 109–15.

39. Harris, *Louisa,* pp. 181, 193, 215; Agee, *Goochland,* pp. 125–34.

40. Gay Neale, *Brunswick County, Virginia, 1720–1975* (Richmond, 1975), p. 94; Brown, *Sketches of Greensville,* pp. 229, 234–35.

41. William Taylor Thom, *The Struggle for Religious Freedom in Virginia; The Baptists* (Baltimore, 1900), pp. 40–41.

42. Wesley Gewehr, *The Great Awakening in Virginia, 1740–1790* (Durham, 1930), pp. 189–94.

43. Schoepf, *Travels,* pp. 90, 102–3.

44. Hunter, *Quebec to Carolina,* p. 281.

45. Francis Lutz, *Chesterfield, an Old Virginia County* (Richmond, 1954), p. 137.

46. Clifford R. Hinshaw, Jr., "North Carolina Canals before 1860," *North Carolina Historical Review,* 25, no. 1 (Jan. 1948), 1–56, esp. 2–3.

47. H. Roy Merrens, *Colonial North Carolina in the Eighteenth Century* (Chapel Hill, 1964), pp. 37–39.

48. Hunter, *Quebec to Carolina,* p. 270.

49. Smyth, *Tour,* I, 102–3.

50. Ibid., pp. 92, 152.

51. Ibid., pp. 83–84; Merrens, *Colonial North Carolina,* pp. 155–56. The best description of Halifax and its social life is in Blackwell P. Robinson, *William R. Davie* (Chapel Hill, 1957), pp. 139–49.

52. Schoepf, *Travels,* pp. 129–30. The papers of Wood Jones Hamlin, NCDH, a planter of Halifax, indicate considerable social interchange with Virginians.

53. Merrens, *Colonial North Carolina,* pp. 147–48; Schoepf, *Travels,* pp. 111–12.

54. Hunter, *Quebec to Carolina,* pp. 270–71, 276; Schoepf, *Travels,* pp. 109–10.

55. Northampton County Bicentennial Committee, *Footprints in Northampton* ([Jackson? N.C.], 1976), pp. 7–10.

56. I have not used the census of 1790 because Washington claimed the North Carolina headcount was worthless. See Henderson, *Washington's Southern Tour,* p. 117.

57. Henderson, *Washington's Southern Tour,* p. 77.

58. Schoepf, *Travels,* pp. 141–43.

59. Smyth, *Tour,* II, 94, claimed that each slave produced £100 to £200 worth of tar annually.

60. Lewis C. Gray, *History of Agriculture in the Southern States to 1860,* 2 vols. (Gloucester, Mass., 1958), I, 157, 539; Merrens, *Colonial North Carolina,* p. 89.

61. Surviving tax lists are: Beaufort (1789), Carteret (1784), Onslow (1787, 1800), Nash (1782), and Wayne (1786), Treasurer's and Comptroller's Papers, NCDH.

62. Charles C. Crittenden, *The Commerce of North Carolina, 1763–1789* (New Haven, 1936), pp. 15–16; Linda Rodman, ed., "Journal of a Tour to North Carolina in 1787 by William Attmore," *James Sprunt Historical Publications,* 17 (1922), 34–35.

63. Merrens, *Colonial North Carolina,* pp. 154–55.

64. Some idea of urbanization (or the lack of it) in North Carolina can be gained from the census figures for 1800 (source: U.S. Census Office, *Return of the Whole Number of Persons with the Several Districts of the United States* [*Second Census*] (New York, 1976), pp. 73–75.

New Bern	2,467	Raleigh	669
Wilmington	1,689	Halifax	382
Fayetteville	1,656	Bath	100
Edenton	1,302		

65. Alonzo Thomas Dill, Jr., "Eighteenth Century New Bern, Part VIII," *North Carolina Historical Review,* 23, no. 4 (1946), 494–535, esp. 515.

66. Blount to Coxe, New Bern, Aug. 9, 1784, Coxe Papers, PaHS.

67. Hunter, *Quebec to Carolina,* p. 286; Smyth, *Tour,* II, 87.

68. Lawrence Lee, *The Lower Cape Fear in Colonial Days* (Chapel Hill, 1965), pp. 282–83; Merrens, *Colonial North Carolina,* pp. 151–52; Hunter, *Quebec to Carolina,* p. 287.

69. Evangeline W. Andrews, ed., *Journal of a Lady of Quality* (New Haven, 1939), pp. 184–85.

70. William Dickson to Rev. Robert Dickson, Duplin, Feb. 24, 1786, Dickson Papers, NCDH: James Gillespie to John Haywood, Philadelphia, Mar. 7, 1796, Ernest Haywood Coll., NCU.

71. Merrens, *Colonial North Carolina,* pp. 57–58, La Rochefoucauld-Liancourt, *Travels,* I, 636–37; Hunter, *Quebec to Carolina,* p. 288.

72. Merrens, *Colonial North Carolina,* pp. 156–57; Henderson, *Washington's Southern Tour,* pp. 117, 326.

73. Tax lists: New Hanover (1782), Brunswick (1784), Sampson (1784), Cumberland (1787), Bladen (1788), Duplin (1788), Treasurer's and Comptroller's Papers, NCDH.

74. Smyth, *Tour,* II, 169, 226, 256, 263; Douglas L. Rights, "The Trading Path to the Indians," *North Carolina Historical Review,* 8, no. 4 (1931), 403–26.

75. Smyth, *Tour,* II, 147–48, 160–61; Merrens, *Colonial North Carolina,* pp. 47, 162; E. S. Vanetta, *Soil Survey of Orange County, North Carolina* (Washington, 1921).

76. Caswell Tax Lists, 1784, 1790, 1796, Treasurer's and Comptroller's Papers, NCDH.

77. Merrens, *Colonial North Carolina,* pp. 56–61.

78. William H. Gehrke, "The Transition from the German to the English Language in North Carolina," *North Carolina Historical Review,* 12, no. 1 (1935), 1–19, esp. 2–3.

79. Rev. Jethro Rumple, *A History of Rowan County, North Carolina* (Salisbury, 1881), p. 46; Merrens, *Colonial North Carolina,* pp. 164–65; Stephen B. Weeks, *Southern Quakers and Slavery* (Baltimore, 1896), pp. 98–99, 103–5.

80. Henderson, *Washington's Southern Tour,* p. 303; Robert W. Ramsay, *Carolina Cradle: Settlement of the Northwest Carolina Frontier, 1747–1762* (Chapel Hill, 1964), p. 202.

81. Joseph Burr to Tench Coxe, Rutherford County, Apr. 15, 1796, Coxe Papers, PaHS; Merrens, *Colonial North Carolina,* p. 113.

82. D. A. Tompkins, *History of Mecklenburg County and the City of Charlotte, from 1740 to 1903* (Charlotte, 1903), pp. 22–25; Clarence W. Griffin, *History of Old Tryon and Rutherford Counties, North Carolina, 1730–1936.*

83. Merrens, *Colonial North Carolina,* pp. 162–64.

CHAPTER THREE   THE POLITICS OF PERSONALITIES, 1781–1783

1. Carroll to Charles Carroll, Jr., Nov. 3, 1800, Henry O. Thompson Papers, MdHS.

2. Only one senator, John Smith, habitually opposed Carroll on Senate roll

calls. Since Smith voted against the impost law of 1782–83 and the commerce amendment in 1785–86, he was probably opposed to the Constitution, but he did not enter the debate over ratification.

3. Merrill Jensen, *The New Nation* (New York, 1950), p. 182; Harold C. Syrett, ed., *The Papers of Alexander Hamilton,* 25 vols., to date (New York and London, 1961–) III, 1n; *Maryland Gazette* [Annapolis], June 30, Aug. 23, 1781.

4. Md, *JHD, 1781* (Jan. 1782); Carroll to Chase, Jan. 8, Feb. 11, 1782, and Chase to Carroll, Feb. 3, 1782, Carroll Papers, MdHS.

5. Jackson T. Main, "Political Parties in Revolutionary Maryland," *Maryland Historical Magazine,* 62 (1967), 1–27, uses a slightly different procedure, but comes to almost exactly the same conclusion.

6. The remaining roll calls involved federal-state relations (4), reorganization of the militia (4), enlargement of the Baltimore city market (2), reform of the state constitution, and an effort to compel better attendance at legislative sessions.

7. From Ogle of Frederick to Brogden of Prince George's, with Rowland of Cecil omitted because he agreed with only one member of the bloc.

8. This particular computer program does not measure disagreements, but they can be checked manually.

9. The regional division described below will be used in the Maryland tables throughout the book, with the exception of the urban category which is dropped at the end of the 1780s because the cities thereafter voted with their adjacent counties. The "Eastern Shore" embraces all the counties on the east side of the bay from Kent southward (Kent, Queen Anne's, Talbot, Caroline, Dorchester, Somerset, and Worcester). The "upper bay" subdivision is applied to the three counties on the northwest shore of the bay—Baltimore, Harford, and Cecil. "Western Shore" means the counties south of Baltimore, including those on the lower reaches of the Potomac: Anne Arundel, Calvert, St. Mary's, Charles, and Prince George's. Anne Arundel and Prince George's, which border on debtor frontier to the north and west, almost deserve a subdivision of their own, for they are internally divided throughout the 1780s. They are lumped with the Western Shore to keep the categories to a minimum, but it should be remembered that they account for most of the "debtor" or "mixed" voting of that region. The "upper Potomac," finally, includes the counties of Montgomery, Frederick, Washington, and (after 1790) Allegany.

10. Md, *SJ, 1782,* 1st sess., p. 42 (Jan. 11, 1783).

11. Randolph to Jefferson, Richmond, May 15, 1784, Julian P. Boyd, ed., *The Papers of Thomas Jefferson,* 19 vols. to date (Princeton, 1950–), VII, 259–61.

12. For particulars of the electoral turnover in Virginia and the methods of roll call analysis used in this state, see: Norman K. Risjord and Gordon Den Boer, "The Evolution of Political Parties in Virginia, 1782–1800," *The Journal of American History,* 60, no. 4 (1974), 961–84, esp. 962–63.

13. This excludes the votes on British debts, in which Henry did not participate. The alignment on them is analyzed in chapter 4. Three other roll calls involve the relief of tax collectors, who were technically obligated to the state even when they were unable to collect from their parishioners. These are exluded because they involved mixed feelings, pro- or anti-collector as well as pro- or anti-debtor.

14. Jefferson to Madison, Tuckahoe, May 7, 1783, Boyd, ed., *Jefferson Papers,* VI, 265–67.

15. Joseph Jones to Madison, Richmond, May 25, June 8, 1783, William T.

Hutchinson, Robert A. Rutland, and William M. E. Rachal, eds., *The Papers of James Madison,* 9 vols. to date (Chicago and London, 1962–), VII, 75–77, 118–21.

16. Robert D. Meade, *Patrick Henry, Practical Revolutionary* (Philadelphia, 1969), pp. 260–61.

17. Va, *JHD, 1783,* 1st sess., p. 4 (May 12, 1783).

18. Lee to Landon Carter, Richmond, June 3, 1783, Lee-Ludwell Papers, VaHS.

19. Edmund Randolph to Madison, Richmond, May 9, 1783, and Joseph Jones to Madison, Richmond, June 8, 1783, Hutchinson, ed., *Madison Papers,* VII, 32–34, 118–21. Lee participated in four roll calls involving debts and taxation, 1782–84, and voted debtor on three of them.

20. James to John F. Mercer, St. James's, Va., May 6, 21, Sept. 23, 1783, Mercer Family Papers, VaHS. During a 1782 attempt in the House of Delegates to censure Arthur Lee and deprive him of his congressional seat, Mercer voted for Lee: Va, *JHD, 1782,* 1st sess., pp. 62, 66, 71 (Dec. 11, 14, 1782). Since Lee was saved by majorities of 50 to 28, 46 to 28, and 48 to 37 it seems likely that these votes reflected Virginians' antipathy to Robert Morris rather than the true strength of the Lee faction. Arthur Lee had few friends in Virginia. Morris resigned in 1784, and Arthur Lee was nominated for the post of Secretary of Finance. The Virginia congressional delegation voted instead for Mercer. They preferred, Monroe explained, "to suffer Arthur Lee to retire from the publick service in the opinion it will be advantageous to the publick": to Madison, Trenton, Dec. 18, 1784, Rutland, ed., *Madison Papers,* VIII, 188–90.

21. Jefferson to Madison, Annapolis, Apr. 25, 1784, Boyd. ed., *Jefferson Papers,* VII, 119.

22. There was only one roll call of significance in 1782, involving an attempt to modify the legislation on lending. On losing, 40 to 41, Tazewell called for the roll call; *JHD, 1782,* fall sess., pp. 37–38 (Nov. 26, 1782). In 1783 there were votes on a bill for the relief of debtors (*JHD, 1783,* 1st sess., p. 70), payment of taxes in commodities (*JHD, 1783,* fall sess., pp. 23–24), and on debts owed British merchants (ibid., pp. 125–26). Agreeing with Tazewell on at least three of these were 12 delegates: 4 voted creditor in the years 1784–86; 2 debtor; 6 became Federalists, 2 Antifederalists. Opposing him were 10 men—2 subsequently became Federalists, 1 Antifederalist.

23. Tazewell to John F. Mercer, Apr. 15, 1783, Mercer Family Papers, VaHS.

24. "Fairfax County Freeholders' Address and Instructions to their General Assembly Delegates," May 30, 1783, Robert A. Rutland, ed., *The Papers of George Mason,* 3 vols. (Chapel Hill, 1970), II, 779–82.

25. On his return from Congress in December 1783 Madison stopped at Gunston Hall and spent an evening with Mason. He subsequently reported to Jefferson that Mason was solid on most domestic issues. "His heterodoxy lay chiefly in being too little impressed with either the necessity or the proper means of preserving the confederacy." Madison to Jefferson, Orange, Dec. 10, 1783, Boyd. ed., *Jefferson Papers,* VI, 377–79.

26. Halifax County Tax Lists, 1784, 1786, 1787, NCDH.

27. Besides Nash the North Carolina congressional delegates in the years 1782–84 were; Samuel Johnston, lawyer-planter of Chowan, William Blount, a

land speculator who favored paper money in the assembly but supported nationalist measures in Congress, Benjamin Hawkins, Roanoke Valley planter and friend
of Madison's, Dr. Hugh Williamson, an Edenton merchant-physician with connections among New York and Philadelphia merchants, William Cumming, an Edenton lawyer who became a federal judge in 1790, and Richard Dobbs Spaight, New
Bern lawyer and political maverick. Evidence of Nash's changed attitude is in Nash
to Iredell, Philadelphia, Jan. 18, 1783, Griffith J. McRee, *Life and Correspondence of
James Iredell*, 2 vols. (New York, 1857–58), II, 35.

28. Only James Madison and Benjamin Hawkins, whose records for continuous public service were similar, could contest the title. None of the three took
much interest in the management of their estates. Bloodworth possessed 800 acres
and 12 slaves at the end of the war; New Hanover County Tax List, 1782, NCDH.

29. John H. Wheeler, *Historical Sketches of North Carolina, from 1584 to
1851. . . .* (Philadelphia, 1851), pp. 383–84.

30. Born in New Jersey and a graduate of Princeton, Martin started his
Carolina career as a merchant in Salisbury, but after some regulators administered a
public whipping he moved to Guilford County. Early in the Revolution he was a
colonel in the Continental Line, but he resigned his commission after being court-
martialed for cowardice at Germantown. Archibald Maclaine indicated he was a
tobacco planter who sold his crop in Virginia: Maclaine to Hooper, Dec. 23, 1783,
Hooper Coll., NCU.

31. In contrast, Hugh Williamson and Benjamin Hawkins conducted regular
tours on their way to attend sessions of Congress, stopping at the homes of
acquaintances like Madison, Washington, and Carroll, and communicating the
latest ideas back home. See note 33 for other evidence of such communication.

32. The terms "Radical" and "Conservative" seem to have originated in the
earliest descriptions of North Carolina politics, and they have been used indiscrim-
inately by historians (see, for instance, Thomas P. Abernethy, *From Frontier to
Plantation in Tennessee* [Chapel Hill, 1932], p. 44; Hugh T. Leffler and Albert R.
Newsome, *North Carolina: History of a Southern State* [Chapel Hill, 1954], pp.
240–41; and Blackwell P. Robinson, *William R. Davie* [Chapel Hill, 1957], p.
149). These terms are value judgments that have little meaning when used to
describe political parties. As descriptions of individuals or ideas they can be useful,
but only when carefully defined. As a result, they will be avoided where possible
throughout this book.

33. The phrase was that of William Cumming, a member of the Lawyers
faction: to Henry Tazewell, Edenton, July 5, 1783, Tazewell Papers, VaSL.

34. Chowan County Tax List, 1786, NCDH: Direct Tax of 1799, copy in
Hayes Collection (microfilm in the Southern Historical Collection, University of
North Carolina, Chapel Hill, from originals in the possession of Mr. John G.
Wood, Edenton, North Carolina).

35. Onslow County, Jones County, Edenton Town Tax Lists, 1783, NCDH.

36. Maclaine to George Hooper, Hillsborough, Mar. 24, Apr. 29, 1783,
Hooper Coll., NCU.

37. Maclaine to George Hooper, May 29, 1783, ibid.

38. The regional division described below will be used in North Carolina
tables throughout the book (see North Carolina county map). The Albemarle
region includes those counties bordering on Albemarle Sound and extending

westward up the Roanoke Valley as far as the falls (Northampton and Halifax counties). The Pamlico region embraces those counties bordering on Pamlico Sound (from Hyde to Onslow) and in the Neuse/Tar River watersheds, extending west as far as Nash and Johnston counties. Cape Fear refers to the southeast corner of the state and extends west as far as Cumberland and Robeson. The Piedmont begins at the Warren-Wake-Richmond line and extends west to Surry, Iredell, and Lincoln. The west is everything west of that, including Tennessee until 1790. North Carolina towns were not counted separately because they usually voted in the same way as their surrounding counties.

   39. McRee, *Iredell*, II, 62–64.

CHAPTER FOUR   DEBTOR RELIEF FOR RICH AND POOR

   1. William Tilghman to Tench Coxe, Chester Town, Apr. 9, 1781, Coxe Papers, PaHS. Another merchant-planter pled an inability to pay his debts because the blockade prevented his shipping flour to Philadelphia: William Hemsley to Tench Coxe, Apr. 14, 1781, ibid.

   2. Merrill Jensen, *The New Nation* (New York 1950) pp. 40, 302; E. James Ferguson, *The Power of the Purse* (Chapel Hill, 1961), pp. 51–52.

   3. Va, *JHD, 1780,* 1st sess., pp. 36–37, 59 (June 6, 22, 1780).

   4. William Waller Hening, *Statutes at Large . . . of Virginia,* 13 vols. (Richmond, 1822), X, 321–24, 429–31, 456–57; Mary T. Armentrout, "A Political Study of Virginia Finance, 1781–1789." (Ph.D. diss., University of Virginia, 1934), pp. 48–49.

   5. Jensen, *New Nation,* pp. 304, 307.

   6. Va, *JHD, 1784,* 2nd sess., pp. 88–90 (Dec. 28, 1784).

   7. Philip A. Crowl, *Maryland During and After the Revolution* (Baltimore, 1943), pp. 44–45; Kathryn L. Behrens, *Paper Money in Maryland, 1727–1789* (Baltimore, 1923), pp. 61–73.

   8. James R. Morrill, *The Practice and Politics of Fiat Finance: North Carolina in the Confederation, 1783–1789* (Chapel Hill, 1969), pp. 19–20.

   9. Hening, *Statues at Large,* XI, 140–42; Walter Clark, ed., *State Records of North Carolina,* 30 vols. (Winston and Goldsboro, N.C., 1896–1917), XXIV, 802–3.

   10. Md, *JHD, 1782,* 2nd sess., pp. 34, 88–89 (Nov. 30, 1782, Jan. 12–13, 1783); *SJ, 1782,* 2nd sess., p. 32 (Jan. 5, 1783).

   11. Randolph to Madison, Richmond, Apr. 26, 1783, Hutchinson, ed., *Madison Papers,* VI, 499–500; Thomas Johnson to Gov. Henry, Jan. 19, 1786, *Calendar of Virginia State Papers and Other Manuscripts,* 11 vols (Richmond, 1875–92), IV, 82.

   12. Legislative Petitions, 1780–83, VaSL.

   13. Va, *JHD, 1781,* 2nd sess., p. 69 (Jan. 3, 1782); St. George Tucker to Theodorick Bland, Jr., Richmond, May 10, 1782, Charles Campbell, ed., *The Bland Papers* (Petersburg, Va., 1840), pp. 81–82. The *Journal* of the House of Delegates for the spring 1782 session is not extant.

   14. Mason to Henry, Gunston Hall, May 6, 1783, Robert A. Rutland, ed., *The Papers of George Mason,* 3 vols. (Chapel Hill, 1970), II, 772.

   15. Va, *JHD, 1783,* 1st sess., pp. 33–34 (May 26, 1783); Jones to Madison,

Richmond, May 31, 1783, and Randolph to Madison, Richmond, May 9, 24, 1783, Hutchinson, ed., *Madison Papers,* VII, 32–34, 72, 74, 99–101.

16. Va, *JHD, 1783,* 2d sess., pp. 23–24 (Nov. 19, 1783); William Wirt Henry, *Patrick Henry: Life, Correspondence, and Speeches* (New York, 1891), II, 212–13. Eight of Tazewell's supporters remained in the House through 1784–85, and all became Madison men.

17. Marshall to Monroe, Richmond, May 15, 1784, Monroe Papers, DLC; Madison, Jr., to Madison, Sr., Richmond, June 15, 1784, Rutland, ed., *Madison Papers,* VIII, 79–80.

18. "Laws of North Carolina—1781," Clark ed., *State Records,* XXIV, 390–94; Johann D. Schoepf, *Travels in the Confederation, 1783–1784* (Philadelphia, 1911), p. 132.

19. Jensen, *New Nation,* 319–20; Samuel A. Ashe, *History of North Carolina,* 2 vols. (Greensboro, 1908–25), II, 5–6; James R. Morrill, *The Practice and Politics of Fiat Finance: North Carolina in the Confederation, 1783–1789* (Chapel Hill, 1969), pp. 173–74. Jensen calls it a "clear-cut fight" between debtor farmers and merchants and a "sweeping victory for the debtors," but more persuasive is Morrill's argument (pp. 57–61) that the emission had broad support in the mercantile community and the main contest in the assembly was whether the money ought to be purely fiat or whether it should be backed with something of a tangible value. William H. Masterson, *William Blount* (Baton Rouge, 1954), pp. 68–74, suggests that merchants like Blount wanted paper money to buy western lands.

20. Richard Caswell to William Caswell, May 4, 1783, Richard Caswell Papers, NCU; Clark, ed., *State Records,* XXIV, 475–78.

21. Morrill, *Fiat Finance,* pp. 59, 62.

22. Griffith J. McRee, *Life and Correspondence of James Iredell,* 2 vols., (New York, 1857–58); II, 60–66; Maclaine to Iredell, Aug. 25, 1783, Iredell Papers, NCDu; Martin to John Gray Blount and Thomas Blount, Sept. 27, 1783, Alice B. Keith and William H. Masterson, eds., *The John Gray Blount Papers,* 3 vols. (Raleigh, 1952–65), I, 127.

23. Morrill, *Fiat Finance,* pp. 70–71, 73.

24. Crowl, *Maryland During and After the Revolution,* pp. 41–63.

25. Md, *JHD, 1780,* fall sess., pp. 101–2, 114–15 (Jan. 26, 31, 1781). The House vote on the Confiscation Act was 20 to 19. Md, *SJ, 1780,* fall sess., pp. 44, 46 (Jan. 30, 31, 1781). The Senate passed the compromise bill without a roll call.

26. Crowl, *Maryland During and After the Revolution,* pp. 49–52, lists the purchasers of the two companies.

27. William Hemsley to Tench Coxe, Queen Anne's County, Mar. 31, 1781, Coxe Papers, PaHS.

28. Md, *JHD, 1782,* 1st sess., p. 95 (Jan. 15, 1783); *JHD, 1782,* 2d sess., pp. 28, 42 (May 21, 28, 1783); *SJ, 1782,* 1st sess., pp. 42, 46 (Jan. 11, 14, 1783).

29. Md, *JHD, 1782,* 1st sess., pp. 60, 90 (Dec. 23, 1782, Jan. 14, 1783); *JHD, 1782,* 2d sess., p. 13 (May 13, 1783).

30. Md, *JHD, 1782,* 1st sess., p. 92 (Jan. 15, 1783).

31. Md, *JHD, 1782,* 1st sess., p. 95 (Jan. 15, 1783); ibid., 2d sess., pp. 28, 42 (May 21, 28, 1783); *JHD, 1783,* p. 83 (Dec. 24, 1783).

32. Md, *SJ, 1783,* p. 32; *JHD, 1783,* pp. 87–88 (Dec. 25, 1783).

33. Md, *JHD, 1783,* pp. 83, 85–86 (Dec. 24, 25, 1783); *SJ, 1783,* pp. 34–35 (Dec. 26, 1783).

34. Julian P. Boyd, ed., *The Papers of Thomas Jefferson,* 19 vols. to date (Princeton, 1950–), II, 171, editor's note.

35. Emory G. Evans, "Planter Indebtedness and the Coming of the Revolution in Virginia," *William and Mary Quarterly,* 3d ser., 19, no. 4 (1962), 511–33, esp. 531.

36. Mason to Patrick Henry, Gunston Hall, May 6, 1783, Rutland, ed., *Mason Papers,* II, 769–73. The quotation was part of a lengthy effort to induce Henry to support repayment in the assembly.

37. Jensen, *New Nation,* p. 278.

38. Among those using the 30,000 figure was Jefferson, who was governor during the British occupation; Jefferson to William Gordon, Paris, July 16, 1788, Boyd, ed., *Jefferson Papers,* XIII, 363–64.

39. George Mason to Arthur Lee, Gunston Hall, Mar. 26, 1783, and Mason to Patrick Henry, Gunston Hall, May 6, 1783, Rutland, ed., *Mason Papers,* II, 765–67, 769–73, esp. 766, 771. It must be admitted that few southerners actually expressed this viewpoint, but they might well have anticipated such a result. By 1787 the ending of paper money, the removal of obstructions against British law suits, and the prospect of a stronger central government all brought a return of British merchants and British capital: see Edward C. Papenfuse, *Pursuit of Profit: The Annapolis Merchants in the Era of the American Revolution, 1763–1805* (Baltimore and London, 1975), ch. 5 passim.

40. William Lee to Thomas Lee, Green Spring, Mar. 26, 1786, Lee-Ludwell Papers, VaHS.

41. Washington to George William Fairfax, Mount Vernon, June 30, 1786, and Washington to David Stuart, Mount Vernon, Nov. 5, 1787, Washington Papers, DLC.

42. Grayson to Madison, New York, May 28, 1786, Rutland, ed., *Madison Papers,* IX, 61–65; Randolph to St. George Tucker, Richmond, Nov. 19, 1784, Tucker-Coleman Papers, VaWM. Concern for the state's honor was also prevalent among westerners who did not owe any debts: "Resolutions of the Freeholders of Frederick County," *Virginia Gazette* [Richmond], Dec. 27, 1783.

43. "Petition of the Subscribers, Inhabitants of the County of Fairfax . . . To the honourable Speaker & Members of both Houses of Assembly" [June 18, 1783], George Mason Papers, VaSL. The Alexandria tax books do not go back before 1787; only three of the subscribers owned lots in Alexandria at that time. Fairfax and Alexandria Tax Lists, VaSL.

44. Washington to George W. Fairfax, June 30, 1786, Washington Papers, DLC; Jefferson to Alexander McCaul, London, Apr. 19, 1786, Boyd, ed., *Jefferson Papers,* IX, 388–90, and editor's note, 397.

45. Pendleton to Madison, Edmundsburg, Mar. 31, 1783, David John Mays, ed., *The Letters and Papers of Edmund Pendleton, 1734–1803,* 2 vols. (Charlottesville, Va., 1967), II, 440–41.

46. Mason to Arthur Lee, Gunston Hall, March 25, 1783, and Mason to Patrick Henry, Gunston Hall, May 6, 1783, Rutland, ed., *Mason Papers,* II, 765–67, 769–73.

47. Hening, *Statutes at Large,* XI, 195; Va, *JHD, 1783,* 1st sess., pp. 61, 70 (June 17, 20, 1783); Thomson Mason to John F. Mercer, Richmond, June 22, 1783, quoted in Kate Mason Rowland, *The Life of George Mason,* 2 vols. (New York, 1892), II, 55–63, esp. 58.

48. Va, *JHD, 1783,* 2d sess., pp. 125–26 (Dec. 17, 1783); Harrison to Virginia Delegates in Congress, Aug. 9, 1783, Governor Benjamin Harrison's Letterbook, VaSL; Isaac J. Harrell, *Loyalism in Virginia* (Philadelphia, 1926), p. 144.

49. Linking the debt issue to slaves and the northwest posts were: Monroe to Harrison, Annapolis, Mar. 26, 1784, and Tyler to Jefferson, Richmond, May 20, 1784, Boyd, ed., *Jefferson Papers,* VII, 47–49, 277–78.

50. Va, *JHD, 1784,* 1st sess., pp. 41, 74–75 (June 7, 23, 1784). A further amendment asking Congress to sanction the policy of withholding part of the debts failed by 33 to 50.

51. Randolph to Jefferson, Richmond, May 15, 1784, Boyd, ed., *Jefferson Papers,* VII, 259–61. Smith's pamphlet was entitled *Observations on the Fourth and Fifth Articles of the Preliminaries for a Peace with Great Britain* (Richmond, 1783).

52. Lee to Madison, Trenton, Nov. 20, 26, 1784, Rutland, ed., *Madison Papers,* VIII, 144–47, 149–51; Marshall to Monroe, Richmond, Dec. 2, 1784, Monroe Papers, DLC; Washington to R. H. Lee, Mount Vernon, Dec. 14, 1784, Washington Papers, DLC.

53. Madison to Monroe, Richmond, Jan. 8, 1785, Rutland, ed., *Madison Papers,* VIII, 220–21; Madison to Jefferson, Richmond, Jan. 9, 1785, Boyd ed., *Jefferson Papers,* VII, 588–98, esp. 595–96.

54. Edmund Pendleton to R. H. Lee, Edmundsburg, Mar. 7, 1785, Mays, ed., *Pendleton Papers,* II, 475–76.

55. The geographical subdivisions delineated here will be used in Virginia tables throughout the book; see Virginia county map. The Northern Neck refers to the counties between the Potomac and the Rappahannock rivers, extending west to the Blue Ridge (Loudoun, Fauquier). The middle Tidewater embraces the counties between the Rappahannock and the James Rivers, and east of the fall line (Caroline, Essex, King and Queen, Hanover). The Piedmont is here defined as the counties immediately to the west of these, also between the Rappahannock and the James, and extending west to the Blue Ridge (Orange, Albemarle, Amherst). The Southside is everything south of the James, from Princess Anne on the Atlantic to Bedford, Franklin, and Henry. The west includes the Great Valley, the Appalachian plateau, and until 1791, Kentucky.

56. The regional lineup and subsequent attitudes toward the Constitution were almost identical in the Senate, which rejected, 6 to 13, a resolution to repeal the laws obstructing the treaty: *Virginia Gazette* [Richmond], July 10, 1784. The vote occurred on June 26.

57. Alexander Henderson, "To the Freeholders of Fairfax County," *Virginia Journal and Alexandria Advertiser* [Alexandria], Mar. 24, 1785.

58. Williams to Dr. Philip Thomas, July 29, 1789, O. H. William Papers, MdHS.

59. Margaret B. Klapthor and Paul D. Brown, *The History of Charles County, Maryland* (La Plata, Md., 1958), pp. 65–66. The judges were John Dent, Samuel

Hanson, Jr., and Walter Hanson. Colonel Samuel Hanson (1783–84) and George Dent (1782–90) were prominent members of the creditor faction in the House of Delegates.

60. Md, *JHD, 1783*, 2nd sess., p. 11 (Nov. 14, 1783).

61. Crowl, *Maryland During and After the Revolution*, pp. 75–76.

62. Md, *JHD, 1785*, pp. 110, 186 (Jan. 24, Mar. 8, 1786).

63. Crowl, *Maryland During and After the Revolution*, 79–80.

64. Md, *SJ, 1786*, p. 53 (Apr. 28, 1787); *JHD, 1786*, pp. 147–49 (May 7, 10, 1787).

65. James F. Shepherd and Gary M. Walton, *Shipping, Maritime Trade, and the Economic Development of Colonial America* (Cambridge, 1972), pp. 131–33*n* list the debts owed British merchants in pounds sterling as follows:

	1776	1790 (5% interest added)
Maryland	£ 289,000	£ 571,000
Virginia	1,164,000	2,305,409
North Carolina	192,000	379,000
South Carolina	347,000	687,954

66. Maclaine to George Hooper, Wilmington, Dec. 30, 1783, Hooper Coll., NCU.

67. Hawkins to Washington, June 10, 1784, Washington Papers, DLC.

68. Maclaine to George Hooper, Wilmington, June 25, 1784, Hooper Coll., NCU.

69. Schoepf, *Travels*, pp. 349–50.

70. "Resolutions of the Freeholders of Frederick County," *Virginia Gazette* [Richmond], Dec. 27, 1783.

CHAPTER FIVE   EMERGENCE OF STATE PARTIES, 1784–1787

1. Correspondence, 1785–86, Washington Papers, DLC.

2. Washington to Mercer, Mount Vernon, Nov. 6, 1786, Washington Papers, DLC.

3. Washington to Charles Lee, Mount Vernon, Apr. 4, 1788; to John Hopkins, Apr. 27, 1788; to David Stuart, Dec. 2, 1788, Washington Papers, DLC.

4. Washington to George Clinton, Mount Vernon, Apr. 12, 20, 1785; to John F. Mercer, Sept. 9, 1786, Washington Papers, DLC.

5. Samuel and John Smith to Wilson Cary Nicholas, Baltimore, Sept. 28, 1786, Carter-Smith Papers, VaU.

6. *Maryland Journal* [Baltimore], Nov. 23, 1784, contains a reprint of the address from Virginia papers.

7. Johann D. Schoepf, *Travels in the Confederation, 1783–1784* (Philadelphia, 1911), p. 131.

8. Lyle Goodwin to Charles Ridgely, Sept. 5, 1784, Ridgely Family Papers, MdHS.

9. Maclaine to George Hooper, Wilmington, Dec. 16, 1783, Hooper Coll., NCU; Iredell to Pierce Butler, Edenton, Mar. 14, 1784, in Griffith J. McRee, *Life and Correspondence of James Iredell*, 2 vols. (New York, 1857–58), II, 93–94.

10. North Carolina state census, 1787, Northampton County, credited him with 110 slaves. The *U.S. Census, 1790,* Northampton, marks him as having 177.

11. Maclaine to George Hooper, Hillsborough, Apr. 29, 1783, Hooper Coll., NCU.

12. Iredell to Mrs. Iredell, Aug. 25, 1781, Charles E. Johnston Coll., NCDH.

13. Blackwell P. Robinson, *William R. Davie* (Chapel Hill, 1957), pp. 137–38, 156–58.

14. Hawkins to Washington, June 10, 1784, Washington Papers, DLC.

15. Warren County Tax List, 1784, NCDH. This holding increased to 4,991 acres and 11 slaves by 1788 but remained at about that level thereafter.

16. Hooper to the North Carolina Congress at Halifax, Philadelphia, Oct. 26, 1776, William L. Saunders, ed., *Colonial Records of North Carolina,* 10 vols. (Raleigh, 1886–90), X, 862–70. Jefferson, who never successfully distinguished between Loyalism and political conservatism exclaimed to John Adams in 1819, ". . . we had not a greater tory in Congress than Hooper." Monticello, July 9, 1819, P. L. Ford, ed., *The Works of Thomas Jefferson,* 12 vols. (New York and London, 1904–5), XII, 131–34, esp. 133.

17. George Hooper, son-in-law of Archibald Maclaine, fled to Charleston after the British captured the city in 1780.

18. Maclaine to George Hooper, Hillsborough, Apr. 21, 1784, Hooper Coll., NCU. Clearly aware of their politics in advance, Maclaine listed each member of the circle and welcomed him as an ally, except for Davie, who was new to him. And he made it clear that they cooperated closely on their political program. He identified Griffith Rutherford and Timothy Boodworth as their main opponents.

19. NC, JHC, 1784, 1st sess., Walter Clark, ed., *State Records of North Carolina,* 30 vols (Winston and Goldsboro), XIX, 555, 566, 576, 602–3, 678 (May 5, 6, 10, 15, 29, 1784). The Senate Journal for spring, 1784 is no longer extant.

20. NC, JHC, 1784, 1st sess., Clark, ed., *State Records,* XIX, 671, 674–75 (May 29, 1784). Though defeated, the repeal bill was published in the House Journal and reprinted in Virginia newspapers together with a statement by those who favored the bill: *Virginia Journal* [Alexandria], Aug. 12, 1784.

21. Maclaine to George Hooper, Wilmington, June 14, 25, 1784, Hooper Coll., NCU.

22. NC, JHC, 1784, 1st sess., Clark, ed., *State Records,* XXIV, 557–59; William R. Davie to Gen. Nathaniel Greene, June 27, 1784, Davie Papers, NCU.

23. NC, JHC, 1784, spring sess., Clark, ed., *State Records,* XIX, 612–14, 642–43 (May 18, 24, 1784); Hooper to Iredell, Hillsborough, July 8, 1784, Iredell Papers, NCDu.

24. The Senate was elected annually, and turnover there was as high as in the Commons. It seldom held roll calls; 1784 was the first year it held enough to permit an assessment of party strength. The Senate Journal for the spring of 1784 is no longer extant.

25. Benjamin Hawkins to Washington, June 10, 1784, Washington Papers, DLC; William R. Davie to Nathaniel Greene, June 27, 1784, Davie Papers, NCU.

26. Neither man trusted the mails; hence they often expressed themselves in vague generalities even in cipher. The importance of conversations is evident throughout their correspondence, if only from things that are left unsaid or only

implied. Madison often did not bother to explain the importance of certain issues; he assumed Jefferson knew. When political friends or foes were discussed (usually in code), their relationship to each other and attitudes toward legislative items were seldom delineated, except in reference to previous positions and problems. Throughout the Jefferson-Madison correspondence there is a mutual understanding of the makeup of Virginia politics and general agreement on what was needed to change it.

27. Madison to Jefferson, Orange, Dec. 10, 1783, Julian P. Boyd, ed., *The Papers of Thomas Jefferson,* 18 vols. to date (Princeton, 1950–), VI, 377–79.

28. Harry Ammon, *James Monroe: the Quest for National Identity,* (New York, 1971), 42–43; Jefferson to Madison, Annapolis, Apr. 8, 1784, Boyd, ed., *Jefferson Papers,* VII, 234.

29. Randolph to Jefferson, Richmond, May 15, 1784; Short to Jefferson, Richmond, May 14, [15], 1784, Boyd, ed., *Jefferson Papers,* VII, 257, 259–61. Randolph predicted help from Madison as early as April 24: ibid., 116–17.

30. The turnover was actually slightly lower than in the two preceding sessions. See tabulation of turnover in the House of Delegates, 1782–1800 in Norman K. Risjord and Gordon Den Boer, "The Evolution of Political Parties in Virginia, 1782–1800," *The Journal of American History,* 60, no. 4 (1974), 961–84, esp. 962.

31. Gov. Benjamin Harrison to Jefferson, Richmond, Apr. 16, 1784; Randolph to Jefferson, Richmond, Apr. 24, 1784, Boyd, ed., *Jefferson Papers,* VII, 102–3, 116–17.

32. Beverley Randolph to Monroe, May 14, 1784, Monroe Papers, DLC; Edmund Randolph to Jefferson, Richmond, May 15, 1784, Boyd, ed., *Jefferson Papers, VII, 259–61.*

33. Also part of this circle were Andrew Ronald, another prominent member of the Richmond bar who represented British plaintiffs when Virginia courts were opened to foreign suits, and his brother William Ronald, a Richmond merchant who owned half a dozen plantations in the counties south of the James; (Robert A. Rutland, ed., *The Papers of George Mason,* 3 vols. (Chapel Hill, 1970), I, glossary, p. xcii. William sat for Powhatan County in the House of Delegates throughout the 1780s.

34. The tax lists for Middlesex County are incomplete for the early 1780s, but he is listed as possessing no land in 1782 and no slaves in 1784. By 1785 he is credited with one slave, by 1787 he held 200 acres and 23 slaves, and by 1792 he owned 750 acres and 22 slaves with another 489 acres in Carolina.

35. Madison to Jefferson, Aug. 20, 1784, Boyd, ed., *Jefferson Papers,* VII, 401–8, esp. 401–2; Madison to Richard H. Lee, Orange, July 7, 1785, Lee Family Papers, VaU.

36. Edmund Randolph noted that Madison introduced the port bill as chairman of this committee: to Jefferson, Richmond, May 15, 1784, Boyd, ed., *Jefferson Papers,* VII, 260–61. I assume Madison deliberately sought the position for this purpose because otherwise it was a relatively minor committee that a young man with ambition might prefer to avoid. Susan Lee Foard, "Virginia Enters the Union, 1789–1792" (M.A. thesis, College of William and Mary, 1966), demonstrates the relationship between house leadership and the committee structure in this period.

37. Madison to Monroe, Orange, June 21, 1785, Madison Papers, DLC.

38. John Marshall to Charles Simms, Richmond, June 16, 1784, Simms Papers, DLC; Edward Carrington to John Breckinridge, Williamsburg, June 19, 1784, Breckinridge Papers, DLC.

39. Va, *JHD, 1784,* 1st sess., p. 61.

40. I am indebted to Gordon Den Boer for pointing out to me the relationship between the port bill and British debts. His dissertation, "The House of Delegates and the Evolution of Political Parties in Virginia, 1782–1789" (University of Wisconsin, 1972) is the best study yet on Virginia politics in the 1780s.

41. British debts will be treated in greater detail in chapters 6 and 10. The purpose here is only to delineate the parties.

42. The regional classifications "middle Tidewater" and "Southside" are maintained in the table to enable comparison with other issues. However, all of those delegates in Madison's column listed as middle Tidewater came from counties along the north side of the James, and those listed as Southside came from the south shore of the James. Thus, this analysis is in close agreement with that of Jackson T. Main, "Sections and Politics in Virginia, 1781–1787," *William and Mary Quarterly,* 3d ser., 12 (1955), 96–112.

43. John Marshall (Fauquier), Wilson Cary Nicholas (Albemarle), Moses Hunter (Berkeley), and Alexander White (Frederick).

44. The cluster matrix for 1783 is not reproduced here because it looks essentially like that of 1782.

45. Since this finding is in complete accord with Jackson Turner Main, *Political Parties Before the Constitution* (Chapel Hill, 1973), pp. 217–22, which examine these issues at some length, it seems unnecessary to go into them further here. Specific problems involving the Maryland debt, confiscation of Loyalist property, and paper money will be examined in chapter 6.

46. With so few votes involved it seems reasonable to raise the threshold, and 75 percent permits comparison with Virginia and North Carolina, where all comparisons had to be done manually because of infrequent roll calls.

47. The Consolidating Act and its implications will be treated in more detail in chapter 6.

48. Md, *SJ, 784,* pp. 32, 60 (Jan. 4, 21, 1785).

49. Chase himself deviated on a few votes involving private debts, where his own interests again may have been affected, but on these he did not even carry his paper money crowd with him.

50. This is on the basis of economic issues alone (25 roll calls), with a minimum agreement threshold of 75 percent. Fourteen delegates did not vote enough to be identified. Because the conclusions are essentially the same, it seems unnecessary to duplicate the tabular analysis of Main, *Political Parties,* pp. 232–36.

51. Md, *SJ, 1785,* pp. 87–88 (Mar. 12, 1786). There is no clue in the *Journal* as to why this matter came up again after both houses apparently approved the reimbursement in 1784.

52. Md, *JHD, 1785,* p. 170 (Mar. 2, 1786).

53. *Maryland Gazette* [Annapolis], Aug. 17, 24, 31, 1786; *Maryland Journal* [Baltimore], Sept. 1, 5, 1786.

54. "A Friend to Paper Money," *To the Voters of Anne-Arundel County,* Sept. 23, 1786, broadside, MdHS; "Algeron," *Maryland Gazette* [Baltimore], Oct. 17, 1786.

55. *Maryland Journal* [Baltimore], Sept. 1, 1786.

56. Somerset and Caroline, previously evenly divided, voted 5 to 1 against paper in 1786.

57. The new Annapolis delegate, Thomas Jenings, was an enemy of Chase's who had helped to expose his wartime frauds. The other Annapolis representative, Allan Quynn, was an old ally of Chase's who had supported paper money in 1785. But he voted against it in 1786, possibly with an eye on the electorate.

58. Philip A. Crowl, *Maryland During and After the Revolution* (Baltimore, 1943), p. 103, saw no sectional incidence in the paper money votes of 1785–86, but Crowl failed to observe the changes in the divided counties (Caroline, Somerset, Baltimore, Montgomery, and Frederick), and he erroneously listed Harford as anti-paper in 1785.

59. The computer matrix for this session shows three vague blocs, but they are quite formless. The reasons are that Chase's schism mixed the voting on several economic issues; votes on taxation involved some special local interests, rather than principle; and voting on social matters (education, religion, slavery) followed no particular pattern.

60. Main, *Political Parties*, pp. 224–25, seems to suggest that the alliance between speculators and debtors held throughout the session. They voted together only when matters of general indebtedness were at stake. When the interests of speculators alone were involved (as, for instance, in the series of votes on the plea of speculators who had purchased the Nottingham furnace: *JHD, 1786*, pp. 153–63), most of the debtor element voted against the Chasites. The three factions can thus be clearly distinguished. The same was true of the solitary vote on relief for speculators in the 1787 session: *JHD, 1787*, p. 45 (Dec. 14, 1789).

61. L. Marx Renzulli, *Maryland: the Federalist Years* (Rutherford, N.J., 1973), p. 39, is the most recent of a long line of writers who have asserted that Ridgely and Chase were political allies (an exception is Forrest McDonald, *We the People: The Economic Origins of the Constitution* [Chicago, 1958], p. 160*n*). Renzulli even goes so far as to describe Chase as Ridgely's "spokesman." Ridgely's voting pattern was mixed but generally pro-debtor on economic issues throughout the 1785–87 period. The only thing he consistently agreed with Chase on was paper money. The two even differed on votes involving confiscated property.

62. Yet another delegate, Richard Bond of Cecil, agreed with Chase on economic issues but voted to unseat Chase on a critical roll call; hence he was classified as "middle."

63. Among those who agreed closely with Chase on economic issues, for instance, was Robert Bowie of Queen Anne's, who subsequently became an Antifederalist and one of the state's earliest Republicans. He entered the House in 1785, and his record in that session was utterly mixed. His agreement with Chase thus seems largely coincidental.

64. Pendleton was conservative in the sense that he opposed a number of the legal reforms proposed by Jefferson, such as abolition of primogeniture and entail: see Dumas Malone, *Jefferson the Virginian* (Boston, 1948), pp. 253–54, 270.

65. Washington to William Carmichael, Mount Vernon, June 10, 1785; to Richard Henry Lee, Mount Vernon, Aug. 22, 1785; Washington to George Mason, Mount Vernon, Oct. 3, 1785; Washington to David Stuart, Mount Vernon, Nov. 30, 1785, Washington Papers, DLC.

66. The Harrison homestead, "Berkeley," is a magnificent mansion in Charles City County on the north side of the James. One can assume mortification on the part of a man who retired as governor, stood for the assembly in a county where he owned much of the land, and was defeated.

67. Pendleton to R. H. Lee, Edmondsburg, Apr. 18, 1785, Lee Papers, VaU; Madison to Jefferson, Apr. 27, 1785, Boyd, ed., *Jefferson Papers,* VIII, 110–16, esp. p. 113.

68. Richard H. Lee to Patrick Henry, New York, Oct. 29, 1785, Lee Papers, VaU; Stuart to Jefferson, Richmond, Oct. 17, 1785, Boyd, ed., *Jefferson Papers,* VIII, 644–47. Stuart finally backed Harrison on the grounds that Tyler was a Henryite: Stuart to John Breckinridge, Richmond, Oct. 24, 1785, Breckinridge Papers, DLC.

69. Va, *JHD, 1785,* pp. 4, 19–22 (Oct. 24, Nov. 2–3, 1785); James Currie to Jefferson, Richmond, Oct. 17, 1785, and Madison to Jefferson, Richmond, Jan. 22, 1786, Boyd, ed., *Jefferson Papers,* VIII, 640–44, IX, 194–95.

70. Gov. Benjamin Harrison to Jefferson, Richmond, Apr. 16, 1784, Boyd, ed., *Jefferson Papers,* VII, 102–3.

71. Va, *JHD, 1785,* pp. 45–46; Madison to Washington, Richmond, Nov. 11, 1785, Washington Papers, DLC; Stuart to John Breckinridge, Richmond, Dec. 7, 1785, Breckinridge Papers, DLC. Breckinridge had been a member of the House in the years 1781–84. In 1784 he and Stuart, both from Botetourt in the upper Valley, were the only westerners who voted with the Madison circle. Paper money does not appear in the legislative journal, but a discussion of it was reported by Nicholas Cabell to John Breckinridge, Richmond, Oct. 26, 1785, ibid.

72. In explaining his change of heart, for instance, on the commerce amendment, which finally induced him to vote in favor of postponement, Madison gave no hint that he expected others to follow him: Madison to Washington, Dec. 9, 1785, Washington Papers, DLC; Madison to Jefferson, Richmond, Jan. 22, 1786, Boyd, ed., *Jefferson Papers,* IX, 194–202, esp. 197–99.

73. On commerce and trade policy Madison identified his main opponents as Harrison, Carter Braxton, and Meriwether Smith; and on law reform Harrison and Mercer: Madison to Washington, Richmond, Nov. 11, 1785, Washington Papers, DLC; Madison to Jefferson, Richmond, Jan. 22, 1786, Boyd, ed., *Jefferson Papers,* IX, 194–202, esp. 195. In addition, Harrison made the usual step of coming down from the Speaker's chair to record his vote in favor of postponing taxes: *JHD, 1785,* pp. 45–46 (Nov. 19, 1785). Strangely enough, John Tyler voted with the Madison men on both taxes and commerce in this session. Perhaps he was voting in opposition to Harrison.

74. Grayson to Madison, New York, Nov. 14, 1785, Rutland, ed., *Madison Papers,* VIII, 410–12; R. H. Lee to Monroe, Monroe Papers, DLC.

75. Va, *JHD, 1785,* pp. 92, 100, 115 (Dec. 14, 20, 28, 1785); Madison to Monroe, Richmond, Dec. 24, 30, 1785, Rutland, ed., *Madison Papers,* VIII, 455–56, 465–66; Madison to Jefferson, Richmond, Jan. 22, 1786, Boyd, ed., *Jefferson Papers,* IX, 199. The vote against postponement was 46 to 55, but the names were not recorded.

76. R. H. Lee to Washington, Trenton, Nov. 20, 1784, Washington Papers, DLC.

77. Stuart to John Breckinridge, Jan. 26, 1786, Breckinridge Papers, DLC.

78. Va. *JHD, 1785,* pp. 66–67 (Nov. 30–Dec. 1, 1785); Madison to Washington, Richmond, Dec. 9, 1785, Washington Papers, DLC. The tax votes involved an amendment for remitting half the taxes for 1785 (passed, 52 to 42), and the vote on final passage (rejected, 48 to 50). Madison voted against both. The measure was later revived and passed without a roll call.

79. Newspapers did report two popular meetings, one in Norfolk and one in neighboring Nansemond County, which adopted instructions to their delegates in 1785. They endorsed the commerce amendment and, somewhat inconsistently, a navigation act that would restrict foreign vessels in Virginia. But they did not mention other elements of the creditor-nationalist program. *Virginia Gazette* [Richmond], Oct. 15, Nov. 12, 1785.

80. Joseph Prentis (1754–1809) had served in the House intermittently since 1776, representing variously Williamsburg, James City, and York. He represented York at this point, although he is not on any York County tax lists for the 1780s. He lived and practiced law in Williamsburg (advertisement in the *Virginia Gazette,* March 29, 1787). He voted debtor in 1782–84; in 1785 he voted against Madison on the commerce amendment and with him on court reform. As a judge of the general court (1788–1809) he favored the Constitution, though apparently with misgivings, and subsequently became a Jeffersonian Republican.

81. Grayson was an able, elderly Northern Neck planter-lawyer, educated in Philadelphia and London. Like Richard Henry Lee, he was excessively fearful of northern merchants, but he did favor strengthening the powers of Congress. Like Monroe, he later opposed the Constitution because it went too far. "Light Horse Harry" Lee was a friend of Washington's from the Northern Neck and a life-long Federalist.

82. Madison to Washington, Richmond, Nov. 8, 1786, Washington Papers, DLC.

83. Madison to Jefferson, Richmond, Dec. 4, 1786, Boyd, ed., *Jefferson Papers,* X, 574–75.

84. Randolph to Jefferson, Richmond, Jan. 28, 1787, ibid., XI, 84–85.

85. Marshall to Arthur Lee, Richmond, Mar. [5], 1787 [copy], Lee Papers, VaHS.

86. Randolph to Madison, Richmond, Mar. 22, Apr. 4, 11, 1787; see also John Dawson to Madison, Fredericksburg, Apr. 15, 1787; Rutland, ed., *Madison Papers,* IX, 328, 364–65, 381–82.

87. Dawson to Madison, Fredericksburg, June 12, 1787, Madison Papers, DLC.

88. Jones to Madison, Richmond, Nov. 22, 1787; Monroe to Madison, Richmond, Dec. 6, 1787; Stuart to Madison, Dec. 2, 1787; all in Madison Papers, DLC.

89. "Address of the Freeholders of Prince George County to their Delegates," *Virginia Gazette* [Richmond], June 28, 1787. None of the signers served in the assembly at any time; it was apparently an expression of local feeling.

90. Jefferson to Monroe, Paris, Aug. 5, 1787, Boyd, ed., *Jefferson Papers,* XI, 687–88.

91. These findings stem from an examination of the county tax lists in the Virginia State Library, Richmond, in collaboration with Dr. Gorden Den Boer. We tabulated the annual totals for all counties with extant records under the headings

taxed: land values (which did not vary much from year to year), white and black population, horses, and cattle. The number of horses seemed to be related to the fluctuations in the white population, but the size of the cattle herd closely followed the business cycle—from a high in 1782 (when most tax records begin) to a low in 1785–86 (the nadir varied from county to county) and a noticeable recovery in 1787. Unfortunately, cattle were not taxed after 1787. The rise in white population and slaves in the Piedmont counties continued in 1788 and 1789, leveling off thereafter.

92. Merrill Jensen, *The New Nation* (New York, 1950), p. 305.

93. There were only three roll calls on economic issues in the 1787 session; hence delegates who served only in that session had to be omitted from table 5.8.

94. John Sitgreaves (1757–1802) was a New Bern lawyer, who was born in England. He served in Congress in 1784–85 and in the Commons, 1786–87. He voted in favor of the Constitution in the 1788 ratifying convention, and President Washington made him a federal district judge in 1789. He married a daughter of Allan Jones and was thus a brother-in-law to William R. Davie.

95. Philemon Hawkins was a friend of Person's from Granville County. Matthew Lock of Rowan is considered by several historians a major leader of the debtor element, though there is little in the record to show it. He was chiefly remarkable for his longevity, having served in the Commons and Senate since 1770. He was an Antifederalist in 1788 and a Republican congressman in the 1790s. Jesse Franklin, of far-western Wilkes, was a newcomer to debtor ranks, having moved south from Virginia at the end of the war. After a long career in the Commons, he entered Congress as a Republican in 1795 and moved to the U.S. Senate in 1799.

96. The state possessed 57 counties and 6 towns by 1787. If each were fully represented, the House would have contained 240 members. In fact, only about a third of that number was present on any given roll call.

97. Main, *Political Parties,* p. 315, suggests that a line drawn from Wilmington north to Halifax would virtually delineate the two parties. Most of the Cosmopolitans (Lawyers) and not a single Localist (debtors) resided east of that line, he discovered. The sectional division, though quite apparent, was not quite that sharply drawn, for there was substantial debtor feeling in the pine woods counties along Pamlico Sound. Using the criteria described earlier in the text to discover party allegiance, I have found 6 debtor (Localist) delegates residing east of that line, 1 from the lower Cape Fear (New Hanover), and 5 from the Pamlico region.

98. Maclaine remained a trenchant commentator on political affairs until his death in 1790, however. He supported the Constitution and the Washington Presidency.

99. He possessed 1,680 acres, 59 slaves, and two lots in Edenton: Chowan County Tax List, 1783, NCDH.

100. Jefferson to Madison, Annapolis, Apr. 25, 1784, Boyd, ed., *Jefferson Papers,* VII, 119. Among the reasons for Jefferson's dismay may have been Spaight's friendship with politically unreliable John Francis Mercer: Spaight to Mercer, New York, Mar. 16, 1785, Etting Coll., PaHS.

101. Maclaine, at least, gave him one of his rare blessings: to Iredell, Aug. 24, 1786, Iredell Papers, NCDu.

102. Spaight later attended the Philadelphia convention, signed the Constitution, and supported it in the state ratifying convention. But his support was so equivocal that Antifederalists nominated him for U.S. senator in 1789 against Samuel Johnston. In three terms as governor, 1792–95, he again received bipartisan support. In 1796 he ran for Congress against a prominent Republican, Nathan Bryan, while standing for the electoral college as a candidate pledged to Jefferson. In 1802 he was killed in a duel by a fellow Jeffersonian, John Stanly.

103. NC, SJ, 1785, Clark, ed., *State Records,* XX, 102 (Dec. 27, 1785); XVIII, 155–56, 184–85 (Dec. 26, 30, 1786).

CHAPTER SIX   DEPRESSION POLITICS, 1784–1787

1. Curtis P. Nettels, *The Emergence of a National Economy, 1775–1815* (New York, 1962), pp. 62–63.

2. The leading sources for prices in this period, Anne Bezanson, *Prices and Inflation During the American Revolution: Pennsylvania, 1770–1790* (Philadelphia, 1951) and Arthur H. Cole, *Wholesale Commodity Prices in the United States, 1700–1861* (Cambridge, Mass., 1938), are confined to the major cities. Except for James River tobacco, which was singled out because it commanded a special price, there is no way of determining where the commodities they list originated. Since the timing and severity of the depression varied in different parts of the nation, it seems useful to construct a price series for the Cheasapeake, incomplete though it be. Newspapers (Richmond and Alexandria *Gazettes*) did not begin systematically reporting prices until 1785 and ceased abruptly at the end of 1787. Manuscript sources include the Tench Coxe Papers, PaHS; Madison Papers, DLC; Webb-Prentis Coll., VaU; Washington Papers, DLC. Table 6.1 indicates that the statement of Gordon C. Bjork in "The Weaning of the American Economy: Independence, Market Changes, and Economic Development," *Journal of Economic History,* 24 (1964), 541–559, esp. 555, that "Tobacco prices continued at a high level until 1790" is simply incorrect.

3. Bezanson, *Prices During the American Revolution,* pp. 104, 138.

4. Ibid., p. 268.

5. Cole begins this particular series in 1784. A Richmond merchant attributed the jump in wheat and flour prices in the spring of 1794 to the purchases of French ships in Norfolk: Robert Pollard to Wilson C. Nicholas, Feb. 23, 1794, Nicholas Papers, VaU.

6. Timothy Pitkin, *A Statistical View of the Commerce of the United States* (New York, 1817), pp. 220, 241–42; Lewis C. Gray, *History of Agriculture in the Southern States,* to 1860, 2 vols. (Gloucester, Mass., 1958), II, 605; Bjork, "Weaning of the American Economy," p. 544.

7. William Cooke to Coxe & Frazier, New Bern, Mar. 11, 1785, Coxe Papers, PaHS.

8. Madison to Jefferson, Orange, Aug. 20, 1784, Julian P. Boyd, ed., *The Papers of Thomas Jefferson,* 18 vols. to date (Princeton, 1950–), VII, 401–8, esp. 402. By "the country" Madison was clearly referring to Virginia.

9. Bezanson, *Prices During the American Revolution,* pp. 260–65.

10. Madison to Jefferson, Orange, Mar. 18, 1786, Boyd, ed., *Jefferson Papers.*

IX, 332–36, esp. 335. With some tortured reasoning Madison then sought to demonstrate that tax postponement caused the currency shortage.

11. Defining as a speculator anyone who purchased more than £100 property on credit, only 103 served in the assembly at any time in the 1780s, and in the crucial 1786 session there were only 17 in the House of Delegates. Figures taken from the Proceedings of the Commissioners for Confiscated Property, 8 vols., MdHR (see my "Note on Sources" for description of each volume). Moreover, speculators did not always vote their interests. Some of the largest purchasers of confiscated property opposed paper money and other forms of debtor relief, among them Thomas Johnson, James Shaw, John H. Stone, James McHenry, Richard Potts, Nathaniel Ramsay, and Dr. Philip Thomas. All were members of the creditor party, and all were Federalists in 1788.

12. Philip A. Crowl, *Maryland During and After the Revolution* (Baltimore, 1943), pp. 96–97; "Steady" in *Maryland Gazette* [Baltimore], Sept. 28, 1787.

13. Md, *JHD, 1784,* pp. 49, 68 (Dec. 17, 29, 1784); Crowl, *Maryland During and After the Revolution,* pp. 61–62.

14. One proposal that arose during the debate appears to have been directed against the speculators. This was an amendment giving the attorney general power to compel the performance of certain contracts. Chase voted against it, but the clause was added to the bill by 26 to 21. The extent of the threat depended on the disposition of the attorney general, and since 1778 Chase's protégé Luther Martin had filled that post. A few days earlier the assembly appointed Martin a delegate to Congress, and the House had voted 30 to 19 that Martin could not serve in Congress without resigning his state position. Chase apparently did not feel he needed Martin's protection because he voted in favor of resignation: *JHD, 1784,* pp. 46, 66 (Dec. 17, 28, 1784). Martin declined the congressional appointment.

15. Md, *SJ, 1784,* p. 39 (Jan. 13, 1785).

16. Gen. O. H. Williams to Philip Thomas, Apr. 7, 1785, Williams Papers, MdHS.

17. Jenifer, untitled broadside dated Dec. 24, 1784, MdHS.

18. *Maryland Journal* [Baltimore], editorials on July 8, 22, 1785; "Sydney" on Aug. 12, and "A Cropper" on Aug. 30, 1785. The *Maryland Gazette* [Annapolis] contained no contributions on paper money before the opening of the legislative session.

19. Md, *JHD, 1785,* pp. 31–32, 48 (Dec. 1, 13, 1785).

20. Ibid., pp. 170, 186, 191 (Mar. 2, 8, 10, 1786).

21. Md, *SJ, 1785,* p. 23 (Dec. 26, 1785).

22. Md, *JHD, 1785,* pp. 41–42, 69–70 (Dec. 9, 29, 1785). One committee, appointed early in the session, exonerated Jenifer of wrongdoing. The change in attitude was clearly due to the change in composition. On the second committee were Philip Key, John DeButts, John Gale, Howes Goldsborough, and Thomas Cramphin, all opponents of paper money.

23. A member of the assembly signing himself "Philagathus" subsequently admitted that the payments to Chase and Stone were the most damning of the revelations: *Maryland Gazette* [Annapolis], Apr. 20, 1786. Stone's speculative holdings are listed in Crowl, *Maryland During and After the Revolution,* p. 104n.

24. Md, *JHD. 1785.* pp. 82, 89–93, 97, 130–33 (Jan. 6, 10, 11, 15, Feb. 9,

10, 1786). Those who sided with Jenifer favored paper money by 15 to 3; his critics opposed paper by 6 to 2. "Philagathus," *Maryland Gazette* [Annapolis], Apr. 20, 1786, claimed that "some of the warmest advocates for continuing that office are largely indebted to the state on account of confiscated property heretofore purchased."

25. The Senate's action suspended the office of Intendant for a year. In the interval the governor made Jenifer state agent for the sale of confiscated property.

26. Md, *JHD, 1785,* pp. 89, 146–49, 155–56 (Jan. 10, Feb. 18, 21, 1786).

27. *Maryland Gazette* [Baltimore], June 20, 1786; *Maryland Journal* [Baltimore], July 21, 1786. The grand jury of the Eastern Shore was sufficiently alarmed to denounce the "dangerous insurrection" in Charles County: *Maryland Gazette* [Annapolis], Sept. 21, 1786.

28. Wallace, Johnson & Muir to Ridgely, Sept. 30, 1786, Ridgely Family Papers, MdHS.

29. *Maryland Journal* [Baltimore], June 13, 20, 23, 27, 30, July 4, 11, 14, 21, 28, Aug. 18, 1786; *Maryland Gazette* [Annapolis], Aug. 17, 24, 31, Sept. 14, 21, 1786.

30. Daniel Dulaney to George Fitzhugh, Jan. 27, 1787, Dulaney Papers, MdHS.

31. Md, *JHD, 1786,* pp. 26–27 (Dec. 12, 15, 1786). The amendment lost by 30 to 31. The final roll call was printed in the *Maryland Journal* [Baltimore], Dec. 19, 1786, as a sort of opening salvo in the propaganda war that ensued.

32. Md, *SJ, 1786,* pp. 17–23 (Dec. 30, 1786, Jan. 5, 1787); *Maryland Journal* [Baltimore], Jan 16, 1787; *JHD, 1786,* p. 60 (Jan. 5, 1787).

33. Md, *SJ, 1786,* pp. 24, 31, 33 (Jan. 6, 15, 17, 1787).

34. Md, *JHD, 1786,* p. 82 (Jan. 15, 1787). The motion passed, 33 to 23, with virtually the same lineup as on paper money. Both Federalists and Antifederalists were divided (Federalists opposed it by 12 to 6; Antifederalists favored it by 15 to 2), so the vote was less a test of attitudes toward federal reform than a device for winning leverage against the Senate on debtor relief. There was leverage to be gained because the federal convention movement was gaining momentum. Virginia's action in appointing deputies was widely reported in Maryland: *Maryland Journal* [Baltimore], Dec. 22, 1786.

35. "Address of the House of Delegates to their Constituents," Jan. 16, 1787, printed broadside, MdHS.

36. William Tilghman to Tench Coxe, Chester Town, Feb. 4, 1787, Coxe Papers, PaHS.

37. Md, *SJ, 1786,* pp. 37–39 (Jan. 20, 1787); *Maryland Journal* [Baltimore], Feb. 6, 1787.

38. *Maryland Gazette* [Annapolis], Feb. 8, 1787. Chase was sufficiently concerned to reply with a discourse on the right of instruction and the obligations of representatives: ibid., Feb. 22, 1787.

39. *Maryland Journal* [Baltimore], Feb. 20, Mar. 6, 20, 1787; *Maryland Gazette* [Annapolis], Mar. 15, 22, 29, Apr. 26, 1787.

40. "REMARKS on the Proposed Plan of an EMISSION OF PAPER and on the Means of Effecting It, Address to the Citizens of Maryland, by 'Aristides,'" broadside, Annapolis, 1786, MdHS.

41. Edward C. Papenfuse, *In Pursuit of Profit: The Annapolis Merchants in the*

Era of the American Revolution, 1763–1805 (Baltimore and London, 1975), pp. 194–97. The ultimate irony is that the boon to Maryland contributed to Morris's own bankruptcy. The French objected to the poor quality of tobacco and stopped payment on a note they had sent to Morris's agents in London. When Maryland merchants heard of this, they quickly sent their Morris notes to Philadelphia for redemption: see Daniel Delozier to O. H. Williams, Baltimore, July 4, 1787, O. H. Williams Papers, MdHS.

42. Carroll to Daniel Carroll of Duddington, Mar. 13, 1787, Harper-Pennington Papers, MdHS.

43. The speculators were back with cap in hand, however. The consortium that purchased the Nottingham Iron Furnace in Harford County informed the assembly that it was unable to meet its obligations and asked the state to take back the property. The request sparked a bitter controversy with opponents demanding roll calls every step of the way. The House finally reached a compromise that permitted the Nottingham purchasers to pay their debts in state paper ("black money") in installments: *JHD, 1786*, pp. 153, 160, 162–66, 170 (May 12, 16–18, 1787). On the 14 roll calls lines were firm, but they bore little relation to voting on other issues. Chasites supported the speculators, but both creditors and debtors were divided. Strongest support for the speculators lay in the upper bay, where the property was located; their main opposition came from the upper Potomac. The controversy does suggest that the speculators could count on little public sympathy. They had to clothe their demands for relief in a popular cause such as paper money. When prosperity undermined that crusade, they were left with nothing. By the end of the year Chase was petitioning the assembly for permission to declare bankruptcy.

44. Randolph to Arthur Lee, Sept. 24, 1785, Lee Coll., VaU.

45. Stuart to Jefferson, Richmond, Oct. 17, 1785, Boyd, ed., *Jefferson Papers,* VIII, 644–47.

46. Washington to R. H. Lee, Mount Vernon, Aug. 22, 1785; R. H. Lee to Washington, New York, July 23, 1785; and Mason to Washington, Gunston Hall, Nov. 9, 1785, all in Washington Papers, DLC; Grayson to R. H. Lee, New York [Jan.–March] 1786, Lee Papers, VaU.

47. One Northern Neck planter reported that specie was quite plentiful in that area: John R. Wood to James Wood, July 8, 1785, Letters to James Wood, VaSL.

48. Nicholas Cabell, who represented the southern Piedmont in the Senate, and Francis Preston, delegate from southwestern Montgomery County, both opposed paper money: Cabell to John Breckinridge, Richmond, Oct. 26, 1785, and Preston to John Breckinridge, Richmond, Nov. 6, 1786, Breckinridge Papers, DLC. The only political leader anywhere in the state that I have found who was willing to advocate paper money, even privately, was John Brown of Kentucky: to John Breckinridge, Danville, Ky., May 20, 1786, ibid. Madison claimed that Meriwether Smith was the "most zealous" partisan of paper money in the assembly: to Jefferson, Jan. 22, 1786, Boyd, ed., *Jefferson Papers,* IX, 199.

49. Madison to Jefferson, Richmond, Jan. 22, 1786, Boyd, ed., *Jefferson Papers,* IX, 194–202, esp. 199–200; David Stuart to Washington, Richmond, Nov. 16, 1785, Washington Papers, DLC; *JHD, 1785,* pp. 43–45 (Nov. 19, 21, 1785).

50. Edmund Pendleton to R. H. Lee, Feb. 28, 1785, David John Mays, ed.,

The Letters and Papers of Edmund Pendleton, 1734–1803, 2 vols. (Charlottesville, Va., 1967), II, 475; Madison to Washington, Richmond, Dec. 9, 1785, Washington Papers, DLC; Madison to Jefferson, Richmond, Jan. 22, 1786, Boyd, ed., *Jefferson Papers,* IX, 199–200.

51. Madison to Monroe, Orange, June 4, 1786, Rutland, ed., *Madison Papers,* IX, 73–74.

52. "Shandy," in *Virginia Journal* [Alexandria], Sept. 28, 1786.

53. Va, *JHD, 1786,* pp. 15, 58 (Nov. 1, 24, 1786); Madison Jr. to Madison Sr., [Richmond], Nov. 24, 1786, Rutland, ed., *Madison Papers,* IX, 178.

54. Madison to Washington, Richmond, Dec. 24, 1786; Madison to Pendleton, Richmond, Jan. 9, 1787; Madison to Jefferson, New York, Feb. 15, 1787; all in Rutland, ed., *Madison Papers,* IX, 224–26, 243–45, 267–70.

55. Robert Morris to Samuel and Jonathan Smith, Philadelphia, Jan. 18, 1787, Samuel Smith Papers, DLC. Morris ordered 200 hogsheads from a merchant in Dumfries. It is assumed that he placed other orders through other agents.

56. James Duncanson to James Maury, Fredericksburg, July 3, 1787, James Maury Papers, VaU; Francis Corbin to Arthur Lee, Middlesex, Aug. 8, 1787, Lee Papers, VaU (photostat from Lee Papers, Harvard College); John Dawson to Madison, Fredericksburg, June 12, 1787, and James McClurg to Madison, Richmond, Aug. 22, Sept. 5, 1787, Madison Papers, DLC.

57. Francis Corbin to Arthur Lee, Middlesex, Aug. 8, 1787, Lee Papers, VaU.

58. Marshall to Arthur Lee, Richmond, Mar. [5], 1787 [copy], Lee Papers, VaHS.

59. Matthew Maury to James Maury, Fredericksburg, Dec. 10, 1787, James Maury Papers, VaU.

60. Stuart to Madison, Richmond, Nov. 9, 1787, Madison Papers, DLC.

61. "Resolutions Condemning the Use of Paper Money," Nov. 3, 1787; and Mason to Washington, Richmond, Nov. 6, 1787, Robert A. Rutland, ed., *The Papers of George Mason,* 3 vols., (Chapel Hill, 1970), 1008–12.

62. Mason to Washington, Richmond, Nov. 6, 1787, ibid.; Va, *JHD, 1787,* pp. 101–2, 105, 120 (Dec. 15, 17, 27, 1787).

63. Stuart to Madison, Nov. 9, Dec. 2, 1787, Madison Papers, DLC.

64. Jones to Madison, Richmond, Dec. 10, 1787, ibid.

65. Mason to Washington, Richmond, Nov. 27, 1787, Washington Papers, DLC; *JHD, 1787,* p. 66 (Nov. 24, 1787).

66. William R. Davie to Spruce Macay, July 13, 1785, Macay-McNeeley Papers, NCU; Maclaine to Samuel Johnston, Dec. 24, 1785, Hayes Coll., NCU; James R. Morrill, *The Practice and Politics of Fiat Finance: North Carolina in the Confederation, 1783–1789* (Chapel Hill, 1969), pp. 74–76.

67. NC, *JHC, 1785,* Walter Clark, ed., *State Records of North Carolina* (Winston and Goldsboro, 1896–1917), 30 vols., XVII, 364–65 (Dec. 19, 1785); Hugh Williamson to Charles Thomson, Edenton, Jan. 14, 1786, Gratz Coll., PaHS.

68. NC, JHC, 1785, Clark, ed., *State Records,* XVII, 366, 405–6 (Dec. 19, 27, 1785); SJ, 1785, ibid., XX, 68, 81, 102 (Dec. 16, 21, 27, 1785).

69. Ibid., XVII, 394–95 (Dec. 24, 1785).

70. Ibid., XVIII, 155–56, 361–62 (Dec. 22, 26, 1786); Morrill, *Fiat Finance,* pp. 84–85.

71. A. Donald to Jefferson, Richmond, Nov. 12, 1787, *Proceedings of the Massachusetts Historical Society,* 2d ser., 17 (1903), 489–90.

72. When courts of assize became a political issue in 1784, Archibald Stuart credited Jefferson with the idea: to Jefferson, Richmond, Oct. 17, 1785, Boyd, ed., *Jefferson Papers,* VIII, 644–47. The 1779 proposals by the Jefferson-Pendleton-Wythe committee for changes in the judicial system are printed in ibid., II, 569–82.

73. Marshall to Charles Simms, Richmond, June 16, 1784, Simms Papers, DLC.

74. Madison to Jefferson, Richmond, Jan. 9, 1785, Boyd, ed., *Jefferson Papers,* VII, 588–89; *Acts Passed at a General Assembly of the Commonwealth of Virginia, October Session, 1784* (Richmond, n.d.), pp. 1–3.

75. Va, *JHD, 1785,* pp. 89–90 (Dec. 13, 1785); Madison to Monroe, Richmond, Dec. 17, 1785, Rutland, ed., *Madison Papers,* VIII, 445–46. Madison did not explain the exact nature of the supplemental legislation, and since it failed to pass it was never published.

76. *Virginia Gazette,* (Richmond), Feb. 22, 1786; Madison to Washington, Nov. 11, 1785, Washington Papers, DLC; Madison to Jefferson, Richmond, Jan. 22, 1786, Boyd, ed., *Jefferson Papers,* IX, 194–202, esp. 197. The revision codified colonial statutes and simplified court procedures.

77. Madison to Edmund Pendleton, Richmond, Nov. 30, 1786; Madison to Jefferson, Richmond, Dec. 4, 1786, Rutland, ed., *Madison Papers,* IX, 185–87, 189–92; Stuart to John Breckinridge, Richmond, Nov. 24, 1786, Breckinridge Papers, DLC.

78. Archibald Stuart to John Breckinridge, Nov. 24, 1786, Breckinridge Papers, DLC; David Stuart to Washington, Richmond, Dec. 25, 1786, Washington Papers, DLC.

79. Madison to Washington, Richmond, Dec. 7, 1786; Madison, Jr., to Madison, Sr., Richmond, Dec. 12, 1786, Rutland, ed., *Madison Papers,* IX, 199–200, 205–6; Va, *JHD, 1786,* pp. 104–7 (Dec. 16, 18, 1786).

80. Madison to Jefferson, New York, Feb. 15, 1787, Boyd, ed., *Jefferson Papers,* XI, 152–5.

81. Va, *JHD, 1787,* pp. 105–6 (Dec. 18, 1787); Jones to Madison, Richmond, Dec. 10, 1787, Madison Papers, DLC.

82. William Waller Hening, *Statutes at Large . . . of Virginia,* 13 vols. (Richmond, 1822), XII, 532–58. The act was replaced by another in the following year, but the judicial organization remained essentially the same: ibid., 730–63.

83. Joseph Prentis, St. George Tucker, Richard Parker, and Gabriel Jones.

84. Blackwell P. Robinson, *William R. Davie* (Chapel Hill, 1957), pp. 159–60.

85. NC, JHC, 1785, Clark, ed., *State Records,* XVII, 269–72, 307–8, 311–12 (Nov. 21, Dec. 3, 5, 1785). The Journal does not describe the nature of the discussion. But it started out on the subject of the governor's message (which did not mention court reform) and ended with the resolution asking Maclaine and Hay to draft a court bill. It is a fair inference that they brought up the subject. The

matter of compiling the law code was taken up in a separate bill drafted by Abner Nash.

86. Samuel A. Ashe, *History of North Carolina,* 2 vols. (Greensboro, 1908–25), II, 45; Maclaine to Samuel Johnston, New Bern, Dec. 24, 1785, Hayes Coll., NCU.

87. Maclaine to Johnston, New Bern, Dec. 24, 1785, Hayes Coll., NCU.

88. NC, JHC, 1785, Clark, ed., *State Records,* XVII, 368 (Dec. 20, 1785); SJ, 1785, ibid., XX, 83 (Dec. 22, 1785); Hooper to Iredell, Hillsborough, Jan. 22, 1786, Iredell Papers, NCDu.

89. Alfred Moore to Iredell, Wilmington, Dec. 14, 1786, Iredell Papers, NCDu; JHC, 1786, Clark, ed., *State Records,* XVIII, 528–29 (Jan. 2, 1787).

90. NC, JHC, 1786, Clark, ed., *State Records,* XVIII, 360–61, 468–69, 471 (Dec. 22, 1786, Jan. 6, 1787). On the second bill the Lawyers' motions were voted down by 31 to 46, 13 to 57, and 19 to 49; on final passage it was 57 to 20.

91. SJ, 1786, Clark, ed., *State Records,* XVIII, 184–85 (Dec. 30, 1786). The regional and party lineup was similar to that in the Commons. Senators from the Piedmont and west supported the amendment by 12 to 4; easterners opposed it by 13 to 4. Subsequent Antifederalists favored it, 7 to 4; subsequent Federalists opposed it, 4 to 3 (all 3 being westerners).

92. Md, *SJ, 1785,* p. 9 (Nov. 24, 1785); *JHD, 1785,* 24–26 (Nov. 28, 1785). The House also held four roll calls on the exact amount of judicial salaries, and it defeated 19 to 33 a motion to pay the judges out of tax arrearages.

93. *JHD, 1785,* pp. 74–75 (Dec. 31, 1785).

94. *JHD, 1786,* p. 72; *SJ, 1786,* pp. 38–39 (Jan. 11, 20, 1787). The House earlier granted leave to bring in a repeal bill by 31 to 28.

95. Md, *JHD, 1786,* pp. 54–57, 98–100; *SJ, 1786,* pp. 37, 40, 42 (Jan. 11, 17, 20, 1787).

96. Md, *JHD, 1787,* p. 8 (Nov. 22, 1787).

CHAPTER SEVEN   TORIES, ANGLICANS, AND SLAVES

1. Ezra S. Tipple, *The Heart of Asbury's Journal* (New York, 1904), p. 199.

2. Throughout the war it was reported that Methodist ministers refused to take Maryland's test oath, and they often encouraged their adherents to resist military service and taxes. One Eastern Shore military leader called them "the greatest stroke the British Ministry ever struck amongst us." Ronald Hoffman, *A Spirit of Dissension: Economics, Politics, and the Revolution in Maryland* (Baltimore and London, 1973), pp. 227–30; Albert W. Werline, *Problems of Church and State in Maryland During the Seventeenth and Eighteenth Centuries* (South Lancaster, Mass., 1948), p. 185.

3. Charles B. Clark, *The Eastern Shore of Maryland and Virginia* (New York, 1950), pp. 414–15; Hoffman, *Spirit of Dissension,* pp. 184–97. Hoffman, following the reports of local officials, calls it "a full-scale insurrection," but the documents he cites talk more of apprehended dangers than real ones. And frequently they intermix the dangers of slave uprising with the problems of Loyalist resistance. If such nameless fears are discounted, the reports of local officials present a picture of verbal hostility and noncooperation, but no organized attempts to aid the British side. Eastern Shore turmoil continued for some years, but after 1777 it seldom amounted to anything more than Methodist-led resistance to military recruiters.

4. Allan Nevins, *American States During and After the Revolution* (New York, 1924), p. 310; Hoffman, *Spirit of Dissension,* pp. 229–30.

5. William Tilghman to Tench Coxe, Chester Town, Feb. 1, 1784, Coxe Papers, PaHS.

6. Md, *JHD, 1784,* p. 99; *SJ, 1785,* pp. 49, 54 (Jan. 14, 15, 18, 1785).

7. Md, *JHD, 1784,* pp. 106–7 (Jan. 16, 1785); David McMechen to "The Electors of Baltimore Town," *Virginia Journal* [Alexandria], Oct. 27, 1785.

8. Md, *JHD, 1784,* pp. 114–16 (Jan. 20, 1785); McMechen, "To the Electors of Baltimore Town," indicated that his vote in favor of the bill had caused some criticism and he felt obliged to defend it.

9. Md, *JHD, 1786,* pp. 41, 49; *SJ, 1786,* p. 17 (Dec. 26, 30, 1786, Jan. 1, 1787). The Senate adopted the amendment by 6 to 5, but there was no pattern to the voting. Carroll this time was in the majority. Supporting the view that the amendment was designed to make the bill more palatable to the Senate is the fact that the same majority rejected an even more stringent amendment that would have excluded Tories from officeholding. The House approved the first amendment by 37 to 16.

10. William Tilghman to Tench Coxe, Chester Town, Feb. 4, 1787, Coxe Papers, PaHS.

11. JC, JHC, 1779, Walter Clark, ed., *State Records of North Carolina* (Winston and Greensboro, 1896–1917), 30 vols., XIII, 991–2 (Nov. 20, 1779).

12. William K. Boyd, *History of North Carolina,* 3 vols. (Chicago and New York, 1919), II, 8–9; William H. Masterson, *William Blount* (Baton Rouge, 1954), p. 55.

13. Maclaine to Hooper, Wilmington, Feb. 19, March 7, May 29, 1783, Hooper Coll, NCU.

14. Boyd, *History of North Carolina,* II, 10–11.

15. Maclaine to Hooper, Wilmington, June 14, 1784, Hooper Coll, NCU; JHC, 1784, spring sess., Clark, ed., *State Records,* XIX, 671–3 (May 29, 1784). Although there is no extant Senate Journal for the session, the act is not listed among the laws passed in the session (ibid., XXIV, 543–649), so it is fair to surmise that the Senate killed it.

16. Johnston to Iredell, Hillsborough, May 1, 1784; Hooper to Iredell, Hillsborough, May 1, 1784, Griffith J. McRee, *Life and Correspondence of James Iredell,* 2 vols. (New York, 1857–58), II, 99–100; JHC, 1784, 1st sess., Clark, ed., *State Records,* XIX, 674–75 (May 29, 1784). There is no extant Senate Journal for this session.

17. Maclaine to Hooper, New Bern, Nov. 25, 1785, Hooper Coll., NCU.

18. Maclaine to Samuel Johnston, New Bern, Dec. 24, 1785, Hayes Coll., NCU; JHC, 1785, Clark, ed., *State Records,* XVII, 322, 345, 350, 419–21 (Dec. 7, 13, 15, 28, 1785). There were no roll calls on Loyalist matters in this session.

19. Iredell to William Hooper, Jan. 29, 1786, Iredell Papers, NCDu.

20. Boyd, *History of North Carolina,* II, 9–10; JHC, 1786, Clark, ed., *State Records,* XVIII, 421–25, 428–29 (Jan. 1, 2, 1787). On the investigating committee were: Archibald Maclaine (chairman), W. R. Davie, William Hooper, R. D. Spaight, J. G. Blount, Jonathan Stokes, and John Sitgreaves.

21. JHC, 1786, Clark, ed., *State Records,* XVIII, 399, 419 (Dec. 29, 30, 1786).

22. *North Carolina Reports* by Francois Xavier Masters (Raleigh, 1843), pp. 42–48.

23. JHC, 1787, Clark, ed., *State Records*, XX, 239–40, 285 (Dec. 15, 21, 1787).

24. John Page to St. George Tucker, Rosewell, Oct. 8, 1783, Tucker-Coleman Papers VaWM; John Breckinridge, speech on the citizenship bill, Jan. 20, 1784, Breckinridge Papers, DLC; Gov. Harrison issued a proclamation on July 2, 1783, barring Loyalists from returning to the state, but he listed no particular reasons other than that the law ought to be enforced until the legislature changed it: *Calendar of Virginia State Papers and Other Manuscripts*, 11 vols. (Richmond, 1875–93), pp. 504–5.

25. Va, *JHD, 1783*, 1st sess., p. 141 (June 21, 1783); R. H. Lee to Landon Carter, Richmond, June 3, 1783, Lee-Ludwell Papers, VaHS; Jones to Madison, Richmond, May 31, 1783, William T. Hutchinson, ed., *The Papers of James Madison*, 9 vols. to date (Chicago and London, 1962–), VII, 99–101.

26. Isaac S. Harrell, *Loyalism in Virginia* (Philadelphia, 1926), p. 138; Edmund Randolph to Madison, Sept. 13, 1783, Hutchinson, ed., *Madison Papers*, VII, 314–15. "Statute staple men" were agents of British mercantile houses, who had been forced to leave Virginia in 1776.

27. Page to Tucker, Rosewell, Oct. 8, 1783, Tucker-Coleman Papers, VaWM; Jones to Monroe, Richmond, Nov. 28, Dec. 29, 1783, Monroe Papers, DLC; Breckinridge, speeches on the citizenship bills, Dec. 1, 1783, Jan. 20, 1784, Breckinridge Papers, DLC.

28. Va, *JHD, 1783*, pp. 76, 110–11 (Dec. 1, 13, 1783); Jones to Monroe, Richmond, Dec. 6, 29, 1783; Beverley Randolph to Monroe, Jan. 2, 1784, Monroe Papers, DLC.

29. "Mentor," in *Virginia Gazette* [Richmond], July 30, 1785. The writer identified himself as coming from Essex County, Smith's home, and Smith liked the pen name "Mentor," although enemies preferred to call him "Fiddlehead."

30. Werline, *Problems of Church and State*, p. 181.

31. Hamilton J. Eckenrode, *Separation of Church and State in Virginia* (Richmond, 1910), pp. 91–92; Madison to Jefferson, Richmond, July 3, 1784, Julian P. Boyd, ed., *The Papers of Thomas Jefferson*, 18 vols. to date (Princeton, 1950–), VII, 360–61.

32. Eckenrode, *Separation of Church and State*, pp. 88–91; Rev. John B. Smith to Madison, Hampden Sydney, June 21, 1784, Rutland, ed., *Madison Papers*, VIII, 80–82; Madison to Jefferson, Richmond, July 3, 1784, Boyd, ed., *Jefferson Papers*, VII, 360–61.

33. Joseph Jones to Monroe, Richmond, Nov. 13, 1784; Beverly Randolph to Monroe, Nov. 26, 1784, Monroe Papers, DLC.

34. Lee to Madison, Trenton, Nov. 26, 1784, Madison Papers, DLC.

35. Va., *JHD, 1784*, fall sess., p. 19 (Nov. 11, 1784); Madison to R. H. Lee, Nov. 14, 1784, Lee-Ludwell Papers, VaHS; Eckenrode, *Separation of Church and State*, pp. 87–88.

36. Va, *JHD, 1784*, fall sess., pp. 27, 29 (Nov. 17–18, 1784); Eckenrode, *Separation of Church and State*, p. 94.

37. Va, *JHD, 1784*, fall. sess., p. 51 (Dec. 2, 1784); Eckenrode, *Separation of Church and State*, pp. 99–100.

38. Va, *JHD, 1784,* fall sess., pp. 65–66, 75, 77–79; (Dec. 11, 18, 20, 22, 1784); Madison to Madison, Sr., Richmond, Jan. 6, 1785, Rutland, ed., *Madison Papers,* VIII, 216–17; Eckenrode, *Separation of Church and State,* pp. 100–1. This vote was 47 to 38.

39. Va, *JHD, 1784,* fall sess., pp. 80–82 (Dec. 22–24, 1784); Madison to Jefferson, Richmond, Jan. 9, 1785, Boyd, ed., *Jefferson Papers,* VII, 594–95; Eckenrode, *Separation of Church and State,* pp. 99–102. The vote on postponement was 45 to 38.

40. Madison to Madison, Sr., Richmond, Jan. 6, 1785, Rutland, ed., *Madison Papers,* VIII, 216–17.

41. Washington to [Zachariah Johnston], May 31, 1785, Johnston Papers, NCDu.

42. Nicholas to Madison, Charlottesville, Apr. 22, 1785, Rutland, ed., *Madison Papers,* VIII, 264–65. Nicholas was undoubtedly acquainted with Madison from earlier service in the assembly. He did not return to the House of Delegates until 1786, when he made himself the spokesman for the debtor element. The friendship resumed in 1788 when Nicholas supported the Constitution (though reluctantly), and his correspondence with Jefferson and Madison continued after he moved to Kentucky.

43. Madison to Monroe, Orange, Apr. 28, May 29, 1785, Ibid., 272–73, 285–86.

44. *Virginia Journal and Alexandria Advertiser,* Mar. 31, Apr. 7, 1785.

45. George Nicholas to Madison, July 7, 1785, and Madison to Edmund Randolph, Orange, July 26, 1785, Rutland, ed., *Madison Papers,* VIII, 316, 327–28; George Mason to Washington, Gunston Hall, Oct. 2, 1785, Washington Papers, DLC; handwritten copy of the "Remonstrance" in Breckinridge Papers, DLC.

46. Eckenrode, *Separation of Church and State,* pp. 106–7; William Taylor Thom, *The Struggle for Religious Freedom in Virginia: The Baptists* (Baltimore, 1900), pp. 77–78.

47. Va, *JHD, 1785,* pp. 93–94, 141–42 (Dec. 16, 17, 1785, Jan. 16, 1786); *SJ, 1785,* p. 61 (Dec. 28, 1785); Madison to Madison, Sr., Richmond, Dec. 24, 1785, and Madison to Jefferson, Richmond, Jan. 22, 1786, Rutland, ed., *Madison Papers,* VIII, 454–55, 472–81. The Senate amendment revising the preamble passed by 10 to 8. The regional division was almost exactly the same as in the House, except for two senators from Patrick Henry's heartland, the southern Piedmont, who voted with the conservatives.

48. Werline, *Problems of Church and State,* p. 151; Merrill Jensen, *The New Nation* (New York, 1950), p. 133.

49. Werline, *Problems of Church and State,* pp. 160–61, 167–68.

50. Ibid., pp. 173–76.

51. Washington to Chase, Mount Vernon, Jan. 17, 1785, Washington Papers, DLC, is a reply to Chase's request for a copy of the Virginia assessment bill. "Timothy Homespun" in *Maryland Journal,* Sept. 15, 1786, admitted that Maryland Episcopalianism looked to Chase for political guidance, and Rev. Patrick Allison identified Chase as the leader of the Episcopalians in the assembly: Allison to James McHenry, Baltimore, Mar. 4, 1784, McHenry Papers, MdHS.

52. Md, *JHD, 1784,* pp. 745, 88–89 (Dec. 31, 1784, Jan. 4, 1785).

53. This view differs slightly from the interpretation offered by Jackson Turner Main, *Political Parties Before the Constitution* (Chapel Hill, 1973), pp. 231–32, who argues (evidently on the basis of only 2 of the 6 votes) that the division was more economic than regional. My tabulation suggests that regional cohesion was stronger than party cohesion.

54. *Maryland Journal* [Baltimore], August–December, 1785, passim.

55. *Maryland Journal* [Baltimore], Feb. 8, Nov. 8, 1785.

56. Nathaniel Ramsey to O. H. Williams, Annapolis [Nov. 19, 1785], O. H. Williams Papers, MdHS; Md, *JHD, 1785,* p. 9 (Nov. 19, 1785).

57. Werline, *Problems of Church and State,* p. 182.

58. Bernard C. Steiner, *History of Education in Maryland* (Washington, 1894), pp. 71–75.

59. Md, *JHD, 1784,* pp. 17, 22, 70 (Nov. 30, Dec. 3, 30, 1784); *Maryland Journal* [Baltimore], Dec. 24, 1784; Tench F. Tilghman, "The Founding of St. John's College, 1784–1789," *Maryland Historical Magazine,* 44 (1949), 75–92.

60. Main, *Political Parties,* pp. 230–31, rejects the notion that opposition to the colleges was religiously motivated. The tabulations here indicate that religion influenced a few delegates, though it remained distinctly secondary to economic considerations.

61. *Maryland Gazette* [Baltimore], Feb. 11, 1785. The controversy continued in the issues of Feb. 23, Apr. 1, and Jun. 17, 1785.

62. *Maryland Journal* [Baltimore], Apr. 29, 1785.

63. Md, *JHD, 1785,* pp. 7, 8, 18, 45–46, 58–59 (Nov. 18, 22, Dec. 10, 20, 1785).

64. Steiner, *History of Education in Maryland,* pp. 98–101; Walter W. Preston, *History of Harford County, Maryland* (Baltimore, 1901), pp. 184–88.

65. Robert McColley, *Slavery and Jeffersonian Virginia* (Champaign, Ill., 1964), pp. 114 ff.

66. Md, *JHD, 1785,* p. 39 (Dec. 7, 1785). The clerk tallied the roll call at 32 to 22. Rolls calls on similar petitions in later sessions produced the same pattern: *JHD, 1786,* pp. 120, 126, 170 (Apr. 25, 28, May 20, 1787); *JHD, 1787,* pp. 35–36 (Dec. 11, 1787).

67. NC, JHC, 1785, Clark, ed., *State Records,* XVII, 312 (Dec. 5, 1785).

68. Samuel A. Ashe, *History of North Carolina,* 2 vols. (Greensboro, 1908–1925), II, 21; JHC, 1786, Clark, ed., *State Records,* XVIII, 317 (Dec. 13, 1786).

69. NC, JHC, 1788, Clark, ed., *State Records,* XXI, 120–21 (Nov. 19, 1788).

70. Maclaine to Edward Jones, Wilmington, Nov. 18, 1790, Maclaine Papers, NCDH.

CHAPTER EIGHT THE WESTERN QUESTION

1. Thomas Perkin Abernethy, *Western Lands and the American Revolution* (Charlottesville, 1937), 217–25. Unless otherwise stated, the factual information in this chapter is taken from this source.

2. Abernethy, *Western Lands,* pp. 255–59; Va, *JHD, 1782,* pp. 58, 64 (Dec. 7, 12, 1782).

3. NC, JHC, 1783, Walter Clark, ed., *State Records of North Carolina* (Winston and Goldsboro, 1896–1917), 30 vols., XIX, 354 (May 14, 1783).

4. William H. Masterson, *William Blount* (Baton Rouge, 1954), pp. 78–79.

5. Ibid., pp. 80–83.

6. Blount and Williamson to Gov. Martin, Oct. 22, 1782, Clark, ed., *State Records*. XVI, 434–41.

7. NC, JHC, 1784, Clark, ed., *State Records*, XIX, 567–68; Hooper to Iredell, Hillsborough, July 8, 1784, Iredell Papers, NCDu; Hawkins to Madison, Botetourt, Va., Sept. 4, 1784, Madison Papers, DLC; Samuel A. Ashe, *History of North Carolina*, 2 vols. (Greensboro, 1908–1925), pp. 34, 37.

8. NC, JHC, 1784, Clark, ed., *State Records*, XIX, 612–13, 621–22 (May 18–24, 1784).

9. Hawkins to Madison, Botetourt, Sept. 4, 1784, Madison Papers, DLC; Maclaine to Hooper, Wilmington, Dec. 1, 1784, Hooper Coll, NCU; NC, JHC, 1784, fall sess., *State Records*, XIX, 773, 794, 804–5 (Nov. 9–18, 1784). For purposes of comparison with earlier roll calls, an early vote of 46 to 23 was used in order to obtain the maximum number of names.

10. Samuel Cole Williams, *History of the Lost State of Franklin* (Johnson City, Tenn., 1924), pp. 26–29. The extent to which Eastern attitudes offended Westerners is enlarged upon in William Cage and others to Gov. Alex. Martin, Jonesboro, Mar. 22, 1785, Clark ed., *State Records*, XXII, 637–40.

11. Joseph Martin to Gov. Patrick Henry, Sept. 19, 1785, *Calendar of Virginia State Papers and other Manuscripts*, 11 vols. (Richmond, 1875–93), IV, 53–54; Sevier to Col. Kennedy, Jan. 2, 1785, in J. G. M. Ramsey, *The Annals of Tennessee* (Chattanooga, 1926), p. 291.

12. Cocke, who was not allied with eastern speculators, was evidently moved by the economic advantages the West would gain through independence. His activities are discussed by Thomas Hutchins: to Gen. Evan Shelby, Apr. 22, 1787, Clark, ed., *State Records*, XX, 679–80.

13. Williams, *Lost State of Franklin*, pp. 29–32; James Montgomery, William Edmiston, and Arthur Bowen to Gov. Patrick Henry, July 27, 1785, *Calendar of Virginia State Papers*, IV, 45–46.

14. Campbell to R. H. Lee, Washington County, Oct. 18, 1784, Lee Papers, VaU.

15. John Preston to John Breckinridge, Nov. 28, 1784, Breckinridge Papers, DLC; Arthur Campbell to Robert Preston, Goodwood, Feb. 7, 1785, Preston Family Papers, VaHS; Breckinridge and Stuart "To the Freeholders & Inhabitants of Botetourt—Montgomery," Jan. 5, 1785, printed broadside in Breckinridge Papers.

16. Masterson, *William Blount*, p. 95, calls Cocke "Arthur Campbell's mouthpiece," but there is no evidence for this. The Virginia Executive Council believed that the Franklinites rejected Campbell's proposals in order to avoid antagonizing Virginia: Joseph Jones to Monroe, Richmond, June 18, 1785, Monroe Papers, DLC.

17. Williams, *Lost State of Franklin*, pp. 29, 38, lists the members of the two conventions. There were 40 delegates to the first and 44 in the second; 15 men served in both. Others not present at the December meeting who were prominent earlier and later in the secession movement were Samuel Doak, Alexander Outlaw, and Landon Carter.

18. Ibid., p. 40.

19. Ibid., pp. 282–329, gives biographical sketches of the important men on each side. Tipton came to North Carolina from southwestern Virginia in 1783. He represented Washington County, Virginia, in the House of Delegates from 1774 to 1780. See Samuel Evans Massengill, "Colonel John Tipton," *Publications of the Historical Society of Washington County, Virginia,* ser. I, bulletin 7 (1942), 83–92.

20. The thesis of Abernethy, *Western Lands,* pp. viii, 290, that land speculators were behind the movement to set up independent states in the West does not hold true for Tennessee. The Franklin movement took the big North Carolina speculators, Blount and Caswell, by surprise, and their agents in Tennessee—Sevier, Donelson, Robertson—dragged their feet on the question of separation.

21. Sevier to Joseph Martin, Mar. 27, 1788, *Calendar of Virginia State Papers,* IV, 416–17; Williams, *Lost State of Franklin,* pp. 54–55.

22. Carl S. Driver, *John Sevier: Pioneer of the Old Southwest* (Chapel Hill, 1932), pp. 87–88.

23. Deposition of George Clark [1785]; deposition of Joseph Cole [1785]; deposition of Robert Preston, Feb. 23, 1786; printed broadside "To the Freemen of Washington County," n.d., inscribed by Governor Patrick Henry, "Recd. June 10, 1785"; James Montgomery, William Edmiston, and Arthur Bowen to Gov. Patrick Henry, Washington County, Jul. 27, 1785; all in Executive Papers, VaSL.

24. Campbell to Henry, Washington County, Mar. 27, July 26, 1785, Executive Papers, VaSL; Campbell to Richard H. Lee, Washington County, Oct. 18, 1784, Lee Family Papers, VaU.

25. "Proclamation of Governor Henry," June 10, 1785; "Deposition of William Russell," Mar. 10, 1786; "Deposition of James Montgomery," Mar. 14, 1786; *Calendar of Virginia State Papers,* IV, 34–36, 99–100, 103–4.

26. Madison to Jefferson, Richmond, Jan. 22, 1786, Julian P. Boyd, ed., *The Papers of Thomas Jefferson,* 19 vols. to date (Princeton, 1950–), IX, 194–202, esp. 200–1; *JHD, 1785,* p. 445 (Jan. 17, 1786). There was no roll call on the bill.

27. Council Minutes, Dec. 13, 1785, Executive Papers, VaSL; *Calendar of Virginia State Papers,* IV, 94–110.

28. On the commission were Joseph Martin and Benjamin Hawkins of North Carolina, Daniel Carroll of Maryland, Andrew Pickens of South Carolina, and Lachlan McIntoch of Georgia. All were nationalists.

29. Masterson, *William Blount,* pp. 102–5.

30. Williams, *Lost State of Franklin,* pp. 97, 102; Evan Shelby to Gen. William Russell, Sullivan County, Apr. 27, 1787; Arthur Campbell to Gov. Edmund Randolph, Apr. 15, 1787, Executive Papers, VaSL.

31. Williams, *Lost State of Franklin,* pp. 115; Caswell to the Inhabitants of Washington, Sullivan, Greene, and Hawkins, May 31, 1787; Caswell to Shelby, May 31, 1787, Clark, ed., *State Records,* XXII, 685–88.

32. Williams, *Lost State of Franklin,* pp. 145–58; Report of a Senate committee on Tipton's election, NC, SJ, 1787, Clark, ed., *State Records,* XX, 322–24.

33. NC, SJ, JHD, 1787, Clark, ed., *State Records,* XX, 202, 379–80 (Dec. 7, 1787).

34. Thomas P. Abernethy, *From Frontier to Plantation in Tennessee* (Chapel Hill, 1932), pp. 81–82; Williams, *Lost State of Franklin,* pp. 186–88; *Maryland*

Journal [Baltimore], Apr. 8, 11, 1788; Tipton to Martin, Mar. 21, 1788, Clark, ed., *State Records*, XXII, 691–93; Driver, *John Sevier*, pp. 92–95.

35. Williams, *Lost State of Franklin*, pp. 205–12.

36. Driver, *John Sevier*, pp. 97–98.

37. In the summer of 1788 Sevier wrote two strange letters to the Spanish minister in the United States, Don Diego Gardoqui, in which he seemed to endorse the idea of an independent republic in the West, but he never pursued the idea. It seems likely that he was searching only for leverage in his struggle with North Carolina. Abernethy, *Western Lands*, pp. 340–43, thinks that Sevier was linked with the "Spanish conspiracy" that infected Kentucky as well. Driver, *John Sevier*, pp. 96–97, concludes that he merely wanted the Spanish to prevent the Indians from attacking the Muscle Shoals settlement.

38. *Journals of the Continental Congress, 1774–1789*, 34 vols. (Washington, 1904–37), XXXIV, 292–93 (July 3, 1788).

39. Williams, *Lost State of Franklin*, pp. 238–9, says Sevier favored the Constitution as early as December 1787, but the petition he cites (Clark, ed., *State Records*, XXII, 705–7) does not mention the Constitution. Sevier's most recent biographer, Carl Driver, does not tackle the question of how and why Sevier became a Federalist; and Abernethy, *Frontier to Plantation*, p. 111, unconvincingly attributes it to the influence of William Blount. Nor does there seem to be any clue in the manuscript correspondence. Hence the explanation presented here is largely conjecture.

40. Of the delegates who can be identified, 7 of the Tennessee Antifederalists were antisecessionists and 4 were Franklinites. Williams, *Lost State of Franklin*, pp. 282–329, provides sketches of the most prominent Franklinites and "Antis."

41. Johnston to Iredell, Fayetteville, Nov. 20, 1788, Iredell Papers, NCDu; NC, SJ, 1788, Clark, ed., *State Records*, XX, 513 (Nov. 17, 1788).

42. NC, JHC, 1788, Clark, ed., *State Records*, XXI, 77, 115 (Nov. 21, 28, 1788); SJ, 1788, ibid., XX, 553–54 (Nov. 27, 1788).

43. Of those Tennessee Federalists who could be identified in the 1789 convention, 6 were Franklinites (all prominent) and 4 were antisecessionists (all obscure). John Tipton was not elected.

44. NC, JHC, SJ, 1789, Clark, ed., *State Records*, XXI, 257, 345–46, 679 (Dec. 11, 12, 1789).

45. Maclaine to Iredell, Wilmington, Dec. 22, 1789, Iredell Papers, NCDu.

46. Patricia Watlington, *The Partisan Spirit: Kentucky Politics, 1779–1792* (New York, 1972), pp. 92–94; Abernethy, *Western Lands*, pp. 249–51.

47. Watlington, *Partisan Spirit*, pp. 95–97.

48. Abernethy, *Western Lands*, pp. 303–9.

49. R. H. Lee to Madison, New York, May 30, 1785, Robert A. Rutland, ed., *The Papers of James Madison*, 9 vols. to date (Chicago and London, 1962–), VIII, 288–89; Madison to Lee, Orange, July 7, 1785, and Lee to Madison, Aug. 11, 1785, Lee Papers, VaU. Other opinions favoring separation included: Washington to David Stuart, Mount Vernon, Nov. 30, 1785, Washington Papers, DLC; John Marshall to George Muter, Richmond, Jan. 7, 1785, *Tyler's Quarterly*, 1 (1919–20), 28; Jefferson to Madison, Feb. 20, 1784, Boyd, ed., *Jefferson Papers*, VI, 544–55, esp 547; William Grayson to Madison, Aug. 21, 1785, Rutland, ed., *Madison Papers*, VIII, 347–49.

50. Va, *JHD, 1785,* p. 136 (Jan. 10, 1786); William Waller Hening, *Statutes at Large . . . of Virginia,* 13 vols. (Richmond, 1822), XII, 37–40.

51. Watlington, *Partisan Spirit,* p. 106; Abernethy, *Western Lands,* p. 319.

52. Watlington, *Partisan Spirit,* pp. 118–21; Abernethy, *Western Lands,* p. 327.

53. Samuel McDowell to William Fleming, Mercer County, Sept. 23, 1787, Fleming Papers, VaSL.

54. Brown's congressional experience greatly expanded his perspective. He even professed to find advantages to Kentucky in the Federal Constitution, which made specific provision for the admission of new states, whereas the Articles of Confederation did not. He also worried that if Kentucky voted against the Constitution, the eastern states would be even less inclined to admit it to the union: John Brown to James Breckinridge, New York, Mar. 17, Apr. 11, June 21, 1788, James Breckinridge Papers, VaU.

55. Levi Todd to Gov. Beverley Randolph, May 27, 1789, *Calendar of Virginia State Papers,* IV, 630; Hening, *Statutes at Large,* XII, 788–91; Thomas Marshall to George Nicholas, Apr. 26, 1789, and Nicholas to Marshall, May 4, 1789, in Harry Innes Papers, DLC.

56. Washington to Jefferson, Mount Vernon, Mar. 29, 1784, Boyd, ed., *Jefferson Papers,* VII, 49–52.

57. Jefferson to Washington, Annapolis, Mar. 5, 1784; Jefferson to Madison, Philadelphia, May 25, 1784; Madison to Jefferson, Orange, Aug. 20, 1784; all in Boyd, ed., *Jefferson Papers,* VII, 25–27, 289, 401–8.

58. Washington to Gov. Benjamin Harrison, Mount Vernon, Oct. 10, 1784; and Harrison to Washington, Nov. 13, 1784, Washington Papers, DLC.

59. *Maryland Journal* [Baltimore], Nov. 9, 1784.

60. The Maryland commissioners were Thomas Stone, Samuel Hughes, and Charles Carroll from the Senate; John Cadwallader, Samuel Chase, John DeButts, George Digges, Philip Key, Gustavus Scott, and Joseph Dashiell from the House of Delegates. Report of the Commissioners, n.d., Washington Papers, DLC.

61. Md, *JHD, 1784,* pp. 65–66; *SJ, 1784,* pp. 24–26 (Dec. 27–28, 1784). The House roll calls were 40 to 9 and 38 to 10; the Senate approved the measures without a roll call.

62. Madison to Jefferson, Richmond, Jan. 9, 1785, Boyd, ed., *Jefferson Papers,* VII, 588–98, esp. 589–91; Patrick Henry to Washington, Richmond, June 18, 1785, Washington Papers, DLC.

63. *Virginia Journal* [Alexandria], May 19, 26, 1785. The chief source for residence and occupations was advertisements in the Alexandria *Journal,* Bartgis' *Maryland Gazette* [Frederick], and the *Maryland Gazette* [Annapolis]. A substantial number are identified in Robert A. Rutland, ed., *The Papers of George Mason,* 3 vols. (Chapel Hill, 1970), Glossary.

64. Washington to Lafayette, Mount Vernon, July 25, 1785, Washington Papers, DLC. For similar political considerations see: George Clendinen to Gov. Patrick Henry, Richmond, Jan. 5, 1785, Executive Papers, VaSL; David McMechen, "To the Electors of Baltimore Town," *Virginia Journal* [Alexandria], Oct. 27, 1785; and Henry Lee to Washington, New York, July 3, Sept. 8, 1786, Washington Papers, DLC.

65. Because the Irishmen kept running away, the company had to shave off their eyebrows so they would be recognizable: advertisements in *Maryland Gazette* [Annapolis], Feb. 16, 1786, and *Maryland Journal* [Baltimore], Oct. 17, 1786.

66. *Virginia Gazette* [Richmond], May 14, June 11, 18, 1789.

67. *Virginia Gazette* [Richmond], June 18, 1789; Bartgis's *Maryland Gazette* [Frederick], Apr. 25, 1793.

68. Lee to Madison, Berkeley County, Sept. 8, 1789, Madison Papers, DLC.

69. Minutes of a meeting of the James River Company, Aug. 20, 1785; Randolph to Washington, Sept. 2, 1785; Washington to Randolph, Mount Vernon, Nov. 5, 1785, all in Washington Papers, DLC.

70. Report of Commissioners to Survey the James River, Oct. 1, 1785, copy in Washington Papers, DLC; George Skillern to Zachariah Johnston, Botetourt, Nov. 10, 1790, Johnston Papers, NCDu.

71. Stuart to Jefferson, Richmond, Oct. 17, 1785, Boyd, ed., *Jefferson Papers*, VIII, 644–47; Samuel Purviance to Washington, Baltimore, Mar. 6, 1786, Purviance-Courtenay Papers, NCDu.

72. Walker to Washington, Albemarle, Jan. 24, 1784; Washington to Gov. Patrick Henry, Mount Vernon, Nov. 30, 1785, Washington Papers, DLC.

73. Henry to Washington, Richmond, June 18, 1785; Washington to Henry, Mount Vernon, June 24, 1785, Washington Papers, DLC.

74. Josiah Parker to Washington, Portsmouth, Sept. 9, 1786; Washington to John Cowper, May 25, 1788, Washington Papers, DLC.

75. Washington to Jefferson, Sept. 26, 1785, and Madison to Jefferson, Richmond, Jan. 22, 1786, in Boyd, ed., *Jefferson Papers*, VIII, 555–57, IX, 201.

76. Henry to Washington, Richmond, Nov. 11, 1785, Jan. 18, 1786, Washington Papers, DLC.

77. NC, JHC, 1786, Clark, ed., *State Records*, XVIII, 350–51 (Dec. 20, 1786).

78. Neither state parties nor national considerations were involved. Men who subsequently became Federalists supported Spaight's motion by 11 to 7; Antifederalists favored it by 16 to 8.

79. NC, JHC, 1788, Clark, ed., *State Records*, XXI, 109–10 (Nov. 27, 1788). The Commons vote was 51 to 40. Again, parties were not involved. Federalists supported the measure, 16 to 13; Antifederalists split evenly, 19 to 19.

80. NC, JHC, 1790, SJ, 1790, Clark, ed., *State Records*, XXI, 781, 929–30, (Nov. 17, 19, 1790).

81. Clifford R. Hinshaw, Jr., "North Carolina Canals Before 1860," North Carolina Historical Review, 25, no. 1 (Jan. 1948), 19–23.

82. Advertisement in *Virginia Gazette and General Advertiser* [Richmond], Jan. 12, 1791.

CHAPTER NINE   THE MOVEMENT FOR FEDERAL REFORM

1. Of the men who served the Chesapeake region in Congress between 1781 and 1789, 42 were nationalists, 10 were antinationalists, and the attitudes of 9 could not be determined.

2. Merrill Jensen, *The New Nation* (New York, 1950), p. 58; Va, *JHD, 1781,* 1st sess., pp. 11–12 (June 7, 8, 1781); NC, JHC, 1781 (MSS, Microfilm, Early State Records series) July 8, 1781; Md; *SJ, 1781,* 2d sess., p. 61 (June 12, 1782).

3. Gov. Harrison to the Virginia congressional delegates, Jan. 4, 1783, Harrison Letterbook, VaSL; Harrison to Washington, Mar. 31, 1783, Washington Papers, DLC; Randolph to Madison, Sept. 13, 1783, William T. Hutchinson, ed., *The Papers of James Madison,* 9 vols. to date (1962–), VII, 317–18.

4. "Circular Letter Addressed to the Governors of all the States on Disbanding the Army," Newburgh, June 8, 1783. W. C. Ford, ed., *Writings of George Washington,* 14 vols. (New York, 1889–93), X, 254–65, esp. 258, 260–61.

5. "Fairfax County Freeholders' Address and Instructions to their General Assembly Delegates," May 30, 1783, Robert A. Rutland, ed., *The Papers of George Mason,* 3 vols. (Chapel Hill, 1970), II, 779–82.

6. Lee to Landon Carter, Richmond, June 3, 1783, Lee-Ludwell Papers, VaHS.

7. Jefferson to Madison, Richmond, May 7, 1783, Julian P. Boyd, ed., *The Papers of Thomas Jefferson,* 19 vols. to date (Princeton, 1950–) VI, 266. Merrill D. Peterson, *Thomas Jefferson and the New Nation* (New York, 1970), p. 267.

8. Jefferson to Madison, Richmond, June 17, 1783, Boyd, ed., *Jefferson Papers,* VI, 277; Randolph to Madison, Richmond, May 9, 15, 1783, Hutchinson, ed., *Madison Papers,* VII, 32–34, 44–46.

9. Thomson Mason to J. F. Mercer, Richmond, June 27, 1783, Mercer Papers, VaHS; Joseph Jones to Madison, Richmond, June 14, 1783, Hutchinson, ed., *Madison Papers,* VII, 143–45; Edmund Pendleton to Madison, June 2, 1783, David John Mays, ed., *The Letters and Papers of Edmund Pendleton, 1734–1803,* 2 vols. (Charlottesville, 1967), II, 449.

10. Randolph to Madison, Richmond, June 28, 1783, and Jones to Madison, Richmond June 28, 1783, Hutchinson, ed., *Madison Papers,* VII, 196–201.

11. Tyler to J. F. Mercer, Sep. 9, 1783, Mercer Papers, VaHS; Breckinridge, "Speech on the Impost," Jan. 27, Feb. 9, 1784, Breckinridge Papers, DLC; William Waller Hening, *Statutes at Large . . . of Virginia,* 13 vols. (Richmond, 1822), XI, 350–52.

12. Jones to Monroe, Spring Hill, Dec. 29, 1783, Monroe Papers, DLC.

13. Walter Clark, ed., *State Records of North Carolina,* 30 vols. (Winston and Goldsboro, 1896–1917), XXIV, 547–49; Maclaine to George Hooper, Apr. 23, 1784, Hooper Coll., NCU.

14. Report of the Secretary of Congress, Jan. 3, 1786, *Journals of the Continental Congress,* 34 vols. (Washington, 1904–37), XXX, 7–9.

15. Madison to Jefferson, Orange, Dec. 10, 1783, Boyd, ed., *Jefferson Papers,* VI, 377–79, records the results of this visit.

16. In his "Circular Letter Addressed to the Governors," June 8, 1783, Washington spoke of the need to add "tone to our federal government" (Ford, ed., *Writings of George Washington,* X, 254–65); and Madison, summarizing the attitudes of the states toward Congress, singled out those who were "friendly to liberal and foederal ideas": to Jefferson, Philadelphia, Aug. 11, 1783, Boyd, ed., *Jefferson Papers,* VI, 334. Jensen, *New Nation,* pp. xiii–xiv, makes a distinction between "nationalists" and "federalists" that is extremely useful to historians, but it should be remembered that those terms were rarely used at the time. Nationalists would

not admit to the name, and their opponents lacked the sense of identity to coin any term prior to the Constitution.

17. The first use of "Antifederal" I have seen is: David Humphreys to Jefferson, Hartford, June 5, 1786, and Washington to Jefferson, Mount Vernon, Aug. 1, 1786, Boyd, ed., *Jefferson Papers,* IX, 609, X, 186–87. In January 1787 William Blount scornfully referred to the New York delegation in Congress as "antifederal peasants": to Richard Caswell, Jan. 28, 1787, in Edmund C. Burnett, ed., *Letters of Members of the Continental Congress,* 8 vols. (Washington, 1921–36), VIII, 532–34.

18. Jensen, *New Nation,* pp. 283–84, 400–1.

19. Ibid., pp. 402–3.

20. Monroe to Jefferson, New York, Apr. 12, June 16, July 15, 1785; and Jefferson to Monroe, Paris, Apr. 15, June 17, 1785, Boyd, ed., *Jefferson Papers,* VIII, 75–80, 88–90, 215–19, 227–33, esp. 228, 296–97.

21. Washington to William Carmichael, Mount Vernon, June 10, 1785, Washington Papers, DLC; Monroe to Madison, New York, July 26, 1785, Madison Papers, DLC; Madison to Jefferson, Orange, Oct. 3, 1785, Boyd, ed., *Jefferson Papers,* VIII, 579–82, esp. 580.

22. Madison to Lee, Orange, July 7, 1785; Lee to Madison, New York, Aug. 11, 1785, Lee Papers, VaU; Grayson to Madison, New York, May 28, 1786, Rutland, ed., *Madison Papers,* IX, 61–65.

23. McHenry to Washington, Aug. 14, 1785, Washington Papers, DLC; Monroe to Jefferson, Aug. 15, 1785, Jan. 19, 1786, Boyd, ed., *Jefferson Papers,* VIII, 381–83, IX, 186–91.

24. Jones to Madison, Richmond, June 12, 1785, Rutland, ed., *Madison Papers,* VIII, 292–93; Jensen, *New Nation,* p. 66.

25. Madison to Jefferson, Richmond, July 3, 1784, Boyd, ed., *Jefferson Papers,* VII, 359–62, esp. 361.

26. Md, *SJ, 1784,* p. 58 (Jan. 19, 1785). Thomas Stone, thanking Monroe for sending him a copy of the committee report on the commerce amendment, reported that he was about to set out for Alexandria, but he gave no indication that he saw any connection between the Potomac conference and the powers of Congress. Instead, he hoped to resolve the Potomac matter quickly while the two states were still on good terms: Stone to Monroe, Annapolis, Mar. 18, 1785, Monroe Papers, DLC.

27. Randolph to Madison, Richmond, July 17, 1785, Rutland, ed., *Madison Papers,* VIII, 324–25.

28. Mason to Madison, Gunston Hall, Aug. 9, 1785, Rutland, ed., *Madison Papers,* VIII, 337–38.

29. Md, *JHD, 1785,* pp. 7–10 (Nov. 18–20, 1785). On the committee were Chase, Peregrine Lethrbury, John DeButts, Joseph Dashiell, and Brice T. B. Worthington. Worthington's voting on economic issues was mixed, but he became a Federalist in 1788. The rest voted solidly creditor. All but Chase supported the Constitution.

30. Later in the session the assembly named commissioners to a tristate meeting with Delaware and Pennsylvania, one that the Marylanders considered as important as their discussion with Virginia: ibid., pp. 150–51 (Feb. 20–21, 1786).

31. Ibid., p. 180; *SJ, 1785,* p. 73 (Mar. 6, 1786). The Senate vote was 8 to 2.

Opposing the impost were John Smith, who consistently opposed granting powers to Congress, and Edward Lloyd, who was never consistent on anything.

32. See other roll calls on relations with Congress: *SJ, 1785,* pp. 79–81, 185.

33. Madison to R. H. Lee, Orange, July 7, 1785, Lee Papers, VaU; Madison to Monroe, Aug. 7, 1785, Rutland, ed., *Madison Papers,* VIII, 333–36.

34. *Virginia Gazette* [Richmond], Oct. 15, Nov. 12, 1785; Madison to Washington, Richmond, Nov. 11, 1785, Washington Papers, DLC.

35. Va, *JHD, 1785,* pp. 66–67 (Nov. 30–Dec. 1, 1785); Madison to Washington, Richmond, Dec. 9, 1785, Washington Papers, DLC. Only two of Madison's nationalist allies, David Stuart and Charles Simms, went with him in his tactical reversal; the rest voted for the bill. But if, as seems likely, the motion to reconsider came from the Madison circle, it probably changed a number of minds among the uncommitted.

36. Va, *JHD, 1785,* pp. 71–72 (Dec. 3–5, 1785); David Stuart to Washington, Richmond, Dec. 18, 1785, Washington Papers, DLC.

37. On the committee (Va, *JHD, 1785,* p. 6) were 8 men who normally sided with Madison and subsequently favored the Constitution, 9 who voted against Madison and became Antifederalists, and 3 whose politics could not be ascertained.

38. There is no extant copy of the Tyler resolution, but in reporting the affair to Jefferson, Madison claimed it was virtually identical to what the House finally approved on January 21: Madison to Jefferson, Richmond, Jan. 22, 1786, Boyd, ed., *Jefferson Papers,* IX, 194–202, esp. 197–99. Julian Boyd's editorial note (ibid., pp. 204–9) argues persuasively that Irving Brant, *James Madison, Nationalist* (Indianapolis and New York, 1948), pp. 379–81, was incorrect in ascribing authorship of the Tyler resolution to Madison. But in focusing on the Madison-Tyler relationship (or rather on the lack of one), Boyd underestimates the importance of the Maryland resolutions as a catalyst and ignores the role of the commerce committee. For a summary of the conventional interpretation of the Annapolis meeting—which I am seeking to revise—see John J. Reardon, *Edmund Randolph: A Biography* (New York and London, 1974), 79–86.

39. Va, *JHD, 1785,* p. 90 (Dec. 13, 1785); Mason to Speaker of the House of Delegates, Mount Vernon, Mar. 28, 1785, Rutland, ed., *Mason Papers,* II, 814–21. For the rest of that month the House was preoccupied with discussion of the Statute for Religious Freedom.

40. The Madison circle, it will be remembered, supported Harrison against Tyler in the contest over the Speakership that year. Their assessment of Tyler is in Archibald Stuart to John Breckinridge, Oct. 24, 1785; Breckinridge Papers, DLC. Tyler, like Monroe and Grayson, favored some modest changes in the Articles of Confederation, but he was no nationalist. During the debates on the Constitution in the Virginia convention he expressed regret for his role in summoning the Annapolis meeting, but offered no explanation for it. Lyon G. Tyler, *Letters and Times of the Tylers* (Richmond, 1884), I, 151.

41. Among those expressing skepticism of conventions besides Madison were: David Stuart to Washington, Richmond, Dec. 18, 1785, Washington Papers, DLC; and Joseph Jones to Jefferson, Richmond, Feb. 21, 1786, Boyd, ed., *Jefferson Papers,* IX, 296–97. Rutland, ed. note, *Madison Papers,* VIII, 406–9, notes Madison's attitude toward conventions, but he does not attempt to unravel the mystery of Virginia's endorsement of the Annapolis meeting.

42. Va, *JHD, 1785,* pp. 113–14, 117–19 (Dec. 27, 29, 30, 1785).

43. Madison to Monroe, Richmond, Jan. 22, 1786, Rutland, ed., *Madison Papers,* VIII, 482–84. To Jefferson he was even more abbreviated, noting only that the Tyler resolution "was left on the table till it was found that several propositions for regulating our trade without regard to other States produced nothing. In this extremity the resolution was generally acceded to. . . ." Madison to Jefferson, Jan. 22, 1785, pp. 472–81, esp. 476–77.

44. In the introduction to his notes on the debates in the federal convention Madison's explanation for the assembly action on Tyler's resolution was that it faced "the alternative of adjourning without any effort for the crisis in the affairs of the Union": Henry D. Gilpin, comp., *The Papers of James Madison,* 3 vols. (Washington, 1840), II, 696.

45. Va, *JHD, 1785,* pp. 136, 139–40 (Jan. 10, 13, 1786). The Senate agreed to the resolutions without change: *SJ, 1785,* p. 94 (Jan. 17, 1786).

46. On January 19 the House appointed commissioners to meet with North Carolina: *JHD,* 149–50.

47. Ibid., p. 153 (Jan. 21, 1786); Madison to Monroe, Richmond, Jan. 22, 1786, Rutland, ed., *Madison Papers,* VIII, 482–84.

48. Jones was a Northern Neck physician who supported the Constitution in 1788 and became a Republican in the 1790s.

49. Madison to Monroe, Richmond, Jan. 22, 1786, Rutland, ed., *Madison Papers,* VIII, 482–84.

50. Ross was a Petersburg merchant and Ronald a Richmond merchant. Ronald supported the Tyler motion in the House and became a Federalist. Only Madison, Randolph, and Tucker actually attended the Annapolis meeting.

51. Madison to Monroe, Richmond, Jan. 22, 1786, Rutland, ed., *Madison Papers,* VIII, 482–84.

52. Randolph to Madison, Richmond, Mar. 1, 1786, ibid., 494–95. Virginians, of course, were not alone in developing either the conception or the nomenclature. The Pennsylvania assembly on March 21 approved resolutions appointing commissioners to "a Convention of the States proposed by the Commonwealth of Virginia": *Calendar of Virginia State Papers and Other Manuscripts,* 11 vols. (Richmond, 1875–92) IV, 116–7.

53. Grayson to Madison, New York, Mar. 22, 1786, Rutland, ed., *Madison Papers,* VIII, 508–10.

54. Madison to Jefferson, Orange, Mar. 18, 1786; Monroe to Jefferson, New York, May 11, 1786, Boyd, ed., *Jefferson Papers,* IX, 332–36, 510–12; Madison to Monroe, Orange, Mar. 19, Apr. 9, 1786, Rutland, ed., *Madison Papers,* VIII, 504–06, IX, 25–26.

55. Washington to Lafayette, Mount Vernon, May 10, 1786; Washington to John Jay, May 18, 1786, Washington Papers, DLC.

56. Md, *JDH, 1785,* p. 185 (Mar. 8, 1786). The commissioners nominated were Thomas Johnson, Samuel Chase, William Paca, Charles Carroll of Carrollton, Daniel of St. Thomas Jenifer, Thomas Stone, John Hall, Robert H. Harrison, William Hemsley, Otho H. Williams, and Tench Tilghman. The last five were wealthy merchants and land speculators who did not serve in the assembly.

57. Md, *JDH, 1785,* p. 195 (Mar. 11, 1786).

58. Ibid., p. 199 (Mar. 12, 1786).

59. Daniel Carroll to Madison, Annapolis, Mar. 13, 1786; Randolph to

Madison, Richmond, June 12, 1786, Rutland, ed., *Madison Papers,* VIII, 496, IX, 75; Madison to Jefferson, Orange, May 12, 1786, Boyd, ed., *Jefferson Papers,* IX, 519.

60. Grayson to Madison, New York, May 28, 1786, Rutland, ed., *Madison Papers,* IX, 61–65.

61. Samuel A. Ashe, *History of North Carolina,* 2 vols. (Greensboro, 1908–25), II, 48. The nominees were Abner Nash, Alfred Moore, Hugh Williamson, John Gray Blount, and Philemon Hawkins. Hawkins was a friend of Thomas Person from Granville County. Nash, who returned from a stint in Congress a moderate nationalist, died later that year. The rest all became Federalists.

62. "Address of the Annapolis Convention," Harold C. Syrett, ed., *The Papers of Alexander Hamilton,* 25 vols. to date (New York and London, 1961–), III, 686–90. Rutland, ed. note, *Madison Papers,* VIII, 115–19, esp. 118, adopts the conventional view that the turnout at the Annapolis meeting was "disappointing" to Madison and other delegates. None of these writers see the significance that I do in the haste with which the meeting adjourned.

63. Tucker to Monroe, [Sept.], 1786, Monroe Papers, DLC; Lee to Tucker, New York, Oct. 20, 1786, Tucker-Coleman Papers, VaWM.

64. Monroe to Madison, New York, Sept. 3, 1786, Rutland, ed., *Madison Papers,* IX, 112–14; Pendleton to Madison, Edmondsburg, Dec. 19, 1786, Mays, ed., *Pendleton Papers,* II, 491–94.

65. Madison to Jefferson, Philadelphia, Aug. 12, 1786, Boyd, ed., *Jefferson Papers,* X, 229–36, esp. 233–34; Henry Lee to [a member of the Virginia assembly], New York, Oct. 28, 1786, Charles Carter Lee Papers, VaSL.

66. Madison to Washington, Richmond, Nov. 1, 1786, Rutland, ed., *Madison Papers,* IX, 155–56.

67. Washington, Henry Lee, and John Marshall saw no objection to keeping the river closed because that would increase the importance of the Potomac and James River routes into the Ohio Valley: Washington to R. H. Lee, Mount Vernon, Aug. 22, 1785; Henry Lee to Washington, New York, Apr. 21, 1786, Washington Papers, DLC; Washington to Henry Lee, Mount Vernon, June 18, 1786, Lee-Ludwell Papers, VaHS; John Marshall to George Muter, Richmond, Jan. 7, 1785, *Tyler's Quarterly,* 1 (1919–20), 28. After the assembly opened, Madison promised Monroe that the House would support navigation of the river "with as much zeal as could be wished": Richmond, Oct. 30, 1786, Rutland, ed., *Madison Papers,* IX, 146. John Marshall reversed his earlier view, denounced Jay's request, and approved the "pointed instructions" passed by the assembly: Marshall to Thomas Marshall, [ca. Jan. 11, 1787], Herbert A. Johnson, ed., *The Papers of John Marshall,* 2 vols. to date (Chapel Hill, 1974–), I, 201–2.

68. Va, *JHD, 1786,* pp. 66–67 (Nov. 29, 1786); Va, *SJ, 1786,* p. 44 (Dec. 7, 1786). The Senate concurred by a vote of 7 to 4, but supporters and opponents of the Constitution were both divided.

69. Madison to Washington, Richmond, Dec. 7, 1786, Rutland, ed., *Madison Papers,* IX, 199–200.

70. "Federal" and "Antifederal" were in common use by the spring of 1787 and frequently referred to as "parties": Madison to Washington, Mar. 18, 1787, Rutland, ed., *Madison Papers,* IX, 314–16, esp. p. 315; Madison to Jefferson, Apr. 23, 1787, and Edward Carrington to Jefferson, Apr. 24, 1787, Boyd, ed., *Jefferson Papers,* XI, 309, 311.

71. Edmund Randolph to Madison, Richmond, Mar. 1, 1787, and Madison to Washington, New York, Mar. 18, 1787, Rutland, ed., *Madison Papers,* IX, 301, 314–16. Hugh Blair Grigsby, *The History of the Virginia Federal Convention of 1788 . . .,* 2 vols. (Richmond, 1890–91: Virginia Historical Society *Collections,* IX–X), I, 32*n,* reports an encounter, obviously handed down by hearsay, between the Rev. John Blair Smith, president of Hampden-Sydney College, and Patrick Henry during the debates in the Virginia Convention. When Smith asked Henry why he had not gone to Philadelphia to obtain a document more to his liking, Henry replied, "I smelt a rat."

72. Randolph to Madison, Richmond, Mar. 22, 1787, Rutland, ed., *Madison Papers,* IX, 325. On the council were James Wood, James McClurg, Joseph Jones, Sampson Matthews, Spencer Roane, Miles Selden, Carter Braxton, and Beverly Randolph. The first four became Federalists, the remainder Antifederalists. McClurg was an arch-nationalist who even favored a federal veto on state legislation: to Madison, Richmond, Aug. 22, 1787, Madison Papers, DLC.

73. Madison to Jefferson [New York], Apr. 24, 1787, Boyd, ed., *Jefferson Papers,* XI, 310.

74. Grayson to Monroe, New York, May 29, 1787, Monroe Papers, DLC.

75. Carroll to Daniel Carroll of Duddington, Mar. 13, 1787, Harper-Pennington Papers, MdHS. A Baltimore merchant agreed that paper money was a dead issue: Robert Lemmon to Councillor Carter of Virginia, Mar. 5, 1787, cited by Kate Mason Rowland, *Charles Carroll of Carrollton,* 2 vols. (New York, 1898), II, 97.

76. Md, *SJ, 1786,* 2d sess., pp. 39, 63, 66 (May 24, 1787). This was apparently not a Chasite maneuver. Chase was present in the House but did not vote. He had both friends and enemies among those trying to start a fight with the Senate.

77. This interpretation evidently originated with Philip A. Crowl, *Maryland During and After the Revolution* (Baltimore, 1943), p. 110, but Crowl, recognizing perhaps the flimsiness of his evidence, merely mentions the possibility without endorsing it. The only evidence for it is a letter of John Brown Cutting, the American chargé in London, to Jefferson, London, July 11, 1788, Boyd, ed., *Jefferson Papers,* XIII, 331–38, esp. 332–33. Cutting felt that the mutual suspicions of Chase and Carroll explained why Maryland sent a second-rate delegation to Philadelphia. But Cutting, it should be noted, was writing more than a year after the event. He was a New Englander who had no known contacts in Maryland. It is easy for persons remote from the situation to explain it in terms of conspiracy.

78. The House nominees were John Henry, Charles Carroll, William Smallwood, Robert H. Harrison, James McHenry, Thomas S. Lee, Daniel of St. Thomas Jenifer, George Gale, Alexander C. Hanson, and Robert Goldsborough. Every one became a Federalist.

79. Md, *SJ, 1786,* 2d sess., pp. 47–49 (Apr. 20–21, 1786).

80. Jenifer's politics, admittedly, are a mystery. As Intendant of Revenue he had become closely linked with the speculators in confiscated property (though he purchased none for himself), and his endorsement of paper money in 1785 seemed to label him a "Chasite." But he had no personal interests at stake, so far as can be determined, and his public service, from a tour in the Continental Congress (1778–81) to the Mount Vernon meeting, was a record of consistent nationalism. At Philadelphia he sided generally with the nationalists, thereby splitting the Maryland

vote since for most of the summer his only colleague was Antifederalist Luther Martin: Bernard C. Steiner, ed., "Papers of James McHenry on the Federal Convention of 1787," *American Historical Review*, 11 (1905–6), 595–624.

81. Md, *SJ, 1786,* 2d sess., pp. 51, 56–57, 59–61 (May 3, 7, 1787).

82. Ibid., pp. 61, 66, 75–76 (May 10, 22, 24, 1787).

83. Mercer to Madison, Annapolis, Jan. 16, 1787, Rutland, ed., *Madison Papers,* IX, 246. Forrest McDonald, *We the People: The Economic Origins of the Constitution* (Chicago, 1958), p. 31, places Mercer in the Chase faction, but his only basis for doing so, it would seem, was Mercer's opposition to the Constitution. During his legislative service in Virginia Mercer was an opponent of congressional power.

84. Max Farrand, ed., *Records of the Federal Convention of 1787,* 3 vols. (New Haven, 1911), III, 589.

85. Steiner, ed., "Papers of James McHenry." The meeting took place on the evening of August 6, the day that Rutledge reported the Constitution out of the Committee of Detail.

86. NC, JHC, 1786, Clark, ed., *State Records,* XVIII, 462 (Jan. 6, 1787); Caswell to William R. Davie, Mar. 1, 1787, and Caswell to William Blount, Apr. 24, 1787, ibid., XX, 627–28, 683–84.

87. A radically different stance by North Carolina would have altered the two most prominent features of the convention on which historians rely for their analyses—the large-state, small-state split and the North-South division.

CHAPTER TEN RATIFICATION WITH OR WITHOUT AMENDMENTS

1. David Robertson, *Debates and Other Proceedings of the Convention of Virginia . . . June 1788 . . .,* 2d ed. (Richmond, 1805), p. 466.

2. Randolph to Madison, Bowling Green, Va., Sept. 30, 1787, Madison Papers, DLC. Madison had journeyed north to attend the fall session of Congress in New York. Chase's address was also reported in the *Maryland Journal* [Baltimore], Sept. 25, 28, 1787.

3. Samuel Chase to ———, Baltimore, June 13, 1788 (photostat of letter in the New York Historical Society), Chase Papers, MdHS.

4. Daniel Carroll to Madison, Near Georgetown, Oct. 28, 1787, Madison Papers, DLC.

5. *Maryland Journal* [Baltimore], Oct. 11, 1787.

6. William Tilghman to Tench Coxe, Chester Town, Nov. 25, 1787, Coxe Papers, PaHS.

7. Md, *JHD, 1787,* p. 10 (Nov. 23, 1787). Antifederalists generally supported the motion; Federalists were evenly divided.

8. "Extract of a letter from a member of the House of Delegates, now sitting in Annapolis, to his friend in this town, dated 1 December 1787," *Maryland Journal* [Baltimore], Dec. 7, 1787. Bernard C. Steiner, ed., "James McHenry's Speech before the Maryland House of Delegates in November, 1787," *Maryland Historical Magazine,* 4 (1909), 336–44.

9. Md, *JHD, 1787,* pp. 12–13 (Nov. 26, 27, 1787); Md, *SJ, 1787,* pp. 5, 7 (Nov. 26, Dec. 1, 1787). House roll calls on the last two resolutions were 31 to 18 and 28 to 21.

10. Md, *JHD, 1787,* p. 45 (Dec. 14, 1787).

11. Orin G. Libby, *The Geographical Distribution of the Vote of the Thirteen States on the Federal Constitution, 1787–1788* (Madison, 1894), p. 66, first advanced the thesis that there was a "correspondence" between the advocates of paper money and Antifederalists. Philip A. Crowl, *Maryland During and After the Revolution* (Baltimore, 1943), pp. 133–51, pointed out that the correspondence was not exact because of the shift in stance of certain counties (though he failed to note that the main shift was in the upper Potomac). Yet he felt that there was "an underlying continuity" among public debtors, paper money, and Antifederalism. Forrest McDonald, *We the People: The Economic Origins of the Constitution* (Chicago, 1958), pp. 154–55, objected to this interpretation on two grounds: (1) both Federalists and Antifederalists held confiscated property, and (2) the paper money laws of 1785–86 provided that the paper could be used only for certain purposes, which did not include payments to the state for confiscated property. Both of McDonald's arguments are flawed. Federalists who possessed Loyalist property were men like Gen. Otho Holland Williams and Thomas Johnson, who could afford their speculations. They did not need relief, nor did they ask for it. Others, such as Samuel Chase and Charles Ridgely, who walked much closer to the line of bankruptcy, had to concern themselves with the Constitution's impact on their interests. As to McDonald's second argument, it is true that the paper money laws limited the usage of the paper to private debts and taxes, but other acts and resolutions of the assembly permitted speculators to discharge their public debts with it. In any case, the issue of more paper, by adding to the total quantity in circulation, relieved the pressure on other forms of currency, thus making more available to debtors of all kinds.

At the same time, Crowl's argument was simplistic because he failed to distinguish among the supporters of paper money. Old debtor party men naturally favored paper money, and most of them became Antifederalists. Among these, for instance, was Charles Ridgely, a major speculator but a man whose voting record was generally debtor throughout the 1780s. Possibly Ridgely's votes throughout conformed to his interests (though he also had a large mercantile business), but most likely Ridgely's interests conformed to those of his back-country Baltimore constitutents.

On the other hand, Crowl was correct in observing that the regional correlation between the parties of 1785–86 and those of 1788 is not precise. The reason for this is the shift of the upper Potomac from debtor to Federalist, owing to circumstances that will be discussed. The correlation among individuals is better. When the electorate in the upper Potomac changed to Federalism it simply elected new men.

12. *Maryland Journal* [Baltimore], Feb. 1, Mar. 21, Apr. 4, 25, 1788.

13. Smith to Tench Coxe, Baltimore, Apr. 13, 1788, Coxe Papers, PaHS. Smith made no mention of speculators or paper money. Eastern Shore lawyer William Tilghman likewise felt that, while "men of peoperty & Integrity are for it," many debtors were "alarmed" at the judiciary provisions because "under the federal system there would be more vigor & dispatch than under the State laws." Tilghman to Coxe, Chester Town, Nov. 25, 1787, ibid.

14. "Farmer and Planter," in *Maryland Journal* [Baltimore], Apr. 1, 1788.

15. Anonymous letter dated Baltimore, Apr. 24, 1788, in *Pennsylvania Gazette* [Philadelphia], Apr. 30, 1788.

16. L. Marx Renzulli, *Maryland: The Federalist Years* (Rutherford, N.J., 1973), p. 101, following an earlier lead by Thomas Perkins Abernethy, *The South in the New Nation, 1789–1819* (Baton Rouge, 1961), pp. 23–25, argues that wheat-growing farmers, in need of new foreign markets, were Federalist, and tobacco-planters, secure in the market and unconcerned about governmental aid, were Antifederalists. I have presented a similar argument in "The Virginia Federalists," *Journal of Southern History,* 33 (1967), 486–515, esp. 496–97. The hypothesis does not stand up under close scrutiny, however. The upper bay–Susquehanna region produced as much wheat and flour as the Potomac, yet it voted Antifederalist. The Patuxent Valley, which grew the finest tobacco in Maryland, was staunchly Federalist. Most farmers in Maryland seem to have raised both tobacco and cereal grains, often side by side. Economic interests shaped attitudes toward the Constitution, but not in such narrow considerations as markets for particular crops. The best single index is land values.

17. There is, unfortunately, no direct contemporary evidence that the possible location of the national capital had any influence on Potomac Federalism in 1787–88. Nevertheless, there were continuous rumors to that effect, and Congress even discussed the possibility that winter. It would seem a fair inference that the prospect increased Federalist feelings in the region.

18. John A. Munroe, *Federalist Delaware, 1775–1815* (New Brunswick, 1954), pp. 102–3, 213.

19. William Tilghman to Tench Coxe, Chester Town, April 6, 11, 1788, Coxe Papers, PaHS.

20. Anonymous contributors in *Maryland Journal* [Baltimore], Apr. 18, 1788, and *Maryland Gazette* [Annapolis], Apr. 22, 1788; Daniel Carroll to Madison, Georgetown, May 28, 1788, Madison Papers, DLC.

21. McMechen's association with Charles Ridgely is evident from his correspondence in the Ridgely Family Papers, MdHS.

22. Samuel Smith to Tench Coxe, Baltimore, April 13, 1788, Coxe Papers, PaHS; *Maryland Gazette* [Baltimore], Apr. 11, 15, 18, 22, 25, 1788. The poll results were:

McHenry 902	Sterett	383
Coulter 958	McMechen	380

23. Crowl, *Maryland During and After the Revolution,* p. 128.

24. The 1783 Baltimore tax list credited Deye with 6 plantations totaling 3,119 acres valued at £5,940, plus 77 slaves.

25. Charles Ridgely to Harry Dorsey Gough, Feb. 27, 1787, H. D. Gough Papers, MdHS. Ridgely accused Gough of plotting with Deye to "leave me out of the representation," and claimed that Deye "placed himself at the head of the opposition to me" in 1786 as well.

26. "A Decided Federalist," in *Maryland Journal* [Baltimore], Mar. 14, 1788. The three were George Lux, Dr. John Cradock, and James Gittings. Only Cradock had prior legislative service—one term, 1782.

27. George Lux "To the Inhabitants of Baltimore County," *Maryland Journal* [Baltimore], Mar. 25, Apr. 4, 1788.

28. "A Decided Federalist" in *Maryland Journal* [Baltimore], Mar. 14, 1788; and "A Real Federalist," in ibid., Mar. 21, 1788.

29. In the *Maryland Journal* [Baltimore], Apr. 4, only four days before the election, Lux listed the Federalist slate as himself, Gough, Cradock, and Gittings.

30. The result, recorded in the *Maryland Gazette* [Baltimore], Apr. 11, 1788, was:

Charles Ridgely	676	Harry D. Gough	192
Charles Ridgely of Wm.	673	James Gittings	183
Edward Cockey	649	John E. Howard	172
Nathan Cromwell	629	Dr. John Cradock	171

31. William Tilghman to Tench Coxe, Chester Town, Apr. 20, 1788, Coxe Papers, PaHs; Daniel of St. Thomas Jenifer to Washington, Annapolis, Apr. 15, 1788, Washington Papers, DLC; Daniel Carroll to Madison, Georgetown, Apr. 28, 1788, Madison Papers, DLC.

32. *Maryland Journal* [Baltimore], Apr. 11, 1788. Three of the Federalists—Johnson, Richard Potts, and Thomas Sim Lee—had impeccable creditor credentials. The fourth, Abraham Faw, had voted with Chase in the assembly. Evidently committed by the convention election, he voted in favor of the Constitution, but he voted Antifederalist when he returned to the assembly in the fall. In 1789 he stood for Congress as an Antifederalist, suffered defeat, and after one more term in the assembly (fall 1789) was never heard from again.

33. Sprigg owned 1,754 acres and 44 slaves: Herbert C. Bell, *History of the Leitersburg District . . .* (Leitersburg, Md., 1898), pp. 54, 224. He was elected to the House of Delegates, 1780–82, but failed to attend the 1782 session, so his views on economic issues are unknown. Stull voted debtor, 1784–86, but was not returned in 1787.

34. Jonathan Albert to Horatio Gates, Frederick Town, Apr. 14, 1788, Gates Papers, NYPL.

35. *Maryland Journal* [Baltimore], Apr. 15, 1788.

36. *Pennsylvania Gazette* [Philadelphia], Apr. 30, 1788; James Tilghman to Tench Coxe, Chester Town, Apr. 19, 1788, Coxe Papers, PaHS.

37. Daniel of St. Thomas Jenifer to Washington, Annapolis, Apr. 15, 1788, Washington Papers, DLC; Daniel Carroll to Madison, Georgetown, Apr. 28, 1788, Madison Papers, DLC.

38. Madison to Daniel Carroll, Orange, Apr. 10, 1788, and to Washington, same date, Madison Papers, DLC; Washington to Thomas Johnson, Mount Vernon, Apr. 20, 1788, and to James McHenry, Apr. 27, 1788, Washington Papers, DLC.

39. Robert Goldsborough of Dorchester and Jeremiah Banning of Talbot were too ill to attend: Daniel Carroll to Madison, Apr. 28, 1788, Madison Papers, DLC.

40. Alexander C. Hanson, "An Address to the People of Maryland," enclosed in Hanson to Madison, June 2, 1788, in A. H. Allan, ed., *Documentary History of the Constitution of the United States,* 5 vols. (Washington, 1905), IV, 645–664, esp. 650.

41. In 1796 to 1798 Lloyd wrote a series of letters to Coxe seeking reimbursement, which he claimed Coxe had promised. Coxe Papers, PaHS. A contributor to the *Maryland Gazette* [Annapolis], May 22, 1788, claimed that Lloyd was

reimbursed at the time by Maryland Federalists as an inducement not to publish the debates, since the only speeches made were by Antifederalists.

42. "A Fragment of Facts . . ." is in Jonathan Elliot, *The Debates in the Several State Conventions on the Adoption of the Federal Constitution . . .,* 5 vols. (Philadelphia, 1901), II, 547–56; Alexander C. Hanson, "An Address to the People of Maryland" is in Allan, ed., *Documentary History,* IV, 645–64. Hanson never published his rebuttal because the Antifederalist exposé was greeted with public indifference, but he did send a copy to Madison to enable him to correct any misapprehensions in Virginia concerning the Maryland convention. Hanson to Madison, Annapolis, June 2, 1788, Madison Papers, DLC. Except where otherwise noted, the narrative is based on these sources.

43. William Smith to O. H. Williams, Baltimore, Apr. 28, 1788, Williams Papers, MdHS.

44. Alarmed at a rumor spread by John F. Mercer that his own "officious" letters had irritated Johnson, Washington wrote to inquire about this motion for adjournment. Johnson assured him that the letters were of great help to the Federal cause, and his action stemmed only from a desire to see some limited amendments. He was, however, "very far from wishing all that was proposed." "Extract of a letter from Doctor Brooke at Fredericksburg to David Stuart," July 10, 1788; Washington to Johnson, Mount Vernon, Aug. 31, 1788; Johnson to Washington, Frederick, Oct. 10, 1788; all in Washington Papers, DLC.

45. Hanson, "Address to the People," Allan, ed., *Documentary History,* IV, 658–63; Hanson to Madison, Annapolis, June 2, 1788, Madison Papers, DLC.

46. "A Fragment of Facts," Elliot, *Debates,* II, 554–55. This address records the vote as 47 to 27, but there are only 26 names in the minority.

47. Madison to Jefferson, Oct. 17, 1788, Julian P. Boyd, ed., *The Papers of Thomas Jefferson,* 18 vols. to date (Princeton, 1950–), XIV, 18. On the basis of past experience, Jefferson would know that he was talking about Patrick Henry and his Southside allies. Washington, also relying on past performance, predicted that the Northern Neck would support the document and most of the opposition would come from the region south of the James and the west: Washington to Gen. Henry Knox, Mount Vernon, Oct. 15, 1787, Washington Papers, DLC.

48. The depredations did not reach Virginia until 1787, but throughout the autumn of that year—just when Virginians were debating the merits of the Constitution—newspapers carried reports of Indian raids deep into present-day West Virginia: *Virginia Gazette* [Richmond], November–December, 1787, passim. The issue of December 27, for instance, described the murder of a family of settlers in Harrison County. The Executive Papers, VaSL, are full of requests from county lieutenants in the west for additional funds to hire "spies" (i.e., scouts) to keep track of the Indians' movements.

49. William McMahan to Gov. Randolph, Ohio County, Dec. 4, 1787, and George Clendinen to Gov. Randolph, Richmond, Jan. 14, 1788, Executive Papers, VaSL. McMahan and Clendinen sat in the House of Delegates at the time; both supported the Constitution.

50. After the Constitution was ratified, Clendinen reported to Gov. Beverley Randolph that westerners were "Confidently relying that the Genl. Government will take the business [of frontier defense] up, as one of their first and greatest

Objects": Clendinen to Randolph, Richmond, Dec. 18, 1788, Executive Papers, VaSL.

51. William Grayson to Madison, New York, May 28, 1786, Madison Papers, DLC; *Virginia Gazette* [Richmond], July 12, 1786.

52. Randolph to Madison, Richmond, Oct. 23, 1787, Madison Papers, DLC. Such expectations were not confined to the governmental elite. One rural lawyer, who chanced to have British connections, anticipated that when the Constitution was approved, "British merchants will be enabled to demand their debts of the people. If it should be the case I intend to offer my services to some of them in the collecting way." Abram Maury to James Maury, Culpeper, Feb. 6, 1788, James Maury Papers, VaU. An anonymous contributor to the Fredericksburg, *Virginia Herald,* Jan. 15, 1789, commenting on the Federalist victories in the first elections, concluded with the punch line: "Strange as it may appear, I am a British debtor and A FEDERALIST."

53. Madison to Coxe, New York, Oct. 26, 1787, Coxe Papers, PaHS.

54. Mason to Washington, Richmond, Nov. 27, 1787, Washington Papers, DLC; Va. *JHD, 1787,* pp. 46–47, 51–52 (Nov. 14, 17, 1787).

55. Monroe to Madison, Richmond, Dec. 6, 1787, Madison Papers, DLC; Madison to Jefferson, New York, Dec. 9, 1787, Boyd, ed., *Jefferson Papers,* XII, 408–12.

56. Mason to Washington, Gunston Hall, Oct. 7, 1787, Washington Papers, DLC.

57. Randolph's public letter listing his objections to the Constitution and the amendments he desired was published in the *Virginia Gazette* [Richmond], Jan. 3, 10, 1788. His change of heart is recorded in Randolph to Madison, Richmond, Apr. 17, 1788, and Madison to Washington, Richmond, June 4, 1788, Madison Papers, DLC.

58. Stuart to Washington, Abingdon, Feb. 17, 1788, in *Proceedings of the Massachusetts Historical Society,* 2d ser., 17 (1903), 496. Robert A. Rutland, ed., *The Papers of George Mason,* 3 vols. (Chapel Hill, 1970), III, 1047–48, traces the hardening of Mason's attitude.

59. Hugh Blair Grigsby, *The History of the Virginia Federal Convention of 1788 . . .,* 2 vols. (Richmond, 1890–91: Virginia Historical Society Collections, IX–X), I 4n.

60. Lee to George Mason, Chantilly, May 15, 1787, Rutland, ed., *Mason Papers,* III, 876–79. His brother Arthur Lee was similarly dismayed with the weakness of Congress and prepared for substantial change: Arthur Lee to Richard H. Lee, [New York], Jan. 13, 1787, Lee Family Papers, VaU.

61. Lee to Francis Lightfoot Lee, New York, July 14, 1787, Lee Family Papers, VaU.

62. Lee to Mason, Chantilly, May 15, 1787, Rutlend, ed., *Mason Papers,* III, 876–79. Lee's analysis of political issues throughout the 1780s is so shallow that one is tempted to doubt his authorship of the highly perceptive *Letters of a Federal Farmer.* Even if the pen was Lee's, were the ideas George Mason's? Washington, for instance, felt that "The political tenets of Col. M. and Col. R. H. L. are always in unison." Washington thought that if either gave "the tone," it must be Lee because he was too stubborn to accept advice from anyone: to Madison, Mount Vernon, Oct. 10, 1787, Washington Papers, DLC. By playing on Lee's vanity, Mason may

have been more effective than Washington realized; surviving correspondence leaves no doubt that he was the more perceptive of the two.

63. Harrison to Washington, Berkeley, Oct. 4, 1787, Washington Papers, DLC.

64. Monroe to Madison, Fredericksburg, May 23, Oct. 13, 1787, Madison Papers, DLC; Monroe to Jefferson, Fredericksburg, July 12, 1788, Boyd, ed., *Jefferson Papers,* XIII, 351–53; Harry Ammon, *James Monroe: The Quest for National Identity* (New York, 1971), 66–69.

65. Randolph to Madison, Bowling Green, Va., Sept. 30, 1787, Madison Papers, DLC; R. H. Lee to Mason, New York, Oct. 1, 1787, Rutland, ed., *Mason Papers,* III, 996–97; Edward Carrington to Madison, Richmond, Jan. 18, 1788, Madison Papers, DLC; Carrington to Jefferson, New York, Apr. 24, 1788, Boyd, ed., *Jefferson Papers,* XIII, 100–3.

66. Charles Lee to Washington, Richmond, Apr. 11, 17, 1788, Washington Papers, DLC.

67. Washington was more cognizant of the impact the Constitution might have on his western holdings. Refusing an offer of two dollars an acre for a tract in southwestern Pennsylvania, he informed an agent the day after the Constitution was signed that "If the Government of this Country gets well-toned, and property perfectly secured, I have no doubt of obtaining the price I have fixed on the land, and that in a short time." Washington to Col. John Cannon, Philadelphia, Sept. 16, 1787, Washington Papers, DLC. This was an isolated bargaining point, however, for there is no other evidence that western lands were a primary consideration. Patrick Henry, for instance, was just as heavily involved in the West as Washington.

68. Stephen to Madison, Berkeley County, Nov. 25, 1787, Madison Papers, DLC.

69. Jefferson to Madison, Paris, June 20, 1787; to Edward Carrington, Dec. 21, 1787; to Alexander Donald, Feb. 7, 1788; all in Boyd, ed., *Jefferson Papers,* XI, 480–84; XII, 445–47, 570–72. See also editor's note, XIII, 354–55.

70. John to James Breckinridge, Grove Hill, Jan. 25, 1788, Breckinridge Papers, DLC; Page to Jefferson, Rosewell, Mar. 7, 1788, Boyd, ed., *Jefferson Papers,* XII, 650–54; Jones to Madison, Richmond, Oct. 29, 1787, Madison Papers, DLC.

71. Henry Lee to Madison [Dec. 1787]; Archibald Stuart to Madison, Richmond, Jan. 14, 1788; and Edward Carrington to Madison, Richmond, Apr. 8, 1788, all in Madison Papers, DLC. Among judges only James Mercer and St. George Tucker remained Antifederalists.

72. Randolph to Madison, Richmond, Feb. 29, 1788; Madison to George Nicholas, Orange, Apr. 8, 1788, Madison Papers, DLC; Grigsby, *Virginia Convention of 1788,* I, 85.

73. Randolph to Madison, Richmond, Oct. 23, 1787; Monroe to Madison, Fredericksburg, Feb. 7, 1788, Madison Papers, DLC.

74. Monroe to Jefferson, Fredericksburg, July 12, 1788, Boyd, ed., *Jefferson Papers,* XIII, 351–53. Voters nevertheless knew where Monroe stood. Wrote one Federalist: "The election in this County last Tuesday ended very unfavorably. Dawson & Col. Monroe carryed agst Page and Spotswood." James Duncanson to James Maury, Fredericksburg, Mar. 11, 1788, James Maury Papers, VaU.

75. John Dawson to Madison, Richmond, Oct. 19, 1787, Feb. 18, 1788, Madison Papers, DLC. Dawson himself seems to have been a victim of electoral pledges. A close associate of Madison in the assembly, he furnished Madison with information on Piedmont politics throughout the ratification campaign, and his letters reflected a generally Federalist slant. Yet, elected to represent heavily Antifederal Spotsylvania County, he ultimately voted against the Constitution. A Federalist neighbor in Fredericksburg, however, thought Dawson was voting with the Henryites because he was deeply in debt: James Duncanson to James Maury, Fredericksburg, Mar. 11, 1788, James Maury Papers, VaU.

76. Mercer to John F. Mercer, Richmond, Dec. 12, 1787, Mercer Papers, VaHS.

77. James McClurg to Madison, Richmond, Sept. 10. 1787, Madison Papers, DLC.

78. *Maryland Journal* [Baltimore], Mar. 28, 1788. Over 600 attended the poll, and the results were: William Cabell 327, Samuel J. Cabell 313, Hugh Rose 23, Samuel Meredith 5.

79. Carrington to Madison, Richmond, Apr. 8, 1788, Madison Papers, DLC.

80. James Duncanson to James Maury, Fredericksburg, Dec. 20, 1787, Mar. 11, 1788, James Maury Papers, VaU.

81. Henry Lee to Madison [Dec. 1787]; Madison, Sr., to Madison, Jr., Orange, Jan. 30, 1788; James Gordon to Madison, Orange, Feb. 17, 1788; Joseph Spencer to Madison, Orange, Feb. 28, 1788; Madison to Jefferson, Orange, Apr. 22, 1788, all in Madison Papers, DLC.

82. James Duncanson to James Maury, Fredericksburg, May 8, 1788, Maury Papers, VaU. The result in Orange was Madison 202, James Gordon 178, and Thomas Barbour 56. *Virginia Herald* [Fredericksburg], Mar. 27, 1788.

83. Lee to Washington, Richmond, Apr. 6, 1788, Washington Papers, DLC; *Virginia Centinel, or the Winchester Mercury,* Apr. 2, 1788. The accuracy of these prognoses was borne out when the convention ratified by 89 to 79.

84. Harry Innes to John Brown, Apr. 4, 1788, Innes Papers, DLC; George Nicholas to Madison, Charlottesville, Apr. 5, 1788, Madison Papers, DLC; James Breckinridge to John Breckinridge, Richmond, June 13, 1788, Breckinridge Papers, DLC.

85. The Executive Papers, VaSL, contain far fewer requests for help from Kentuckians in this period than from county lieutenants in (West) Virginia. Gen. James Wilkinson, a member of the "court" party, journeyed to New Orleans in 1787 and succeeded in obtaining trade concessions, at least for himself. He returned just as Kentuckians were discussing the Constitution and openly opposed it. Thomas Perkins Abernethy, *Western Lands and the American Revolution* (Charlottesville, 1937), pp. 346–48.

86. James Breckinridge to John Breckinridge, Richmond, June 13, 1788, Breckinridge Papers, DLC; Harry Innes to John Brown, Apr. 4, 1788; David Stuart to Innes, Richmond, June 29, 1788; Madison to Innes, New York, July 5, 1789, all in Innes Papers, DLC.

87. John Brown to James Breckinridge, New York, Dec. 16, 1787, May 14, June 21, 1788, James Breckinridge Papers, VaU.

88. Patricia Watlington, *The Partisan Spirit: Kentucky Politics, 1779–1792* (New York, 1972), pp. 149–56. This division held firm in the final vote. One

Kentucky delegate, Notley Conn, failed to vote, but his subsequent record in the assembly was Antifederal.

89. James Duncanson to James Maury, Fredericksburg, June 8, 1788, James Maury Papers, VaU.

90. Stuart to John Breckinridge, Richmond, June 19, 1788, Breckinridge Papers, DLC.

91. Washington to James McHenry, Mount Vernon, July 31, 1788, Washington Papers, DLC; Madison to Washington, Richmond, June 23, 1788, Madison Papers, DLC. Two days before the final ballots, Francis Corbin, anticipating that amendments incorporating vital changes in the Constitution would be voted upon before the ratification roll call, predicted that the amendments would lose by four or five votes and that the Constitution would then be ratified by a comfortable margin. This suggests that efforts to analyze voting behavior continued throughout the convention. But it also suggests that the Henryites could not get a majority to support a conditional ratification (i.e., one conditioned on certain amendments). This would explain why the votes on substantive amendments actually came *after* the ratification roll call: Corbin to Tench Coxe, Richmond, June 23, 1788, Coxe Papers, PaHS.

92. The delegate who shifted positions was David Patteson of Southside Chesterfield, who was elected as an Antifederalist.

93. David Robertson, *Debates and Other Proceedings of the Convention of Virginia . . . June 1788 . . .*, 2d ed. (Richmond, 1805), pp. 470–75.

94. Richard Beeman, *The Old Dominion and the New Nation, 1788–1801* (Lexington, Ky., 1972), pp. 11–13, considers this vote evidence that there remained a substantial number of "undecided" delegates even after the vote on the Constitution.

95. Madison philosophically explained to Washington that, although several of the amendments were "highly objectionable," they "could not be parried": Richmond, June 27, 1788, Madison Papers, DLC.

96. Supporters of the Constitution who supported the tax amendment were:

	Region	*Subsequent Party*
Edmund Randolph	Piedmont	Federalist/Republican
Edmund Pendleton	Middle Tidewater	Republican
William Fleming	West	Unknown
Paul Carrington	Southside	Federalist
David Patteson	Southside	Republican
William O Callis	Piedmont	Republican
Cole Digges	Middle Tidewater	Unknown
Miles King	Middle Tidewater	Federalist
Burwell Bassett	Middle Tidewater	Federalist
Solomon Shepherd	Southside	Federalist
William Clayton	Middle Tidewater	Federalist
Walker Tomlin	Northern Neck	Federalist
Andrew Moore	West	Republican
Willis Riddick	Southside	Republican
John H. Cocke	Southside	Federalist or Republican Quid (supported Monroe in 1808)
William McKee	West	Federalist

97. Archibald Stuart to John Breckinridge, Charlottesville, June 30, 1788, Breckinridge Papers, DLC; Jones to Madison, Richmond, Aug. 3, 1788, *Proceedings of the Massachusetts Historical Society,* 2d ser., 17, 509–10.

98. There are some surviving election poll lists, which can be checked against tax records for voting by wealth, but other influences on popular voting behavior cannot, by presently available methodology, be retrieved: see Norman K. Risjord, "How the Common Man Voted in Jefferson's Virginia," John B. Boles, ed., *America, The Middle Period: Essays in Honor of Bernard Mayo* (Charlottesville, 1973), pp. 36–64.

99. Norman K. Risjord, "Virginians and the Constitution: A Multivariant Analysis," *William and Mary Quarterly,* 3d ser., 31 (1974), 613–32. The data and evaluations in regard to Virginians given here are taken from this article.

100. Jackson Turner Main, *Political Parties Before the Constitution* (Chapel Hill, 1973), pp. 33–35, has an excellent discussion of the quality and variety of these sources. See Risjord, "Virginians and the Constitution," for a discussion of the particular sources for Virginians. There is no Maryland source comparable to E. G. Swem, comp., *Virginia Historical Index,* 2 vols. (Roanoke, 1934–36), but there are a number of relatively new and fairly competent county histories. In addition, the *Maryland Historical Magazine* is indexed volume by volume.

101. The particular program used, called Regan II, is available only in the University of Wisconsin Data Processing Library. However, any stepwise regression program can be adapted to this purpose. Multiple classification was used because the various attributes (independent variables) are nominal, and there is no linear regression.

102. The multiple Virginia regions used in earlier tables are reduced for this purpose to three—Tidewater, Piedmont, and west (otherwise there could have been too few in each category for meaningful calculations). The four Maryland regions used earlier are retained here.

103. See Risjord, "Virginians and the Constitution," pp. 617–18, for an explanation of this.

104. The exception to this is the arbitrary assignment of a slaveholding index number to a dozen Marylanders (7 Federalists, 5 Antifederalists) whose holdings, unaccountably, seem to be understated by the census. Gov. John E. Howard, for instance, is credited with only 4 slaves in the census, although every contemporary source indicates he possessed vast estates. Thus, the Maryland figures are more an index of wealth than simple slaveholdings, and this may explain why the percentages do not vary much when other factors, such as occupation, are taken into account.

105. McDonald, *We the People,* pp. 161, 281–83.

106. This is the central thesis of Crowl, *Maryland During and After the Revolution,* ch. 5, passim. Crowl, however, contents himself with a list of the largest purchasers and makes no effort to ascertain how many members of the ratifying convention purchased little or no British property. McDonald, *We the People,* p. 161, in concluding that there were four and a half times as many Antifederalist speculators as Federalist speculators, used Crowl's partial list, rather than examining the original records. The "Proceedings of the Commissioners for Confiscated British Property," 8 vols., are in the Hall of Records, Annapolis, and are available on microfilm. See the "Note on Sources" for a description of the contents of each volume.

107. One of the volumes of the "Proceedings" (see the preceding note), entitled "Agent's Ledger, 1786–1789," is an accounting of payments made into the treasury and the dates of payment. Unfortunately, I am not able to be more specific as to exactly how many still owed the state money in 1788 because payments were partial and do not always add up to the amount of the original debt. Moreover, by then property that had been returned to the state for insolvency was being resold and continued to be sold until about 1795. Payments for this property were still being made as late as 1817. To untangle all of this completely would require a separate monograph.

108. The seven were: Samuel and Jeremiah T. Chase, Thomas Gantt, Luther Martin, Capt. Charles Ridgely, Charles Ridgely "of William," and Samuel Sterett. All but the Ridgelys were Chasites in the assembly. But it should also be noted that two of Chase's closest political allies, William Pinkney and Allan Quynn, made no purchases of British property (David McMechen of Baltimore made some small purchases for which he paid cash).

109. Most of the heavily Antifederal "unknowns" in Maryland were probably planters. They came from counties in the upper bay and upper Potomac where, because of the lack of newspapers, occupation was difficult to determine. They were also missing from the census data.

110. Stanley Elkins and Eric McKitrick, "The Founding Fathers, Young Men of the Revolution," *Political Science Quarterly,* 76 (1961), 181–216, and McDonald, *We the People,* p. 260*n*7.

111. Age was the most difficult characteristic to ascertain. Even genealogists seem to regard it as irrelevant. In some cases the birthdate was inferred from the date of matriculation in college. The calculation was based on each man's age in 1790.

112. Each delegate was recorded only once—for the highest level he achieved or the farthest he went geographically. Sources for attendance at British universities are W. Connely, "List of Colonial Americans in Oxford and Cambridge," *American Oxonian,* 29 (1942), 6–17, 75–77; Samuel Lewis, "List of the American Graduates in Medicine in the University of Edinburgh," *New England Historical and Genealogical Register,* 62 (1888), 159–65; J. G. deRoulhac Hamilton, "Southern Members of the Inns of Court," *North Carolina Historical Review,* 10 (1933), 273–86. William and Mary students in the period 1753 to 1778 are listed in the *William and Mary Quarterly,* 2d ser., 1 (1921), 27–41, 116–30. Virginians who attended Princeton in the period 1749 to 1824 are listed in ibid., 1st ser., 6 (1897–98), 218–19; 7 (1898–99), 2–9. Virginians who attended the College of Philadelphia are listed ibid., 1st ser., 6 (1897–98), 180; 7 (1898–99), 4–8. Swem's *Index* lists by name 52 Virginia academies, and some of these references contain lists of students and dates of attendance.

113. Main, *Political Parties,* pp. 265–66, reaches essentially the same conclusion, although his quantitative method is somewhat different.

114. The coefficient of determination for the Virginia model (Net_a) is 0.1770, which suggests that all of the personal attributes taken together account for only about 17 percent of a delegate's voting behavior. This figure rises to 0.3052 when region is taken into account. The comparable coefficients for the Maryland model are 0.2204 and 0.2217, which indicates that region was not quite as important in Maryland as in Virginia. If all of these figures seem disappointingly low, they serve as a standing reminder of the limitations of quantitative analyses of human behavior.

115. North Carolina legislators were not included in the foregoing quantitative analysis because not enough biographical information could be gained on them. Because of the nature of the parties in that state, however—the one urban, mercantile, and professional, the other overwhelmingly agrarian—there is good reason to suppose that the attributes found to be important in Virginia and Maryland would also be important in North Carolina.

116. Williamson to Iredell, Philadelphia, July 8, 1787, and Maclaine to Iredell, Wilmington, Aug. 29, 1787, Iredell Papers, NCDu.

117. Davie to Iredell, Halifax, Sept. 5, 1788, and Maclaine to Iredell, Wilmington, Dec. 25, 1787, ibid.

118. Thomas Alderson to John Gray Blount, Bath, Oct. 8, 1787, John Gray Blount Papers, NCDH.

119. Washington to Madison, Mount Vernon, Jan. 12, 1788, Washington Papers, DLC.

120. NC, JHC, 1787, Walter Clark, ed., *State Records of North Carolina,* 30 vols. (Winston and Goldsboro, 1886–1907), XX, 194–97 (Dec. 5–6, 1787); NC, SJ, 1787, ibid., XX, 369–72 (Dec. 5–6, 1787).

121. Maclaine to Iredell, Wilmington, Dec. 25, 1787, Iredell Papers, NCDu; Griffith J. McRee, *Life Correspondence of James Iredell,* 2 vols. (New York, 1857–58), II, 220.

122. Hawkins to Madison, Warrenton, Feb. 14, 1788, Madison Papers, DLC.

123. Hugh Williamson to Iredell, New York, June 11, 1788; William Hooper to Iredell, Hillsborough, July 8, 1788; and W. R. Davie to Iredell, Halifax, July 9, 1788, all in Iredell Papers, NCDu.

124. Elliot, *Debates,* IV, 250–54.

CHAPTER ELEVEN   FEDERALISTS TRIUMPHANT

1. McHenry to Madison, Baltimore, July 26, 1788, Madison Papers, DLC: Washington to McHenry, Mount Vernon, July 31, 1788, Washington Papers, DLC.

2. Henry to R. H. Lee, Richmond, Nov. 15, 1788, Patrick Henry Papers, DLC.

3. Washington to Madison, Mount Vernon, Sept. 23, 1788, Washington Papers, DLC.

4. Jones to Madison, Richmond, Nov. 21, 1788; Edward Carrington to Madison, Richmond, Oct. 24, 1788; and Monroe to Madison, Richmond, Oct. 26, 1788, all in Madison Papers, DLC.

5. Randolph to Madison, Richmond, Aug. 13, 1788; Madison to Randolph, New York, Aug. 22, 1788, Madison Papers, DLC.

6. Edward Carrington to Madison, Jan. 18, 1788, Madison Papers, DLC.

7. John Dawson to Madison, Fredericksburg, Sept. 30, 1788; Edmund Randolph to Madison, Richmond, Oct. 23, 1788; Alexander White to Madison, Dec. 4, 1788, Madison Papers, DLC; Edmund Custis to John Cropper, Richmond, Dec. 3, 1788, Cropper Papers, VaHS; Alexander Donald to Jefferson, Richmond, Nov. 24, 1788, Jan. 16, 1789, Julian P. Boyd, ed., *The Papers of Thomas Jefferson,* 18 vols. to date (Princeton, 1950–), XIV, 280–84, 457–58.

8. Va, *JHD, 1788,* p. 17 (Oct. 30, 1788); Carrington to Madison, Richmond, Nov. 15, 1788; Madison Papers, DLC; Richard B. Lee to Madison, Richmond, Oct. 29, 1788, R. B. Lee Papers, DLC. Lee complaimed that the Federalists'

leaders were too young and inexperienced to cope with Patrick Henry. Except for Lee himself, who was only 27, the leading Federalists (Edward Carrington, John Page, Francis Corbin) were veterans of Madison's creditor party. More likely, what Lee meant was that none of them had as yet come to the forefront.

9. Bland to Lee, Richmond, Oct. 28, 1788, Lee Papers, VaU.

10. Carrington to Madison, Oct. 19, Nov. 9, 1788; Madison to Randolph, Nov. 2, 1788; Va, *SJ, 1788,* p. 20 (Nov. 10, 1788).

11. Bland to R. H. Lee, Richmond, Nov. 9, 1788, Lee Papers, VaU.

12. Madison to Edmund Randolph, Nov. 2, 1788, Madison Papers, DLC.

13. Va, *JHD, 1788,* p. 40 (Nov. 13, 1788); Carrington to Madison, Richmond, Nov. 9, 1788, Madison, Papers, DLC. Though writing before the vote took place, Carrington anticipated defeat because several Federalists had told him they thought the proviso was correct; by implication he had made a mistake in moving to delete it.

14. Theodorick Bland to R. H. Lee, Nov. 9, 1788, Lee Papers, VaU; Va, *JHD, 1788,* pp. 43–44 (Nov. 14, 1788). The House clerk listed the vote as 50 to 72, but only 71 names were recorded.

15. Francis Corbin to Madison, Nov. 12, 1788; Carrington to Madison, Nov. 15, 1788, Madison Papers, DLC.

16. *JHD, 1788,* pp. 50–51 (Nov. 18, 1788); Carrington to Madison, Richmond, Nov. 9, 18, 1788, ibid.

17. Madison to Jefferson, Philadelphia, Dec. 8, 1788, Boyd, ed., *Jefferson Papers,* XIV, 339–42, esp. 340.

18. Va, *JHD, 1788,* p. 115 (Dec. 22, 1788); Carrington to Madison, Richmond, Dec. 19, 1788, Madison Papers, DLC. The bill passed by 82 to 26.

19. Lee to Madison, Stratford Hall, Dec. 8, 1788, Madison Papers, DLC.

20. Madison to Jefferson, Philadelphia, Dec. 8, 1788, Boyd, ed., *Jefferson Papers,* XIV, 340.

21. Madison to Jefferson, Philadelphia, Dec. 8, 1788, and Monroe to Jefferson, Fredericksburg, Feb. 15, 1789, Boyd, ed., *Jefferson Papers,* XIV, 340, 557–59.

22. Richard B. Lee to Madison, Richmond, Dec. 12, 1788; Carrington to Madison, Dec. 30, 1788; Henry Lee to Madison, Marmion, Jan. 14, 1789; Gen. Edward Stevens to Madison, Culpeper, Jan. 31, 1789; all in Madison Papers, DLC.

23. *Virginia Herald* [Fredericksburg], Jan. 15, 1789.

24. The poll, taken from the *Virginia Herald* [Fredericksburg], Feb. 5, 12, 1788 was:

	Stand on Constitution	Madison	Monroe
Spotsylvania	A	215	189
Culpeper	A	256	103
Orange	F	216	9
Albemarle	F	174	105
Amherst	A	145	246
Fluvanna	A	42	63
Goochland	A	132	133
Louisa	A	228	124
		1,308	972

The Madison quotes are from Madison to Jefferson, New York, Dec. 8, 1788, Boyd, ed., *Jefferson Papers,* XIV, 339–42, esp. 342.

25. For an elaboration of this approach see Norman K. Risjord, "How the Common Man Voted in Jefferson's Virginia," in John B. Boles, ed., *America: The Middle Period: Essays in Honor of Bernard Mayo* (Charlottesville, 1973), pp. 36–64.

26. Lee to Madison, Stratford, Dec. 8, 1788, Madison Papers, DLC: Duncanson to Maury, Fredericksburg, Feb. 17, 1789, James Maury Papers, VaU.

27. "To the Freeholders of Gloucester, Middlesex, Essex, King and Queen, King William, Caroline, Westmoreland, Richmond, Northumberland, and Lancaster," printed handbill, n.d., and Arthur Lee to R. H. Lee, New York, Jan. 13, 1787, and Alexandria, Feb. 19, 1788, all in Lee Papers, VaU; Henry Lee to Madison, Jan. 14, 1788, Madison Papers, DLC.

28. Washington to Henry Lee, Mount Vernon, Dec. 12, 1788, Washington Papers, DLC.

29. Isaac Avery to John Cropper, Dec. 29, 1788, Jan. 30, 1789, Cropper Papers, VaHS.

30. Edmund Randolph to Madison, Williamsburg, July 23, 1789, Madison Papers, DLC. In a congressional career that lasted until 1801 Parker remained a maverick, shifting from one party to the other with the flow of public opinion.

31. Carrington to Madison, Dec. 19, 30, 1788, Madison Papers, DLC; Bland to St. George Tucker, Feb. 8, 1789, Tucker-Coleman Papers, VaWM.

32. *Virginia Gazette* [Richmond], Jan. 29, 1789; Madison to Jefferson, New York, Mar. 29, 1789, Boyd, ed., *Jefferson Papers,* XV, 5. The newspaper report omitted one elector, Samuel Kello of Southampton, a Federalist.

33. Carrington to Madison, Richmond, Nov. 9, 1788, Madison Papers, DLC.

34. Theodorick Bland to St. George Tucker, Feb. 8, 1789; John Page to Tucker, New York, July 23, 1789, Tucker-Coleman Papers, VaWM.

35. *Virginia Gazette* [Richmond], Feb. 5, 1789; Madison to Jefferson, New York, Mar. 29, 1789, Boyd, ed., *Jefferson Papers,* XV, 5.

36. *Maryland Journal* [Baltimore], May 23, Aug. 1, 1788; *Maryland Gazette* [Baltimore], June 3, 6, 27, July 11, 1788.

37. McHenry to Madison, Baltimore, July 26, 1788, and Madison to Washington, New York, July 21, 1788, Madison Papers, DLC; McHenry to Washington, Baltimore, July 27, 1788, Washington Papers, DLC; Robert Smith to Tench Coxe, Baltimore, July 31, 1788, Coxe Papers, PaHS.

38. James Buchanan to Tench Coxe, Baltimore, Aug. 24, 1788, Coxe Papers, PaHS.

39. *Maryland Journal* [Baltimore], Aug. 10, 1788.

40. *Maryland Journal* [Baltimore], Sept. 12, 23, 1788; O. H. Williams to [Dr. Philip Thomas], Baltimore, Sept. 20, 1788, Williams Papers, MdHS.

41. *Maryland Journal* [Baltimore], Oct. 4, 7, 1788.

42. Ibid., Oct. 14, 17, 24, 1788. The results were: McHenry 635, Coulter 622, Chase 505, McMechen 494. Unfortunately, newspapers did not record the popular vote in previous assembly elections, so comparisons of turnout cannot be made.

43. Md, *JHD, 1788,* pp. 5, 15, 18–19, 24 (Nov. 6, 14, 21, 26, 1788).

44. There were a total of 74 roll calls in the session, but most involved local interests or nonpartisan social issues. The 12 roll calls used involved the Baltimore contested election (4) and arrangements for the congressional election (8).

45. McHenry to Washington, Annapolis, Dec. 10, 1789, Washington Papers,

DLC: "Our house of Delegates though not very federal have joined heartily and unanimously with me in a prayer" for the President's good health.

46. Md, *JHD, 1788,* pp. 29–30 (Dec. 3, 1788). The vote was 41-24.

47. *Maryland Journal* [Baltimore], Dec. 19, 1788.

48. Ramsey to O. H. Williams, Sept. 24, Dec. 29, 1788, Williams Papers, MdHS.

49. Seney voted against some features of Hamilton's funding system, but he remained a Federalist until he resigned from Congress in 1792 to become a state circuit judge. A Presidential elector in 1792, he voted for Washington and Adams.

50. Ramsey to O. H. Williams, Dec. 29, 1788, Williams Papers, MdHS.

51. "Friends to Amendments," broadside, MdHS; *Maryland Gazette* [Baltimore], Dec. 30, 1788. Another broadside entitled "No Party" had a slightly different list of candidates, which may have been intended to confuse the electorate.

52. Done was still a Federalist in 1796 when he was elected Presidential elector on the Adams ticket.

53. Tilghman was a firm party man who frequently sought political advice from Tench Coxe in Philadelphia. Tilghman to Coxe, Chester Town, Jan. 2, 25, Feb. 9, Coxe Papers, PaHS. The Antifederalists' other electoral college candidate from the Eastern Shore, Henry Waggaman of Somerset, was also a Federalist.

54. Faw was a small farmer (two slaves by the census of 1790), who had invested in some confiscated property (Philip A. Crowl, *Maryland During and After the Revolution* [Baltimore, 1943], p. 130*n*). In 1785–86 assembly sessions he voted creditor on all economic matters except paper money, which he endorsed. He voted Federalist on 4 of 5 roll calls in the 1788 session, and Antifederalist on 3 of 3 in 1789.

55. Rawlings to O. H. Williams, Hagerstown, Jan. 8, 1789, Williams Papers, MdHS. Antifederalists did not replace Rawlings, probably for lack of time, and when George Thomas of St. Mary's withdrew (for reasons unclear, since he voted Antifederalist in the assmbly), their Presidential ticket was two electors short.

56. Dr. Richard Pindell to O. H. Williams [Hagerstown], Jan. 6, 1789; John Stull to Williams, Milsbury [Milsborough, Washington County], Jan. 9, 1789, Williams Papers, MdHS.

57. Stull to O. H. Williams, Milsbury, Jan. 9, 11, 1789, Williams Papers, MdHS.

58. The Baltimore results were printed in the *Virginia Herald* [Fredericksburg], Jan. 15, 1789. Unless I overlooked them, they were not published in the Maryland papers, a curious omission. The Harford poll listed the candidates by party; the Baltimore poll did not.

59. Harford County Presidential Poll List, 1789, Harford County Papers, MdHS. The lack of abstentions among Antifederalists is a puzzle. The 3 Federalists who were unopposed received 441, 444, and 439 ballots respectively, so a couple of voters, at least, saw fit to abstain. But abstention did not occur to the majority. This was true of all Virginia poll lists examined as well. Perhaps it was considered discourteous to ignore a candidate altogether.

60. Robert Smith to Tench Coxe, Baltimore, Jan. 21, 1789, Coxe Papers, PaHS.

61. William Tilghman to Tench Coxe, Chester Town, Jan. 2, 25, Feb. 9, 1789, Coxe Papers, PaHS.

62. Davie to Iredell, Halifax, Sept. 8, 1788; Maclaine to Iredell, Wilmington, Oct. 27, 1788, Iredell Papers, NCDu.

63. Hooper to Iredell, Hillsboro, Sept. 2, 1788, Iredell Papers, NCDu; Maclaine to Edward Jones, Wilmington, Nov. 14, 1788, Hooper Coll., NCU. Hooper remarked on the shift in the western counties but did not attempt to explain it.

64. Maclaine to Iredell, Wilmington, Nov. 17, 1788, Iredell Papers, NCDu.

65. NC, JHC, 1788, Walter Clark, ed., *State Records of North Carolina,* 30 vols. (Winston and Goldsboro, 1886–1907) XXI, 52, 68, 130 (Nov. 15, 19, Dec. 1, 1788); SJ, 1788, ibid., XX, 514 (Nov. 17, 1788).

66. Maclaine to Edward Jones, Wilmington, Nov. 14, 1788, Hooper Coll., NCU; Benjamin Hawkins to Madison, Warren, June 3, 1789, Madison Papers, DLC.

67. Hugh Williamson to Madison, May 21, 24, 1789, Madison Papers, DLC; Memorial of Hugh Williamson to Congress, Aug. 31, 1789, North Carolina State Papers, NCDH.

68. Davie to Madison, Halifax, June 10, 1789; Benjamin Hawkins to Madison, Warren, June 1, 1789; Hugh Williamson to Madison, July 2, 1789; all in Madison Papers, DLC.

69. Madison to Johnston, New York, June 21, 1789, Hayes Coll., NCU.

70. Williamson to Madison, Edenton, May 24, 1789; Hawkins to Madison, Warrenton, Aug. 27, 1789, Madison Papers, DLC.

71. Maclaine to Iredell, Wilmington, Sept. 15, 1789, Iredell Papers, NCDu. The delegate that Maclaine mentioned, Richard Clinton of Sampson, voted against the Constitution at Fayetteville anyway. Forgiving voters returned him to the Senate for the next five years.

72. Of the 84 Federalists at Hillsborough 37 attended the Fayetteville convention; of the 184 Hillsborough Antifederalists, 57 went to Fayetteville—35 voted against the Constitution again, 22 switched.

73. This thesis is extremely tentative, pending identification of more of the Tennessee delegates. There is, moreover, no literary evidence to substantiate it. Antisecessionists outnumbered Franklinites by 7 to 4 at the 1788 convention, but all 4 Franklinites voted against the Constitution. In 1789 Franklinites outnumbered the antisecessionists by a bare 6 to 4, and all 4 of the antisecessionists favored the Constitution. All that can be said, pending further investigation, is that Sevier was conspicuously absent in 1788, and the Tiptons stayed home in 1789.

74. The election was not mentioned either in newspapers or in private correspondence. The first congressman to reach New York, Hugh Williamson, took his seat on March 19, 1790.

75. Of these, only Steele has not been previously introduced. He was a 35-year-old lawyer from Salisbury, who entered the assembly in 1789 and voted consistently Lawyer-Federalist.

CHAPTER TWELVE   THE DEATH OF ANTIFEDERALISM

1. Bland to St. George Tucker, New York, Apr. 15, 1789, Tucker-Coleman Papers, VaWM.

2. Lee to Madison, Alexandria, June 10, 1789, and Joseph Jones to Madison, Fredericksburg, May 28, 1789, Madison Papers, DLC; Pendleton to Madison, Apr.

7, 1789, David John Mays, ed., *The Letters and Papers of Edmund Pendleton, 1734–1803,* 2 vols. (Charlottesville, 1967), II, 555–56; John Page to Tucker, New York, July 23, 1789, Tucker-Coleman Papers, VaWM.

3. Stuart to Washington, Abingdon July 14, 1789; Washington to Stuart, New York, July 20, 1789, Washington Papers, DLC.

4. Bland to Tucker, New York, Apr. 15, 1789, Tucker-Coleman Papers, VaWM.

5. [Arthur Lee] to [R. H. Lee], Baltimore, May 9, 1789, Lee Papers, VaU. Richard H. Lee was equally critical: to Samuel Adams, New York, May 10, 1789 [photostat from Adams Papers, Yale University], ibid.

6. Chase to Richard H. Lee, Baltimore, July 2, 1789 [photostat from Chase Papers, American Philosophical Society, Philadelphia], Lee Papers, VaU; Grayson to Henry, New York, Sept. 29, 1789, Henry Papers, DLC; Henry Lee to Madison, Alexandria, June 10, 1789, Madison Papers, DLC.

7. John C. Miller, *The Federalist Era, 1789–1801* (New York, 1960), p. 16. I have not been able to locate the original source of the Madison quote.

8. There were a number of head counts in the House of Representatives on minor features, such as the exact amount of levy on particular items, and this tariff bill did generate the first roll call in the federal Congress, which by 41 to 8 approved a motion to extend the expiration date beyond the two years originally contemplated. *Debates and Proceedings of the Congress of the United States, 1789–1824,* (Washington, 1834–56), pp. 365–66 (May 16, 1789): hereinafter cited as *Annals of Cong.* The opposition were all northerners, which suggests solid southern support for the bill.

9. *Annals of Cong.* I, 409 (May 26, 1789).

10. Monroe to Madison, Fredericksburg, July 19, 1789, and Carrington to Madison, Powhatan, May 27, 1789, Madison Papers, DLC.

11. Johnston to ———, Edenton, Sept. 12, 1789, Hayes Coll., NCU.

12. *Annals of Cong.,* I, 617–19 (July 1, 1789).

13. Ibid., p. 50 (July 17, 1789); Miller, *Federalist Era,* pp. 28–29; Charles A. Beard, ed., *The Journal of William Maclay* (New York, 1927), p. 85.

14. *Annals of Cong.,* I, 809–12, 822–27, 1894 (Aug. 29, 31, Sept. 17, 1789).

15. Washington to Joseph Jones, New York, Nov. 30, 1789; Randolph to Washington, Williamsburg, Aug. 2, 1789. Edward Carrington similarly began a recommendation: "I well know that no considerations but those of public fitness and propriety will influence your Excellency in the appoints. . . ." To Washington, Powhatan, May 11, 1789, Washington Papers, DLC.

16. Washington to O. H. Williams, Nov. 22, 1789, Washington Papers, DLC. Italics are Washington's.

17. Washington to Gouverneur Morris, New York, Oct. 13, 1789, ibid.

18. O. H. Williams to Washington, Oct. 10, 1789, ibid.; McHenry to Hamilton, Baltimore, Oct. 27, 1789, Harold C. Syrett, ed., *The Papers of Alexander Hamilton,* 25 vols. to date (New York and London, 1961–), V, 471–72.

19. Applications for office occupy 32 volumes (ca. 600–700 letters) in the Washington Papers, DLC, and almost half date from the year 1789. It was not deemed worthwhile to examine every one. The letters are arranged alphabetically by name of applicant; those whose names began with A, B, or C constituted the

sample. It totaled 109 letters, including both the individuals' applications and the letters of recommendation from friends.

20. Washington's initial appointments under the Judiciary Act are listed in the Senate *Journal: Annals of Cong.,* I, 86–87 (Sept. 24, 1789).

21. For Chase's political conversion see below.

22. McHenry advised that Paca's appointment might have "political good consequences," and would be "generally acceptable" to Maryland Federalists: to Washington, Annapolis, Dec. 10, 1789, Washington Papers, DLC.

23. Nelson voted with the Federalists four times and with Antifederalists twice in the House of Delegates, 1788–89. His influence on the lower Williamsburg peninsula is evident from the number of popular meetings he chaired later in the 1790s when this device became common. The meetings he attended through 1795 were Federalist.

24. "Recommendations for Federal Offices in North Carolina and the Southwestern Government" [before June 7, 1790], Julian P. Boyd, ed., *The Papers of Thomas Jefferson,* 18 vols. to date (Princeton, 1950–), XVI, 476–78, 478*n.* Davie declined and was replaced by William Hill, about whom nothing is known. Washington's appointments for the major posts in the Southwest Territory (Tennessee) were also Federalists.

25. Neither Washington's correspondence nor Hamilton's contains extant evidence of efforts to solicit advice on treasury nominations.

26. Appointments listed in *Virginia Herald* [Fredericksburg], Feb. 25, 1790.

27. Chase to Lee, Baltimore, May 16, 1789, Lee Papers, VaU.

28. Chase to Lee, Baltimore, July 2, 1789 [Photostat of original in American Philosophical Society, Philadelphia], ibid.

29. Smith to O. H. Williams, Baltimore, Jan. 9, 1783, Williams Papers, MdHS.

30. Chase to Washington, Baltimore, July 19, 1789, Washington Papers, DLC.

31. Chase to Washington, Baltimore, Sept. 3, 1789, Gratz Coll., PaHS.

32. Ridley to Jay, Susquehanna, Sept. 7, 22, 1789, Samuel Chase Papers, VaHS. The mutual recommendations between Chase and Ridley are in the Chase Transcripts, MdHS.

33. Jonathan Elliot, *The Debates in the Several State Conventions on the Adoption of the Federal Constitution . . . ,* 5 vols. (Philadelphia, 1901), III, 622.

34. Madison to Jefferson, Philadelphia, Dec. 8, 1788, Boyd, ed., *Jefferson Papers,* XIV, 339–42.

35. William Tilghman to Tench Coxe, Chester Town, Jan. 2, 1789, Coxe Papers, PaHS.

36. Robert A. Rutland, *The Birth of the Bill of Rights, 1776–1791* (Chapel Hill, 1955), pp. 197–215.

37. Lee to Henry, May 28, 1789; Grayson to Henry, June 12, 1789, Patrick Henry Papers, DLC.

38. R. H. Lee to Francis Lightfoot Lee, Sept. 13, 1789, James C. Ballagh, ed., *Letters of Richard Henry Lee,* 2 vols. (New York, 1911–14), II, 500–1; Lee to Henry, Sept. 14, 1789, and Grayson to Henry, Sept. 29, 1789, Henry Papers, DLC.

39. Mason to Jefferson, Gunston Hall, Mar. 16, 1790, Boyd, ed., *Jefferson Papers*, XVI, 232–34.

40. Madison to Washington, Orange, Dec. 5, 1789, enclosing Lee-Grayson broadside of Sept. 28, 1789, Washington Papers, DLC.

41. Madison to Washington, Orange, Nov. 20, 1789, Madison Papers, DLC.

42. Carrington to Madison, Richmond, Dec. 20, 1789, ibid.

43. Henry Lee to Madison, Richmond, Nov. 25, 1789; Hardin Burnley to Madison, Richmond, Nov. 28, 1789; Madison to Washington, Orange, Dec. 5, 1789; all in Madison Papers, DLC.

44. Va, *JHD, 1789,* pp. 62–67 (Dec. 12, 1789); Hardin Burnley to Madison, Richmond, Nov. 5, 1789, and Carrington to Madison, Richmond, Dec. 20, 1789, Madison Papers, DLC.

45. Va, *SJ, 1789,* pp. 62–67 (Dec. 12, 1789); Hardin Burnley to Madison, Richmond, Nov. 5, 1789, Madison Papers, DLC; John Dawson to Tench Coxe, Richmond, Dec. 25, 1789, Coxe Papers, PaHS.

46. Dawson to Madison, Richmond, Dec. 17, 1789, and Carrington to Madison, Richmond, Dec. 20, 1789, Madison Papers, DLC.

47. When Washington's election was announced Monroe hastened to congratulate him and enclosed a copy of his observations on the Constitution. Washington genially replied that he expected that the actions of the new government would quiet Monroe's fears. He replied in similar fashion to a peace overture from John Dawson. Washington to Monroe, Mount Vernon, Feb. 25, 1789, and Washington to Dawson, March 5, 1789, Washington Papers, DLC.

48. Maclaine to Iredell, Wilmington, Nov. 26, 1789, Iredell Papers, NCDu.

49. Davie to Iredell, Fayetteville, Nov. 16, 1789; Johnston to Iredell, Nov. 23, 1789, ibid.

50. Maclaine to Iredell, Wilmington, Nov. 26, 1789, ibid.

51. Hugh Williamson to Gov. Johnston, Sept. 29, 1789, Governor's Papers, XVII, NCDH.

52. James R. Morrill, *The Practice and Politics of Fiat Finance: North Carolina in the Confederation. 1783–1789* (Chapel Hill, 1969), pp. 45–47, treats the measure as a victory for the inflationists. But the number of Federalists who supported it on the Senate roll call, and the argument advanced by the Senate opponents (most of them debtor-Antifederalists), suggest that they considered the new currency fiscally sound.

53. NC, SJ, 1789, Walter Clark, ed., *State Records of North Carolina,* 30 vols. (Winston and Goldsboro, 1886–1907) XXI, 696, 726–27 (Dec. 16, 22, 1789). William Lenoir and Richard Singleton, both Antifederalists, did not sign the address.

54. NC, SJ, Clark, ed., *State Records,* XX, 519 (Nov. 18, 1788), XXI, 801–2 (Nov. 25, 1790); JHC, ibid., XXI, 74 (Nov. 20, 1788), 233–34, 294 (Nov. 13, Dec. 1, 1789).

55. NC, JHC, 1791, p. 38; (Jan, 4, 1792), *SJ, 1791,* pp. 27, 30. (Jan. 5, 1792). Proceedings after 1790 are published individually by session. They are available on microfilm in the Early State Records series.

56. Albemarle-Pamlico delegates consistently opposed efforts to remove the capital to Hillsborough in the 1780s; JHC, 1782 (microfilm edition, May 8, 1782); Clark, ed., *State Records,* XIX, 334 (May 10, 1783), XVII, 354–55 (Dec. 16, 1785).

57. JHC, Clark, ed., *State Records,* XXI, 47 (Nov. 14, 1788); 969–70 (Nov. 26, 1790), 1011–12 (Dec. 7, 1790).

58. JHC, 1791, pp. 43, 45–46 (Jan. 7, 10, 1792).

59. William Dickson to Rev. Robert Dickson, Goshen, Dec. 28, 1790, Dickson Papers, NCDH.

CHAPTER THIRTEEN   THE CHESAPEAKE WINS THE CAPITAL

1. Johnston to Iredell, New York, Mar. 11, 1790, Griffith J. McRee, *Life and Correspondence of James Iredell,* 2 vols. (New York, 1857–58) II, 285. In the House John Steele reached a similar conclusion: to Joseph Winston, June 20, 1790, Henry M. Wagstaff, ed., *The Papers of John Steele,* 2 vols. (Raleigh, 1924), I, 64–65.

2. John F. Mercer to Madison, Trenton, Nov. 12, 1784, Madison Papers, DLC.

3. Grayson to Madison, New York, May 28, 1786, Madison Papers, DLC; Grayson to Monroe, New York, May 29, 1787, Monroe Papers, DLC.

4. Madison to Hamilton, Orange, Nov. 19, 1789, Harold C. Syrett, ed., *The Papers of Alexander Hamilton,* 25 vols. to date (New York and London, 1961–), V, 525–27.

5. Treasurer's Reports in Va, *JHD. 1784,* pp. 88–90, and *JHD. 1790,* p. 123.

6. *Annals of Cong.,* 1st Cong., 2d sess., p. 1298; William L. Smith, *The Politicks and Views of a Certain Party, Displayed* (n.p., 1792), p. 8. Theodorick Bland was undoubtedly the maverick Virginian (see below, note 20). Scott (Pa.), Stone (Md.), and Jackson (Ga.) sided with Madison in the debate.

7. Williams to Dr. Philip Thomas, Baltimore, Jan. 26, 1790, Williams Papers, MdHS.

8. Stuart to Washington, Abingdon, Mar. 15, 1790, Washington Papers, DLC; Stuart to Richard B. Lee, Abingdon, May 23, 1790, R. B. Lee Papers, DLC. Edward Carrington similarly thought Madison's proposal was full of "mischief": to Madison, Richmond, Mar. 2, 1790, Madison Papers, DLC.

9. Stephen to Madison, Martinsburg, Mar. 3, 1790, Madison Papers, DLC. Among those who remained Federalists throughout the 1790s only Henry Lee approved of Madison's discrimination plan: Lee to Madison, Stratford, Mar. 4, 13, 1790, ibid.

10. Randolph to Madison, Baltimore, Mar. 2; Fredericksburg, Mar. 6; Williamsburg, Mar. 10, 1790; Jones to Madison, Fredericksburg, Mar. 25, 1790; John Dawson to Madison, Richmond, Mar. 14, 1790; all in Madison Papers, DLC.

11. Randolph to Madison, Williamsburg, May 20, 1790, Madison Papers, DLC.

12. Smith to Williams, New York, Feb. 25, 1790, O. H. Williams Papers, MdHS.

13. E. James Ferguson, *The Power of the Purse* (Chapel Hill, 1961), pp. 296–97, 304, 308–11. Actually none of the three suffered. When Virginia's claim was settled in 1794, she was credited with 35 million dollars, more than any other state and a sum about equal to the remaining state debt.

14. Stuart to Washington, Abingdon, Jun. 2, 1790, Washington Papers, DLC.

15. Lee to Madison, Berry Hill, Apr. 3, 1790, and Carrington to Madison, Richmond, Apr. 30, 1790, Madison Papers, DLC.

16. Johnston to Iredell, New York, Apr. 6, 1790, McRee, *Iredell,* II. 286; Hawkins to the North Carolina House of Commons, Philadelphia, Nov. 20, 1792, Legislative Papers Coll., NCDH.

17. *Annals of Cong.,* 1st Cong., 2d sess., pp. 1489–90, 1493, 1496–97, 1525; Williamson to Gov. Martin, Mar. 6, 20, May 13, 1790; Samuel Johnston and Benjamin Hawkins to Gov. Martin, Apr. 11, 1790; all in Executive Letterbooks, NCDH.

18. Timothy Bloodworth to Gov. Martin, June, 19, 1790, Executive Letterbooks, NCDH; Charles A. Beard, ed., *The Journal of William Maclay* (New York, 1927), pp. 204, 219–20; *Annals of Cong.,* 1st Cong., 2d sess., pp. 1480, 1525. Sen. Maclay later stated that the votes of the North Carolinians, including Williamson, "settled the business" against assumption (*Maclay Journal,* p. 246). Among Pennsylvanians, Maclay noted that only FitzSimons, Clymer, and Hartley voted in favor of assumption on April 12, thereby implying that the rest opposed it or failed to vote (ibid. pp. 230–31). At least one of those (Scott) had supported assumption in the floor debate.

19. *Annals of Cong.,* 1st Cong., 2d sess., pp. 1287, 1396, 1409, 1417–18; Beard, ed., *Maclay Journal,* p. 209.

20. Forrest McDonald, *We the People: The Economic Origins of the Constitution* (Chicago, 1958), p. 277. Bland's wife had a long-standing feud with Madison, the origins of which are not entirely clear. Illness may also have been a factor; Bland died on June 2.

21. *Annals of Cong.,* 1st Cong., 2d sess., pp. 1101–2, 1399–1401 (Seney), 1365–67 (Stone), 1347–48, 1510–13 (Moore), 1497–99 (Page). The other congressmen from the three states did not enter the debate, except for Lee and White (see the next note).

22. Ibid., pp. 1299–1300, 1394–95 (Lee), 1229–39, 1342–45, 1355–56, 1396 (White); Beard, ed., *Maclay Journal,* p. 200.

23. *Annals of Cong.,* 1st Cong., 2d. sess., pp. 1531–32; Williamson to Gov. Martin, Mar. 6, Apr. 24, May 13, Aug. 9, 1790, Executive Letterbooks, NCDH. Named to the committee, besides FitzSimons and Williamson, were William Smith of Maryland and two northerners. The Pennsylvania-Chesapeake alliance thus had firm control. The committee was set up on April 20.

24. Ibid., p. 1545. Besides FitzSimons, George Clymer (1316), Thomas Hartley (1505–6), and Thomas Scott (1419) favored assumption in the debate. Only Daniel Hiester among Pennsylvanians had voiced opposition to assumption (1374–75).

25. Ibid., pp. 1623–26.

26. James Mercer to John F. Mercer, St. James's, Va., July 15, 1783, Mercer Papers, VaHS.

27. Benjamin Harrison to the Virginia Delegates in Congress, Oct. 25, 1783, and "Documents Concerning the Residence of Congress" [Oct.–Dec., 1783], Julian P. Boyd, ed., *The Papers of Thomas Jefferson,* 19 vols. to date (Princeton, 1950–), VI, 345–47, 361–68; James Mercer to John F. Mercer, St. James's, Va., Sept. 23, 1783, Mercer Papers, VaHS.

28. Md, *SJ, 1783,* pp. 66–67 (May 25, 1783).

29. Daniel Carroll and James McHenry to Gov. Paca, Princeton, Oct. 23, 1783, Revolutionary Transcripts, MdHS.

30. *Journals of the Continental Congress,* 34 vols. (Washington, 1904–37), XXVII, 704.

31. Thomas Johnson to Washington, Annapolis, Dec. 11, 1787, Washington Papers, DLC.

32. *Journals of the Continental Congress,* XXIX, 734–35.

33. Ibid., XXXIV, 359–60.

34. Madison to Washington, New York, Aug. 11, 1788, Washington Papers, DLC.

35. Williams to David Ross, Baltimore, Sept. 1, 1788, Williams Papers, MdHS.

36. Coxe to Madison, Phila., Sept. 10, 1788, and Madison to Randolph, New York, Sep. 14, 1788, Madison Papers, DLC.

37. *Journals of the Continental Congress,* XXXIV, 515–8.

38. Beard, ed., *Maclay Journal,* p. 86.

39. [Arthur Lee] to [F. L. Lee], Aug. 29, 1789 [photostat from Lee Papers, Harvard College Library], Lee Papers, VaU. Lee was in New York wrapping up the affairs of the old Board of Treasury. On that same day Smith of Maryland told Sen. Maclay about the Philadelphia-Potomac arrangement. Maclay, who had been absent for several weeks, knew nothing about it, and, on inquiry, his Pennsylvania colleagues denied any knowledge of it. The fact that Smith's information coincided with Lee's, however, indicates that some, at least, of the Pennsylvanians had been discussing a bargain. It may have been expedient to deny it in the light of Morris's negotiations with New Englanders (see below, note 41): *Maclay Journal,* pp. 135–36.

40. *Annals of Cong.,* 1st Cong., 1st sess., p. 786.

41. Beard, ed., *Maclay Journal,* pp. 135–36, 142–43. Morris told Maclay that the arrangement had been made in early August while Maclay was out of town. On the evening of August 28, Hamilton, newly appointed Secretary of the Treasury, appeared at a meeting of the Pennsylvania delegation with proposals from New Englanders in favor of a Pennsylvania site.

42. Beard, ed., *Maclay Journal,* 142–43.

43. *Annals of Cong.,* 1st Cong., 1st sess., pp. 835–36; *Maclay Journal,* pp. 145, 147.

44. *Annals of Cong.,* 1st Cong., 1st sess, pp. 849–52, 855, 859, 875.

45. Ibid., p. 875; *Maclay Journal,* p. 146.

46. *Annals of Cong.,* 1st Cong., 1st sess., pp. 881–84.

47. Ibid., pp., 884–85. The maverick was Daniel Hiester, the Pennsylvanian who seemed to be most independent of Morris (Beard, ed., *Maclay Journal,* pp. 143, 204, 231). He subsequently became a Republican.

48. *Annals of Cong.,* 1st Cong., 1st sess., pp. 886, 911.

49. Beard, ed., *Maclay Journal,* pp. 158–62; William Smith to O. H. Williams, New York, Sept. 25, 1789, Williams Papers, MdHS.

50. Beard, ed., *Maclay Journal,* pp. 162, 164–65.

51. Madison to Washington, Orange, Nov. 20, 1789, Washington Papers, DLC.

52. Dawson to Madison, Richmond, Dec. 17, 1789, Madison Papers, DLC.

53. Beard, ed., *Maclay Journal,* pp. 169–70, 185–86. Maclay was a problem to his Pennsylvania colleagues because he favored the Susquehanna (his home was

Harrisburg), but was willing to back any location in Pennsylvania. He refused, however, to make any sort of deal, feeling that if an honest choice were made Pennsylvania would get the prize because of its central location. Since he also opposed assumption of state debts, Morris and FitzSimons left him out of many of the negotiations that spring. So far as his information went, however, Maclay's account seems to be accurate; his own self-righteousness did not seriously interfere with his reporting. The following account therefore rests heavily on his journal.

54. Ibid., pp. 217–18.

55. Ibid., pp. 224–25. Charles Beard, editor of Maclay's *Journal,* felt that this meant "a voter for Hamilton," implying that Jackson was a member of Congress. The only Jackson in the First Congress, however, was a stridently anti-administration representative from Georgia. Maclay probably picked up the phrase from capital gossip. During the Revolution, Washington, imitating a practice used by his first commander, General Edward Braddock, occasionally referred to his military aides as his "family." Maclay's use of the phrase may have been a scornful reference to Maj. William Jackson's continued use of his military rank and his known connections with the administration.

56. Broaddus Mitchell, *Alexander Hamilton: The National Adventure, 1788–1804* (New York, 1962), p. 709n51.

57. Beard, ed., *Maclay Journal,* pp. 225, 227–28.

58. John Steele to Gov. Martin, New York, May 17, 1790, Executive Letterbooks, NCDH.

59. Beard, ed., *Maclay Journal,* pp. 230–32.

60. Ibid., pp. 237–38. Maclay referred only to "the Philadelphians," but Clymer and FitzSimons were the only members of the delegation who resided in the city.

61. Ibid. pp. 242–43.

62. Williamson to Martin, New York, May 13, 1790, Executive Letterbooks, NCDH.

63. Beard, ed., *Maclay Journal,* pp. 256–57. Maclay inserted the italics, evidently to show his surprise.

64. Ibid., pp. 237–38. Since Lee had just arrived in town, he may not have been privy to the negotiations, and it is possible that Madison (who undoubtedly spoke for the Virginians) did not trust him.

65. Ibid., p. 262.

66. Ashe to Gov. Martin, May 2, 1790, Executive Letterbooks, NCDH.

67. Letters home by North Carolinians during the crucial months of June and July, when the "compromise of 1790" was consummated, give no hint of discussions with Virginians or awareness that the capital and funding issues were connected. See Benjamin Hawkins to Gov. Martin, New York, June 13, 1790, and John Steele to Gov. Martin, New York, June 20, July 19, 1790, Executive Letterbooks, NCDH.

68. Beard, ed., *Maclay Journal,* pp. 265–68; *Annals of Cong.,* 1st Cong., 2d sess., pp. 978–80.

69. *Annals of Cong.,* 1st Cong., 2d sess., pp. 1623–26. Beard, ed., *Maclay Journal,* p. 270, noted that Clymer and FitzSimons had visited the New Englanders the night before and threatened to back the Potomac if they failed to win Philadelphia. Since this was the threat implicit in the Pennsylvania-Virginia alliance

anyway, it seems unlikely that it had much affect on the New Englanders. There is no way of knowing what Morris and Maj. Jackson were telling the Massachusetts men.

70. Beard, ed., *Maclay Journal,* pp. 273–74.

71. McDonald, *We the People,* p. 39.

72 Beard, ed., *Maclay Journal,* pp. 262, 265. Maclay also referred to Langdon as "the old and intimate friend of Mr. Morris" (p. 173).

73. Ibid., pp. 273–74; *Annals of Cong.,* 1st Cong., 2d sess., p. 981. On the committee were Butler (S.C.), Johnston (N.C.), Henry (Md.), Lee (Va.), and Dalton (Mass.).

74. Jefferson to Short, New York, June 6, 1790, Boyd, ed., *Jefferson Papers,* XVI, 475–76. On May 14, Maclay recorded the suspicion that the New Yorkers were pushing the admission of Rhode Island in order to get two more Senate votes "on the question of residence": Beard, ed., *Maclay Journal.* p. 257.

75. Davies to Gov. Beverly Randolph, New York, June 20, 1790, *Calendar of Virginia State Papers and Other Manuscripts,* 11 vols. (Richmond, 1875–92), V, 170–72; *Annals of Cong.,* 1st Cong., 2d sess., pp. 1626–28.

76. Jefferson to Coxe, June 6, 1790, Coxe Papers, PaHS.

77. The Coxe Papers, PaHS, contain letters from both FitzSimons and Maclay on the residence controversy during May. The inference that Coxe joined Jackson in the bargaining is drawn from the fact that both were present at the crucial meeting of the Pennsylvania delegation on June 11 (see below).

78. Some two years later Jefferson wrote a memorandum, probably intended for Washington, in which he explained that the capital-assumption bargain was struck between Hamilton and Madison at a dinner arranged by Jefferson. Although Jefferson never sent the memorandum, he incorporated it in his autobiographical *Anas,* which was published in 1829. Julian Boyd dates the memorandum to the fall of 1792: *Jefferson Papers,* XVII, 205–8. Historians have accepted the story, even to the point of assigning June 20 as the date for the dinner. The only serious doubt thrown on Jefferson's account is by Jacob E. Cooke, who feels that the dinner-table bargain involved only the residence; assumption was another matter which neither Madison nor Hamilton could control: "The Compromise of 1790," *William and Mary Quarterly,* 3d ser., 27, no. 4 (1970), 523–45. Because it omits more than it explains, Jefferson's account seems rather a grossly oversimplified summary of terribly complex negotiations, designed primarily to obscure Jefferson's own role in the business. There were probably a number of dinners, as well as other private meetings that summer, and if Hamilton was present at any of them it probably made little difference because his interests were represented by trusted friends, Jackson and Coxe. On the other hand, for reasons that should be clear throughout this narrative, I cannot agree with Professor Cooke that the residence and assumption questions were unconnected. Though oversimplified, that part of Jefferson's narrative was correct. By overlooking the Jefferson invitation of June 6 (the only contemporary document involving Jefferson), Cooke failed to see the importance of Jefferson's role and the significance of his contacts with the Treasury through Coxe.

79. *Annals of Cong.,* 1st Cong., 2d sess., pp. 1634, 1644–46.

80. Beard, ed., *Maclay Journal,* pp. 276–77.

81. *Annals of Cong..* 1st Cong., 2d sess., pp. 984–86.

82. Ibid., pp. 1635–37; Beard ed., *Maclay Journal*, p. 282; Jefferson to William Hunter, Jr., to Nicholas Lewis, and to George Mason, New York, June 13, 1790, Boyd, ed., *Jefferson Papers*, XVI, 491–94.

83. Beard, ed., *Maclay Journal*, pp. 282, 284–85.

84. Cooke, "Compromise of 1790," p. 532, says that "Hamilton had asked for what Morris could not deliver; Morris, in turn, proposed what Hamilton was unable to grant." He therefore concludes that the capital-assumption bargain never materialized, and that the capital removal was achieved by the Pennsylvania-Virginia coalition without involving assumption. He assumes, however, that Morris's negotiations were limited to the Pennsylvania delegation, which did prove immovable. But he could also have talked to the Virginians, and in view of Jefferson's changed attitude on June 13 (see below) that seems likely. Cooke's neglect of Jefferson's correspondence leads him to brand as inaccurate Maclay's critically important description of a Morris-Jefferson contact on June 15 (see below also).

85. Beard, ed., *Maclay Journal*, p. 285.

86. Historians usually date this dinner on June 20 (cf. Cooke, "Compromise of 1790," p. 535), but June 12 or 13 seems more likely in view of Jefferson's letter to George Mason on the 13th (see below). Julian Boyd, ed. note, *Jefferson Papers*, XVII, 163–83, esp. 170, places the dinner on June 14, the day on which the Baltimore resolution was postponed and on which Hamilton had to inform Morris that his friends would not hear of a bargain. Boyd's view seems equally reasonable, and it squares with Jefferson's offer of a Philadelphia-Georgetown compromise to Morris on the 15th.

87. Beard, ed., *Maclay Journal*, pp. 284–85.

88. The Rhode Island legislature instructed its senators, Theodore Foster and Joseph Stanton, to vote against assumption, but they proved susceptible to Hamilton's persuasion.

89. Jefferson to Mason, New York, June 13, 1790, Boyd, ed., *Jefferson Papers*, XVI, 493–94.

90. Beard, ed., *Maclay Journal*, p. 286. Maclay went on to observe that "Jefferson vouched for nothing," implying that he had queried Jefferson on the offer. Morris might have fabricated such an offer privately to Maclay, but he would not have taken it to the entire Pennsylvania delegation, from whence it was certain to get back to Jefferson. Jefferson, in talking to Maclay, was trying to keep his own role in the negotiations as unobtrusive as possible, the more so, it seems likely, to a puritan like Maclay, who could create difficulties but was not involved in the solution.

91. Beard, ed., *Maclay Journal*, p. 287.

92. In the absence of evidence there is no answer to this question. But it is obvious that Washington's close supervision of the federal district in the 1790s helped insure the ultimate relocation. Perhaps it's fairer to ask what might have happened to the federal district had the first President been John Adams. In any case, the Virginians' sense of self-assurance when everyone else was quarreling over the temporary seat suggests some long-range planning.

93. This is pure conjecture, but it does fit with Jefferson's account of the switched votes by Richard B. Lee and Alexander White. These votes, obtained because the Virginians knew what was in the final settlement bill, were Jefferson's

trump. By assuring the ultimate passage of assumption, they were to hold in line various members—New Hampshire's, for instance—who had earlier made assumption-for-residence bargains with Robert Morris. Additional evidence for this hypothesis lies in Senator Maclay's account of the Pennsylvanians' discussion of the "Potomac contract." By June 24 the deal with the Virginians was firm enough so that Maclay could be informed and brought into it. He gave his old objections to any sort of bargain, but then acquiesced on the grounds that Pennsylvanians ought to stick together. To his surprise, Morris and FitzSimons then attacked him for not giving in earlier. Had he been less intransigent earlier, Morris declared, they could have won 15 years for Philadelphia. As it was, the deal with Virginia called for only a 10 years' stay (Beard, ed., *Maclay Journal*, pp. 297–98). This clearly implies that Virginia's leverage lay in the Senate vote. Had Maclay been more dependable, Morris felt he could have obtained more from the Virginians. The only Senate votes on the residence question that were not dictated by regional interest were New Hampshire's and possibly North Carolina's. Since North Carolina also opposed assumption, there was no bargain to be made there (unless Williamson was playing a double game). Of the New Hampshire senators, Langdon was a friend of Morris's, but Wyngate was an independent. The price of their votes on the residence question may have been assurances on assumption in the House of Representatives. That is where Virginia's leverage lay. Hamilton had once stated that he needed 5 votes in the House, and Virginia could offer only 2 (though an outright reversal actually amounted to 4, since 2 would be subtracted from the opposition). Even so, the Virginians were important because with that kind of margin every vote was crucial, and Hamilton had several irons in the fire. On June 14 Morris noted that Hamilton was counting on the arrival of the Rhode Islanders, but, he added, "I think he has some other assurances" (ibid., p. 285).

94. Boyd, ed., *Jefferson Papers*, XVI, 536–38.

95. South Carolina's senators, Butler and Izard, reversed themselves and supported the Philadelphia-Potomac coalition from June 28 on. Butler held no securities, though he was deeply in debt to Dutch merchants, and Izard possessed over £20,000 worth. McDonald, *We the People*, pp. 81–82, 223.

96. Beard, ed., *Maclay Journal*, pp. 297–89.

97. R. B. Lee to Theodorick Lee, New York, June 26, 1790, R. B. Lee Papers, DLC.

98. *Annals of Cong.*, 1st Cong., 2d sess., pp. 995–97.

99. King to Caleb Strong, June 30, 1790, quoted in Charles R. King, *Life and Correspondence of Rufus King*, 6 vols. (New York, 1894–1900), pp. 384–85. Although King's memorandum is dated June 30, it seems likely, in view of the change in Massachusetts on June 29, that the meeting took place on the night of the 28th.

100. Beard, ed., *Maclay Journal*, pp. 305–6, 312.

101. Cooke, "Compromise of 1790," notes 45 and 56, argues that Massachusetts could not have entered the bargain because her House delegation continued to vote for New York. The crucial shift, which did take place, was in the votes of her two senators. The Pennsylvania-Potomac alliance did not need Massachusetts' support in the House. They had the votes there, so long as they could keep the Marylanders in line. Hamilton and Morris were working on individuals; they probably never hoped to win commitments from entire delegations.

102. *Annals of Cong.,* 1st Cong., 2d sess., pp. 998–1002.

103. Beard, ed., *Maclay Journal,* p. 306.

104. R. B. Lee to Theodorick Lee, New York, June 26, 1790, R. B. Lee Papers, DLC.

105. Charles Carroll to Mary Caton, New York, July 11, 1790, Carroll-McTavish Papers, MdHS; William Smith to O. H. Williams, Jan. 24, 1791, Williams Papers, MdHS. Smith, still bitter over Baltimore's loss, grumbled that the Virginians would somehow turn it to their advantage even though the buildings were to be on the Maryland side of the Potomac.

106. *Annals of Cong.,* 1st Cong., 2d sess., p. 1672.

107. Ibid., pp. 1660–64, 1672.

108. Ibid., pp. 1673–76, 1678–80.

109. Beard, ed., *Macley Journal,* pp. 305–6. Rufus King later told Maclay that Carroll's vote was part of the residence bargain. When King threatened to vote against assumption if the capital were moved from New York, Morris and Hamilton persuaded Carroll to switch in order to neutralize King—or so King thought (ibid., pp. 312–3).

110. Ibid., pp. 313, 315–16; Ferguson, *Power of the Purse,* p. 321. The amount ultimately voted by Congress was $21,500,000.

111. William Davies to Gov. Beverly Randolph, New York, July 2, 7, 12, 1790, *Calendar of Virginia State Papers,* V, 179–80, 182–85; Beard, ed., *Maclay Journal,* pp. 307–9.

112. New Hampshire, Rhode Island, and Georgia all registered formal complaints about their allotments, but the rest remained strangely silent about the bonanza given Virginia: Ferguson, *Power of the Purse,* p. 321.

113. Beard ed., *Maclay Journal,* pp. 315–17, prints the Carroll committee report.

114. *Annals of Cong.,* 1st Cong., 2d sess., p. 1016; Beard, ed., *Maclay Journal,* pp. 314–16; William L. Smith to Edward Rutledge, July 14, 17, 1790, as quoted by George C. Rogers, *Evolution of a Federalist: William Loughton Smith of Charleston* (Columbia, S. C., 1962), p. 197. The actual settlement reached by Congress on the matter of interest was more complex, but it retained the variable rates demanded by the opponents: Ferguson, *Power of the Purse,* pp. 321–22.

115. *Annals of Cong.,* 1st Cong., 2d sess., pp. 1710–12.

116. Cooke, "Compromise of 1790," p. 543. An exact comparison is impossible, in any case, because the April 12 vote did not list names. Nor would it be reasonable to compare it with the April 26 roll call postponing assumption, since that apparently involved much tactical voting.

117. Gale and Daniel Carroll were the only Marylanders who favored assumption. Carroll benefited from the Potomac compromise, but since he supported assumption in the March debate it is unlikely that he switched votes. Gale had sat silent throughout. When he was defeated for reelection later that year, Hamilton made him a tax collector. Neither Huger nor Sumter took a stand in debate. Huger did not participate in the July 25 vote; Sumter switched, voting to reject the bill on the 25th, but supporting assumption on the 26th. Sumter was an Antifederalist and subsequently a Republican.

118. Irving Brant, *James Madison,* 6 vols. (Indianapolis and New York, 1941–61), III, 317.

119. Boyd prints an extract from a member of Congress to a gentleman in Alexandria, July 28, 1790, from the *New York Daily Advertiser,* Aug. 13, 1790, in *Jefferson Papers,* XVII, 182. The letter explains that the modifications "have either removed, or greatly lessened, my original objections." Boyd conjectures that the letter was written by either White or Lee. The latter seems most likely since he had numerous contacts in Alexandria.

120. *Annals of Cong.,* 1st Cong., 2d sess., pp. 1719–21; Ferguson, *Power of the Purse,* pp. 323–24.

CHAPTER FOURTEEN   RISE OF THE REPUBLICANS

1. Dawson to Madison, Richmond, July 4, 1790, Madison Papers, DLC.

2. Dawson to Tench Coxe, Richmond, May 28, 1790, Coxe Papers, PaHS.

3. Lee to Madison, Berry Hill, Apr. 3, 1790, Madison Papers, DLC.

4. Lee purchased land at the falls of the Potomac in 1788, anticipating that completion of the Potomac Company's canal would enhance their value. He greeted the arrival of the capital with glee and tried to interest Madison in further speculations, but Madison pled a shortage of funds. Washington to Madison, Nov. 17, 1788, Washington Papers; Lee to Madison, Aug. 6, 24, Dec. 8, 1791; Madison to Lee, Dec. 18, 1791, Madison Papers, DLC.

5. Carrington to Madison, Richmond, Dec. 24, 1790, Madison Papers, DLC; Va, *JHD, 1790,* p. 36 (Nov. 3, 1790); *SJ, 1790,* pp. 77–78 (Dec. 24, 1790). The House clerk recorded the vote as 75 to 52.

6. There is ample testimony that residents of the Potomac Valley anticipated rich benefits from the capital location. General Adam Stephen, leading figure in the lower Shenandoah Valley, thought it would reinforce westerners' Federalism: Stephen to Madison, Berkeley County, Sept. 12, 1789, Madison Papers, DLC. Henry Lee reported that westerners even anticipated federal aid in improving the Potomac as a result of the capital: Lee to Madison, Berkeley County, Sept. 8, 1789, ibid. Samples of Potomac "boosterism" in connection with the capital are: David Stuart to Washington, Nov. 18, 1791, Washington Papers, DLC, and "Address of John Hopwood," *Maryland Gazette,* [Frederick] Aug. 14, 1792.

7. Dorothy Brown, "Party Battles and Beginnings in Maryland" (Ph.D. diss., Georgetown University, 1962) has an excellent quantitative analysis of the realignment, but rather exaggerates the break with previous factions. L. Marx Renzulli, *Maryland: The Federalist Years* (Rutherford, N.J., 1973), pp. 149 ff., relies heavily on Brown but confuses the issue by imposing a "liberal-conservative" interpretation on the conflict.

8. *Maryland Gazette* [Baltimore], June 25, 1790.

9. It is preserved in the Chase Papers, MdHS.

10. Md, *JHD, 1790,* p. 54 (Nov. 30, 1790); *SJ, 1790,* pp. 19, 23, 32–33, 39 (Dec. 1, 3, 13, 17, 1790). The vote was 38 to 10. Supporting it were several former foes of Chase, including William Vans Murray, Harry D. Gough, and George Plater.

11. *Maryland Journal* [Baltimore], Sept. 28, 1790; *Virginia Gazette and Alexandria Advertiser* [Alexandria], Sept. 30, 1790.

12. Jackson Turner Main, *Political Parties Before the Constitution* (Chapel Hill; 1973), p. 235, calls him a "Cosmopolitan," but his record on economic issues in

1784–85 was thoroughly mixed. In 1787, he voted with the pro-Constitution people three out of four times. Renzulli, *Maryland: Federalist Years,* p. 151, seems to confuse him with his cousin Philip Barton Key, whom Renzulli labels an "arch-conservative."

13. *Maryland Journal* [Baltimore], Sept. 28, 1790. O. H. Williams claimed that the Potomac ticket was formed first "by the junto at Georgetown," but he was trying to demonstrate that Baltimore had not instigated the factionalism: Williams to Dr. Thomas, Baltimore, Oct. 16, 1790, Williams Papers, MdHS.

14. J. R. Pole, "Constitutional Reform and Election Statistics in Maryland, 1790–1812," *Maryland Historical Magazine,* 55 (1960), 275–92, esp. 277.

15. Noble E. Cunningham, Jr., *The Jeffersonian Republicans: The Formation of Party Organization, 1789–1801* (Chapel Hill, 1957), pp. 267–72.

16. Md, *JHD, 1790,* p. 93 (Dec. 18, 1790). It was simply listed as Bill No. 16.

17. The state received 8 congressional seats under the census of 1790, and Republicans won 3 of them in the election of 1792.

18. Md, *JHD, 1790,* pp. 86–87 (Dec. 16, 1790). Dent's legislative record is chiefly distinguished for its inconsistency. He voted creditor in the mid-1780s, and in the middle in 1788 (8 Antifederalist, 4 Federalist votes). He was on the Antifederalist ticket for Congress in 1789, and when he finally entered Congress in 1793 he voted more or less at random. After 1795 he moved into the Republican camp, and was a Jeffersonian Presidential elector in 1800.

19. Renzulli, *Maryland: Federalist Years,* pp. 131–32, attributes the reversal to the influence of speculators, and points, in particular to the "politically promi-nent" firm of Forrest and Stoddert.

20. Even the 5 delegates whose record on the first three ballots was mixed split on the final one (2 voted yea, 3 nay).

21. It is possible, of course, that they were induced to go home by specula-tors, but there is no evidence for this.

22. McHenry to Washington, Baltimore, Jan. 6, 1791, Washington Papers, DLC.

23. An "Extract of a Letter from Fayetteville," *Virginia Gazette* [Richmond], Jan. 19, 1791, said that a Dr. John Leigh of Tarboro had assumed leadership of the Federalist party. This was Leigh's first term in the assembly.

24. JHC, 1790, Walter Clark, ed., *State Records of North Carolina,* 30 vols. (Winston and Goldsboro, 1886–1907), XXI, 946, 961–62 (Nov. 20, 24, 1790). The roll call on the postponed resolution was 46 to 37.

25. Ibid., p. 1021 (Dec. 9, 1790).

26. Ibid., p. 1055 (Dec. 15, 1790); Griffith J. McRee, *Life and Correspondence of James Iredell,* 2 vols (New York, 1857–58), II, 303.

27. NC, SJ, 1790, Clark, ed., *State Records,* XXI, 815 (Nov. 30, 1790). Of the late arrivals, Antifederalists outnumbered Federalists by 7 to 2.

28. Ibid., p. 860 (Dec. 14, 1790).

29. Ibid., pp. 862, 876–78 (Dec. 14–15, 1790).

30. Because the issue at stake in each roll call is not always clear, two model groups were created, each internally consistent, and each consistently opposed to the other.

31. Hay to Iredell, Fayetteville, Dec. 16, 1790, Iredell Papers, NCDu.

32. Irving Brant, *James Madison,* 6 vols. (Indianapolis and New York, 1941–61), III, pp. 328–33; Jones to Monroe, Fredericksburg, Jan. 27, 1791, Monroe Papers, DLC; Jones to Madison, Fredericksburg, Apr. 6, 1792, Madison Papers, DLC; Hugh Williamson to Gov. Martin, Philadelphia, Feb. 7, 1791, Williamson Papers, PaHS.

33. *Annals of Cong.,* 1st Cong. 3d sess., 1960. The vote on final passage was 39 to 20. The third Virginia Federalist, Samuel Griffin, did not vote.

34. Smith to O. H. Williams, Philadelphia, Feb. 5, 1791, Williamson Papers, MdHS; Carroll to Madison, Georgetown, Apr. 23, 1791, Madison Papers, DLC.

35. Hamilton forestalled further opposition in Maryland by delaying the establishment of a branch of the federal bank in Baltimore and by depositing treasury funds in the Bank of Maryland: Hamilton to O. H. Williams, Philadelphia, Mar. 28, 29, 1792, Harold C. Syrett, ed., *The Papers of Alexander Hamilton,* 25 vols. to date (New York and London, 1961-), XI, 204–6.

36. *Annals of Cong.,* 1st Cong., 3d sess., pp. 1748, 1766.

37. Timothy Bloodworth to Gov. Martin, New York, June 19, 1790, Executive Letterbooks, NCDH.

38. See speech of Josiah Parker, *Annals of Cong.,* 1st Cong. 3d sess., pp. 1859–60.

39. Ibid., p. 1846.

40. Ibid., p. 1884. There was no roll call in the Senate.

41. Carrington to Madison, Richmond, Feb. 26, Apr. 20, Sept. 21, 1791; Jefferson to Madison, Philadelphia, June 21, 1791, Madison Papers, DLC.

42. Corbin to Madison, Richmond, Oct. 25, 1791, ibid. There is no evidence of a Madison reply, and no further correspondence between the two.

43. Jefferson to Madison, Philadelphia, June 21, 1791, and Randolph to Madison, Philadelphia, July 21, 1791, Madison Papers, DLC; William Polk to Hamilton, Wilmington, Aug. 20, 1791, Syrett, ed., *Hamilton Papers,* IX, 84–85.

44. Cunningham, *Jeffersonian Republicans,* pp. 8–9.

45. Lee to Monroe, Chantilly, Jan. 15, 1791; Henry to Monroe, Prince Edward, Jan. 24, 1791, and Tucker to Monroe, Williamsburg, Feb. 18, 1791, Monroe Papers, DLC. Richard Henry Lee was not the one to perceive the inconsistency between his distress at the funding system and his subsequent support for the Bank.

46. Jefferson to Mason, Feb. 4, 1791, Julian P. Boyd, ed., *The Papers of Thomas Jefferson,* 18 vols. to date (Princeton, 1950-), XIX, 214–42; Jefferson to Madison, Georgetown, Oct. 1, 1792, Madison Papers, DLC. In early 1792 Monroe also opened a correspondence with Mason on political matters: Robert A. Rutland, ed., *The Papers of George Mason,* 3 vols. (Chapel Hill, 1970), III, 1252, 1254–60.

47. Tazewell to Monroe, Feb. 14, Nov. 28, 1792, Monroe Papers, DLC; Monroe to Breckinridge, Philadelphia, Apr. 6, 1792, Breckinridge Papers, DLC.

48. Lee to [a member of Congress], Richmond, Jan. 8, 1792 [copy], Charles Carter Lee Papers, VaSL; Lee to Madison, Jan. 8, 23, 1792, Madison Papers. On the back of Lee's January 23 letter Madison wrote some years later, "Evidence of General H. Lee's disaffection to the policy & measures of the Federal Government during several of the early years of Washington's Administration and of his partiality for Freneau's National Gazette."

49. Lee to Washington, Richmond, Dec. 16, 1791, Washington Papers, DLC.

50. John Dawson to Madison, Richmond, Nov. 12, 1792, Madison Papers, DLC.

51. Hamilton to Carrington, May 26, 1792, Syrett, ed., *Hamilton Papers*, XI, 426–45.

52. Robert Rutherford to Washington, Berkeley County, Dec. 15, 1790, Washington Papers, DLC.

53. George Clendinen to Washington, Philadelphia, June 25, 1791, and David Stuart to Washington, Nov. 18, 1791, Washington Papers, DLC. Land prices in the lower valley were still "rising rapidly" in 1796: Smith to Coxe, Winchester, Jan. 4, 1796, Coxe Papers, PaHS. "The rise of land in Berkeley astonish me much," wrote Solomon Bedinger to Henry Bedinger, Norfolk, Apr. 10, 1798, Danske-Dandridge Papers, NCDu.

54. "Address of John Hopwood," *Maryland Gazette* [Frederick], Aug. 14, 1792. In 1790 the people of Williamsport were so confident that the federal district would be located in their vicinity that they used it as an advertising inducement in selling city lots: Thomas J. C. Williams, *A History of Washington County, Maryland . . . ,* 2 vols. (2nd ed., Baltimore, 1968), I, 90. If they were disappointed at Washington's ultimate choice, it was probably only temporary. They clearly understood the relationship between the capital and land prices.

55. Corbin to Madison, Richmond, Oct. 25, Nov. 22, 1791, Jan. 7, 1791 [2]; and Charles Carter to Madison, Academy, Dec. 16, 1791, Madison Papers, DLC; Va, *JHD, 1791,* p. 144, (Dec. 20, 1791).

56. Madison to Jefferson, Fredericksburg, Oct. 23, 1792, Madison Papers, DLC.

57. William to James Madison, Richmond, Dec. 3, 1791; James to William, Philadelphia, Dec. 13, 1791, Madison Papers DLC.

58. Frank Cassell, *Merchant Congressman in the Young Republic: Samuel Smith of Maryland, 1752–1839* (Madison, 1971), pp. 71–72.

59. McHenry to Washington, Nov. 14, Dec. 10, 1789, Washington Papers, DLC; McHenry to Hamilton, Nov. 19, 1791, Jan. 31, 1793, Hamilton Papers, DLC.

60. McHenry to William Perry and William Hindman, July 15, 1792, McHenry Papers, MdHS.

61. The Federalists were William Vans Murray, William Hindman, Samuel Smith, and Thomas Sprigg. Republicans were Gabriel Christie, George Dent, and John F. Mercer. The Federalists regained control of Baltimore (Smith replaced Samuel Sterett, who had shifted with Chase to the Federalist side anyway), but lost the new district on the lower Western Shore (Dent, previously a waverer, voted Republican after 1793). The maverick was Uriah Forrest, a Georgetown merchant and speculator in confiscated property. Forrest's voting record in the assembly was creditor in 1786, Antifederalist in 1788, and Republican (i.e., against assumption of state debts) in 1790. The *Biographical Directory of the American Congress, 1774–1949* (Washington, 1950), p. 1173, states that he was elected as a Federalist in 1792 but gives no evidence. He did not participate in the proceedings enough to reveal a stand and resigned in 1794. By the end of this session two of the Federalists, Samuel Smith and Thomas Sprigg, would desert to the Republicans, giving the opposition a majority of the delegation by 1795.

62. McHenry to Hamilton, Annapolis, Nov. 18, 1792, Syrett, ed., *Hamilton Papers,* XIII, 157. Hamilton did not make the appointment, a fact that McHenry

attributed, apparently without rancor, to other influences. McHenry to Hamilton, Apr. 14, 1793, ibid., XIV, 316–17.

63. NC, JHC, 1792, pp. 9, 40, 52 (Nov. 22, Dec. 17, 26, 1792). The Federalist leaders were David Stone and Willis Alston, both young men just embarking on lengthy political careers. Both eventually became Republicans, but as late as 1798 they described themselves as Federalists in running for seats in Congress.

64. The model was a bloc of known Federalists who agreed with each other 100 percent. Republicans were assumed to be the reverse. Threshhold: 3 votes, 75 percent.

65. NC, JHC, 1792, 24, 27, 33 (Dec. 4, 6, 12, 1792); William J. Dawson to Samuel Johnston, New Bern, Dec. 15, 1792, Hayes Coll., NCU.

66. The new Federalist was Benjamin Williams of Johnston County. In the western Piedmont John Steele yielded to Joseph McDowell, a Virginia-born Antifederalist. In the lower Pamlico, Thomas Blount won election as a Federalist (defeating Republican John B. Ashe and Federalist John Leigh), but he sided with the Republicans once he reached Philadelphia. For William Dawson's political beliefs see W. J. Dawson to Samuel Johnston, Dec. 15, 1792, Hayes Coll., NCU.

67. *The North Carolina Journal* [Halifax], Jan. 16, 1793, listed all the candidates but did not identify any by party. Party affiliation, nevertheless, was known, at least among the politicians themselves. Before the new Congress opened Federalist John Steele promised to describe the new men to Hamilton so the secretary would know "what sort of Materials he has the misfortune to work with." Steele to Hamilton, Salisbury, Apr. 30, 1793, Syrett, ed., *Hamilton Papers,* XIV, 358–60.

68. Cunningham, *Jeffersonian Republicans,* pp. 13–18.

69. *National Gazette* [Philadelphia], Jan. 23, 1792.

70. Richard Hofstadter, *The Idea of a Party System* (Berkeley and Los Angeles, 1969), pp. 80–84.

71. *National Gazette,* [Philadelphia], Apr. 2, 1792.

72. Jefferson to Washington, Philadelphia, May 23, 1792, Washington Papers, DLC; Jefferson to Madison, Philadelphia, June 29, 1792, Paul Leicester Ford, *The Works of Thomas Jefferson,* 12 vols. (New York and London, 1904–5), VII, 129–31.

73. McHenry to Hamilton, May 3, Oct. 15, Nov. 19, 1791, Syrett, ed., *Hamilton Papers,* VIII, 321–22, IX, 386, 510–11. Gen. O. H. Williams, collector at the port of Baltimore, might have given Hamilton better-informed advice, but Williams's communications held strictly to business.

74. McHenry to Hamilton, Aug. 16, Sept. 30, Oct. 19–23, 1792, ibid., XII, 212–13, 509–11, 602–4.

75. Lee addressed his criticisms directly to Hamilton while reaffirming his friendship: Lee to Hamilton, Alexandria, Aug. 12, 1791, ibid., IX, 31–32.

76. Hamilton to Carrington, Philadelphia, May 26, 1792, ibid., XI, 426–45. As early as the spring of 1791 Hamilton began enclosing private notes to Carrington along with his official correspondence. The contents can only be guessed since the documents themselves have not been found: ibid., VIII, 207, 240.

77. Cunningham, *Jeffersonian Republicans,* pp. 24–27; Harry Ammon, *James Monroe: The Quest for National Identity* (New York, 1971), pp. 93–95.

78. "A Candid State of Parties" and "Who Are the Best Keepers of the People's Liberties?" *National Gazette,* [Philadelphia], Sept. 26, Dec. 20, 1792.

79. Cunningham, *Jeffersonian Republicans,* pp. 11–12; Brant, *Madison,* III, 337–40.

80. Jefferson to Madison, June 21, 1792, and Monroe to Jefferson, July 17, 1792, Jefferson Papers, DLC.

81. Monroe to Madison, Oct. 9, 1792, Madison Papers, DLC.

82. Monroe and Madison to Melancthon Smith and Marinus Willet, Oct. 19, 1792, Monroe Papers, DLC.

83. Beckley to Madison, Oct. 17, 1792, Madison Papers, NYPL.

84. Clinton also obtained the electoral votes of New York and Georgia, giving him a total of 50 to Adam's 77.

85. *Maryland Journal* [Baltimore], Oct. 16, 23, 1792; McHenry to Hamilton, Annapolis, Oct. 19–23, 1792, Syrett, ed., *Hamilton Papers,* XII, 602–4.

86. Benjamin Stoddert to Tench Coxe, Dec. 6, 1792, Coxe Papers, PaHS.

CHAPTER FIFTEEN   THE POLITICS OF NEUTRALITY, 1793–1794

1. Republicans, nevertheless, were gaining ground. After surveying results of the election of 1792, Jefferson thought the new Congress would be more to his liking: Jefferson to Thomas Mann Randolph, Nov. 2, 16, 1792, and Jefferson to Thomas Pinckney, Dec. 3, 1792, P. L. Ford, *The Works of Thomas Jefferson,* 12 vols. (New York and London, 1904–05), VI, 128, 134, 143. Most of those gains must have been in the North, for Maryland and North Carolina returned delegations divided approximately as before. On the other hand, the huge increase in congressmen granted Virginia under the census (19 instead of 10) augured well for Republicans when that state voted in April 1793.

2. The controversy can be traced in Harold C. Syrett, ed., *The Papers of Alexander Hamilton,* 25 vols. to date (New York and London, 1961–), XII, 481–89.

3. *Maryland Gazette* [Annapolis], Sept. 20, 1792; "To the Voters of Anne-Arundel and Prince Georges Counties," Sept. 26, 1792, broadside, DLC; McHenry to Hamilton, Aug. 16, 1792, Syrett, ed., *Hamilton Papers,* XII, 212–13.

4. Antifederalists won Anne Arundel (the key county in the district) by a mere 50 votes in 1788, but William Pinkney expanded that substantially in the congressional election of 1790 (though precise figures are not available). And when Pinkney was declared ineligible, Mercer was elected with no apparent opposition: L. Marx Renzulli, *Maryland, Federalist Years* (Rutherford, N.J., 1973), p. 152.

5. Irving Brant, *James Madison,* 6 vols. (Indianapolis and New York, 1941–61), III, 368.

6. Broaddus Mitchell, *Alexander Hamilton: The National Adventure, 1788–1804* (New York, 1962), pp. 248–49.

7. Giles could have laid claim to the distinction that he had started under the tutelage of Patrick Henry and ended under that of John C. Calhoun. Although there is no evidence that he was actually a Nullifier, he was an ardently "states rights" governor of Virginia, 1827–30. In the interval, however, he underwent several political gyrations that revealed no particular ideological commitment.

8. *Annals of Cong.,* 2d Cong., 2d sess., pp. 835–40.

9. Madison to Pendleton, Feb. 23, 1793, Gaillard Hunt, ed., *Writings of James Madison,* 9 vols. (New York, 1900–10), VI, 123–25.

10. Mitchell, *Hamilton: National Adventure,* p. 253.

11. *Annals of Cong.,* 2d Cong., 2d sess., pp. 895, 899–900, 955–56 (Feb. 27, 28, Mar. 1, 1790).

12. Jefferson's draft and the resolutions Giles introduced are both printed in Ford, ed., *Works,* VI, 168–71.

13. Carrington to Hamilton, Richmond, Feb. 15, 1793, Syrett, ed., *Hamilton Papers,* XIV, 80. There is no indication that Hamilton made a similar effort to influence opinion in any other state.

14. Carrington to Hamilton, Richmond, Mar. 26, 1793, ibid., 247–48. Federalists nevertheless thought they had the best of the contest in the end. Reporting on a popular meeting over a year later in Giles's own district, William Heth claimed that Giles was "mute as a fish" on the subject of the Treasury Secretary, while Carrington was "huzzad and applauded." William Heth to Hamilton, Shillelah, July 6, 1794, ibid., XVI, 570–71.

15. "Fabricus," "A Freeholder of Albemarle," and "Gracchus," *Virginia Gazette and General Advertiser* [Richmond], Jan. 30, Feb. 27, Mar. 6, 1793. The "Freeholder" had raised the Antifederalist issue by accusing the first writer of being a "Daw in borrowed feathers," a reference to John Dawson, Monroe's law partner in Fredericksburg and an opponent of the Constitution. The victorious candidate was Francis Walker of Albemarle, who had supported the Constitution in the assembly. He apparently let his newspaper supporters do his talking, for Madison, unsure of his current politics, visited him shortly after the election and reported to Jefferson that he would "go . . . right": Madison to Jefferson, Orange, Apr. 12, 1793, Madison Papers, DLC. Newspaper contributors did not mention the name of his opponent, but he was probably Samuel Jordan Cabell, who had represented Amherst in the assembly for eight years and won the congressional seat in 1795. Cabell voted against the Constitution in the Ratifying convention.

16. Madison to Jefferson, Orange, Apr. 12, 1793, Madison Papers, DLC. Suspecting the mails, Madison was exceedingly cautious and avoided mentioning names insofar as he could. He was so cryptic that he even confused Jefferson. Wrote Madison, "The vote at the election stood thus—for R. 886—S. 403— [code] 276." Jefferson decoded the name as "Hite," which was a prominent political name in the neighborhood (Hampshire County). But the initials and statistics make sense only if Madison meant "White." White's opponents were Robert Rutherford, and John Smith, a Frederick County planter. Smith, who had lost to two Federalists in the election to the ratifying convention, was probably a former critic of the Constitution. Federalist leaders in Congress felt acutely the loss of White, whom they regarded as "the only good Member" in the delegation. William Loughton Smith to Hamilton, Apr. 24, 1793, Syrett, ed., *Hamilton Papers,* XIV, 338–41, esp. 341.

17. Rutherford to Madison, Aug. 22, 1789, Madison Papers, DLC.

18. Rutherford, a resident of Frederick County, enlisted the support of Henry Bedinger, Berkeley Federalist, to help him carry the neighboring county: Henry Bedinger to George M. Bedinger, Shepherd's Town, June 16, 1793, Danske-Dandridge Papers, NCDu. For Rutherford's congressional record see Manning J. Dauer, *The Adams Federalists* (Baltimore, 1953), p. 286.

19. Neville only served one term; he sided with Madison on the question of

commercial retaliation against Britain. Otherwise his politics are unknown. Hancock served two terms, 1793–97, voting Federalist at first, and drifting to the Republicans after the Jay Treaty: Dauer, *Adams Federalists,* pp. 292, 296. The *Biographical Directory of Congress* says he was elected as a "Democrat" without offering evidence, and the sketch of him in Robert D. Stoner, *A Seed-bed of the Republic...* (Roanoke, 1962), pp. 294–96, seems generally confused.

20. Fisher Ames to T. Dwight, Jan. 1793, quoted in Brant, *Madison,* III, p. 368.

21. Washington to Gouverneur Morris, New York, Oct. 13, 1789, Washington Papers, DLC.

22. Lee to Washington, Apr. 29, 1793, and Washington to Lee, May 6, 1793, Washington Papers, DLC; Lee to Hamilton, May 6, 1793, Syrett, ed., *Hamilton Papers,* XIV, 416. Edward Carrington reported that although he considered the execution of the king an act of "unprincipled cruelty," Virginians in general embraced the "cause of France": to Hamilton, Richmond, Apr. 26, 1793, Syrett, ed., *Hamilton Papers,* XIV, 346–52. For other pro-French sentiment after the outbreak of war and prior to the arrival of Genet see Benjamin Hawkins to Tench Coxe, Warren, N.C., Apr. 29, 1793, Coxe Papers, PaHS. On the other hand, William Vans Murray, Maryland Federalist, expected France to degenerate into a tyranny after the execution of "Lewis the last": to Tench Coxe, Cambridge, Apr. 19, 1793, Coxe Papers, PaHS.

23. Hamilton to Jay, Philadelphia, Apr. 9, 1793, Syrett, ed., *Hamilton Papers,* XIV, 297–98.

24. The story of the cabinet discussions on French policy has been often told, but it is particularly interesting to compare the different viewpoints of two sympathetic but able biographers: Broaddus Mitchell, *Hamilton: National Adventure,* pp. 222–26, and Merrill D. Peterson, *Thomas Jefferson and the New Nation* (New York, 1970), pp. 482–85.

25. Harry Ammon, *The Genet Mission* (New York, 1973), pp. 44–45, 52.

26. Jefferson to Madison, Philadelphia, Apr. 28, 1793, Ford, ed., *Works,* VII, 301–2; Madison to Jefferson, Orange, May 8, 1793, Madison Papers, DLC.

27. Steele to Hamilton, Salisbury, Apr. 30 [1793], Syrett, ed., *Hamilton Papers,* XIV, 358–60.

28. Madison to Jefferson, Orange, May 27, 1793, Madison Papers, DLC.

29. Ammon, *Genet Mission,* pp. 54–55.

30. Randolph to Washington, Richmond, June 24, 1793, Washington Papers, DLC. Madison, who kept watch on Randolph's movements, commented scornfully that one is certain to misconstrue the sentiment of Virginia if he listens only to "the heretical tone of conversation in the towns on the post road": to Jefferson, Orange, July 30, 1793, Hunt, ed., *Writings,* VI, 139.

31. Jefferson to Madison, Philadelphia, July 7, 1793, Ford, ed., *Works,* VII, 436–37.

32. Davis's *Virginia Gazette and General Advertiser* [Richmond], Aug. 21, Sept. 4, 11, 25, Oct. 2, 1793; "Resolutions of the Inhabitants of Petersburg & Vicinty," Sept. 2, 1793; "Resolutions of the County and Borough of York," Sept. 2, 1793; "Resolutions of the City of Williamsburg," Sept. 11, 1793; "Resolutions from James City County," Sept. 12, 1793; all in Washington Papers, DLC.

33. Madison to Jefferson, Albemarle (Monroe's), Aug. 27, 1793; and same to same, Orange, Sept. 2, 1793; Monroe to Madison, Albemarle, Sept. 25, 1793; all

in Madison Papers, DLC. That Monroe was exaggerating his success in Federalist Staunton seems likely in view of his utter failure in neighboring Rockingham County where a Republican meeting was canceled when nobody appeared: Monroe to Madison, Sept. 25, 1793.

34. Madison to Jefferson, Orange, Sept. 2, 1793, ibid.

35. Taylor to Madison, Bowling Green, Sept. 25, 1793, ibid.; *Virginia Gazette and General Advertiser* [Richmond], Sept. 25, 1793. Several counties altered Madison's resolutions, usually in efforts to strengthen them, but the variations do not seem terribly significant and probably made little difference to voters: *Virginia Gazette and General Advertiser* [Richmond], Sept. 4, 25, Oct. 2, 30, Nov. 6, 23, 1793; *Virginia Herald* [Fredericksburg], Nov. 14, 1793.

36. Ammon, *Genet Mission,* pp. 106–7.

37. Eugene P. Link, *Democratic-Republican Societies, 1790–1800* (New York, 1942), pp. 13–16, found only 7 societies in the Chesapeake area in the entire decade, though he feels that there may have been more that went unreported in the newspapers.

38. *Virginia Gazette and Richmond Chronicle,* June 8, 1793. Richard Beeman, *The Old Dominion and the New Nation, 1788–1801* (Lexington, Ky., 1972), p. 121, says that the society "accused the Federalist administration of using the Proclamation to obstruct the French cause," but in fact it never mentioned either the administration or the Neutrality Proclamation.

39. Thomas Newton, Sr., had represented Norfolk in the assembly intermittently since the convention of 1776. He voted with the creditor element in the mid-1780s and probably supported the Constitution. Thomas, Jr., served in the House of Delegates, 1796–99 and voted consistently Republican. He entered the U.S. House of Representatives in 1801, and in a congressional career that spanned three decades he was a faithful adherent of the Republican administrations, becoming a National Republican in the 1820s.

40. Washington to Thomas Newton, Jr., Mount Vernon, Apr. 9, 1786, Washington Papers, DLC.

41. John Stewart to Genet, Richmond, May 10, 1793, quoted in Link, *Democratic-Republican Societies,* p. 127n.

42. Henry Bedinger to George M. Bedinger, Shepherd's Town, June 16, 1793, Danske-Dandridge Papers, NCDu.

43. Lee to [Washington], Richmond, Sept. 17, 1793, Lee Papers, VaU (copy).

44. This conversation was recorded by Jefferson in his autobiographical "Anas," Ford, ed., *Works,* I, 256–59.

45. Ammon, *Genet Mission,* p. 106.

46. Washington to Henry Lee, Mount Vernon, Oct. 16, 1793, Washington Papers, DLC.

47. Va, *JHD, 1793,* p. 31 (Nov. 1, 1793).

48. Ibid., pp. 56–57 (Nov. 8, 1793).

49. Ibid., pp. 117–18 (Dec. 6, 1793).

50. Ibid., pp. 121–22, (Dec. 9, 1793); Dawson to [The House of Delegates], Dec. 7, 1793, Monroe Papers, DLC.

51. The 111 to 13 division was omitted from the table 15.1 figures as too lopsided. There were a total of 8 roll calls in the session. The other 3 involved salaries and taxes, on which there was no party division.

52. *North Carolina Gazette* [New Bern], Sept. 28, 1793. This meeting of New Bern merchants was the only one reported, but extant issues of North Carolina newspapers are very rare for 1793 and it is likely that other meetings were held that cannot be confirmed.

53. Steele to Hamilton, Salisbury, Sept. 17, 1793, Syrett, ed., *Hamilton Papers,* XV, 338–39; Steele to Tench Coxe, Fayetteville, Dec. 23, 1793, Coxe Papers, PaHS. The roll call to which Steele referred was not entered into the published journal, but the day after his letter the House approved the resolutions by a roll call of 97 to 12: JHC, 1793, p. 32 (Dec. 24, 1794).

54. Murray to Coxe, Cambridge, May 2, 1793, Coxe Papers, PaHS.

55. Neither the Baltimore nor the Annapolis newspapers mentioned Genet's passage through the state.

56. *Maryland Gazette* [Annapolis], July 11, 1793.

57. Smith to Hamilton, Baltimore, Aug. 20, 1793, Syrett, ed., *Hamilton Papers,* XV, 254–55.

58. William Vans Murray organized a meeting at Cambridge to draft an address on the proclamation, predicting that "The most respectable will be there & are all unanimous": Murray to Tench Coxe, Cambridge, Aug. 19, 1793, Coxe Papers, PaHS. The Richmond resolutions were published in the *Maryland Journal* [Baltimore], Aug. 27, and the *Maryland Gazette* [Annapolis], Aug. 29, 1793. On September 5 an Annapolis meeting, chaired by Alexander Contee Hanson, approved the proclamation and denounced "the intervention of any foreign minister to correct supposed abuses in our government": *Gazette,* Sept. 26, 1793.

59. Smith to Hamilton, Baltimore, Aug. 27, 1793, Syrett, ed., *Hamilton Papers,* XV, 300–1. See also John E. Howard to Hamilton, Aug. 26, 1793, ibid., pp. 278–79.

60. The *Gazette* [Annapolis] published the Caroline resolutions on Oct. 10, 1793, but not once during the autumn did it report a similar meeting in Maryland.

61. William Tilghman to Tench Coxe, Annapolis, Dec. 2, 1793, Coxe Papers, PaHS. There were no roll calls on the resolutions.

62. Brant, *Madison,* III, 389; John C. Miller, *The Federalist Era, 1789–1801* (New York, 1960), pp. 140–44. The *Report* was sent to Congress on December 31; *Annals of Cong.,* 3rd Cong., 1st sess., 152.

63. *Annals of Cong.,* 3d Cong., 1st sess., pp. 155–58 (Jan. 3, 1794).

64. Roane to Monroe, King and Queen, Jan. 25, 1794, Monroe Papers, DLC.

65. *Annals of Cong.,* 3d Cong., 1st sess., p. 422. The *Journal* actually records the motion to strike as passing by 51 to 46, but in light of the subsequent motion to postpone for a month (which does not make sense unless the motion to strike was defeated) and the 51 to 47 roll call in Madison's favor, it seems likely that the recorder became confused on the first roll call and was reporting House sentiment on the resolution itself.

66. After departing from Philadelphia, Jefferson had some "pleasing expectations" of the disposition of the House on the basis of "one or two leading votes," but he was not certain which side had the majority: to Archibald Stuart, Monticello, Jan. 26, 1794, Ford, ed., *Works,* VIII, 137. Noble E. Cunningham, Jr., *The Jeffersonian Republicans: Formation of Party Organization* (Chapel Hill, 1957), pp. 67–68, (who ignores the 51 to 46 roll call) infers from Jefferson's statement that members of Congress were not committed party men before they went to Con-

gress, i.e., that party divisions had not yet affected the general public. A more reasonable explanation is that Jefferson and Madison had neither time nor facilities to contact every new member of Congress (the House had increased that session from 65 to 105), so they anxiously scanned the early roll calls. At least in the Chesapeake, there is every indication that most men were committed to a party when elected.

67. *Annals of Cong.,* 3d Cong., 1st sess., pp. 431–32 (Feb. 5, 1794). Samuel F. Bemis, *Jay's Treaty: A Study in Commerce and Diplomacy* (rev. ed., New Haven, 1962), p. 264*n*16, says news of the seizures began to arrive in February.

68. Smith to O. H. Williams, Philadelphia, Mar. 6, 1794, Williams Papers, MdHS. Shenandoah Valley Federalist Alexander White came to much the same conclusion: to Madison, Woodville, Mar. 31, 1794, Madison Papers, DLC.

69. Madison to Jefferson, Philadelphia, Mar. 14, 24, 26, 1794, Madison Papers, DLC; *Annals of Cong.,* 3d Cong., 1st sess., pp. 529–30 (Mar. 25, 1794).

70. *Annals of Cong.,* 3d Cong., 1st sess., pp. 561, 596–97, 604–6, (Apr. 7, 16, 17, 25, 1794).

71. Miller, *Federalist Era,* p. 151, considers Dayton's proposal evidence of Federalist "Anglomania," but given the extraordinary efforts Dayton and other Federalists were making to avoid war, it seems more likely that it was a half-serious slap at the Virginians.

72. Madison to Jefferson, Philadelphia, May 25, 1794, Hunt, ed., *Writings,* VI, 215–17.

73. Quoted in Cunningham, *Jeffersonian Republicans,* p. 70. The pamphlet was dated Apr. 5, 1794.

74. Renzulli, *Maryland: Federalist Years,* p. 168.

75. Bernard C. Steiner, *The Life and Correspondence of James McHenry* (Cleveland, 1907), pp. 159–68; John T. Scharf, *History of Maryland,* 3 vols. (Baltimore, 1879), II, 594–95.

76. Harry Ammon, *James Monroe: The Quest for National Identity* (New York, 1971), p. 112.

77. White to Madison, Apr. 26, 1794, Madison Papers, DLC; Carrington to Hamilton, Richmond, July 9, 1794, Syrett, ed., *Hamilton Papers,* XVI, 580–1; see also William Barry Grove to John Haywood, Philadelphia, Apr. 24, 1794, Ernest Haywood Coll., NCU.

78. Madison to Jefferson, Philadelphia, Apr. 28, 1794, Madison Papers, DLC.

79. *Columbian Mirror* [Alexandria], June 19, 1794.

80. Link, *Democratic Societies,* p. 131. The resolutions were adopted on May 8, apparently the first organized criticism of the nomination.

81. *Virginia Gazette* [Richmond], July 23, Aug. 20, 1794.

CHAPTER SIXTEEN   THE POLITICS OF TAXES
AND TREATIES, 1794–1795

1. *Annals of Congress,* 1st Cong., 3d sess., pp. 1890–1934 (Jan. 5–27, 1791). The only Chesapeake congressmen who strongly opposed it in debate were Josiah Parker and Michael J. Stone. Madison appeared to favor the measure as did William Branch Giles, though Giles ultimately voted against it. The bill passed 30

to 21; most of the opposition came from Pennsylvania and the South. It was more a regional opposition than a partisan one.

2. Hawkins to Tench Coxe, Warren, Aug. 29, 1792, Coxe Papers, PaHS.

3. Henry M. Brackinridge, *History of the Western Insurrection* (Pittsburgh, 1859), p. 17.

4. The region was represented in Congress by John Smilie and William Findlay, two of Madison's most loyal adherents. Albert Gallatin replaced Smilie in the Fourth Congress.

5. The exception was Monongalia County, Virginia (Morgantown), where one delegate, John Evans, voted against the Constitution. In view of the solidly Federalist stance of the remainder of the West, however, it seems likely that Evans did not reflect the sentiment of his county.

6. *Pennsylvania Gazette* [Philadelphia], Sept. 2, 1794.

7. *Virginia Gazette and General Advertiser* [Richmond], Aug. 27, 1794. This is probably a reference, from a different perspective, to the Morgantown incident reported by the *Pennsylvania Gazette* on Sept. 2. (see above, note 6).

8. *Virginia Gazette and General Advertiser* [Richmond], Aug. 27, 1794. Since Gallatin had yet to take his seat in Congress, Davis's reference must have been to Smilie and Findlay.

9. Burgess Ball reported to the President from the Valley (Bath, Aug. 28, 1794, Washington Papers, DLC) that no coercion was necessary in Frederick and Bath counties because there were plenty of volunteers. [West] Virginia counties alone contributed a thousand men to Gov. Lee's army: Thomas C. Miller and Hu Maxwell, *West Virginia and Its People,* 3 vols. (New York, 1913), I, 206.

10. Page to St. George Tucker, Rosewell, Sept. 22, 1794, Tucker-Coleman Papers, VaWM.

11. John Jeffers to Joseph Jones, Petersburg, Aug. 22, 1794, enclosed in Jones to Gov. Henry Lee, Aug. 26, 1794; Jones to Lt. Col. William Maclin, Petersburg, Sept. 17, 1794; and Lt. Gov. James Wood to Jones, in council, Sept. 30, 1794, all in Joseph Jones Papers, NCDu.

12. Murray to Tench Coxe, Cambridge, Aug. 28, 1794, Coxe Papers, PaHS, John Davidson to Gen. Samuel Smith, Governor's Council, Sept. 18, 1794, Carter-Smith Papers, VaU.

13. *Daily Intelligencer* [Baltimore], Sept. 4, 1794; Md, *JHD, 1794,* pp. 12–13, 15 (Nov. 12, 14, 1794).

14. Herbert C. Bell, *History of Leitersburg District, Washington County, Maryland* (Leitersburg, 1898), p. 223.

15. Allegany County, created in 1790, was Federalist through 1793. Its delegates in 1794–95 could not be identified for lack of party roll calls; in 1796 it sent three Republicans and one Federalist to the assembly. Hampshire and Harrison voted solidly Federalist in 1794 (roll call of Nov. 21, see note 18). In 1795 each county replaced one Federalist with a Republican, and by 1796 they were both solidly Republican.

16. Thomas Evans to John Cropper, Richmond, Nov. 30, 1794, Cropper Papers, VaHS. Evans was a Federalist reporting on Republican opinions.

17. Va, *JHD, 1794,* pp. 5–6 (Nov. 12, 1794).

18. Ibid., p. 28 (Nov. 21, 1794); Joseph Jones to Madison, Fredericksburg, Nov. 16, 1794, and Madison to Monroe, Philadelphia, Dec. 4, 1794, Madison

Papers, DLC; Evans to Cropper, Richmond, Nov. 30, 1794, Cropper Papers, VaHS. Brooke's record in the assembly, 1791–94, was firmly Republican.

19. That it was a party contest was clearly understood. "The Jacobins have succeeded in the choice of a Governor," wrote Francis Corbin to Tench Coxe, Richmond, Nov. 19–20, 1794, Coxe Papers, PaHS.

20. Roane to Monroe, King and Queen, Feb. 24, 1794, Monroe Papers, DLC; Tazewell to Monroe, Richmond, Apr. 13, 1794, Mar. 9, 1795, and Madison to Monroe, Philadelphia, Dec. 4, 1794, Monroe Papers, DLC.

21. Corbin to Coxe, Richmond, Nov. 19–20, 1794, Coxe Papers, PaHS. Even before the session began Corbin was determined to assert leadership of the Federalists and lead a movement in defense of administration policies. Corbin to Coxe, Virginia Middlesex, Oct. 10, 1794, ibid.

22. Corbin to Coxe, Virginia Middlesex, Oct. 10, 1794, ibid.

23. John Dawson to Madison, Richmond, Mar. 2, 1794, and Madison to Monroe, Dec. 4, 1794, Madison Papers, DLC.

24. Bassett and his father (who died in 1793) were both Federalists in 1788. A letter to Washington (Nov. 26, 1797, Washington Papers, DLC), indicates that Bassett considered himself a Federalist in 1797, and in the 1798 Senate he voted Federalist on two out of three roll calls. His switch came apparently in 1799 when he voted in favor of renewing the Virginia Resolutions of 1798. In 1805 he was elected to Congress as a Republican.

25. The New Kent county tax list for 1791 credits him with no land and 6 slaves. His father was prosperous enough, however, to send him to the College of Philadelphia for schooling.

26. Madison to Monroe, Philadelphia, Mar. 27, 1795. Rutherford was elected as a Federalist in 1793, but sided with Madison in the House: Manning J. Dauer, *The Adams Federalists* (Baltimore, 1953), p. 286.

27. "Protest of John Hay and Others," 1794, Legislative Papers Coll., NCDH.

28. *Columbian Mirror* [Alexandria], June 19, 1794.

29. Jones to Madison, Fredericksburg, Nov. 16, 1794, Madison Papers, DLC. For Jones's role in the debt suit see: Daniel L. Hylton to Jones, Richmond, Jan. 17, 1795, Joseph Jones Papers, NCDu.

30. Madison to Jefferson, Philadelphia, Feb. 15, 1795, Madison Papers, DLC.

31. This is the view first expressed by Joseph Charles, *Origins of the American Party System* (Williamsburg, 1956), Part III, and repeated, somewhat less forcefully, by numerous other scholars.

32. Samuel F. Bemis, *Jay's Treaty: A Study in Commerce and Diplomacy* (rev. ed., New Haven, 1962), p. 353; Madison to Monroe, Mar. 26, 1795, and Madison to _____, Aug. 23, 1795, Madison Papers, DLC.

33. Isaac S. Harrell, *Loyalism in Virginia* (Philadelphia, 1926), 162.

34. Hardin Burnley to Madison, Dec. 3, 1791, and Francis Corbin to Madison, Jan. 7, 1792, Madison Papers, DLC: James Iredell to Samuel Johnston, May 29, 1793, Hayes Coll., NCU.

35. *Ware, Administrator of Jones,* v. *Hylton,* Order Book I, United States Circuit Court, Richmond, Va., pp. 141 ff. (May 1793).

36. W. W. Henry, *Patrick Henry: Life Correspondence, and Speeches,* 3 vols. (New York, 1891), II. 473.

37. *Ware* v. *Hylton et al.,* 1796 (3 Dallas 199), B. R. Curtis, *Reports of the Decisions of the Supreme Court of the United States,* 57 vols. (Boston, 1855–56), I, 164–229. By then Jay had resigned from the court. Justices Chase, Cushing, Patterson, and Wilson formed the majority. Iredell adhered to his earlier opinion.

38. Bemis, *Jay's Treaty,* pp. 438–39. The American commissioners were James Innis of Richmond and Thomas FitzSimons of Philadelphia. In 1802 the Jefferson administration negotiated a convention under which the federal government paid Britain a lump sum of £600,000 to discharge all debts.

39. Bemis, *Jay's Treaty,* pp. 436–37.

40. Henry Tazewell to Monroe, Philadelphia, June 27, 1795, enclosing a list of senators' votes. Against the treaty were Tazewell and Mason of Virginia, Martin and Bloodworth of North Carolina. Maryland's Federalists, Henry and Potts, favored it. Monroe Papers, DLC.

41. Madison to Monroe, Philadelphia, Dec. 20, 1795, Madison Papers, DLC. Madison was referring primarily to Virginia. Northern Republicans reacted a bit more slowly, and there was more concert among them: Eugene P. Link, *Democratic-Republican Societies, 1790–1800* (New York, 1942), p. 132.

42. *Virginia Gazette and General Advertiser* [Richmond], Aug. 1, 1795; Madison to Jefferson, Orange, Aug. 6, 1795, Madison Papers, DLC.

43. The addresses were printed in all the newspapers; originals are in the Washington Papers, DLC. The committees, which numbered between 6 and 10 men, contained a large number of current and future members of the assembly.

44. *Virginia Herald* [Fredericksburg], Sept. 1, Nov. 10, 1795.

45. Mason to Henry Tazewell, Raspberry Plain, Oct. 6, 1795, Tazewell Papers, VaSL.

46. *Virginia Herald* [Fredericksburg], Oct. 20, 1795, reporting on a New Bern meeting of October 3.

47. Absalom Tatom to John Haywood, Philadelphia, May 9, 1796, Ernest Haywood Coll., NCU.

48. *Virginia Herald* [Fredericksburg], Aug. 4, 1795, reports the Baltimore meeting, but neither the Baltimore nor the Annapolis papers mentioned it. The *Maryland Journal,* July 27, 1795, however, did carry a notice of a meeting to sign an address critical of the treaty, a document presumably drafted at the earlier meeting. The address itself was not printed.

49. Neville to Madison, Hardy County, Dec. 8, 1795, and Arthur Campbell to Madison, Washington County, Jan. 24, 1796, Madison Papers, DLC. Campbell also wrote a series of letters in defense of the treaty under the pseudonym "Atticus," *Virginia Centinel* [Winchester], Nov. 7, 9, 16, 1795.

50. Joseph Jones to Madison, Oct. 29, 1795, *Proceedings of the Massachusetts Historical Society,* 25 (1901–2), 150–51.

51. *Annals of Cong.,* 3d Cong., 2d sess., pp. 861–62 (June 24, 1795). See also Thomas J. Farnham, "The Virginia Amendments of 1795: An Episode in the Opposition to Jay's Treaty," *Virginia Magazine of History and Biography,* 75, no. 1 (1967), 75–88.

52. Va, *JHD, 1795,* pp. 27, 29 (Nov. 20, 21, 1795); Jones to Madison, Fredericksburg, Nov. 22, 1795, Madison Papers, DLC.

53. Va, *SJ, 1795,* Nov. 24, 1795. The manuscript Journal is not paginated. The three absent were Francis Peyton from the Northern Neck, Hugh Holmes from the Valley, and Thomas Wilson from the Northwest.

54. Va, *JHD,* pp. 91–92 (Dec. 12, 1795).

55. Va, *SJ, 1795,* Dec. 15, 1795).

56. Because of the procedural moves, the issue at stake in each roll call is not always clear, so an ideal party model could not be constructed. John Marshall, who participated in all six roll calls, was used as the Federalist model; voting the reverse of his record were Wilson Cary Nicholas and several other prominent Republicans.

57. Even the ten delegates still in the middle may not be evidence of organizational failure. All ten came from counties that were themselves divided, counties that often send delegates of opposite opinions to the House. These then may have been intentionally nonpartisan.

58. *Virginia Centinel* [Winchester], May 6, 1796. The idea was picked up by the Federalist *Columbian Mirror* [Alexandria], May 10, June 21, 1796, but nothing came of it.

59. He was not following congressional districts because, with the exception of George Hancock, the Virginia delegation was solidly Republican in the Fourth Congress. Dauer, *Adams Federalists,* p. 292, lists Page, Parker, and Rutherford as Federalists, but his own table shows that all three voted Republican in the Fourth Congress. Page's own correspondence indicates he was a Republican, and Madison clearly considered Rutherford an ally. Parker switched sides so many times he is unclassifiable, except by congressional session.

60. Madison to Monroe, Philadelphia, Dec. 20, 1795, Madison Papers, DLC.

61. This was Pinkney's first legislative service since 1791 when he was an active Antifederalist. The 1795 session (he represented Anne Arundel, his birthplace) was his last elective office until he went to Congress in 1815. Anne Arundel was a predominantly Republican county, and the voters may have been unaware of his switch.

62. Md, *JHD, 1795,* pp. 36–37 (Nov. 25, 1795). The Senate, which contained no Republicans, also approved it unanimously: *SJ, 1795,* p. 13 (Nov. 25, 1795).

63. Md, *SJ, 1796,* pp. 37–38 (Dec. 21, 1796); *JHD, 1796,* pp. 88–89 (Dec. 22, 1796).

64. North Carolina newspapers are spotty, but in the extant issues there are no articles on the treaty.

65. Person to Wood J. Hamlin, Nov. 15, 1796, Hamlin Papers, NCDH.

66. NC, *JHC, 1795,* p. 53 (Dec. 8, 1795). Since this was the only roll call on a matter of national policy between 1792 and 1798, there is no way of analyzing it. The minority, presumably all Republicans, came from all sections of the state.

67. J. Rives Childs, "French Consul Martin Oster Reports on Virginia, 1784–1796," *Virginia Magazine of History and Biography,* 76, no. 1 (1968), 27–40, esp. 38.

68. *Annals of Cong.,* 4th Cong., 1st sess., 759, 782 (Mar. 24, Apr. 7, 1796); Noble E. Cunningham, *The Jeffersonian Republicans: Formation of Party Organization* (Chapel Hill, 1957), pp. 80–83.

69. *Annals of Cong.,* 4th Cong., 1st sess., pp. 1280, 1282, 1289–90 (Apr. 29–30, 1796); Madison to Jefferson, Philadelphia, May 1, 1796, Madison Papers, DLC. Chesapeake Republicans who broke ranks and voted against the resolution were Dent of Maryland, Claiborne, Heath, and Parker of Virginia, and Bryan of North Carolina. Samuel Smith, still unpersuaded, also voted against it.

70. Ibid., p. 1291 (Apr. 30, 1796).

71. Voting in favor of the treaty were 4 Federalists from the Chesapeake (Grove, Hancock, Hindman, and Murray), and against it were 26 Republicans (18 from Virginia, 7 from North Carolina, 1 from Maryland). Historical analysis of these roll calls has been negligent. Cunningham, *Jeffersonian Republicans,* pp. 80–85, does not analyze them at all, even though the amount of switching is central to his interpretation (it was wavering Federalists who were switching, not Republicans). Dauer, *Adams Federalists,* pp. 389–92, uses only 3 of the 4 roll calls and hence misses some crucial changes. L. Marx Renzulli, *Maryland: Federalist Years* (Rutherford, N.J., 1973), pp. 175–77, has the sequence—and hence the explanation—muddled.

72. Frank A. Cassell, *Merchant Congressman in the Young Republic: Samuel Smith of Maryland, 1752–1839* (Madison, 1971), pp. 67–72.

73. Monroe apparently had the assignment of contacting Antifederalists. At the end of 1793, for instance, he wrote Spencer Roane, Henry's son-in-law, and next to John Taylor the leading Antifederalist in the middle Tidewater. It was evidently their first contact in some time, for Monroe misaddressed the letter, causing it to be delayed: Roane to Monroe, King and Queen, Jan. 25, 1794, Monroe Papers, DLC. The result was an intermittent exchange that lasted for some years, with Roane providing advice and political intelligence. For contacts with other Antifederalists see: George Tucker to Monroe, Williamsburg, Dec. 15, 1793, Monroe Papers, DLC.

74. Washington to Lee, Germantown, Aug. 26, 1794, Lee-Ludwell Papers, VaHS. This letter refers to an earlier communication from Lee (not found), and it recalls a conversation with Lee about Henry in the fall of 1792. Lee had written Henry earlier to urge him to accept a seat in the U.S. Senate, apparently in place of John Taylor: Lee to Henry, Richmond, July 11, 1794, Lee Papers, VaU.

75. Randolph to Henry, Philadelphia, Aug. 28, 1794 (copy), William Wirt Henry Papers, VaHS.

76. Bernard C. Steiner, *The Life and Correspondence of James McHenry* (Cleveland, 1907), pp. Steiner, 159–68.

77. *Hylton* v. *United States,* 3 *Dallas* 171 (1796).

78. Lee to Henry, Stratford, Sept. 30, 1795, and Henry to Washington, Campbell County, Oct. 16, 1795, Henry Papers, DLC.

79. Washington to Carrington, Oct. 9, 1795, and Washington to Henry, Oct. 9, 1795, Washington Papers, DLC; Washington to Lee, Philadelphia, Jan. 11, 1796 (copy), Lee-Ludwell Papers, VaHS.

80. Marshall to Rufus King, Richmond, May 24, 1796, King Papers, NYHS.

81. Henry to his daughter, Red Hill, Aug. 20, 1796 (copy), William W. Henry Papers, VaHS.

82. Jefferson to Monroe, July 10, 1796, Monroe Papers, DLC.

83. Va, *SJ, 1796,* Nov. 25, 1796; Henry to Nicholas, Red Hill, Nov. 29, 1796, Henry Papers, VaSL.

CHAPTER SEVENTEEN   PROSPERITY SOLVES MANY PROBLEMS

1. See index heading under "ethnicity and voting behavior" for the various references to this question.

2. Md, *JHD, 1789,* pp. 80, 86–91 (Dec. 16, 19, 20, 1789).

3. Md, *JHD, 1790,* pp. 60–61, 100, 106–7 (Dec. 2, 20, 21, 1790).

4. Edmund Randolph to Madison, Richmond, Sept. 12, 1788, Madison Papers, DLC.

5. The model was the record of Matthew Cheatham of Chesterfield, an Antifederalist who had been in the debtor element in the mid-1780s. He was chosen because he participated in 6 of the 7 roll calls.

6. Va, *JHD, 1792,* pp. 93–5, 203 (Oct. 31, Nov. 1, Dec. 20, 1792). Party correlations are difficult because there were no party-determining roll calls in this session.

7. NC, JHC, Clark, ed., *State Records of North Carolina,* 30 vols. (Winston and Goldsboro, 1886–1907), XXI, 160 (Dec. 4, 1788), 371–72 (Dec. 16, 1789), 402–3 (Dec. 19, 1789), 927, 937 (Nov. 16, 18, 1790); SJ, ibid., XX, 545–46 (Nov. 24, 1788), XXI, 696 (Dec. 16, 1789), 815, 839 (Dec. 7, 1790); SJ, 1791, pp. 44 (Jan. 17, 1792).

8. Samuel Johnston to ———, Edenton, Sept. 12, 1790, Hayes Coll., NCU; W. R. Davie to Alexander Martin, Nov. 1, 1790, Davie Papers, NCU; Hay to Iredell, Fayetteville, Dec. 16, 1790, Iredell Papers, NCDu; Davie to John Haywood, Halifax, Jan. 15, 1791, Ernest Haywood Coll., NCU; JHC, 1790, Clark, ed., *State Records,* XXI, 1013 (Dec. 7, 1790).

9. Voting was also random on all other legal-judicial questions that arose in the 1790–91 sessions: JHC, 1790, Clark, ed., *State Records,* XXI, 980 (Nov. 30, 1790); JHC, 1791 (Early State Records Series Microfilm), p. 42 (Jan. 7, 1792); SJ, 1790, Clark, ed., *State Records,* XXI, 846 (Dec. 9, 1790); *SJ, 1791,* p. 16 (Dec. 22, 1791), p. 38 (Jan. 12, 1792).

10. NC, JHC, 1794, p. 57 (Feb. 7, 1795). The Journal recorded the vote as 53 to 28, but only 52 names were listed.

11. Md, *JHD, 1796,* pp. 6–7, 38–39, 45–46 (Nov. 29, 1796).

12. Hamilton to Williams, Philadelphia, Mar. 28, 1792, and Williams to Hamilton, Baltimore, Apr. 5, 1792, Harold C. Syrett, ed., *The Papers of Alexander Hamilton,* 25 vols. to date (New York and London, 1961-), XI, 204, 239–40.

13. *Virginia Gazette and Alexandria Advertiser,* June 23, 1791. The one exception was Stevens Thomson Mason, who may have been chosen simply for his wealth and position. Occupations were obtained from advertisements in the newspaper.

14. Randolph to Washington, Philadelphia, Sept. 10, 1792, Washington Papers, DLC. Randolph thought the new bank would be located in Richmond. The assembly's choice of Alexandria clearly suggests that it was trying to counteract the Alexandria petition.

15. Va, *JHD, 1792,* pp. 128–30 (Nov. 19, 20, 1792); Dawson to Madison, Richmond, Nov. 27, 1792, Madison Papers, DLC.

16. John Taylor, *An Examination of the Late Proceedings in Congress Respecting the Official Conduct of the Secretary of the Treasury* (Richmond, 1793).

17. Taylor to Madison, Caroline, Aug. 5, 1793, and Madison to Jefferson, Orange, Aug. 11, 1793, Madison Papers, DLC.

18. Va, *JHD, 1795,* p. 79 (Dec. 8, 1795); *JHD, 1796,* pp. 80–81 (Dec. 15, 1796).

19. The only branch that the first Bank of the United States opened in

Virginia was located in Norfolk in 1800. Bray Hammond, *Banks and Politics in the United States from the Revolution to the Civil War* (Princeton, 1957), p. 127, states that its establishment "was preceded by a long and acrid controversy," but he offers neither details nor evidence.

20. Thomas Swann to Charles Simms, Richmond, Dec. 24, 1799, Jan. 29, 1800, Simms Papers, DLC.

21. Hammond, *Banks and Politics,* p. 127.

22. Hammond, *Banks and Politics,* pp. 164–71, makes no mention of North Carolina in a survey of state banks opened prior to the War of 1812.

23. Md, *JHD, 1795,* p. 52 (Dec. 5, 1795). The bill passed the House of Delegates by 39 to 33. In the previous year (*JHD, 1794,* p. 74), the House rejected a similar bill by 23 to 44. The only support for it came from Baltimore and its environs.

24. The move does coincide with Samuel Smith's conversion to Republicanism, and Smith had been one of the prime movers in the Bank of Maryland. Moreover, he subsequently became a member of the Board of Directors of the Bank of Baltimore. But there is no direct evidence of politics in the chartering of the second bank. Frank A. Cassell, *Merchant Congressman in the Young Republic: Samuel Smith of Maryland, 1752–1839* (Madison, 1971), pp. 42, 166, does not even raise the question. Evidently there was not enough evidence even to arouse his curiosity.

25. Md, *JHD, 1796,* pp. 93–94, 108 (Dec. 24, 29, 1795); James Buchanan to Tench Coxe, Baltimore, Dec. 20, 1796, Coxe Papers, PaHS.

26. In 1797 a resolution that the state invest $66,000 in the Bank of Baltimore passed the House of Delegates, 42 to 33, but it was apparently blocked in the Senate (*JHD, 1797,* p. 65).

27. Md, *JHD, 1799,* pp. 80, 86 (Dec. 24, 27, 1799).

28. Md, *JHD, 1796,* pp. 62–63 (Dec. 13, 1796).

29. The governor was John Francis Mercer, who had been a Republican. But Mercer had a rather equivocal voting record in his last year in the assembly (1800), and was probably elected with Federalist support. The first truly Republican governor was Robert Bowie in 1802.

30. Md, *JHD, 1801,* pp. 18, 82–83, 103–4 (Nov. 10, Dec. 17, 26, 1801); *SJ, 1801,* p. 49 (Dec. 27, 1801). The Senate approved the bill by 6 to 4. Provisions of the statues are in Frederick Green, comp. *Laws of Maryland, 1796* (Annapolis, 1797), ch. 43, and idem., *Laws of Maryland, 1801* (Annapolis, 1802), ch. 74.

31. Md, *JHD, 1795,* pp. 43, 48–49, 65, 68–69 (Nov. 28, Dec. 2, 11, 14, 1795).

32. Md, *JHD, 1797,* pp. 11, 60, 75 (Nov. 13, Dec. 6, 15, 1797).

33. Ibid., pp. 102–3, 108–9, 117–18, 121–22, 125–27, 129 (Dec. 28, 31, 1797, Jan. 5, 9, 11, 13, 1798).

34. Md, *JHD, 1799,* p. 42 (Dec. 4, 1799). The Chesapeake-Delaware Canal bill passed by 50 to 15; the Potomac resolutions by 37 to 29, and the Susquehanna bill by 38 to 29.

35. Va, *JHD, 1795,* p. 124 (Dec. 24, 1795). The clerk recorded the tally as 65 to 24.

36. Va, *JHD, 1796,* pp. 23–24 (Nov. 18, 1796). The Appomatox project did arise in the 1795 session with a bill that would codify the various acts concerning

the river, but it was defeated, 45 to 59 (*JHD, 1795*, p. 133). Since the issues at stake are not clear, the vote is not very meaningful.

37. NC, *JHD, 1792*, p. 46 (Dec. 21, 1792); *JHC, 1793*, pp. 51–52 (Jan. 7, 1794).

38. NC, *JHC, 1795*, p. 40 (Dec. 1, 1795). The clerk recorded the tally as 37 to 65, but the roll call adds up to 36 to 62.

CHAPTER EIGHTEEN   REFORM WITH RESTRAINT

1. Md, *JHD, 1788*, pp. 75–76, 90–95 (Dec. 19, 22, 1788); *SJ, 1788*, pp. 33–35.

2. Md, *JHD, 1792*, p. 76 (Dec. 12, 1792).

3. Md, *JHD, 1795*, p. 20 (Nov. 16, 1795).

4. The only one was in 1791 when the House of Delegates approved a bill incorporating a Presbyterian congregation in Queen Anne's by 46 to 9: *JHD, 1791*, pp. 93–94.

5. Md, *JHD, 1797*, p. 2 (Nov. 8, 1797). Rev. Wyeth is not mentioned in any histories of Annapolis or of Maryland Anglicanism. He may have been Methodist, since that was the only other church in Annapolis at the time.

6. Md, *JHD, 1794*, p. 99 (Dec. 23, 1794); Frederick Green, comp. *Laws of Maryland* 1794 (Annapolis, 1795), XLIX.

7. Md, *JHD, 1795*, 28 (Nov. 20, 1795). The vote was 40 to 28.

8. Md, *JHD, 1797*, 144 (Jan. 20, 1798). The vote was 33 to 12.

9. Md, *JHD, 1801*, 101 (Dec. 26, 1801).

10. Hamilton J. Eckenrode, *Separation of Church and State in Virginia* (Richmond, 1910), pp. 133–34; *JHD, 1787*, p. 82 (Dec. 4, 1787). The vote on postponement was 69 to 58.

11. Eckenrode, *Separation of Church and State*, pp. 135–37; *JHD, 1789*, p. 113 (Dec. 9, 1789).

12. Eckenrode, *Separation of Church and State*, pp. 137–41; *JHD, 1790*, pp. 73–74 (Nov. 19, 1790); *JHD, 1791*, pp. 106–7 (Dec. 6, 1971); *JHD, 1792*, p. 177 (Dec. 8, 1792).

13. *JHD, 1794*, pp. 48–49 (Nov. 28, Dec. 2, 1794); *JHD, 1795*, pp. 47–48, 101 (Nov. 27, Dec. 16, 1795).

14. Eckenrode, *Separation of Church and State*, pp. 142–44.

15. John C. Hunter "To the Freeholders of Fairfax County," *Columbian Mirror* [Alexandria], Mar. 23, 1797; Augustus J. Smith "To the Freeholders of Fairfax County," ibid., Apr. 4, 1797; poll results in ibid., Apr. 18, 1797. Neither candidate can be identified politically, so it is uncertain whether parties were involved in the contest.

16. The clerk tallied the roll call at 97 to 51: *JHD, 1797*, pp. 80–81 (Jan. 5, 1798); S. M. Hamilton, ed., *The Writings of James Monroe*, 7 vols. (New York and London, 1898–1903), II, 97*n*.

17. Va, *JHD, 1798*, p. 84 (Jan. 18, 1799).

18. Richard Beeman, *The Old Dominion and the New Nation, 1788–1801* (Lexington, Ky., 1972), pp. 198–99, examines only the 1798 roll call and thus perhaps overestimates the amount of partisanship on the issue. The difference between his figures and mine concerning the party lineup is not significant. It is

sometimes a matter of where the agreement threshhold is placed for assigning a man to a party.

19. Md, *JHD, 1792,* pp. 33, 40–41 (Nov. 23, 28, 1792).

20. Party figures should be used cautiously, for there were no clear-cut party roll calls in the 1792 or 1793 sessions. Party assignments were made on the basis of other evidence or post-1793 performance.

21. Md, *JHD, 1793,* pp. 22, 64, 70–74, 76–77 (Nov. 19, Dec. 10, 13, 14, 16, 1793).

22. Md, *SJ, 1793,* pp. 32, 41–42.

23. Md, *JHD, 1793,* pp. 107–8; *SJ, 1793,* p. 32 (Dec. 26, 1793).

24. Md, *JHD, 1794,* pp. 28–29 (Nov. 24, 1794); *JHD, 1796,* p. 93 (Dec. 24, 1796); *SJ, 1797,* p. 32 (Dec. 20, 1797).

25. Md, *JHD, 1797,* pp. 57–59 (Dec. 5, 1797); *SJ, 1797,* p. 32 (Dec. 20, 1797).

26. Md, *JHD, 1798,* pp. 90, 131–32.

27. Md, *JHD, 1798,* pp. 92–93 (Dec. 31, 1798); *Laws of Maryland, 1798,* ch. 107. There were a total of 9 roll calls on educational matters in this session, 7 of which were used to form the analysis (2 were duplicative).

28. Davie to Martin, Nov. 1, 1790 (copy), Davie Papers, NCU.

29. NC, JHC, 1794, p. 46 (Feb. 2, 1795).

30. Grove to Coxe, Congress Hall, May 16, 1796, Coxe Papers, PaHS.

31. Va, *JHD, 1792,* p. 179 (Dec. 10, 1792); *JHD, 1794,* p. 99 (Dec. 16, 1794); and *JHD, 1799,* p. 88 (Jan. 15, 1800).

32. NC, JHC, 1794, p. 11 (Jan. 7, 1795). The clerk recorded the vote as 84 to 24. There was no roll call in the Senate.

33. NC, JHC, 1796, p. 29 (Dec. 14, 1976); *JHC, 1797,* p. 20 (Dec. 6, 1797). Both roll calls were used in the following compilation to obtain a maximum sample. Only 7 legislators changed their minds between the two.

34. Md, *JHD, 1791,* pp. 106–7 (Dec. 21, 1791). Since there were no party-determining roll calls in this session, party assignments had to be made on the basis of earlier and subsequent sessions. This introduces much uncertainty; those who failed to fit obviously into categories were placed among the "unknowns."

35. Md, *JHD, 1790,* p. 80 (Dec. 13, 1790).

36. Md, *JHD, 1791,* pp. 116–17 (Dec. 24, 1791). The action was taken without a roll call vote.

37. Md, *JHD, 1792,* p. 16 (Nov. 15, 1792). McHenry to Hamilton, Annapolis, Nov. 18, 1792, Syrett, ed., *Hamilton Papers.* XIII, 157.

38. In 1796 the House of Delegates rejected by substantial margins proposed changes in the constitution in regard to the method of appointing sheriffs and the composition of the governor's council. Although the exact nature of the changes cannot be ascertained, they do not appear important. Voting followed neither a partisan nor a regional pattern. Md, *JHD, 1796,* pp. 26, 35–36, 69–70, 97–98, 102.

39. Chilton Williamson, *American Suffrage from Property to Democracy, 1760–1860* (Princeton, 1960), pp. 159 ff., says reform in the northern states was boosted by party competition. On the other hand, his story of the Maryland suffrage reform movement (pp. 140–50) is hopelessly muddled because he begins with the

assumption that "the distinction between Federalist and Republican had been drawn only in national and not state politics."

40. Md, *JHD, 1797,* p. 96 (Dec. 25, 1797); *SJ, 1797,* p. 38 (Dec. 26, 1797), L. Mark Renzulli, *Maryland: Federalist Years,* (Rutherford, N. J., 1973) p. 215*n*, erroneously states that the bill was defeated by 30 to 21; hence his explanation is valueless. The question of Negro enfranchisement is a curious one. In 1803 Congressman Joseph H. Nicholson (who had been a new Delegate from Queen Anne's in 1797) wrote a letter to his constituents defending himself against the accusation that he had been opposed to suffrage reform in the assembly. He said he voted against the 1797 law only because of the Negro suffrage provision, and that the following year he introduced a bill to abolish the property qualification, but for whites only. (Cited in Frederic Emory, *Queen Anne's County,* p. 367). Nicholson, it would seem, was using political hindsight. If many legislators were aware of the Negro enfranchisement provision, it would not have gotten the overwhelming support it did. If Nicholson did introduce a reform bill in 1798, the House ignored it (see below).

41. Md, *JHD, 1798,* pp. 97–98, 114–15, 128, 138 (Jan. 2, 3, 11, 17, 19, 1798); *SJ, 1798,* pp. 54, 56 (Jan. 15, 1799).

42. Md, *JHD, 1799,* p. 72 (Dec. 22, 1799); *SJ, 1799,* p. 25 (Dec. 24, 1799).

43. *JHD, 1799,* pp. 10, 15, 34 (Nov. 13, 14, 29, 1799).

44. Ibid., p. 92 (Dec. 30, 1799).

45. On the three questions of election regulation, manhood suffrage, and the secret ballot, there were 4 roll calls; 2 were repetitive.

46. Md, *JHD, 1801,* p. 90 (Dec. 21, 1801).

47. Md, *JHD, 1800,* p. 51 (Dec. 3, 1800).

48. "Notes of a Speech on the State Constitution of Virginia" [June, 1784], Madison Papers, DLC.

49. Va, *JHD, 1784,* pp. 70–71 (June 21, 1784); Madison to Jefferson, Richmond, July 3, 1784, Julian P. Boyd, ed., *The Papers of Thomas Jefferson,* 18 vols. to date (Princeton, 1950), VII, 359–62, esp. 360.

50. White to Madison, Bath, Aug. 16, 1788. Archibald Stuart earlier reached the same conclusion: to Madison, Richmond, Oct. 21, 1787. Madison Papers, DLC.

51. John Dawson to Madison, Richmond, Dec. 17, 1789, and Randolph to Madison, Williamsburg, Mar. 23, 1790, Madison Papers, DLC.

52. *Virginia Gazette* [Richmond], Aug. 29, 1792.

53. "To the Freemen of Culpeper," *Columbian Mirror and Alexandria Gazette,* Jan. 24, 1797. Suffrage was the only thing Banks specifically advocated.

54. *Virginia Centinel,* May 6, 1796; *Columbian Mirror,* June 21, 1796.

55. Va, *JHD, 1796,* p. 47 (Nov. 28, 1796); *SJ, 1796,* Dec. 9, 1796. The House vote was 86 to 56. The Senate tied 8 to 8, whereupon Speaker Ludwell Lee (a Northern Neck Federalist and son of Richard Henry) broke the impasse in favor of reform. Supporting the resolution in the Senate were 4 Federalists and 4 Republicans; opposing it were 1 Federalist and 7 Republicans.

56. "Analyticus," *Columbian Mirror and Alexandria Advertiser,* Dec. 15, 1796.

57. Va, *JHD, 1797,* p. 87 (Jan. 9, 1798).

58. NC, *JHC, 1795,* p. 34 (Nov. 26, 1795).

59. NC, *JHC, 1797*, pp. 19, 21 (Dec. 5, 7, 1797); *JHC, 1798*, p. 10 (Nov. 23, 1798); *JHC, 1799*, pp. 11, 18–19 (Nov. 25, 29, 1799).

CHAPTER NINETEEN   A YANKEE PRESIDENT

1. Charles Simms, "Address to the Freeholders of the Counties of Prince William, Stafford, and Fairfax," *Columbian Mirror* [Alexandria], Sept. 29, 1796, and *Federal Gazette* [Baltimore], Oct. 4, 1796. That Simms was a Federalist is without doubt. A former aide-de-camp to Washington and a member of the ratifying convention, Simms had a soldily Federalist record in the assembly (1792 and 1796). In 1798 he was placed on a list of politically approved applicants for army commissions, Washington Papers, DLC.

2. Leven Powell, "To the Freeholders of the Counties of Loudoun and Fauquier," *Columbian Mirror* [Alexandria], Oct. 1, 1796.

3. See statements by Thomas Griffin and Ralph Wormeley in *Virginia Gazette and General Advertiser* [Richmond], Oct. 12, 1796. Griffin was a Yorktown attorney who sought to represent the Richmond-Williamsburg peninsula. He was a firm Federalist in the assembly, and as late as 1803 ran for Congress as a Federalist. Wormeley was a planter with vast estates in Tidewater counties between the Rappahannock and the York, a member of the colonial governor's council, a pardoned Loyalist, and a Federalist of 1788 (in the House of Delegates—he was elected to the ratifying convention but did not vote). He had been in political limbo since 1790.

4. "A Farmer," and "A Citizen of Loudoun" in *Columbian Mirror* [Alexandria], Sept. 27, Oct. 20, 1796.

5. Albert Russell, "To the Freeholders of the Counties of Loudoun and Fauquier," *Columbian Mirror*, Sept. 20, 1796; Daniel C. Brent "To the Freeholders of Prince William, Stafford, and Fairfax," ibid., Oct. 18, 1796; "A Young Columbian," ibid., Oct. 20, 1796; "A Freeholder," *Richmond and Manchester Advertiser*, Oct. 12, 1796; William Munford to Joseph Jones, May 18, 1796, Jones Papers, NCDu.

6. Powell was a merchant from Middleburg, Loudoun County, a town he had founded himself on his own land. It lay on the road that led up to Ashley's Gap in the Blue Ridge, approximately halfway between Alexandria and Winchester. It quickly became an important stopover in the overland trade between the Shenandoah Valley and the Potomac, paralleling the water route developed by the Potomac Company. Powell's associates in founding Middleburg were prominent Northern Neck Federalists — Francis Peyton, Burr Powell, and Richard Bland Lee. See Harrison Williams, *Legends of Loudon* (Richmond, 1938), p. 166. The development of party organization is inferred from the stranglehold Federalists had on the county (both in the House of Delegates and in Congressional balloting) from this time until the War of 1812. Prior to 1796 the county had been evenly divided. With its heavy concentration of Germans and Quakers, Loudoun was more socially akin to the Shenandoah Valley than to eastern Virginia. Anti-French feeling among Loudoun Germans also served the Federalist cause.

7. Loudoun and Berkeley were newly developed counties in 1790, and most of the statements cited in chapter 14, note 53 concerning the dramatic rise in land values in the 1790s referred to those counties. The part of the Northern Neck

below Alexandria did not benefit from the river improvements, and, being longsettled, witnessed no dramatic change attributable to the capital.

8. The only Federalist besides Leven Powell that Republicans worried about was Littleton Eyre on the Eastern Shore. The only other ones even mentioned were Griffin and Wormeley: Joseph Jones to Madison, Fredericksburg, Nov. 23, 1796, Madison Papers, DLC.

9. McHenry never openly endorsed the scheme, but he may have been behind some of the newspaper essays obviously written by Federalists and critical of Adams: L. Marx Renzulli, *Maryland, Federalist Years* (Rutherford, N.J., 1973), pp. 184–86. William Vans Murray evidently considered McHenry in on it, for he chastized him with heavy-handed sarcasm: Murray to McHenry, Oct. 2, 9, Nov. 2, 1796, in Bernard C. Steiner, *Life and Correspondence of James McHenry* (Cleveland, 1907), pp. 198–201.

10. Carroll to McHenry, Dec. 12, 1796, Steiner, *McHenry,* p. 206.

11. "Eastern Shore," in *Maryland Journal,* Oct. 19, 1796; Murray to McHenry, Nov. 2, 9, 1796, Steiner, *McHenry,* p. 201.

12. *The Federal Gazette and Baltimore Daily Advertiser,* Oct. 29, Nov. 1, 1796.

13. Murray to McHenry, Nov. 15, 22, 1796, Steiner, *McHenry,* pp. 201–2.

14. Carroll to McHenry, Nov. 28, Dec. 5, 1796, ibid., pp. 202–5. Carroll actually resided in Prince George's, but that divided county was lumped with Montgomery in this election. Francis Deakins stood for the pair; he was the son of a prominent Georgetown merchant and a firm Federalist. Rather than divide the party, Carroll apparently moved over to Anne Arundel, as he had in earlier elections, relying on his reputation to carry him through. Plater had voted Republican in earlier legislative service (1790–93).

15. That Murray was responsible is conjecture, since there is no way of knowing which Federalists voted for Henry. But Murray's concern for the Pinckney threat and his assurance that the Eastern Shore had chosen "excellent & trusty" men when the election was over make it highly likely that the mavericks were his Eastern Shore compatriots. Potomac Federalists, on the other hand, showed little evidence of concern, or even awareness, of the Pinckney conspiracy. Bartgis's *Federal Gazette* [Frederick] carried no letters on the subject during the campaign.

16. The popular vote in this contest, published in the *Federal Gazette,* Sept. 15, 1796, shows the locus of party strength in the district:

	George Baer "Federalist"	Samuel Ringold "Independent"
Frederick Town	709	16
Washington Country	634	615
Allegany County	449	61

Residence was still a factor, though less important than party. Baer resided in Frederick; Ringold in Washington. Frederick County was joined with Montgomery in another congressional district.

17. Generalization is hazardous because few copies of North Carolina newspapers have survived. But the scattered copies of the *North Carolina Journal* [Halifax], the *State Gazette of North Carolina* [Edenton], and the *North Carolina Gazette* [New Bern] that are extant do not contain the heavy polemics that filled Maryland and Virginia papers in the early 1790s.

18. *State Gazette of North Carolina,* Oct. 20, 27, Nov. 3, 1796; *North Carolina Journal,* Nov. 28, 1796.

19. Spaight to James J. Jasper, New Bern, June 16, 1796, John H. Bryan Papers, NCDH; *North Carolina Gazette,* July 9, 11, Aug. 6, 1796. Leonard H. Richards, "John Adams and the Moderate Federalists: the Cape Fear Valley as a Test Case," *North Carolina Historical Review,* 43 (1966), 14-30, esp. 20, argues that the Highland Scots of the upper Cape Fear/Fayetteville area were Federalists out of gratitude for Maclaine's and Iredell's efforts on behalf of Loyalists in the 1780s. The argument would be more persuasive if the Cape Fear had been more firmly Federalist early in the 1790s. The Scots' sympathy for Britain in the European war is a more likely explanation. The Fayetteville area remained Federalist until the War of 1812.

20. Va, *SJ, 1796,* Nov. 25, Dec. 6, 1796; *Columbian Mirror* [Alexandria], Dec. 3, 15, 1796; Thomas Evans to John Cropper, Richmond, Dec. 6, 1796, Cropper Papers, VaHS.

21. Much of this is conjecture because no contemporary observers indicated that it was a party contest. The only contemporary comment was by a back bencher from the Shenandoah Valley who favored Wood's election and in the next breath expressed the hope that Jefferson would win the Presidential election: William Lemon to Henry Bedinger, Richmond, Nov. 23, 1796, Danske-Dandridge Papers, NCDu.

22. The list, in the Washington Papers, DLC, is undated, but it was obviously drafted during the army buildup of 1798–99. Though nominally a loyalty check, it is in reality a political check because party firmness was the primary criterion used to ascertain loyalty. The comments of the person who drew up the list (possibly Charles Lee of Alexandria, who was then U.S. Attorney General) as well as Washington's own marginal notes, make this clear. The list will be referred to again because it is the best index of Federalist leadership in the entire Chesapeake.

23. *Columbian Mirror* [Alexandria], Nov. 24, 1796; Evans to Cropper, Richmond, Dec. 6, 1796, Cropper Papers, VaHS. Evans mistakenly records Mason's opponent as John Breckinridge (a Republican), but he had moved to Kentucky in 1793.

24. Evans to Cropper, Richmond, Dec. 6, 1796, Cropper Papers, VaHS.

25. Hancock to Breckinridge, Philadelphia, Feb. 10, 1797, James Breckinridge Papers, VaU.

26. Jefferson to Madison, Philadelphia, May 18, June 8, 1797, Madison Papers, DLC.

27. Marshall to Iredell, Richmond, Dec. 15, 1796, Griffith J. McRee, *Life and Correspondence of James Iredell,* 2 vols (New York, 1857–58), II, 482–43; Marshall to Charles Lee, Richmond, Apr. 20, 1797 [copy from Adams Papers, Massachusetts Historical Society], Marshall Transcripts, VaWM. I am indebted to Stephen Kurtz, first editor of the Marshall Papers, for letting me see the transcripts.

28. *Virginia Gazette* [Richmond], May 24, 1797; Merrill D. Peterson, *Thomas Jefferson and the New Nation* (New York, 1970), p. 605. The charge is published in McRee, *Iredell.* II, 505–11.

29. *Virginia Gazette* [Richmond], June 14, 1797.

30. W. C. Ford, Ed. *Writings of George Washington,* 14 vols. (New York, 1889–93), VII, 158-64; Richard Beeman, *The Old Dominion and the New Nation, 1788–1801* (Lexington, Ky., 1972), p. 171.

31. Va, *JHD, 1797,* p. 63 (Dec. 28, 1797).

32. Madison to Jefferson, Orange, Jan. 21, 1798, Madison Papers, DLC.

33. Because these were, as Madison noted, the only party votes in the session, it is possible that the rigidity of voting represented firmness only on this issue. The only way to test Madison's charge that the Rebulicans were confused and divided is to identify individuals by their behavior in the 1798 session (which had 13 party roll calls). This cross-check confirms the fact that each party in 1797 was internally united. Because the identification relies in part on 1798 behavior, no tabular analysis of the assembly will be made until the 1798 session is discussed.

34. Md, *JHD, 1796,* p. 34 (Nov. 25, 1796).

35. Md, *JHD, 1796,* p. 103 (Dec. 28, 1796). Federalist actions are inferred from the fact that the House adjourned immediately after the vote, and the *Journal* makes no further mention of the amendments.

36. Bartgis's *Federal Gazette* [Frederick], Sept. 6, 13, 20, 1797.

37. Ibid., Oct. 11, 1797.

38. Population and election statistics for these years are published in J. R. Pole, *Political Representation in England and the Origins of the American Republic* (London and New York, 1966), p. 556.

39. Admittedly, there may have been some hidden switching—switchers going one direction canceling out those going the other way. But even if the percentage figure is doubled or tripled, it is still infinitesimal.

40. Joseph Charles in a doctoral dissertation that was posthumously published as *The Origins of the American Party System: Three Essays* (Williamsburg, 1956) was among the first to question Beard's continuity theme, and his views were supported with only minor variations by Noble E. Cunningham, Jr., *The Jefferson Republicans: The Formation of Party Organization, 1789 - 1801* (Chapel Hill, 1957). The best statement of the importance of foreign policy in the formation of parties is Harry Ammon, *The Genet Mission* (New York, 1973).

41. Jefferson to Madison, Philadelphia, Feb. 15, 1798, Madison Papers, DLC; Jefferson to Monroe, Philadelphia, Mar. 8, 1798, Monroe Papers, DLC; William Hindman to Rufus King, Apr. 12, 1798, Charles R. King, ed., *Life and Correspondence of Rufus King,* 6 vols. (Boston, 1894–1900), II, 314. The roll call on which everyone relied, prior to the publication of the XYZ dispatches, was apparently an amendment by Republican leader John Nicholas on a foreign intercourse bill. The motion lost, 48 to 52: *Annals of Cong.,* 5th Cong., 2 sess., p. 1234 (Mar. 5, 1798).

42. *Annals of Cong.,* 5th Cong., 2 sess., p. 1371.

43. Jefferson to Monroe, Philadelphia, Apr. 19, 1798, Monroe Papers, DLC.

44. Jefferson to Madison, Philadelphia, Apr. 26, 1798, W. C. Ford, ed., *Writings of George Washington,* 14 vols. (New York, 1889–93), VII, 244.

45. Cunningham, *Jeffersonian Republicans,* p. 125, says that the Republicans, "helpless and dispirited, lost heart for a fight," citing Jefferson's letter. Actually their numbers held up quite well, and they conducted a spirited fight against the military preparedness bills, winning a number of roll calls. The subsequent departure of Daniel Morgan, James Machir, and Josiah Parker, moreover, offset the Republicans' losses. Among all southern congressmen, Republican losses during the session exceeded Federalists' by only 2 (one of which was due to the death of Nathan Bryan of North Carolina in June).

46. Manning J. Dauer, *The Adams Federalists* (Baltimore, 1953), pp. 304–9,

tabulates the roll calls of the Fifth Congress, second session. I am accepting his assessment of which ones involved party loyalty.

47. *Annals of Cong.,* 5th Cong., 2 sess., p. 1521 (Apr. 20, 1798).

48. Ibid., pp. 1553–54 (Apr. 25, 1798).

49. Ibid., pp. 1769–72 (May 17, 18, 1798). The two Republican motions passed by 56 to 35 and 53 to 35. In each case the same Federalists crossed over.

50. Dauer, *Adams Federalists,* pp. 174 ff.

51. *Annals of Cong.,* 5th Cong., 2d. sess., pp. 1834, 1868 (May 26, June 1, 1798). Maryland lines held firm.

52. Ibid., p. 1890 (June 8, 1798).

53. James Morton Smith, *Freedom's Fetters: The Alien and Sedition Laws and American Civil Liberties* (Ithaca, 1956), tells the story of this legislation in complete detail. I have relied on his account except where otherwise noted.

54. *Annals of Cong.,* 5th Cong., 2d sess., p. 1796. The vote to recommit the bill to committee was 46 to 44.

55. For party assignments among Congressmen outside the Chesapeake I am relying on Dauer, *Adams Federalists,* pp. 306–9. The one question mark is a Rhode Island congressman, Thomas Tillinghast, who voted for the act and whom Dauer lists as a Republican. However, since by Dauer's own count he voted Federalist 19 times and Republican on only 9 occasions, he would be best described as a waverer.

56. I am inferring that they left for home (rather than simply abstaining) from the fact that Machir participated in no roll calls after the June 4, and Morgan in none after the June 15. Although neither opened his mouth in debate during the session, both gave staunch support to the military preparedness bills. Morgan may have left because of illness. He declined to run for reelection the following spring on grounds of ill health and died in 1802. Machir retired from politics for a time, but when he returned to the assembly during the War of 1812 he was still a Federalist.

57. Forrest to McHenry, Dec. 6, 1797, in Steiner, *McHenry,* p. 206.

58. Smith, *Freedom's Fetters,* pp. 94–111.

59. The debate is ably summarized in ibid., pp. 112 ff.

60. *Annals of Cong.,* 5th Cong., 2d sess., p. 2171 (July 10, 1798).

61. This is accepting Dauer's classification of Bullock as a Federalist (*Adams Federalists,* pp. 171, 306–7), although by his own count Bullock voted Federalist 18 times and Republican 10 times in this session.

CHAPTER TWENTY   MOBILIZING THE ELECTORATE: 1800

1. *Columbian Mirror* [Alexandria], Apr. 14, May 12, 1798. The statements came from candidates in Alexandria, Hanover, Chesterfield, Gloucester, York, and Fauquier, so it would seem an independent development, not an imitation of Maryland.

2. Carrington to Washington, Richmond, June 4, 1798, Washington Papers, DLC; Robert Gamble to John Cropper, Richmond, July 11, 1798, Cropper Papers, VaHS.

3. Va, *JHD, 1798,* pp. 18–19 (Dec. 11, 1798); Randolph to St. George Tucker, Richmond, Dec. 13, 1798, Tucker-Coleman Papers, VaWM; Samuel

Shield to Tazewell, Richmond, Dec. 13, 1798, Tazewell Papers, VaSL. Names were not listed in the head count.

4. For details of this meeting see: Adrienne Koch and Harry Ammon, "The Virginia and Kentucy Resolutions: An Episode in Jefferson's and Madison's Defense of Civil Liberties," *William and Mary Quarterly,* 3d ser., 5 (1948), 145–76.

5. Nicholas to Jefferson, Oct. 4, 1798, and Jefferson to Nicholas, Oct. 5, 1798, Jefferson Papers, DLC.

6. Delbert H. Gilpatrick, *Jeffersonian Democracy in North Carolina, 1789–1816* (New York, 1931), pp. 96–99.

7. Hindman to Rufus King, Dec. 13, 1798, Charles R. King, ed., *Life and Correspondence of Rufus King,* 6 vols. (Boston, 1894–1900), II, 492. Hindman was obviously counting all the new members (5 of the 10) as Federalists, plus Richard Dobbs Spaight, who was reelected after filling out the term of deceased Republican Nathan Bryan. Spaight's recent switch to the Republicans may not have been known in the North. Grove, who was also reelected, made 7.

8. NC, *JHC, 1798,* pp. 77–78 (Dec. 24, 1798).

9. The Piedmont was divided so as to pinpoint the locus of western Federalism. The western Piedmont is defined as those counties drained by the Yadkin or Catawba rivers. Most of the eastern Piedmont drained into the Albemarle, Pamlico, or Cape Fear basins.

10. NC, *SJ, 1798,* p. 77 (Dec. 24, 1798).

11. When the Virginia and Kentucky resolutions came before the North Carolina assembly the following year, they were discussed briefly and dropped. Madison ascribed the failure to a lack of Republican leadership: to Jefferson, Richmond, Dec. 29, 1799, Madison Papers, DLC. It is true that the old Antifederalist leadership—Thomas Person, Alexander Mebane, James Gillespie, Nathan Bryan, and Wyatt Hawkins—retired (Bryan died) in 1798–99. And converts from Federalism, such as Alexander Martin and Richard D. Spaight, had little talent for party management. A new generation of Republicans was on the way—Nathaniel Macon, David Stone, Richard Stanford—but at this point all were in Congress.

12. *Resolutions of Virginia and Kentucky . . . and Debates in the House of Delegates of Virginia . . .* (Richmond, 1832), pp. 174–76.

13. Jefferson to W. C. Nicholas, Monticello, Nov. 29, 1798, Paul L. Ford, *Writings of Thomas Jefferson,* 10 vols. (New York and London, 1892–99), VII, 312–13; Taylor to Jefferson, Richmond [1798], W. E. Dodd, ed., *John P. Branch Historical Papers of Randolph-Macon College,* 5 vols. (Richmond, 1901–18), II, 277.

14. *Debates in the House of Delegates, upon . . . the Alien and Sedition Laws* (Richmond, 1818), pp. 67–74, 79.

15. Va, *JHD, 1798,* pp. 31–32 (Dec. 21, 1798).

16. Ibid., p. 59 (Jan. 4, 1799).

17. In the absence of popular vote tallies, a narrow margin in a county electorate is assumed if the county had recently switched party allegiance or if it chose delegates on opposite sides.

18. Richard Beeman, *The Old Dominion and the New Nation, 1788–1801* (Lexington, Ky., 1972), pp. 195–97, summarizes the addresses and identifies the authors, though he mistitles Madison's.

19. Marshall to Timothy Pickering, Richmond, Aug. 11, 1798 [copy from

Pickering Papers, Mass. Historical Society], Marshall Transcripts, VaWM. He publicly admitted that the laws were "useless" in "Answer to a Freeholder," *Times and Virginia Advertiser* [Alexandria], Oct. 11, 1798.

20. Va, *JHD, 1798,* pp. 88–96 (Jan. 22, 1799).

21. Va, *JHD, 1798,* pp. 90–96 (Jan. 22, 1799). There were two other roll calls on this issue which were not included in the calculations. One was a second Federalist effort at postponement, which went down by an even bigger margin, 31 to 108, and probably reflected weariness, rather than party attitudes. The other involved an amendment to Madison's "Address" recounting the wrongs inflicted on the Republicans who wanted to keep Madison's format intact.

22. The Senate, which held 7 roll calls on the various party resolutions sent to it from the House, divided in similar fashion. Federalists were a little stronger than in the House because the Tidewater districts combined strong Federalist counties with ones that were evenly divided. Using the same agreement standard (except for Speaker Ludwell Lee, a Federalist who did not vote), there were 14 Republicans, 8 Federalists, and 1 unknown (Burwell Basset, Jr., who cast two Federalist and one Republican vote). Only one Federalist was a westerner; the rest came from the Northern Neck, Eastern Shore, and Lower James and York rivers. Va, *SJ, 1798,* Dec. 24, 1798, Jan. 10, 24, 1799.

23. Bartgis's *Federal Gazette* [Frederick], Aug. 1, Sept. 13, 1798; *Federal Gazette* [Baltimore], July 13, Sept. 1, Oct. 2, 1798. L. Marx Renzulli's discussion of this election, *Maryland: Federalist Years* (Rutherford, N.J., 1973), pp. 201–2, intermingles quotations over a two-year span, including some that refer to the Virginia resolutions, and thus confuses the issues.

24. Hindman to McHenry, Talbot County, Aug. 12, 1798, McHenry Papers, MdHS.

25. George Salmon to McHenry, Baltimore, Sept. 25, 1798, ibid.

26. Hindman to McHenry, Talbot, Aug. 12, 1798, ibid.

27. Salmon to McHenry, Baltimore, Sept. 25, 1798, ibid.

28. Gov. John Henry, who may not have been aware of Smith's tough stand against the Sedition Act, urged him to run for reelection: Henry to Smith, Aug. 9, 1798, quoted in Renzulli, *Maryland: Federalist Years,* pp. 203–4.

29. James Ash to McHenry, Aug. 24, 1798, B. C. Steiner, *Life and Correspondence of James McHenry* (Cleveland, 1907), pp. 333–34.

30. George Salmon to McHenry, Baltimore, Oct. 7, 1798, and David Stewart to McHenry, Baltimore, Sept. 15, 1798, McHenry Papers, MdHS.

31. Robert Smith replaced Chasite David McMechen in 1797, and the city's delegation was Republican thereafter. Baltimore county, Antifederalist and Republican in the early part of the decade, did send some Federalists to the assembly in the mid-1790s, but by 1798 it was Republican again.

32. *Federal Gazette* [Baltimore], Oct. 8, 1798.

33. Smith to John Adams, Aug. 2, 1798, and Smith "To the Voters of the City and County of Baltimore," [Sept. 7, 1798], Samuel Smith Papers, DLC.

34. One of McHenry's informants claimed that, although Baer was opposed by a newcomer from Pennsylvania and had the support of "all the Friends of Government," nevertheless "the contest appears doubtful." Salmon to McHenry, Baltimore, Sept. 25, 1798, McHenry Papers, MdHS.

35. Ibid.

36. Md, *JHD, 1798,* pp. 32–33 (Nov. 27, 1798).

37. Ibid., pp. 34–35 (Nov. 28, 1798).

38. Ibid., pp. 82, 86–87 (Dec. 28, 1798).

39. Ibid., pp. 124–25 (Jan. 16, 1798).

40. Md, *SJ, 1798,* p. 12 (Dec. 7, 1798); *JHD, 1798,* pp. 57–58 (Dec. 11, 1798).

41. Marshall to Washington, Richmond, May 16, 1799, Washington Papers, DLC.

42. Marshall's figure of 8 evidently included Josiah Parker, who, continued to vote erratically (though he may have been elected as a Federalist) and Edwin Gray, who was claimed by both sides in the election but subsequently voted Republican.

43. "New" in this context means any member who did not serve in the previous session, even though he might have served some time earlier. The rate of turnover had been declining steadily since the early 1780s when 55 to 60 percent was common. From 1793 to 1796 it averaged about 40 percent, then jumped to 51 percent in 1797. By 1800 it was back to 40 percent. If the increased turnover reflected heightened public feelings during the French crisis, it is apparent from the stability of party strength that the various influences (e.g., XYZ correspondence, Sedition Act) canceled each other in the state as a whole.

44. Henry chose, curiously, to stand for Charlotte County, which he had never represented before. Charlotte was in the western Piedmont, adjacent to predominantly Federalist Bedford; perhaps he thought his chances better there. His old "stamping grounds," Prince Edward County, was also Randolph's home.

45. Bartgis's *Federal Gazette* [Frederick], Sept. 25, 1799. There was, interestingly, no attempt to balance the ticket ethnically. All four candidates were of English origin. On the other hand, there is no firm evidence that ethnicity was a factor in Maryland elections. Of those who served in the House of Delegates between 1798 and 1800 from all of the upper Potomac counties, Germans, Scots-Irish, and English are about evenly distributed between the parties. It may have been a negative factor—in the sense that parties were careful not to offend an ethnic segment—but there is no evidence that ethnic segments associated en masse with one party or the other. In 1797 a meeting at this same tavern, which nominated the same slate of men, published a list of those attending. Three-fourths of the names appear to be English in origin, one-fourth were German. *Federal Gazette,* Sept. 13, 1797.

46. Ibid. On the Republican ticket were three men with English surnames and one German.

47. *North Carolina Mercury* [Salisbury], June 27, 1799.

48. Robert Park to Hamlin, Warren, June 17, 1798, and Thomas Person to Hamlin, Personton, July 1, 1799, Wood Jones Hamlin Papers, NCDH.

49. Chase Papers, MdHS.

50. The only other variations between the list and actual behavior were one Federalist (he had been a Federlist in the previous session) who voted Republican in this session, and one Republican who voted Federalist. Two others listed as Republicans mixed their votes.

51. In Maryland this was the chronological order in which the counties were established.

52. Series 4 Washington Papers, DLC. A similar list of North Carolina

applicants contains no partisan comments, but the only persons making the recommendations (and, presumably, the only ones Washington solicited) were the Federalist congressmen William B. Grove and Archibald Henderson.

53. Hindman to McHenry, Talbot County, Aug. 12, 1798, McHenry Papers, MdHS.

54. Taylor to Tench Coxe, Caroline, Feb. 1, 1798, Coxe Papers, PaHS.

55. Taylor to Jefferson, Caroline, Feb. 15, 1799, W. E. Dodd, ed., "Letters of John Taylor," *John P. Branch Historical Papers of Randolph-Macon College,* II, 278–81.

56. John Guerrant to Monroe, Goochland, Oct. 14, 1799, Monroe Papers, DLC.

57. Lisle A. Rose, *Prologue to Democracy: The Federalists in the South, 1789–1800* (Lexington, Ky., 1968), pp. 222–23, thinks the establishment of this paper "one of the most significant advances" in party development in the decade. This is a gross overstatement. The move was hardly novel, since both parties in all parts of the country had been establishing party papers for a decade. At the time and thereafter the *Columbian Mirror* of Alexandria was the chief Federalist organ in the state. Davis's *Gazette* always bore a pretense of neutrality, but it was more likely to print Federalist commentary at the beginning of the decade and Republicans comments at the end.

58. The remark is actually by Wise's great-grandson, Barton H. Wise, evidently from family hearsay: Barton H. Wise, *Life of Henry A. Wise* (New York, 1899, p. 6. That there is some substance to it is indicated by a letter Jefferson wrote to Wise, Feb. 12, 1799, admitting that he had denounced Wise to his friends as a "tory" and explaining what he meant by it. Wise, in an action that would certainly have confirmed Jefferson's suspicions, had he known, sent the letter to James McHenry. B. C. Steiner found it among McHenry's papers and published it in the *Virginia Magazine of History and Biography,* 12 (1904–5) 257–59.

59. Va, *JHD, 1799,* p. 3 (Dec. 2, 1799); *Virginia Gazette* [Richmond], Dec. 6, 1799.

60. Va, *JHD, 1799,* p. 10 (Dec. 5, 1799). The Republican *Virginia Gazette* [Richmond], Dec. 10, 1799, reported the result as 111 to 44; the Federalist *Columbian Mirror* [Alexandria], Dec. 12, 1799, reported it as 101 to 66. No vote was recorded in the House *Journal.*

61. Va, *JHD, 1799,* p. 88 (Jan. 15, 1800). The lineup correlates closely with party divisions on other roll calls. Party affiliation was not mentioned in the committee report, but the four candidates—William McKinley, John Morgan, Benjamin Biggs, and Ebenezer Zane—can be identified by their voting records in this and earlier sessions.

62. Thomas Swann to Charles Simms, Richmond, Dec. 24, 1799, Simms Papers, DLC.

63. Beeman, *Old Dominion and the New Nation,* p. 213. Beeman also presents a good summary of the *Report,* on pp. 213–15.

64. Va, *JHD, 1799,* p. 72 (Jan. 8, 1800); Madison to Jefferson, Richmond, Jan. 12, 1800, Madison Papers, DLC.

65. Beckley to Tench Coxe, Philadelphia, Jan. 24, 1800, Coxe Papers, PaHS. Party leaders in Richmond, Beckley told Coxe, had replied that all his recommendations either had been or would be approved.

66. Va, *JHD, 1799,* p. 79 (Jan. 10, 1800).

67. Ibid., pp. 81–83 (Jan. 11, 1800).

68. Ibid., p. 93 (Jan. 18, 1800); Madison to Jefferson, Dec. 29, Jan. 12, 18, 1800, Madison Papers, DLC. There is no extant Senate *Journal* for 1799.

69. The change had been under discussion for some time. Alexander Smyth, political novice from far-western Wythe County, had suggested the previous year that the assembly change the electoral law to "secure a Unanimous vote to our state." Smyth to Nicholas, Wythe, Dec. 15, 1798, Wilson Cary Nicholas Papers, VaU.

70. Va, JHD, 1799, p. 91 (Jan. 17, 1800). The Federalist accusation was in the *Virginia Federalist* [Richmond], Mar. 19, 1800. It is assumed that similar charges were made on the House floor.

71. Madison to Jefferson, Richmond, Jan. 18, 1800, Madison Papers, DLC.

72. Charles C. Pinckney to Hamilton, Shepherd's Town, Va., July 17, 1800, Hamilton Papers, DLC.

73. Ogle had served on the governor's council since 1783; he never held elective office. There is no indication even that he was a Federalist, other than his selection by the assembly to be governor in 1798.

74. Renzulli, *Maryland: Federalist Years,* p. 214, summarizes the newspaper controversy over the electoral law.

75. James McHenry abandoned hope for the plan of choosing electors by the legislature when after the fall election he concluded that the lower house had an "antifederal majority": to Wolcott, Oct. 12, 1800, Steiner, *McHenry,* p. 470.

76. *Calendar of Virginia State Papers and Other Manuscripts,* 11 vols. (Richmond, 1875–93), IX, 74–75.

77. Ibid., pp. 75–87. See also Harry Ammon, "The Richmond Junto, 1800–1824," *Virginia Magazine of History and Biography,* 61 (1953), 395–418.

78. Austin never held office of any kind, so far as can be determined; nothing is known of him.

79. Broadside, signed William Austin, Secretary of "The Committee Entrusted with the Ticket of the Minority," Feb. 11, 1800, and Austin, "An Address to the Voters for Electors of President and Vice President of the United States, in the State of Virginia," May 26, 1800, John Cropper Papers, VaHS.

80. Noble E. Cunningham, *The Jeffersonian Republicans: Formation of Party Organization, 1789–1801* (Chapel Hill, 1957), pp. 194–95.

81. Dawson to Coxe, Fredericksburg, Sept. 28, 1800, Coxe Papers, PaHS.

82. 'Renzulli, *Maryland: Federalist Years.* pp. 214–16.

83. Smith to Hall, Baltimore, Aug. 6, 8, 1800, Benedict Edward Hall Papers, Harford County Coll., MdHS.

84. The assembly election was annually held on the first Monday in October; choosing of Presidential electors was scheduled for November 10, 1800.

85. Charles P. Polk to Madison, Fredrick, June 20, 1800, Madison Papers, DLC; *Federal Gazette* [Baltimore], Aug. 11, Oct. 3, 1800.

86. *Columbian Mirror* [Alexandria], Oct. 9, 11, 1800. Because the *Mirror* was a Federalist sheet, it perversely referred to the parties as "Federalists" and "Antifederalists."

87. McHenry to Hamilton, Nov. 1800, Steiner, *McHenry,* pp. 478–79.

88. Benjamin Stoddert to John Rutledge, Jr., Washington, D. C., Oct. 2,

1800, and Robert G. Harper to Rutledge, Baltimore, Sept. 4, 1800, Rutledge Papers, NCU; Harper to Hamilton, Baltimore, June 5, 1800, Hamilton Papers, DLC.

89. Henry Lee to Hamilton, Philadelphia, Mar. 5, 20, 1800; Edward Carrington to Hamilton, Richmond, Aug. 30, 1800, Hamilton Papers, DLC.

90. Renzulli, *Maryland: Federalist Years,* pp. 221–22, cites a letter of McHenry's on the eve of the election stating "we shall make little or no exertions for the federal candidate" as evidence that the party split ruined morale. McHenry does not cite that reason for his discouragement, however, and in any case he was speaking for himself. Others, including Samuel and Jeremiah Townley Chase and Robert G. Harper, made strenuous exertions.

91. Beckley to Tench Coxe, Philadelphia, Sept. 29, 1800, Coxe Papers, PaHS. Carroll and Harper both expected to get all but three of the state's votes: Carroll to Hamilton, Aug. 27, 1800, and Harper to Hamilton, June 5, 1800, Hamilton Papers, DLC.

92. Exact statistics are not available, but the district included Prince George's, which voted Federalist in the assembly election a month earlier. So the Republican margin in Anne Arundel had to be big enough to carry the district.

93. County votes in the Presidential contest were not recorded. The conclusion is drawn from the fact that Washington and Frederick both chose Republican slates for the assembly in the October election. In that contest Republicans carried Washington county by 470 votes and Frederick by 50 or 60: *Columbian Mirror* [Alexandria], Oct. 11, 1800. Allegany, Republican after the Whisky Rebellion, returned to Federalism in 1798.

94. *Columbian Mirror,* Nov. 13, 1800. This was the first time in Maryland that a city's vote was broken down by wards. Curiously, the results were not printed in the Maryland press. See also Richard M. Bernard, "A Portrait of Baltimore in 1800: Economic and Occupational Patterns in an Early American City," *Maryland Historical Magazine,* 69, no. 4 (1974), 341–60.

95. *Columbian Mirror,* Oct. 9, 11, 1800.

96. Richmond, Williamsburg, and Norfolk. Alexandria's vote was merged with that of Fairfax County, which went for Jefferson by 240 to 218.

97. Various newspapers carried partial tallies of the voting, but the most complete list was published in the *Annual Register and Virginia Repository for 1800* (Petersburg, n.d.), p. 174. Only the returns from far-western Kanawha and Wood counties are missing.

98. This result tends to substantiate my basic thesis that parties did exist in the state legislatures and the roll call methods used to identify them.

99. The five were Henry (where Patrick Henry resided), Powhatan (where Edward Carrington had some influence), Campbell on the edge of the mountains (which like neighboring Bedford had some spillover migrants from the Valley), Lunenburg, and Mecklenburg. The latter two had periodically sent Federalists to the House of Delegates in the mid-1790s. They were in the Roanoke Valley, not far from Federalist Halifax.

100. Campbell to Madison, Washington County, Mar. 23, 1801, Madison Papers, DLC.

101. Manning J. Dauer, *The Admas Federalists* (Baltimore, 1953), p. 329, calls Willis Alston of Albemarle a Federalist also, apparently because he was elected in

1798 on a pledge to support the administration. However, he voted Republican in the Sixth Congress and continued to do so through a congressional career that lasted until 1831.

102. John Stanly did reappear in the Eleventh Congress, elected, one supposes, as a protest against the embargo, and he voted with John Randolph and the Republican dissidents.

103. Voting figures are from the *North Carolina Mercury* [Salisbury], Aug. 21, 1800.

104. Harper's original piece, signed "Civis," appeared in the *Federal Gazette* [Baltimore] Oct. 15, 1800. The exchange of letters from October 21 to December 19, 1800, is in the Harper-Pennington Papers, MdHS.

105. Md, *JHD, 1800,* pp. 16, 19, 62, 64 (Nov. 11, 13, Dec. 9, 1800). The initial House ballot to delay the election was a party vote of 42 to 35. The Senate apparently compromised, rather than leave the seat vacant: *SJ, 1800,* p. 25 (Dec. 9, 1800).

106. Md, *JHD, 1801,* p. 22; *SJ, 1801,* p. 10 (Nov. 10, 1801). Names on the roll call were not recorded.

107. Md, *JHD, 1801,* pp. 21, 33, 35, 40–41, 67–68 (Nov. 18–24, Dec. 10, 1801).

108. Because the purpose of some proposals is not clear from the *Journal,* the record of Robert Bowie, who was elected Republican governor in 1803, was used as the model.

109. Md, *JHD, 1800,* pp. 10–14 (Dec. 3, 1800); *SJ, 1800,* p. 85, (Dec. 19, 1800). The House vote in favor of the bill was 57 to 11. See Chapter 18 for analysis of these votes.

110. Md, *JHD, 1801,* p. 73, 90 (Dec. 12, 21, 1801).

111. Ibid., pp. 18, 51, 72, 82–83, 93, 103 (Nov. 10, Dec. 1, 12, 17, 22, 26, 1801). There were 10 roll calls on these matters.

112. There were a total of 70 roll calls in the House of Delegates in 1801; 22 were omitted in constructing the matrix because they were lopsided or of purely personal interest. This is the first time since 1784 that partisan votes were a majority of those taken. Computerized cluster analysis of the intervening sessions revealed no patterns.

A Note on Sources

A LIST OF all the published books, articles, and newspapers I have consulted would add many pages to a book that is already overly long. The reader who wishes to pursue certain topics can glean bibliographical citations from my notes. I feel that the interests of future scholars will be better served by an annotated list of manuscripts available in various depositories or on microfilm.

DISTRICT OF COLUMBIA

LIBRARY OF CONGRESS

The papers of Washington, Jefferson, Madison, Monroe, and George Mason are all indispensable, and all available on microfilm or in printed editions. Also on microfilm are the Wilson Cary Nicholas Papers and the Samuel Smith Papers. Both are exclusively business and family correspondence with no political information prior to 1800.

Breckinridge Family Papers. 20 volumes beginning in 1752. Superb col-
lection of agricultural business records, and the political correspon-
dence of John and James Breckinridge and Archibald Stuart.
Patrick Henry Papers. A small but usefull collection.
Harry Innes Papers. 28 volumes. Excellent on Kentucky politics.
Richard Bland Lee Papers. Small but useful.
Charles Simms Papers. 7 volumes. Mostly legal correspondence. An
interesting political exchange with Leven Powell begins in 1799.

MARYLAND

MARYLAND HISTORICAL SOCIETY, BALTIMORE

The William Wirt Papers, 1786–1860, 9,000 items, available on
microfilm, are disappointing for the period prior to 1800. Also
available on microfilm are the county tax lists for 1783 and the
federal tax of 1798.

Bland Family Papers, 1757–1860, 11 boxes. Of no value for the period
1782–1800.
Charles Carroll of Carrollton Papers, 1658–1883, 30 boxes. Almost no
political correspondence, 1781 to 1800. Carroll's Journal (1792–
1802) is a splendid source for anyone who wants to chart Maryland's
weather.
Carroll-Harper Papers, 1753–1880. Little of interest prior to 1800.
Samuel Chase Letters. One portfolio, 1741–1811. Contains a few originals, photocopies of Chase letters in the Virginia Historical Society,
and transcripts of others in various depositories. The collection is
scant, but the best we have.
Harry Dorsey Gough Papers. One box, 1681–1835. There is one gem
from Charles Ridgely; the rest is family and legal correspondence.
Alexander Contee Hanson Collection. Has disappointingly little politics.
Harford County Collection. Contains election returns for period 1789–
1829 for Harford. There are some restrictions on the collection.
Robert Goodloe Harper Papers. 1,000 items, 1748–1880. Nearly all
business correspondence prior to 1800, though there are a few letters
from Charles and Daniel Carroll.
Harper-Pennington Papers. Family memorabilia prior to 1800, except for
a few letters of Charles Carroll.

John Edgar Howard Papers. Two volumes and 15 boxes, 1752–1827. Of no value for the period of 1782–1800.

Francis Scott Key Papers, in the Howard Family Collection. Of no value.

James McHenry Papers. Mostly transcripts, with nothing that cannot be found in B. C. Steiner's biography.

Ridgely Family Papers. Includes the accounts and mercantile correspondence of Captain Charles Ridgely.

Tench Tilghman Papers, 1731–1808. Disappointing for the period after the Revolution.

William Tilghman Papers. 270 items. Strictly legal correspondence.

Otho Holland Williams Papers. 9 boxes. The best collection in the society for Maryland politics in the post-Revolutionary years. It also has a WPA-compiled guide containing reliable summaries of letters.

MARYLAND HALL OF RECORDS, ANNAPOLIS

The Proceedings of the Commissioners for Confiscated British Property are available on microfilm. All volumes are indexed. The contents of the volumes are as follows:

Proceedings of the Commissioners, 1781–82. A journal of procedures for the evaluation of property.

Sales Journal, 1781–85. A list of purchasers and the items bought in chronological order.

Sales Ledger, 1781–85. Lists the accumulated holdings of each purchaser with references to pages in the Sales Journal. It also gives the method of payment, whether by cash, sale of other property, or personal bonds.

Intendent of Revenue: Property Sold in 1785. A list of purchasers in that year.

Agent's Ledger, 1786–89. Accounts of debtors to the state paying off their bonds and the dates of payment.

Auditor's General Sale Book, 1792–95. Purchases made in the 1790s, evidently of property that had been recovered by the state when initial purchasers failed to pay.

Governor and Council Sale Book, 1803–17. Apparently a continuation of the previous book.

Auditor-General List of Claims against Confiscated British Property, 1787–89. A list of creditors to whom Loyalists owed money prior to confiscation, and the liens they placed on the confiscated property.

NEW YORK

NEW YORK HISTORICAL SOCIETY, NEW YORK CITY

Available on microfilm, done by the society or by the Library of Congress, are the Papers of Thomas Jefferson, Albert Gallatin, James Madison, and John Jay.

Horatio Gates Papers. 30 boxes, 1750–99. Available on microfilm. Disappointing for his post-Revolutionary residence in Virginia.

Rufus King Papers. 36 boxes and 37 volumes, 1786–1826. Excellent correspondence among northern Federalists, with a few letters from Henry Lee.

Miscellaneous Manuscripts. Contains a few letters of John Marshall, Bushrod Washington, and Charles Fenton Mercer.

NEW YORK PUBLIC LIBRARY, NEW YORK CITY

Emmet Collection. 10,800 pieces. An autograph collection with many famous names and little information.

James Monroe Papers. 1,297 pieces. Not very useful for pre-1800 period.

Myers Collection. Includes one volume of papers of General Dan Morgan.

NORTH CAROLINA

NORTH CAROLINA DEPARTMENT OF ARCHIVES AND HISTORY, RALEIGH

The Archives have scattered tax lists for about half of North Carolina's counties. The state census of 1787 includes 11 counties for which there are no tax lists in this period. None of this data is on microfilm.

John Gray Blount Papers, 1770–1931. 11 cubic feet. Published by the North Carolina Historical Commission.

John H. Bryan Papers, 1773–1906. 3 cubic feet. Only a dozen letters prior to 1800.

William R. Davie Papers, 1778–1817. 0.5 cubic foot. Disappointingly thin, except for material on his 1799 mission to France.

Wood Jones Hamlin Papers, 1769–1835. Contains a couple of rare letters from Thomas Person.

James Iredell Papers, 1770–1829. 0.25 cubic foot. Everything of importance is printed by Griffith J. McRee in his biography.

Montfort Stokes Papers, 1790–1811. 0.5 cubic foot. Contains nothing of interest prior to 1800.

John Walker Papers, 1736–1909. 150 items. The Tory-baiter of Wilmington left nothing of value for posterity.

WILLIAM R. PERKINS LIBRARY, DUKE UNIVERSITY, DURHAM

Campbell Family Letters. The focus is on Governor David Campbell, but there are a few letters from his uncle Arthur Campbell.

John Clopton Papers. 6 vols., 1629–1915. Family and business papers for the early period, but rich in politics after 1796.

Danske-Dandridge Papers. 5,508 items, 1752–1954. For the 1790s it is mostly the letters of the Bedinger Family of Berkely/Jefferson county, Virginia. There are also a few letters of General Adam Stephen and Congressman Robert Rutherford.

James Iredell Papers. 125 items, 1767–1856. Nearly all the political letters are published in McRee's biography.

James Jackson Papers. The early senator from Georgia. Only a few scattered letters on politics, but they are worth seeing.

Zachariah Johnston Papers. Generally thin, but there are a few political letters for the 1790s. Some good discussions of agricultural methods and transportation problems in the Shenandoah Valley.

Joseph Jones Papers. Mostly business records and military affairs until 1794, when some good political commentary begins.

North Carolina State Papers, 1788–89: Ratification of the Constitution. Contains petitions favoring ratification with long lists of names.

William and John Preston Papers. Mostly business records and land surveys. Not equal to the Preston papers at the Virginia Historical Society.

Purviance-Courtenay Collection. 2,328 items, 1776–1920. For the 1790s the collection includes the papers of Samuel D. Purviance, merchant of Baltimore. The mercantile information is good, but there is little on politics.

UNIVERSITY OF NORTH CAROLINA, CHAPEL HILL

The Simpson-Bryan Papers, Macay-McNeely Papers, and Morris Family Papers, all described below, are in the North Carolina Collection. The remainder are in the university's superb Southern Collection.

Thomas Burke Papers. 315 pieces, 1744–89. Available on microfilm, but contains little after 1782.

Preston Davie Autograph Collection. Contains a few letters of Alexander White of Winchester, Virginia, and Samuel Johnston.

William R. Davie Papers. One volume and 124 pieces, 1758–1819. Mostly copies of letters in other collections.

William Gaston Papers. 1,407 pieces, 1744–1914. The important material begins in 1800.

James Gillespie Papers. 701 pieces, 1720–1877. Nothing but family gossip for the 1790s.

William Barry Grove Letters, 1792–1802. Sixteen letters to James Hogg, which have been published in the *James Sprunt Papers,* vols. VIII and IX.

Hawkins Family Papers. Mostly commercial and legal materials for this period.

Hayes Collection. The most valuable collection of political correspondence relating to North Carolina in this period. Available on microfilm. Reels 4 and 5 contain most of the Samuel Johnston and James Iredell letters for the 1780s and 1790s. There are some restrictions on use of the collection.

Ernest Haywood Collection. 38 boxes, 1752–1846. There are letters to and from numerous political figures in the 1790s.

Archibald Henderson Papers. Of little political interest for this period, except for one folder of materials on Matthew Lock.

Hooper Collection. Ranks with the Hayes Collection in value. Marvelous letters of Archibald Maclaine on the politics of the 1780s.

E. Vernon Howell Collection, 1725–1929. Contains the correspondence of Richard Henderson and the papers of the Transylvania Company. All business transactions; no politics.

James Iredell Papers. 23 volumes, 1759–89. Exclusively legal correspondence.

Jonathan Jacocks Papers. Folder 1 includes the correspondence of the first Jonathan Jacocks, 1732–1822. Of no real value.

Samuel Johnston Papers. 26 microfilm reels, 1676–1865. Mostly taken, so far as I could tell, from the Johnston materials in the Hayes Collection.

Edmund Jones Papers. Addition E contains 26 tax lists for Wilkes County, 1791–1802.

Lenoir Family Papers. An immense collection with around 8 folders for the period 1782–1800. Mostly plantation operations and land transactions.

Macay-McNeely Papers, 1746–1918. The papers of Judge Spruce Macay are nearly all legal documents, but there are some political letters of Allan Jones in the collection.

Morris Family Papers. 100 items, 1764–1827. Contains some political letters from John Hay of Cumberland County.

Simpson-Bryan Papers. Most valuable are the Papers of Samuel Simpson, 1788–1815, 169 items. There are several letters on elections between 1789 and 1800.

John Steele Papers, 1764–1815. The collection contains a number of letters that are not in the volumes of his correspondence published by the North Carolina Historical Commission.

Swann Papers. Five folders. Includes the letters of John Swann, 1790–1801.

PENNSYLVANIA

HISTORICAL SOCIETY OF PENNSYLVANIA, PHILADELPHIA

Tench Coxe Papers. An enormous collection recently made available to scholars. It is now available on microfilm from the society. There is some political correspondence for the 1790s, but most of it is mercantile exchanges.

Hugh Williamson Papers. A useful collection of letters to and from this North Carolina congressman who settled in Philadelphia.

VIRGINIA

UNIVERSITY OF VIRGINIA, CHARLOTTESVILLE

The university's Jefferson, Madison, and Monroe collections, all indispensable, are all available on microfilm or in printed editions. Publication of the papers of George Washington and James Madison is currently in process.

Barbour Family Papers. Contain a few items of interest for the 1790s, but most of it is post-1800.

James Breckinridge Correspondence. 150 items. A dandy collection for its size, it contains letters from Congressmen John Brown of Kentucky, Francis Preston, and George Hancock.

Bryan Family Papers. 719 items. Nearly all family exchanges prior to 1800; thereafter rich in John Randolph of Roanoke materials.

Carter-Smith Collection. A fine collection, but better for the post-1800 period. General Samuel Smith's letters have been microfilmed along with his Library of Congress Papers.

Cocke Family Papers. 9,000 items. Nothing of political importance in the pre-1800 period.

Edgehill-Randolph Papers. The heart of this collection has been removed to form a special Jefferson Collection, leaving mostly family interchanges.

Lee Family Papers. A few letters, though not very consequential, have been inserted since this collection was microfilmed.

James Maury Papers. A sleeper in the university's collections. Maury was a Virginian residing in Liverpool. His extensive correspondence with planters of the Rappahannock gives a rare view of men who were intensely interested in politics, but not actively involved. Some interesting mercantile exchange, as well.

Wilson Cary Nicholas Papers. Prior to 1800 they are nearly all business records of a man in chronic financial difficulties.

Creed Taylor Papers. 33 items. Small collection, and better after 1800 than before.

Webb-Prentis Collection. Contains an impressive amount of material on the nineteenth century, but not of much value before 1800.

VIRGINIA HISTORICAL SOCIETY, RICHMOND

Charles Campbell Papers. Contains mostly the letters of Theodorick Bland, which Campbell collected and published.

Paul Carrington Letters. 110 items, 1755–92. Of no apparent value.

John Cropper Papers. 8 boxes. A superb exchange among eastern Virginia Federalists.

Hugh Blair Grigsby Papers. Generally disappointing, except for a folder of Patrick Henry letters.

William Wirt Henry Papers. 1,000 items, 1776–1878. The only interesting materials are two folders of Patrick Henry letters, most of them copies made by Henry's numerous descendants.

Ludwell Lee Papers. A splendid collection, and none of it, so far as I could tell, is reproduced in the microfilm edition of the Lee Family Papers.

Mercer Family Papers. There is a useful assortment of letters from James and John F. Mercer down to 1799.

Preston Family Papers. This collection contains mostly land surveys and transfers, but there are some good letters of William, Robert, and James P. Preston in the 1790s.

Stuart Family Papers. Contains about 80 items of Archibald Stuart correspondence, nearly all of it concerning legal matters.

VIRGINIA STATE LIBRARY, RICHMOND

The glory of this archival collection is the tax lists, wills, and deed books for nearly every county, dating from the mid-eighteenth century (most tax lists series begin in 1782) to recent times. The tax records, both personalty and realty, are currently being microfilmed.

Corbin Family Papers. 30 items. Mostly family gossip.

Executive Correspondence. A huge collection containing letters to and from the governor and council. Nearly all, so far as I could tell, was published in the *Calendar of Virginia State Papers*.

William Fleming Papers. Contains nothing of importance.

Charles Carter Lee Papers. 1,917 items, 1780–1871. The collection is under restrictions, but it contains a few interesting letters to and from Henry Lee. Most of it is nineteenth-century material.

John Marshall Papers. 30 items. Mostly photostats of letters in other collections, and nothing of importance prior to 1800.

General Daniel Morgan Letters. 26 items, 1763–1800. Nearly all business papers.

Tazewell Family Papers. 14 volumes, 1740–1867. Mostly legal and business correspondence prior to 1800, but a few political letters beginning in the mid-1790s.

THE COLLEGE OF WILLIAM AND MARY, WILLIAMSBURG

Richard Corbin Family Papers. 3 vols, 1746–1818. There may be some good Revolutionary materials here on this Virginia Loyalist, but the post-Revolutionary correspondence is disappointing.

Tucker Family Papers, including the Tucker-Coleman Papers. 24,000 pieces, 1768–1860. The best of this collection is nineteenth century, but there is a good 1790s exchange between John Page and St. George Tucker. I understand that a number of useful letters have been added to the Tucker-Coleman Collection since I last saw it.

WISCONSIN

STATE HISTORICAL SOCIETY OF WISCONSIN, MADISON

The famous Draper Collection is available on microfilm, and the society has published an index. For the purposes of my story the following sets were most valuable: the Virginia Manuscripts, 16 volumes (volume I contains the letters of Philip Doddridge of Brooke County, volume V the papers of Thomas Madison of Botetourt County, and volume VIII has letters concerning various Valley politicians); the Preston Family Papers; the David Shepherd Papers (which contain some letters of Alexander White); the Benjamin Biggs Papers (particularly valuable for the Whisky Rebellion); and General Daniel Morgan's letters.

Index

DATE DUE

#47-0108 Peel Off Pressure Sensitive